T0231370

# New Directions in Internet Management

# THE AUERBACH

## BEST PRACTICES SERIES

## AUERBACH PUBLICATIONS

www.auerbach-publications.com

**TO ORDER**: Call: 1-800-272-7737 • Fax: 1-800-374-3401
E-mail: orders@crcpress.com

# New Directions in Internet Management

*Editor*

## Sanjiv Purba

# AUERBACH PUBLICATIONS

A CRC Press Company

Boca Raton   London   New York   Washington, D.C.

## Library of Congress Cataloging-in-Publication Data

New directions in Internet management / [edited] by Sanjiv Purba.
     p.  cm. — (Best practices)
  Rev. ed. of: Internet management. 2000 ed. c2000.
  Includes bibliographical references and index.
  ISBN 0-8493-1160-8 (alk. paper)
    1. Business enterprises—Computer networks—Management. 2. Internet. I. Purba,
Sanjiv. II. Internet management. III. Best practices series (Boca Raton, Fla.)

HD30.37.I56 2001
658′.054678—dc21                                    2001046222

**Visit the Auerbach Publications Web site at www.auerbach-publications.com**

© 2002 by CRC Press LLC
Auerbach is an imprint of CRC Press LLC

No claim to original U.S. Government works
International Standard Book Number 0-8493-1160-8
Library of Congress Card Number 2001046222
Printed in the United States of America 1 2 3 4 5 6 7 8 9 0
Printed on acid-free paper

# Contributors

Leilani Allen, *Partner, Summer Point Consulting, Mundelein, Illinois*

Mary Ayala-Bush, *Principal, Computer Sciences Corp., Dallas, Texas*

Nijaz Bajgoric, *Faculty Member, Bogazici University, Istanbul, Turkey*

Charles Banyay, *IT Professional, Toronto, Ontario, Canada*

Michael Bieber, *Assistant Professor, Information Systems, New Jersey Institute of Technology, Newark, New Jersey*

Janet Butler, *Consulting Editor, Auerbach Publications, Rancho de Taos, New Mexico*

Chao-Min Chiu, *Assistant Professor, Information Management, National Kaohsiung First University of Science and Technology, Kaohsiung, Ye chao, Taiwan*

Carlson Colomb, *Director, Host Access Marketing, Eicon Technology, Baie d'Urfe, Quebec, Canada*

Frank Cullen, *Principal, Blackstone and Cullen, Atlanta, Georgia*

Harry Demaio, *President, Deloite & Touche Security Services LLC, Deerfield, Illinois*

Eran Feigenbaum, *Manager, PricewaterhouseCoopers LLP, Los Angeles, California*

Frederick Gallegos, *CISA, CDE, CGFM, Faculty Member, Computer Information Systems, California State Polytechnic University, Pomona, California*

Daniel Gonneau, *Founder, Zephyr Networks, New York, New York*

Anura Gurugé, *Independent Technical Consultant, Meredith, New Hampshire*

Barbara J. Haley, *Doctoral Student, Management and Information Systems, University of Georgia, Athens, Georgia*

Gilbert Held, *Director, 4-Degree Consulting, Macon, Georgia*

Kelly Mega Hilmer, *Doctoral Student, Management and Information Systems, University of Georgia, Athens, Georgia*

Mark G. Irving, *CISA, Information Systems Auditor, Minnesota Power, Duluth, Minnesota*

## Contributors

RALPH L. KLIEM, *President, Practical Creative Solutions, Inc., Redmond, Washington*

KEITH G. KNIGHTSON, *Technology Consultant, Kanata, Ontario, Canada*

R. KOCHAREKAR, *World Bank, Washington, D.C.*

WALTER KUKETZ, *Performance Engineering Group, Consulting and Systems Integration, Computer Sciences Corp., Dallas, Texas*

CAROL L. LARSON, *Freelance Desktop Publisher, Hillsboro, Oregon*

JAMES A. LARSON, *Senior Software Engineer, Intel Architecture Lab, Hillsboro, Oregon*

CHANG-YANG LIN, *Ph.D., Professor, Computer Information Systems, Eastern Kentucky University, Richmond, Kentucky*

CHIN-FENG LIN, *Instructor, Business Administration, National Chin-yi Institute of Technology and Commerce, Taiping, Taichung, Taiwan*

LISA M. LINDGREN, *Independent Consultant, Meredith, New Hampshire*

ANDRES LLANA, JR., *Telecommunications Consultant, Vermont Studies Group, Inc., King of Prussia, Pennsylvania*

PHILLIP Q. MAIER, *Program Manager, Lockheed Martin Secure Network Initiative, San Francisco, California*

MICHAEL MCCLURE, *Vice President, Marketing, Marketwave Corporation, Seattle, Washington*

DOUGLAS C. MERRILL, *Ph.D., Senior Manager, Pricewaterhouse Coopers LLP, Los Angeles, California*

NATHAN J. MULLER, *Independent Consultant, Huntsville, Alabama*

JUDITH M. MYERSON, *Author, Philadelphia, Pennsylvania*

FRED NEUFELD, *National Data Warehouse System Engineer, Sun Microsystems of Canada, Inc., Markham, Ontario, Canada*

BOB PACKER, *Founder and Chief Technical Officer, Packeteer, Inc., Cupertino, California*

SRINIVAS PADMANABHARAO, *Consultant, Deloitte Consulting, Toronto, Ontario, Canada*

MIKE PREVOST, *DBsign Product Manager, Gradkell Systems, Inc., Huntsville, Alabama*

TERINIA REID, *Canadian Networking Manager, Deloitte Consulting, Oakville, Ontario, Canada*

DAVE SCHUETTE, *E-Business Solutions Director, Paragon Computer Professionals, Inc., Cranford, New Jersey*

E. EUGENE SCHULTZ, *Ph.D., Program Manager, SRI Consultants, Menlo Park, California*

JOHN SEASHOLTZ, *Business Consulting Director, Free Range Media, Seattle, Washington*

YASH SHAH, *Co-Founder, President, and Chief Technology Officer, InteQ Corporation, Burlington, Massachusetts*

ANTONIO SI, *Assistant Professor, Department of Computing, Hong Kong Polytechnic University, Hong Kong*

CAROL A. SIEGEL, *Chief Security Officer, American International Group, Inc., New York, New York*

EDWARD SKOUDIS, *Account Manager and Technical Director, Global Integrity, Howell, New Jersey*

LOUISE L. SOE, *Ph.D., Associate Professor, Computer Information Systems, California State Polytechnic University, Pomona, California*

SZU-YUAN SUN, *Instructor, Department of Information Management, National Kaohsiung First University of Science and Technology, Kaohsiung, Ye chao, Taiwan*

WAYNE THOMAS, *Vice President, DataSoft, Markham, Ontario, Canada*

PAT THOMAS, *Technical Communication Manager, Packeteer, Inc., Cupertino, California*

BHAVANI THURAISINGHAM, *Principal Engineer, Advanced Information Systems Center, MITRE Corp., Bedford, Massachusetts*

HOLLIS TIBBETTS, *Marketing Director, OnDisplay, Inc., San Ramon, California*

JOHN R. VACCA, *Information Technology Consultant, Pomeroy, Ohio*

PETE WELTER, *Senior Software Engineer, Freshwater Software, Inc., Boulder, Colorado*

# Contents

*Contents*

Contents

# Introduction

The principles of Internet management are in the process of evolving with the rest of the Internet business model, which is itself becoming more focused on financial profit and loss rather than gaining market share over competitors. Some questions that are commonly asked in the business and technology communities include: Will users be willing to pay for Internet-based services? Who will pay for enhancements? What is the business model for making money on the Internet? The answers to these questions will determine the shape of the Internet over the near term.

The Internet has existed since the 1960s. It is based on networked computers that use telephone networks to create a highly redundant global web of computing devices. It was founded by financial investments made by governments, universities, think tanks, and other public sources. In the late 1990s and at the turn of the century, venture capitalists (VCs) sensed an unprecedented opportunity to shape a market that was believed to be on the verge of replacing all that had gone before.

VCs invested hundreds of millions, if not billions, of dollars into the Internet, World Wide Web, and related solutions. While a lot of this investment clearly did not produce any meaningful returns, the cumulative effect of the investment was to generate a substantial amount of public awareness, interest, and acceptance of some notable killer apps (e.g., e-mail, search engines, and some portals). This alone has demonstrated the value of the Internet to businesses and consumers worldwide. In the process, most major applications from the 1990s (e.g., ERP and CRM) are still being reengineered to produce more Internet touch points.

Product vendors are not the only source of capital for future innovation on the Internet. VC capital has not disappeared from the Internet space. It is just more difficult to obtain and requires more traditional and reasoned business models. This means that we can continue to safely expect the emergence of more business applications and services on the Internet.

Another substantial source of revenue for the Internet is expected to be the end-user community on a fee-for-service basis. This has several implications. For one, future innovation on the Internet will be closely linked to profits and usability. This means that every solution being built will need to have a buyer somewhere—very quickly. Another implication is that cost control is going to be imperative to generating profits. This is of primary interest to the subject of Internet management.

## PURPOSE OF THIS BOOK

The purpose of this book is to focus on managing Internet infrastructure to support future business and personal user requirements. This infrastructure supports the types of business and Web solutions that will continue to fuel the growth of this powerful medium.

Given the implosion of the dot.com markets, it is critical for the industry to understand and respect the future of the Internet. In some ways, the Internet frenzy at the turn of the century was fueled by an original underestimation of the Internet's capabilities. The panic resulted when many people began to understand the medium's usefulness and started to question everything they knew about the way business was conducted. In an effort to catch up, the panic led to a public feeding frenzy. Today, the opposite is arguably happening. Again, there is some underestimation of the Internet's capabilities. Even though this is understandable as a reaction to the fervor of the last few years, it leaves us exposed to another feeding frenzy in the future. This book supplies readers with the information they need to leverage Internet technology while abiding time-honored business practices.

## SCOPE OF THIS BOOK

The scope of this book focuses on managing Internet infrastructure. This includes examining future trends, strategic issues, business issues, Internet infrastructure from the ground up, system integration opportunities, wireless and mobile solutions, Web site management, information management, Internet security, operations, and other post-implementation considerations.

## INTENDED AUDIENCE

This book is intended to be read by IT practitioners and technically inclined business users. This includes executives, managers, business analysts, data analysts, architects, LAN administrators, operators, developers, consultants, methodologists, Web masters, and testers.

## GETTING THE MOST FROM THIS BOOK

Section I, "Internet Trends," examines opportunities to overcome the obstacles facing the IT industry in the current Internet environment. This includes a reexamination of the information superhighway, application service providers, management service providers, and E-commerce based on acquired knowledge.

Section II, "Strategic and Business Issues," explains some of the strategic and business issues that are confronting the Internet. This includes an examination of measuring return on investment in terms of Internet-related expenditures, reducing operating costs, understanding Web and language issues, reducing risk, and allowing users to access Internet services more seamlessly.

Section III, "Internet Infrastructure from the Ground Up," takes a low-level view of some components that make up the global Internet infrastructure. This includes developing an end-to-end architecture, understanding the Internet protocol (IP), implementing voice applications for IP, bridging strategies for LAN Internets, and making product selections in building up a suitable Internet infrastructure.

Section IV, "System Integration," identifies some opportunities to integrate different and disparate business applications or Web services. This includes Web-to-host connectivity, case studies of Web-host integration, information system integration to the World Wide Web, building an integrated reporting architecture, and converting host data to HTML.

Section V, "Internet Variations and Applications" examines a few popular alternatives to a public Internet, including extranets and intranets. A cross section of implementation and support issues are discussed. Risk issues in this space are also included in this section.

Section VI, "Wireless and Mobile Solutions: Expanding the Internet Infrastructure," focuses on several wireless infrastructure options and alternatives. This includes such topics as voice and data, wireless data networking, wireless technology impacts on the enterprise network, mobile database interoperability, and a review of some Internet standards.

Section VII, "Web Site Management," explains considerations for managing a Web site before, during, and after development—but before permanent full-scale implementation of a solution. This section includes Web site design considerations for managers, managing Web content, and opportunities to control or restrict data flow and volume rates.

Section VIII, "Managing Information on the Internet," examines opportunities to create and manage various types of information in this space. This includes topics such as creating Internet server documents with HTML, Java-enabled data warehousing, bridging legacy data with XML, publishing data on the Web, including images and sounds in Web-accessible database tables, and other data management challenges on the Web.

Section IX, "Internet Security," explores a concern that is of utmost importance to many corporate executives and users of the Internet. This section reviews Internet security concepts, Internet security architecture, risk-mitigation strategies, digital signatures, computer virus protection, firewalls, and an extensive primer on how to prevent cracking.

Section X, "Operations and Post-Implementation Considerations," discusses methods to support a Web site after it is implemented into production. This includes a review of operational processes, monitoring a Web site, analyzing Web traffic, guaranteeing Internet service levels, Web site auditing procedures, and using intelligent agents to improve the benefits of the Web site.

The appendix provides a list of vendors and organizations that are helpful at various stages of the application development cycle.

SANJIV PURBA
June 2001

# Section I
# Internet Trends

Internet trends over the short term have experienced fundamentally different types of shifts in direction and industry expectations. At first, the business community did not know what to make of this far-reaching technology. Before too long, everyone — organizations and individuals alike — wanted a personal Web presence with lots of contact with Internet users. Comments such as "How would you like to have 1 million customers visiting your store every day?" were often repeated and always added to the passion that fueled the Internet frenzy. Almost any idea that dealt with the Internet was believed to be brilliant and worthy of a multimillion dollar investment.

In hindsight, it seems that many of the initiatives undertaken by dot.com organizations in the past couple of years were based on shaky premises. In fact, I remember speaking to several dot.com specialists about the need for a portal dedicated to male hair-care products. I was told by several people that the idea was worth millions and that a stop at several venture capital companies (VCs) was warranted. Before I could do anything about this, the market conditions changed, and suddenly everyone started asking legitimate questions about company profitability, products, sales plans, and marketing initiatives.

The frenzied Internet environment changed dramatically within a short period of time and the pendulum swung definitively in the other direction. The panic to get involved with the Internet disappeared with every significant stock plunge of business-to-consumer (B-to-C) and business-to-business (B-to-B) companies. At first, only B-to-C stocks were affected by the downturn, while the general consensus was that B-to-B, the "infrastructure" stocks, would continue to prosper. This turned out to be as inaccurate as the original assumption that the Internet would replace brick-and-mortar stores within a few years. In fact, excitement about the Internet's capabilities arguably waned too much in too short a time and really good opportunities started being missed.

We have now entered a more rational period for Internet expectations that will probably last for a couple of years. The Internet always offered another strong channel for computer services. This fact took a backseat to the unfounded Internet expectations for a time, but the rationality has resurfaced. Knowing how to leverage the Internet properly is not an easy task and involves cooperation from a myriad of stakeholders, including end-user organizations, individuals, and the Internet suppliers themselves. This new period of adjusted and more realistic expectations of the Internet is expected to see a lot more cooperation between these more "humble" players.

In the new period, the Internet is experiencing several trends as discussed in the chapters contained in this section. This includes business-to-business solutions such as cooperative marketplaces, enterprise integration (which includes removing islands of technology by using messages between internal business applications), and application service providers to reduce overall support costs and to manage risk. There is also a lot of interest in finding the next killer application, something that can be as far-reaching as e-mail.

"Turning E-Business Barriers into Strengths" explains how organizations can overcome internal and external inhibitors that are stopping them from fully leveraging innovations on the Internet. This chapter shows how organizations can overcome common barriers on the Internet.

"The Superhighway: Information Infrastructure Initiatives" examines how organizations can join the information infrastructure that offers global access and interoperability. This vision requires an infrastructure that integrates communications, computer, and entertainment technology which, in turn, requires cooperation of different bodies worldwide.

"Application Service Providers: A 'New' CIO Option" details the advantages that organizations can achieve by looking outside their corporate boundaries. Although application service providers (ASPs) are not for everyone, they provide an innovative solution for some.

"The Management Service Provider Option" (MSP) shows how organizations can leverage subscription-based external services that manage infrastructure resources and applications. They employ some of the basic principles of application service providers. The key is to reduce the overall cost of ownership or to leverage outside capital to meet required service levels.

"K-Commerce" examines the synergy between E-commerce and knowledge management. This includes linking transactions that are external to an organization, along with internal corporate initiatives to provide a better foundation of information.

# Chapter 1
# Turning E-Business Barriers into Strengths

*Dave Schuette*

DESPITE ALL THE POSITIVE STORIES ABOUT THE INTERNET, BUSINESS HAS A LONG WAY TO GO BEFORE IT CAN REAP ITS FULL BENEFITS. A variety of internal and external inhibitors are preventing many companies from keeping up with the pace of innovation on the Internet. As mobile commerce and other emerging technologies are used to conduct business on the Internet in the future, companies will be forced to embrace them quickly, or succumb to their more techno-savvy, and often younger and smaller competitors. The key to success in the emerging economy will involve identifying and strategically turning organizational barriers to E-business into strengths.

The simple fact is that E-business is becoming the way people conduct business, just as industrialization, electricity, the telephone, and a multitude of other inventions have transformed commerce. By the end of this decade, the terms "E-commerce" and "E-business" will fade into the history books as virtually all companies use computers, the Internet, and Internet-related technologies not only to sell their products, but also to manage their intellectual capital and business processes.

Business will never be the same. By as early as 2005, 25 percent of consumer spending and 70 percent of business-to-business commerce will involve the Internet, according to the Gartner Group.

No one knows for sure exactly how the Internet and E-business will change commerce, yet many pundits are beginning to paint pictures. In a series of articles in the *Harvard Business Review,* four observers offer their thoughts:

1. Harvard business professors Clayton Christensen and Richard Tedlow agree that E-commerce will change the basis of competitive

advantage in retailing, where the critical mission has always been getting the right product to the right place at the right time.

2. Nicholas Carr, a senior editor of the *Review*, takes issue with the widespread notion that the Internet will usher in an era of "disintermediation," in which producers of goods and services bypass wholesalers and retailers to connect directly with customers. Carr says that business is undergoing precisely the opposite phenomenon, which he calls "hypermediation." Transactions over the World Wide Web will routinely involve all sorts of intermediaries, who, Carr argues, are positioned to capture most of the profits.

3. Adrian Slywotzky, a vice president at Mercer Management Consulting, points out that the Internet will overturn the inefficient push model of supplier–customer interaction, and predicts that in all sorts of markets, customers will use choiceboards — interactive online systems that let people design their own products by choosing from a menu of attributes, prices, and delivery options. Companies will change the way they compete, as the customer is transformed from a passive recipient to an active designer.

No matter how one looks at it, virtually all the experts agree that the Internet is already transforming the way people conduct business. From retail Web sites to Internet-enabled systems for supply purchasing management, procurement, human resources, and knowledge management, many companies are in a frenzy to achieve the massive increases in productivity offered by Internet technologies. In fact, a study by the Internet Research Group and SRI Consulting in early 2000 estimated that U.S. companies spent $153 billion on building up their E-business infrastructure during 1999, and that by 2003, this total will rise to $348 billion.

Although that is a big number, it seems rather small when one considers that the nation spent an estimated $100 billion on remediating the Year 2000 bug alone. It is going to take a lot more investment. As Bill Laberis writes in *ComputerWorld*, "We've barely begun. Very few E-commerce systems have been built to date. Instead, by using the high-tech equivalent of spit and baling wire, IT architects have retrofitted legacy systems to accommodate applications they were never built to handle."

Unfortunately, the willingness to jump right in and invest and innovate at many organizations is hampered by a series of cultural, logistical, and technical issues. Increasingly, these issues are being identified. In reporting on a recent KPMG survey, *InternetWeek* notes that, "The message from survey participants was loud and clear: They are acutely aware of the need to execute a Web strategy to complement existing business models. But numerous forces undermine the effectiveness of those efforts." Clearly, these forces must be addressed from both internal and external perspectives before these firms can take full advantage of E-business efficiencies.

## THE CULTURAL STUMBLING BLOCK

The advent of the Internet is forcing the business world to go though a massive, unprecedented exercise in managing change. Established companies in traditional industries are just beginning to grapple with the nature and magnitude of such changes. Today and into the future, a company's success requires challenging traditional assumptions about organization, communication, decision-making, operating style, and managerial behavior. By far, cultural issues represent the biggest E-business stumbling block that many organizations will continue to face — and often internal and external cultural barriers will be at odds with one another.

Internally, the organization may not be staffed and structured properly for the E-business transition. In our change-resistant society, many employees often fear that E-business will change their jobs. Conversely, others may want to jump on the exciting E-commerce bandwagon to work on some "cool Internet stuff," but at the expense of supporting underlying strategic systems that must continue to be maintained.

Clearly, many individuals lack a clear understanding of E-business and a vision for its potential in their organizations. Business managers frequently view E-business as just E-commerce, or the marketing and purchasing of goods over the Internet. They have yet to appreciate the efficiencies created by using the technology to manage business processes and knowledge acquisition, storage, and retrieval.

Even if they understand the full scope of E-business activities, they may have difficulty envisioning how they apply to their businesses. Take, for example, an executive at a pharmaceutical research group who only saw the Internet as a product delivery mechanism. It took a lot of time and energy to convince him that the Internet could be used to manage knowledge and ultimately speed up the introduction of new drugs to the marketplace. By creating an Internet-based repository of research information, the group enabled pharmaceutical companies to collaborate more quickly on research results, helping to shorten the research and development cycle. And, according to the rule of thumb in the research-intensive, heavily regulated drug business, a company can save approximately $1 million for each day it cuts off the cycle.

If management appreciates such benefits, their efforts to implement an E-business plan may be hampered by rank-and-file employee concerns over their own privacy, because the nature of E-business is collaboration, including information sharing and decision-making. Suddenly, employees' become obsessed with the Big Brother thought that "people can see what I am doing every day."

In some cases, rivalries between units may also make it difficult to innovate. This may especially be the case if the company creates an internal E-business start-up. Other units may resent the resources that the new venture is consuming, and the new venture may have trouble fitting into the stodgy corporate environment, and want to break loose.

A bad previous experience with new technology increases reluctance to change, or sometimes managers feel that they have too many other problems to solve before tackling the Internet. Conversely, past successes can also create a cultural barrier. After all, why change a good thing that has been making money?

Getting over these internal cultural barriers will not be easy. It requires a top-down commitment to change management. Line managers and the rank-and-file will not appreciate the strategic importance of the Internet unless they see senior management leading the effort, and practicing what they preach.

Companies that try to force the issue with employees should be prepared for rapid turnover. Instead, these companies can define current and future business models, educating their workers on how the Web can empower them, and illustrating that they can control E-business processes.

## THE EXTERNAL PERSPECTIVE

A major external inhibitor for many companies is how the Internet will change the company's business model, and affect relationships with customers and sales intermediaries. The perception that a company intends to sell directly to end users and cut out the middlemen — whether they are retailers, manufacturers' reps, distributors, or agents — can present serious financial consequences. This is particularly true in such highly competitive industries as insurance, in which independent agents tend to represent several different insurers. If independent insurance agents believe that one company is beginning to cut them out of the loop, they will take their business to its competitors. Likewise, retailers who believe they are now competing against manufacturers will no longer want to carry their products.

Furthermore, cutting out the middleman and selling the product on the Web, with its vast repository of information and tools to conduct searches, encourages price comparisons and the commoditization of products. When prices increase, consumers can easily gravitate toward similar, more competitive products. Innovative concepts such as Priceline.com also turn traditional purchasing upside-down by empowering consumers to set prices they are willing to pay for a product, without regard to brand.

There are several solutions to such external cultural inhibitors. First, it is important for a company to establish a strong digital brand to attract individual and business consumers to a Web site, and to distinguish itself and its products from others.

In many other cases, companies can partner with intermediaries to offer products over the Internet. This concept will be increasingly embraced in the future, as customers view intermediaries as "purchasing consultants."

Another way to avoid alienating the salesforce is to create some differentiation among products offered on a retail and direct basis. Compaq, for example, sells PCs on its own Web site as well as via the telephone. But the models it offers are custom-built, primarily for the more sophisticated computer user who would not want to buy the off-the-shelf models available in retail stores.

## LOGISTICAL NIGHTMARES

After culture, logistical issues are the next major category of inhibitors to E-business development. These barriers can be found in four key areas: fulfillment, customer service, the global economy, and business process reengineering.

The existing fulfillment process may conflict with an E-business approach, and orders may not be fulfilled as advertised. No one needs to be reminded of numerous media reports of E-tailers failing to deliver on time during the 1998, 1999, and 2000 holiday seasons. Toys "R" Us was unable to fulfill some offers placed on its Web site before December 10, 1999, its deadline for Christmas delivery by standard mail. As a result, it dished out $100 coupons to disappointed Internet shoppers who did not get their gifts in time for the holiday.

If a company does not meet the expectation of customers by filling orders correctly and delivering items on time, customers will be turned off to using its Web site. That resentment may also spill over into the company's storefront operations.

In addition to facing consumers' wrath, companies will increasingly face class-action lawsuits along with scrutiny and penalties by regulators. In fact, the Federal Trade Commission has warned E-commerce companies that they appear to be in violation of its Mail Order Rule, which was created in 1975 to govern the performance of mail-order sales generated by direct mail, as well as telephone, fax, or computer. The rule states that mail-order companies must ship purchases within the time specified in their advertising, or, in the absence of a shipment date, within 30 days of receiving a properly completed order. It also requires companies to notify consumers if an order cannot be shipped on time, and to provide them with a new shipping date. The customer must then be given an opportunity to cancel the order, and receive a full refund if any payment has been made.

Fulfillment can also be a problem when the company is accustomed to shipping all its goods to retailers and business customers on palettes. Individual Web site sales may mean that it now has to ship individual items to multiple locations. And, in the case of certain products, which were shipped unassembled to distributors in the past, the company may now have to assemble the product before shipping. Or, if a customer purchases several products that are manufactured in more than one location, it will have the challenge of coordinating one delivery.

Similarly, because the company is dealing with many more customers, it will need to have a substantially larger trained customer service operation. As part of providing good customer service, companies will need to post ordering and merchandise return policies on their sites. Furthermore, they need to better coordinate returns between dot.com sites and the organization's bricks-and-mortar stores.

Outsourcing customer service and fulfillment obligations to a third party may provide a viable solution to these substantial E-business inhibitors. Package delivery and logistic companies have vast experience in running warehouses, and in filling orders for companies that do not want to handle those complicated tasks on their own. Recently, companies such as United Parcel Service have begun to invest heavily in operations that can run the entire back end of a company, ranging from plucking orders off a warehouse shelf to handling phone calls and returns from customers.

Furthermore, because the Web has no geographical boundaries, the site owner must be prepared to deal with orders not only from out of state, but perhaps from all over the world. On top of the shipping fulfillment and customer service issues, the company now has to deal with foreign currencies and related pricing issues. Conversely, do not expect a great reception if launching a site in such areas as Latin America, where antiquated back-office computer systems, inefficient distribution networks, and widespread credit-card fraud have kept many businesses from jumping online.

In many cases, the best alternative is to partner with companies in foreign markets that understand the local cultural and technical issues. In addition, these partners can handle local logistical issues, eliminating such problems as currency conversion.

Finally, there is the logistical challenge associated with reengineering business processes to dovetail with Internet activities. The company needs to determine if it should extend existing business processes, or completely rethink them. This can be a particularly difficult task when employees and customers resist, and need to be educated on changes.

Just consider what happened when various units at a telecommunications company rushed to put some 50 forms online for customers. Customers placed service orders using the form; but because they were not tied in with back-end systems, they were just spit out as paper on the receiving end.

Chaos can be avoided when a company takes a more holistic and planned approach to E-business projects. Before launching a new online activity, any strategy should be validated. Initially, a prototype should be built, and project leaders should get buy-in from management and consumers before they build it out, and then integrate it with other systems. Simply put, people need to feel and touch the product before they can trust it.

## TECHNICAL HURDLES

Obviously, without the technology and the technical talent, no company is going to get its E-business plan off the ground. And in this regard, companies often face considerable challenges. Large companies typically will have a more difficult and longer time implementing new technologies. This can put them at a substantial disadvantage compared to smaller, entrepreneurial firms that are operating at Internet speed. As previously discussed, many companies have chosen to solve this problem by turning their E-business operations into a separate entity.

To be effective, any E-business system must be integrated with legacy systems. Web site ordering must often be connected to the back-room mainframes involved with billing, inventory control, customer service, and other functions. Unfortunately, life cycles in the legacy world tend to be longer, and orchestrating systems integration is difficult. The solution involves developing separate Internet deliverable schedules, and then integrating them with the legacy life cycle.

Retooling to an E-business environment will likely require companies to staff up. That is no small challenge considering the demand for IT talent in an already tight job market. Staff shortages are further compounded by the fact that many organizations lack a central decision-maker for E-business. In fact, according to a KMPG survey, 75 percent percent of respondents did not have a central decision-maker. Many companies have multiple departments involved in E-business initiatives, all competing for talent and funding, and to be the leader.

Selecting the right tools is another formidable inhibitor. There are so many different tools to choose from, and providers update them constantly. Researching differences among applications and the company's existing expertise with them are a good way to solve the problem. This may also prove beneficial, particularly for smaller and mid-sized organizations, to partner with an applications service provider (ASP). For a monthly fee, the ASP will allow the company to test out an application before the company determines to purchase it. However, keep in mind that an ASP provides little scalability, and few legacy integration capabilities.

In addition to improving technical capabilities, site owners must continually update content, as well as look-and-feel. Users must be able to expediently navigate around a site and find the content they desire. And, especially in light of the recent denial-of-service attacks by hackers, organizations must employ state-of-the-art security measures. Users must feel secure enough to divulge information or perform a transaction. Company or property information must remain secure from external or other unauthorized access.

Finally, if business unit and IT managers are going to get the financial support for E-business initiatives, they must continue to convince management that E-business systems are worthwhile investments. The return on investment needs to be measured and communicated. It is important to consider how well a site is doing, how many orders are being processed, and how it can be improved.

These are steps necessary to build support and trust for E-business activities among management, rank-and-file employees, product distributors, and customers. Trust is fundamental — and it is perhaps the one challenge to E-commerce that cuts across all of the others. It is not easy to obtain.

The company must back E-business activities with a strong commitment, and technical and logistical management. Otherwise, it will all be a foolish investment that not only does not pay off, but costs the organization its credibility and competitive position.

Too many companies make minor mistakes that chip away at their credibility. A survey by a provider of error-detection and prevention tools, for example, revealed that Web sites are riddled with errors. The survey found an average of one link error per 3.5 pages, and more than 12 HTML errors per page. Such errors can be easily avoided.

Even when an organization tries hard to maintain trust, it must be prepared for the unknown. Take the experience of the head of an online loan site, who knew people would be wary of supplying their salaries, savings, and other financial information over the Internet. Encryption systems were employed so hackers could not intercept loan applications; more than $250,000 was spent for outside security audits; and consumers were assured that their privacy was the top concern. And, although the site was secure, little did the site owner know that his customers' confidence has been violated: an auto loan site his company purchased and linked to its site used cookies to track every visitor.

Clearly, surviving in the new E-business environment will not be simple. Just consider how many companies failed to meet the challenges brought on them by industrialization and electrification a century ago. Many could not grasp that these innovations were going to change the essential processes for manufacturing and selling products. They did not adapt; so they did not survive. But those companies that did adapt, grew into today's superpowers of industry.

# Chapter 2
# The Superhighway: Information Infrastructure Initiatives

*Keith G. Knightson*

MANY COUNTRIES AND ORGANIZATIONS HAVE DEVELOPED INITIATIVES AIMED AT ESTABLISHING AN ELECTRONIC HIGHWAY, SUCH AS THE NATIONAL INFORMATION INFRASTRUCTURE (NII) IN THE UNITED STATES AND THE EUROPEAN INFORMATION INFRASTRUCTURE (EII). To cover global aspects, a Global Information Infrastructure (GII) is being developed. The outcome of these initiatives depends on the changes taking place in the information and communications industries because of converging technologies, deregulation, and business restructuring or reorganization based on economic considerations. This chapter explores some of the possibilities and problems associated with information infrastructures.

## WHAT IS AN INFORMATION INFRASTRUCTURE?

The term *information infrastructure*, which is used interchangeably with the term *information superhighway* in this chapter, describes a collection of technologies that relate to the storage and transfer of electronic information, including voice, data, and images. It is often illustrated as a technology cloud with user devices attached, including broadband networks, the Internet, and high-definition TV.

However, problems emerge when users attempt to fit technologies together. For example, in the case of videophone service and on-demand video service, it is not clear if the same display screen technology can be used, or if a videophone call can be recorded on a locally available VCR. This example illustrates the need for consistency between similar technologies and functions.

### Relevance of the Information Infrastructure

The information infrastructure is important because it provides an opportunity to integrate technologies that have traditionally belonged to specific industry domains, such as telecommunications, computers, and entertainment. (Integration details are discussed later in this chapter.) The information infrastructure also presents an opportunity to greatly improve the sharing and transferring of information. New business opportunities abound that are related to the delivery of new and innovative services to users.

### Goals and Objectives of Information Infrastructures

The goals of most information infrastructures are to achieve universal access and global interoperability. Without corporate initiatives, the information infrastructure could result in conflicting and localized services, inefficient use of technology, or greater costs for fewer services. Some of the elements necessary to achieve such goals, including standards and open technical specifications that ensure fair competition and safeguard user interests, have yet to be adequately addressed.

### BACKGROUND: TECHNOLOGY TRENDS

Two factors are often cited as driving the technology boom: the increase in computer-processing power and the increase in the amount of available memory. Advances in these areas make a greater number of electronic services available for lower costs. This trend is expected to continue.

### Bandwidth Pricing Issues

Unfortunately, comparable gains of higher bandwidths and decreasing costs are not as evident in the communications arena. Whether this is because of the actual price of technology or because of pricing strategies is debatable. Many applications requiring relatively high bandwidths have yet to be tariffed.

On-demand video is an interesting test case for the pricing issue. To be attractive, this service would have to be priced to compete with the cost of renting a videotape. However, such a relatively low price for high bandwidth would make traditional low-bandwidth phone services seem extremely expensive by comparison. Asynchronous transfer mode (ATM)-based broadband Integrated Services Digital Network (B-ISDN) is likely to emerge as the vehicle for high-speed, real-time applications that require constant propagation delay.

The lack of higher bandwidths at inexpensive prices has inhibited the growth of certain applications that are in demand. The availability of inexpensive high bandwidth could revolutionize real-time, on-demand applications, not only in the video entertainment area but also in the electronic publishing area.

### Decoupling Networks and Their Payloads

One factor that is influencing the shape of the superhighway is the move toward digitization of information, particularly audio and video. Digitization represents a total decoupling between networks and their payloads.

Traditionally, networks have been designed for specific payloads, such as voice, video, or data. Digital networks may become general-purpose carriers of bit streams. In theory, any type of digital network can carry any type of information in digital format, such as voice, video, or computer data, thus banishing the tradition of carrying video on special-purpose cable TV networks and telephone service only over phone company networks. All forms of information are simply reduced to bit streams.

### The Service-Oriented Architecture

The separation of information services from bit-delivery services leads to the concept of a new service-oriented architecture as shown in Exhibit 1. The most striking aspect of this service-oriented architecture is that the control and management entity may be provided by either a separate service organization or a distributed set of cooperating entities from different service organizations. The architecture represents a move away from the current world of vertical integration toward one of horizontal integration.

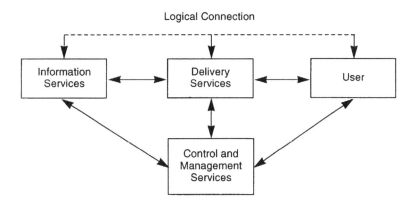

**Exhibit 1.   Service-Oriented Architecture**

Deregulation of communications also plays a part in this scenario. Deregulation often forces an unbundling of components and services, which creates a business environment ideally suited to a service-oriented architecture.

## KEY ISSUES IN CREATING THE SUPERHIGHWAY

Achieving a singular, seamless information highway is going to be a challenge, and whether users can influence development remains to be seen. Unless all interested parties act in harmony on the technical specifications (i.e., standards), market sharing, and partnering issues, the end user may be the biggest loser.

For provision of a given service (e.g., voice or data), it should not matter whether a user's access is through the telephone company, the cable company, or the satellite company. Similarly, it should not matter whether the remote party with whom a user wants to communicate has the same access method or a different one.

Several common elements exist in any end-to-end service. For example, there is a need for agreed-on access mechanisms, network platforms, addressing schemes, resolution of inter-provider requirements, and definition of universal services. The development of a generic framework would help to ensure that service requirements are developed equitably and to introduce innovative new services.

### The User's Role

Users are becoming more technology literate. The use of technology in the home in recent years has increased. Many users already benefit from what can be achieved through the convergence and integration of user-friendly technologies. User perspectives, rather than those of a single industry or company, should be thoroughly considered in the development of infrastructure initiatives.

### Government's Role

The private sector takes most of the risks and reaps most of the rewards for development of the information superhighway. However, government should assert some influence over the development of universally beneficial user services. The role of the government mainly involves

- Encouraging industry to collaborate and develop universally beneficial user services
- Mediating between competing industry factions
- Solving problems involving cultural content, cross-border and customs issues, protection of the individual, obscene or illegal material, and intellectual property and copyrights

### Industry's Role

Three dominant technology areas — telecommunications, computers and related communications, and the entertainment industry — are converging. Although there has already been some sharing of technology among industries, a single integrated system has not been created.

For example, many existing or planned implementations of videophone service invariably involve a special-purpose terminal with its own display screen and camera. For a home or office already equipped with screens and loudspeakers for use with multimedia-capable computers, the need for yet another imaging system with speakers is a waste of technology. Apart from the cost of duplication associated with industry separations, there is the problem of lack of flexibility. For example, if a VCR is connected to a regular TV, it should also be able to record videophone calls.

A plug-and-play solution may soon be possible in which the components are all parts of an integrated system. In such case, screens, speakers, recording devices, computers, and printers could be used in combination for a specific application. The components would be networked and addressed for the purpose of directing and exchanging information among them. Similar considerations apply to computing components and security systems. Using the videophone example, if the remote videophone user puts a document in front of the camera, the receiving party should be able to capture the image and print it on the laser printer.

Plug-and-play integration is not simple; yet, if the convergence is not addressed, the result will be disastrous for end users, who will be faced with a plethora of similar but incompatible equipment that still fails to satisfy their needs.

**The Dream Integration Scenario**

Exhibit 2 shows what the ideal configuration might look like when a high degree of convergence has been achieved. Ideally, there would be only one pipe into the customer's premises, over which all services — voice, video, and data — would be delivered. User appliances could be used interchangeably. In this scenario, videophone calls could be received on the home theater or personal computer and recorded on the VCR.

**The Nightmare Scenario**

Exhibit 3 shows what user networks might look like if convergence is not achieved. Customer premises would include many pipes. Some services would be available only on certain pipes and not others. The premises would have duplicate appliances for generating, displaying, and recording information. End-to-end services would be extremely difficult to achieve because all service providers would not choose to use the same local- or long-distance delivery services. In addition, all the local- and long-distance networks would not be fully interconnected.

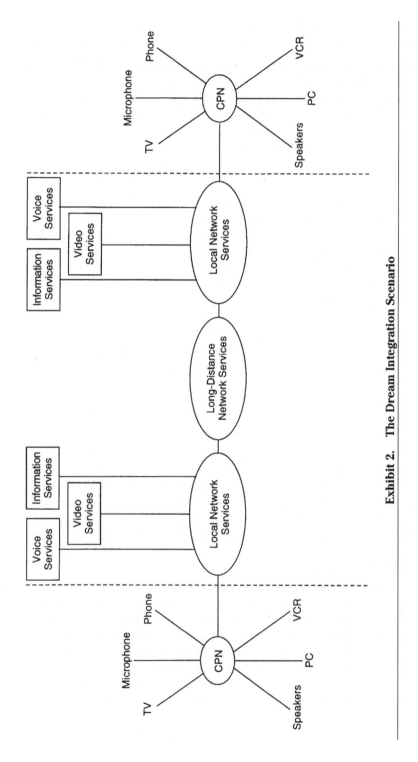

**Exhibit 2.   The Dream Integration Scenario**

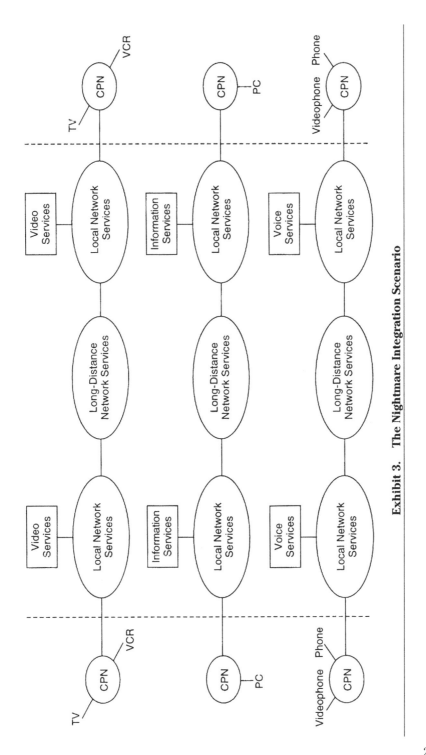

**Exhibit 3.  The Nightmare Integration Scenario**

Purveyors of technology and services may argue that this means they can all sell more of their particular offerings, which is good for business. Users, on the other hand, are more likely to feel cheated, because they are being forced to subscribe to different suppliers for slightly different services.

## Corporate Networks

Large corporations create networks that are based on their preferred supplier of technology. They are usually extremely conservative in their technology choices because many of their business operations depend totally on the corporate network.

Two factors are causing this traditional, conservative approach to be questioned:

- *The cost of maintaining private networks.* In many cases, several private networks operate within a single corporation, such as one for voice, one for IBM's Systems Network Architecture network, and one for a private internet using TCP/IP or Novell's Internetwork Packet eXchange. The change taking place is sometimes referred to as consolidation. Consolidation involves network sharing by operating the different systems protocols over the same physical network.
- *The need for global communications.* Corporations cannot afford to remain electronically isolated from their customers. As every business tackles cost cutting by increasing the use of information technology, the need for intercompany communication increases. Companies now need to communicate electronically with the banking industry, their suppliers, their customers, and the government to carry out their business.

## THE INTERNET AND B-ISDN

Many users consider the Internet the only true information highway. In many ways, this is true — the Internet is the only highway, at least in the sense that it is the only worldwide, seamless, and consistent end-to-end digital networking facility available. In addition, it has become a place where certain standardized applications can be used. It has a globally unique, centrally administered address space. The Internet provides national and international switched data services on a scale that would usually be associated with the major telecommunications carriers.

Not surprisingly, not everyone agrees that the Internet is the only highway. Technically, the Internet is a connectionless packet network overlaid on a variety of network technologies, such as leased lines, frame relay, ATM, and local area networks (LANs). However, it is difficult to imagine that at some point in the future, all voice and video traffic would be carried over such a network rather than directly over a B-ISDN.

Thus, there may be a battle between the Internet and the traditional telecommunications carriers for control of the primary switching of data. The carriers may try to establish B-ISDN as the primary method of switching data end to end, using telephone company–oriented number/addressing plans such as E.164.

The Internet community is interested in the use of broadband ISDN, primarily as a replacement for leased lines between Internet switching nodes (i.e., routers) where the real switching occurs. The deployment of broadband ISDN within the Internet may result in the migration of routers to the edges of the Internet, eliminating the need for intermediate routers. In any event, the interaction between the traditional router-based Internet style of operation and the emerging broadband ISDN switched services will be closely watched by corporate users.

The anarchic nature of the Internet will also be put to the test by commercial users who will want better service guarantees and accountability for maintenance and recovery. Despite these known deficiencies, the Internet remains the predominant information highway and it is difficult to imagine that it will lose its dominance in the near future.

## TELECOMMUNICATIONS AND CABLE TV

Deregulation in many countries now permits cable TV companies to offer services traditionally offered by the telephone companies. One of the scenarios under consideration in many countries is shown in Exhibit 4.

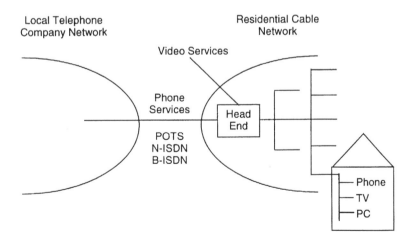

**Exhibit 4.   Telephone Company and Cable TV Network Interconnection**

The cable companies are just beginning to form plans on how new two-way services should be offered. Access to the telephone company network would also provide access to other services, such as the Internet.

A major issue is the kind of interface to be provided on the cable network for associated telephone apparatus. It is not clear whether a traditional phone could simply be plugged into the cable system. Other issues, such as numbering and access to 800 service, need to be resolved. Whether traditional modem, telephony, or ISDN interfaces could be used or whether new cable-specific interfaces would be developed is also under consideration. Both solutions could coexist through provision of appropriate conversion units.

Cable systems usually consist of a head end with a one-way subtending tree and branch structure. Whether the head end would provide local switching within the residential area has not been determined. Other topologies, such as rings, may be more appropriate for new services.

Conversely, deregulation also permits the telephone companies to offer services previously offered by the cable companies. In such a case, a video server would be accessed by the telephone company network, probably using broadband ISDN and ATM technology, as shown in Exhibit 5.

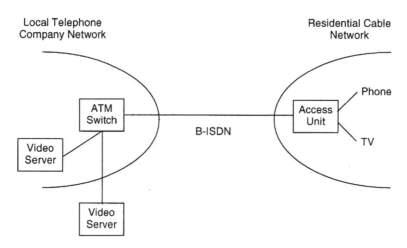

**Exhibit 5.   Telephone Company-Provided Video Services**

## COMPUTER-INTEGRATED TELEPHONY

Computing and telecommunications are coming together in several ways. Computers can now be attached to telecommunications lines to become sophisticated answering machines, autodialers, and fax machines.

The availability of calling and called-line identification permits databases to be associated with telephone calls. For example, calling line identification can be used to automatically extract the appropriate customer record from a database so that when the call is answered the appropriate customer information becomes available on a screen.

Computer-integrated telephony allows a variety of telephone service features to be controlled by the customer's computers. Intelligent network architectures that facilitate the separation of management and control are ideally suited to external computer control.

Public switched data networks have not been very efficient because of the costs of building separate networks and because the scale and demand for data proved nothing like that for voice services. A single digital network, such as narrowband Integrated Services Digital Network (N-ISDN) or broadband ISDN, changes the picture significantly when coupled with the new demand for digital services.

## COMPUTING AND ENTERTAINMENT

Most personal computers on the market have audiovisual capabilities. Movies and audio clips can be combined with text for a variety of multimedia applications. Video or images can be edited as easily as text.

With the advent of high-definition TV and digital encoding of TV signals, it is easy to imagine a system in which the traditional TV screen and the PC monitor would be interchangeable. Computers are already being used to produce movies and as a playback medium, even providing the possibility of real-time interaction with the users.

Integrating all the appliances into a single architecture is the difficult part. Home theater systems provide simple forms of switching between components, for example, video to TV or VCR, or audio from TV to remote speakers. Soon, no doubt, the personal computer will be part of this system.

## NATIONAL AND INTERNATIONAL INITIATIVES

Many countries have prepared recommendations for their respective National Information Infrastructure (NII), including the United States, Canada, Europe, Japan, Korea, and Australia, among others. The major differences in each country's initiatives seem to revolve around the extent government will fund and regulate the information infrastructure.

### The United States

The Information Infrastructure Task Force (IITF) launched the NII initiative in early 1993. The IITF is composed of an advisory council and committees on security, information policy, telecommunications policy, applications, and technology. Government funding is being made available for the development of NII applications.

The IITF's goal is that the information infrastructure become a seamless web of communications networks, computers, databases, and consumer electronics. The NII initiative is also closely associated with the passage of a new communications act, which outlines principles for the involvement of the government in the communications industry. According to the communications act, the government should

- Promote private sector investment.
- Extend the universal service concept to ensure that information resources are available at affordable prices.
- Promote technological innovation and new applications.
- Promote seamless, interactive, user-driven operation.
- Ensure information security and reliability.
- Improve management of the radio frequency spectrum.
- Protect intellectual property rights.
- Coordinate with other levels of government and with other nations
- Provide access to government information and improve government procurement

**International Initiatives**

The G7 countries (Britain, Canada, France, Germany, Italy, Japan, and the United States) are considering developing an information infrastructure that would offer, among others, the following services:

- Global inventory
- Global interoperability for broadband networks
- Cross-cultural education and training
- Electronic museums and galleries
- Environment and natural resources management
- Global emergency management
- Global health care applications
- Government services online
- Maritime information systems

## STANDARDS AND STANDARDS ORGANIZATIONS

It is difficult to imagine how objectives such as universal access, universal service, and global interoperability can be achieved without an agreed-on set of standards. However, some sectors of industry prefer that fewer standards be established because this gives them the opportunity to capture a share of the market with proprietary solutions. Regardless, several national and international standards development organizations (SDOs) throughout the world are initiating activities related to the information infrastructure.

## ISO AND ITU

Both the International Standards Organization (ISO) and the International Telecommunications Union (ITU — formerly the International Telegraph and Telephone Consultative Committee) are embarking on information infrastructure standards initiatives. The ISO and ITU have planned a joint workshop to address standards issues.

### American National Standards Institute Information Infrastructure Standards Panel (ANSI IISP)

The ANSI IISP goals are to identify the requirements for standardization of critical interfaces (i.e., connection points) and other attributes and compare them with national and international standards already in place. Where standards gaps exist, SDOs will be asked to develop new standards or update existing standards as required.

ANSI IISP is developing a database to make standards information publicly available. The process of identification and the structure of the IISP are illustrated in Exhibit 6. In its deliberations, the ANSI IISP has been reluctant

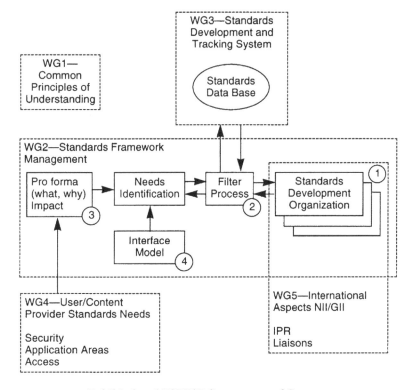

**Exhibit 6.   ANSI IISP Structure and Process**

to identify specific networking architectures or interconnection arrangements and appears to be confining its efforts to a cataloguing process.

### Telecommunications Standards Advisory Council of Canada (TSACC)

The TSACC is an umbrella organization for all the standards organizations in Canada. It is a forum where all parties can meet to discuss strategic issues. The objectives of TSACC, with respect to the Canadian Information Infrastructure and the Global Information Infrastructure (GII), are similar to those of the ANSI IISP. However, TSACC considers the identification of specific networking architectures and associated specific access and interconnection points essential to achieving the goals of universal access, universal service, and interoperability.

### European Telecommunications Standards Institute (ETSI)

The Sixth Review Committee (SRC6) of ETSI published a report on the European Information Infrastructure (EII) that emphasizes the standardization of the EII. Many of the recommendations in the report concern the development of reference models for defining the particular services and identifying important standards-based interface points. B-ISDN is recommended as the core technology for the EII.

### The Digital Audiovisual Council (DAVIC)

DAVIC was established in Switzerland to promote emerging digital audiovisual applications and services for broadcast and interactive use. DAVIC, which has a very pro-consumer slant, believes that these services will be affordable only through sufficient standardization. The council has formed technical committees in the following five areas:

- Set-top units
- Video servers
- Networks
- Systems and applications
- General technology

DAVIC may be the only forum in which home convergence issues can be solved.

### ALTERNATIVE INITIATIVES

Following are two interesting U.S.-based information infrastructure initiatives.

### EIA/TIA

The Electronic Industries Association (EIA) and its affiliate, Telecommunications Industry Association (TIA), have just released version 2 of their white paper titled "Global Information Infrastructure: Principles and Promise." The basic principles conclude that

- The private sector must play the lead role in development
- Enlightened regulation is essential
- The role of global standards is critical
- Universal service and access must support competitive, market-driven solutions
- Security and privacy are essential
- Intellectual property rights must support new technologies

### The Computer Systems Policy Project (CSPP)

The CSPP is not a standards organization but an affiliation of the chief executive officers of several American computer companies. The CSPP has published a document titled "Perspectives on the National Information Infrastructure: Ensuring Interoperability." The CSPP document identifies the following four key points-of-presence as candidates for standardization:

- The interface between an information appliance and a network service provider
- The applications programming interface between an information appliance and emerging NII applications
- The protocols that one NII application, service, or system uses to communicate with another application, service, or system
- The interfaces among and between network service providers

### CONCLUSION

The technical challenges of creating a GII are not insurmountable. The main difficulties arise from industries competing for the same business rather than sharing an expanding business, and from the lack of agreement on necessary open standards to achieve universal access and global interoperability that would expand the total business.

Interoperability requires agreed-on network architectures and the associated standards that could, in some cases, stifle innovation. A balance must also be struck between government regulation and private sector control over GII development. However, if each camp can cooperate, it is possible that in the future the communications, information, and entertainment industries could merge technology to provide plug-and-play components integrated into a single, coherent system that offers exciting new services that exist now in only the wildest imaginations.

# Chapter 3

# Application Service Providers: A "New" CIO Option

*Leilani Allen*

For those who have been in the technology field for some time, the phrase "everything old is new again" is particularly meaningful nowadays. One of the current hot concepts for managing information resources is that of the ASP (application service provider). This notion hearkens back, literally, to the early 1970s, when it was known as "time-sharing." In those days, computers were expensive and the expertise required to program and maintain them was scarce. Also, companies were not as dependent on computers as they are today. They might only need the computer to run month-end payrolls or inventory reports. So, rather than purchase an entire configuration, they purchased part of one. Much like the borrower who does not need a vacation home at the beach all year-round, but rather for two weeks in July, and decides on a time-share, so too could companies purchase just the computer power they needed when they needed it.

The time-share concept eventually diminished as computers dropped in price, and, especially, as companies went from batch to online processing. Once most of the users were accessing the computers during most of the day, it did become cost-effective to have one's own data center with one's own computer staff. That was the heyday of mainframe computing, as companies built proprietary applications designed for their specific needs.

Along came client/server, which helped decentralize computing and, in many cases, turned over the development of software and the management of computer hardware to the business units. Instead of a $20 million mainframe, a department could now buy a minicomputer or server, for prices that easily fit into its budget. Everyone was gung-ho to create the latest and greatest client/server applications.

So what about the mainframe applications? Over time, a majority of industries had standardized on a couple of operating system/subsystem choices, with IBM's MVS/ESA and CICS being the leading combination. Once this was accomplished, the care and feeding of the operating environment became largely generic. This meant that knowledge of the particular business was presumably no longer essential.

Thus began the era of *outsourcing* — when companies large and small outsourced their data center and their core applications to companies such as IBM, EDS, CSC, and a host of system integrators. Outsourcing was particularly welcome in the 1980s, when organizations sought to become "lean and mean," and eliminate all "unnecessary" headcount. How much easier it was to turn over the whole responsibility to someone else.

Outsourcing took at least three forms. The first model was to outsource all of information technology (IT) — network, hardware, and software development — keeping only a skeleton staff to manage the contract with the vendor and do strategic technology analysis. The most common approach was to outsource the first two components but keep software development in-house, and thus more responsive to the particular business. A third approach was to turn to outsourcers (service bureaus) for specific applications such as accounting or payroll.

As usual, no technology solution is completely satisfactory. Companies soon found that the outsourcers often underbid the contract for the first one or two years of operation, but that, over time, the cost exceeded the original in-house installation. Also, many employees who really knew the applications were lost in the shuffle, making maintenance and enhancement a real challenge. Indeed, one of the reasons that the cost for year 2000 (Y2K) remediation was so large was that so many people who had built the applications in the first place were no longer available.

Unfortunately, one of the downsides of outsourcing for the technology industry was that innovation in mainframe technology largely disappeared. The last thing an outsourcer wants is new and different technology to which to migrate its clients.

Thus, outsourcing gave an indirect boost to client/server technology. Firms found that, with their core production (legacy) applications safely in the hands of outsourcers, the remaining IT staff was free to focus on strategic systems that utilized the newest technology. A lot of innovation occurred at the level of departmental applications. True, with innovation came a lot of failures that gave client/server a bad reputation for a while. As time went by, however, the client/server architectures became more stable and reliable, and IT became more skilled and knowledgeable in this technology as well.

So today, there is a whole new layer of mission-critical production systems that are now built on client/server technology. They are often very complex, involving multiple servers and network connections. They are usually built upon databases that require special expertise to design and maintain. And, as before, there has been a good deal of standardization in the languages and tools used to create these systems.

This is another opportunity to outsource. Oracle Corporation President Larry Ellison has declared his firm to be the world's largest and fastest-growing ASP. He says, "The software industry is in the process of a huge change, a tectonic change. Software is on its way to becoming a service." And software companies are becoming service providers.

## DEFINITION OF AN ASP

An ASP can be defined as a firm that "implements and provides ongoing support of application software for customers on one or more computer platforms and networks." The term ASP was supposedly coined by International Data Corp. of Framingham, Massachusetts, in 1998 in a study on the future of outsourcing. By May 1999, 25 companies had joined a newly formed ASP Industry Consortium. By November, 178 companies had joined. At the Consortium's first conference in Denver, Colorado, almost all of the technology industry heavyweights spoke in favor of the concept.

For example, Compaq and Cable and Wireless (a U.K.-based telecommunications firm) announced a global network of data centers that would host applications, and provide help desk services, systems integration, and market strategy. On the software side, Microsoft unveiled Office Online to deliver its popular suite of productivity products to users across an Internet connection. Corel already rents WordPerfect for $9.95 per user per month, while Sun Microsystems began giving away its StarOffice suite last year. Indeed, Gene Banman, a Sun executive, says, "Hosted application services will replace boxed software sales altogether in the next decade."

Hardware vendors are equally enthusiastic. IBM is repositioning its venerable AS/400 minicomputer as an ASP platform. Hewlett-Packard and KPMG are working to build CyberCenters to host data warehouses. Novell, Inc., recently acquired Just-On, Inc., a Web-based file management business. PC maker Acer, Inc., in Taiwan is partnering with software giant Computer Associates in Islandia, New York, to offer ASP services. Cisco Systems and Sun Microsystems are developing standards and practices guidelines for ASPs, including a certification program.

The latter point is particularly important. Just as there were no strict rules about the services that an outsourcer once offered, there is no strict definition of an ASP. Many firms do not yet have documented contracts in place, and have not really worked through their economic model. Services, performance, and availability of applications are also fairly restrictive.

There are at least three models of ASPs, in descending order of popularity:

1. Internet Service Providers (ISPs) provide access to individuals and firms for Internet services. ISPs vary widely in terms of services provided, but most are still confined to hosting Web sites and providing e-mail capabilities. Market researcher Input in Mountain View, California, expects Internet management outsourcing to grow 76 percent annually between 1998 and 2003.
2. An emerging group of companies are what this author refers to as Bundled Service Providers (BSPs), essentially service bureaus hosting a handful of interrelated applications. The most popular are enterprise resource planning (ERP) systems from such firms as SAP, PeopleSoft, or Baan; or customer relationship management (CRM) systems that bind together telephone, computing, and Internet technologies to support telemarketing sales and service centers.
3. Finally, there is the Proprietary Service Provider (PSP), usually a software firm that will make its software available on a shared basis. Instead of paying for the software outright and running it on their own computers, customers contract with the PSP to connect to the vendor's architecture. PSPs vary widely on the ancillary services available to customers.

## WHY ASP?

There are already a number of ASP success stories from firms as varied as Monsanto, Volvo, Fleetwood Retail, Robert Mondavi Winery, and Barnes & Noble. Cynthia Morgan, writing in *Computerworld*, finds that ASPs make sense for larger firms when:

1. The application requires expertise lacking in the existing IT staff
2. IT has more pressing projects
3. A neutral party is needed to merge and centralize services
4. An application needs extremely rapid deployment
5. Users will be widely scattered, often with only a handful at a particular site
6. Users are outside the firewall

Almost all experts agree that the ASP solution is primarily for smaller companies that want to use a world-class application but cannot afford the up-front costs of acquisition, or the ongoing personnel burden of maintenance. Because they are most susceptible to swings in market conditions, smaller companies like the fact that ASPs usually charge on a variable price basis. If volume diminishes, the monthly bill declines, although the actual cost per transaction (or loan) may increase because volume discounts no longer apply.

Not surprisingly, the cost-effectiveness of ASPs is similar to that of any leasing arrangement. The longer one expects to keep a given vehicle, the less it makes sense to lease, because the cost of ownership can be amortized over a longer period of time. On the other hand, in the world of technology, long-term relationships are not the norm, and a firm can expect to change its technology every three to five years.

Continuing with the car analogy, leasing a car requires the dealer to be responsible for maintenance and repairs, recalls, and model obsolescence. Similarly, it is the ASP that must worry about system maintenance and performance, capacity, and technology obsolescence. The ASP must contend with vendors, dealing with bugs and sweating through the installation of new releases and issues of system compatibility.

Most importantly, the ASP must worry about recruiting and retaining knowledgeable staff. At the moment, there are an estimated 300,000 technology jobs going begging. Even small firms are finding that the cost of IT professionals is beyond their means, with a typical programmer/analyst earning as much as senior managers in the business units, and specialists such as database administrators or Web masters earning the same as executive vice presidents. It is almost impossible for many firms today to find these people, provide sufficient technical challenges and financial incentives to keep them, and have appropriate management to make sure they are doing the right things. Thus, ASPs are an attractive alternative.

Another factor fueling ASPs is the fact that implementation times can be a lot quicker. The organization need not build an infrastructure to handle the application; the infrastructure is already in place. A firm's representatives can visit the service bureau, see the servers and network configurations already in place, presumably happily serving other customers. More and more, ASPs are also providing an electronic commerce (E-commerce) infrastructure for companies that want a fast path to Internet viability.

The argument in favor of ASPs is neatly summed up by Craig Kinyon, CFO for Reid Hospital and Health Care Services, Inc., of Richmond, Indiana: "The ASP model takes care of what I call the 'Tylenol factors' of applications — the maintenance, support, upgrades, and hardware. And we don't have to find and pay for staff to handle the applications." (*Information-Week*, February 21, 2000)

## A CASE EXAMPLE

A small mortgage company (less than 300 employees) has offered government (FHA/VA) and conventional (Fannie Mae/Freddie Mac) loans primarily to first-time homebuyers in the northeastern United States. Its loan origination and servicing technology was written by a third-party provider to run on a DEC platform. Two or three staff members were hired to work with the third party to run the hardware and maintain the software.

Mortgage lending is an industry where there are a great number of regulatory changes — not exciting work, but necessary. The IT staffers who were brought on board quickly became bored and left. Maintenance of the hardware was outsourced to a contractor; maintenance of the software largely ceased because it was too difficult to find the right technical skill set. The third-party provider (essentially a one-man shop) moved on.

To compound matters, this is a period when mortgage lenders are fundamentally reexamining their processes and approach to the marketplace, wishing to include such facilities as workflow and Internet lending. To stay competitive, the firm must update its technology. Needless to say, the existing platform will not accommodate such profound enhancements.

The firm evaluated third-party mortgage lending packages and found three that had the functionality it desired. All the packages used relational database technology and ran on NT servers. However, there would still be some customization required. So, once again, the firm was confronted with the task: Who would customize and maintain the software on a go-forward basis? Where would the firm get the NT expertise to run the hardware?

One of the software firms raised the concept of an ASP. It offered to customize the software and maintain it, as well as operate the hardware (the database server from its own data center, and the application server on site). In addition, the vendor could provide database, help desk, security, and disaster recovery services. The cost? A setup charge, as well as a fee per user per month.

To the mortgage lender, it seemed an attractive alternative. The firm would overcome its personnel problem by having the vendor's staff perform the work. Recruiting, training, management, and retention would all be someone else's problem. The vendor would be responsible for regulatory and other software modifications, as well as keeping abreast of technology changes.

The executives liked the idea that they would not have to pay the full cost of the hardware and software up front (approximately $1 million), but rather could "lease" the technology on a pay-as-you-go basis. This is especially important in a highly cyclical industry such as mortgage, where interest rate fluctuations bring feast or famine volumes. Assuming that the number of users generally reflects the volume of work, the firm could translate its technology cost from fixed (if it owned the technology) to variable.

Not everyone was pleased with the proposal. Some of the managers were concerned about not having on-site support. They also did not like the fact that the firm would not own the software, but merely lease it. The hardware contractor began a campaign of denigrating the supposed reliability and performance of NT.

Moreover, the vendor's sales representative was only lukewarm to the concept. Part of this was lack of familiarity; part of it was the impact on their wallet. After all, salespeople are traditionally paid commission based on the value of the signed contract. In an ASP mode, the total amount of the sale is unknown; commission would be calculated on an amount to be paid out over time based on usage. Not as attractive a proposition. This is a factor that software-companies-cum-ASPs will have to consider.

Thus, a firm that would appear to be an ideal candidate for an ASP still has hesitations about whether the model will work. And the vendor still has some homework to do on selling its own people.

## THE FUTURE

Will every technology company become an ASP, or call itself one? Probably, for a while. However, a number of software firms will undoubtedly find that running reliable "data (cyber) centers" is more difficult than imagined. For one thing, the ASP concept calls on a different set of expertise than what they have used to develop whiz-bang applications. Many of today's current software developers have little understanding of, or appreciation for, such issues as performance analysis, tuning, and capacity planning. In the past, if the application grew too big or obstreperous, the solution was simple — buy a bigger box. To maintain profitability, ASPs will not be able to simply resort to this practice. They will need to have a rigorous program of configuration management that is constantly evaluating and improving the reliability and performance of their hardware and networks.

And, as recent experience has shown, the software firms-come-ASPs will have to take the same rigorous approach to security management that was the norm for the big outsourcers, with multiple layers of security and disaster recovery. After all, an individual firm's computer center was not much of a target for hackers; however, an ASP handling business for dozens or hundreds of firms is far more inviting. Indeed, a *Computerworld* poll found that 96 percent of respondents had concerns about security. On the other hand, an ASP is more likely to have access to security experts than a typical small company.

Also, as anyone who has ever endured the torture of calling a software provider's customer support line knows, these firms have a dismal record in post-market support. Staffing a competent help desk is no easy task, but will be mandatory for a successful offering as an ASP. The firms are hosting mission-critical applications, and users will need quick and accurate answers. Yet finding the source of a problem will prove very difficult for those ASPs who try to integrate software from several different vendors.

Another key problem for an ASP firm is finding the appropriate price model. For example, CenterBeam, Inc., in Santa Clara, California, is offering a Lucent Technologies-based network, a PC running Windows 2000 and Microsoft Office applications, a wireless LAN service, a public Web site, a company intranet, high-speed DSL Internet access, daily data backup, and 24×7 technical support for less than $200 per user. BSP firms will have higher prices than this because of the database and storage costs for high-end applications.

Dataquest in Redwood City, California predicts a $22 billion ASP market by 2003.

## EVALUATING ASPs

Not every ASP will be successful. How does one know if one is dealing with the right firm? Generally speaking, it is better to deal with an ASP that offers a focused group of applications. This will be a learning experience; and the greater the number of variables, the greater the chances of failure. It is important to find an ASP that has developed the offering as part of a natural evolution of its product or industry, rather than one that is just a case of "me too." The range of issues to consider is lengthy, but a preliminary list includes:

- Expertise. Just what are the provider's qualifications? Has it built infrastructures before, or is it simply a software developer? Has it run a 24×7 operation? What is its motivation in doing this? How does it expect to make money? Will the provider be in it over the long haul? Obviously, the greater the expertise, the better. Also, the financial expectations should be realistic and should include an honest assessment of the costs. And it is essential that the provider has an understanding of system performance and capacity planning.
- Service. When is the system available? What response time is guaranteed? What happens if service degrades? What happens if there is a system failure? The more competent the ASP, the more guarantees of service it will offer, and the more likely it will be to offer compensation for its errors.
- Help desk. How are people trained on the help desk? What questions do they handle — technical only or application specific? What is the allowable wait time for a response? Is the response received over the phone or via e-mail? What hours does the help desk work? What happens after hours? The help desk will be the only real contact most of a client's users have with the ASP, so support must be of the highest possible caliber.
- Security. How is this handled? Will your auditor be comfortable? What happens in the event of a security breech, and who is accountable for damages?

- Special services. Does the ASP provide database administration, disaster recovery planning/testing, project management? Is some of this built into the standard contract, or is each service separate? The former method is preferred. Otherwise, one gets the "nickel-and-dime" effect.
- Licensing. Who pays, and on what basis? Can software be made "rent to own"? If the intention is to utilize the ASP for less than three years, then negotiating to own the licenses at the end of the contract is important.
- Scalability. Can the infrastructure grow to handle your needs? Who decides when upgrades are necessary, and how is payment handled? This is especially important if a number of clients are sharing a configuration.
- Software maintenance/enhancement (especially for BSPs). How are new releases handled? What if one does not want to move to the new release? How does one request enhancements, and who gets a vote on setting priorities? How are enhancements tested? It is important that the ASP have a rigorous system life-cycle methodology, and a careful method of deciding which enhancements will be part of the standard release, and which are truly custom. Otherwise, the costs can be prohibitive.
- Pricing. Is the charge per user or per transaction, and how is the transaction defined? For example, for the mortgage lender, is the charge per user, per loan application, or per closed loan? The cost models of each industry will differ. And the ASP should provide guidance in helping the client get the most bang for the buck.
- Implementation. What is the process for getting up and running? What does the provider do? What does the client do? Is there a sample contract? Is there a significant choice of offerings, and the ability to negotiate a customized deal? Flexibility is good, but beware the ASP that claims to provide all things to all people. Part of the deal in sharing a resource is learning to live with limitations; both the client and the ASP have to understand this. And that will be the most difficult lesson of all.
- Administration. How is billing done? One may wish to pay on a quarterly or monthly basis. Can the provider accommodate this? One should ask to see a variety of performance reports each month: availability, response time, help desk call resolution times, etc. The ASP should have a mechanism in place to routinely survey its customers, and it should be willing to share the results of internal audits. There should be a user group or advisory council in place where customers can routinely influence the ASP's direction. The more willing the ASP is to shine a light on its own operation, the more confident one can feel in its capabilities.

- Termination. There is no point in maintaining a relationship if one partner is unhappy. As much as the ASP will want to lock one in for the long term, there should be a relatively painless and graceful way of terminating the contract if expectations are not met. Look for provisions that provide reasonable notice (no more than 90 days) and reasonable penalties (no more than the equivalent of six months' lost revenue, but try for something even better).

## CONCLUSION

ASPs offer clear advantages to firms large and small that are contending with the problem of too many initiatives and too little talent. ASPs offer an efficient way to utilize hardware, software, network, and human resources. However, a shared platform often results in catering to the lowest common denominator. Therefore, the more different or innovative a firm wants to be, the less likely it will be comfortable with the ASP as a long-term solution.

The best advice? Perform due diligence with particular care, and find a vendor that has good solid business reasons for being an ASP, as well as a plan that makes it a long-term player. If one decides to take the plunge, take advantage of being an early customer by ensuring that one has a voice in how the ASP is run, and how it develops its products, prices, and services over time. And monitor, monitor, monitor the ASP's performance — not only in the reports it provides, but by surveying one's users. Remember that — outsourced or insourced — to your business peers, technology is still your responsibility.

# Chapter 4
# The Management Service Provider Option

*Janet Butler*

CONVENTIONAL WISDOM WARNS COMPANIES AGAINST OUTSOURCING THEIR CORE COMPETENCIES AND, AT ONE TIME, MANAGEMENT FELL INTO THIS CATEGORY. Now, however, especially with the rise of E-business, organizations require exceptional management to survive. Because this is not always available in-house, management service providers (MSP) are springing up to fill the need.

MSPs are an emerging type of vendor that lets customers outsource various aspects of information technology (IT) management. If an MSP can guarantee that an organization's network or applications will remain up and running, and downtime will be nearly or completely eliminated, an organization should seriously consider this option.

MSPs appeal, in particular, to small and mid-sized companies, as well as E-businesses, as an alternative to the expense of building their own management systems. While these businesses might require 24×7 availability, they do not have the resources to ensure this uptime by doing their own management. However, an MSP can do so, notifying the customer of potential problems or slowdowns.

In fact, some analysts predict that 50 to 70 percent of organizations will use a service provider to assist in building or hosting their E-commerce applications. In-house management costs are steep, and include management platforms and point products; management integration tools such as a central console; and staff to install, configure, test, and maintain systems. Businesses must also gauge the cost of downtime.

The cost savings attributed to MSPs can be substantial. Companies save not only the hefty price of the software itself, but the cost of internally hosting management software, which is estimated at three to nine times the cost of the software, plus ongoing staff costs.

Still, in turning to MSPs, IT managers give up some control and visibility into their infrastructure. Also, because the services might lack the functionality of traditional management platforms, flexibility is an issue; it becomes difficult to add new technologies and systems to the IT infrastructure. Therefore, if IT is critical to the organization, such as in the financial services and telecommunications industries, companies might want to retain management control.

According to one analyst, there are approximately 70 vendors in the management service provider category. These include Manage.com, Luminate.net, SilverBack Technologies, NetSolve, Envive Corp., Freshware, StrataSource, and SiteLine.

Major management solution providers are also beginning to offer MSP services, including Computer Associates and Hewlett-Packard; the latter has a new HP OpenView service provider unit. Some vendors such as TriActive are changing their marketing message from application service provider (ASP) to MSP. And other management software vendors, such as BMC, are forging alliances with MSPs, and buying companies with point products.

## MSP BENEFITS

MSP drivers include the shortage of skilled professionals, the increasing complexity of network and systems management, the rapid evolution of technology, and the need to monitor on a 24×7×365 basis. An MSP offers organizations a subscription-based external service to manage their infrastructure resources or applications. The MSP vendor provides tool implementation and external tool hosting, or hosting within the customer environment. MSPs predominantly target E-business applications and small to mid-sized companies.

In addition to cost advantages, MSPs offer these organizations rapid time to value, due to quick implementation; an ongoing relationship, to ensure subscription renewal; supplementation of staff resources with additional expertise; and an outside perspective. Because the MSP hosts the solution, the organization can be up and running quickly. This rapid implementation contrasts sharply with the long implementation times required for an organization to host a solution in-house.

The MSP model also supplements the IT staff in new technology areas — specifically, in E-commerce application management. By doing the repetitive work, MSPs free the IT staff to focus on higher-level, value-added programs.

One analyst group recently estimated that the demand for IT professionals exceeds the supply by 30 percent. The labor shortage is particularly acute in network and systems management, which people have not been trained for, and which does not represent a growth path.

Frameworks have failed to solve the labor shortage problem. Enterprise management tools from the likes of Compuware, Tivoli, and Computer Associates are too expensive, too difficult to implement, and require too many people. So the management solution becomes a management problem in and of itself, whereby enterprise software is partially implemented, it becomes shelfware, or its use is not widespread across all environments. When its champions leave the company, the tools are seldom used.

By contrast, the MSP allows people to manage via the Internet on a subscription basis, so a $100,000 to $150,000 up-front cost is not required. Not only is there a low cost of entry, but payment on a monthly basis means the work comes out of the services budget, rather than that of capital acquisition. Therefore, organizations do not get caught up in budget/approval cycles, where different price points require different authorizations. The monthly basis keeps the sale lower in the organization, helping both vendors and users.

In addition, the MSP bears the initial and continuing costs of investing in hardware and software infrastructure, while the customer company simply pays a monthly fee. There is also relatively low risk to companies that choose an MSP solution. If the provider is not meeting its needs, the organization can cancel the subscription and go elsewhere.

## SOURCING APPROACHES

In managing their IT environments, organizations have traditionally focused on enterprise tools, purchasing them via perpetual license, and taking advantage of volume discounts. The tools range from point products to comprehensive management frameworks, providing the entire range of systems management functionality. In addition, organizations often augment their tool purchases with vendor-supplied implementation services.

The MSP offers an alternative model that takes different forms. For example, the MSP might sell directly to enterprises, or it might package its offerings with another service provider, such as an ASP or Internet service provider (ISP).

Some organizations have turned to the "legacy MSP." Here, the management service provider functions as a layer between the complexity of an enterprise management framework and the user. The MSP takes traditional enterprise software, installs it, and runs it for the organization, with both the customer and MSP operating the software. Characteristically, there is dedicated hardware for each customer.

For example, MSPs such as TriActive might run the Tivoli environment for a user, wrapping their technical expertise around it. In this hosted model for enterprise software, the customer gets the benefit of the framework, while being shielded from its complexity, and attains faster implementation of the software, and lower up-front costs than with a software-based approach.

However, there is a higher cost of entry than with other types of MSPs. While users pay on a monthly basis, they must commit to the cost over a longer period of time. In addition, users are still limited by the inherent disadvantages of frameworks, including the software's functionality, complex deployment, and scalability. After all, these are classic client/server products that have been extended to the Internet and tend to focus on such processes as network node management and software distribution, rather than offering service level agreements, application management, or performance management.

The turnkey MSP, which might be considered a variant or subset of the legacy MSP, is a service whereby the MSP installs products on the client site and remotely manages the infrastructure. Such MSPs will manage entire systems, an entire application, or an entire management process, such as the help desk. The turnkey MSP is subscription based and process focused, although enabled by tools — which generally come from traditional software vendors.

When these MSPs provide a holistic end-to-end systems strategy, they might be considered to be "Tivoli in MSP format." However, while the MSPs are now selling Tivoli capabilities, they could change vendor, because they all work with numerous vendors. The product partner of the moment is unknown to the end user, who just gets the required management reports or service delivery.

Turnkey MSPs that offer a complete enterprise system management solution include SilverBack, TriActive, MimEcom, and InteQ. For its part, StrataSource manages an entire application. While such providers get much of their technology from traditional vendors, such as Micromuse, BMC, and Computer Associates, the MSPs add value through their technology and processes.

While the software is often installed at the client site, the MSP vendor is responsible for implementation, maintenance, and ongoing use. In most cases, the MSP staff is located off-site, with secure connections to customer hardware.

Small and medium-sized enterprises with 50 to 300 servers are best suited to turnkey MSPs. Larger organizations would find them too costly because they have greater scalability and customization requirements, which bring high failure potential. However, for small and mid-sized businesses, turnkey MSPs will likely expand their offerings to include Internet-enabling infrastructure functions such as load balancing, cache management, and content distribution.

For its part, the **Internet MSP** is a subscription service of three, six, or nine months, whereby companies pay a monthly service fee for the management of a specific aspect of systems or applications, such as Internet monitoring or content delivery. This is what most people refer to when talking about a management service provider. Designed to manage and run over the Internet, these quick-to-install MSPs provide high functionality, although they are not appropriate for all functions. As their name implies, Internet MSPs primarily focus on managing Internet-based applications. They offer such functions as monitoring, storage, security, end-user self-help, and marketing.

These MSPs tend to sell to two camps. The first, classical example, is that of mature companies that understand what they do not know, as well as what it takes to run an IT organization, including hardware, and a network infrastructure. Here, MSPs are dealing with technical folks. The second customer camp consists of dot.coms, which are small, or do not realize they cannot do it themselves. In this case, business rather than technical people are generally involved.

Internet MSPs usually offer a service that is based on point tools that target a single management concern. Internet MSPs use brand-new technology and applications that were built to exploit the Internet. They target E-business applications, and require little or no technology to be deployed internally. Because customers need not buy and install large frameworks or applications, Internet MSPs offer a low barrier to entry, and low cost.

Internet MSPs offer specific services. For example, Keynote, Freshwater, Luminate, and Mercury Interactive provide infrastructure monitoring and testing. They can generally view application performance from outside, simulating the users' perspective. Internet MSPs also provide security testing, software maintenance, and external storage networks for storing and managing data.

As for the disadvantages, Internet MSPs are "very niche"; that is, all the functionality is not there yet. While they provide application and server management, they do not offer software distribution or help-desk functions, although broader functionality is expected in the future. In addition, use of a framework limits the number of vendors with which a company must work. Because the MSP space is new, companies might have to deal with more vendors, for example, to attain network performance functions in addition to infrastructure monitoring.

Some analysts anticipate the development of "integration MSPs," which will allow ISPs and ASPs to share real-time infrastructure events and alarms with their customers. If, as some believe, data gathering is becoming a commodity, MSPs must differentiate themselves from competitors. To do so, MSP vendors such as Ganymede, Luminate, and Manage.com are giving away a tool or service to gain customers. The free tools monitor an element or process, allowing IT departments to try them out. The MSPs hope that these organizations will then become customers and start using their other services, such as data integration.

Another approach to MSPs is that offered by service providers, which add management tools to their contracted service offerings. Operating on a subscription basis, these providers focus on performance monitoring, and delivering to service level agreements. However, flexibility is an issue because they only offer a few standard configurations.

As ISPs and ASPs become commodities, they must distinguish themselves from the competition. To do so, some are looking at offering customers services that are similar to MSPs, whereby the ISP acts as middleman. Other ISPs have acquired MSPs because of their management value; for example, Exodus acquired Service Metrics to provide response time management. In general, analysts anticipate MSP consolidation, with ISPs and ASPs acting as the primary consolidators.

Partnerships are becoming common, for example, those between Keynote and Digix, and between Keynote and UUNet. ASPs are also partnering with tool vendors and MSPs to provide management services similar to those of ISPs; for example, PeopleSoft with Qwest, and Corio with Marimba. From their side, organizations must gauge whether these management services are sufficient, or if they should be supplemented.

## A NEW BUSINESS MODEL: SERVICE VERSUS PRODUCT

At present, software vendors still generate the majority of Web site management products, which have comprehensive capabilities that provide testing, internal performance benchmarking, and site monitoring management tools. However, those considering an investment in an enterprise management system should consider the new business model in town. While vendors have traditionally productized enterprise management, the market for network, systems, and Web site management can now be segmented into service and software.

Luminate, for example, initially sold enterprise management as a product, but is now trying to reposition it as a service. As it moves from a pure enterprise application software provider to a service provider, it is managing applications and the Internet infrastructure. The MSP offers a series of services that let IT managers monitor the health of their E-business infrastructures, using a small downloadable tool and a subscription to Luminate.net.

The MSP is giving away a sizable piece of its offering by letting customers download its Mamba performance monitoring tool for free. The MSP expects that buyers will then plug into more advanced tools online for a monthly fee.

Mamba's package of Web server software and Java servlets tests events, performance, and availability. It can automatically discover network assets and do real-time testing — without a major deployment and without installing agents. Thousands of copies of Mamba for SAP R/3 have already been downloaded. Luminate also offers Mamba for Windows NT and Mamba for Oracle databases. Prices range from $50 per server per month for the Windows version, to $350 per server per month for R/3, to $500 per server per month for Oracle.

To motivate Mamba users to become paying customers, Luminate provides small software bundles called "energizers," by which the software communicates with Luminate.net. When customers plug into the Luminate.net site, they obtain expanded views of the data that Mamba collects, including graphical reports of performance over weeks or months. They also receive daily e-mail hotlists, which indicate trouble spots in the enterprise.

Via Luminate.net, subscribers can drill down into specific reporting areas, and access a library of help and support files. The service allows customers to monitor effectively, and retain important data, which would otherwise be very time-consuming and difficult to do.

For its part, major MSP Keynote has an approach that sells only services — not software. And NetSolve offers management services that focus specifically on network performance and availability, rather than application behavior. As for the main enterprise management vendors, they will either buy management service companies, or provide a management service with their own tools, as an offshoot of their services organization, thereby productizing it. However, this is not their strong suit.

### MOVING TOWARD STANDARDS

There are already so many MSPs that they cannot all survive, so there will be consolidation. Companies have the need to manage all elements; monitoring their response time, and all protocols to and from them. Correlating all this presents a problem, and the solution is not available as a holistic tool. Therefore, organizations need an integration point, such as a performance repository or response time event console. While this is not holistic, the information is integratable, and Micromuse, for one, can serve as an integration point.

In addition, Extended Markup Language (XML) will enable data-sharing among multi-vendors. To this end, the Distributed Management Task Force, Inc. (DMTF) provides a Web-based Enterprise Management (WBEM) roadmap to give customers the ability to manage all their systems, regardless of instrumentation type, through the use of a common standard.

On October 19, 1998, the DMTF announced the first version of its XML Encoding Specification, to encode the Common Information Model (CIM) schema in XML. The specification defines XML elements, which can be used to represent CIM classes and instances. It will enable companies to leverage Web technologies to manage enterprise systems. Thus, XML lets industry groups worldwide rapidly define and implement standards for interoperability across diverse computing environments and technologies. WBEM was initiated by BMC, Cisco, Compaq Intel, and Microsoft, but was later incorporated into the DMTF.

## THE MSP FUTURE

Organizations have an increasingly complex, expanding infrastructure to manage. Even if the corporate infrastructure is manageable, the E-business environment presents new management challenges. In the recent past, efficient management provided E-businesses with a competitive advantage. Today, however, availability is no longer an option. If sites are not as or more available than the competition, organizations are no longer in business. So companies realize that management and availability have gone from being a competitive advantage to a mission-critical necessity.

The MSP premise used for the Web has helped the infrastructure management business. In the past, most organizations saw systems and applications management as a blackbox. Companies knew they needed it, but did not understand the bottom-line focus. Now they understand the business significance of management.

MSPs represent a growth market. Analysts predict that every Global 2000 company will have an MSP by the end of 2001. They also anticipate that MSPs will represent a multibillion dollar market in the next few years, reaching the $4 to $5 billion range.

### The Self-integration Imperative

However, because systems, applications, and Web management represent a niche market, companies will likely use a combination of MSPs, rather than working with a single company. For example, while they might use BMC for performance monitoring, they would still subscribe to Keynote for Web management. In choosing MSP vendors, companies should prepare to do self-integration in three to four years, identifying and covering all their systems management needs. For example, they should determine what access to tools they need for internal process integration, so they can deal with alarms internally.

### Problem Resolution

Most MSPs today find potential problems and notify the customer company, which then fixes the problems. Very few of today's MSPs actually fix the problems they uncover. Some analysts believe MSPs are therefore missing a key component. If the company has neither the time nor money to invest in monitoring business-critical networks or applications to ensure they are all up and running, it might not have the means to fix mission-critical problems.

Partnering with an E-support provider could shore up this gap, whereby MSPs form solid partnerships with such E-support companies as Motive Communications and Support.com. MSPs would thereby gain competitive advantage and a stronger customer relationship. E-support providers would gain entrée into a new business market — and customers could fix problems in a timely manner, thereby keeping their business running. In addition to E-support providers, newer MSPs are emerging, which offer both problem identification and problem resolution; one such is SiteLite.

**Market Shakeout**

Given the market need for MSPs, the future will undoubtedly see a lot more vendors, venture capital, and functionality. In fact, some analysts predict an explosion of new MSP entrants, followed by a shakeout and a lowering of prices as vendors commoditize — thus providing capabilities for dollars.

Because the MSP is an unproven model, some vendors will go under. They will find the cost of tool ownership and the number of failures high. In addition, customers can easily change MSP allegiance, because there is a low switching cost — especially when compared with traditional software and services.

Furthermore, when customers pay a service fee, they simply get a service level agreement (SLA) as a commitment. For example, while an MSP might specify 100 percent availability, speed is not mentioned, so the vendor is only policing SLAs.

Some MSPs offer free service during the time of an outage. However, an ISP can lose $100,000 an hour every eight hours it is down, while a power company could lose $1.5 million. In such cases, the free $1000 service provides no equity.

This will have to change so that MSPs add more management capabilities and monitoring tools and shore up their service levels, backing it up by a rock-solid environment. Because this will cost more to do, it will kill some vendors. However, a number of large ones will remain.

**Differentiating Offerings**

Not only will MSPs have to deploy a pretty comprehensive network, but every ISP will have to offer management services. In addition, as ASPs move into the Web site management space, both ASPs and MSPs will potentially offer services ranging from Web speed monitoring to commercial transaction tracking and usage analysis. When software vendors and service providers compete for the same customers, services and products will converge, and MSPs will bundle their services with the appropriate software products.

MSPs are already acquiring such products. For example, Keynote Systems recently acquired Velogic, a provider of load testing simulation services. Keynote already offers E-commerce customers quality-of-service reporting on performance criteria such as downloading speeds, and the demand for this service is high. Velogic expands Keynote's services so the two are strategically complementary. Companies can now test their Web sites before going live, measure real-time performance after the site is up and running, and subsequently perform diagnostic maintenance.

**Of Control and Value**

Organizations moving to MSPs give up some control, so companies are just starting to trust them. It helps that MSPs sometimes provide a free tool for organizations to try out. Still, IT cannot give up control completely because people know they will be fired if the E-business site goes down.

While management platforms provide an all-encompassing solution for all operations, MSPs tend to be based on point products; offering help desk, performance management functions, and the like for people to use on a day-to-day basis. Thus, MSPs are generally niche players, largely providing a departmental rather than an enterprisewide solution.

MSPs' unique value is in providing functions that are difficult for an organization to do on its own, such as building enough storage space or performing security intrusion testing. And, although innovations are coming, companies using MSPs are already seeing value today.

# Chapter 5
# K-Commerce: Knowledge-Based Commerce Architecture with Convergence of E-Commerce and Knowledge Management

*R. Kocharekar*

THERE IS SYNERGY BETWEEN E-COMMERCE AND KNOWLEDGE MANAGEMENT. E-COMMERCE IS ABOUT TRANSACTIONS WITH EXTERNAL STAKEHOLDERS. Knowledge management is about internal collaborative endeavors and the sharing of information and experience. K-commerce is the collaboration and sharing of knowledge with external stakeholders.

Organizations are currently embarking on two different projects — knowledge management and E-commerce. Both undertakings are complex by themselves, but seem unrelated at this time. Quite expectedly, this creates some level of confusion as to the significance of the two undertakings and their relative importance. This chapter describes the challenges involved in these two undertakings and outlines the architecture that will bring about the convergence.

Only a few years ago, organizations struggled to consolidate all their internal transactional systems into one or two enterprise-level resource planning systems. Possibilities of Y2K problems in the existing system hastened the migration. The migration was a highly structured project with a clear understanding of the end goals. It was, however, not a trivial exercise by any account because of the enormity of the project and its impact on the business and IT environments within the organization.

Many lessons were learned from the ERP implementation project, the foremost perhaps the challenge of managing organizational change. Business process reengineering and ERP implementations were, to a degree, exercises that were comparable to Taylor's efficiency exercises in the industrial world. Just as Taylor measured and streamlined the manufacturing operations manual processes, BPR and ERP streamlined the organization's back-end processes. However, with sole focus on processes, they neglected the management of human resources. This resulted in a backlash against the BPR process, with subversion or sometimes outright resistance to these projects.

Even before the ERP project could be concluded, organizations and their IT departments were confronting two different new issues:

1. The growing presence of the Internet in the business environment meant moving almost all of the organization's business onto the Internet. Pressures from dot.com companies aggravated the situation and, within a short time, brick and mortar companies were thought of as dinosaurs, doomed for extinction. They were compared to IBMs of the mainframe computer world or Ma Bell of the telephone monopoly world.
2. With the realization that the organization's intellectual capital now substantially surpassed the physical capital, organizations faced the task of better managing, investing in, and harvesting the intellectual capital. Also, with increased availability of computing and communication technologies, it became possible to overcome the geographical boundaries, if not the organizational boundaries, in managing knowledge.

Exhibit 1 depicts the organization's initial state and its responses to these two challenges. In the initial state, organizations focused on streamlining internal transaction processes through BPR and consolidating fragmented transaction systems into ERP packages. Exhibit 1 also shows how the two response initiatives differ from each other. The response to the first challenge is the E-commerce initiative, in which organizations are linking internal transactional processes and systems to the outside world. The response to the second challenge is to focus on internal knowledge management, in which the shift is away from the transactional processes to collaboration and knowledge sharing. The focus of knowledge management,

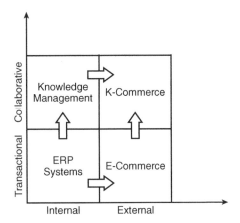

**Exhibit 1.   IS Evolution Path**

however, remains primarily internal within the organization. What are the challenges organizations face in connection with these two issues?

As mentioned previously, with the consolidation of business systems within the organization, it is now possible to leverage the ERP infrastructure to conduct electronic business with partners. Many models of E-commerce are being implemented. Some are parallel in nature to the existing commerce in the physical world; others are new.

Exhibit 2 shows the different possibilities. Both the business-to-business (B2B) and business-to-consumer (B2C) models can be implemented using the push model, in which sellers bid (push) for products and services to match the buyers' or consumers' requirements. They could also use the pull model, in which sellers advertise products and services and buyers select (pull) what they need from the vendor's offering based on the buyer's purchasing power. Finally, both buyers and sellers could participate in market-based models, in which many suppliers and buyers come together to transact, leveraging their aggregate buying power.

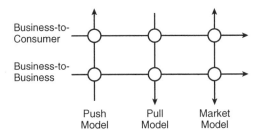

**Exhibit 2.   E-Commerce Models**

Organizations face several issues in choosing and implementing E-commerce models from both business and technology perspectives. From the business perspective, one of the biggest challenges is to decide on which of the two models is applicable for what purposes. It is also necessary to understand the impact of implementing a particular model on the current distribution and supply channels. The particular model may augment current channels or it may entirely replace them, causing a substantial shift in the organization's own resources and surrounding processes. Implementation of a particular model has cascading effects across the value chain. For example, if B2C E-commerce is implemented and current ERP and ordering systems are linked, supply channels could also be changed to map the new E-commerce strategy. E-commerce not only influences vertical integration, but also opens up the possibility of horizontal integration, in which organizations can buy or sell auxiliary products or services.

The technology to support the E-commerce framework is rapidly evolving. XML has emerged as the standard that replaces the earlier EDI. However, different industries are adapting different exchange formats to exchange industry-specific information. Some, like Commerce.net, have taken an innovative approach with the common business library (CBL) that attempts to encompass all these standards. In the past, internal IT architecture and system choices had a relatively limited impact on the organization's business interfaces to the external world, good or bad. Wrong choices resulted primarily in higher costs in support, but the organization's external business interfaces still could be carried out, as very few processes in this area were automated in real-time fashion. Now, it is no longer possible to hide internal information and technology architectures and systems behind the organization's firewalls. These systems are interfacing with the external market-based systems and are dynamically affected by external changing environments. For example, in financial payment systems, there is no longer any need for the delayed settlement clearing process between different financial organizations. It is possible to process these transactions in real-time mode. This substantially reduces the systemic risks (i.e., risks in failure of the financial market due to the cascading effect of default of one or two financial organization), but simultaneously puts a heavy burden on organizations to ensure that their information systems remain accessible.

Even though IT infrastructure technologies have advanced enough, ensuring continuous system accessibility remains a challenge because external access substantially enhances existing exposures or creates new ones. For example, transaction workload or number of external users accessing a system remains largely unpredictable, and the possibility of malicious attacks requires new security management. Infrastructure capacity and performance needs to be enhanced continuously through different ways such as multitier architectures with caching, replications, and failover mechanisms.

There is no doubt that the E-commerce models will rapidly evolve. Internal management will have little control over when and how these changes are incorporated, as they will be driven by market demand and direction. The information systems and technology therefore will need to be flexible and extensible to incorporate the changes. In addition, the systems need to incorporate new software and hardware enhancements or repair features without any system outages. This is where object-based software technology will derive its greatest benefits. Finally, many different IT support sourcing options are now possible in the new Internet age, ranging from ASPs to offshore sourcing to insourcing. Selecting the right support sourcing model is critical.

Even though substantial business and technology challenges exist in E-commerce space, they remain primarily focused on efficiency in transaction processes through automation. However, in knowledge management, effectiveness is the name of the game. As mentioned before, while BPR completely ignored the human element, knowledge management focuses directly on the most valuable aspect of human resource — its intellectual capital.

Thorstein Veblen, the famous institutional economist, had recognized the potential of intellectual capital and the power of knowledge workers (whom he called technicians) as early as 1920. He saw a power struggle between knowledge workers and capitalists. Today, we do not see the struggle that Veblen described; rather, we see the interdependence between management and knowledge workers. There is no doubt that the knowledge workers today command power that matches that of the organization's management. This is evident in the popularity of employee stock option plans and the flat organization model with self-managed teams.

Still, the knowledge management program has been difficult to communicate within an organization and even to senior management. There is little disagreement at the conceptual level, but articulating tangible results is a challenge. Pilot case studies and story-telling constitute one of the promising approaches. How are the organizations managing knowledge effectively to gain maximum benefits? They have been experimenting with various approaches, not necessarily mutually exclusive. Some, like Microsoft, have created a skills inventory of all employees, hoping that rather than managing knowledge, knowing who knows what would add more value. Some, like the World Bank, have been implementing communities of practices. These communities cross organization boundaries to bring practitioners and function experts together and are managed in an informal manner. Some organizations have focused on creating the right incentives for people to share their knowledge.

Many believe that knowledge management is not really a technology issue, like E-commerce. Others have heavily relied on technology to implement knowledge management practices. Many different technologies are falling into the knowledge domain. Business intelligence systems or intelligent data mining systems cover the analytical toolsets. Collaborative tools such as Notes-based applications are being used to aid self-managed teams. Content management tools try to keep the enterprise information fresh. Intranet portals attempt to bring all this information together. Challenges remain in designing information taxonomy or ontology maps. Distance learning and collaborative learning methods foster learning within organizations.

Because effectiveness is always more difficult to measure than efficiency, assessment of knowledge management exercises remains a key challenge. However, in spite of the initial difficulties, knowledge management will continue to dominate organizational activities in the near future. As Peter Drucker has said, productivity of knowledge employees will be the key challenge in the twenty-first century.

As mentioned previously, organizations are currently managing the two initiatives quite separate from each other. As depicted in Exhibit 1, they are orthogonal to each other from the organization boundary and nature of process perspective. The IS department is definitely at the forefront of the E-commerce initiative, if not leading it altogether. On the other hand, the knowledge management initiative may not have high-level IS department involvement. This may be for political reasons, as senior management may not want to concede that knowledge management is a technology issue, or it may be for lack of sufficient skill in the IS department to manage such an initiative.

Will the two initiatives eventually converge? The answer, of course, is yes. As enough experience is gained in the two initiatives, organizations will converge the two initiatives to the right-hand upper quadrant in Exhibit 1. At this stage, they will implement and practice knowledge-based commerce — K-commerce for short. K-commerce combines the experience and features of the two initiatives to build a new architecture. K-commerce will be collaborative, involving internal as well as external stakeholders. Even though all the details of this new architecture may not be clear, it is essential to have some idea about it, as it will help in implementing both initiatives today. It also acts as a guide in planning the convergence of the two initiatives.

What are the basic ingredients of this K-commerce architecture? Simplistically put, they are processes, information, and communication channels. Processes create and enhance information and communicate across channels. Exhibit 3 shows the sets of processes connected through communication flows. One vertical stack consists of the internal organization while the other represents different partner organizations. Partners could be suppliers, consumers, or other stakeholders. The term "supplier" is used in the broadest sense that includes not just raw material providers or parts suppliers but also financial, human resource, marketing, distributor, or IT support service suppliers. Each process within the vertical stack is linked to its counterpart process in the partner organization and forms the layer. It is not necessary that the communication channels are directly linked to the two partners. They may be linked through brokers or market intermediaries, who may add value to the communication and information flows by augmenting them. Understanding of the information processed and communicated within each layer as well as between the layers indicates what systems and technology infrastructure must be put in place.

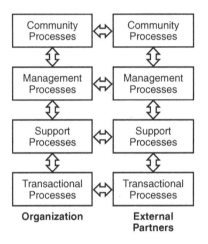

**Exhibit 3.    K-Commerce Architecture**

At the bottom layer, there are transactional processes such as procurement. These are mostly automated through information systems. However, it should be noted that these systems are not passive in nature. They will have built-in intelligence to adapt to the changing environment. They will have the capability to automatically negotiate transactions such as procurements based on the constraints and guidelines set. The closest models that exist today are the systems that buy and sell equities, through predefined parameters. The bottom layer is what E-commerce primarily consists of today.

As much as the transaction layer is adaptive to the changing environment with built-in intelligence, there must be a support layer above that extracts information from transaction processes, gleans trends, and continuously guides the transaction processes in the right directions. The support layer therefore consists of function experts as well as monitoring and analytical systems. They receive the vital statistics from the transaction layer, but also have communication links and information flows to partners. Finally, they feed information to the upper management layer and receive directions on long-term strategic directions.

The upper management process is, in turn, focused on the strategic directions with input from the support processes, from management of business partners, and from industry or sector community-at-large on the top. They will have business intelligence and decision support systems to facilitate the process. Management as well as support layers will also include other knowledge management processes for lessons learned and best practices.

Finally, at the top layer, the sector community exists that incorporates stakeholders including government regulators, competitors, trade associations, lobbies, and non-governmental organizations. This community has some common interests, including managing the health of the overall sector, articulating its value to society, and mitigating its detrimental side effects. The community needs information and communication channels as well as knowledge-sharing to thrive.

One may not notice any difference between this model and the current business architectures at the onset. Indeed, it is the foundation of any business. However, closer inspection reveals gaps in current business models. The following analogy might help to draw the distinction between the K-commerce model and current business architecture. Think of the assembly level programming in the early days of computers, and then think of the sophistication in existing programming languages such as inheritance, encapsulation, and reuse. Both are programming languages, but it is the level of sophistication in abstraction that differentiates the two. The level of abstraction in modern programming languages has increased their power substantially, or to put it in economic terms, the programmers' productivity has increased multifold with modern languages.

Currently, these processes are not integrated with information systems and communication flows. The resistance between the layers is too high for communication to take place. Relevant forms of communication flows between the processes within the organization are key. Take, for example, prenegotiated procurement transactions. How are these transactions monitored? How are the remedial actions being taken if transactions fall out of set constraints? Are these processes and corresponding information systems linked? Similarly, analyze what level of communication takes place across counterpart processes in the same layer. How do they encounter and address organizational and cultural barriers? How do they build trust across organizations?

Like the communication flows, the processes must be examined to see how they are performed currently. Do they have adequate information and knowledge to carry out the process? How is this knowledge managed? As these issues are explored, the information and knowledge management architecture that needs to be in place will become evident. It will be possible to design taxonomies and knowledge maps for each process and communication channel and to recognize the wide gaps in where we are today and where we need to be.

Building the new K-commerce architecture will not be without difficulties. First, promising initiatives may fail to scale up, not because those initiatives are poorly designed or managed, but because the underlying infrastructure will not be mature. It may be necessary to redefine what constitutes the organization's wealth or stock. Also, the revenue models will need to change from what they are today. Finally, the definition of what constitutes an organization will change in practice, if not in legal terms. Concepts such as virtual organization are already in the current vocabulary.

In conclusion, much has been learned from the BRP and ERP exercises. Experience has been gained in collaborative processes and technologies. A lot more can be learned about E-commerce and knowledge management initiatives. Managers will also learn to manage organizational processes and systems in an environment where they will not have full control over them, because of their close coupling with processes and systems of outside partners. These initiatives will also supply new technologies and systems that will form the foundation blocks for the K-commerce environment. Once these component blocks are in place, the K-commerce structure can be put in place. Therefore, in moving forward in developing and integrating the necessary building blocks, the K-commerce architecture will continue to be refined even further.

# Section II
# Strategic and Business Issues

The chapters in this section examine the strategic and business issues facing the Internet. These issues includes cost reduction, funding, and measuring the value proposition of Internet solutions. Evolving technology issues and functional alternatives are also considerations in this space.

"Return on Internet Investment: Measuring the Success of Online Business Solutions" examines how to measure an organization's return on investment in the Internet environment.

"Using the Internet to Improve Competitive Position and Reduce Costs" discusses opportunities for reducing operating costs. This is a critical driver in the current information technology environment and it is likely to retain the same level of importance in the future.

"Web and Java Risk Issues" examines opportunities to reduce risk caused by external customers accessing internal corporate data. This discussion is provided in the context of the Java programming language.

"Managing Risk in Electronic Commerce" provides a general purpose methodology for organizations to leverage in evaluating their security technologies, standards, and requirements.

"Single Sign-On for the Enterprise" explains the advantages and approaches for supporting a single sign-on for a suite of applications across an organization. This chapter examines password synchronization, shared systems, authentication, password change policies, and integration of techniques.

# Chapter 6
# Return on Internet Investment: Measuring the Success of Online Business Solutions

*John Seasholtz*

CORPORATIONS BUILDING ONLINE BUSINESS SOLUTIONS are beginning to recognize the value of measuring Return on Internet Investment (ROI2) early. Determining methods to measure ROI2 needs to be one of the first major steps in the up-front planning process, and continually evaluated and applied throughout the entire project life cycle. ROI2 provides a foundation for corporations to determine the success of their online business solutions and develop future plans to bring the projects to the next level.

This chapter examines return on investment and how it has traditionally been applied to measure business initiatives. It will explain how ROI2 applies to every online business solution or Web project (Internet, intranet, and/or extranet sites). This chapter will

- Bring greater clarity to ROI2
- Help companies define their goals so they can anticipate ROI2 for their Web sites
- Present ideas and concepts about how to measure ROI2, with a special emphasis on measuring indirect returns

By considering these issues at the very onset of the project, a company will have a greater understanding of how its online business solution has met its objectives. Plans to measure ROI2 will be different for every corporation, and companies should include only the measures that make sense.

This chapter proposes a framework that companies can use to help determine what to expect from their investment in a Web site.

## TRADITIONAL RETURN ON INVESTMENT

No matter what the situation, individuals and businesses alike ask a series of questions to help them figure out what return on investment to expect. At its simplest level, use these four questions as a framework for thinking about rate of return:

- What is my goal?
- What situations or events will I use to know that I've met my goal?
- How many of these situations or events will show me I've met my goal?
- How will I measure/count these situations or events?

Obviously, there is not just one set of answers to these questions. Each goal might have more than one kind of situation or event that can assess how well the goal has been met.

ROI2 should be considered in the same manner. Some returns a company may look for are direct; some are indirect. A direct return, for example, might be the dollars a company makes as a result of selling products via its Web site. An indirect return might be retaining customers because they find it easier to order products from the Web site than to try to reach the company's sales people by phone. The recipe for determining ROI2 is different for every company.

## RETURN ON INTERNET INVESTMENT (ROI2)

There is no cookie-cutter formula for ROI2 and it is different for every company. It should be stressed that ROI2 is the end result of an effective Web strategy. The Web strategy should support corporate objectives and should have a clear plan for measuring its effectiveness. Identifying planned benefits and a means to measure them is a critical first step to measuring ROI2.

ROI2 should be seen as a compilation of both direct and indirect returns. Direct returns can be measured and linked to a Web solution. Indirect returns are "softer" and are realized over a longer period of time.

### Direct Returns

In its purest form, direct ROI2 can be expressed as the incremental dollar benefits resulting from a Web solution divided by the Web investment. Optimally, the return is greater than the company's cost of borrowing and/or greater than returns that could be earned on other business opportunities.

$$ROI2 = (\text{Incremental Dollar Benefits/Web Investment}) - 1$$

Incremental dollar benefits can be split into revenue enhancement benefits and expense and capital reduction benefits.

Incremental Dollar Benefits = Incremental Increases in Revenue +

Reduction in Expenses

**Direct Revenue Benefits.** Businesses can develop an online store or catalog where customers can actually browse products and product literature, download demos, as well as purchase items without having to pick up the phone or go to a store. Selling via the Web reduces overall cost, turnaround time, and the ability to update. Selling over the Web is often referred to as E-commerce.

E-commerce Web solutions usually provide the most obvious revenue benefits. These solutions build marketing and selling capabilities into a Web site. Incremental revenues are those sales that would not normally have taken place if the Web solution had not been implemented.

E-commerce allows online marketers to personalize Web sites to individual customers. This practice is often referred to as one-to-one marketing and it helps facilitate a sense of community for surfers. These Web sites may pull information from other sites that is of particular interest to a customer. Chat rooms are another means of building a community as surfers can chat online with others that share similar interests.

As surfers register to obtain membership for Web sites, request a demo download, or purchase a product, information is gathered. This information can be used by online marketers to further refine their target markets and thus implement more effective online or offline marketing campaigns.

Other revenue benefits can result from more efficient sales lead processing, increased purchase frequency, and average order size. The Web makes purchasing easier and more repeatable. Therefore, purchase frequency may rise as a result of Web selling.

For example, 1-800-FLOWERS allows visitors to its Web site to view and choose a flower arrangement online, add the item to a shopping cart that stores all of the items chosen, fill out a form online for billing and shipping information, and process the request. So, if a visitor buys a flower arrangement for $29.95, a direct ROI2 is the $29.95 minus the costs of arranging and delivering the flowers. Traditionally, 1-800-FLOWERS would have had the extra costs of paying a customer services representative to take the call and process all of the information manually. Additionally, 1-800-FLOWERS also saved costs in that it did not have to pay for printing and shipping a catalog — the visitor was able to view the flower arrangements online.

**Expense Reduction Benefits.** Another way to measure a direct ROI2 is to calculate how the Web site has reduced corporate expenses. For instance, the costs for paper, printing, postage, software distribution, mailing, order processing, documentation, corporate licensing, etc. will all be significantly less if information and documentation can be accessed online.

Business processes that utilize large quantities of paper and time, such as procurement or the order and delivery process for supplies, can be made more efficient and cost effective. Traditional procurement systems entail having an employee search for and find the supply he or she needs, fill out the paperwork for a supply, send the paperwork through an approval process, wait for a check to be cut and sent, and then wait for the supply to be shipped and delivered.

Purchasing over the Web also enables companies to streamline the fulfillment process by implementing electronic catalogs that provide pricing, availability, shipping, configuration, and detailed product information online. This reduces the time from order to delivery, making the process more efficient, and reducing administrative costs.

Using the Web, companies can also open new lines of distribution for ordering products, checking order status, receiving advice, and obtaining shipping and/or billing information by developing an extranet for their distributors and partners. Doing these activities via the Web reduces the need for printed manuals, lessens the overhead costs needed to maintain a customer service representative answering phone calls, and makes information that is in the corporate database immediately accessible online as opposed to having a representative search for it.

For example, Sun Microsystems was able to measure a direct ROI2 by calculating the amount of money it saved by publishing online its 700-page catalog of books on Sun and Sun-related technologies. The cost of the Web site at $5000 was much less expensive than the printing and distribution of a 700-page paper catalog. In addition, the number of accesses of the Web book catalog increased by threefold during its first year.[2]

Overhead expenses for maintaining personnel dedicated to customer service, technical support, reception, administration, etc. can all be saved as a result of bringing business to the Web. Companies can also save money by downloading tools and products off the Internet, and sharing and reusing tools internally. For example, Swedish Medical Center, the largest and most comprehensive medical center in the Pacific Northwest, saves more than $6 in staff cost for each online referral to a physician, compared to a telephone referral. Online referrals are also bringing in more than $40,000 in new revenue each month. Calculating the overhead expenses saved, a direct monetary return allowed Swedish to measure its ROI2.

Online business solutions provide a wealth of information for customers, employees, and business partners. For example, the Web makes the distribution of marketing materials much more effective, saving both time and money. Leads are most often worked manually — a call comes in, the inside sales rep takes down the information, then enters it into the customer management database and sends a note to the field representative. The field representative then puts an information packet together, mails it, and follows up. Using the Web, the customer can obtain the exact information he or she requires anytime of the day and from anywhere in the world. This not only satisfies the customer but saves the company printing and distribution costs.

Making processes easier and faster to execute saves everything from paper and printing costs to the overhead expenses for having a full-time staff member executing the process. For example, an inevitable part of running an effective business is making the delivery process for supplies more efficient. Traditional procurement systems entail having an employee search for and find the supply he or she needs, fill out the paperwork for a supply, send the paperwork through an approval process, wait for a check to be cut and sent, and then wait for the supply to be shipped and delivered.

**Reduced Capital Benefits.** It is quite feasible that Web solutions will allow companies to significantly reduce capital expenditures in the future. Capital expenditures typically include plant and building equipment that are carried on a company's balance sheet.

Let us say that a company implements a global sales and marketing extranet from which customers can gather product information, negotiate prices, and receive training and customer service. Previously, this company may have used field offices to coordinate the selling process. These offices can now be significantly reduced or even eliminated, generating significant benefits through reduction in capital expenditures for buildings, land, vehicles, and computer equipment.

**Elements of the Web Investment.** Before direct ROI2 can be measured, the dollar value of the Web investment must be calculated. According to Forrester Research Inc., companies spend approximately $300,000 for a purely promotional site and $3.4 million for a transactional site. Salaries for Web masters and other dedicated personnel add to ongoing expenses. There are also costs associated with design and gathering content, which often take time from existing employees unless the company decides to outsource to consultants. Content collection can become expensive, especially on global sites where translation is necessary.

**Exhibit 1. Metrics and Goals**

| Web Benefit | Metric(s) | Goal |
|---|---|---|
| More efficient customer service | Cost per customer response | Reduce from $10 to $5 per response |
| Reduced time for sales cycle | Cost per customer acquisition | Reduce from $500 to $400 per customer acquisition |
| Increased sales | Web site revenues | $500 Incremental sales per week |
| Employee empowerment of benefits management | Time required to access benefits data and cost per employee contact | Reduce time from five hours to two hours per month and costs of contact from $12 to $6 per employee contact |

**Measuring Direct Returns.** A direct return is a return on investment that produces or saves dollars as a result of the investment. Direct sales and money saved in corporate costs and expenses can all be direct measurements of an online business solution. If a company pays $100,000 to build a Web site and saves $20,000 per month in overhead for customer service representatives by having customer service and support online, the ROI2 for its site is approximately 140 percent for the year.

Businesses must identify the process metrics before the Web site is implemented. A baseline must be established before the efficiency of the site can be measured. Some examples of metrics and goals are shown in Exhibit 1.

## Indirect Returns

Many companies view Web investments as "costs of doing business" much like having an ad in the Yellow Pages or an 800 number to gather customer feedback. Some companies have adopted "balanced scorecards," as shown in Exhibit 2, that outline "softer" goals that will help them achieve their strategies. Financial measures only make up a portion of these goals, whereas the others are more indirect and harder to place dollar values on.

Typical indirect goals include customer loyalty, employee satisfaction, supplier relations, learning, and innovation. Shareholder value is measured using direct ROI2, although indirect benefits also affect shareholder value. It is beneficial for companies to put weights on these metrics and evaluate each Web solution to see where it will benefit. We will elaborate on customer retention and employee satisfaction below.

**Customer Retention.** Marketing initiatives can be tailored and personalized on the Web. Rather than treating all customers the same, online marketing enables companies to use the Web for more personalized one-to-one

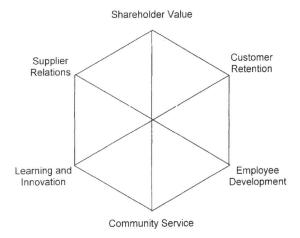

Shareholder Value

Supplier Relations

Customer Retention

Learning and Innovation

Employee Development

Community Service

**Exhibit 2.   A Hypothetical Balanced Scorecard**

marketing. Each visitor is treated as a unique individual and will only view the information he or she cares about vs. getting advertisements, brochures, products, and other materials that are created for the general public. Electronic marketing enables companies to provide unique and tailored information at an efficient price.

Greater customer service is almost always a number one business priority, and the best example of an indirect return. Traditional measures taken to improve customer service include providing an 800 number for toll-free customer service calls, more customer service representatives to take telephone calls, and automated answering machines to help customers direct their own questions, complaints, and suggestions to the correct departments.

Online customer service has continued this progression of customer self service. By using the Web for customer service, companies empower customers to serve themselves at their own convenience. Not only can customers access general information online, but also online support centers, enabling the end user to log complaints, search for status on a problem, or look up solutions. This creates community by enabling customers not only to use, but also add to a shared knowledge base, facilitating exchange of information. The company benefits by limiting the number of customer support representatives needed and reducing the costs of training and documentation.

**Employee Satisfaction.** One important aspect of every business is effective internal communication and sharing of knowledge. Information on medical benefits, 401(k) plans, vacation, holidays, sick days, emergency contacts, etc. should be made readily available to every employee. Traditionally, this information is usually stored in pamphlet or brochure form with the human resources department. The pamphlets are often just general information. In order to find confidential information (for example, information on company stock options or specific medical coverage), it is often necessary for employees to ask a human resources representative to locate the material and then explain how it can apply to them.

Intranets offer employees quick and confidential access to the information they need. In addition to posting the general brochure information, companies can also post more company-specific information. An intranet allows businesses to gain more control over internal processes by providing faster, more accurate updates to contact information, detailed statements, and summaries, and is an efficient method for posting key corporate communications messages. It also streamlines project management efforts and sharing of resources. Web solutions can improve the quality, frequency, and clarity of communication throughout the company.

Training and recruitment are other areas where the Web offers benefits. National training programs can be rolled out simultaneously and feedback can be given through e-mail and chat rooms. Job openings are posted on Web sites, which increases the reach of the company and makes the job search easier for prospective employees.

Another indirect benefit is improved learning and innovation. It is also one area where Web solutions can offer the greatest benefits. Collaborative working environments have become the norm and productivity increases as a result. Files can be sent and stored on Web applications, which enables employees to work together no matter the time or location. Enhanced communication that results from the ease of Web-based applications improves employee skills, develops new relationships, and provides a platform for solving complex problems.

**Measuring Indirect Returns.** It is much more difficult to obtain benchmarks to measure indirect benefits. For example, how will a company measure whether or not a new intranet is improving employee morale? There are metrics such as monitoring employee turnover that can track its effectiveness, as shown in Exhibit 3. However, an employee satisfaction survey may be the best way to track its impact. It is important that such a survey is instituted before the site goes live, so that employee reaction can be tracked after it is up and running. Employee feedback should be used to further refine and improve the intranet.

Web solutions also often enhance communication. Besides direct benefits such as reduced communications expenses, improved communication enhances planning and morale. For example, improved communication between suppliers and buyers through an extranet allows for the sharing of sales projections and allows for more efficient planning and scheduling.

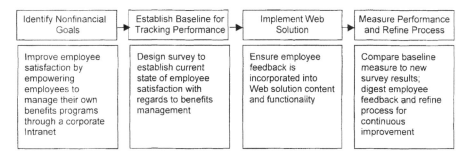

**Exhibit 3.   Measuring Indirect Benefits**

Like direct benefits, metrics should be identified for each set of indirect goals before a Web solution is implemented. Examples of some indirect goals and potential metrics are shown in Exhibit 4.

Surveys, focus groups, and interviews are some of the tools that will allow managers to establish baselines and measure changes going forward. Questions regarding customer or employee attitudes and behaviors, learning, and innovation are common baseline measures for tracking the effectiveness of a Web solution.

## CASE STUDY: SWEDISH MEDICAL CENTER

Swedish Medical Center is the largest, most comprehensive medical center in the Pacific Northwest. Home to companies like Microsoft, Boeing, Amazon.com, and Teledesic, the Pacific Northwest has a work force that is well educated and computer literate, and Seattle is the fifth most-wired city in the country. Swedish decided that an Internet solution was critical to strengthening its business position in a rapidly expanding and technically sophisticated economy. After the launch of its site in July 1997, Swedish immediately received a ROI2.

**Exhibit 4.   Indirect Goals and Potential Metrics**

| Goals | Metric(s) |
|---|---|
| Customer retention | • Average time per customer relationship |
| | • Customer attitudes toward company |
| Employee development | • Performance appraisal ratings |
| | • Employee loyalty |
| Learning and innovation | • Decisions made and problems solved |
| | • Successful projects completed |
| Community service | • Community attitudes toward company |

## Strategic Planning

Swedish Medical Center crafted a strategic plan for an online business solution with clear, measurable objectives.

- Reach a premium, technically sophisticated audience and generate incremental revenues through online referrals
- Provide the same information and ease of use as the toll-free 1-800-SWEDISH telephone service
- Enhance the well-being of patients and build ongoing relationships with clients by providing a superior Web experience
- Maintain consistency with existing marketing campaigns in print and other media

Through a collaborative and interactive process, Swedish was able to focus its Internet strategy.

## Building the Solution

Swedish's solution was developed using Microsoft technologies including Windows NT, Microsoft SQL Server, and Active Server Pages (ASP). These technologies enabled a solution that was scalable, flexible, and interactive. Using ASP to generate custom Web pages from criteria submitted by users, visitors to the Swedish site are able to search and select various titles or links to books from Swedish's "Book Store," services from their "Guide to Services," and physicians from Swedish's "Physician Referral" program.

## Measuring ROI2

The Swedish Website went live in July 1997, on time and on budget. The Web solution rendered a ROI2 above and beyond Swedish's expectations.

## Direct Benefits

- Incremental Revenues. Online referrals are bringing in more than $40,000 in new revenue each month.
- Reduction in Expenses. Each online referral to a physician saves more than $6 in staff cost, compared to a telephone referral.

## Indirect Benefits

- Improved Target Marketing. In February 1998, there were 1500 Web site visits from Microsoft employees alone. Total visitors numbered nearly 8000 and the volume is growing at 30 percent per month.
- Improving the customer's experience. Online referrals offer the same information as 1-800-SWEDISH. As a result, the number of online referrals is now greater than the number of telephone referrals. Prospective clients can now get referrals directly from the Web, and Web referrals are more private than telephone referral since there is no need to confide any medical details to an operator.

- Better information on promotional effectiveness. When a visitor links to the Swedish Web site, Swedish can see from what company the visitor is linking. This helps Swedish track which marketing campaigns — and which communications channels — are most effective. The site is carefully organized so users can self-navigate through a large amount of material. Content is served dynamically according to the requests of each visitor. This engages visitors and at the same time captures demographic information that helps Swedish understand its customer base.
- More effective human resources management. Swedish is planning additional cost-saving initiatives as a result of the site's success. The Human Resources department, which has already seen a reduction in its paperwork costs and staff time as an effect of the successful site, will now be able to focus more directly on the core tasks of selecting, hiring, and training the best people.
- Enhanced community service. The Volunteer Services department has also benefited from online volunteer recruitment. Without any promotion whatsoever, it has been able to recruit several high-quality volunteers each week through the Web site.

"Building long-term success on the Web is not done by just momentarily grabbing people's attention," said Douglas D. Waite, Chief Financial Officer of Swedish Medical Center. "A successful site should not only provide immediate results, but should be built on a foundation that allows for future growth and development."

## SUMMARY

Measuring return on investment has traditionally been difficult to define because it is different for every situation. People calculate their return on investment for situations in their lives every day — from choosing which brand of paper towels to buy in the supermarket, to deciding how their business would profit with the installation of new technology. ROI2 needs to be weighed in a similar manner — taking into consideration both direct and indirect returns. When a company is determining whether it would be profitable to invest in an Internet, intranet, or extranet business solution, it needs to factor in everything from direct sales and cost savings, to better customer experience and more effective internal communication. Internet, intranet, and extranet sites benefit customers, employees, and partners, respectively — ROI2 entails both tangible and intangible benefits and costs. Companies need to figure out which balance would best fit their online business objectives.

### Notes

1. Return on Internet Investment (ROI2) is a trademark of Free Range Media, Inc. All product and company names should be considered trademarks of their respective companies.
2. See other examples of how Sun Microsystems saves money using Internet technologies at http://www.sun.com:80/960101/feature1/index.html.

# Chapter 7
# Using the Internet to Improve Competitive Position and Reduce Costs

*Hollis Tibbetts*

TODAY, THE INTERNET CAN BE USED BY COMPANIES THAT WISH TO DIFFERENTIATE THEM-SELVES IN THE MARKETPLACE. These companies will achieve a competitive advantage by improving customer service, offering better products, and making better use of working capital, while simultaneously reducing costs.

The Internet facilitates this by providing a universally available backbone for sharing information among customers, distributors, manufacturers, and suppliers — the so-called "supply chain." All businesses leverage a variety of information to deliver products, plan for resource needs, and manage the overall business. This information can take many forms — the content that businesses leverage to achieve competitive advantage has traditionally included structured, nondynamic data like databases and delimited or fixed-field data files. Increasingly, organizations need to further leverage the nonstructured information served up by technology such as ERP-packaged solutions, legacy operational systems, e-mail systems, business reporting systems, and middleware frameworks. With the advent of the Internet, this has grown to include dynamic, nonstructured information such as Web information (HTML, XML), content-management systems and Web-enabled applications (such as catalogs). Those companies that are able to share timely information across the entire supply chain will become the new leaders in their industries or will increase their lead on their less nimble competitors. In some industries, laggards risk being driven out of business completely, as some industries will be so transformed by the Internet as to make its adoption as a core business platform a requirement for doing business.

0-8493-1160-8/02/$0.00+$1.50
© 2002 by CRC Press LLC

This chapter discusses the market dynamics that are shaping business Internet usage, how this information sharing involves linking various disparate applications and data sources across enterprises, the various different types of software packages and information sources that are linked, and the emerging technologies and standards that are involved in the process.

## MARKET DYNAMICS

There are a number of market forces which are the impetus behind the adoption of Internet technologies for integrating customers and their suppliers.

### Consumer Demand

Increased demands from customers, both individuals as well as businesses, for product delivery that is faster, cheaper, and better is creating a need to improve corporate agility and efficiency.

**Improved Inventory Management.** Several industries, most notably high-technology and automotive, are aggressively seeking to decrease inventory. The impetus in high-tech is the rapid obsolescence of inventory. In the automotive industry the motivation is for suppliers to provide JIT services to the major manufacturers. In both instances, the "carrying costs" of inventory are a significant factor as well.

**Limitations of Traditional Technology.** In the past, traditional technologies such as EDI defined electronic commerce. However, its batch personality, lack of message flow control, complex and expensive implementation issues, and fixed message formats have limited its utility.

EDI has fallen short for large hubs needing to get smaller trading partners on board due to the costs and complexity of implementation. For a large company, only about 20 percent of its trading partners typically participate in traditional EDI.

### Increased Outsourcing

Companies are increasingly outsourcing noncore functions such as manufacturing, warehousing, and logistics. This new business model will realize its full potential, both in terms of efficiency and profitability, when it is based upon tightly integrated electronic business partner systems.

Because of these dynamics, the need to integrate operational systems such as electronic catalogs, purchasing applications, financial systems, supply chain planning (SCP) systems, and ERP (enterprise resource planning) systems between organizations is rapidly growing. By linking these systems, organizations achieve competitive advantage through automated, collaborative processes and shared information. Internet technologies, which offer vast potential for open information exchange, further enable the evolving concept of supply chain integration.

## Internet "Ground Zero" Industries

Some industries, more than others, will be at the forefront of the Internet commerce movement. These are industries which are undergoing fundamental shifts, either because of market conditions, regulatory conditions, or technological innovation. These industries are characterized by short product life cycles, changing consumer demand, and rapid technology innovation — factors that break down corporate inertia and reward the adaptation and agility that collaboration brings.

## Media and Publishing

Media and publishing are truly at the forefront of the Internet (and information) revolution — precisely because media and publishing are information. Organizations in this area will be driven by competitive pressures to leverage the Internet to gather, host, and re-purpose information from a variety of sources. The companies involved here range from newspapers, classified ad companies, entertainment, and travel-related organizations to business information providers such as consulting firms.

## Distributors

Companies in this category have a pressing need to exchange data with many business partners, both upstream and downstream. These frequent interactions make a real-time communication infrastructure cost effective. By sharing real-time information with trading partners, entrepreneurial manufacturers and distributors can improve their efficiency to gain a competitive advantage. For example, a manufacturer or distributor can closely track inventory levels, so when inventories dip, the system will trigger automatic replenishment from an online supplier. Collaborative information exchange with business partners can also help streamline business processes and improve customer satisfaction. For instance, by sharing sales forecasts with preferred suppliers, manufacturers can strive for JIT (just in time) manufacturing.

## High-Tech Manufacturing

Adoption of outsourcing is common in the high-technology industry, which is defined by cutthroat competition, short selling cycles, and rapid technological churn. High-tech companies are also aggressive technologically, looking to reduce inventory and increase speed-to-market. This stems from the need to minimize inventory depreciation costs by better inventory and manufacturing management, particularly in the PC and semiconductor segments. Companies can no longer afford to carry inventory that may within days become obsolete.

## Commodity Goods

Vendors of commodity goods will be driven to the electronic commerce space by falling profit margins, which will be brought on by increased competition and increased ability by consumers and businesses to "comparison shop" using the Internet. Faced with declining margins and the inability to compete based on product differentiation (almost by definition), manufacturers of commodity goods will seek differentiation through brand awareness (advertising and marketing) and through providing added-value goods and services over the Internet. Examples of this might be an office supply vendor using the Internet to "manage" a client company's stocks of office supplies, or a commodity product vendor building a "super site" by providing its products, as well as products from other vendors, in an effort to capture mindshare from its customers.

## Configurable or Customizable Goods

Due to the nature of their business, manufacturers of customizable or configurable products — for example, the telecommunications, PC, electronics, and office furniture markets are typically constrained by the availability of components rather than by their ability to assemble or manufacture the final goods. By sharing information among the manufacturer, the end customer, and the suppliers to the manufacturer, the assembly and manufacturing cycle time for products can be greatly reduced.

## TACTICAL VS. STRATEGIC COMPETITIVE ADVANTAGE

The Internet can be employed for both tactical and strategic advantage. The tactical approach is taken to either reduce costs or achieve incremental increases in revenue without impacting the core business processes or primary business relationships of the company. This path is typically taken based on a Return on Investment (ROI) approach, and as such, represents the majority of Internet projects undertaken in the business world at this time.

Achieving long-term strategic advantage, i.e., to dominate new markets, change the way products are created from conception to final customer delivery, fundamentally change the relationship between the customer and the vendor, or even recast the nature of an entire market typically require a substantial overhaul in the way a company thinks, is organized, and does business. This path is typically taken by either upstart visionaries (like Amazon.com) that succeed in shaking up an entire industry, or by companies in industries that are in the midst of tremendous upheaval — because of competitive, technological, sociological, or regulatory forces. These are visionary undertakings, with the possibility (but certainly not the guarantee) of tremendous ROI. From this perspective, companies that embark on this route are the ones with everything to gain, or conversely, everything to lose.

Attention must also be paid to the electronic commerce undertakings of the competition. From this perspective, it is important to understand to what degree the proposed E-commerce initiatives are simply catching up to the industry leaders, or even to the industry "norm" (i.e., maintain market share), and to what extent they are designed to increase market share (i.e., become an innovator). In the end, those solutions that integrate best with the organization's operational systems (financial, customer service, order entry, etc.), require the fewest changes in organizational structure and process, and those with the lowest acquisition and total ownership costs are the most appropriate ones for implementation, as shown in Exhibit 1.

## ACHIEVING STRATEGIC COMPETITIVE ADVANTAGE

The extended enterprise concept has been advocated by industry analysts as the model organization of the future, and the Internet is by far the most likely candidate for being the "glue" that holds the components of this model together. The extended enterprise represents a shift away from the traditional vertical integration business model and toward a model where each organization focuses on its core competencies, and forges strong partnerships to "complete" the enterprise.

The extended enterprise, illustrated in Exhibit 2, is really a continuum. There are different degrees of "extendedness," depending on the level to which an organization is willing to commit. The vertically integrated company maintains arms-length relations with its trading partners, whereas the virtual enterprise sticks to its core competency and outsources many functions. Virtual companies act as relationship managers and brand marketers — they manufacture little or nothing. To adapt to changes in demand, they need to have excellent, real-time visibility into their trading partners' capabilities and current activities.

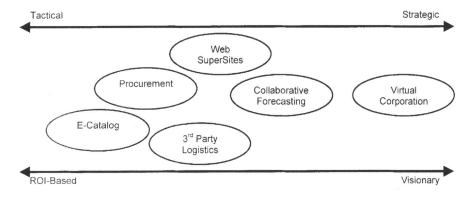

**Exhibit 1.   Tactical versus Strategic Implementations**

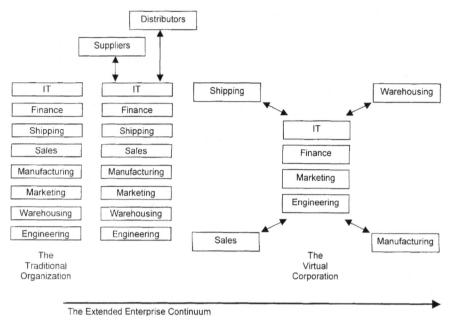

**Exhibit 8.2.    The Extended Enterprise Continuum**

"High Tech" companies like Monorail Computer Corp. are examples of virtual enterprises. Monorail Computer Corp. was founded in 1995 by a number of computer industry executives to provide high-quality products and services for practical computing needs. Monorail Computer Corp. focuses on management, design, and vision (its core competencies) and outsources functions such as manufacturing, support, and logistics.

The model leverages key partnerships with industry leaders that offer world-class expertise in logistics, service, and support and manufacturing. These partnerships deliver extremely efficient operations, maintain a flexible, variable cost model, and continually deliver outstanding products and services to the customer, all the while maintaining lower overhead costs. The result is high-quality, world-class-managed PC products at industry-leading prices.

Monorail's variable cost growth model ties almost all of its corporate expenses directly to sales volume and eliminates the large overhead carried by its competitors. Monorail has accomplished this by working with world-class firms who *can accomplish certain tasks with more efficiency and effectiveness* than Monorail.

FedEx, the acknowledged leader in overnight delivery services and logistics, provides a variety of services related to order entry, shipping, and delivery. Through FedEx's Logistics, Electronic Commerce & Catalog (LEC&C) Division, *Monorail's channel partners can reduce inventory stocking levels from eight weeks to as little as eight days*, greatly increasing inventory turns, significantly reducing the costs associated with obsolescence, and substantially *improving cost competitiveness*.

SCI, based in Huntsville, Alabama, is Monorail's desktop and minitower manufacturing partner. SCI is a global leader in computer component and system assembly. This relationship allows Monorail *to leverage SCI's vast experience and scale in ordering, warehousing, and assembly* of the units. The result is *world-class quality and timely delivery*.

SunTrust Bank, Inc. is a premier financial services company based in Atlanta. The Factoring Division of SunTrust acts as Monorail's credit department, collections department, and accounts receivable department. Through factoring its accounts, *Monorail has instant access to cash and can fund very high growth rates* with little additional financing.

These unique relationships have enabled Monorail to create a business model whereby most of Monorail's costs are tied to sales volume. Additionally, by *avoiding the investment associated with high-cost, low-value-add activities, Monorail can scale its business to very high volumes in a very short period of time*. The result is unparalleled responsiveness and efficiency, all of which allows Monorail to deliver the best products at the best prices.

In summary, benefits realized from the extended enterprise model include improved time to market for products, shortened manufacturing cycles, more efficient inventory management, reduced waste, better use of working capital, more accurate forecasting, and improved customer satisfaction.

The Internet is clearly the technology platform of choice for realizing the full potential of this business model.

## ACHIEVING TACTICAL COMPETITIVE ADVANTAGE

Tactical advantage is achieved by automating and integrating systems, and for the most part require no significant changes to corporate processes, structure, or mind set. The areas that offer the fastest payback are usually purchasing (often starting with office supplies) and online selling (via an online catalog). The growing trend for products in these areas is demonstrated by the June 1998 announcement of the Online Retail Store and Business-to-Business Procurement products by the software Titan SAP.

Although the word "tactical" often has a negative connotation, using the Internet for tactical advantage should not be viewed in a negative light — companies can impact the bottom line significantly by employing so-called "tactical" techniques. For example, Global 2000 companies typically spend about a third of their revenues on nonstrategic/nonproduction goods and services such as communications and capital equipment, computer hardware and software, industrial and office supplies, and MRO (maintenance, repair, and operating) supplies. Typically, these purchasing processes are loosely managed and monitored and labor intensive, which result in high costs and little opportunity for optimization.

Case studies have consistently shown that companies can realize savings in the 15 percent range by automating, coordinating, and monitoring these purchasing activities. The Internet provides a natural mechanism for automating these processes. These savings are then passed directly on to the bottom line in the form of increased profitability. Tactical? Yes. Insignificant? Hardly. Industry analysts have generally predicted that nearly all "Global 2000" organizations, as well as a fairly large number of small and mid-size businesses will have implemented some level of automated purchasing using the Internet within the next four years, with the rapid ROI providing the justification for these projects.

### Automating Purchasing

For many companies, automating purchasing represents the first logical step in Internet-enabled electronic commerce. The key to the success of this kind of project is to provide enough flexibility and ease of use so that it can be used by the majority of corporate employees, and so that the "masses" do not subvert its effectiveness by going outside the system. ROI is achieved by having an automated system that typically aggregates purchases (reducing accounting and administrative overhead) and then places these orders with the lowest-cost vendor (typically, comparison shopping over the Internet). ROI is also significantly enhanced by having a full reporting system which allows for spending trends to be viewed, allowing better "preferred customer" prices to be negotiated.

The costs associated from automating purchasing in this fashion can be expensive — large companies can easily face project costs in the millions of dollars, regardless of whether this automation is achieved by purchasing a package or whether a solution is custom developed; however these costs are typically recovered in 12 to 18 months.

### Setting up Shop Online

The logical complement to automating purchasing using the Internet is selling via the Internet. These "sell-side" solutions were the first to appear in the electronic commerce space. Many of these sites will grow to become "Supersites," where the catalog content will consist not only of products from the company, but also from other companies. An example of this would be an office supply company that wishes to sell computers, office furniture, and business books online as a method of offering additional value to its customers. The company would create a Supersite where all of the product information from the various vendors would be aggregated, and all purchases could be executed through the single site.

Selling online typically involves engaging either a catalog hosting service, or purchasing catalog software. The price range spans from a few thousands of dollars to hundreds of thousands of dollars, depending upon need. Because of the potential expenditure, and a number of publicized "failures," where returns were not as high as expected, decisions to implement these sell-side solutions typically need to be justified on an ROI basis. Before investing in any of these technologies, organizations must evaluate the appropriateness of sell-side electronic commerce technologies to their sales and marketing strategies, customer needs, and customer management agendas. Businesses must evaluate their customers' (or potential customers') needs and profiles, and craft a value proposition that reflects true business needs. Efforts targeted at customers who are unlikely to interact online, or offering no additional value through ease of transaction or incremental benefits such as price discounts or extra/additional products, should not be undertaken as they are almost certain to disappoint.

The benefits of a sell-side E-commerce implementation will fall into the two categories: cost savings and revenue enhancements. Cost savings are primarily driven by reduced costs of doing business — for example, orders can be taken and tracked without "human" intervention. Revenue enhancements come from the potential to increase the customer base and market share by creating an E-commerce site that offers compelling business value and makes it easy for customers to interact with it. Aside from these somewhat measurable benefits, there is also the reality that without such an E-commerce presence, many organizations will find it difficult to compete in their markets. An example of this is the office supplies market, where the E-commerce presence is rapidly becoming a "ticket to entry." Those companies who are looking to make the E- commerce sales channel a more strategic investment will be the ones who view this decision in light of factors such as business cycle acceleration, preservation of existing client base, and market (and new market) penetration.

## ISSUES AND CHALLENGES

For E-commerce to thrive, a number of technical and cultural issues must be addressed.

### Information Sharing

E-commerce requires that we link applications and share information with upstream and downstream supply chain partners, regardless of computing and information storage environments. For instance, information once reserved for internal company use, such as inventory or product availability, now needs to be shared with supply chain partners in the context of an electronic commerce system.

Corporations must also be able to integrate their business systems with the business systems of their partners and suppliers without requiring modifications to a partner's applications. Some of the barriers to implementing these cross-organizational processes are beginning to fade, with the Internet providing a low-cost, ubiquitous network connecting business partners. An ongoing challenge, however, is that all supply chain partners need a far simpler approach to data integration and information sharing. The limiting factor is that supply chain partners have had to develop and maintain additional APIs or object interfaces, significantly increasing the cost of electronic cooperation between companies, because these applications were never designed to work with one another.

The bottom line is that information developed by all supply chain partners for inventory management, forecasting, and sales force automation needs to be shared and updated. Prepackaged solutions currently do not exist for this kind of implementation, so market leaders will need to look at the emerging category of Internet-focused software solutions that allow data from multiple unstructured data sources of all types. This need fits into the category of "Content Integration," which is the ability to leverage all of the data and information that a company uses by integrating it with existing operational systems, such as ERP and E-commerce applications (Exhibit 3).

The content businesses leverage to achieve competitive advantage has traditionally included structured, nondynamic data such as databases and delimited or fixed-field data files. Increasingly, organizations need to further leverage the nonstructured information served up by ERP packaged solutions, legacy operational systems, e-mail systems, business reporting systems, and middleware frameworks. With the advent of the Internet, this has grown to include dynamic, nonstructured information such as Web information (HTML, XML), content management systems, and Web-enabled applications, such as catalogs.

Leveraging this content, to date, has been a process which has been largely manual, involving a hodge-podge of different tools and custom-written programs, some of which support structured nondynamic data, some of which support interfaces into operational systems, and some of which support Web information. None of these tools supports the challenges of data inconsistency, changing schemas, or varying data formats — issues that are typically resolved manually or by writing complex custom applications.

## Electronic Catalog Implementation

Catalogs are key repositories of information in E-commerce. In the case of the sell-side implementation, the E-catalog must be populated with

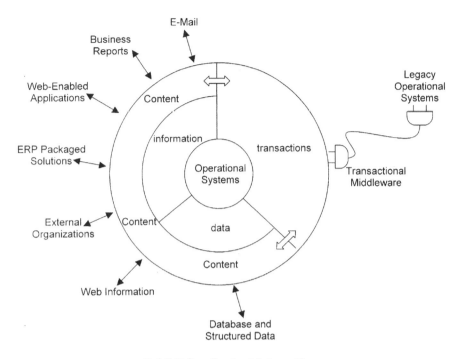

**Exhibit 3.  Content Integration**

product information, and that information must be kept current on a regular basis with regards to pricing, features, and inventory status. This implies interfaces with systems as far ranging as Quark (where the paper equivalent of the electronic catalog may have been created) to SAP (where the inventory information may be stored) to Vantive (where the customer service information is kept). In the case of the buy-side implementation, an E-catalog is usually kept locally. Information on products must be loaded into that catalog, either by having that information presented in one of the several evolving "standard" formats such as CIF, or by other means. Emerging products in the content integration space can provide a valuable bridge between these different worlds.

### "Operational Systems" Integration

Electronic commerce requires integration with the applications which traditionally "run the business." These "operational systems" are made up of both "back office" systems, i.e., finance, human resources, and purchasing, as well as "front office" systems such as customer service. Depending on the sophistication of the E-commerce system, information such as inventory status, prices, payments, purchase orders, and customer and supplier information must be integrated. For procurement systems, information from HR systems is valuable, to help determine who is allowed to purchase and who is allowed to approve purchases. This integration can be done manually (through custom-developed scripts, and usually a "batch-loading" methodology), by using products from "processware" vendors who focus on automating the integration of certain processes between certain software vendors packages — for example, automating the ability of a customer-service package to deal with a customer return, and send the appropriate information to the financial package for a credit and to the inventory management system to update inventory. This is also an area where content integration software can be helpful, as none of the "processware" packages can support all combinations of processes and packages to interface.

## Structural Issues

Scalability and reliability are key "structural" requirements for any serious electronic commerce application. Many commerce applications have failed because they became victims of their own success, i.e., the application or Web site became significantly more popular than originally anticipated. This unanticipated load results in crashed servers and unacceptable response times. Generally, the flaws that result in lack of scalability and reliability are structural in nature — and generally cannot be resolved by adding more hardware or making quick "fixes" to the software. By the time the issues are addressed in the application, the initiative has typically been declared a failure. It is important "up front" to have a clear picture of how many tens, hundreds, thousands, or millions of hits this application will need to cope with, both initially and down the road, and to have a clear understanding of how well the application can scale to handle the anticipated transaction levels.

Similarly, interoperability and manageability are structural issues that are important to address during the design phase of a project. Electronic commerce systems never operate in a vacuum — they must (one way or another) interface with systems both internal and external to the enterprise — for example, financial applications, inventory systems, customer care applications, human resource packages, and EDI implementations. These interfaces may be built into the E-commerce package, which is occasionally the case, or left up to the end customer to either manually move information from one to the other (for example, manually rekey product orders that come in via EDI or manually extract the employee list from the HR system and load it into a procurement application), write custom software to do this automation, or leverage information integration types of software for more rapid implementations. Manageability is core to any enterprise-class software implementation. Issues that arise are the ability to diagnose problems, make and manage changes to the applications functionality, "tune" the application for optimal performance online, etc.

**Cultural and Organizational Issues**

The largest impediments to the success of E-commerce are cultural and organizational in nature. These impediments vary, but include:

- The mistrust of suppliers, reluctance to cede "control" to outsourcers, and other insular behaviors
- The view that the Internet is not strategic to the business
- Lack of understanding of the customer or market needs
- Overreliance (or underreliance) on cost justification for Internet projects
- Attempts to implement E-commerce "on the cheap," without examining the ramifications of a poorly planned and poorly executed system
- Lack of holistic planning — where Internet-related projects are not coordinated across different business units and departments, are at cross-purposes with each other, and end up lacking important support from departments within the enterprise

## SUMMARY

Clearly, the Internet is reshaping the way that business is done. We are at the beginning of a transformation that will possibly prove as significant as the industrial revolution. The Internet "revolution," like the industrial revolution, is about the automation of processes. They both create tremendous gains in wealth by providing for tremendous efficiencies in the economy. Almost every entity, from entrepreneurs to government to major corporations, have or will experience major paradigm shifts because of this.

This global revolution is creating a single-market world. This pace of change continues to accelerate as the information float collapses further, bringing the sender and receiver instantly together. With the collapse of the information float, the financial float has also collapsed (i.e., the time it takes to move money around the world). Money, like information, is now only data.

Eventually, every organization will harness the power of these new technologies. We are just at the starting point of this metamorphosis — the technology is young, the markets are nascent, and the risks are high. In the end, every business will need to analyze the risks and rewards as it positions itself as a leader or follower in the race for competitive advantage.

# Chaper 8
# Web and Java Risk Issues

*Louise L. Soe*
*Frederick Gallegos*

THE INTERNET HAS BEEN AROUND FOR YEARS, BUT PRIVATE INDUSTRY ONLY BECAME INTER-ESTED IN ITS COMMERCIAL POSSIBILITIES AFTER THE GRAPHICAL WORLD WIDE WEB EMERGED DURING THE EARLY 1990s. The Web version of the Internet offered a potentially inexpensive and platform-independent network over which to conduct business and disseminate information. In addition, companies grew excited about the possibility of developing intranets (internal Internets) that would give them access to all of their legacy data via one simple Internet browser interface.

All of this was to be enabled by a programming language, Java, that would work on any operating system or computing platform. In addition, this language could be used to deliver to client machines the program and data elements (in the form of a Java applet) that the client needed to use at any given time. Companies envisioned desktops equipped with Internet appliances that would not need to contain expensive copies of application programs such as word processors and spreadsheets. It is little wonder that corporations were ready to embrace both the Internet and Java, and to build such high expectations about these technologies. These expectations have not died. Many corporate executives and managers expect these technologies to drive economic growth well into the next century.

## THE PERCEIVED RISKS

However, the Internet and its most promising language, Java, present an interesting mix of opportunities and risks to organizations. On the one hand, organizations want to stay competitive and embrace technologies that provide so much promise. Yet, both corporations and individuals still perceive the Internet as insecure and the use of Java applets as unsafe. Corporations are wary of the very serious security threats from outside hackers to which a connection to the Internet might expose them. Individual users of the Internet are wary of the possible destructive use of Java applets that they download to their computers over the Internet. Thus, while the promise of the Internet and Java pushes companies toward expectations of free and open communication over the Internet, fear pushes companies toward isolation because they want to protect their information assets from theft, corruption, or destruction.

The remainder of this chapter discusses ways in which corporations can use the Internet in a secure fashion by implementing security measures that are currently available. It also discusses the Java programming language, which is still somewhat immature, and the measures that are being taken to strengthen its security so that it will become the powerhouse language of the Internet.

## INTERNET SECURITY

Security tools and procedures exist right now to reduce risk when a company gives its customers access to business resources over the Internet. Security measures are available to provide access security to protect the company's own computers, disks, memory, and other computing equipment from outside interference, and transaction security to ensure that two individuals or organizations on the Internet can privately and safely execute a transaction.

Properly implemented, these security mechanisms will:

- Protect the company from intruders who attempt to enter the internal network from the Internet
- Provide authorized users with access to Internet services such as HTTP, FTP, Telnet, and Gopher
- Deliver required Internet applications from the internal network to the Internet
- Deliver SMTP and Netnews services to the internal network from the Internet
- Prevent unauthorized use of resources on the internal network
- Give users an easy way to understand network security status without being Internet security experts
- Ensure expert round-the-clock, seven-day-a-week monitoring and response to security events, and
- Maximize protection from the Internet and minimize the cost of operating and monitoring protective devices, such as the application proxy firewall

## SECURITY TOOLS AND TECHNOLOGIES

Effective security solutions rely on several tools and technologies designed to protect information and computers from intrusion, compromise, or misuse: encryption technologies, security policies and procedures, and various types of firewalls.

**Encryption Technologies**

Encryption technologies electronically store information in an encoded form that can only be decoded by an authorized individual who has the appropriate decryption technology and authorization to decrypt. Encryption provides a number of important security components to protect electronic information:

- Identity.............................Who are you?
- Authentication.................. Can you prove who you are?
- Authorization................... What can you do?
- Auditing............................ What did you do?
- Integrity............................ Is it tamper proof?
- Privacy.............................. Who can see it?
- Nonrepudiation................ Can I prove that you said what you said?

When information is encoded, it is first translated into a numerical form, and then encrypted using a mathematical algorithm. The algorithm requires a number or message, called a key, in order to encode or decode the information. The algorithm cannot decode the encrypted information without a decode key.

**Security Policies and Procedures**

In the rush to establish an Internet presence, many companies have overlooked perhaps the most important foundation piece in an effective security solution: a sound security policy that identifies who has access to a company's electronic resources, and under what circumstances they have access. Many companies have overlooked this strategy in the rush to establish an Internet presence. Thus, security policies are almost nonexistent in some companies and clearly defined in others. For example, the use of stateless filters means that the organization is relying on defaults set by the vendor of the security package, whereas the use of state-maintained filters means the organization is actively ensuring certain types of activity or patterns are reviewed to prevent possible intrusion or loss.

Security policies fall along a continuum that ranges from promiscuous at one end to paranoid at the other. The promiscuous policy allows unchecked access between the Internet and the organization's internal network to everyone. The paranoid policy refuses access between these two networks to everyone. In between are two more palatable alternatives, the permissive policy and the prudent policy.

The permissive policy allows all traffic to flow between the internal network and the Internet except that which is explicitly disallowed. Permissive policies are implemented through packet-filtering gateways, where stateless filters prevent individual packets of data from crossing the network boundary if the packet is coming from or going to a specific computer, network, or network port. There are two major drawbacks to a permissive policy, however. First, it requires an exhaustive set of filters to cover all possible addresses and ports that should be denied access. Second, it is virtually impossible to block certain undesirable packets without also blocking other desirable and necessary packets, because network protocols are dynamic and often change network port numbers, depending on the protocol state.

A prudent policy, on the other hand, selectively allows traffic that is explicitly permitted by the protocol and excludes any other. Prudent policies are implemented by a set of application proxies that understand the underlying application protocol and can implement a set of state-maintaining filters that allow specific application data to pass from one network to the next. Because the filters can follow the state of the protocol, they can change dynamically when the protocol changes state. This way, rules allow only properly authorized data to flow across the network boundary. Prudent policies are implemented through application proxy firewalls.

Because prudent and permissive policies act as the network boundaries, they are referred to as perimeter security solutions.

Once a company selects the appropriate security policy, the policy can be implemented according to a strict set of procedures with the support of software systems. These security procedures, which include a documented set of rules governing the management and administration of the security system and its generated events, record a trail of all modifications to the security system (auditing) and set off signal alarms when someone attempts to violate the policies. Properly followed, they protect an organization from all types of security violations, including accidental administrative mistakes, human factor attacks (i.e., people characteristics) and unauthorized modifications to the security policy.

To reduce the risk of "inside" break-ins, many companies also require a background check of security systems personnel, and separate security management and auditing to prevent an administrator from altering the audit of management actions.

### Internet Firewalls

An Internet application proxy firewall is a prudent perimeter security solution. These systems sit between the Internet and the organization's internal network, and control the traffic flow between the Internet and a company's internal resources. A firewall provides application proxies for most popular Internet applications as well as support for a more restrictive prudent policy. This policy might restrict the establishment of network connections from within the company outward to the Internet. In addition, rather than forwarding packets between networks, the firewall can require the application client to establish an application service connection to the firewall. The firewall then maintains the connection with the outside server. The firewall will only pass data for applications that it currently supports, which eliminates most security holes.

Security holes created by incorrectly configured computers on the internal network are not visible to the Internet and therefore cannot be exploited by external Internet users. The organization's own Internet application servers then sit outside the firewall in what is called the demilitarized zone. This eliminates the need for outside traffic to travel through the firewall into the organization's internal network when it is using Web, FTP, or Telnet services.

To maintain the integrity of the perimeter, the firewall must be constantly monitored for potential security breaches. Should a breach occur, an Internet security expert must be available to survey the damage and recommend a solution.

### Internet Firewall Configurations

**Bastion Host.** This is the only host on the customer's internal network that is visible to the Internet. It has no customer-accessible accounts for logging into the bastion host.

Customer communications travel through the bastion host via proxy applications. This is the most secure method of performing perimeter security today.

In the popular dual-homed bastion host configuration, the toolkit software is installed on a host with two network interfaces. The toolkit software provides proxy services for common applications like FTP and TELNET, and security for SMTP mail. Since the bastion host is a security-critical network strong point, it is important that the configuration of the software on that system be as secure as possible.

Dual-homed gateways provide an appealing firewall, since they are simple to implement, require a minimum of hardware, and can be verified easily. Most Berkeley-based UNIX implementations have a kernel variable _ipforwardign, which can be set to indicate to the operating system that it should not route traffic between networks, even if it is connected to them (which would normally cause the system to act as a gateway router). By completely disabling routing, the administrator can have a high degree of confidence that any traffic between the protected network and any untrusted network has to occur through an application that is running on the firewall. Since there is no traffic transferred directly between the internal network and the untrusted network, it is not necessary to show any routes to the protected network over the untrusted network. This effectively renders the protected network invisible to any systems except the bastion host. The only disadvantage of this type of firewall is that it implicitly provides a firewall of the type in which that which is not expressly permitted is prohibited. This means that it is impossible to weaken the firewall's security to let a service through should one later decide to do so. Instead, all services must be supported via proxies on the firewall.

**Choke Router/Screened Host.** The choke router reinforces the bastion host, enforces security policy, and isolates the internal network from the Internet.

A screened host gateway relies on a router with some form of packet screening capacity to block off access between the protected network and the untrusted network. A single host is identified as a bastion host, and traffic is permitted only to that host. The software suite that is run on the bastion host is similar to a dual-homed gateway; the system must be as secure as possible, as it is the focal point for attack on the network. Screened host gateways are a very flexible solution, since they offer the opportunity to selectively permit traffic through the screening router for applications that are considered trustworthy, or between mutually trusted networks.

The disadvantage of this configuration is that there are now two critical security systems in effect: the bastion host and the router. If the router has access control lists that permit certain services through, the firewall administrator has to manage an additional point of complexity. Verifying the correctness of a screened host firewall is a bit more difficult. It quickly becomes increasingly difficult as the number of services permitted through the router grows. Screened host firewalls also introduce management risks; because it is possible to open holes in the firewall for special applications or influential users, the firewall administrator must be careful to resist pressure to modify the screening rules in the router.

In a screened subnet firewall, a small isolated network is placed between the trusted network and the untrusted network. Screening rules in routers protect access to this network by restricting traffic so that both networks can only reach hosts on the screened subnet. Conceptually, this is the dual-homed gateway approach applied to an entire network. The main utility of this approach is that it permits multiple hosts to exist on the outside network (again referred to as the demilitarized zone). An additional advantage to the screened host subnet is that the firewall administrator can configure network routing in a way that does not advertise routes to the private network from the Internet, or internal routes to the Internet. This is a powerful means to protect a large private network, since it becomes very difficult for an outsider to direct traffic toward the hidden private network. If the routing is blocked, then all traffic must pass through an application on the bastion host, just as it must in the dual-homed gateway.

**Firewalls in a Partitioned Network.** Not every network is a single, isolated network attached to an untrusted network. As the use of large-scale networks continues to increase, businesses increasingly form business partnerships and transmit sensitive corporate information over public networks. In addition, single corporations seek to establish a common security perimeter among multiple facilities connected over a public backbone. In this type of situation, a business can effectively combine a firewall with network-level encryption hardware (or software) to produce a virtual network, with a common security perimeter.

A company can establish a common security perimeter between two facilities, over a public Wide Area Network (WAN). The encryption is separate from the router, but need not be if integrated encrypting routers are available. Currently, there are several products that act as encrypting bridges at a frame level. These products work by examining the source and destination address of all packets arriving via one interface and retransmitting the packet out via another interface. If the encrypting bridge/router is configured to encrypt traffic to a specific network, the packet data is encrypted, and a new checksum is inserted into the packet header. Once the packet is received at the other computer, the peer encrypting bridge/router determines that it is from a network with which the router is encrypting traffic, and decrypts the packet, patches the checksum, and retransmits it.

Anyone intercepting traffic between the two encrypting networks would see only useless cipher text. An additional benefit of this approach is that it protects against attempts to inject traffic by spoofing the source network address. Unless attackers know the cipher key that is in use, their packets will be encrypted into junk when they go through the encrypting bridge/router. If the encrypting bridge/router gets traffic for a network with which it does not have an encryption arrangement, traffic is transmitted normally. In this manner, a firewall can be configured, with encrypted tunnels to other networks. For example, a company could safely share files via NFS or safely use weakly authenticated network login programs, such as rlogin over their encrypted link, and still have a strong firewall protecting access between the corporate perimeter and the rest of the world. Two companies that wanted to establish a business connection for proprietary information could apply a similar approach, in which traffic between the firewall bastion host on one corporate network and the firewall bastion host on the other corporate network was automatically encrypted.

## PRACTICAL WEB SECURITY SOLUTIONS

Thus, it is easy to see that businesses need not be intimidated into bypassing the opportunities available to them on the Internet. Several security solutions exist immediately to reduce or remove the risk involved in connecting to the Internet. We list and summarize a few of them.

### A Back Door Connection

This method connects the Internet server (Web server, List server, etc.) to other company computer systems through a dial-up link, which is not made available anywhere on the Internet.

A back door data transfer method might include setting up a program like ProComm Plus (by Datastorm) on a computer connected to the Web Server. The company's other computer systems then periodically dial into that back door computer via ProComm to upload files that are then imported to the Web server's database via a custom import program. This same method works well for sending order or questionnaire data in batches from a Web server to other computers within the company.

In using this approach, the communications lines between the company's computers and its Internet presence are severed most of the time. Even when the link is established between computers, it does not use an insecure network protocol like TCP/IP, which is easy for hackers to penetrate. This prevents Internet hackers from drilling through to vital company systems and information.

### A Network Firewall

A network firewall connects the Internet server into the company's existing computer network system via a permanent firewall router.

Firewall routers are sold by a growing number of network hardware and software companies. They serve as a security barrier between network systems. By placing such a barrier between the company's Web server and the rest of the company's network, a network administrator can restrict the flow of network data packets between these segments. The firewall could restrict all inbound packets to those generated by the Web server itself; thus only the Web server can access internal information.

A good hacker can get through a firewall, although attempting to gain access beyond the firewall would require the use of sophisticated IP source-address spoofing techniques. These techniques fool the firewall into believing that the hacker's connection has the same network address as the Web server or some other privileged user. At this point, the hacker would need sufficient motivation to expend the effort and time to get through.

Any time a company plans to connect its in-house computer network directly to an Internet server, a firewall should be used to deter casual hacking and other less malicious security risks.

### A Pseudo-Firewall

A pseudo-firewall connects the Internet server into the company's existing computer network system via standard router equipment, but segregates network traffic with different network protocols (i.e., TCP/IP and IPX/SPX).

The main security problem on the Internet exists due to certain flaws in the Internet network protocol (TCP/IP). Thus, using a different protocol to connect the company's internal computers to its Internet server solves this problem.

For example, if a company's Internet server used a Pentium PC running Microsoft Windows NT as its Web server over a leased line connected to an Internet Service Provider, this method would entail running two network protocols on the Web server. The Web server must use TCP/IP to connect to the Internet. Yet, to access information on internal computer networks, that same Web server could be configured to use something else, such as IPX/SPX, which is native to Novell's Netware. The hacker could spoof the TCP/IP address, but would find no other network connections beyond the Web server.

This method is not proven to work more effectively than a firewall. However, its appeal is that it can provide a similar level of security to a firewall router, at lower cost.

Our discussion now moves to the application language, Java, and the risks and opportunities it provides to organizational computing.

### JAVA RISK ISSUES

Another area for management review in corporate use of the World Wide Web is the use of Java. Java is an object-oriented programming language in which small programs (called applets) can be compiled and run on any computing platform. Within an internal intranet, applets could deliver software and data to client workstations only as needed. The applet would only need to include the functions of a software application and the data that the client needed to accomplish a specific task. Thus, corporations could save on software licenses and workstation computing power across the enterprise. On the Internet, Java applets are downloaded by the client from a server on the Internet. However, many individuals fear the destructive potential of Java applets from unknown sources. Current browsers allow users to refuse Java applets or accept them only from trusted sources.

Although Java provides benefits and cost-effective measures to a corporation, the current versions of Java are not mature enough to satisfy the needs of corporate security. Java may be fine for building Windows applets, but it is not yet a real tool for mission-critical programs that draw on legacy data. The earlier Java tools provided weak data validation and relied too heavily on object linking and embedding (OLE). These older Java tools were geared too much toward Windows and often lacked some of the key features such as debuggers and compilers that are essential in a workbench.

Recent studies by universities and private industry groups have identified three areas that pose the most significant risks to Java applications: (1) the lack of audit trails, (2) the variances between Java language and bytecode semantics, and the (3) deficiencies in the design of the language and byte code format and the input/output object classes.

Presently, the Java environment does not provide a standard or default mechanism to produce audit trails. The developer must customize all verification into the application. Java needs built-in accountability functions to maintain protected and selective auditing information much like an audit log, which identifies the parties responsible for various actions performed on the computer.

Users also need to understand that they do not control a Java applet once it is downloaded into the local environment. For example, users may not necessarily know that an applet has been downloaded or may not have information on how many applets are in operation, unless they set up adequate security on their Internet browsers. A common form of malicious applet can continue running on the client and force the user to restart the system.

There are other security problems as well. Today, compiler languages such as C or Ada can produce bytecode that looks like Java bytecode to the verifier. If the verifier erroneously accepts the non-Java bytecode, it is unlikely to follow Java's language restrictions and it may allow performance of illegal procedures. For example, a hostile applet could be used to create a classloader containing unacceptable statements. The classloader, which is responsible for defining namespace seen by other classes, could then allow the attacking applet to customize the user's computer environment.

Finally, from an IS audit standpoint, Java input/output object classes are public. Even though this feature improves the usefulness of Java, it provides hackers with a way to deliver damage. This major weakness of Java makes the use of audit tools critical to safe use of Java programs.

For the average corporate IS developer, accustomed to Visual Basic and similar drag-and-drop development tools, the early Java environments seemed to take two steps backwards. Therefore, Java's competitors took advantage of this weakness and prepared a second generation of Java toolsets to resolve some of the weaknesses of the Java programming language. These tools were intended to give corporate IS developers the same warm, fuzzy feeling of confidence they get from other visual development environments.

Corporate IS developers want to build Web applications for the long term. Many corporate and government IS departments are caught up in testing new Web-based development technologies, primarily centered on Java-based development. These include tools such as Visix's-eleven, and emerging technologies such as remote method invocation (RMI) and object serialization. One of the documented weaknesses that most toolsets do not redress is Sun's implementation of the abstract Windowing Toolkit for building user interface features. Developers are still working to resolve this problem.

## JAVA SECURITY IMPROVEMENTS

Java has additional shortcomings in the area of security. Most companies that use Java will not yet use it for security-sensitive data because it lacks the necessary security functions. Development experts describe the programming language as "a few cups short of a full pot." Unresolved issues revolve around database access, security, bi-directional communication, and the way in which Java handles compound documents. Sun Microsystems has several initiatives to make Java more suitable for utilizing security-sensitive data. These include creation of several API programs for encryption, digital signatures, authentication, and support for a key management system.

The latest version of the Java tools addresses many concerns by offering:

- Strong memory protection. Java applications and applets cannot gain unauthorized memory access to read or change accounts because Java removes the possibility of either maliciously or inadvertently reading and/or corrupting memory locations outside boundaries of the programs.
- Encryption and signatures. Java uses powerful encryption technology to verify that an applet came from an authorized source and has not been modified.
- Rules enforcement. Java objects and classes make it simple to represent corporate information entities, and the rules governing their use are embedded within the objects themselves. The result is that the introduction of ad hoc access and manipulation methods can be controlled.
- Runtime Code verification. The Java run-time verification system inspects all code for viruses and tampering before running it, ensuring that all applications and applets downloaded to the client do not violate the integrity of the environment.

Even with these improvements, there is no singular approach to solve the major concerns with Java.

Recently, Microsoft Corporation and Netscape announced a security plan, which includes a series of security techniques for forthcoming products. These include ways to verify authorship, improvements to proxy-server and firewalls, and an information database on the security status of Java applets. However, the continued competition between Microsoft and other companies over definition of Java language standards may not be doing much to contribute to the development of a mature, stable Java programming language.

## CONCLUSIONS

For CIOs and CEOs, the new millennium promises many exciting opportunities and risks in information technology. As unsettling and unnerving as many of these changes are, managers must employ common sense and informed business judgement to understand both risks and benefits. We have attempted to provide an overview of Web and Java security issues facing business today. We understand the technical complexities and encourage decision-makers to carefully weigh the investment in security against the potential risks. We also reiterate that there are answers and solutions for many of the security issues we discuss. Effective measures exist to protect both access security and transaction security over the Internet. As improvements are made to Java and as the programming language matures, we can also expect that it will incorporate more and better security measures, because Java language developers realize that security is critical to the acceptance and success of the language.

Java provides an entirely new kind of cross-platform computing environment that can be used to integrate and work with an organization's existing systems and networks. As Java matures, it may well replace costlier, less efficient elements in existing computing systems and make feasible the continued use of existing legacy systems. This is especially important today, when multiple incompatible platforms and legacy systems are typical in global corporate and private information systems infrastructures. The Web and Java hold great promise for organizations that want to integrate their existing, incompatible applications and make them available through one common user interface, an Internet browser.

Web platforms and application platforms are incredibly complex and resource-intensive, expensive to buy and maintain, and costly to update or expand. But, as troublesome as these existing systems may be, the CEO and CIO have to consider whether they can afford to scrap huge corporate investments in existing information systems. It is very costly to replace systems, convert databases that contain invaluable information, and retrain workers in new computing environments and techniques.

Throughout the business and personal computing world, industry leaders, software vendors, and software developers are showing utmost support for Java, the programming language that they believe will transcend all barriers. Most business organizations will benefit by using adaptable application architecture. This new technology can save a company millions of corporate dollars per fiscal year on hardware, software, and systems development by converting a "custom fat client" into a "thin client."

While Web technology and Java are still somewhat immature, there is no doubt that they are here to stay. Major software developers continue to give credence to Java's future, and have addressed user concerns by announcing plans to embed Java in future versions of their operating systems. As other higher-order tools are built up around it, Java should become one of the best enablers on the market. Those higher-order tools are on their way to the marketplace now, so sit tight, and be prepared to embrace the Web and the Java revolution.

# Chapter 9
# Managing Risk in Electronic Commerce

*Carol A. Siegel*

A<small>S THE USE OF</small> I<small>NTERNET-RELATED ELECTRONIC COMMERCE</small> (EC) <small>INCREASES, THE POTEN-</small>
<small>TIAL FOR PROBLEMS INCREASES WITH IT.</small> The major concern for organizations doing business over the Internet is the security of their systems and operations. Corporations are worried that their internal networks may be threatened by hackers or other violations of security. Financial institutions are at substantial risk because they are responsible for protecting the assets of their customers as well as their own.

This chapter presents a general methodology for corporations to use to evaluate EC solutions, along with key security technologies necessary to make EC safe. It also discusses the Internet standards organizations that can help corporations evaluate individual security solutions.

## A METHODOLOGY FOR EVALUATING E-COMMERCE SOLUTIONS

To reduce the risk in transacting business on the Internet, organizations must use a methodology for evaluating EC solutions from a security perspective. This is a circular process: as the needs change, the whole process must be reevaluated. The methodology is made up of four components, involving business needs, security objectives, security solutions, and EC solutions.

### Step One: Define Business Needs

The process begins with a comprehensive needs analysis for conducting E-commerce on the Internet. Individual business units should develop their own plans. All plans must then be integrated into a cohesive enterprisewide plan. Some areas may want to advertise only on the Internet; others may want to go to transactional processing or to providing full financial services. Next, a timeframe for getting to the specified objectives must be developed and resource requirements must be identified.

0-8493-1160-8/02/$0.00+$1.50
© 2002 by CRC Press LLC

## Step Two: Establish the Security Objectives

One of the most important elements of this process is establishing a clear security policy. First, the level of acceptable risk must be determined. The risk is not only security risk, but also business risk, which includes legal and financial risk. Adequate levels of security can be identified by asking and answering questions on specific security situations, such as

- How would the organization's reputation be damaged if a break-in to the company was announced on the six o'clock news?
- If the organization's systems became inoperative because of a "denial of service" attack or a virus outbreak, how long could it survive using manual procedures?
- What would the organization do if it were responsible for infecting a business partner network with a virus, thereby causing it hardship and loss of business?

After addressing potential security scenarios and issues such as these, an organization will have a good idea of the level of protection it needs in its systems and networks. The Department of Defense's *Rainbow Series*, specifically "The Orange Book," is a good reference for assisting with the process of identifying levels of security associated with various systems and tools. In general, for commercial institutions, level C2 is adequate, whereas for government installations, B1 or B2 may be required. The higher the level of protection required, the higher the associated cost. An organization's security policy should be a balance of all three levels.

## Step Three: Evaluating the Security Solutions

Each specific security solution must be evaluated on the basis of specific criteria. The classic security services as defined by the International Standards Organization (ISO) standard are appropriate guidelines, although other standards may apply. The organization should examine and evaluate each solution on the basis of how it implements the following:

- *Identification and authentication.* Establish and confirm who or what the entity is. The "who" may be a user, an application, a system, or data.
- *Access Control.* Authorize the "who" to have and use specific rights or permissions.
- *Data integrity.* Ensure that information has not been modified, added to, or deleted during storage or transit.
- *Data Confidentiality.* Ensure that information is protected and is not disclosed to unauthorized parties.
- *Data Availability.* Ensure that information is present, accessible, and fit for use.
- *Auditability.* Ensure the existence of adequate audit trails that provide records of activity.

- *Nonrepudiation.* Ensure that parties in a transaction cannot deny that they performed that specific transaction at that exact time and place.

A critical part of the evaluation process is live system testing. Not only should the organization perform a test with real data at the company's labs, but any cryptographic application or algorithm also should be tested by industry professionals. The implementation of any security solution is as important as the theory behind the solution.

**Step Four: Evaluate the Complete E-Commerce Solution**

The E-commerce solution should be considered in its entirety and evaluated according to the following criteria:

- *Secure*—as it relates to the security objectives.
- *Interoperable*—it is compatible with existing systems, and it can be integrated into the enterprise architecture.
- *Flexible*—it can be customized.
- *Scaleable*—it supports multiple services and large networks.
- *Efficient*—it supports micropayments.
- *Open*—whether it relies on specific technologies, proprietary solutions, or protocols.

To assess different types of solutions, an in-depth knowledge of key security technologies is mandatory. It is important to have an understanding of security mechanisms, in addition to knowing how they are implemented. A poor implementation can render any system ineffective. New technologies and standards are emerging at an incredible rate, so that keeping current is almost a full-time job. Participating with organizations that focus on security standards can help with the evaluation process. Reading technical publications, attending conferences, and conducting open discussions with vendors will provide the continuing education required to identify the critical issues. Some of the security technologies that are essential ingredients to any E-commerce security strategy are listed below.

**Cryptography.** Encryption is a critical part of the security process. Elements of a thorough cryptography program are

- *Public Key Cryptography.* Public key cryptography can be used for confidentiality, integrity, and nonrepudiation. Digital signature requires that the verifier is certain that he or she has the public key belonging to the signer. The verifier's confidence in the signature is only as good as his or her confidence in the ownership of the public key.
- *Certification.* A certificate is a digital document containing identification information and a public key. It binds a public key to an identity. Certificates generally have a common format, usually based on the ITU-T X.509 standard. This still leaves the problem of ensuring that a

certificate is genuine and not forged. One way to accomplish this is by using certificate authorities.

- *Certificate Authority.* Certificate authorities (CAs) are used to verify digital certificates. They must be trusted entities and willing to accept liability. It is for this reason that financial institutions are considered to be excellent candidates for CAs.
- *Digital Signature.* A method based on public key encryption that is used to verify identities over a network.

**Key Management.** Systems for key management include

- The Internet Security Key Management Protocol (OAKLEY/ISAKMP)
- Simple Key Exchange Protocol (SKIP), developed by Sun Microsystems
- Photuris Session Key Management Protocol (PSKMP), developed by Qualcomm

**Security Protocols.** Specific systems for the critical areas of data exchange and payment are

- Data exchange
  — Internet Protocol Security (IPSec), developed by a working group of the Internet Engineering Task Force (IETF).
  — Secure Socket Layer, developed by Netscape Communications.
  — Secure HyperText Transfer Protocol, developed by Enterprise Information Technologies (EIT).
- Payment
  — Internet Keyed Payment Protocol (IKP), developed by IBM.
  — Private Communication Technology (PCT), developed by Microsoft.
  — Secure Electronic Transactions (SET) specification, developed by Visa and MasterCard in conjunction with other organizations, including Terisa Systems and Netscape Communications. SET is a combination of the old SEPP (MasterCard/Netscape) and STT (Visa/Microsoft) protocols. The purpose of SET is to enable secure bankcard transactions over the Internet. SET is also approved by the Amex and Discover. This is probably the most important protocol for Internet-based secure credit-card transactions, and will undoubtedly start to be integrated into most products and platforms. SET is based on RSA public key cryptography standards, allows multiparty payment schemes, and securely routes information to both the acquirer and issuer.

The key point is that all of these technologies must be integrated into the overall enterprise architecture. These technologies enable security services and should be part of the security architecture. Building them into the technical architecture can literally take years in large organizations, as they may bring about infrastructural changes. These changes require project planning and budgeting. Before dollar resources can be allocated, senior management must first believe in and support their indispensability. Because of the technical sophistication of these concepts, the need for functionality may not be perceived by senior management for a long time.

Another problem is that some of these functions, such as the CA, have never been used in traditional organizations. Specialized firms, such as VeriSign, are addressing this need by providing CA services to companies. Some organizations, such as the U.S. Postal Service, are offering digital notarization and electronic postmarking of electronic documents. For organizations that want to act as their own CA until issues concerning standards and cross-certification become clear, the question then becomes: Where will this function reside in the company, and who will champion it? If this issue is not swiftly addressed, the window of competitive opportunity may pass before an organization establishes its presence. Organizations should select solutions that integrate these standards into their platforms. When analyzing these technologies, managers should remember the Netscape lesson: it is not only what is used, but how it is implemented. By incorporating these standards into an organization's technologies, they are building tomorrow's architecture.

## ORGANIZATIONS AND ALLIANCES

Here are some of the major organizations and alliances that play a significant role in shaping Internet EC solutions. These organizations develop standards, controls, and guidance. They can identify if a solution has been sanctioned by the industry and if it will be integrated into popular platforms.

- IETF, which develops standards for the Internet. Each standard starts as requests for comments (RFCs) and is posted on the Internet.
- Internet Activities Board (IAB), the governing body of the IETF.
- NIST's ANSI committees that develop standards for the following:
  — Digital Signature Algorithm (DSA)
  — Secure Hash Algorithm (SHA)
  — Public Key using RSA for the financial services industry
  — Elliptic Curve Digital Signature for the financial services industry
  — Key management
  — Key agreement
  — Certificate management (X.509)

Other organizations include the Internet SOCiety, the World Wide Web Consortium (W3C), ISO, and International Information Integrity Institute (I4). The EMV group is composed of Europay, MasterCard International, and Visa. They are working on developing standards for microchips in money cards. Members of the Smart Card Forum, initiated by Citibank, Bellcore, and the U.S. Treasury, include American Express, AT&T, IBM, Microsoft, MCI, MasterCard, Visa International, numerous other banks and smart-card vendors. Other organizations include the Financial Services Technology Consortium (FSTC) and CommerceNet, a nonprofit consortium of technology-oriented companies and organizations, including many financial service organizations. Its focus is on promoting E-commerce on the Internet. It recently performed the controversial demographic Internet Usage Study with Nielsen Media Research, in which some industry experts think that Internet usage was overreported. The Joint Electronic Payments Initiative (JEPI), formed by CommerceNet and W3C, aims to develop an open standard for payment method negotiation for the Web.

By integrating the standards of industry-approved committees into computer platforms, companies demonstrate a positive indication of business prudence, which is important in determining management liability. Companies need to take responsible precautions to protect their computer systems and preserve their stockholders' investments.

## CONCLUSION

Recent advances in technology offer great new opportunities for organizations to extend the reach of their business. Implementing the appropriate methodology to conduct E-commerce ensures that organizations will thrive and expand, and prepares them for exploration of other new areas as the occasion arises. As the world becomes increasingly technically oriented, so must the companies and the people. The differentiation becomes not between the haves and the have-nots, but between the technically savvy and the technically illiterate. Organizations must realize that this is not the time to resist the technical revolution—it is the time to make the most of it.

# Chapter 10
# Single Sign-On for the Enterprise

*John R. Vacca*

As IT SYSTEMS PROLIFERATE TO SUPPORT ENTERPRISE PROCESSES, USERS AND SYSTEM ADMINISTRATORS ARE FACED WITH AN INCREASINGLY COMPLICATED INTERFACE TO ACCOMPLISH THEIR JOB FUNCTIONS. Users typically have to sign-on to multiple systems, necessitating an equivalent number of sign-on dialogues, each of which can involve different usernames and authentication information. System administrators are faced with managing user accounts within each of the multiple systems to be accessed in a coordinated manner in order to maintain the integrity of security policy enforcement. This legacy approach to user sign-on to multiple systems is illustrated in Exhibit 1.

Historically, a distributed system has been assembled from components that act as independent security domains. These components comprise individual platforms with associated operating system and applications.

The components also act as independent domains in the sense that an end user has to identify and authenticate himself or herself independently to each of the domains with which he or she wishes to interact; this scenario is illustrated in Exhibit 1. The end user interacts initially with a primary domain to establish a session with that primary domain. This is termed the "primary domain sign-on" as shown in Exhibit 1, and requires the end user to supply a set of user credentials applicable to the primary domain (e.g., a username and password). The primary domain session is typically represented by an operating system session shell executed on the end user's workstation within an environment representative of the end user (process attributes, environment variables, and home directory). From this primary domain session shell, the user is able to invoke the services of the other domains, such as platforms or applications.

To invoke the services of a secondary domain, an end user is required to perform a "secondary domain sign-on." This requires the end user to supply a further set of user credentials applicable to that secondary domain. An end user has to conduct a separate sign-on dialogue with each secondary domain that the end user requires to use. The secondary domain

0-8493-1160-8/02/$0.00+$1.50

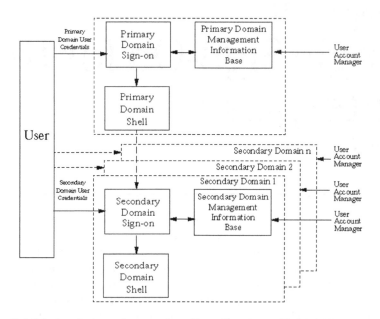

**Exhibit 1.  Legacy Approach to User Sign-On to Multiple Systems**

session is typically represented by an operating system shell or an application shell, again within an environment representative of the end user. From the management perspective, the legacy approach requires independent management of each domain and the use of multiple user account management interfaces. Consideration of both usability and security gives rise to a need to coordinate and, where possible, integrate user sign-on functions and user account management functions for the multitude of different domains now found within an enterprise. A service that provides such coordination and integration can provide real cost benefits to an enterprise through:

- Improved security via the enhanced ability of systems administrators to maintain the integrity of user account configuration, including the ability to inhibit or remove an individual user's access to all system resources in a coordinated and consistent manner
- Improved security via the reduced need for a user to handle and remember multiple sets of authentication information
- Reduction in the time taken, and improved response, by systems administrators in adding and removing users to the system or modifying their access rights
- Reduction in the time taken by users in sign-on operations to individual domains, including reducing the possibility of such sign-on operations failing

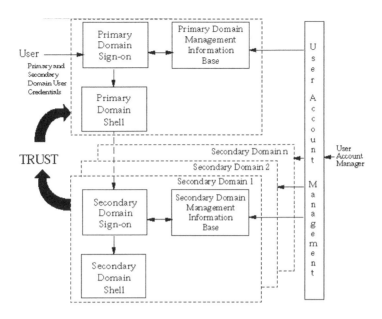

**Exhibit 2. Single User Sign-On to Multiple Services**

Such a service has been termed "single sign-on" after the end-user perception of the impact of this service. However, both the end-user and management aspects of the service are equally important. This approach is illustrated in Exhibit 2. In the single sign-on approach, the system is required to collect from the user, as part of the primary sign-on, all the identification and user credential information necessary to support the authentication of the user to each of the secondary domains that the user may potentially require to interact. The information supplied by the user is then used by single sign-on services within the primary domain to support the authentication of the end user to each of the secondary domains with which the user actually requests to interact. The information supplied by the end user as part of the primary domain sign-on procedure can be used in support of secondary domain sign-on in several ways including:

- *Directly*: the information supplied by the user is passed to a secondary domain as part of a secondary sign-on
- *Immediately*: to establish a session with a secondary domain as part of the initial session establishment (this implies that application clients are automatically invoked and communications established at the time of the primary sign-on operation)
- *Indirectly*: the information supplied by the user is used to retrieve other user identification and user credential information stored within the single sign-on management information base; the retrieved information is then used as the basis for a secondary domain sign-on operation

- *Temporarily stored or cached:* and then used at the time a request for the secondary domain services is made by the end user

From a management perspective, the SSO model provides a single user account management interface through which all the component domains can be managed in a coordinated and synchronized manner. Two significant security aspects or approaches to SSO systems are:

1. Authentication credentials must be protected when transferred between the primary and secondary domains against threats arising from interception or eavesdropping leading to possible masquerade attacks.

2. The secondary domains must trust the primary domain to:
   a. Correctly assert the identity and authentication credentials of the end user,
   b. Protect the authentication credentials used to verify the end-user identity to the secondary domain from unauthorized use.

With that in mind, this chapter discusses how security enterprises such as The Open Group, Mercury Information Technology, Inc., Platinum Technology IP, Inc.,[1] Syllogic B. V., and Schumann Security Software, Inc. are developing industry-wide product standards and new technologies for single sign-on (SSO) — starting with The Open Group.

## SCOPE OF THE SINGLE SIGN-ON STANDARD

The Open Group defines the scope of the Single Sign-On Standard (SSOS) as services in support of the development of applications to provide a common, single end-user sign-on interface for an enterprise, and as services in support of the development of applications for the coordinated management of multiple user account management information bases maintained by an enterprise.

### Functional Objectives: User Sign-On Interface

The following functional objectives have been defined for the SSOS in support of a user sign-on interface. For example, change of user-controlled authentication information shall be supported. This is interpreted as initially being restricted to change of user password, although capability for future extension shall not be precluded.

Furthermore, provision of a service to enable a caller to notify the SSOS implementation of a change of user-controlled authentication information by an application other than the SSOS implementation is an optional requirement and may be supported. Also, SSOS shall not predefine the timing of secondary sign-on operations.

In addition, support for the initiation of cleanup services on session termination, or sign-off, shall be supported. Also, support shall be provided for a caller to establish a default user profile. User selection from a set of available user profiles is not required to be supported, but shall not be precluded as a future extension. Finally, the interface shall be independent of the type of authentication information handled.[2]

### User Account Management Interface

The following functional objectives have been defined for the SSOS in support of a user account management interface:

- Creation, deletion, and modification of user accounts shall be supported
- Setting of attributes for individual user accounts shall be supported
- Attributes to be supported shall include as a minimum those necessary to support the SSOS

### Nonfunctional Objectives

The nonfunctional objectives of the SSOS are, for example, that the SSOS shall be authentication technology independent. The interface shall not prescribe the use of a specific authentication technology, nor preclude the use of any appropriate authentication technology.[3]

SSOS shall be independent of platform or operating system. Also, SSOS shall not preclude the integration of common desktops or common servers, including mainframes. Finally, there is no expectation that such desktops or servers shall be capable of integration within SSOS without modification.

### Security Objectives

There many security objectives to be met by an implementation of SSOS. These objectives are:

- An SSOS implementation shall audit all security relevant events that occur within the context of the SSOS.
- An SSOS implementation shall protect all security relevant information supplied to or generated by the SSOS implementation such that other services may adequately trust the integrity and origin of all security information provided to them as part of a secondary sign-on operation.
- SSO shall not adversely affect the resilience of the system within which it is deployed.
- SSOS shall not adversely impact the availability of any individual system service.
- SSOS shall not provide access by principals to user account information to which they would not be permitted access within the controlling security domain for that information.

- The SSOS shall provide protection to security-relevant information when exchanged between its own constituent components and between those components and other services.

**Out of Scope**

Finally, there are also many aspects that are not considered to be within the current scope of SSOS. These aspects include:

- Configuration and management of alternative sets of user profiles
- Graphical and command line user interfaces to SSOS-based services; these are the province of applications written to utilize the SSOS
- Maintenance of the integrity of the single sign-on user account information base with underlying individual service user account information bases when those underlying user account information bases are modified by means other than SSOS-provided functionality
- Selection of alternative user profiles on user sign-o
- Support for single sign-on across enterprise system boundaries
- User-initiated change of non-user configured authentication information (e.g., magnetic badges, smart cards, etc.)

Now we will discuss how Mercury Information Technology, Inc.[2] is developing an industry-wide product standard and technology for single sign-on (SSO). This part of the chapter briefly defines two authentication-related technologies developed by Mercury Information Technology, Inc.: password synchronization and single sign-on. It describes how each fits into the process of user authentication and their individual strengths and weaknesses. But first, take a look at shared systems.

**SHARED SYSTEMS**

Mercury Information Technology, Inc. defines enterprise networks as including servers that provide the following services to multiple users:

- Database management
- Electronic messaging
- File sharing
- Printer sharing
- Remove access
- Run centralized applications

Most of these systems require users to identify themselves before servicing their requests.

**Authentication**

Shared systems on a network are either open to all users or are restricted to access by authorized users only. When systems are restricted to authorized use only, they normally determine whether a given user can access a specific function based on that user's identity.

For access control based on user identity to be effective, users must be reliably identified. Authentication is the process of identifying users in a manner that makes it difficult for one user to impersonate another.

A number of technologies are available for user authentication. The most popular authentication systems include:

- Biometric devices (fingerprints, retina scans, head scans, etc.)
- Secret passwords
- Smart cards

### Password Synchronization

Most shared systems use passwords to authenticate users. In a network where users access multiple shared resources, they must remember a password for every system they access. Users frequently forget their passwords and must ask the enterprise help desk to reset their passwords. Also, password synchronization software is used to ensure that each of a user's multiple passwords is set to the same value, so that users need not remember multiple passwords for multiple systems.

**Advantages of Password Synchronization.** Password synchronization is characterized by the following advantages:

- **Improved security:** A user must still enter his or her password to access a shared system. If a workstation is left unattended, only the systems currently being accessed are vulnerable to access by someone who can reach the workstation. By implementing a single point from which passwords are changed, it is possible to apply stringent requirements for what constitutes a valid password, and thus make passwords much more difficult to guess.
- **Less intrusive:** Password synchronization does not require any new servers on the network. Furthermore, password synchronization can be implemented without installing any new software on existing servers.
- **Lower cost:** Finally, password synchronization can be implemented for about one tenth the cost of single sign-on technology.

### Single Sign-on

Single sign-on programs are used to allow a user to authenticate himself or herself once, and from then on be able to access additional network resources without providing additional passwords. In practice, most single sign-on systems operate as follows.

117

First of all, the user provides a user ID and password to a primary login program, which authenticates the user against a *master* system. Once authenticated, the user can request access to additional systems. When he or she does so, the single sign-on system retrieves the user's password for the new system, and starts a session with the new system using that password.

**Advantages of Single Sign-on.** On the other hand, SSO is characterized by the advantages of convenience and centralized administration. The advantages include:

- **Convenience:** Using single sign-on, users only have to type their password once when they first log in. Users can also access additional systems by just pressing a button — without entering their ID and password again.
- **Centralized administration:** Some single sign-on systems are built around a unified server administration system. These systems allow a single administrator to add and delete accounts across the entire network from one user interface.

Platinum Technology IP, Inc. is developing an industry-wide product standard and technology for single sign-on (SSO). Take a look at Platinum Technology IP, Inc.'s SSO solution: ProVision AutoSecure Single Sign On (SSO) remote log-on and password protection, as well as other authentication techniques and how to use an enterprise SSO.

## AN SSO ENTERPRISE SOLUTION

The benefits of the client/server revolution have brought a new generation of challenges and security risks. The Platinum SSO solution (like many of the SSO solutions just discussed) addresses the shift toward distributed computing that has dispersed information traditionally stored in a central mainframe into a network of interconnecting LANs — with multi-vendor servers, many different applications and services, complex log-in routines, and a multitude of passwords. Platinum's ProVision AutoSecure Single Sign-On (SSO), further addresses these problems by:

- Enforcing password security policy by managing the password change process and ensuring that content rules are maintained
- Increasing user productivity by allowing users to access all their authorized applications and services with a single user name and password — without having to log into each individually
- Protecting information by authenticating all users and authorizing which applications and services they can use
- Reducing administrator and help-desk workloads by cutting the number of passwords a user needs — and by logging users transparently into the applications and services they need to use

- Reducing the system administrator's workload by providing facilities that allow an unskilled administrator to set up and delete user accounts on different platforms from a single point

### Using an Enterprise SSO

With an enterprise SSO, the user signs on to the SSO client using his or her SSO user name, SSO password, and (optionally) a role. The SSO client sends the information (in encrypted form) to that user's security server, where it is validated against defined security policies. Successful authentication means that the user's credentials are acceptable and that the user is allowed that role from that particular workstation.

Following this, the user is presented with a desktop containing all the applications which, in that role, he or she is authorized to use. Desktops are constructed in user-friendly GUI or text format, depending on the type of terminal or workstation being used.

The user can then select an application or service from the desktop and be transparently logged into that application or service by the Service Access Procedures (SAPs). No further authentication is needed. Users can also, optionally, be logged on to network servers.

If authentication fails, the enterprise SSO prevents the user from gaining access to the enterprise's applications and services. The defined security policy determines whether or not the user is given an explanation for the failure. After a predetermined number of consecutive failed log-on attempts by the user, the workstation can be disabled pending specific intervention by the local administrator.

### Remote Log-On

An enterprise SSO offers its entire set of capabilities to mobile users who can log on to the network via a modem from remote locations. They should be presented with their own desktops, enabling them to use their usual set of applications.

### Password Protection

To protect its passwords from interception and misuse, an enterprise SSO offers a range of controls and encryption techniques. Where security requirements are less stringent, the requirement for password authentication can be overridden by defining roles whose users can simply log on through a user name.

### Enforcing Password Change Policy

An enterprise SSO provides options as to how password changes are handled. The system can be set up to allow users to select the passwords to their applications and services. An enterprise SSO can also be used to generate random passwords on their behalf. In the latter case, the user never knows the passwords to the individual applications and services. This can provide increased security, because the only way a user can gain access is via the enterprise SSO system, thereby preventing backdoor access.

Facilities are also available to accommodate an enterprise that wants all the passwords for a user's applications and services to be the same. This approach, however, is not recommended because it can undermine security by providing a means of access that circumvents the enterprise SSO systems and the associated auditing and alert processes.

### Auditing and Alarms

An enterprise's SSO audit capability keeps track of all the actions carried out by users. Auditing capabilities ensure that security policies are enforced and that users are accountable for their activities. For example, the security policy may specify a maximum of three password attempts to log on to the network. When an enterprise SSO senses the fourth attempt, it will take whatever action has been stipulated. It could, for example, close the workstation down or raise an alert; an enterprise SSO can even raise a *silent* alert that allows the attacker to continue the break-in attempt unaware that he or she has been detected. This allows time to trace the offender.

The record of events can be analyzed to identify where breaches of security and policy may have occurred. For events where immediate attention is required, the audit facility can trigger alarms that can be directed to any number of places, including administrator workstations, a pager or e-mail system, or an event management system. Examples of information that can be audited include:

- End of a user session
- Failed log-on attempts
- Inactivity periods for workstations
- Lock-outs of users and terminals
- Services and applications used
- Start of a user session and role adopted by the user
- System start-up and close-down
- Use of administration utilities

A logged event can also specify the user, role, and workstation or terminal used, as well as the date, time, and session used. Audit administrators have considerable control over configuration of alarm capabilities and can set parameters on some 600 events to trigger the following actions:

- Enter the event in an audit file
- Ignore the event
- Raise an alert

In addition to the deterrent effect of audit facilities, the audit log can be used to assess damage and recover data caused by breaches of security. It can also provide insight into the method of attack used, which can form the basis of effective future defense.

Furthermore, the security administration tools provide methods to access the audit file via various filters. In addition, the audit data can be moved into popular databases where ad hoc inquiries and various reports can be run.

### SSO Encryption

All enterprise SSO components include encryption facilities that the system uses to enhance security. Techniques used include one-way encryption algorithms for password protection and two-way algorithms for functions such as password access control (PAC) and script-variable protection.

### Integration of Other Authentication Techniques

An enterprise SSO itself offers standard authentication via password. It can also support additional or alternative authentication techniques, such as magnetic stripe cards and smart tokens (Security Dynamics SecurID card). If required, these may be associated with specific roles. In addition to an enterprise SSO password authentication method, it also provides APIs to other authentication facilities to enable an enterprise to integrate its own choice of authentication method.

There are other single sign-on solutions. In particular, consider next Syllogic B. V.'s single sign on product SSO+.

### OTHER SSO SOLUTIONS

With the proliferation of client/server technologies over the past years, information has gradually migrated from centralized computers to heterogeneous, distributed environments. This trend toward open and diverse systems has impacted today's enterprises by requiring that end users remember a number of IDs and passwords to gain access to various computing platforms and applications. The necessity for multiple passwords, while designed to increase security, has instead compromised enterprise productivity and security, as well as increased the costs of managing a diverse computing environment.

How can multiple passwords compromise both productivity and security?[4] The amount of time it takes for a user to recall and enter multiple passwords to access various platforms and applications can translate to tens of thousands of dollars a year. Users who desire to be more *efficient* by writing down their numerous passwords for swift recall can create a significant security breach. Add to both these scenarios the fact that today's help-desk administrators routinely claim that up to 50 percent of their time is spent resetting forgotten passwords. It all translates into a waste of time and productivity in a system that is far less secure than anyone can imagine.

Syllogic B.V.'s SSO+ is one of several SSOs described in this article that also addresses these concerns. As previously discussed, SSO reduces the frustration of end users by enabling them to easily access multiple platforms and applications through the use of a single password. It eases the burden of password administration for the help desk or system administrators by consolidating user account administration. It also offers enterprises the assurance that access across distributed computing environments remains secure.

For example, SSO+ is a product developed by IBM in The Netherlands and at Syllogic. It was designed to offer single log-on, additional security, and central user management, including authorizations in existing heterogeneous client/server environments, without having to make changes to the existing applications.

Single log-on is achieved using pass tickets. It allows the existing authentication methods of the server to continue to be used. This offers the advantage that during the implementation of SSO, no modifications need to be made to the existing security repositories. This way, a step-by-step implementation at the user or application level is provided.

Standards and standard components have been used as much as possible in constructing SSO+. The use of SSO+ has a number of advantages for both users and IT managers. Users only have to log in once and can subsequently start any application for which they are authorized.

## Choosing the Right Single Sign-On Solution

The truth is, there are not many single sign-on solutions designed to fully adapt to the number of diverse operating systems and authentication methods available today. SSOs should be capable of handling a diverse security infrastructure, and provide a seamless interface across platforms and applications to allow administrators to learn one system, rather than many. The following are key components that should be part of any well-designed single sign-on solution:

- Open architecture
- Open authentication
- Support for multiple log-in methods, including one-time passwords
- Credentials forwarding
- Support for multiple servers, clients, and hosts
- Seamless user and administrative interface
- Central administration

**Open Architecture.** An SSO solution designed for today and tomorrow is based on open standards. Open architecture ensures that the solution can be easily extended as an enterprise's security policy evolves. As standards change, an open architecture adapts with them.

**Open Authentication.** Support for a diverse range of authentication methods is critical. Popular platforms must be supported, such as Net-Ware, UNIX, and Windows NT. Broker-based authentication such as digital certificates must be supported, along with hardware (smart card) and software token-based methods. And — perhaps even more critical — such support must be easy to weave into an existing security infrastructure, because many enterprises are planning to move to one or more of these systems in the near future.

**Support for Multiple Log-in Methods.** With all of the diverse systems in use today, SSO must support log-in methods from passwords to tokens. Due to the all-too-common use of *sniffers* to detect passwords sent in plain text over the Internet and intranet, support for one-time passwords (OTPs) is an important means of providing enhanced system security.

**Credentials Forwarding.** In the past, SSO solutions relied on scripts to forward passwords to various and diverse applications and platforms. Today's solutions use Application Programming Interfaces (APIs) and easy-to-use Login Dialogs instead. A well-designed solution must allow these forwarding methods to work in parallel to suit the needs of a heterogeneous computing environment.

**Support for Multiple Servers, Clients, and Hosts.** Today's most popular platforms, including UNIX, Windows (3.x, 95, 98, 2000, XP, and NT), and MVS, must be supported. Legacy systems must be supported as well.

**Seamless User and Administrative Interface.** A Windows 95/NT, 98/NT, or 2000/NT, XP *look-and-feel* eases the learning curve for administrators and end users. The SSO solution should maintain a consistent *look-and-feel* across platforms. It must appear integrated with the operating system and transparent to the end user.

**Central Administration.** Finally, security or system administrators must be able to manage the SSO solution from a central location. The interface, again, must be seamless with the operating system, enabling the administrator to easily learn the process and become proficient quickly and efficiently.

## CONCLUSION AND SUMMARY

In today's heterogeneous computing environments, end users frequently need access to applications and network resources running on multiple platforms and systems to perform their day-to-day responsibilities. As a result, end users must use multiple sign-on routines, user IDs, and passwords. This cumbersome management problem impedes productivity and compromises security when end users resort to writing down their passwords in an effort to keep track of them.

With that in mind, this chapter is directed toward enterprise executives, IT managers, security administrators, and others who want to know more about how different types of SSOs are designed to be simple to administer in even the largest, most complex networks. Different types of SSO tools are presented that allow effective administration of:

- Applications
- Menus
- Roles
- SAP variables
- Users
- Workstations

SSOs should provide a highly flexible set of rules that enable a clear definition of users' access authority, as well as the construction of roles that encompass numerous capabilities. Relationships between the different administrative functions should be a vital element in an SSO's ability to define which services can be accessed by individual users. The system should embody these relationships in the following ways:

- An application definition can refer to SAP variables (SVs).
- Any role can be restricted to a single application or initial menu.
- Applications and menus are allocated to these roles.
- Menus contain lists of applications and other menus.
- SAP variable values can be assigned to users, roles, or specific applications.
- Users are allocated roles according to their needs.
- Workstations identifiable by an SSO server can be permitted or denied access by specific roles; users can only use such workstations to run roles permitted on that workstation.

Also presented in this article is a high-level overview of SSO technology requirements to meet the diverse needs of the end user, the help-desk/security administrator, and the security officer who sets overall enterprise security policy. The enterprise SSO should be able to meet these needs by increasing user productivity, reducing administrative overhead, and increasing overall security throughout the enterprise. Its flexible, open architecture should ensure that it is designed to meet the requirements of today's ever-evolving computing environment.

SSOs should also be able to automate user log-in to applications and platforms by supplying an application *launch pad* that acts as a familiar desktop for users and simplifies log-in, reducing it to a simple *point-and-click* process. End users authenticate once, and are presented with a customized desktop of authorized applications that they can access quickly and efficiently. This simple process should enable an enterprise to flexibly move from password-based log-ins to strong authentication methods without visibly impacting the log-in process for the end user.

SSOs should be able to consolidate security administration by providing a centralized database of user IDs, application dialogs, access paths, and preferred credentials-forwarding information. An additional tier of administration enables central management of user access to applications and platforms across the enterprise.

An SSO should also be able to act as a mediator between users and applications, matching the best-available security with application capabilities and requirements. Most of the SSOs discussed in this article offer a hybrid approach to support SSO for a wide range of applications and systems, from legacy applications requiring proprietary passwords to one-time passwords to encrypted tickets. Finally, their architecture should be able to meet the requirements of the most complicated computing environments by providing a secure method of single sign-on that includes:

- A flexible use of current credentials-forwarding methods and adaptability to future security standards
- The ability for a phased implementation approach to ease the introduction of enhanced security standards across an enterprise
- An effective and secure response that meets the SSO expectations of end users, administrators, and security officers alike

**NOTES**

1. Platinum Technology, Inc. was purchased by Computer Associates, which is located at World Headquarters, Computer Associates International, Inc., One Computer Associates Plaza, Islandia, New York 11749.
2. This means that SSOs shall not require that all sign-on operations be performed at the same time as the primary sign-on operation. This would result in the creation of user sessions with all possible services although those services may not actually be required by the user.
3. Some authentication technology (e.g., those based on challenge-response mechanisms of which a user-held device is a component) may not be appropriate for use as part of secondary sign-on functions.
4. The Schumann answer for the dilemma of multiple sign-ons is Secure Single Sign-On (SAM/SSSO). This fully scalable solution uses a tamper-proof smart card (other tokens are possible) and a single sign-on PIN to access any environment from client/server to legacy. All log-ins and passwords are encrypted into the card's integrated circuit. Only possession of the card and knowledge of the single sign-on PIN will allow it to function. The smart card operates by presenting all log-ins and passwords immediately and automatically to applications in use, creating large gains in productivity and security.

# STRATEGIC AND BUSINESS ISSUES

## Addresses of Entities

The Open Group, 1010 El Camino Real, Suite 380, Menlo Park, California 94025-4345.

M-Tech Mercury Information Technology, Inc., Suite 750, 910 7th Avenue S.W., Calgary, Alberta, T2P 3N8, Canada.

Platinum Technology IP, Inc., 1815 South Meyers Road, Oakbrook Terrace, Illinois 60181-5241.

Security Dynamics Technologies, Inc., 20 Crosby Drive, Bedford, Massachusetts 01730.

Syllogic B.V. Hoefseweg 1, 3821 AE Amersfoort, The Netherlands.

Schumann Security Software, Inc., 8101 Sandy Spring Road, Laurel, Maryland 20707.

BM Nederland NV, Johan Huizingalaan 765, Post Office Box 9999, 1066 CE Amsterdam, The Netherlands.

# Section III
# Internet Infrastructure from the Ground Up

The chapters in this section examine the different components of Internet infrastructure. They include a review of the overall strategic principles and offer a ground-up examination of protocols, middleware, servers, and other emerging building blocks.

"Developing an E-Business Architecture" explains the requirements for an E-business and explores some major trends in the marketplace. This is done in the context of a sound business model and effective management processes.

"Understanding the Internet Protocol: The IP in TCP/IP" shows how network managers can improve their decision making in maintaining their local networks and how they interoperate with the Internet using the IP protocol.

"Expanding Internet Support with IPv6" examines the characters of the v6 release of this protocol. This provides an understanding of the major characters of the release and identifies some opportunities and approaches for migration. Devices connected to the Internet have a unique IP address that is used by other Web services to communicate with the device. IP addresses can be temporarily assigned upon log-in (e.g., for laptops) or be permanent (e.g., for desktops and other Internet devices). The current IP address scheme can support in the low billions of unique IP addresses. This requirement (like telephone area codes) is expected to grow exponentially into the half-trillion range over the next decade or so. Of course, all of this is based on a variety of assumptions that demand the continued popularity of the Internet. Although it may not change the way you buy pizza, it is still expected to grow in popularity. IPv4 has been in place since 1983. It was designed by Dr. Vint Cerf. APARnet was created by the U.S. government in 1969 and preceded Dr. Cerf's creation. V6 was approved as a global standard in 1999. IPv6 has the capability to support billions and billions of unique addresses. This standard also improves security (something executives are talking a lot about), addressing capacity, and automatic configuration.

"Implementing Voice Over IP" discusses approaches for using common TCP/IP application tools and logical networking techniques to improve the opportunity of implementing a successful voice-over-IP implementation solution.

"Bridging Strategies for LAN Internets" explains methods of interconnecting dissimilar host systems and LANs in the context of the Internet.

"Choosing and Equipping an Internet Server" examines how to select an Internet server and application software that best suits the needs of different users and organizations. The server is arguably the most important component of an Internet-based solution.

"Gracefully Transitioning from SNA to IP: Why, How, and When?" identifies conditions for migrating from SNA-based networks to TCP/IP. Case studies and an examination of suitable migration tools are also discussed.

# Chapter 11
# Developing an E-business Architecture

*Srinivas Padmanabharao*

WHAT IS AN E-BUSINESS? All definitions that are floating out there strive to distinguish "E-business" from "E-commerce." The former refers to the process of using the Internet and associated technologies to transform every business process and E-enable all parts of the organization's value chain from acquiring, serving, and retaining customers to interacting with employees, partners, and the world at large. "E-commerce" can safely be considered one vital but small part in the overall E-business architecture.

There are two basic categories of businesses conducted over the Internet. The first category is the Business-to-Consumer (B2C) segment, which includes the popular, Wall Street-friendly businesses like Amazon, E*Trade, etc. The second is the Business-to-Business (B2B) segment, which is increasingly overshadowing the B2C segment and includes such names as Chemtex and AutoExchange. Despite fundamental differences in the business models of these two categories, they share one common key aspect — use of Internet technologies to manage all aspects of the business. This chapter presents an integrated architecture for these Internet technologies so that organizations can effectively implement whichever type of business model they choose.

## REQUIREMENTS

An effective E-businesss architecture must satisfy a basic set of requirements. The following sections discuss these requirements.

### Multiple Access Channels

While the past decade has seen the use of the Internet as the point of contact with the customer as distinguished from the traditional channels, businesses are increasingly finding that customers are using multiple channels to satisfy their needs. This includes the Internet, handheld devices like Palm Pilots, mobile communication devices like the cell phone, and set-top boxes for cable. A business must be capable of providing the customer the same high level of service irrespective of the channel used by the customer. However, each channel comes with its own unique set of technological challenges and it may not be cost-effective for a business to address each of these individually.

### Single View of Customer

Irrespective of the mode of accessing the business, there is only one customer. Businesses need to be able to consolidate all information regarding a customer and develop a holistic view of the customer. This includes having access to all products and services used by the customer to provide opportunities for cross-selling of products and services. In addition, it lets business personalize the entire interaction with the customer by allowing for customer self-care and allowing the customer to dictate the nature of the interaction.

### The World Wide Web

In addition to the fact that customers are using multiple access channels, the boundaryless nature of the Internet opens up the entire world as a potential market for one's business. While this is a very attractive proposition, it throws up challenges of the kind few businesses have had to contend with in the past. The obvious issues that come to mind include the multiplicity of languages, customer habits, legal environments, and business practices.

### Security and Privacy

One of the fundamental requirements of a successful business is its ability to establish an environment of trust between its customers and itself. The Internet has renewed fears about this traditional issue by creating the impression that the Internet is an unregulated jungle in which evil-minded hackers roam free with the power to tap into information databases and eavesdrop on transactions between the customer and the business. However, businesses need to be prudent regarding issues of security and privacy of customer information and evaluate the level of protection they wish to establish.

### Scalability, Availability, Flexibility, and Reliability

It is sometimes said in the Internet world that businesses can die of starvation or die of indigestion — that is, no customers or too many customers. Recent public attention on downtimes at eBay further highlights this point. Most E-businesses start small but, if successful, experience growth rates that have never been seen before. So, the architecture must provide the ability to start small and grow rapidly to meet business needs. The electronic storefront and the associated channels are the modes of contact with the customer and, hence, reliability of these applications is vital.

### The Entire Value Chain

While many of the aspects thus far have focused on the interaction between the customer and the enterprise, the remaining interactions between the business and its partners and employees also need to be considered. Its internal operational support systems (appropriate to the specific business), along with e-mail, financial, human resources, and other systems, need to be integrated into the overall architecture.

### Integrating the Enterprise

There are very few applications that satisfy all the functional needs of a business. It is most common to adopt a "best-of-breed" approach that utilizes different applications to address specific functional needs. However, this approach creates silos of information within the enterprise and hinders the seamless processing of business functions. In addition, it is necessary to have a unified logical view of the business and customer information to be able to quickly respond to the fast-moving marketplace. Hence, there is a need to integrate all these applications to the fullest possible extent to allow for fast and accurate performance of business functions.

### Leveraging the Legacy Applications

While most companies in the news these days are companies that did not exist ten years ago, some of the biggest initiatives in the field of E-business have recently come from old, traditional companies like Ford, GM, and GE. Most of these companies already have billions of dollars invested in their current systems and they would like to leverage this investment as a part of their strategy to move into the E-business space.

## A PROPOSED ARCHITECTURE FOR E-BUSINESSS

The proposed architecture is based on a few key concepts, including:

- **A best-of-breed approach** — The proposed architecture does not make any assumptions as to the suitability of any particular application to satisfy specific functional need. It is generic and must be customized to meet the particular needs of an enterprise. Hence, companies are free to adopt a best-of-breed approach to choosing which applications best suit their needs.
- **The use of middleware** — To meet the requirements of scalability and flexibility, and to be able to best leverage legacy applications, the

architecture uses a middleware platform as the central piece. This middleware incorporates business process intelligence as an integral piece of its functioning. This would involve the use of software adapters to connect different applications into this middleware, and the middleware will provide the capabilities of information routing and workflow automation.

A high-level view of the proposed architecture is outlined in Exhibit 1. The functions of the various components of the architecture are:

1. **Customer information manager:** This is the application that acts as the single repository of information about all aspects of the customer. A typical example of such a system is a CRM package.
2. **Billing manager:** This system is the invoicing application that stores all information on rates and charges for the various products about the customer and handles all aspects of revenue management, including generating feeds for the General Ledger.
3. **Channel manager:** This system manages all interactions with the external world — especially customers. Either the channel manager or the customer information manager itself can handle the interface with the Web.

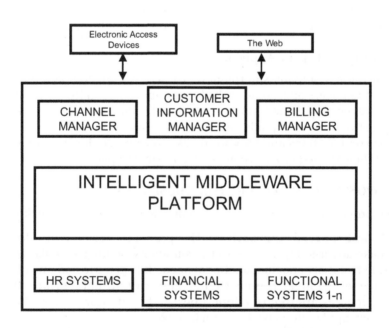

**Exhibit 1.    E-Business Architecture**

## A QUICK SURVEY OF THE MARKETPLACE

This section presents a quick review of the available systems in the marketplace today that can be used to build this architecture.

### Channel Manager

One of the companies in the marketplace today that provides a software solution that can function as a channel manager is 724 Solutions. 724 Solutions' software provides financial institutions and other content providers with a device-independent, operating system-independent, and network-independent channel to their own customers. The current applications of 724 Solutions' software solution will evolve to include additional services available on an increased variety of devices, such as set-top boxes, game consoles, and other emerging Internet access devices.

This company has partnered with some of the leading financial institutions of the world (e.g., Bank of America) to provide wireless financial banking capabilities. The bank's customers are able to access up-to-the-minute account balances and transaction details, conduct real-time fund transfers from one bank account to another, and make bill payments using wireless banking services. Customers can do this not only from their PCs, but also by simply touching a few buttons on their Web-enabled wireless phones or Palm computing devices.

While the company is currently focused on the financial services industry, the same concept can be adapted to meet the needs of any other industry. The key would be the development of a lightweight, XML-based information framework coupled with a presentation mechanism that is appropriate to the needs of handheld/wireless devices.

Further information on the company can be obtained at http://www.724solutions.com.

### Billing Manager

Infranet® from Portal Software, Inc., is one of the leading customer care and billing packages for Internet businesses. It was designed to accelerate the implementation of complex, multi-service Internet business models for IP telephony, wireless data, E-commerce, dial-up and broadband access services, online content and gaming, Web and application hosting, branding, e-mail and unified messaging, and other next-generation communication services.

Infranet® delivers a totally integrated real-time solution that enables one to rapidly develop, price, and provision as many new services as one needs to take advantage of the multitude of possible revenue opportunities. In addition, sophisticated rating engine and flexible account administration facilities of Infranet® enable one to more effectively manage customer usage and billing. Some of the features include support for real-time rating and billing, flexible pricing plans, and customizable business policies.

Infranet® was designed with the scalability to support millions of customers while also providing secure, reliable service — putting no limits on how large an Internet business can grow. Portal enables service providers to rapidly create and deploy a variety of Internet services, with flexible bundling and pricing options that enable businesses to stay one step ahead of changing market demands. The architecture of Infranet® is built to be extensible; it enables companies to add new, value-added services to their menus of offerings.

Further information on the company and Infranet® can be obtained at http://www.portal.com.

## Intelligent middleware

**BusinessWare® from Vitria Technologies.** BusinessWare® is an E-business infrastructure software from Vitria Technologies that provides companies with a tool that enables them to integrate various applications across the entire enterprise, potentially spread across the world. In addition to enabling application integration, BusinessWare® allows for business process intelligence to be embedded into the integration framework.

The different components of BusinessWare® that work together to provide a complete solution include:

1. **Automator:** This tool provides a graphical user interface for businesses to depict business process intelligence into the automation framework.
2. **Communicator:** This tool is the messaging backbone that allows the applications to exchange information. It is built around the publish-and-subscribe mechanism and is designed for high reliablility.
3. **Connectors:** These are pieces of code that are built to provide the connectivity between individual applications and the messaging platform. Each application that needs to be integrated into the end-to-end solution has its own connector.
4. **Analyzer:** This tool enables businesses to monitor and analyze business processes in real-time. The analyzer can be used to gain visibility into key business metrics to enable more efficient management of the overall business.

The following are the steps that need to carried out in order to achieve a full-scale integrated E-businesss solution:

1. Define the information needs
2. Select the individual application

3. Define the information exchange formats
4. Build the connectors
5. Define the process models using Automator
6. Establish the communication framework in Communicator
7. Deploy the individual applications, connectors, and the business process models

Further information on Vitria Technologies and the product can be found at http://www.vitria.com.

**TIB/Active Enterprise® from TIBCO Software.** TIB/ActiveEnterprise® from TIBCO can be used to integrate Internet applications, packaged applications/solutions from a variety of application vendors, and combine them with custom legacy applications to form the required E-business infrastructure. The resulting architecture can support business information flow at the global enterprise scale.

TIB/ActiveEnterprise® is a comprehensive suite of products that delivers an Internet and enterprise infrastructure. TIB/ActiveEnterprise® has the following major categories of products that work in conjunction to provide a comprehensive business integration platform.

- **TIB/Rendevous, TIB/ETX, TIB/ObjectBus:** These products provide the messaging platform for reliable, guaranteed, and transactional messages.
- **Adapters.** These are used for integration with third-party packaged products such as E-commerce applications and databases.
- **TIB/Integration Manager, TIB/ContentBroker:** These applications provide the basis for business process automation and automated workflow.
- **TIB/Hawk:** This application enables a business to monitor its businesses to achieve 24×7 reliability

Further information on the company and the products can be found at http://www.tibco.com.

## CONCLUSION

The business environment is undergoing rapid changes, enabled by the technological changes fostered by the growth of Internet and wireless technologies. Businesses need to adapt their infrastructures to successfully compete in this environment. Firms that adopt an approach that provides them with the flexibility to pick the solutions that best meet their functional needs while managing to achieve enterprise-wide integration for real-time information management are best positioned to succeed in the next millennium.

# Chapter 12
# Understanding the Internet Protocol: The IP in TCP/IP

*Gilbert Held*

THIS CHAPTER FOCUSES ON THE FIRST LAYER OF THE TCP/IP PROTOCOL SUITE. The Internet Protocol (IP) is the primary protocol most people associate with the network layer. Two related protocols should be considered when discussing the TCP/IP protocol suite: the Address Resolution Protocol (ARP) and the Internet Control Message Protocol (ICMP), are not discussed here.

This chapter focuses on what this author commonly refers to as the Network Layer Troika of the TCP/IP protocol suite: IP, ARP, and ICMP. In examining the Internet Protocol, particular attention is paid to the structure of the IP header and its fields, which are examined by routers as a mechanism for making forwarding decisions.

This chapter focuses on IP and including its use for routing datagrams across a network and between interconnected networks. The composition of the IP header and the use of different fields in the header are examined in detail.

Once accomplished, attention is directed to the role and operation of the Address Resolution Protocol (ARP), which includes examining the rationale for a little-known ARP technique that can considerably facilitate the operation of delay-sensitive transmissions such as Voice-over-IP.

## THE INTERNET PROTOCOL

The Internet Protocol (IP) represents the network layer of the TCP/IP protocol suite. IP was developed as a mechanism to interconnect packet-switched TCP/IP-based networks to form an internet. Here, the term "internet" with a lowercase "i" is used to represent the connection of two or more TCP/IP-based networks.

0-8493-1160-8/02/$0.00+$1.50

### Datagrams and Segments

IP transmits blocks of data referred to as datagrams, and receives upper layer protocol data containing either a TCP or UDP header, referred to as a TCP segment or UDP datagram. The prefix of an IP header to the TCP segment or UDP datagram results in the formation of an IP datagram. This datagram contains a destination IP address that is used for routing purposes.

### Datagrams and Datagram Transmission

To alleviate potential confusion between datagrams and an obsolete transmission method referred to as datagram transmission, a few words are in order. When the ARPANet evolved, it experimented with two methods of packet transmission. One method was referred to as datagram transmission and avoided the use of routers to perform table lookups. Under datagram transmission, each node in a network transmits a received datagram onto all ports other than the port on which the datagram was received. While this technique avoids the need for routing table lookup operations, it can result in duplicate datagrams being received at certain points within a network. This results in the necessity to develop software to discard duplicate datagrams, adding an additional level of complexity to networking. Thus, datagram transmission was soon discarded in favor of the creation of virtual circuits that represent a temporary path established between source and destination. As such, datagram transmission will actually be referencing the transmission of datagrams via a virtual circuit created between source and destination.

### Routing

The actual routing of an IP datagram occurs on a best-effort or connectionless delivery mechanism. This is because IP by itself does not establish a session between the source and destination before it transports datagrams. When IP transports a TCP segment, the TCP header results in a connection-oriented session between two Layer 4 nodes transported by IP as a Layer 3 network protocol.

The importance of IP can be noted by the fact that routing between networks is based on IP addresses. As discussed later in this chapter, the device that routes data between different IP addressed networks is known as a router. Because it would be extremely difficult — if not impossible — to statically configure every router in a large network to know the route to other routers and networks connected to different routers, routing protocols are indispensable to the operation of a dynamic series of interconnected IP networks. The best way to obtain an appreciation for the operation of IP is through an examination of the fields in its header.

| 0 4 8 16 31 | | | | |
|---|---|---|---|---|
| Vers Hlen Service Type | | Total Length | | |
| Identification | | Flags | Fragment Offset | |
| Time to Live Protocol | | Header | Checksum | |
| Source IP Address | | | | |
| Destination IP Address | | | | |
| Options + Padding | | | | |

**Exhibit 1.   The Ipv4 Header**

## The IP Header

The current version of IP is version 4, resulting in IP commonly referred to as IPv4. The next generation of IP is IPv6. This section focuses attention on IPv4.

Exhibit 1 illustrates the fields contained in the IPv4 header. In examining this header, note that the header consists of a minimum of 20 bytes of data, with the width of each field shown with respect to a 32-bit (4-byte) word.

**Bytes versus Octets.** In this chapter, the term "byte" refers to a sequence of eight bits used in a common manner. During the development of the TCP/IP protocol suite and continuing today, most standards documents use the term "octet" to reference a collection of eight bits. The use of the term "octet" is due to differences in the composition of a byte during the 1960s.

During the early development of computer systems, differences in computer architecture resulted in the use of groupings of five to ten bits to represent a computer byte. Thus, the term "byte" at that time was ambiguous, and standards-making bodies decided to use the term "octet" to reference a grouping of eight bits. Because all modern computers use 8-bit bytes, the term "byte" is no longer ambiguous. Thus, the term "byte" is used throughout this chapter.

To obtain an appreciation for the operation of IP, one can examine the functions of the fields in the header. In doing so, and when appropriate, the relation of certain fields to routing and security is discussed.

**Vers Field.** The Vers field is four bits in length and is used to identify the version of IP used to create an IP datagram. The current version of IP is v4, with the next generation of IP assigned as version 6 (v6).

| Exhibit 2. | Assigned Internet Version Numbers |
|---|---|
| **Numbers** | **Assignment** |
| 0 | Reserved |
| 1–3 | Unassigned |
| 4 | IP |
| 5 | Streams |
| 6 | IPv6 |
| 7 | TP/IX |
| 8 | P Internet Protocol (PIP) |
| 9 | TUBA |
| 10–14 | Unassigned |
| 15 | Reserved |

The four bits in the Vers field support 16 version numbers. Under RFC 1700, a listing of Internet version numbers can be obtained and a summary of that listing is included in Exhibit 2. In examining Exhibit 2, note that the reason the next-generation Internet Protocol is IPv6, rather than IPv5 relates to the fact that Version 5 was previously assigned to an experimental protocol referred to as the Streams 2 Protocol.

**Hlen Field.** The length of the IP header can vary due to its ability to support options. To allow a receiving device to correctly interpret the contents of the header from the remainder of an IP datagram requires the receiving device to know where the header ends. This function is performed by the Hlen field, the value of which indicates the length of the header.

The Hlen field is four bits in length. In examining Exhibit 1, note that the IP header consists of 20 bytes of fixed information followed by options. Because it is not possible to use a four-bit field to directly indicate the length of a header equal to or exceeding 320 bytes, the value in this field represents the number of 32-bit words in the header. As an example, the shortest IP header is 20 bytes, which represents 160 bits. When divided by 32 bits, this results in a value of 160/32 (or 5), which is the value set into the Hlen field when the IP header contains 20 bytes and no options.

**Service Type Field.** The Service Type field is an 8-bit field commonly referred to as a Type of Service (ToS) field. The initial development of IP assumed that applications would use this field to indicate the type of routing path they would like. Routers along the path of a datagram would examine the contents of the Service Type byte and attempt to comply with the setting in this field.

Exhibit 3 illustrates the format of the Service field. This field consists of two sub-fields: Type of Service (ToS) and Precedence. The Type-of-Service

| 7 | 6 | 5 | 4 | 3 | 2 | 1 | 0 |
|---|---|---|---|---|---|---|---|
| R | Type of Service | | | | Precedence | | |

where:
R represents reserved

Precedence provides eight levels, 0 to 7, with 0 normal and 7 the highest.

Type of Service (ToS) indicates how the datagram is handled.

0000  Default
0001  Minimize monetary cost
0010  Maximize reliability
0100  Maximize throughput
1000  Minimize delay
1111  Maximize security

**Exhibit 3.   The Service Type Field**

sub-field consists of bit positions that, when set, indicate how a datagram should be handled. The three bits in the Precedence sub-field allow the transmitting station to indicate to the IP layer the priority for sending a datagram. A value of 000 indicates a normal precedence, while a value of 111 indicates the highest level of precedence and is normally used for network control.

The value in the Precedence field is combined with a setting in the ToS field to indicate how a datagram should be processed. As indicated in the lower portion of Exhibit 3, there are six settings defined for the ToS field. To understand how this field should be used, assume that an application is transmitting digitized voice that requires minimal routing delays due to the effect of latency on the reconstruction of digitized voice. By setting the ToS field to a value of 1000, this would indicate to each router in the path between source and destination network that the datagram is delay sensitive and its processing by the router should minimize delay.

In comparison, because routers are designed to discard packets under periods of congestion, an application in which the ability of packets to reach their destination is of primary importance would set the ToS sub-field to a value of 0010. This setting would denote to routers in the transmission path that the datagram requires maximum reliability. Thus, routers would select other packets for discard prior to discarding a packet with its ToS sub-field set to a value of 0010.

Although the concept behind including a Service Type field was a good idea, from a practical standpoint it is rarely used. The reason for its lack of use is the need for routers supporting this field to construct and maintain multiple routing tables. While this is not a problem for small networks, the creation and support of multiple routing tables can significantly affect the level of performance of routers in a complex network such as the Internet.

Although routers in most networks ignore the contents of the Service Type field, this field is now being used to map IP datagrams being transmitted over an ATM backbone. Because ATM includes a built-in Quality of Service (QoS) that, at the present time, cannot be obtained on an IP network, many organizations are transmitting a variety of data to include voice-over-IP over an ATM backbone, using the Service Type field as a mechanism to map different IP service requirements into applicable types of ATM service. A second emerging application for the Service Type field is to differentiate the requirements of the various applications as they flow into an IP network. In this situation, the Service Type byte is renamed as the DiffServe (Differentiated Service) byte. The Internet Engineering Task Force is currently examining the potential use of the DiffServe byte as a mechanism to define an end-to-end QoS capability through an IP network.

**Total Length Field.** The Total Length field indicates the total length of an IP datagram in bytes. This length indicates the length of the IP header, to include options, followed by a TCP or UDP header (or another type of header discussed below), as well as the data that follows that header. The Total Length field is 16 bits in length, resulting in an IP datagam having a maximum defined length of $2 \times 10^{16}$ (or 65,535) bytes.

**Identification and Fragment Offset Fields.** Unlike some types of clothing where one size fits all, an IP datagram can range up to 65,535 bytes in length. Because some networks only support a transport frame that can carry a small portion of the theoretical maximum-length IP datagram, it may become necessary to fragment the datagram for transmission between networks. One example of this would be the routing of a datagram from a Token Ring network to another Token Ring network via an Ethernet network. Token Ring networks that operate at 16 Mbps can transport approximately 18 Kbytes in their Information field. In comparison, an Ethernet frame has a maximum-length Information field of 1500 bytes. This means that datagrams routed between Token Ring networks via an Ethernet network must be subdivided, or fragmented, into a maximum length of 1500 bytes for the Ethernet to be able to transport the data.

The default IP datagram length is referred to as the path MTU (Maximum Transmission Unit). The MTU is defined as the size of the largest packet that can be transmitted or received through a logical interface. For the previous example of two Token Ring networks connected via an Ethernet network, the MTU would be 1500 bytes. Because it is important to commence transmission with the lowest common denominator packet size that can flow through different networks, and, if possible, adjust the packet size after the initial packet reaches its destination, IP datagrams use a default of 576 bytes when datagrams are transmitted remotely (off the current network).

Fragmentation is a most interesting function because it allows networks capable of transmitting larger packets to do so more efficiently. The reason efficiency increases is due to the fact that larger packets have proportionally less overhead. Unfortunately, the gain in packet efficiency is not without cost. First, although routers can fragment datagrams, they do not reassemble them, leaving it to the host to perform reassembly. This is because router CPU and memory requirements would considerably expand if they had to reassemble datagrams flowing to networks containing hundreds or thousands of hosts. Second, although fragmentation is a good idea for boosting transmission efficiency, a setting in the Flag field (see below) can be used to indicate that a datagram should not be fragmented. Because many routers do not support fragmentation, many applications, by default, set the Do Not Fragment Flag bit and use a datagram length that, while perhaps not most efficient, ensures that a datagram can flow end to end because its length represents the lowest common denominator of the networks it will traverse.

When an IP datagram is fragmented, this situation results in the use of three fields in the IP header: Identification, Flags, and Fragment Offset.

The Identification field is 16 bytes in length and is used to indicate which datagram fragments belong together. A receiving device operation at the IP network layer uses the Identification field as well as the source IP address to determine which fragments belong together. To ensure fragments are put back together in their appropriate order requires a mechanism to distinguish one fragment from another. That mechanism is provided by the Fragment Offset field, which indicates the location where each fragment belongs in a complete message. The actual value in the Fragment Offset field is an integer that corresponds to a unit of 8 bytes, which indicates the offset from the previous datagram. For example, if the first fragment is 512 bytes in length, the second fragment would have an offset value that indicates that this IP datagram commences at byte 513. Using the Total Length and Fragment Offset fields, a receiver can easily reconstruct a fragmented datagram.

**Flag Field.** The third field in the IP header directly associated with fragmentation is the Flag field. This field is four bytes in length, with two bits used to denote fragmentation information. The setting of one of those bits is used as a direct fragment control mechanism, because a value of "0" indicates the datagram can be fragmented, while a value of "1" indicates the datagram should not be fragmented. The second fragment bit is used to indicate fragmentation progress. When the second bit is set to a value of "0," it indicates that the current fragment in a datagram is the last fragment. In comparison, a value of "1" in this bit position indicates that more fragments follow.

**Time to Live Field.** The Time to Live (TTL) field is eight bits in length. The setting in this field is used to specify the maximum amount of time that a datagram can exist. It is used to prevent a mis-addressed datagram from endlessly wandering the Internet or a private IP network, similar to the manner by which a famous American folk hero was noted in a song to wander the streets of Boston.

Because an exact time is difficult to measure, the value placed into the TTL field is actually a router hop count. That is, routers decrement the value of the TTL field by 1 as a datagram flows between networks. If the value of this field reaches zero, the router will discard the datagram, and depending on the configuration of the router, generate an ICMP message that informs the originator of the datagram that the TTL field expired and the datagram, in effect, was sent to the great bit bucket in the sky.

Many applications set the TTL field value to default of 32, which should be more than sufficient to reach most destinations in a very complex network, to include the Internet. In fact, one popular application referred to as traceroute will issue a sequence of datagrams commencing with a value of 1 in the TTL field to obtain a sequence of router-generated ICMP messages that enables the path from source to destination to be noted.

**Protocol Field.** An IP header prefixes the transport layer header to form an IP datagram. While TCP and UDP represent a large majority of Layer 4 protocols carried in an IP datagram, they are not the only protocols transported. In addition, even if they were, one would need a mechanism to distinguish one upper layer protocol from another that is carried in a datagram.

The method used to distinguish the upper layer protocol carried in an IP datagram is obtained through the use of a value in the Protocol field. For example, a value of decimal 6 is used to indicate that a TCP header follows the IP header, while a value of decimal 17 indicates that a UDP header follows the IP header in a datagram.

The Protocol field is eight bits in length, permitting up to 256 protocols to be defined under IPv4. Exhibit 4 lists the current assignments of Internet protocol numbers. Note that although TCP and UDP by far represent the vast majority of TCP/IP traffic on the Internet and corporate intranets, other protocols can be transported and a large block of protocol numbers is currently unassigned. Also note that under IPv6, the protocol field is named the Next Header field.

Exhibit 4.   Assigned Internet Protocol Numbers

| Decimal | Keyword | Protocol |
|---|---|---|
| 0 | HOPOPT | IPv6 Hop-by-Hop Option |
| 1 | ICMP | Internet Control Message |
| 2 | IGMP | Internet Group Management |
| 3 | GGP | Gateway-to-Gateway |
| 4 | IP | IP in IP (encapsulation) |
| 5 | ST | Stream |
| 6 | TCP | Transmission Control Protocol |
| 7 | CBT | CBT |
| 8 | EGP | Exterior Gateway Protocol |
| 9 | IGP | any private interior gateway (used by Cisco for its IGRP) |
| 10 | BBN-RCC-MON | BBN RCC Monitoring |
| 11 | NVP-II | Network Voice Protocol Version 2 |
| 12 | PUP | PUP |
| 13 | ARGUS | ARGUS |
| 14 | EMCON | EMCON |
| 15 | XNET | Cross Net Debugger |
| 16 | CHAOS | Chaos |
| 17 | UDP | User Datagram |
| 18 | MUX | Multiplexing |
| 19 | DCN-MEAS | DCN Measurement Subsystems |
| 20 | HMP | Host Monitoring |
| 21 | PRM | Packet Radio Measurement |
| 22 | XNS-IDP | XEROX NS IDP |
| 23 | TRUNK-1 | Trunk-1 |
| 24 | TRUNK-2 | Trunk-2 |
| 25 | LEAF-1 | Leaf-1 |
| 26 | LEAF-2 | Leaf-2 |
| 27 | RDP | Reliable Data Protocol |
| 28 | IRTP | Internet Reliable Transaction |
| 29 | ISO-TP4 | ISO Transport Protocol class 4 |
| 30 | NETBLT | Bulk Data Transfer Protocol |
| 31 | MFE-NSP | MFE Network Services Protocol |
| 32 | MERIT-INP | MERIT Internodal Protocol |
| 33 | SEP | Sequential Exchange Protocol |
| 34 | 3PC | Third-Party Connect Protocol |
| 35 | IDPR | Inter-Domain Policy Routing Protocol |
| 36 | XTP | XTP |
| 37 | DDP | Datagram Delivery Protocol |
| 38 | IDPR-CMTP | IDPR Control Message Transport Protocol |
| 39 | TP++ | TP++ Transport Protocol |
| 40 | IL | IL Transport Protocol |
| 41 | IPv6 | Ipv6 |
| 42 | SDRP | Source Demand Routing Protocol |
| 43 | IPv6-Route | Routing Header for IPv6 |
| 44 | IPv6-Frag | Fragment Header for IPv6 |
| 45 | IDRP | Inter-Domain Routing Protocol |
| 46 | RSVP | Reservation Protocol |

Exhibit 4.    Assigned Internet Protocol Numbers (Continued)

| Decimal | Keyword | Protocol |
|---------|---------|----------|
| 47 | GRE | General Routing Encapsulation |
| 48 | MHRP | Mobile Host routing Protocol |
| 49 | BNA | BNA |
| 50 | ESP | Encap security Payload for IPv6 |
| 51 | AH | Authentication Header for IPv6 |
| 52 | I-NLSP | Integrated Net Layer Security |
| 53 | SWIPE | IP with Encryption |
| 54 | NARP | NBMA Address Resolution Protocol |
| 55 | MOBILE | IP Mobility |
| 56 | TLSP | Transport Layer Security Protocol (using Krypto-net key management) |
| 57 | SKIP | SKIP |
| 58 | IPv6-ICMP | ICMP for IPv6 |
| 59 | IPv6-NoNxt | No Next Header for IPv6 |
| 60 | IPv6-Opts | Destination Options for IPv6 |
| 61 | | any host internal protocol |
| 62 | CFTP | CFTP |
| 63 | | any local network |
| 64 | SAT-EXPAK | SATNET and Backroom EXPAK |
| 65 | KRYPTOLAN | Kryptolan |
| 66 | RVD | MIT Remote Virtual Disk Protocol |
| 67 | IPPC | Internet Pluribus Packet Core |
| 68 | | any distributed file system |
| 69 | SAT-MON | SATNET Monitoring |
| 70 | VISA | VISA Protocol |
| 71 | IPCV | Internet Packet Core Utility |
| 72 | CPNX | Computer Protocol Network Executive |
| 73 | CPHB | Computer Protocol Heart Beat |
| 74 | WSN | Wang Span Network |
| 75 | PVP | Packet Video Protocol |
| 76 | BR-SAT-MON | Backroom SATNET Monitoring |
| 77 | SUN-ND | SUN ND PROTOCOL-Temporary |
| 78 | WB-MON | WIDEBAND Monitoring |
| 79 | WB-EXPAK | WIDEBAND EXPAK |
| 80 | ISO-IP | ISO Internet Protocol |
| 81 | VMTP | VMTP |
| 82 | SECURE-VMTP | SECURE-VMPT |
| 83 | VINES | VINES |
| 84 | TTP | TTP |
| 85 | NSFNET-IGP | NSFNET-IGP |
| 86 | DGP | Dissimilar Gateway Protocol |
| 87 | TCF | TCF |
| 88 | EIGRP | EIGRP |
| 89 | OSPFIGP | OSPFIGP |
| 90 | Sprite-RPC | Sprite RPC Protocol |
| 91 | LARP | Locus Address Resolution Protocol |
| 92 | MTP | Multicast Transport Protocol |
| 93 | AX.25 | AX.25 Frames |

**Exhibit 4.    Assigned Internet Protocol Numbers (Continued)**

| Decimal | Keyword | Protocol |
|---|---|---|
| 94 | IPIP | IP-within-IP Encapsulation Protocol |
| 95 | MICP | Mobile Internetworking Control Protocol |
| 96 | SCC-SP | Semaphore Communications Sec. Protocol |
| 97 | ETHERIP | Ethernet-within-IP Encapsulation |
| 98 | ENCAP | Encapsulation Header |
| 99 | | any private encryption scheme |
| 100 | GMTP | GMTP |
| 101 | IFMP | Ipsilon Flow Management Protocol |
| 102 | PNNI | PNNI over IP |
| 103 | PIM | Protocol Independent Multicast |
| 104 | ARIS | ARIS |
| 105 | SCPS | SCPS |
| 106 | QNX | QNX |
| 107 | A/N | Active Networks |
| 108 | IPPCP | IP Payload Compression Protocol |
| 109 | SNP | Sitara Networks Protocol |
| 110 | Compaq-Peer | Compaq Peer Protocol |
| 111 | IPX-in-IP | IPX in IP |
| 112 | VRRP | Virtual Router Redundancy Protocol |
| 113 | PGM | PGM Reliable Transport protocol |
| 114 | | any 0-hop protocol |
| 115 | L2TP | Layer 2 Tunneling Protocol |
| 116 | DDX | D-II Data Exchange (DDX) |
| 117–254 | | Unassigned |
| 255 | Reserved | |

**Header Checksum Field.** The Header Checksum field contains a 16-bit cyclic redundancy check (CRC) character. The CRC represents a number generated by treating the data in the IP header field as a long binary number and dividing that number by a fixed polynomial. The result of this operation is a quotient and remainder, with the remainder being placed into the 16-bit Checksum field by the transmitting device. When a receiving station reads the header, it also performs a CRC operation on the received data, using the same fixed polynomial. If the computed CRC does not match the value of the CRC in the Header Checksum field, the receiver assumes the header is in error and the packet is discarded. Thus, the Header Checksum field, as its name implies, provides a mechanism for ensuring the integrity of the IP header.

**Source and Destination Address Fields.** Both the Source and Destination Address fields are 32 bits in length under IPv4. The Source Address represents the originator of the datagram, while the Destination Address represents the recipient.

Under IPv4, there are five classes of IP addresses, referred to as Class A through Class E. Classes A, B, and C are subdivided into a network portion and a host portion and represent addresses used on the Internet and private IP-based networks. Classes D and E represent two special types of IPv4 network addresses.

### Additional Reading

Gilbert Held, "Working with TCP/IP Utilities," *Data Communications Management,* June 1999 (51-10-99).

Gilbert Held, "Understanding IP Addressing," *Data Communications Management,* April 2000 (52-20-31).

Gurugé, Anura, "Gracefully Transitioning from SNA to IP," *Data Communications Management,* June 1999 (51-10-95).

# Chapter 13
# Expanding Internet Support with IPv6

*Gilbert Held*

A<small>N</small> <small>APPRECIATION FOR THE FUNCTIONALITY OF</small> IP<small>V</small>6 <small>IS BEST OBTAINED BY COMPARING ITS</small> <small>HEADER TO THE</small> IP<small>V</small>4 <small>HEADER.</small> Exhibit 1 provides this comparison, showing the IPv4 header at the top of the illustration, with the IPv6 header below.

In comparing the two headers shown in Exhibit 1, one notes that IPv6 includes six fewer fields than the current version of the Internet Protocol. Although at first glance this appears to make an IPv6 header simpler, in actuality the IPv6 header includes a Next Header field that enables one header to point to a following header, in effect resulting in a daisy chain of headers. While the daisy chain adds complexity, only certain routers need to examine the contents of different headers, facilitating router processing. Thus, an IPv6 header, which can consist of a sequence of headers in a daisy chain, enables routers to process information directly applicable to their routing requirements. This makes IPv6 packet processing much more efficient for intermediate routers when data flows between two Internet locations, enabling those routers to process more packets per second than when the data flow consists of IPv4 headers.

A close examination of the two IP headers reveals that only one field kept the same meaning and position. That field is the Version field, which is encoded in the first four bits of each header as a binary value, with 0100 used for IPv4 and 0110 for IPv6.

Continuing the comparison of the two headers, note that IPv6 does away with seven IPv4 fields. Those fields include the Type of Service, Identification, Flags, Fragment Offset, Checksum, Options, and Padding. Because headers can be daisy chained and separate headers now identify specific services, the Type of Service field is no longer necessary. Another significant change between IPv4 and IPv6 concerns fragmentation, which enables senders to transmit large packets without worrying about the capabilities of intermediate routers. Under IPv4, fragmentation required the use of Identification, Flags, and Fragment Offset fields. Under IPv6, hosts learn the maximum acceptable segment size through a process referred to as path

0-8493-1160-8/02/$0.00+$1.50
© 2002 by CRC Press LLC

IPv4

| Ver | IHL | Types of Service | Total Length | |
|---|---|---|---|---|
| Identification | | | Flags | Fragment Offset |
| Time to Live | | Protocol | Header Checksum | |
| Source Address | | | | |
| Destination Address | | | | |
| Options | | | Padding | |

IPv6

| Ver | Priority | Flow Label | | |
|---|---|---|---|---|
| Payload Length | | Next Header | Hop Limit | |
| Source Address | | | | |
| Destination Address | | | | |

**Exhibit 1.    Comparing IPv4 and IPv6**

MTU (maximum transmission unit) discovery. Thus, this enabled the IPv6 designers to remove those three fields from the new header.

Another difference between IPv4 and IPv6 headers involves the removal of the header Checksum. In an era of fiber backbones it was thought that the advantage obtained from eliminating the processing associated with performing the header Checksum at each router was considerably more than the possibility that transmission errors would go undetected. In addition, since the higher layer (transport layer) and lower layer (IEEE 802 networks) perform checksum operations, the risk of undetected error at the network layer adversely affecting operations is minimal. Two more omissions from the IPv4 header are the Options and Padding fields. Both fields are not necessary in IPv6 because the use of optional headers enables additional functions to be specified as separate entities. Since each header follows a fixed format, there is also no need for a variable Padding field, as was the case under IPv4.

Perhaps the most widely publicized change is the increase in source and destination addresses from 32-bit fields to 128-bit fields. Through the use of 128-bit addressing fields, IPv6 provides the potential to supply unique addresses for every two- and four-footed creature on Earth and still have enough addresses left over to assign a unique address to every past, present, and future appliance. Thus, the extra 96 bit positions virtually ensure that one will not experience another IP address crunch such as the one now being experienced with IPv4.

## NEW AND RENAMED IPV6 FIELDS

IPv6 adds three new fields while relabeling and slightly modifying the use of Total Length and Time to Live fields in Ipv4. Concerning the renamed and revised fields, the Total Length field in IPv4 was changed to a Payload Length. This subtle difference is important, as the use of a payload length now specifies the length of the data carried after the header instead of the length of the sum of both the header and data. The second revision represents the recognition of the fact that the Time to Live field under IPv4, which could be specified in seconds, was difficult — if not impossible — to use due to a lack of time-stamping on packets. Instead, the value used in that field was decremented at each router hop as a mechanism to ensure packets did not endlessly flow over the Internet, since they are discarded when the value of that field reaches zero. In recognition of the actual manner by which that field is used, it was renamed the Hop Limit field under IPv6.

The Priority field is four bits wide, enabling 16 possible values. This field enables packets to be distinguished from one another based on their need for processing precedence. Thus, file transfers would be assigned a low priority, while realtime audio or video would be assigned a higher priority.

Under IPv6, priority field values of 0 through 7 are used for traffic that is not adversely affected by backing off in response to network congestion. In comparison, values 8 to 15 are used for traffic that would be adversely affected by backing off when congestion occurs, such as realtime audio packets being transmitted at a constant rate. Exhibit 2 lists the priority values recommended for different types of congestion-controlled traffic.

Priorities 8 through 15 are used for traffic that would be adversely affected by backing off when network congestion occurs. The lowest priority value in this group, 8, should be used for packets one is most willing to

**Exhibit 2.  Recommended Congestion-Controlled Priorities**

| Priority | Type of Traffic |
| --- | --- |
| 0 | Uncharacterized traffic |
| 1 | Filter traffic, such as Netnews |
| 2 | Unattended data transfer (i.e., e-mail) |
| 3 | Reserved |
| 4 | Attended bulk transfer (i.e., FTP, HTTP) |
| 5 | Reserved |
| 6 | Interactive traffic (i.e., telnet) |
| 7 | Internet-controlled traffic (i.e., SNMP) |

discard under congestion conditions. In comparison, the highest priority, 15, should be used for packets one is least willing to have discarded.

The Flow Label field, also new to IPv6, allows packets that require the same treatment to be identified. For example, a realtime video transmission that consists of a long sequence of packets would more than likely use a Flow Label identifier as well as a high priority value so that all packets that make up the video are treated the same, even if other packets with the same priority arrive at the same time at intermediate routers.

## HEADER CHAINS

The ability to chain headers is obtained through the use of the IPv6 Next Header field. Currently, the IPv6 specification designates six extension headers. Those headers and a brief description of the functions they perform are listed in Exhibit 3.

To illustrate how the Next Header field in IPv6 is actually used, one can use a few of the headers listed in Exhibit 4 to create a few examples. First, assume that an IPv6 header is followed directly by a TCP header and data, with no optional extension headers. Then, the Next Header field in the IPv6 header would indicate that the TCP header follows as indicated in Exhibit 4A.

For a second example, assume that one wants to specify a path or route the packet will follow. To do so, one would add a Routing Header, with the IPv6's Next Header field containing a value that specifies that the Routing Header follows. Then, the Routing Header's Next Header field would contain an appropriate value that specifies that the TCP header follows. This header chain is illustrated in Exhibit 4B.

**Exhibit 3.    IPv6 Extension Headers**

| Extension Header | Description |
| --- | --- |
| Hop by hop options | Passes information to all routers in a path |
| Routing | Defines the route through which a packet flows |
| Fragment | Provides information that enables destination address to concatenate fragments |
| Authentication | Verifies the originator |
| Encrypted security payload | Defines the algorithm and keys necessary to decrypt a previously encrypted payload |
| Destination options | Defines a generic header that can obtain one or more options identified by options type that can define new extensions on an as-required basis |

A.

| IPv6 Header | TCP |
|---|---|
| Next Header=TCP | Header + Data |

B.

| IPv6 Header | Routing Header | TCP |
|---|---|---|
| Next Header=Routing | Next Header=TCP | Header + Data |

C.

| IPv6 Header | Routing Header | Encryption Header | TCP |
|---|---|---|---|
| Next Header=Routing | Next Header=Encryption | Next Header=TCP | Header + Data |

**Exhibit 4.  Creating a Daisy Chain of Headers**

For a third example, assume one wants to specify a route for each packet as well as encrypt the payload. To accomplish this, one would change the TCP Header's Next Header field value from the previous example, where it indicates that there are no additional headers in the header chain, to a value that serves to identify the Encryption Header as the next header.

Exhibit 4C illustrates the daisy chain of IPv6 headers that would specify that a specific route is to be followed and the information required to decrypt an encrypted payload. Now that one has an appreciation for the general format of the IPv6 header, the use of its header fields, and how headers can be chained to obtain additional functionality, one can focus attention on addressing under IPv6.

## ADDRESSING

Under IPv6, there are three types of addresses supported: unicast, multicast, and anycast. The key difference between IPv6 and IPv4 with respect to addressing involves the addition of an anycast type address and the use of 128-bit source and destination addresses.

An anycast address represents a special type of multicast address. Like a multicast address, an anycast address identifies a group of stations that can receive a packet. However, under an anycast address, only the nearest member of a group receives the packet instead of all members. It is expected that the use of anycast addressing will facilitate passing packets from network to network as it allows packets to be forwarded to a group of routers without having to know which is the one nearest to the source. Concerning the actual 128-bit address used under IPv6, its expansion by a factor of four over IPv4 resulted in the necessity to introduce methods to facilitate the notation of this expanded address. Thus, the methods by which IPv6 addresses can be noted can be examined.

## IPV6 ADDRESS NOTATION

Under IPv4, a 32-bit IP address can be encoded as eight hexadecimal digits. The expansion of the IP address fields to 128 bits results in a requirement to use 32 hexadecimal digits. However, because it is fairly easy to make a mistake that can go undetected by simply entering a long sequence of 32 digits, IPv6 allows each 128-bit address to be represented as eight 16-bit integers separated by colons (:). Thus, under IPv6 notation, one can represent each integer as four hexadecimal digits, enabling a 128-bit address to be encoded or noted as a sequence of eight groups of four hexadecimal digits separated from one another by a colon. An example of a IPv6 address follows:

AB01:0000:OO1A:000C:0000:0000:3A1C:1B1F

Two methods supported by IPv6 addressing can be expected to be frequently used by network managers and administrators when configuring network devices. The first method is zero suppression, which allows leading zeros in each of the eight hexadecimal groups to be suppressed. Thus, the application of zero suppression would reduce the previous IPv6 address as follows:

AB01:0:1A:C:0:0:3A1C:1B1E

A second method supported by IPv6 to facilitate the use of 128-bit addresses recognizes that during a migration process, many IPv4 addresses carried within an IPv6 address field will result in a considerable sequence of zero bit positions that cross colon boundaries. This zero density situation can be simplified by the use of a double colon (::), which can replace a single run of consecutive zeros. Thus, one can further simplify the previously zero suppressed IPv6 address as follows:

AB01:0:1A:C::3A1C:1B1E

Note that the use of the double colon can only occur once in an IPv6 address. Otherwise, its use would produce an ambiguous result because there would be no way to tell how many groups of four hexadecimal zeros a double colon represents.

## ADDRESS ASSIGNMENTS

With $2^{128}$ addresses available for assignment, IPv6 designers broke the address space into an initial sequence of 21 address blocks, based on the use of binary address prefixes. As one might surmise, most of the address blocks are either reserved for future use or unassigned because even a small fraction of IPv6 address space is significantly larger than all of the IPv4 address space. Exhibit 5 provides a list of the initial IPv6 address space allocation. Of the initial allocation of IPv6 address space, probably the most important will be the provider-based unicast address. As noted in

**Exhibit 5.    Initial IPv6 Address Space Allocation**

| Address Space Allocation | (binary) | Prefix Fraction of Address Space |
|---|---|---|
| Reserved | 0000 0000 | 1/256 |
| Unassigned | 0000 0001 | 1/256 |
| Reserved for NSAP allocation | 0000 001 | 1/128 |
| Reserved for IPX allocation | 0000 010 | 1/128 |
| Unassigned | 0000 011 | 1/128 |
| Unassigned | 0000 1 | 1/32 |
| Unassigned | 0001 | 1/16 |
| Unassigned | 001 | 1/8 |
| Provider-based unicast address | 010 | 1/8 |
| Unassigned | 011 | 1/8 |
| Reserved for geographic-based unicast addresses | 100 | 1/8 |
| Unassigned | 101 | 1/8 |
| Unassigned | 110 | 1/8 |
| Unassigned | 1110 | 1/16 |
| Unassigned | 1111 0 | 1/32 |
| Unassigned | 1111 10 | 1/64 |
| Unassigned | 1111 110 | 1/128 |
| Unassigned | 1111 1110 0 | 1/512 |
| Link local use addresses | 1111 1110 10 | 1/1024 |
| Site local use addresses | 1111 1110 11 | 1/1024 |
| Multicast addresses | 1111 1111 | 1/256 |

Exhibit 5, the prefix for this allocated address block is binary 010 and it represents one eighth ($^1/_8$) of the total IPv6 address space. The provider-based unicast address space enables the registry that allocates the address, the Internet service provider (ISP), and the subscriber to be identified. In addition, a subscriber can subdivide his or her address into a subnetwork and interface or host identifiers similar to the manner by which IPv4 class A through class C addresses can be subdivided into host and network identifiers. The key difference between the two is the fact that an extension to 128 bits enables an IPv6 address to identify organizations that assigned the address to include the registry and ISP. Concerning the registry, in North America, the Internet Network Information Center (Internet NIC) is tasked with distributing IPv4 addresses and can be expected to distribute IPv6 addresses. The European registry is the Network Coordination Center (NCC) of RIPE, while the APNIC is responsible for distributing addresses for networks in Asian and Pacific countries.

## MIGRATION ISSUES

After considerable deliberation by the Internet community, it was decided that the installed base of approximately 20 million computers using IPv4 would require a dual-stack migration strategy. Instead of one giant cutover sometime in the future, it was recognized that a considerable amount of existing equipment would be incapable of migrating to IPv6. Thus, an IPv6 Internet will be deployed in parallel to IPv4, and all IPv6 hosts will be capable of supporting IPv4. This means that network managers can decide both if and when they should consider upgrading to IPv6. Perhaps the best strategy is, when in doubt, to obtain equipment capable of operating a dual stack, such as the one shown in Exhibit 5. In addition to operating dual stacks, one must consider one's network's relationship with other networks with respect to the version of IP supported. For example, if an organization migrates to IPv6, but its ISP does not, one will have to encapsulate IPv6 through IPv4 to use the transmission services of the ISP to reach other IPv6 networks. Fortunately, two types of tunneling — configured and automatic — have been proposed to allow IPv6 hosts to reach other IPv6 hosts via IPv4-based networks. Thus, with the use of a dual-stack architecture and configured and automatic tunneling, one will be able to continue to use IPv4 as the commercial use of IPv6 begins, as well as plan for an orderly migration.

## RECOMMENDED COURSE OF ACTION

An organization can prepare itself for Ipv6 use by ensuring that acquired hosts, workstations, and routers can be upgraded to support IPv6. In addition, one must consider the fact that the existing Domain Name Server (DNS) will need to be upgraded to support IPv6 addresses, and one must contact the DNS software vendor to determine how and when to implement IPv6 addressing support. By carefully determining the software and possible hardware upgrades, and by keeping abreast of Internet IPv6-related RFCs, one can plan a migration strategy that will allow an organization to benefit from the enhanced router performance afforded by IPv6 addressing.

# Chapter 14
# Implementing Voice-over-IP

*Gilbert Held*

THE ABILITY TO IMPLEMENT A VOICE-OVER-IP SOLUTION DEPENDS ON THE ONE-WAY LATENCY OR DELAY BETWEEN THE ORIGINATOR AND RECIPIENT OF THE CALL. This delay is variable and depends on several parameters, some of which are under one's control and others that, when using a public network, may be beyond one's control.

Exhibit 1 lists the major components associated with the end-to-end analog-to-digital coding, transmission, and conversion back to voice of a packet carrying a digitized portion of a conversation. Note that the fixed and variable delays associated with the end-to-end transmission of a packet can generally range between approximately 60 and 289 ms. To put this time in perspective, a typical human ear can accept up to 250 ms of delay every once in a while before the conversation becomes annoying. While full-duplex transmission is desirable for most data applications, it is not useful and in fact creates problems when voice is carried over a network. This is because two rational humans do not have a conversation by talking at the same time. Instead, rational humans wait for one party to finish talking before the other party to the conversation begins a response. If the latency or delay begins to exceed a quarter of a second for significant portions of a conversation, the conversation will begin to resemble a CB-radio conversation, with each party having to say "over" to inform the other party it is all right to talk. Otherwise, the delay will result in one party periodically thinking the other has finished talking when they have not, resulting in a full-duplex conversation that requires one party to stop and the other party to begin anew. In fact, the International Telecommunications Union (ITU) standard for one-way delay for a voice call requires a maximum latency of 150 ms, which ensures that the call will not turn into a full-duplex conversation. For most organizations, a maximum latency of 200 ms and a mean latency approaching or under 150 ms should be sufficient to provide good quality of reconstructed voice.

0-8493-1160-8/02/$0.00+$1.50
© 2002 by CRC Press LLC

**Exhibit 1.    Packet Network Delays**

| Fixed and variable delays (ms) | Minimum | Maximum |
|---|---|---|
| Compression (voice coding) | 10 | 45 |
| Inter-process (origin) | 10 | 10 |
| Network access at origin | 0.25 | 7 |
| Network transmission delay | 20 | 200 |
| Network egress at destination | 0.25 | 7 |
| Buffer (configurable) | 10 | 10 |
| Decompression | 10 | 10 |
| Total fixed and variable delays | 60.50 | 289 |

For those curious about the latency associated with the use of the public switched telephone network (PSTN), it can be considered almost negligible. That is, telephone company switches introduce delay measured in microseconds (μs), one thousandth of a millisecond (ms). Similarly, pulse code modulation (PCM) and adaptive differential pulse code modulation (ADPCM) have a coding delay of a few microseconds, which represents a thousandth of the delay associated with the use of low-bit voice encoding methods. With an appreciation for the amount of one-way delay a voice-over-IP application can tolerate, examine the component of delay listed in Exhibit 1. In doing so, there are several techniques one can use to modify or adjust certain delays.

## COMPRESSION

There are numerous low-bit rate compression or coding methods one can select. In fact, most equipment vendors typically support between four and six voice coding methods. Most of these methods are members of the code excited linear prediction (CELP) family of voice coders. The original CELP voice coder was a hybrid, incorporating both waveform coding similar to PCM and ADPCM and linear predictive coding. Although the first CELP voice coder operated at a relatively low bit rate in comparison to PCM and ADPCM, its coding delay was relatively high, approaching 60 ms. Since the first CELP voice coder was introduced, numerous variations have been developed, with approximately half a dozen now standardized by the ITU. Two of the more popular members of the CELP family are the low-delay (LD) CELP (G.723) that operates at 16 Kbps but has a delay of 10 ms, and the G.729.1 multicoder that operates at both 5.3 and 6.3 Kbps and has a coding delay of approximately 30 ms. Other coders have delays up to 45 ms.

By carefully examining the specification sheets associated with different voice coding techniques, one will note that there is normally a direct relationship between the coder bit rate and its mean optimum score (MOS), the latter a measurement of voice quality; that is, the higher the bit rate, the higher the MOS. There is also an inverse relationship between the coder's bit rate and its coding delay; that is, the higher the resulting bit rate produced by the coder, the lower the coding delay. Thus, one technique to consider when making a voice-over-IP application work when there is too much latency is to consider changing the voice coding method. In general, changing the coder from one that operates at 5.3/6.3 Kbps to 8 Kbps will reduce the coding delay by approximately 10 ms. If one changes the coder to an LD-CELP coder, one can remove an additional 10 ms of delay. While 20 ms is not earth shattering, it may be enough to ensure that the quality of reconstructed voice is acceptable for one's voice-over-IP application. In addition, if one saves a few milliseconds here and a few milliseconds with other techniques, the cumulative effect of these savings will really add up. The effect of changing these settings may be sufficient to provide an acceptable level of reconstructed voice that might otherwise preclude one's organization from implementing a voice-over-IP application.

## INTERPROCESSING DELAY

The interprocessing delay represents the time required to form an IP datagram from each segment of digitized voice produced by a voice coder and route the resulting datagram to a router connected to the IP network. The total interprocessing delay is approximately 10 ms and represents a series of delays that can be variable due to the fact that the level of utilization of the LAN that connects the voice gateway to the router governs the gateway-to-router delay. In addition to the gateway-to-router delay, the gateway itself has some processing delay as it forms an IP datagram. Similarly, the router must process each datagram prior to sending it on its way toward its destination. Although this author used 10 ms for the total interprocess delay at the origin, it is possible to slightly reduce this time. To do so, consider obtaining a faster processor for the voice gateway.

Most voice gateways are modular devices, with voice processing boards that are inserted into a PC. Although each voice processing board contains its own processor, which enables support for different voice coding methods and actually performs the analog-to-digital conversion, the formation and movement of datagrams through the gateway is a function of its main processor. This means that the use of a Pentium III 700 MHz system will have less delay and support the faster movement of datagrams through the gateway and onto the LAN than a Pentium III 500 MHz-based system. Tests performed by this author showed that the replacement of the gateway system with a faster processor can be expected to shave 1 ms per extra 100 MHz of processor power.

A second method one can consider using to reduce the interprocess delay is to upgrade the LAN if it is operating at a level of utilization beyond 50 percent. Based on this author's experience, the replacement of an Ethernet LAN operating at slightly over a 50 percent level of utilization by a Fast Ethernet network reduced delay by approximately 1 ms. Thus, by upgrading the gateway process from a 500 MHz system to a 700 MHz system and the Ethernet network that connects the gateway to the router by a Fast Ethernet network, one may be able to shave approximately 3 ms off the end-to-end delay.

## NETWORK ACCESS AT ORIGIN

A digitized voice conversation consists of a stream of very small datagrams to reduce the impact of one or more being lost. If the router is connected to the Internet at 56 Kbps and the average datagram length is 49 bytes, then the network access delay at the origin becomes (49 bytes × 8 bits/byte)/56 Kbps, or 7.0 ms.

Of the 49 bytes in a typical datagram, 20 represent the IP header and 8 represent the UDP header, resulting in 21 actual bytes transporting digitized voice. Although one may encounter references to the use of TCP and UDP for transporting voice, in actuality TCP is used for the connection setup while UDP is used for the actual transport of digitized voice. Because one cannot retransmit lost or erroneous datagrams, UDP is used to transport digitized voice because it is a connectionless, best-effort protocol. Because it is extremely important to ensure that call setup information such as the number dialed is received correctly, TCP, which is a connection-oriented error-free protocol, is used to transport call setup information.

If the access line is upgraded to a T1 line operating at 1.544 Mbps, then the network access delay becomes (49 bytes × 8 bits/byte) (1.536 Mbps), or 0.25 ms. Note that a divisor of 1.536 Mbps was used instead of 1.544 Mbps for the T1 line because 8 Kbps is used for framing and is not available for data transfer.

In examining the network access delay at the origin, it becomes possible to reduce the latency associated with moving datagrams from the local network into the Internet by upgrading the access line. As shown by the previous computations, moving from a 56 Kbps access line to a T1 access line can reduce latency by almost 7 ms. If the cost of a T1 is prohibitive, one can consider different types of fractional T1 (FT1) access lines that operate between 56 Kbps and 1.544 Mbps and could be used to reduce network access delays.

## NETWORK TRANSMISSION DELAY

Because it is very rare to use voice-over-IP for intra-city communications, assume that the IP network will route data between dissimilar geographical areas. Because there will then be at least two backbone routers involved in the routing process, one can expect a minimum delay of 20 ms.

Because most network transmission delays are under 200 ms, the range of delays is listed in Exhibit 1 as 20 to 200 ms.

One of the key tools that can be used ahead of time to determine the viability of a voice-over-IP application is the Ping utility program. Exhibit 2 illustrates the basic format of Ping implemented under different versions of Microsoft Windows. Note that one can simply enter Ping with a host name or IP address, or one can enter one or more of the options listed in Exhibit 2. Although the primary use of Ping is to determine the operational status of the target host or address, it will also provide the round-trip delay from originator to destination.

Exhibit 3 illustrates the use of the Ping utility to determine the round-trip delay time between the author's computer and the Web server operated by Yale University. In examining Exhibit 3, note that the Microsoft implementation of Ping results in the transmission of a sequence of four echo-request packets to the target. The target will respond with an echo-reply to each echo-request, with the originating station computing the round-trip delay. If a response is not received within 250 ms, which is the default timeout value, the originating station will consider its request to have timed out and will generate its next echo-request.

In Exhibit 3, note that the initial round-trip delay was 156 ms, while the second and fourth round-trip delays were computed to be 125 ms and 110 ms, respectively. One of the most common mistakes many persons make when using Ping is to use the first round-trip delay time. In actuality, if one enters a host name that was not previously resolved, the resolution of the host name into an IP address will result in the first round-trip delay being longer than subsequent delays. The only exception to this is when traffic or processing at a router reaches the point where it results in significant delays that cause Ping to timeout. This is illustrated by the third line after the "Pinging" message in Exhibit 3.

Thus, when using Ping to determine the round-trip delay through a network, one should always discard the first delay as it can include time for a host-to-IP address resolution. In addition, one should consider running Ping throughout the day to determine if there are one or more periods of time when delays escalate. One can either write a script to run Ping at different times, or use the -t option to run it continuously during the day. If one pipes the results to a file, one can then read the file into a spreadsheet and easily determine the mean, peak, and average values, as well as other statistics about round-trip delay. For example, the following DOS command would run Ping on the target www.yale.edu continuously and pipe its output to the file test:

```
Ping -t www.yale.edu >test
```

```
Command Prompt

Microsoft(R) Windows NT(TM)
(C) Copyright 1985-1996 Microsoft Corp.

C:\>ping

Usage: ping [-t] [-a] [-n count] [-l size] [-f] [-i TTL] [-v TOS]
            [-r count] [-s count] [[-j host-list] : [-k host-list]]
            [-w timeout] destination-list

Options:
    -t             Ping the specifed host until interrupted.
    -a             Resolve addresses to hostnames.
    -n count       Number of echo requests to send.
    -l size        Send buffer size.
    -f             Set Don't Fragment flag in packet.
    -i TTL         Time To Live.
    -v TOS         Type Of Service.
    -r count       Record route for count hops.
    -s count       Timestamp for count hops.
    -j host-list   Loose source route along host-list.
    -k host-list   Strict source route along host-list.
    -w timeout     Timeout in milliseconds to wait for each reply.

C:\>
```

Exhibit 2.  Displaying the Format of Ping by Entering the Command without Any Options

**Command Prompt**

```
C:\>ping www.yale.edu

Pinging elsinore.cis.yale.edu [130.132.143.21] with 32 bytes of data:

Reply from 130.132.143.21: bytes=32 time=156ms TTL=241
Reply from 130.132.143.21: bytes=32 time=125ms TTL=241
Request timed out.
Reply from 130.132.143.21: bytes=32 time=110ms TTL=241

C:\>_
```

**Exhibit 3.   Pinging the Web Server at Yale University**

If the response to a series of Pings issued over a period of time indicates the network delay is too great to allow a voice-over-IP application to have an overall delay under 200 ms, many people would be tempted to give up on the application. Instead, one should consider the use of a second TCP/IP application tool built into Windows and other operating systems. That tool is the traceroute application, which is named tracert under Windows.

Tracert operates by initially transmitting a series of packets with the time-to-live (TTL) field value set to 1. Routers automatically decrement the TTL field value. If its value then equals zero, the packet is discarded and the router returns an error message to the originator, along with the IP address of the router and many times textual information about the router and its network connection. The originator then transmits a new series of packets with the TTL field value incremented by 1 to 2. The packets flow through the first router on the path to the destination, where the TTL field value in each packet is decremented by 1 to 1. Thus, the second router in the packet to the destination discards the series of packets and returns error messages to the originator. This process continues until a sequence of packets either reaches its destination or the maximum default TTL value is reached. Under Windows, the default maximum TTL value is 30 hops.

Exhibit 4 illustrates the format of the Microsoft Windows version of traceroute called tracert. Note that one can change the maximum number of hops in one's search for the route to a target via the use of the -h option.

Because Ping was used to determine the round-trip delay to the Web server at Yale University, now use tracert to trace the path to the Web server. Exhibit 5 illustrates the resulting display from the use of tracert. Note that a total of 15 hops were required to reach the destination. Also note that the Microsoft version of traceroute issues a sequence of three packets for each TTL value used, resulting in three round-trip delay computations. On the 12th hop, the second packet had a response time that exceeded 250 ms, resulting in an asterisk (*) being displayed to indicate a timeout condition.

If the use of Ping indicates a periodic delay that exceeds the amount of latency required for a voice-over-IP application to work, one can use tracert to determine if there are one or more routers abnormally contributing to the delay. If so, it may be possible to request one's Internet service provider (ISP) to reroute the path packets must take, or perhaps the ISP would be willing to upgrade or replace a router that acts as a bottleneck. In carefully examining Exhibit 5, one notes that the routers at hops 11, 12, and 13 represent bottlenecks. If planning a voice-over-IP application to the Yale campus, this author would certainly bring this to the attention of his ISP.

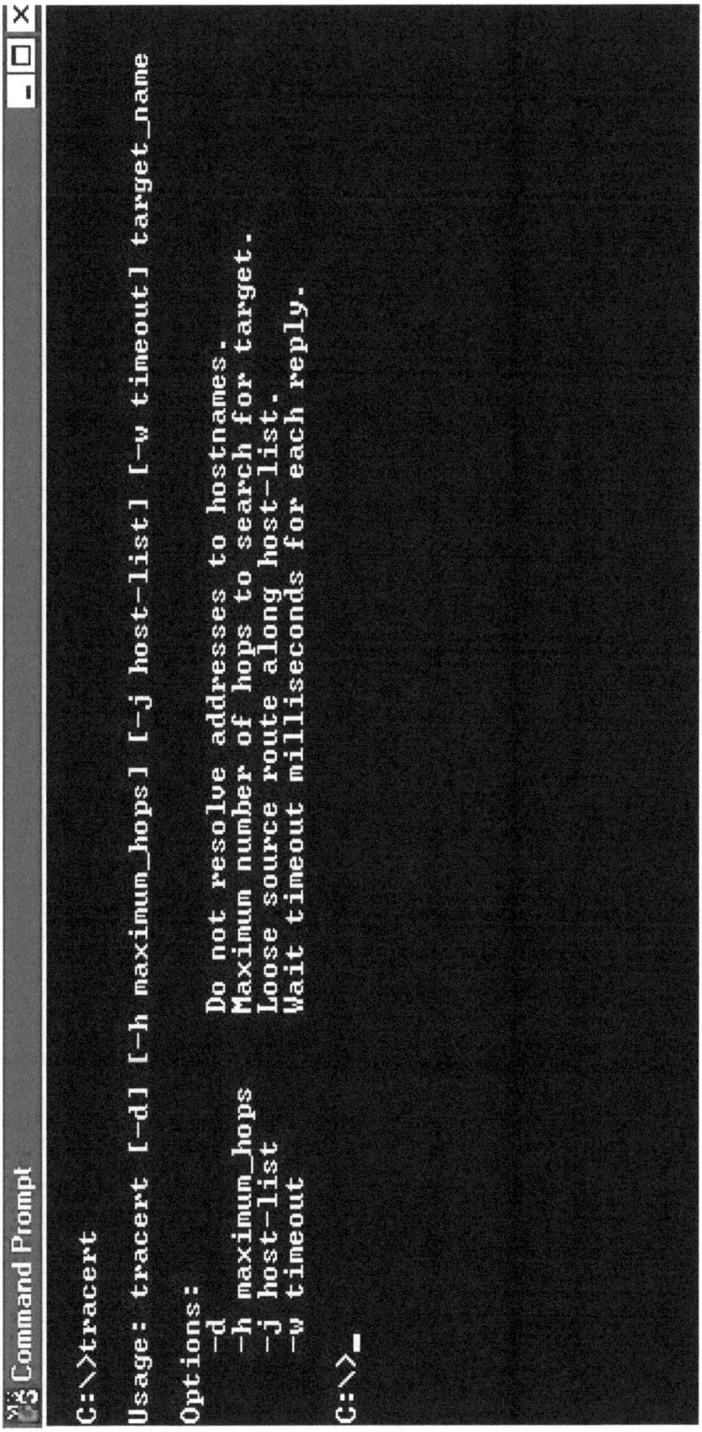

```
Command Prompt                                          - □ X

C:\>tracert

Usage: tracert [-d] [-h maximum_hops] [-j host-list] [-w timeout] target_name

Options:
    -d                 Do not resolve addresses to hostnames.
    -h maximum_hops    Maximum number of hops to search for target.
    -j host-list       Loose source route along host-list.
    -w timeout         Wait timeout milliseconds for each reply.

C:\>_
```

Exhibit 4.   The Format of the Microsoft Windows Version of Traceroute, Called Tracert

## NETWORK EGRESS AT DESTINATION

Returning to Exhibit 1, note that the latency or delay for datagrams flowing from the Internet is shown to be between 0.25 ms and 7 ms. Once again, this range represents the variance in delay resulting from the use of a T1 access line (0.25 ms) and a 56 Kbps access line (7 ms). Thus, by upgrading one or both access lines, it becomes possible to reduce end-to-end delay.

## BUFFER

As a person talks, a voice coder produces a series of datagrams with a uniform time delay between each datagram. As the datagrams flow through the Internet, they experience random delays at each node in the network based on the flow of traffic to the router as well as the state of its queues. By the time the datagrams exit the Internet and flow toward the destination gateway, the gaps between datagrams have random delays. If these datagrams were directly used to reconstruct voice, the result would be awkward-sounding gaps between each small segment of voice. Thus, instead of being directly converted back to analog voice, the datagrams are first moved into a jitter buffer. Then they are removed in order with a uniform time delay between extractions, resulting in natural sounding voice when the contents of the datagrams are converted back into analog voice.

Most jitter buffers can be set from 0 (disabled) to a maximum of 255 ms. Because one needs to reduce the random delays between received datagrams, the jitter buffer should never be set to a value of 0. Similarly, because the human ear can only tolerate 200 ms of delay and there are many other delays that must be considered, the jitter buffer should never be configured anywhere near its maximum value. Instead, a good rule of thumb is to initially set its value to a delay of 10 ms. If the total delay to include the jitter buffer delay is well under 200 ms, one can then experiment and gradually increase the jitter buffer delay to determine if doing so makes reconstructed voice sound better.

## DECOMPRESSION

Unlike voice coding delays that can significantly vary based upon the coding technique, decompression is relatively fixed at approximately 10 ms, regardless of method used. Thus, while there are minor differences in decompression time between voice coding methods, a good rule of thumb is to use a 10-ms delay for compression.

## RECOMMENDED COURSE OF ACTION

As indicated in this chapter, there are seven major components associated with the end-to-end delay or latency of datagrams transporting voice. While some components are relatively fixed and there is little to be gained by altering their parameters, other delay components are quite variable

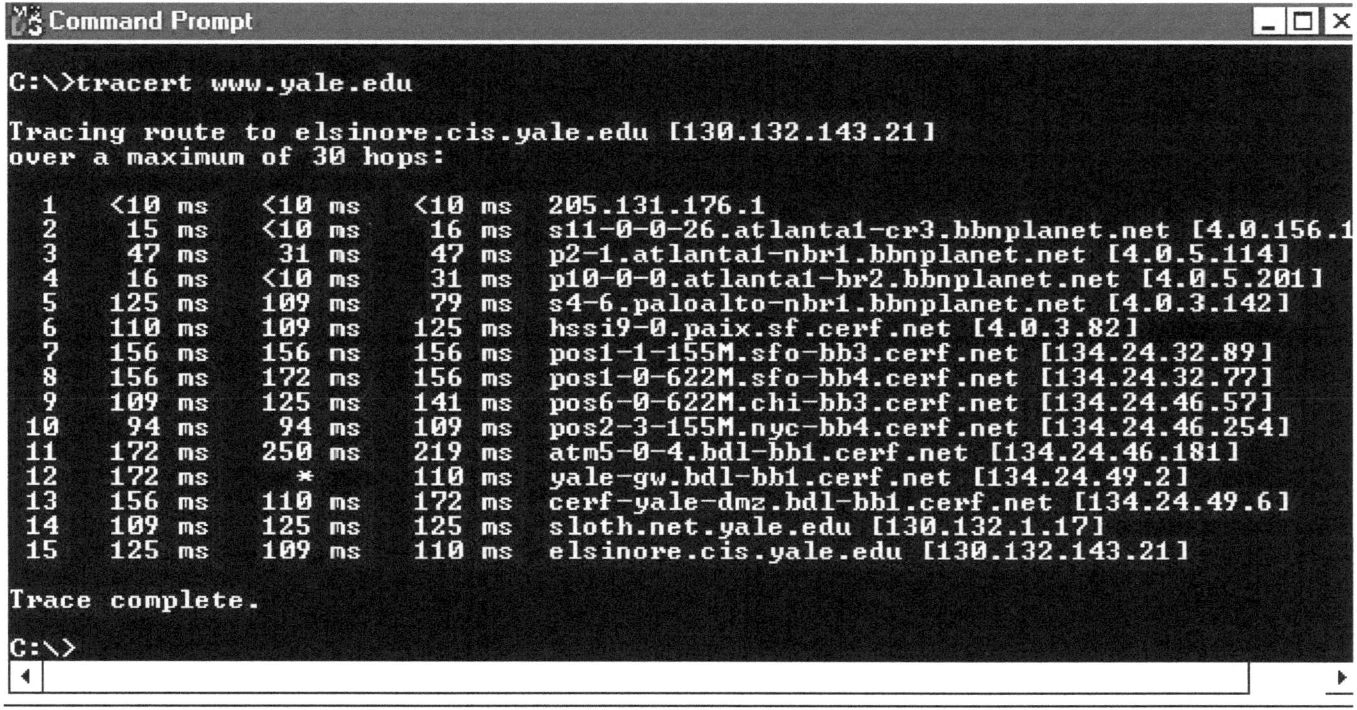

**Exhibit 5.   Tracing the Route to the Yale University Web Server**

and there are several techniques for altering their contributions to overall delay. In addition, through the use of Ping and tracert, one obtains the tools to examine the major contributing factor to end-to-end delay — network transmission delay. By carefully examining each component of delay and using applicable tools, it becomes possible to successfully implement voice-over-IP applications that otherwise might never become a reality.

# Chapter 15
# Bridging Strategies for LAN Internets

*Nathan J. Muller*

THE DEVICES THAT FACILITATE THE INTERCONNECTION OF HOST SYSTEMS AND LANS FALL INTO THE CATEGORIES OF REPEATERS, BRIDGES, ROUTERS, AND GATEWAYS. Repeaters are the simplest devices; they are used to extend the range of LANs and other network facilities by boosting signal strength and reshaping distorted signals. Gateways are the most complex devices; they provide interoperability between applications by performing processing-intensive protocol conversions.

In the middle of this "complexity spectrum" are bridges and routers. At the risk of oversimplification, one could say that traditional bridges implement basic data-level links between LANs that use identical protocols; traditional routers can be programmed for multiple network protocols, thereby supporting diverse types of LANs and host systems over the same wide area network (WAN) facility. However, in many situations the use of routers is overkill and needlessly expensive; routers cost as much as $75,000 for a full-featured, multiport unit, compared with $6,000 to $30,000 for most bridges.

The price difference is attributable to the number of protocols supported, the speed of the central processing unit, port configurations, WAN interfaces, and network management features. Some vendors bundle selected functions of both devices into the same unit, permitting concurrent bridging and routing at a reasonable cost. Bridge and router applications are summarized in Exhibit 1.

Although many companies are implementing LAN/WAN networks based on such vendor-neutral protocols as the transmission control protocol and Internet protocol (TCP/IP) and Open Systems Interconnection (OSI), these same companies have considerable investments in Systems Network Architecture (SNA) equipment and applications. With many vendors providing connectivity to IBM's Token Ring LANs and the SNA environment, it is worthwhile to review IBM's method of bridging and contrast it with the available alternatives.

0-8493-1160-8/02/$0.00+$1.50
© 2002 by CRC Press LLC

**Exhibit 1.    A Comparison of Bridge and Router Applications and Costs**

| Bridge Applications | Router Applications |
| --- | --- |
| • Best for point-to-point and simple mesh topologies<br>• Easier to install and maintain than routers<br>• Operate independently of higher-level protocols<br>• Offer a flexible method for filtering traffic according to source-destination addresses, protocol type, and application | • Accommodate several data links and can exploit complex mesh topologies in cases of link failure and congestion<br>• Support multiple network and router layer protocols at the same time<br>• Offer advanced administration and control services based on network and subnetwork addresses |
| **Cost: $6,000 to $30,000** | **Cost: As much as $75,000** |

## CONNECTIVITY CONCERNS

IBM System Network Architecture is still a dominant architecture, but it is no longer able to meet the networking demands of the majority of users. Consequently, its host-controlled, hierarchical structure, with all information flowing through a central point, is rapidly being displaced by distributed computing and peer-to-peer networking over LANs.

Although IBM very effectively addresses these needs with its Token Ring LANs, its preferred method for interconnecting them — source routing — for a variety of reasons is unsuitable for building large networks. Nor does source routing support other popular internetworking protocols (e.g., TCP/IP and Novell's IPX/SPX), making it unsuitable for multiprotocol networks.

Although users appreciate LANs for their efficiencies and economies, older SNA equipment still provides dependable service and may not yet be fully depreciated. Therefore, another problem faced by users is how best to eliminate parallel networks by integrating ssynchronous data link control and binary synchronous communications (BSC) serial SNA protocols with LAN traffic on a single network.

## BRIDGING METHODS

Several bridging methods are currently available: source route bridging, preferred by IBM; transparent bridging, a basic method of LAN interconnection supported by most bridge makers; and source routing transparent (SRT), a relatively new standard that allows source routing and transparent bridging to be used together on the same network.

## Source Routing

Source route bridging is a method of internetworking Token Ring LANs that uses a process called route discovery to find the optimal path for communications between end stations. The route between end stations is discovered using "explorer packets" that are sent between the source and destination end stations. When the explorer packet reaches its destination, the end station responds by issuing a packet containing the routing information. If multiple routes are available, this packet is sent back to the source over all the routes. The originating station selects as the best route the one with the fewest hops to the destination station.

One problem with source routing is that in mesh networks it creates a significant amount of overhead, which can bog down network performance. The amount of overhead increases as more stations and links are added to the network.

Because the end stations are involved in route selection, they may not have up-to-date knowledge of the best path, especially if the network is temporarily congested. In not being able to implement adaptive routing, source routing bridges are not able to dynamically reroute traffic around failed links. To do this, a new route discovery sequence must be initiated. Source routing bridges also cannot balance the traffic load in response to congestion.

## Transparent Bridging

Transparent bridging originated in the Ethernet environment. It enables stations, regardless of location, to communicate as if they were on the same LAN. In a process called *filtering*, the bridge looks at the destination address to see if it is listed in the table of source addresses. If not, the packet is sent over the bridge to the next LAN. If a match is found, the bridge simply ignores the packet.

In a process called *learning*, the bridge examines all the packets originating on the LAN to build and update its table of source addresses. A table is maintained for each LAN connected to the bridge. The tables are updated when new packets are detected or when addresses expire from nonuse after a specified time.

If a packet contains an address that has not yet been learned, it is sent out over all active links. The best path is determined by an industry-standard spanning-tree algorithm, based on such factors as the number of hops from the designated root bridge and speed of the links. Any redundant paths are put in standby mode and used only in case of primary link failure.

## SOURCE ROUTING TRANSPORT BRIDGING (SRT)

The SRT bridging method combines source routing and transparent bridging, permitting the data of both to be passed over the same network.

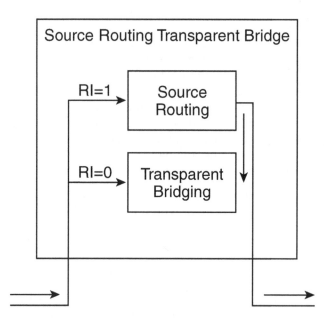

**Exhibit 2.  The SRT Bridge is Capable of Both Source Routing and Transparent Bridging.**

With SRT, the routing information field indicator is used to distinguish between frames using source routing and frames using transparent bridging. Transparent bridges, including those supporting Ethernet, do not alter the routing indicator, but source routing bridges do change the routing indicator, setting it to 1. By inspecting the routing indicator, the SRT-compliant device can determine whether the frame requires transparent bridging or source routing (Exhibit 2). In supporting both bridging methods, SRT-compliant devices eliminate the need for multiple types of internetworking equipment and separate network facilities.

## RAMIFICATIONS OF SRT

In several key areas, SRT enhances the capabilities of source routing and transparent bridging, providing compelling advantages to users.

### Route Discovery

Transparent bridging employs a simple method of forwarding packets and it can "learn" other locations based on newly encountered addresses. With source routing, the originating device sends out explorer packets to discover the route between source and destination end stations. SRT not only supports both methods, but also uses less route discovery overhead than source routing because both the source and destination end stations can simultaneously discover the route.

## Congestion and Load Balancing

Source routing does not automatically reroute around congested or failed links or perform load balancing. Transparent bridging does not make use of idle standby paths during normal operation or offer load balancing in the event of congestion.

SRT makes more efficient use of the available bandwidth by switching to standby paths in case of a failure on the primary link.

## Network Consolidation

SRT-compliant devices support both 4M-bps and 16M-bps Token Ring LANs and can consolidate Ethernet and Token Ring over shared WAN facilities.

## Platform for Interoperability

Although SRT does not translate packets, its support of both source routing and transparent bridging provides an internetworking platform and makes possible the use of applications that will perform such translations.

SRT-compliant bridges do not solve the problem of consolidating System's Network Architecture and Token Ring traffic over the same network. This is an important concern for many users who want to carry forward their considerable investments in fully functional System's Network Architecture equipment, yet take advantage of Token Ring LANs for peer-to-peer networking. The optimal solution lies in choosing an SRT-compliant internetworking device that also supports a capability known as SDLC pass-through.

## SDLC Pass-Through

Much of the installed base of SNA equipment has not been upgraded to support Token Ring connectivity, so the support of SDLC traffic is a significant feature of today's internetworking devices. Before SDLC support, expensive adapters were required to attach, for example, a 3174 cluster controller to a Token Ring LAN. Alternatively, the two traffic types had to be separately routed over the WAN. The latter solution entailed an overhead burden and the cost of two separate networks.

With internetworking devices that support SDLC traffic, users are finally able to consolidate parallel networks into a single multiprotocol backbone. Among the benefits of this arrangement is that it encompasses the SNA environment without any modification to the installed base of cluster controllers and front-end processors (FEPs). Thus, SDLC pass-through is useful for integrating different generations of equipment.

In combining SDLC serial traffic from SNA devices with LAN traffic — as well as supporting such commonly used non-SNA protocols as NetBIOS, transmission control protocol (TCP)/IP, and IPX/SPX — communication costs can be greatly reduced.

SDLC pass-through also provides an economical migration path from older SNA cluster controllers and FEPs to Token Ring peer-to-peer networking. Cluster controller and FEP performance is improved by speeding up the communication lines from the slow 4.8K- and 9.6K-bps serial lines employed by SNA to WAN link speeds of 64K bps.

Reliability is also improved because the SDLC data stream is encapsulated within the Token Ring frame format for routing across the WAN. This allows the advantageous use of redundant routes not available under SNA. If a line fails, traffic can be rerouted in an average of three seconds — well within the timeout threshold of SNA sessions.

SDLC pass-through also allows a permanent virtual circuit (PVC) to be predefined between network endpoints. Some vendors allow 16,000 unique virtual circuit numbers in either a point-to-point topology involving a FEP and controller, or multidrop topology involving as many as 255 cluster controllers. Each connection has a station number as well as an assigned circuit number. Token Ring frames containing the encapsulated SDLC frames are routed to the appropriate network port.

## NETWORK MANAGEMENT

Selecting the right internetworking equipment vendor can actually facilitate network management. Not only can the vendor's management system monitor and control its own internetworking devices, but there also may be enough flexibility to manage Token Rings, TCP/IP networks, and devices compatible with the simple network management protocol (SNMP). Compatibility with IBM's LAN and host management systems — LAN Manager 2.0 and NetView — is another advantage of a good equipment choice.

Of particular benefit to IBM users would be the network management system's built-in protocol analyzer features for troubleshooting the integrated network. Protocol analysis is not an inherent feature of IBM's network management systems, so users must typically spend $25,000 or more for a third-party solution. When protocol analysis is an integral feature of the internetworking equipment vendor's network management system, the cost is only $3,000 to $4,000.

## A CASE STUDY

Recently, one brokerage services firm implemented a plan to upgrade its network. A key component of the plan was to move from Systems Network Architecture to LANs to achieve greater efficiencies and economies in service delivery. The resulting network would have to serve multiple departments, including real estate, tax, ordering, unit trust, information systems development, futures trading, personal financial management, investment banking, and retail sales.

### Competitive Environment

Trading companies rely heavily on their networks to serve customers better and stay competitive. Consequently, more and more brokerage houses are forgoing the traditional SNA architecture, with its single-protocol, low-speed analog lines and polled, multidrop modems. One byproduct of consolidation activity in the brokerage industry is the diversity of protocols that must be accommodated on the enterprise network. Another byproduct is that the redesign of corporate networks opens up the opportunity to employ more modern network protocols (e.g., Novell's NetWare).

The integration of a variety of microcomputers and protocols (e.g., IBM's SNA/3270, Digital Equipment's DECnet and Local Area Transport, and TCP/IP) gives brokerage firms the networking flexibility needed to meet the current and emerging demands of their customers.

### Evaluating the Products

To achieve this level of integration, the products of many internetworking vendors are typically evaluated. Most brokerage houses with mixed-vendor environments disqualify IBM's source-routing bridges at the start because they cannot support non-IBM protocols. Furthermore, IBM bridges operate on a PS/2 platform and the presence of a keyboard invites tampering, representing a potential security problem. Traditional routers are also usually disqualified early in the evaluation process because they do not operate well enough in the SNA environment. A bridge represents a good choice in the multiprotocol networking environment precisely because it overcomes these problems and because it is economical and relatively easy to install.

### The Brokerage Network

This New York brokerage house has more than 300 offices worldwide connected through modems to the network at its headquarters in Manhattan. There, a star network links six home-office buildings (Exhibit 3). Each building has its own LANs, which are interconnected over different media at the T1 rate (1.5M bps), at minimum. Because higher-rate private lines in large cities are so expensive, there are 10M-bps and 45M-bps (Ethernet and T3 speeds) microwave links between several hubs. The T3 facilities support dual 16M-bps Token Ring LANs and miscellaneous other traffic, for example, 3270 terminal traffic and voice. Gateways are used for translation of Novell's Internetwork Packet eXchange and IBM's NetBIOS protocols, among others, between the Token Rings and the SNA host.

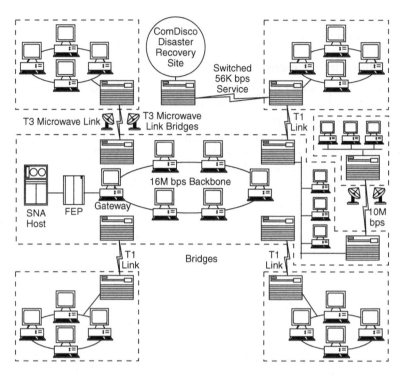

**Exhibit 3.   The Brokerage's Backbone Network**

Then there is the need to pass information between Token Ring and Ethernet LANs. This is effectively handled by a bridge that operates independently of the protocols being used. Such bridges facilitate the interconnection of the two LAN types. This is no small task because there are more than 1000 connections on Token Ring and Ethernet LANs at this brokerage house. Although some traditional routers also offer this capability, they do so at a premium price. This brokerage firm did not need the routing capability, so spending more for devices that would have been used primarily for their protocol conversion capabilities was not justified.

The rule among brokerage firms is to protect their networks against the potential loss of vital information. The New York brokerage firm implemented its disaster recovery plan in association with ComDisco (Foster City, CA). Every night, all data from the home-office locations is sent to a ComDisco backup facility in New Jersey. Within ten minutes of a computer failure on the company's Internet, lost data can be retrieved from the backup site.

### Network Management

The bridge's network management system can isolate problems across the distributed computing environment. It actually does a better job of

178

troubleshooting in such an environment than host-based management systems, despite residing on a single workstation. From the management console, any bridge can be remotely configured, performance statistics gathered, and real-time alarms observed. Moreover, the enterprise network can be quickly diagnosed with a segment-by-segment connectivity test to determine whether a problem is in the network or application software.

For example, a remote bridge can be instructed to test the integrity of the connection between itself and a questionable server. Then the bridge can test the connection between the management system and the remote bridge, completing the network test. Any segment of the network can be tested in this way without the need for extra equipment and without dispatching technicians to remote locations.

These management features achieve greater network uptime, configuration flexibility, and economies in equipment and personnel. Specifically, the brokerage firm can accommodate incremental growth, mitigate congestion, and better protect itself against potential disasters.

### THE OPTIMAL SOLUTION

Companies of all types and sizes are turning to LAN Internets to obtain the operational efficiencies and economies they require to meet the informational needs of a diverse and demanding constituency that often includes consumers, shareholders, regulators, subsidiaries, and strategic partners.

For users in mixed-vendor environments, with a large installed base of Systems Network Architecture equipment, the benefits of SRT-compliant internetworking devices that also support SDLC pass-through are clear. They provide access to and management of a broad range of computing resources from a single workstation or personal computer. And they provide organizations with the performance advantages and configuration flexibility needed to cope with the new economic and competitive realities — advantages that source route bridging and transparent bridging alone do not provide when information must be passed between diverse systems in multivendor environments.

# Chapter 16
# Choosing and Equipping an Internet Server

*Nathan J. Muller*

THE INTERNET IS A GLOBAL COLLECTION OF SERVERS INTERCONNECTED BY ROUTERS OVER VARIOUS TYPES OF CARRIER-PROVIDED LINES AND SERVICES. It consists of more than 4 million hosts on about 100,000 networks in 160 countries. Approximately 30 million people have access to the Internet, a number that was expected to have grown here to 200 million by 2001. The Internet includes databases that have a combined capacity that can only be measured in terabytes — more information than has ever been printed on paper. It is accessed and navigated by PCs and workstations equipped with client software such as Mosaic and Netscape.

## INTERNET AND INTRANET SERVICES

One of the most popular and fastest-growing services on the Internet is the World Wide Web, also known as WWW or simply "the Web." The Web is an interactive, graphically oriented, distributed, platform-independent, hypertext information system. Browser software such as Netscape and Mosaic make it easy for users to find information published on Web servers, which can be configured for public or private access. When configured for private access, companies can create virtual private networks or "intranets" to facilitate information exchange among employees, customers, suppliers, and strategic partners.

Of all the services that can be accessed over the Internet, the Web holds the greatest promise for electronic commerce. Using catalogs displayed on the Web, customers can order products by filling out forms transmitted through e-mail. Often the transactions include buyers' credit card numbers, which require a secure means of transmission. Other electronic commerce applications include online banking and stock trading.

0-8493-1160-8/02/$0.00+$1.50
© 2002 by CRC Press LLC

With a Web server, an organization can leverage Web technology for internal communication on an intranet by producing online documentation of corporate materials, automating sales force activities, providing training-on-demand, or using data warehousing capabilities to analyze large amounts of data or complex data.

The factor driving these activities is the same in every case: providing users access to information. As companies use the Web to deliver new services, they need solutions that are capable of storing, managing, and organizing all their existing data. Furthermore, these mechanisms need to tie into existing applications and be reliable, scalable, and open.

Early Web implementations focused on providing access to static data, mostly in the form of simple text and graphics. As Web-based interactions become more complex, the next step must be the creation of real-world applications that can manipulate, input, modify, analyze, and apply this content to everyday tasks. The need for live, online applications that can manipulate dynamic, constantly changing data is driving the Web into the next phase of its evolution.

## PLATFORM CONSIDERATIONS

The key to delivering services over the Internet is the server. The Internet is a true client/server network. Integration into this client/server environment requires servers with strong connectivity capabilities suitable for high-traffic and mission-critical applications. The server must have ease-of-use functionality that allows corporate users to access information quickly and easily. The server must have security features that enable users to share confidential information or conduct encrypted electronic transactions across the Internet. Finally, the server must be able to support the many applications that have become the staple of the Internet, including electronic mail and newsgroups.

### Processor Architecture

A high-performance server is a virtual requirement for any company that is serious about establishing a presence on the Internet. There are basically two choices of processor architectures: Reduced Instruction Set Computing (RISC)-based or Complex Instruction Set Computing (CISC)-based. RISC processors are usually used on high-end UNIX servers; CISC processors, such as Intel's Pentium Pro, are used on Windows NT machines. The performance of the Pentium Pro rivals that of RISC processors and costs less.

Because of the volume of service requests — sometimes tens of thousands a day — the server should be equipped with the most powerful processor available. The more powerful the processor, the greater the number of service requests (i.e., page lookups, database searches, and forms processing) the server will be able to handle.

**SMP Servers.** Servers with symmetric multiprocessing (SMP) enable the operating system to distribute different processing jobs among two or more processors. All the central processing units (CPUs) have equal capabilities and can handle the same tasks. Each CPU can run the operating system as well as user applications. Not only can any CPU execute any job, but jobs can be shifted from one CPU to another as the load changes. This capability can be very important at high-traffic sites, especially those that do a lot of local processing to fulfill service requests.

Some servers come equipped with multiple RISC or CISC processors. Users should be aware, however, that the added cost of a system modification program (SMP) server is not merely a few hundred dollars per extra processor. There are costs for additional hardware resources as well — such as extra RAM and storage space — that can add several thousand dollars to the purchase price. However, as needs change, users can upgrade SMP servers incrementally without having to buy a new system. In this way, performance can be increased and the original hardware investment can be protected. This requirement is especially critical in the rapidly evolving Internet market in which organizations want to implement new applications on their servers that require increasing database and search performance.

### Operating System: UNIX versus NT

When choosing a server, the operating system deserves particular attention. The choices are usually between UNIX and Windows NT. Although some vendors offer server software for Windows 3.1 and Windows 95, these are usually intended for casual rather than business use.

Most Internet servers are based on UNIX, but Windows NT is growing in popularity and may overtake UNIX in the near future. A Windows NT server offers performance and functionality comparable to a UNIX server and is easier to set up and administer, making it the platform of choice among developers of new sites.

Like UNIX, Windows NT is a multitasking, multithreaded operating system. As such, NT executes software as "threads," which are streams of commands that make up applications. At any point during execution, NT's process manager interrupts (or preempts) a thread to allow another thread some CPU time. Also like UNIX, Windows NT supports multiple processors. If the server has more than one CPU, NT distributes the threads over the processors, allowing two or more threads to run simultaneously.

## Fault Tolerance

If the server is supporting mission-critical applications over the Internet, several levels of fault tolerance merit consideration. Fault tolerance must be viewed from both the systems and subsystems perspectives.

**Site Mirroring.** From the systems perspective, fault tolerance can be implemented by linking multiple servers together. When one system fails or must be taken offline for upgrades or reconfigurations, the standby system is activated to handle the load. This is often called "site mirroring." An additional level of protection can be obtained through features of the operating system that protect read and write processes in progress during the switch to the standby system.

**Hot Standby.** At the subsystem level, there are several server options that can improve fault tolerance, including ports, network interfaces, memory expansion cards, disks, tapes, and I/O channels. All must be duplicated so that an alternate hardware component can assume responsibility in the event of a subsystem failure. This procedure is sometimes referred to as a "hot-standby solution," whereby a secondary subsystem monitors the tasks of the primary subsystem in preparation for assuming such tasks when needed.

If a component in the primary subsystem fails, the secondary subsystem takes over without users being aware that a changeover has taken place. An obvious disadvantage of this solution is that companies must purchase twice the amount of hardware needed, and half of this hardware remains idle unless a failure occurs in the primary system.

Because large amounts of data may be located at the server, the server must be able to implement recovery procedures in the event of a program, operating system, or hardware failure. For example, when a transaction terminates abnormally, the server must be able to detect an incomplete transaction so that the database is not left in an inconsistent state. The server's rollback facility is invoked automatically, which backs out of the partially updated database. The transaction can then be resubmitted by the program or user. A roll-forward facility recovers completed transactions and updates in the event of a disk failure by reading a transaction journal that contains a record of all updates.

**Load Balancing.** Another means of achieving fault tolerance is to have all hardware components function simultaneously, but with a load-balancing mechanism that reallocates the processing tasks to surviving components when a failure occurs. This technique requires a UNIX operating system equipped with vendor options that continually monitor the system for errors and dynamically reconfigure the system to adapt to performance problems.

**Hot Swapping.** Hot swapping is an important capability that allows the network administrator to remove and replace faulty server modules without interrupting or degrading network performance. In some cases, standby modules can be brought online through commands issued at the network management workstation or automatically upon fault detection.

**Uninterruptible Power Supply.** To guard against an onsite power outage, an uninterruptible power supply (UPS) can provide an extra measure of protection. The UPS provides enough standby power to permit continuous operation or an orderly shutdown during power failures, or to change over to other power sources such as diesel-powered generators. Some UPSs have SNMP capabilities, so network managers can monitor battery backup from the central management console. For example, using SNMP, every UPS can be instructed to test itself once a week and report back if the test fails.

## INTERNET APPLICATION SOFTWARE

An Internet server must be equipped with software that allows it to run various Internet applications. Some server software supports general communications for document publishing over the World Wide Web. Often called a communications server or Web server, this type of server can be enhanced with software specifically designed for secure electronic commerce. Server software is available for performing many different functions, including implementing newsgroups, facilitating message exchange (i.e., e-mail), improving the performance and security of communications, and controlling traffic between the Internet and the corporate network.

Sometimes a server is dedicated to a single application such as e-mail, newsgroups, or electronic commerce. At other times, the server supports multiple Internet applications. The specific configuration depends on such factors as available system resources (i.e., memory, disk space, processing power, and port capacity), network topology, available bandwidth, traffic patterns, and the security requirements of the organization.

### Communications Software

A communications server enables users to access various documents and services that reside on it and retrieve them using HTTP. These servers support the standard multimedia document format — HTML — for the presentation of rich text, graphics, audio, and video. Hyperlinks connect related information across the network, creating a seamless web. Client software such as Mosaic and Netscape is used for navigation. Some vendors offer servers preconfigured with these Internet protocols, allowing them to be quickly installed and put into operation.

A key service performed by any Internet server is the translation of complex Internet protocol (IP) addresses to simpler Software Defined Networks (SDNs). When a user requests the URL of a certain Web page, for example, the DNS replies with the numeric IP address of the server the user is contacting. It does this by checking a lookup table that cross-references SDNs and IP addresses.

For example, the domain name ddx might stand for "dynamic data exchange." This domain name might translate into the IP address 204.177.193.22. The translation capability of the IDNS makes it easy for users to access Internet resources by not requiring them to learn and enter long strings of numbers. To access the Web page of Dynamic Data Exchange, the user would enter the URL as http://www.ddx.com, which contains the domain name ddx.

## Commerce Software

- *Server authentication*. A commerce server is used for conducting secure electronic commerce and communications on the Internet. It permits companies to publish hypermedia documents formatted in HTML and to deliver them using HTTP. To ensure data security, the commerce server provides advanced security features through the use of the secure socket layer (SSL) protocol, which provides server authentication. Any SSL-compatible client can verify the identity of the server using a certificate and a digital signature.
- *Data encryption*. The privacy of client/server communications is ensured by encrypting the data stream between the two entities.
- *Data integrity*. SSL verifies that the contents of a message arrive at their destination in the same form as they were sent.

As with other types of Internet servers, vendors offer commerce servers preconfigured with the protocols necessary to support electronic commerce.

## News Software

A news server lets users create secure public and private discussion groups for access over the Internet and other TCP/IP-based networks using the standard network news transport protocol (NNTP). The news server's support of NNTP enables it to accept feeds from popular Usenet newsgroups and allows the creation and maintenance of private discussion groups. Most newsreaders are based on NNTP; some support SSL for secure communication between clients and news servers.

A news server should support multipurpose Internet mail extensions (MIME), which allows users to send virtually any type of data across the Internet, including text, graphics, sound, video clips, and many other types of files. Attaching documents in a variety of formats greatly expands the capability of a discussion group to serve as a repository of information and knowledge to support workgroup collaboration. Colleagues can download documents sent to the group, mark them up, and send them back.

## Mail Software

Client/server messaging systems are implemented by special mail software installed on a server. Mail software lets users easily exchange information within a company as well as across the Internet. Mail software has many features that can be controlled by either the system administrator or each user with an e-mail account.

The mail software should conform to open standards, including HTTP, MIME, SMTP, and Post Office Protocol Version 3 (POP3). MIME lets organizations send and receive messages with rich content types, thereby allowing businesses to transmit mission-critical information of any type without loss of fidelity. The SMTP ensures interoperability with other client/server messaging systems that support Internet mail or proprietary messaging systems with Internet mail gateways. POP3 ensures interoperability with such popular client software as Zmail, Eudora, Pegasus Mail, Microsoft Exchange client (with the Microsoft "Plus" pack), and most other Internet-capable mail products.

## Proxy Software

To improve the performance and security of communications across the TCP/IP-based Internet, many organizations use a proxy server. This kind of software offers performance improvements by using an intelligent cache for storing retrieved documents.

The proxy's disk-based caching feature minimizes use of the external network by eliminating recurrent retrievals of commonly accessed documents. This feature provides additional "virtual bandwidth" to existing network resources and significantly improves interactive response time for locally attached clients. The resulting performance improvements provide a cost-effective alternative to purchasing additional network bandwidth. Because the cache is disk based, it can be tuned to provide optimal performance based on network usage patterns.

The proxy server should allow dynamic process management, which allows the creation of a configurable number of processes that reside in memory waiting to fulfill HTTP requests. This feature improves system performance by eliminating the unnecessary overhead of creating and deleting processes to fulfill every HTTP request. The dynamic process management algorithm increases the number of server processes, within configurable limits, to efficiently handle periods of peak demand, resulting in faster document serving, greater throughput delivery, and better system reliability.

### Firewall Software

An application-level firewall acts as a security wall and gateway between a trusted internal network and such untrustworthy networks as the Internet. Access can be controlled by individuals or groups of users or by system names, domains, subnets, date, time, protocol, and service.

Security is bidirectional, simultaneously prohibiting unauthorized users from accessing the corporate network while also managing internal users' Internet access privileges. The firewall even periodically checks its own code to prevent modification by sophisticated intruders.

The firewall gathers and logs information about where attempted break-ins originate, how they got there, and what the people responsible for them appear to be doing. Log entries include information on connection attempts, service types, users, file transfer names and sizes, connection duration, and trace routes. Together, this information leaves an electronic footprint that can help identify intruders.

## WEB DATABASE CONSIDERATIONS

Internet servers are the repositories of various databases. These databases can be set up for public access or for restricted intracompany access. In either case, the challenge of maintaining the information is apparent to information system (IS) professionals charged with keeping it accurate and up to date.

Vendors are developing ways to ease the maintenance burden. For example, database management vendors such as Oracle Corp. offer ways of integrating an existing data warehouse with the Internet without having to reformat the data into HTML. The data are not sent until a request is received and validated.

In addition, the server supports HTTP-type negotiation, so it can deliver different versions of the same object (e.g., an image stored in multiple formats) according to each client's preferences. The server also supports national language negotiation, allowing the same document in different translations to be delivered to different clients.

The database server should support the two common authentication mechanisms: basic and digest authentication. Both mechanisms allow certain directories to be protected by user name/password combinations. However, digest authentication transmits encrypted passwords and basic authentication does not. Other security extensions that may be bundled with database servers include S-HTTP and SSL standards, which are especially important in supporting E-commerce applications.

## Maintenance and Testing Tools

The maintenance of most Web databases still relies on the diligence of each document owner or site administrator to periodically check for integrity by testing for broken links, malformed documents, and outdated information. Database integrity is usually tested by visually scanning each document and manually activating every hypertext link. Particular attention should be given to links that reference other Web sites because they are usually controlled by a third party who can change the location of files to a different server or directory or delete them entirely.

**Link Analyzers.** Link analyzers can examine a collection of documents and validate the links for accessibility, completeness, and consistency. However, this type of integrity check is usually applied more as a means of one-time verification rather than as a regular maintenance process. This check also fails to provide adequate support across distributed databases and for situations in which the document contents are outside the immediate span of control.

**Log Files.** Some types of errors can be identified by the server's log files. The server records each document request and, if an error occurred, the nature of that error. Such information can be used to identify requests for documents that have moved and those that have a misspelled URL, which are used to identify the location of documents on the Internet. Usually only the server manager has access to that information, however. The error is almost never relayed to the person charged with document maintenance, either because it is not recognized as a document error or because the origin of the error is not apparent from the error message.

Even with better procedures, log files do not reveal failed requests that never made it to the server, nor can they support preventive maintenance and problems associated with changed document content. With a large and growing database, manual maintenance methods become difficult and may eventually become impossible.

**Design Tools.** New design tools are available that address the maintenance and testing issue by providing the means to visualize the creation, maintenance, and navigation of whole collections of online documents. Where traditional Web tools such as browsers and HTML editors focus on the Web page, these tools address the Web site, which may be either physical or logical in structure. These tools include a system to identify which pages are included in the site and another to describe how the pages are interconnected. The construction of a site is facilitated by providing templates for creating pages and scripts and linkage to tools for editing and verifying HTML documents.

189

In addition to offering high-level views of a site — either graphical or hierarchical — the design tools check for stale links (either local or remote), validate the conformance level of HTML pages, and make broad structural changes to the site architecture by using a mouse to drag and drop sections of the Web hierarchy into a different location.

**Agents or Robots.** Although design tools address document creation and maintenance at the site level, they do not comprehensively address the maintenance needs of distributed hypertext infrastructures that span multiple Web sites. This task can be handled by special software known as agents or robots. These programs can be given a list of instructions about which databases to traverse, whom to notify for problems, and where to put the resulting maintenance information. For example, the agent or robot may be tasked to provide information about the following conditions that typically indicate document changes:

- *A referenced object has a redirected URL* (i.e., a document has been moved to another location).
- *A referenced object cannot be accessed* (i.e.,there is a broken or improperly configured link).
- *A referenced object has a recently modified date* (i.e., the contents of a document have changed).
- *An owned object has an upcoming expiration date* (i.e., a document may be removed or changed soon).

To get instructions, the agent or robot reads a text file containing a list of options and tasks to be performed. Each task describes a specific hypertext infrastructure to be encompassed by the traversal process. A task instruction includes the traversal type, an infrastructure name (for later reference), the "top URL" at which to start traversing, the location for placing the indexed output, an e-mail address that corresponds to the owner of that infrastructure, and a set of options that determines which identified maintenance issues justify sending an e-mail message.

## COMMON GATEWAY INTERFACE (CGI)

An Internet server should support CGI, which is a standard for interfacing external applications with information servers, such as HTTP or Web servers. Gateway programs handle information requests and return the appropriate document or generate one spontaneously. With CGI, a Web server can provide information that is not in a form readable by the client (i.e., an SQL database) and act as a gateway between the two to produce something that clients can interpret and display.

Gateways can be used for a variety of purposes, the most common of which is the processing of form requests, such as database queries or online purchase orders.

Gateways conforming to the CGI specification can be written in any language that produces an executable file, such as C and C+. Among the more popular languages for developing CGI scripts are Practical Extraction and Report Language (PERL) and Tool Command Language (TCL), both derivatives of the C language.

An advantage of using PERL and TCL is that either language can be used to speed the construction of applications to which new scripts and script components can be added without the need to recompile and restart, as is required when the C language is used. Of course, the server on which the CGI scripts reside must have a copy of the program itself — PERL, TCL, or an alternative program.

## CONCLUSION

The client/server architecture of the Internet and its use of open protocols for information formatting and delivery make it possible for any connected computer to provide services to any other computer. With this capability, businesses can extend communications beyond organizational boundaries and serve the informational needs of all users.

The types of services that are available depend on the application software that runs on one or more servers. A server may be dedicated to a specific Internet application or multiple applications, depending on such factors as system resources and the specific needs of the organization. A careful evaluation of the hardware platform, operating system, and application software in terms of features and conformance to Internet standards ensures that the current and emerging needs of the organization and its users are met in an efficient and economical manner.

# Chapter 17
# Gracefully Transitioning from SNA to IP: Why, How, and When?

*Anura Gurugé*

WHEN EVALUATING THE MERITS AND IMPLICATIONS OF TRANSITIONING TO A TCP/IP-CENTRIC IT INFRASTRUCTURE, IT HELPS TO REFLECT ON THE TALE OF THE GREAT KING CANUTE OF ENGLAND AND DENMARK (C. 1016) WHO TRIED TO DEMONSTRATE TO HIS ADORING SUBJECTS THAT THERE WERE POWERS THAT EVEN HE COULD NOT CONTROL BY SHOWING THEM THAT HE WAS POWERLESS TO STOP THE TIDE FROM COMING ASHORE. Just as was the case with PCs and LANs, TCP/IP is now an unstemmable technological tide; possibly even a tidal wave. Whether one likes it or not, relishes it or fears it, TCP/IP is here to stay — and will dominate worldwide computing for at least the next two decades, thanks to the endorsement and kudos it receives on a daily basis as the sustaining force behind the Internet miracle.

Mainframe shops today cannot claim unfamiliarity with TCP/IP. Without exception, corporations that use mainframes for their MIS now have a TCP/IP-based intranet in addition to their traditional SNA/APPN or multiprotocol-oriented enterprise network. Most, furthermore, already have a presence on the Internet in the form of a home page, and many are actively exploring the possibilities of using the Internet for electronic commerce, customer support, public relations, product promotions, and global remote access. Not missing out on the tantalizing potential of E-commerce over the Internet, next to that of Y2K concerns, is indubitably the most pressing MIS issue that is being discussed at the highest levels of corporations, starting at the Board Room. In parallel, intranet-to-intranet communications via extranets are being viewed as the most effective means of streamlining and expediting enterprise-to-enterprise

0-8493-1160-8/02/$0.00+$1.50
© 2002 by CRC Press LLC

transactions. All of this intranet and Internet (i.e., i·net) activity means that TCP/IP is already being widely used alongside mainframe-based computing systems.

Installing TCP/IP on a mainframe is no longer a difficult, nerve-racking, or laborious undertaking. Extensively proven, extremely efficient, highly scalable, and extremely reliable TCP/IP stacks for mainframes are readily available. IBM claims that more than half of the mainframes running MVS or OS/390 already have TCP/IP installed. Installing TCP/IP on a mainframe facilitates its integration with intranets or the Internet; permits fast, high-speed bulk data transfers with TCP/IP clients or other systems; and, moreover, positions it as a data server for Web-based applications. Once TCP/IP is installed, one could, if required, even have the mainframe acting as a high-capacity Web server. Companies, such as $9.5B Lafayette Life Insurance (Lafayette, IN), already have Web servers running on their mainframes; Lafayette uses an IBM 9672-R24, 3rd generation CMOS-based S/390 Parallel Enterprise Server.

There are significant strategic and tactical advantages to installing TCP/IP on a mainframe and moving toward a TCP/IP-centric computing environment. For a start, it provides a solid basis for any and all E-commerce-related initiatives. It can also reduce, sometimes quite significantly, overall capital and operational costs. For example, the browser-based access to SNA solutions that is now readily available from over 40-odd credible vendors for providing unrestricted SNA terminal access across i·nets, totally eliminates the considerable cost associated with installing, managing, and periodically upgrading SNA/3270 emulation software on each and every PC/workstation that needs access to SNA applications.

Using TCP/IP all the way into the mainframe, and then performing SNA conversion at the mainframe per the tn3270(E) standard, also ensures that one no longer needs highly expensive, SNA-oriented communications controllers like the 3745 or the 3746-950. Instead, one can profitably utilize high-performance, low-cost, channel-attached routers such as the IBM 2216-400, Cisco 7500/CIP, or Cisco 7200/CPA as the means of interconnecting the mainframe to the network. Then there are networking-related cost savings. With a TCP/IP-centric infrastructure, one can, albeit with the appropriate security measures (e.g., firewalls), gainfully use the Internet as a way to realize extremely cost-effective remote access for far-flung remote offices, agents, telecommuters, and overseas distributors. Intranets, given that they are based on widely available commodity technology, are also invariably less costly to implement than comparable SNA/APPN or multiprotocol networks. Exhibit 1 illustrates a TCP/IP-centric environment.

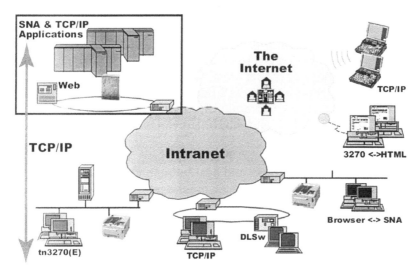

**Clients have access to both TCP/IP and SNA resources across an intranet as well as the Internet.**

**Exhibit 1.  TCP/IP-Centric Environment**

## DISPELLING YOUR CONCERNS

Before the advantages of moving to a TCP/IP-centric infrastructure, with TCP/IP on the mainframe, are articulated any further, it is best to allay any concerns one may have about moving away from SNA.

- Security is no longer the roadblock it used to be with highly proven, bulletproof TCP/IP-specific security solutions for mission-critical commercial computing systems.
- Total unencumbered access to mission-critical SNA/APPN applications running on mainframes or AS/400s is in no way compromised, jeopardized, or even inconvenienced by the installation of TCP/IP on a mainframe and the standardization on a TCP/IP-centric infrastructure. There is a plethora of well-established, standards-based SNA-to-TCP/IP integration technologies, such as tn3270(E) and Data Link Switching (DLSw), that ensure unrestricted SNA access and end-to-end SNA transport across TCP/IP networks.
- Installing TCP/IP on a mainframe and using a TCP/IP centric i·net for all mainframe access does not prevent one from having ACF/VTAM on that same machine as well. Therefore, one can continue to have the same level of APPN/HPR support that is on one's mainframe today to guarantee that mission-critical SNA/APPN applications will continue to work without any problems.

- Today's TCP/IP stacks for mainframes deliver exceptional throughput and are highly optimized to maximize efficiency and scale and easily support tens of thousands of concurrent users. TCP/IP is not the CPU hog that it was portrayed to be a few years ago. Mainframe TCP/IP is so efficient these days that some corporations run, without any difficulty or degradation in overall performance, multiple stacks on the same mainframe to gain added throughput and ensure that different applications (e.g., FTP and tn3270(E)) can each have its own dedicated stack.
- Incisive, sophisticated, and comprehensive TCP/IP-based network, application, TCP/IP-stack, and system management is now possible with mainframe-resident management systems such as Interlink's e-Control. e-Control provides TCP/IP-centric management tools and facilities for problem determination, performance management, change management (i.e., the configuration and administration of mainframe TCP/IP resources), and capacity planning.
- With today's mature router technology, it is now possible to realize TCP/IP-based networks that are sufficiently resilient and robust to provide high-availability networking with uptimes in excess of 98(+) percent. Today's TCP/IP-centric networks are significantly more reliable and stable than the bridge/router-based multiprotocol networks currently used for transporting SNA/APPN traffic.
- Traffic prioritization between different classes of applications, vis-à-vis the TCP/IP network, is no longer an issue with today's router software offering functions such as Quality of Service (QoS), Bandwidth Reservation Protocol (RSVP), and highly customizable queuing schemes (e.g., Cisco's Custom Queuing). For those few situations where there is a need to support SNA LU 6.2 Class-of-Service (COS) prioritization on an end-to-end basis, IBM offers a scheme known as Enterprise Extender that permits APPN/HPR routing across IP.
- The continued presence of ACF/VTAM on the mainframe alongside TCP/IP ensures total, uncompromised support for parallel sysplex operation — including multi-node persistent sessions (MNPS), workload balancing, and generic resources.
- High-performance, highly efficient, full-duplex TCP/IP transfers across ESCON channels is not a problem with the TCP/IP-specific CLAW protocol that permits two subchannels to be grouped together for high-throughput and simultaneous bidirectional communications. If anything, TCP/IP channel transfers are significantly faster than SNA/APPN transfers with both IBM or Cisco channel-attached solutions such as the IBM 2216-400 and the Cisco 7500/CIP.
- Mainframe-based TCP/IP printing is not an impediment with tn3270(E) now supporting host print, and with products such as Interlink's very comprehensive Enterprise Print Services (EPS).

## CASE AGAINST A LAST MINUTE SNA REVIVAL

Despite the daily mounting evidence to the contrary, there are still some who believe that IBM will not allow SNA/APPN to succumb to IP, and that there will be a concerted attempt to reestablish SNA/APPN-based networking. IBM recognizes that the role SNA/APPN plays in the future will be restricted to the mainframe in the context of mission-critical applications and that TCP/IP, unassailably, will be the networking fabric of the future. The following four examples alone should convince the reader that IBM is not just reconciled to, but in reality one of the greatest advocates of, TCP/IP-centric networking.

- In June 1998, IBM announced an ESCON channel-attachment capability for its flagship, 12.8Gbps throughput 8265-17S Nways ATM Switch, which can support 622Mbps ATM uplinks. The only protocol supported across this channel attachment is IP.
- In March 1998, IBM discontinued the 2217 Nways Multiprotocol Concentrator, which was an APPN/HPR-based router that permitted TCP/IP, IPX/SPX, and NetBIOS to be routed end to end across an SNA network. The 2217 was the antithesis of a conventional TCP/IP-based router. By discontinuing the 2217, IBM tacitly admitted that there was no call or future for IP-over-SNA routing.
- IBM is avidly promoting the notion of APPN/HPR-over-IP routing with its Enterprise Extender technology, which is now available on the IBM 2216, 2212, and 2210. Cisco, Bay/NT, and others also are expected to support this capability. By promoting the notion of routing APPN/HPR-over-IP, which is the exact opposite of the routing scheme employed by the 2217 that IBM discontinued, IBM is making it very clear that the only WAN networking role it sees for APPN/HPR in the future is within the context of it being used on top of IP.
- The IBM 2216-400 can be attached to an IBM 3746 via an expansion chassis known as the Multi-access Enclosure (MAE). If one only wants to transfer IP traffic into the mainframe, MAE offers a native, high-speed coupling facility between the 2216-400 and the 3746. If one insists on wanting support for SNA, the best that IBM can offer is a dual Token-Ring connection between the 2216-400 and the 3746. When factoring this in with the 8265 IP-only channel-attachment scheme, discussed above, it becomes clear that IBM is already positioning itself for an era when most of the mainframe channel traffic is IP based.

## THE PRIMARY ADVANTAGES OF MOVING TO MAINFRAME IP

- Enables seamless integration of one's fast-growing intranet with one's mainframe, given that at least 70 percent of the corporate data that one's in-house intranet users require is still on a mainframe rather than on a Web server, NT server, or UNIX system.

- Decisively positions one to exploit all the rich potential of E-commerce over the Internet by ensuring that all of the applications and data one may require to enable such commerce is now TCP/IP-ready and can be easily integrated with the necessary Web technology. Business-to-business E-commerce over the Internet is expected to be in excess of $30B by the year 2002.

- Permits one to exploit the Internet as an extremely low-cost means of realizing global remote access to mainframe applications, including all mission-critical SNA applications, as shown in Exhibits 2 and 3. In addition to browser-based access, extremely secure Virtual Private Networking (VPN) solutions — such as those provided by Interlink's NetLOCK V.2.0 — can be used to realize enterprise-specific remote access over the Internet.

- Facilitates and expedites the File Transfer Protocol (FTP)-based file downloads and uploads that one is likely now doing on a daily basis with all of one's distributed servers.

- Allows one to quickly open up mainframe applications for new, Internet-based services such as home banking, online investment, personal travel reservation, and Web-based status checking (e.g., querying the status of an expedited mail item or a cargo shipment), as demonstrated in Exhibit 4.

- Greatly minimizes the cost of SNA access by using tn3270(E) or browser-based access to SNA solutions. The browser-based access solutions will eliminate the considerable costs associated with installing, managing, and regularly updating SNA/3270 emulation software on individual PCs/workstations by using either an applet-based scheme where the applet is dynamically downloaded from a Web server, or a 3270-to-HTML conversion scheme as shown in Exhibit 4, which only requires a browser to be present within the client PC/workstation.

- Enables one to quickly phase out the very expensive, SNA-oriented IBM 3745 or IBM 3746 communications controllers in favor of high-performance, low-cost channel gateways such as the IBM 2216-400, Cisco 7500/CIP, or Cisco 7200/CPA.

- Permits one to use the mainframe as a high-capacity, very low-cost-per-user Web server for intranet, extranet, or even Internet applications.

- Greatly simplifies the integration of mainframe data with the new Web applications that are being developed using tools such as NetDynamics 4.0, Bluestone Sapphire/Web, and ColdFusion.

- Eliminates the need for external, low-capacity tn3270(E) gateways such as Microsoft's SNA server by using integrated, highly scalable, mainframe-resident tn3270(E) servers such as the one included within Interlink's e-Access TCPaccess TCP/IP software.

- Gain better channel throughput by using TCP/IP across the channel to a mainframe-resident tn3270(E) server. Phase out the cost and

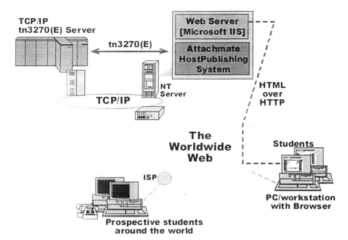

Existing and prospective students are provided with access to mainframe-resident SNA applications over the Web using a totally TCP/IP-centric infrastructure, including TCP/IP and tn3270(E) server on the mainframe.

**Exhibit 2.    Ohio State University Diagram**

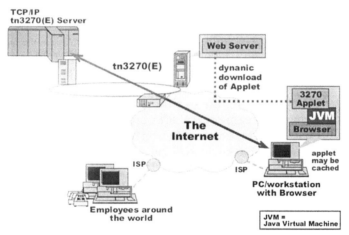

This system is currently being tried out by a $18B U.S. conglomerate to ensure that telecommuters and mobile users around the world have access to mainframe-resident SNA applications across the Internet.

**Exhibit 3.    A Totally TCP/IP-Based System**

complexity of doing business-to-business transactions using SNA Network Interconnection (SNI) by moving toward a secure, low-cost extranet scheme.

**This was used by a mainframe-centric, Internet-based home banking system realized using browser-based access in the form of 3270-to-HTML conversion.**

**Exhibit 4.    Actual Screen Shot of a Rejuvenated 3270 User Interface**

## PROVEN TECHNOLOGY TO FACILITATE THE TRANSITION FROM SNA TO IP

The good news is that highly proven and stable technology, from more than 40 credible vendors including Interlink, Cisco, OpenConnect Systems, IBM, Attachmate, Wall Data, Eicon Technology, Novell, Farabi Technology, Client/Server Technology, Blue Lobster etc., is now readily available to facilitate TCP/IP on the mainframe and the standardization on a TCP/IP-centric networking infrastructure — although one still relies on quite a few mainframe-resident, mission-critical SNA applications. The technologies available will enable one to integrate the current SNA/APPN-based environment with the new TCP/IP-centric world in a seamless and synergistic manner.

Athough it may feel like it, one will not be a lone pioneer beating across hitherto uncharted territory. The move from SNA to IP is happening, with accelerating pace, around the world. In reality, this transition has been happening for the last few years. Enterprises around the world — such as GM, FedEx, Sabre/American Airlines, The Library of Congress, Ohio State University, Royal Jordanian Airlines, Nestles, The Chickering Group, National Van Lines, the state of Idaho, Lafayette Life, Lincoln National Reinsurance, Swiss Air, Al Rajhi Banking & Investment Corp. (Saudi Arabia's largest bank), and Gazprom (a $30B natural gas company in Russia) to name but just a few — have already started to integrate their data center resources with TCP/IP-centric i·nets. Exhibit 5 illustrates the solution deployed by Lincoln National Reinsurance.

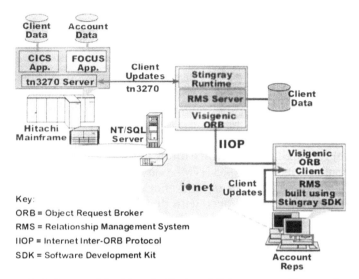

This system is being used by Lincoln National Reinsurance Companies, one of the largest reinsurers in the world, to provide its account reps with up-to-date client information across the Web.

**Exhibit 5.    Mainframe TCP/IP-Based System**

To be of use, the technology that enables the transition from SNA to IP must be able to accommodate an extremely broad and disparate population of client equipment and functionality. Just some of the entities that need to be dealt with vis-à-vis this transition include PCs; UNIX workstations; coax-attached 3270/5250 terminals; printers; minicomputers; SNA applications that communicate program to program using LU 6.2 or LU-LU Session Type 0-based protocols; SNA-only devices (e.g., IBM 4700 Financial Systems); and legacy control units. The PCs, workstations, and printers at remote sites may work in either SNA or TCP/IP mode. Consequently, one will need SNA access technologies to deal with TCP/IP clients, in particular PCs and workstations, and SNA transport technologies to deal with SNA-only clients. This is not a problem. Today, there is a wealth of solid, well-established, field-tested technologies to realize both SNA access and SNA transport in the context of mainframe TCP/IP — and a totally TCP/IP-based network.

Some of the key technologies that will permit an easy transition from SNA to IP include:

- *tn3270(E):* widely used, ten-year-old IETF standard-based access scheme that enables low-cost TCP/IP clients to access SNA applications via a mainframe-resident tn3270(E) server. Today, tn3270(E) is being used by more than ten million SNA users. tn3270(E) clients are ubiquitously available from all of the traditional SNA/3270 emulation vendors. All examples shown in Exhibits 2, 3, and 5 utilize tn3270(E) in some form.

- *Browser-based access with 3270-to-HTML conversion:* a thin-client solution (as shown in Exhibit 2) where a server-resident SNA-Web gateway performs 3270 datastream-to-HTML conversion, replete with some amount of user interface rejuvenation, so that mainframe SNA applications can be accessed directly from a browser across an i-net. The rejuvenated user interface for home banking (shown in Exhbit 4) was realized using 3270-to-HTML conversion. Secure Sockets Layer (SSL)-based authentication and encryption, as available with contemporary browsers, is used with this scheme to provide end to end data encryption.
- *Browser-invoked Java or ActiveX applets:* dynamically downloadable applets that can optionally be cached on a PC/workstation hard disk, that provide tn3270(E) client emulation. This was the technique used in the system shown in Exhibit 3. User interface rejuvenation, as well as end to end data encryption, is also possible with this technique.
- *Application-specific Web solutions:* such as Interlink ActiveCICX, IBM CICS Web Interface, Interlink ActiveIMX, and Interlink OPEN-IMS, that expeditiously integrate mainframe-resident applications with the Web.
- *Programmatic (or middleware) solutions:* such as IBM MQSeries, Blue Stone Sapphire/Web, or Blue Lobster Stingray SDK, etc., that permit mainframe applications to be interfaced with TCP/IP or Web applications.
- *Data link switching:* like tn3270(E), is a ubiquitous, IETF standards-based encapsulation scheme, performed by bridge/routers, that permits any kind of SNA/APPN traffic, independent of session type, to be transported end to end across a TCP/IP WAN. DLSw ensures that any kind of legacy SNA device or application can be nondisruptively and gracefully accommodated within a TCP/IP-based infrastructure
- *High-performance routing-over-IP:* an alternative to DLSw, championed by IBM, whereby APPN/HPR-oriented routing is performed across IP. This scheme has the advantage over DLSw in that it can permit APPN-based routing between multiple data centers, and is capable of supporting LU 6.2 COS prioritization on an end-to-end basis over an IP network.

By using one or more of the above technologies, one can gracefully transition from SNA to IP without losing the services of any current mission-critical SNA/APPN applications, sacrificing any functionality, or compromising security or reliability.

## THE BOTTOM LINE

With the rapid growth of intranets and the daily increasing significance of the Internet as the next frontier for commerce, the hold that TCP/IP has on commercial sector networking continues to solidify. Even IBM has acknowledged that the role of SNA, APPN, and HPR will be relegated to the mainframe as the basis for mission-critical applications. Many of the concerns that MIS professionals had in the past about TCP/IP — such as its security, reliability and efficiency — are no longer germane. Solid and highly proven TCP/IP solutions are now available from multiple vendors for all aspects of mainframe-oriented computing — whether it be TCP/IP stacks, tn3270(E) servers, security packages, management platforms, applications, channel gateways, or network infrastructures. There really are no impediments to transitioning from SNA to IP. Thousands of companies around the world have already started to standardize on an end-to-end, mainframe-to-PC, TCP/IP fabric. Increasing numbers have already started to use the Internet for remote access and information dissemination. The technology required to successfully and gracefully transition from SNA to IP, such as tn3270(E), browser-based access, and DLSw, is here, is widely available, is cost effective, and is remarkably solid. E-commerce beckons. What are you waiting for?

## THE BOTTOM LINE

# Section IV
# System Integration

This section focuses on integrating Web solutions with other applications within an organization. As the Web becomes a more integral tool in communicating with customers and external business partners, integration with back-end or existing applications will be needed to streamline the overall process. For example, getting a purchase order on the Web can also automatically feed the requisition and order fulfillment processes by connecting several applications within the organization.

"Web-to-Host Connectivity Tools in Information Systems" provides a framework for implementing tools for accessing host or legacy data from different applications within an organization.

"Real-Life Case Studies of Web-to-Host Integration" offers a set of case studies of organizations that have successfully implemented Web-to-host solutions.

"Integrating Information Systems into the World Wide Web" explains how to supplement applications with hypertext support through the World Wide Web. The concept of "dynamic relationship mapping" is explained as an effective way to add additional hypertext support to applications.

"Integrating the Web and Enterprisewide Business Systems" examines issues related to enterprisewide business applications in the context of the World Wide Web. The chapter also discusses issues related to intranet solutions.

"Publishing Host Data Using 3270-to-HTML Conversion" explains how organizations can use 3270-to-HTML conversion products to access host-based information for their employees, partners, suppliers, and customers. This will extend the useful life of host-based applications and reduce overall computing costs in an organization.

# Chapter 18
# Web-to-Host Connectivity Tools in Information Systems

*Nijaz Bajgoric*

IN INFORMATION TECHNOLOGY (IT) HISTORY, THE INVENTION OF THE GRAPHICAL USER INTERFACE (GUI) WAS A REVOLUTIONARY STEP IN IMPROVING BOTH THE EFFICIENCY AND EFFECTIVENESS OF IT END USERS. The GUI has become dominant not only in operating systems, but also in application software. After introducing Web technology in 1994, it turned out that a Web browser is the most convenient way of using computers for end users because it is completely based on a mouse-click operation. Of course, this became possible thanks to HTTP, HTML, and other Internet/Web-related facilities.

The job of IT people, both IT vendors and information system (IS) staff, in organizations is to make information technology seamless and easy, so that end users can do their jobs as easily and efficiently as possible. From the perspective of ease of use, it is the Web technology that can help. Web-to-host connectivity tools are software products that ease the process of connecting to several types of host data (also known as legacy data), both from end users and state-of-the-art client/server (c/s) applications.

## FRAMEWORK FOR IMPLEMENTATION OF WEB-TO-HOST ACCESS TOOLS

Today, Web technology can be used in contemporary IS in three modes:

1. For Internet presence, intranet and extranet infrastructures
2. For improving access to corporate data, both legacy and c/s applications
3. For rapid application development

Also, Web technology can significantly cut the costs of accessing systems and reduce the time required to connect users to corporate data. The role of Web technology in improving data access can be considered from the following perspectives:

- End-users' perspective: with the main objective defined as how to provide end users with efficient access to corporate data
- Application developers' perspective: how to improve applications' efficiency using:
  - Web technology in creating middleware and gateway applications that provide more efficient access to the existing applications (legacy data and c/s apps)
  - Web technology in development of Web-enabled c/s applications with the primary aim to provide a "thinner" client side (based only on Web browser)
  - Web technology in creating dynamic Web pages for corporate intranet and extranet infrastructures (dynamic HTML, ASP, etc)

Exhibit 1 represents a framework for implementation of Web-to-host connectivity tools in an IS.

The IS subsystems that can be accessed via Web technology are:

- Transaction processing system, which usually consists of legacy data and c/s data
- Messaging system
- Document management and workflow system
- Business intelligence system
- ERP system (if IS infrastructure is based on an integrated ERP solution)

The remainder of this article provides some examples of Web-to-host tools that connect to these systems.

## WEB-TO-LEGACY DATA

According to a recent study (http://www.simware.com/products/salvo/articles_reviews/linking.html), about 80 percent of all enterprise data is in legacy data structures, and rules for access are within legacy applications. The Gartner Group (www.gartner.com) also estimates that 74 percent of all corporate data still resides on legacy mainframes.

Legacy systems (legacy data or legacy applications) refer to older or mature applications that were developed from the late 1950s to the early 1990s. Such systems are primarily mainframe systems, or distributed systems where the mainframe plays the major processing role and the terminals or PCs are used for application running and data uploading-downloading.

Access to legacy data through user-friendly applications (standard c/s applications and Web-based applications for intranets and the Internet) requires a processing layer between the applications and the data.

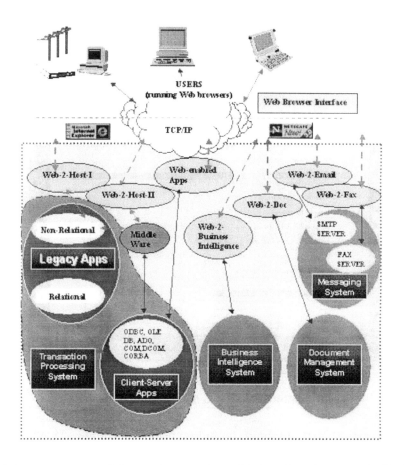

**Exhibit 1. Framework for Implementation of Web-to-Host Connectivity Tools**

Web-to-host technology makes it possible for users to access the data stored on legacy hosts just by clicking a Web link. Moreover, it cuts the costs of software ownership through centralized management.

**Example: WRQ Reflection EnterView (www.wrq.com).** Reflection Enter-View is a Java-based legacy host access program from WRQ. As can be seen from Exhibit 2, it gives users easy access to IBM, UNIX, and Digital hosts — right from their desktop browsers.

**Example: Network Software Associates' Report.Web (www.nsainc.com).** Report.Web is another Web-to-legacy program and intranet report distribution tool from Network Software Associates, Inc. At the heart of Report.Web is the enterprise server, a powerful and robust engine that automates the entire process of delivering host-generated reports to the

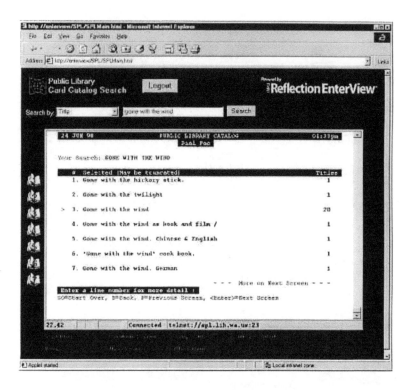

**Exhibit 2.    WRQ Reflection EnterView**

Web — from almost any host, including IBM mainframes, AS/400s, DEC VAXs, and PC LAN servers, to the corporate intranet/extranet.

Report.Web provides a variety of Web-accessible outputs, including:

- Spreadsheet output
- WRF (Web reporting format) output
- HTML output
- PDF output
- Thin client (all reports published by the enterprise server are readable by standard Web browsers)

See Exhibit 3.

Report.Web supports also distributing ERP-generated reports across the corporate intranet, without deploying ERP clients at every desktop.

## WEB-TO-MESSAGING SYSTEMS

**Example: Web-to-Mail (www.mail2web.com).** The Web2Mail or Mail2Web program is a service that lets users use their POP3 e-mail accounts through

host
web reports
REPORT.WEB

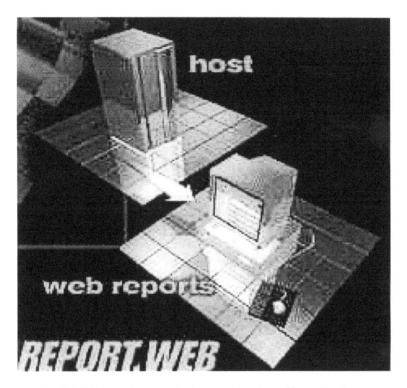

**Exhibit 3. Network Software Associates ReportWeb**

an easy Web interface. If this program is installed on the server side (SMTP server), then the only program users need on the client side is a Web browser. They do not need any e-mail program like Eudora, Pegasus, MS Exchange Client, MS Outlook, or character-based telnet-pine program. From the end-users' perspective, this is very important because the Web browsers' GUI is based on a very simple "point-and-click" interface. Hence, this approach is more user friendly. As an example, Mail2Web URL address is a public site that allows people to use a Web-based interface to their

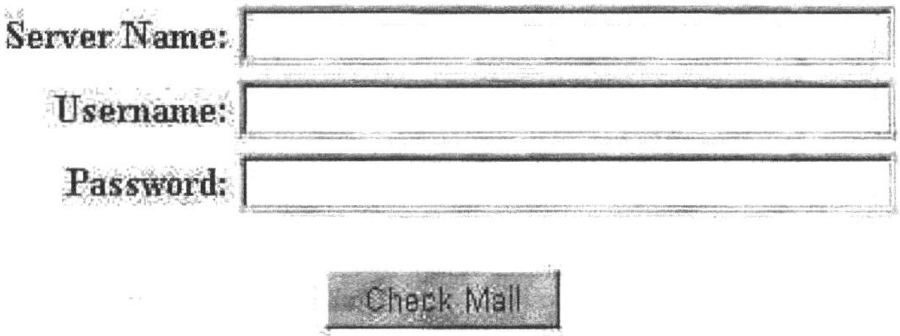

Server Name:
Username:
Password:
Check Mail

**Exhibit 4. Web2Mail Interface**

e-mail accounts (for those SMTP servers without the Web2Mail program). See Exhibit 4.

**Example: Web-to-Fax (http://www-usa.tpc.int ).** The Web2Fax program, which is very similar to Web2Mail, gives an opportunity of sending and receiving fax documents from Web browsers with no additional software (see Exhibit 5).

## WEB-TO-DOCUMENT MANAGEMENT AND WORKFLOW SYSTEMS

### Web-Based Index-Search Tools

**Example: Microsoft's Index Server (www.microsoft.com).** Microsoft Index Server is the Microsoft content-indexing and searching solution for Microsoft Internet Information Server (IIS) and Peer Web Services (PWS). Index Server can index documents for both corporate intranets and for any drive accessible through a uniform naming convention (UNC) path on the Internet. Users can formulate queries using the Web browser. Index Server can index the text and properties of formatted documents, such as those created by Word or Excel (see Exhibit 6).

Even the Office97 package includes Web-searching facilities. Its Web Find Fast is a search utility that allows a Web server to search HTML files and summary properties of Office97 documents (Author, Title, Subject, etc.) (see Exhibit 7).

**Example: Compaq's AltaVista Search Intranet (http://altavista.software.digital.com/).** AltaVista Search Intranet is search and retrieval software that provides search and retrieval for information in several formats, including HTML, Microsoft Word, Adobe PDF, and many other formats (more than 150) of files located on Internet and intranet Web servers, Lotus Domino Servers, and Windows LANs. AltaVista Search also includes multinational support (see Exhibit 8 ).

### Web-Enabled Document Management and Workflow Software

**Example: Keyfile from Keyfile Corporation (www.keyfile.com).** Keyfile document management application provides Web-based access to user documents. It also supports integration with Microsoft Exchange/Outlook messaging system. The client side does not need any extra software installed other than a Web browser (see Exhibit 9).

**Example: FileNET Panagon and Waterflow (http://www.filenet.com).** FileNET Panagon is enterprisewide integrated document management software that represents a solution for capturing, accessing, managing, utilizing, and securing business information. Information is also available via Web interface (see Exhibit 10).

Exhibit 5.   Web2Fax Interface

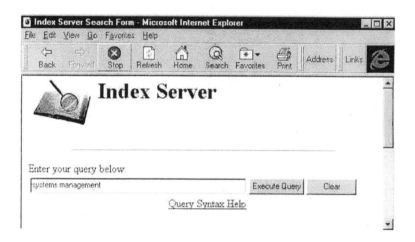

**Exhibit 6. Microsoft Index Server**

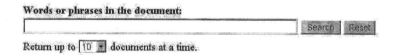

**Exhibit 7. Microsoft Office97 Web Find Fast**

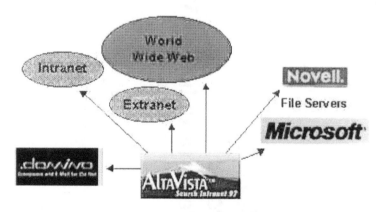

**Exhibit 8. Compaq AltaVista Search Intranet**

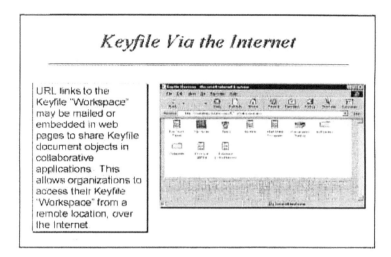

**Exhibit 9. Keyfile Web-Based Interface**

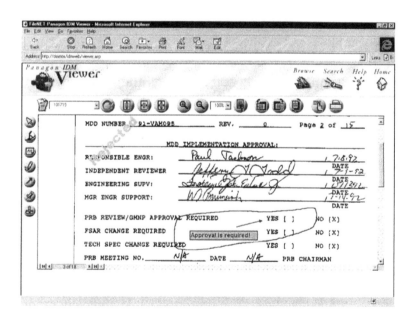

**Exhibit 10. FileNET Panagon**

**Example: SAP Internet-Based Workflow (www.sap.com/internet/index.htm).**
SAP Business Workflow module is another example of a Web-enabled work-flow management system. With SAP Business Workflow, a user can initiate a workflow (via Internet/intranet application components, BAPIs, forms),

track his or her work via the Internet application component "Integrated Inbox," respond to requests from other users, or review the workflow history via the Internet application component "Workflow Status Reports."

## WEB-TO-BUSINESS INTELLIGENCE SYSTEMS

Browser-based access to so-called business intelligence systems (decision support systems, executive information systems, data warehousing systems, etc.) is very important for decision makers because of its ease of use.

### Web-Enabled Desktop DSS Tools

Decision modeling is now available via the Web browser. The decision maker can use a model that is already created and stored on a server from his or her computer through the Web browser.

**Example: Vanguard DecisionPro Web Edition (www.vanguardsw.com).** The Web version of DecisionPro, a powerful desktop DSS tool, allows decision makers to run DecisionPro models remotely. They do not need special software on their computers other than a standard Web browser. For example, a model developed to assist salespeople in determining prices dealing with customers can be installed on a server and run remotely on a salesman's notebook computer.

What follows is an example of "loan qualification model," a model developed with DecisionPro and accessed through the Web browser. Users explore information with a browser so there is no client software to deploy (see Exhibit 11).

### Web-Enabled EIS (Reporting)

Executive information systems (EIS) or reporting applications provide user-friendly access to corporate data. These applications are usually DBMS-based and can contain both direct data from c/s applications or extracted and converted data from legacy systems. This conversion can be done manually or automatically through middleware or gateway programs (e.g., ISG Navigator, http://www.isg.co.il/home.asp).

**Example: Cognos Impromptu Web Reports (www.cognos.com).** Cognos Impromptu Web Reports delivers reporting facilities over the Web, providing end users with quick and easy access to the latest company reports — directly from their browser (see Exhibit 12).

### Web-to-Enterprisewide DSS

In addition to Web access to desktop DSS tools, such GUI interfaces are supported by enterprisewide decision support systems as well.

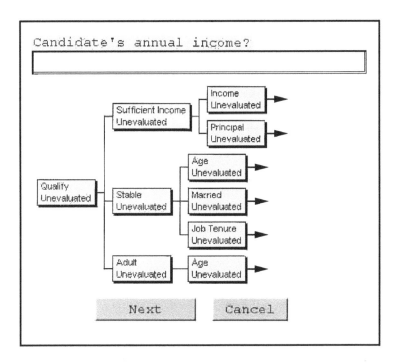

**Exhibit 11.    Web-Based Modeling Feature of Decision Pro**

**Example: Business Objects' WebIntelligence (www.businessobjects. com).**
Business Objects' WebIntelligence is a multi-tier, thin-client decision support system (DSS) that provides end users with ad hoc query, reporting, and analysis of information stored in corporate data warehouses (see Exhibit 13).

**Example: MicroStrategy's DSS Web (www.strategy.com).** MicroStrategy DSS Web is a user-friendly interface that connects corporate data warehouse across the World Wide Web (see Exhibit 14).

## WEB TO ERP

**Example: SAP R/3 System (www.sap.com).** The SAP R/3 application suite includes Internet application components that enable linking the R/3 System to the Internet. These components enable SAP users to use the R/3 System business functions via a Web browser. SAP R/3 Internet applications can be used as they are, or as a basis for creating new ones. SAP R/3 architecture is based on a three-tier client/server structure, with distinct layers for presentation, application, and database (see Exhibit 15).

219

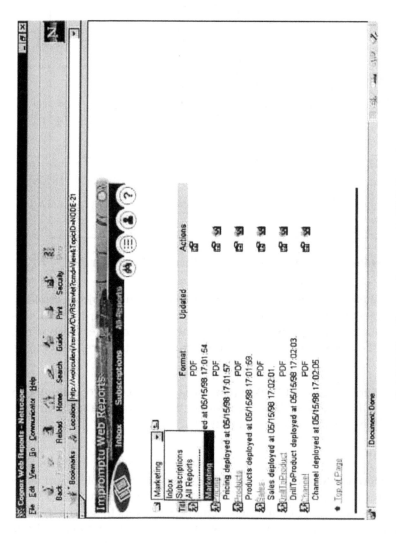

**Exhibit 12.   Cognos Impromptu Web Reports**

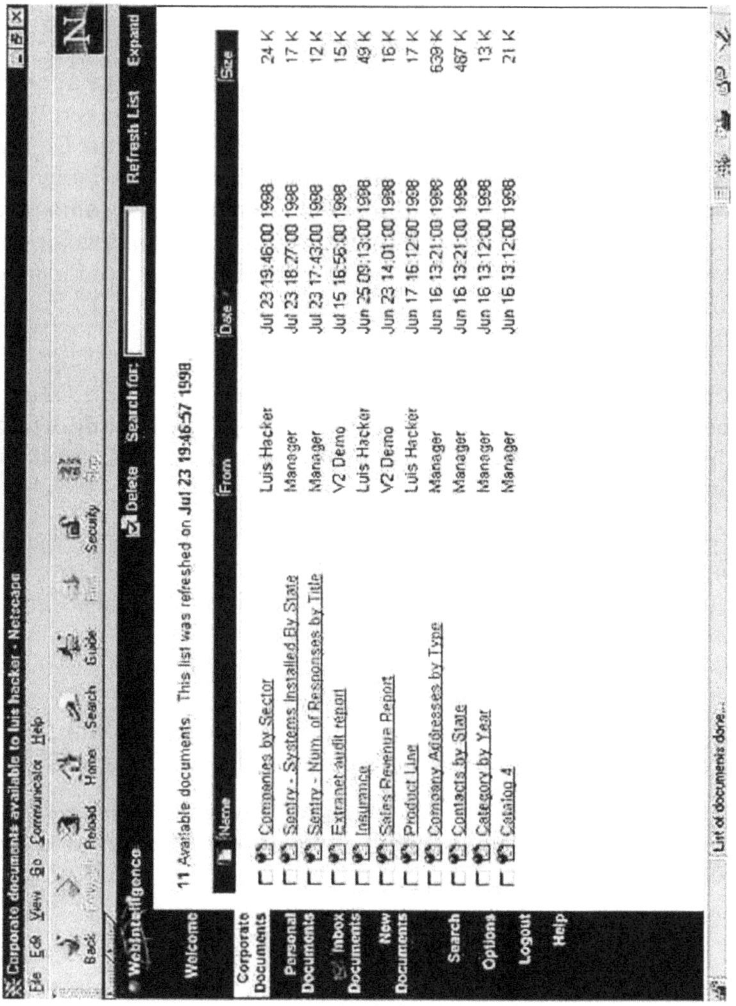

**Exhibit 13.   Business Objects' WebIntelligence**

## WEB-TO-HOST MIDDLEWARE AND RAD DEVELOPMENT TOOLS

Efficient access to legacy data is important from an application developer's perspective as well. The development of new c/s applications that will exchange data with existing legacy systems requires a type of middleware that overcomes the differences in data formats. Different data access middleware products exist and they are specific to a single platform: for example, RMS files on OpenVMS machines, IBM mainframes, or different UNIX machines. Two examples are given.

**Example: ISG Navigator (www.isg.co.il).** ISG Navigator is a data access middleware tool that provides an efficient data exchange between Windows platform and several host platforms such as OpenVMS for Digital Alpha and VAX, Digital UNIX, HP-UX. Sun Solaris and IBM AIX. ISG Navigator (Exhibit 16) enables access to nonrelational data in almost the same way that relational data is accessed. More importantly, application developers can build new Internet-based applications that will use data from legacy systems by using data integration standards such as OLE DB, ADO, COM, DCOM, RDMS, CORBA, etc.

**Example: ClientBuilder Enterprise (www.clientsoft.com).** ClientSoft ClientBuilder Enterprise and other solutions provide the following important capabilities in the development of Web-enabled c/s applications and their integration with legacy data:

- Data integration between desktop Windows applications and legacy data from IBM S/390 and AS/400 machines
- Developing GUI interface to existing host-based legacy applications
- Provides ODBC support to relational databases
- Provides access to applications residing on IBM systems through the use of wireless communications technologies
- Provides access to IBM host machines through the use of Web technologies within the electronic commerce systems (see Exhibit 17)

While middleware products serve as a data gateway between legacy systems and Windows-based c/s and desktop applications, Web-based application development products support building Web-enabled c/s applications.

Microsoft Visual InterDev (www.microsoft.com) is a rapid application development tool for building dynamic Internet and intranet applications based on the ASP feature of Microsoft Internet Information Server. It is available as a stand-alone product or as a part of Microsoft's Visual Studio integrated application development suite. Visual InterDev provides Web-based access to databases supporting ODBC standard (see Exhibit 18).

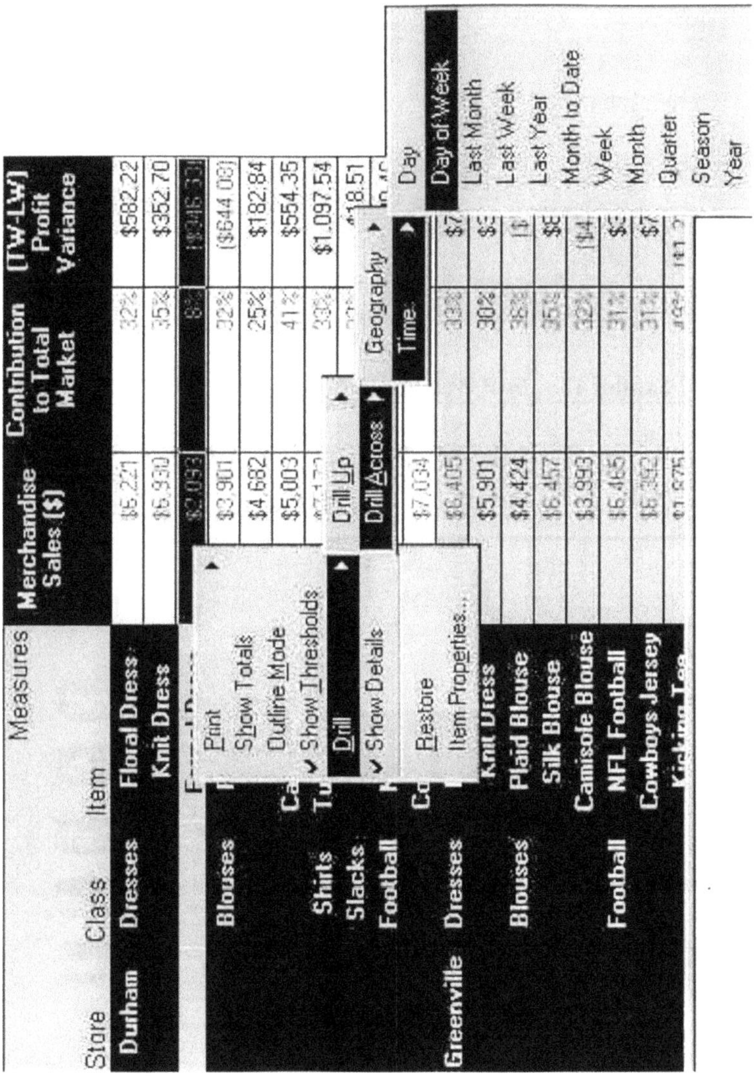

**Figure 14.   MicroStrategy's DSS Web**

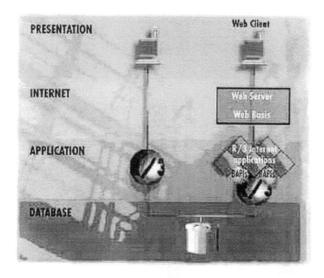

**Exhibit 15.  SAP Web-Based Infrastructure**

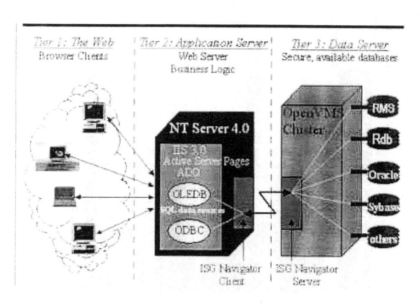

**Exhibit 16.  ISG Navigator**

**Exhibit 17.    ClientSoft**

In addition to specific Web development tools, most contemporary standard rapid application development tools provide features for developing Web-enabled applications. Exhibit 19 illustrates such features supported by Borland C++ Builder (www.inprise.com).

## CONCLUSIONS

This chapter presented a framework for an effective integration of Web-to-host connectivity and development tools in information systems. This issue was considered from both end-user and developer perspectives. This means that an emphasis is put on how to improve data access and data exchange, no matter where that data comes from: standard legacy data, e-mail or fax message, document, business model, report, ERP module, etc. The IS subsystems in which these tools can be used were identified, and some examples of software packages that can be found on the market were presented.

**References**

- www.simware.com
- www.gartner.com
- www.wrq.com
- www.nsainc.com
- www.mail2web.com
- www.tpc.int
- www.microsoft.com
- www.altavista.software.digital.com
- www.keyfile.com
- www.filenet.com
- www.sap.com
- www.vanguardsw.com
- www.isg.co.il
- www.cognos.com
- www.businessobjects.com
- www.strategy.com
- www.clientsoft.com
- www.microsoft.com

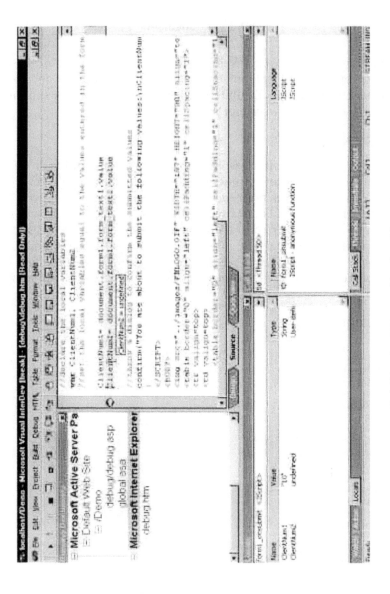

**Exhibit 18. Microsoft's Visual InterDev**

**Exhibit 19.    Borland C++ Builder: Internet Component Bar**

# Chapter 19
# Real-Life Case Studies of Web-to-Host Integration

*Anura Gurugé*

COMPARED TO OTHER DATA CENTER TECHNOLOGIES, WEB-TO-HOST INTEGRATION SOLUTIONS, WHICH ONLY CAME INTO BEING IN MID-1996 WITH THE INTRODUCTION OF THE FIRST 3270-TO-HTML CONVERSION PRODUCT, ARE A VERY RECENT ENTRANT INTO THE RATHER CONSERVATIVE MAINFRAME AND AS/400 ARENA. Nonetheless, the appeal, and applicability — not to mention the return on investment (ROI) — of these TCP/IP-centric solutions are so cogent and obvious that by mid-1999 nearly a thousand corporations around the world had successfully adopted Web-to-host integration, despite the major distraction of Y2K concerns. Many of the early adopters of Web-to-host integration were well-known "blue-chip" companies such as General Motors, FedEx, American Airlines, Trans World Airlines (TWA), Bank of America, Charles Schwab, Nestlé, and Del Monte Foods. Charles Schwab, the world's largest discount brokerage, now does more than 60 percent of its trades online, across the Internet, using Web-to-host technology coupled to six IBM mainframes. The adoption of rate of Web-to-host integration will increase even further when data center professionals, around the globe, recover from their Y2K travails.

This chapter sets out to help future adopters of Web-to-host integration technology by describing in detail six salutary case studies – each using a different type of Web-to-host solution. Each of these case studies clearly demonstrates the viability, potency, and stability of today's Web-to-host integration technology. The Lafayette Life and The Farmers Mutual Protective Association of Texas case studies, both from the insurance sector, dramatically highlight the incontrovertible cost benefits of using the Internet as the means of providing remote access to data centers. Lafayette Life

0-8493-1160-8/02/$0.00+$1.50
© 2002 by CRC Press LLC

reduced its remote access costs by more than 90 percent by moving from a public Frame Relay network-based access scheme to a Web-to-host solution that enabled it to securely and reliably realize the same host access — but this time across the public Internet. Although a very successful, 98-year-old insurance company with 300 sales agents, The Farmers Mutual Protective Association of Texas could only justify online, remote access for these 300 agents when it discovered a Web-to-host integration solution that supported unrestricted AS/400 access across the Internet. The remaining four case studies demonstrate other advantages of Web-to-host integration, such as the cost savings of thin-client access, business-to-business E-commerce over the Internet, and the "zero-lead-time" attribute of using the Internet as a means for host access.

The key characteristics of these six case studies are summarized in Exhibit 1.

**Exhibit 1.  Key Characteristics**

| Customer | Industry Sector | Web-to-Host Technology | Key Payoff | Solution Provided by | Rejuvenated User Interface |
|---|---|---|---|---|---|
| Lafayette Life Insurance | Insurance | 3270-to-HTML | Reduce remote access costs | Sterling Software | Yes |
| The Farmers Protective Assoc. of Texas | Insurance | Java applet-based tn5250 emulation | Enable remote access | ResQNet.com | Yes |
| Sabre (UK) | Transport | 3270-to-HTML | Minimize installation and maintenance cost with thin-client | Novell | Yes |
| Charleston County Court | Local Government | 3270-to-HTML | Public access to mainframe | Intelligent Environments | Yes |
| Navarre Corp. | Entertainment | Java applet-based tn3270(E) emulation and 3270-to-HTML | Business-to-business E-commerce over the Internet | ICOM Informatics | Limited |
| The Chickering Group | Insurance | Java applet-based tn5250 emulation | Zero lead time for implementing host access | Farabi Technology | No |

## LAFAYETTE LIFE INSURANCE

Lafayette Life Insurance (Lafayette, Indiana), founded in 1905, is a \$9.5B super heavyweight operating in 48 states plus Washington, D.C. In addition to traditional life insurance products, it offers a broad range of insurance and financial planning services. Lafayette's growing business is sustained by a large corporate staff in Indiana, augmented by approximately 1000 field agents across the country.

All of the field agents plus the corporate staff have real-time, online access to policy information, customer records, beneficiary status, marketing material, as well as all necessary forms and documentation. High-quality, responsive customer service, instantaneous quotes on policies, and "on-the-spot" information provision are imperative to success in today's competitive insurance and financial planning markets. Lafayette excels in, and is totally committed to, ensuring that its agents have access to all of the information they need, around the clock, to help them be successful. To this end, Lafayette has developed an in-house Policy Information System — written in S/370 Assembler to maximize performance and efficiency. This system, known as the New On Line Administration System (NOLAS) provides online access to all of the requisite information, forms, and documentation. Lafayette is a VM/SP shop that currently has a two-processor unit, IBM 9672-R24, S/390 Parallel Enterprise Server.

Field agents initially gained access to NOLAS via IBM's Advantis Global Network. But this soon became an expensive proposition that cost Lafayette \$6.50 per hour for every agent logged on. Agents who were not served by a local access number for Advantis were forced to use a 1-800 number that cost Lafayette \$6.00 per hour per user. Proactively containing costs is vitally important in today's competitive insurance market, with any measures that reduce the cost per policy typically reflected, positively, on the company bottom line. To dramatically slash these access costs, Lafayette decided to pursue an Internet-based access solution.

Lafayette chose Sterling's VM:Webgateway 3270-to-HTML conversion offering as the means to provide browser-based access, replete with user interface rejuvenation, to NOLAS. Exhibit 2 shows the architecture of this VM:Webgateway host access solution.

VM:Webgateway is a highly scalable and secure, VM-based, 3270-to-HTML conversion product. Contrary to its name, VM:Webgateway is not a VM-only solution. Instead, think of it as a very high-capacity 3270-to-HTML offering that happens to run on a VM server, as opposed to an NT or Novell server. It can be used profitably to Web-enable any SNA/3270 application running on a MVS, OS/390, VM, VSE, or TPF system. All that is required are

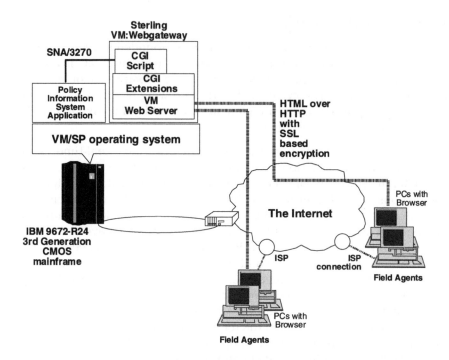

**Exhibit 2. Mainframe-Centric 3270-to-HTML Conversion, Based on Sterling Software's VM:Webgate, as Used by Lafayette Life Insurance**

standard SNA connections between the VM system running VM:Webgateway and the other mainframes containing the SNA/3270 applications. VM:Webgateway includes a built-in, full-function Web Server that supports SSL-based security as well as Java and ActiveX applets.

On a medium-size mainframe, VM:Webgateway can support a couple of thousand concurrent sessions, replete with screen rejuvenation, without any problem. A scalability number that is in the thousands, as opposed to tens of thousands, might appear to be incongruous vis-à-vis SNA access. However, in the case of 3270-to-HTML one has to factor in all the processing associated with the bi-directional conversions involved, as well as the overhead of performing the rejuvenation specific functions — such as that of executing the scripts that do the actual user interface customization. Consequently, many of the 3270-to-HTML offerings that run on NT-based PCs do not typically advertise concurrent session counts that are in excess of a thousand. Hence, the mainframe-based VM:Webgateway approach is definitely, and not unexpectedly, more scalable than most other 3270-to-HTML solutions.

With VM:Webgateway, the 3270-to-HTML conversion is done via individually created Common Gateway Interface (CGI) scripts that are written using IBM's REXX (i.e., Restructured Extended Executor Language) "job" scripting language. The CGI scripts gain access to the mainframe applications that are to be Web-enabled by logging on to them using standard, mainframe userid/password logon conventions. Sterling does provide an automatic tracing facility that records — in terms of a CGI script — the navigation process employed by a user to access and interact with 3270 screens. A skeleton CGI script obtained via this tracing scheme can then be fleshed out to provide the complete rejuvenated user interface. In addition, Sterling also provides CGI scripts that will automatically apply a set of default transformations, such as background and buttons, to any "green-on-black'" 3270 screen. To ensure session integrity and security, VM:Webgateway uses "hidden" HTML FORM fields to store session ID numbers.

Given that it is a long-standing, dedicated VM shop, Lafayette did not hesitate in opting for a VM-based mainframe solution for its Web server, as well as its Web-to-SNA gateway. Implementing NT or UNIX servers in order to realize Web enablement was viewed as an unnecessary distraction and overhead — especially since Sterling could provide them with a highly integrated, VM-resident solution. The conversion to Internet-based access was expedited by Lafayette's use of VM Assist, Sterling's professional services partnership program.

Web enablement has been a huge success — and Lafayette now openly and readily endorses the advantages of Internet-based mainframe access at every opportunity. The Internet-based remote access slashed Lafayette's remote access costs by nearly 94 percent, which has resulted in millions of dollars in cost savings each year.

## THE FARMERS MUTUAL PROTECTIVE ASSOCIATION OF TEXAS

The Farmers Mutual Protective Association of Texas (RVOS), based in Temple, Texas, is a successful mutual insurance company that provides farmers in Texas with property coverage protection against fire, theft, vandalism, etc. RVOS' forte is handling farm property insurance needs that the big, national companies are unwilling or unable to handle.

RVOS was established in 1901 by a group of nine people of Czech heritage, in Bell County, Texas, for the purpose of providing mutual assistance to one another in the event of loss by fire, lightning, and windstorms. The acronym RVOS refers to the company's name in Czech. RVOS has grown steadily over the years and now has 300 sales representatives spread throughout Texas. This case study is all about providing these 300 sales reps with online AS/400 access across the Internet using tn5250 emulation, with built-in user interface rejuvenation, via a Java applet provided by ResQNet.com.

Until March 1999, RVOS' 300 sales reps did not have any type of direct online access to the policy, claim, and financial applications that were being run on an AS/400 Model 510. Policy and claim information, prior to that, was sent to the sales reps via mail and fax. In addition, the sales reps would telephone corporate headquarters in Temple when they needed online information. As with so many companies, RVOS realized a couple of years ago that the Internet was the optimal, most expeditious, and a highly cost-effective way to provide its 300 (and growing) sales reps with direct online access.

In September 1998, Lewis Wolfe, RVOS' Computer Services Manager, saw ResQNet technology at an IBM E-business show in Las Vegas. Wolfe was impressed and initially thought that ResQNet was indeed IBM-developed technology because it was being demonstrated at an IBM booth. (ResQNet provides IBM and others with user interface rejuvenation technology. The Screen Customizer capability of IBM's Host On-Demand Java applet is based on ResQNet technology.) After the show, Wolfe visited the ResQNet Web site (www.resqnet.com) and downloaded an evaluation copy.

RVOS' decision to go with ResQNet was based on the following two important criteria:

1. **Ease of installation, implementation, and maintenance.** RVOS, which has a small MIS department, wanted a solution that was easy to deploy and did not require too much maintenance. ResQNet sent an SE to RVOS in March 1999 and the entire project, including the design of some 20 customized screens, was successfully realized in three days.

2. **AutoGUI capability.** ResQNet automatically detects PF key assignment strings (such as PF3 for exit), and automatically converts these strings to action buttons. ResQNet also recognizes numbered menus and automatically converts them into button-driven menus. Given that RVOS had many menu-type screens, this was of particular interest and value. Given that this AS/400 access scheme was being implemented explicitly for its dispersed sales force, RVOS wanted to deliver a welcoming, user-friendly interface that would not intimidate, frustrate, or hamper the sales reps. RVOS also wanted to minimize, if not eliminate, help-desk calls from users confused about how to "drive" the system. The ResQNet user interface rejuvenation technology compellingly addressed all of these requirements.

The architecture of RVOS' ResQNet solution is shown in the Exhibit 3. It is a classic "two-tier," client-to-host architecture. Printing, which is not a major issue, is restricted to screen prints.

ResQNet uses just one applet for both 'tn' host connectivity and user interface rejuvenation. This applet is typically around 500 KBytes — although it is possible to configure even smaller applets. In general, RVOS uses ResQNet's caching feature, where the applet is cached in the browser's cache after the initial download. This greatly expedites applet invocation (without sacrificing the dynamic and automatic applet version checking) and precludes the need for continual applet downloads across the Net.

Although RVOS uses IBM's firewall technology within the AS/400 to restrict access to the Web server, the company was not comfortable with the potential security risk of having its production AS/400 system directly accessible over the Web. The primary — and justifiable — fear was that a hacker might disrupt the mission-critical production host. To get around this, RVOS acquired a new AS/400 Model 170 in early 1999 — for the explicit purpose of acting as an Internet server for Web-based access. The low-profile, low-cost 170s, referred to by IBM as "E-servers," are positioned as scalable alternatives to NT and UNIX boxes for E-commerce, Java, and Internet applications.

As shown in Exhibit 3, all of the Web server, tn5250 server, and firewall software used by RVOS is a part of OS/400 and resides on the Model 170. This is another factor that simplified the overall implementation and kept costs to a minimum. At present, there is no direct connection between the production Model 510 and the Model 170. Data between the two systems are updated every night using tapes. This guarantees the isolation and security sought by RVOS. Wolfe plans to integrate the two systems to eliminate the need for data replication in the future.

Web-based AS/400 access using the ResQNet tn5250 applet, replete with user interface rejuvenation, provided RVOS with the following advantages:

- Simple, straightforward, low-effort installation in a matter of days
- Easy user interface rejuvenation with many automated features
- Trouble-free, low-maintenance operation
- Cost-compelling, Web-based access with no toll-call charges or the need for Remote Access Server equipment
- Ready extensibility in the future to support Secure Sockets Layer-based authentication and encryption
- Scalable, very clean, two-tier architecture that utilizes standard, highly proven, built-in components in OS/400

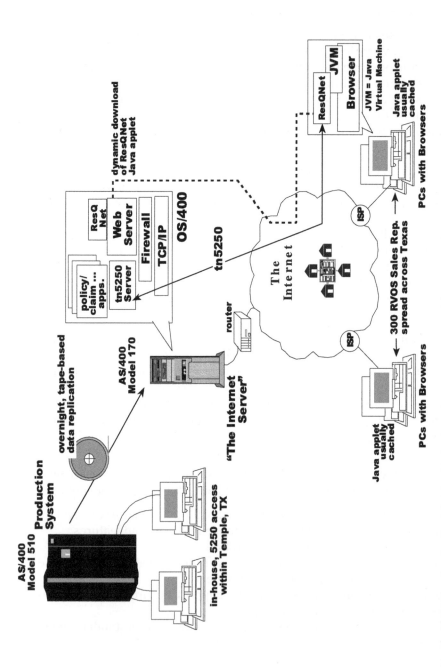

Exhibit 3. ResQNet Applet-Based AS/400 Access over the Internet, Replete with Customized and AugoGUI Screens, as Used by The Farmers Mutual Protective Association of Texas

RVOS is extremely happy with its Web-to-host solution. This is yet another resounding win-win for today's Web-to-host technology.

## SABRE, INC.

Sabre is synonymous with travel reservation systems. Sabre, which was American Airlines' reservation system, was the pioneer in computerized reservation systems. Now an independent entity, Sabre is the world leader in electronic services and products for the travel and transportation industry.

Just as with the above two case studies, this is yet another example of using browser-based SNA access over the Internet to provide agents with "near-zero-cost" remote access to data centers. However, this was not the only pivotal business driver in this instance. Sabre was also looking for a thin-client solution that would significantly minimize client software installation, upgrade, and maintenance costs.

Sabre's U.K. regional office in London needed a means to provide low-cost, low-maintenance remote access to some of its European travel agents. With some 2700 travel agents involved, spread across three countries, it was imperative that the access scheme chosen would not require installation and maintenance on a per-desktop basis — and that it was reliable, rugged, and intuitive so as to minimize training, support, and administration costs. In essence, Sabre required a thin-client, Web-to-mainframe solution.

Sabre initially evaluated an NT-based solution but was unhappy with its reliability and manageability. It then turned Novell's HostPublisher — a highly scalable and feature-rich 3270-to-HTML conversion product that offers more value-added functionality (e.g., bona fide support for light-pen operation) than any of its many competitors. Sabre started a pilot project using HostPublisher in mid-1998.

Given its 1998 roots, the current implementation used by Sabre (as shown in Exhibit 4) is based on NetWare 4.11 and NetWare for SAA 3 — in essence, one release behind the versions available today. The current levels of these products are NetWare 5 and NetWare for SAA 4. Nonetheless, Sabre is ecstatic about the success of this Web-to-host project that uses straightforward 3270-to-HTML conversion to realize mainframe access. The beauty of such an HTML-centric solution is that the only software required on the client machines to realize host access is just a standard browser. 3270-to-HTML conversion is thus the "thinnest" of the thin-client solutions.

This very thin-client host access was exactly what Sabre wanted. With this solution, there was no client-side software that had to be installed, regularly updated, or maintained. All of the travel agents who were being brought online already had browsers on their PCs through Windows 95.

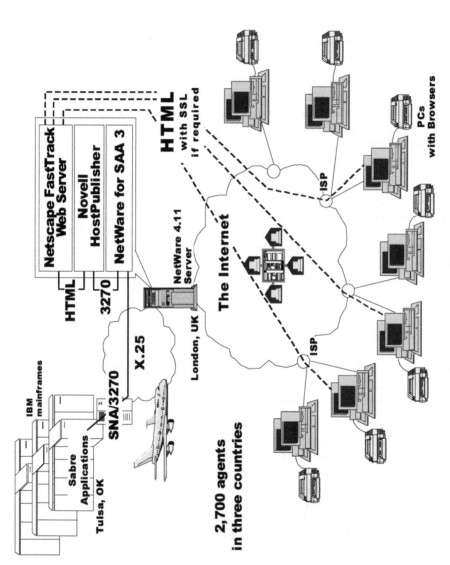

Exhibit 4. The Novell-Centric 3270-to-HTML Employed by Sabre, U.K.

Consequently, nothing had to be done on or installed at the client machine. Everything required to achieve this browser-based mainframe access is self-contained on a server — in this case, a Novell NetWare server running NetWare for SAA and HostPublisher.

The staff and Sabre U.K. love the reliability and the rejuvenated point-and-click user interface. Sabre's praise of 3270-to-HTML conversion can be paraphrased as: *It is colorful. It is point-and-click. It is pretty. And it works.*

This HostPublisher solution has also proved to be extremely scalable. A test conducted in April 1999 showed that HostPublisher was handling around 4200 hits per hour. Also note that this PC server-based solution is expected to handle up to 2700 travel agents. With NetWare 5 and NetWare for SAA 4, this same configuration will be able to handle 4000 to 5000 concurrent sessions.

## CHARLESTON COUNTY COURT

This case study clearly highlights how today's Web-to-host integration technology — in particular, 3270-to-HTML conversion, which is the "thinnest" of 'thin client solutions, — can be effectively and profitably used to provide the general public with authorized access to public records. It also showcases this technology vis-à-vis local and state government applications. All forms of state and local government are extremely promising and receptive candidates for Web-to-host technology given that they are heavy users of mainframes and AS/400s — and moreover, have a public mandate, in many cases instituted as a high-profile election promise by the governor (or similar), for making as much of their information and services as possible Web-accessible. Because the overriding goal of such Web-to-host projects is to provide the general public with easy access to host data, the most germane technology, invariably, proves to be 3270/5250-to-HTML conversion.

The Courts of Common Pleas and General Sessions for Charleston County in South Carolina are located at the Charleston County Judicial Center in North Charleston, South Carolina. This court is a part of the Circuit Court of South Carolina — where Charleston County in conjunction with Berkely County form the 9th Judicial Circuit of the state's 16 circuits.

The Court of Common Pleas is the civil branch of the Circuit Court and has jurisdiction over all civil cases in Charleston where the amount in dispute is in excess of $5000. The Court of General Session handles criminal cases — except most misdemeanor cases, which are usually heard in the Magistrates' Courts.

Case records of the Courts of Common Pleas and General Sessions, as well as those of the Small Claims Courts and out-of-county judgments, are deemed to be public domain information that the general public has a right to access and peruse. The Clerk of Court is responsible for maintaining and managing these records.

Up until mid-1999, the general public, paralegals, or lawyers who required access to Charleston County legal documents or case records could only do so by actually visiting one of two county offices. This was obviously not that convenient — particularly for the average citizen, unless they happened to live or work close to one of these offices and were freely mobile.

Charleston County Clerk of Court, Julie J. Armstrong, took it upon herself, in 2000, to provide access to court documents over the Web. This online access to court documents and information is through the County Court Web site,. www3.charlestoncounty.org. Given that the case records were maintained on a mainframe, the Charleston County Court needed a sound and solid Web-to-host solution in order to realize its goal. The solution opted for, which has proved to be extremely successful, was Intelligent Environments' feature-heavy and scalable ScreenSurfer offering that does 3270/5250-to-HTML conversion, on-the-fly — replete with extensive user interface rejuvenation. See Exhibit 5.

ScreenSurfer is a high-end 3270/5250-to-HTML conversion solution. Its attractive features include:

- Session integrity (i.e., persistence) and session time-out control through the use of cookies
- Function key support via an ActiveX applet
- One-step light-pen selection through the use of clickable Graphical Interchange Format (GIF) tags
- Integrated Web server
- Support for Microsoft Active Server Page (ASP) technology for enhancing Web pages
- Optional user authentication
- Correct alignment of all host-generated columns and tables
- Support for at least 1000 concurrent sessions when installed on a typical NT-server configuration through extensive use of multi-threading

Given this feature set, ScreenSurfer credibly competes with Novell's Host-Publisher and Eicon's Aviva Web-to-Host Server for top honors in this arena — with the only caveat being that ScreenSurfer relies on ActiveX for some of its value-adds, thus becoming Windows-specific in some instances, whereas the other two use Java for their value-adds to realize platform independence.

The Charleston County MIS Department was able to develop and deploy the ScreenSurfer-based Web-to-host access in just eight weeks — and that included the extensive rejuvenation of quite a few mainframe screens.

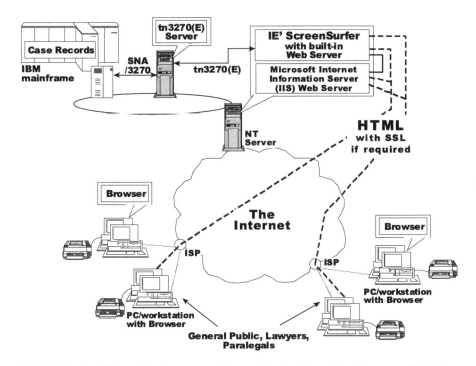

**Exhibit 5   Intelligent Environments' ScreenSurfer-Based Architecture Used by Charleston County Court**

Today, ScreenSurfer is handling around 2800 mainframe access requests a day. (Charleston County Court currently has a license for 100 concurrent sessions.) This is another resounding success and endorsement for the power and simplicity of today's Web-to-host technology.

## NAVARRE CORPORATION

This exemplary case study shows how Web-to-host integration technology can be gainfully used to realize online E-commerce on a business-to-business basis across the Internet. E-commerce will exceed $1 trillion per annum by 2002. Being able to effortlessly harness existing, highly proven, host-resident, mission-critical applications via Web-to-host technology, à la this case study, to access E-commerce applications will expedite the adoption of E-commerce and reduce implementation costs by obviating the need to develop new software.

Navarre Corporation, of New Hope, Minnesota, is one of the largest distributors of consumer software, music, DVDs, and home videos to traditional retailers and the so-called "E-trailers." Navarre, for example, supplies Amazon.com, one of the pioneers of E-commerce, with software.

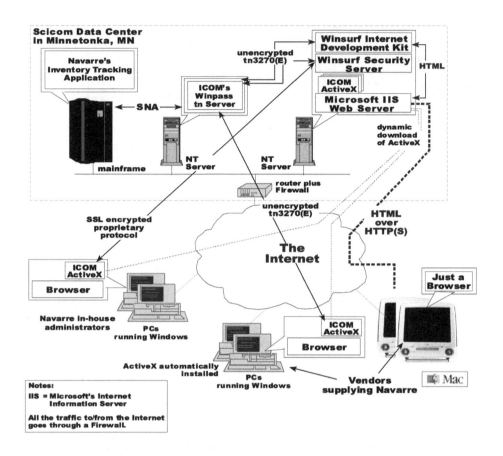

**Exhibit 6.** Navarre's Outsourced Inventory Tracking Mainframe Application That is Accessed by Various Vendors to Check Their Re-stocking Needs Using ICOM's Winsurf Mainframe Access (WMA)

Navarre was one of the first companies to develop a Web site to facilitate *business-to-business* E-commerce à la an extranet application. Navarre, which does about $250 million in net sales at present, went public on December 16, 1993, on NASDAQ. Most of Navarre's business transactions are E-commerce-based and, as such, Navarre is a heavily into electronic data interchange (EDI) and online *supply chain management*. Vendors who wish Navarre to act as a distributor of their wares have no choice but to conduct most of their dealings with Navarre electronically — typically through their navarre.com Web site. Navarre's inventory tracking system is maintained on a mainframe — and outsourced at that. This case study shows how Navarre uses ICOM Informatics' Winsurf Mainframe Access (WMA) product to provide its vendors with access to the mainframe application. WMA offers both ActiveX-based tn3270(E) emulation as well as on-the-fly 3270-to-HTML conversion.

In keeping with Navarre's all-electronic philosophy, Navarre's vendors are expected to ascertain their re-stocking needs and schedules online by interacting with Navarre's inventory tracking application. This inventory tracking application is outsourced by Navarre to a neighboring company — Scicom in Minnetonka, Minnesota. Exhibit 6 shows the architecture of the WMA-centric solution adopted by Navarre.

The WMA server in the Scicom data center is configured such that vendors using Internet Explorer on a PC will realize their access via the ActiveX emulator, while users of all other platforms (in particular, Macs) will rely on WMA's 3270-to-HTML conversion to achieve their mainframe access. Although SSL-based security is available for the ActiveX-based access via the Winsurf Security Server, this option is currently not used by Navarre. Navarre's in-house administrators, however, do use the security server for all their interactions.

Scicom, which acts as the outsourcer for this application, is also an ICOM distributor. With some help from ICOM (U.S.), Scicom implemented this WMA access scheme as a turnkey solution for Navarre as a part of the outsourcing agreement. This WMA solution has now been active for some time and is heavily used — with the system being extremely stable and reliable.

This case study also demonstrates that applet-based emulation and 3270/5250-to-HTML, rather than being mutually exclusive approaches, are oft-times complementary solutions that should be used in tandem to address different categories of users; for example, power users versus casual users, intranet users versus Internet users, and data entry users versus enterprise resource processing (ERP) users.

## THE CHICKERING GROUP

The Chickering Group, based in Cambridge, Massachusetts, provides a great example of a fast-striding corporation that is gainfully exploiting a highly secure, three-tier, Web-to-AS/400 integration over the Internet to rapidly expand its customer base by offering a zero-lead-time access solution. Moreover, by implementing this Web-based AS/400 access solution in 1997, The Chickering Group became one of the very early adopters of Web-to-host integration.

The Chickering Group is a leading provider of health insurance products and services to students pursuing higher education. In 1999, it was providing insurance to approximately 220,000 students spread across more than 120 college and university campuses in the United States. Health insurance in general, and student health insurance in particular, is a highly competitive and price-sensitive industry. Health insurance providers such as The Chickering Group are thus continually and aggressively looking at means to reduce costs, improve efficiency, provide more services, and be more responsive to the changing needs of their clientele. Consequently, corporations such as The Chickering Group are highly motivated and unhesitant when it comes to regularly reengineering their business processes to garner all possible benefits from promising new technology.

The spread of the Internet and the availability of technology to enable browser-based access to SNA applications running on AS/400s provided The Chickering Group with a wonderful opportunity to reduce its operational costs, while at the same time significantly increase its reach into the student population. Whenever possible, The Chickering Group has tried to provide universities and colleges with the ability to remotely access its AS/400-centric computing system to obtain real-time information on insurance plans, insurance coverage, and insurance participant data. Such remote access was originally provided via either dial-up systems or leased point-to-point connections in the case of the larger institutions. Offering this type of remote access is a relatively expensive proposition — particularly as the number of remote sites that have to be supported starts to increase at a rapid clip. The cost issues become even more exacerbated if the client base at some of the remote sites is relatively small. The lead-time required to provide a connection to the customer was also increasing and approaching three to four weeks.

What The Chickering Group desperately needed was an alternate means of providing remote access that was flexible, scalable, cost-effective, and secure — and furthermore, did not require much setup at the data center, thus minimizing the time taken to bring a new customer online. The Internet proved to be the ideal solution, particularly because all of its clients, being academic institutions, already had excellent access to the Internet. Using browser-based access over the Internet, The Chickering Group could cost-effectively and securely connect their branch office employees and scholastic clients to its AS/400-centric healthcare insurance system.

The Chickering Group opted for a three-tier Farabi HostFront solution, given that Farabi Technology is a major provider of AS/400 access solutions. The architecture of the AS/400 access scheme used by The Chickering Group is shown in Exhibit 7. The configuration as shown in Exhibit 7 is constrained to 128 concurrent sessions. As its client base grows, The Chickering Group is planning to install another server to double this capacity. Farabi will use a Microsoft-supplied Windows NT utility to load balance the applet TCP connections between the two servers.

When clients or remote site employees connect to The Chickering Group's home page, they are presented with a user-friendly menu that

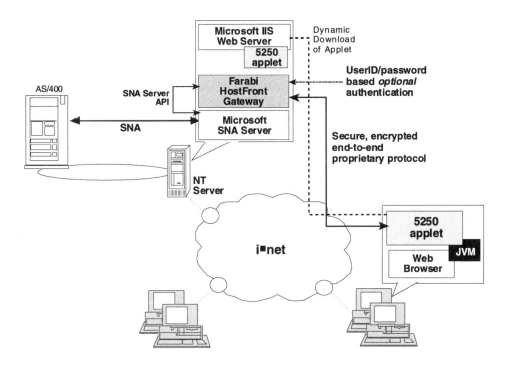

**Exhibit 7. Architecture of the Farabi HostFront-centric AS/400 Access Solution Being Used by The Chickering Group**

provides an option to access either public domain information or the company's internal secure site. If the latter option is chosen, HostFront authenticates the user, downloads a Web-based thin-client interface, in the form of a Java applet or ActiveX control, and then establishes a secure end-to-end connection. Once this connection has been established, the remote Web browser users are able to initiate secure AS/400 host sessions over the Internet.

## THE BOTTOM LINE

These six real-life case studies conclusively demonstrate that Web-to-host integration technology is indeed very real, proven, stable, and more than ready for prime time. These case studies were explicitly chosen to show the diversity of solutions that are possible and the wide spectrum of applications that can be addressed with today's Web-to-host technology. The two case studies pertaining to providing insurance agents with access to host applications, Lafayette Life and RVOS, shows how the same successful end result is achieved using two very disparate techniques — 3270-to-HTML conversion by Lafayette Life and Java applet-based tn3270(E) emulation in the case of RVOS. The Navarre case study, which showcases

E-commerce and business-to-business interactions over the Web, on the other hand, uses both of these techniques in parallel. The Sabre and Lafayette case studies both prove that this technology can indeed be scalable, given that both configurations support over a thousand concurrent sessions. The bottom line is thus very simple and straightforward: Web-to-host integration technology can be very profitably used in conjunction with mission-critical applications and, as demonstrated by these case studies, is indeed already being actively used in such scenarios.

# Chapter 20

# Integrating Information Systems into the World Wide Web

*Chao-Min Chiu*
*Michael Bieber*
*Chin-Feng Lin*
*Szu-Yuan Sun*

THE OVERALL GOAL OF THIS CHAPTER IS TO PROVIDE HYPERTEXT FUNCTIONALITY THROUGH THE WORLD WIDE WEB (WWW) TO HYPERTEXT-UNAWARE INFORMATION SYSTEMS (IS) WITH MINIMAL CHANGES TO IS. Information systems dynamically generate their contents and thus require some mapping mechanism to automatically map the generated content to hypertext constructs (nodes, links, etc.).[1] Information systems include financial information systems, accounting information systems, database management systems, geographic information systems, expert systems, and decision support systems.

What benefit do users gain from providing information systems with hypertext support? Hypertext streamlines access to and provides rich navigational features around related information, thereby increasing user comprehension of information and its context.[2] Augmenting information systems with hypertext support results in new ways to view and manage the information system's knowledge by navigating among items of interest and annotating with comments and relationships (links).[3]

The WWW is mainly used to browse predefined HTML files. However, the WWW has the opportunity to integrate hypertext support into information systems. There are many potential approaches for integrating Web servers with information systems: CGI, server API, server-side Java, ASP, etc. No

0-8493-1160-8/02/$0.00+$1.50
© 2002 by CRC Press LLC

systematic approach exists, however, for integrating an analytical information system into the WWW and giving users direct access to its interrelationships. This research contributes a systematic dynamic-mapping mechanism and a set of guidelines for IS integration on the WWW.

## SYSTEM ARCHITECTURE

As shown in Exhibit 1, a conceptual architecture is proposed that emphasizes the integration of Web servers with information systems, providing hypertext functionality to each.

- The master handler coordinates schema mapping and message passing among different IS domains, thus aiding IS-to-IS integration. It also provides IS command mapping rules.
- An IS handler translates and routes messages between its IS and the Web server. It also provides its system's object mapping rules.
- An IS is an application system with which users interact to perform some task, which dynamically produces output content for display.
- A knowledge database stores commands for accessing various relationships on IS objects and information that cannot be accessed directly from information systems (e.g., relationships in E-R diagrams).
- A linkbase stores user-created comments and *ad hoc* links.

Note that the master handler and IS handlers can be implemented using CGI scripts, server APIs, ASP, etc.

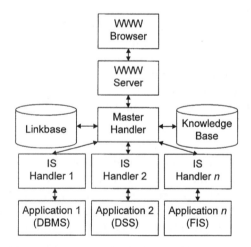

**Exhibit 1.  A Conceptual Architecture for Integrating Information Systems into the WWW**

## BUILDING MAPPING RULES

This section discusses the process of analyzing information systems and building mapping rules. These rules would reside in and become invoked by the master handler or IS handler. Each is explained using a prototype (i.e., a financial information system built using MS-Excel) as the target IS.

### Step 1: Identify Objects

This step is to identify data objects of interest. In the prototype, objects include workbooks, worksheets, and cells.

### Step 2: Identify Relationships

Bieber and Vitali[3] identify several types of relationships for system objects, including those below. Identifying explicit and implicit relationships forces developers to consider which information users are interested in and then build mapping rules to access this.

Each of the following relationships gives the user easy access to some aspect of an object.

- Schema relationships: access to the kind of domain-specific relationships one finds in a schema or application design.
- Operational relationships: direct access to information about IS objects using operational commands supported by the IS. In the prototype, this includes Excel commands over specific objects.
- Structural relationships: access to related objects based on the application's internal structure. In the prototype, these include "contains" links among workbooks, worksheets, and cells.
- Meta information relationships: access to attributes of and descriptive information about IS objects. In the prototype, these include its formula, explanation, cell type, etc.
- Occurrence relationships: access to all manifestations of a given object. In the prototype, for example, one might want to access other worksheets that have the same cell title.
- Annotative relationships: relationships declared by users instead of being inferred based on system structure. All users should be able to annotate objects even when without direct write access. A linkbase will store user-created comments.

### Step 3: Identify Commands for Accessing Relationships on IS Objects

Commands underlie the links that give users direct access to various relationships on IS objects. Exhibit 2 lists some of these commands for sheet and cell relationships. One can classify commands into three categories: common, comment, and formula.

**Exhibit 2.    Commands Underlying Sheet and Cell Relationships**

| Objects | Relationships | Categories | Commands | Functionality |
|---------|---------------|------------|----------|---------------|
| Sheet | Operational | Common | drawChart | Draw a chart based on values of the selected sheet |
| Sheet | Structural | Common | showData | Show contents of a sheet |
| Sheet | Annotative | Comment | add | Create comments on a sheet |
| Sheet | Annotative | Comment | view | View comments on a sheet |
| Sheet | Operational | Common | newSheet | Create a new Excel sheet |
| Cell | Operational | Common | update | Change the value of a cell and do a what-if analysis |
| Cell | Meta information | Common | explain | Get the explanation and formula of a cell |
| Cell | Annotative | Comment | add | Create comments on the selected cell |
| Cell | Annotative | Comment | view | View comments on the selected cell |
| Cell | Meta information | Formula | display | Display the formula (in Excel format) of a cell |

## Step 4: Build Mapping Rules

The main purpose of mapping rules is to infer useful links from the output dynamically generated by an IS and commands for operating on IS objects. Note that one set of mapping rules can serve all instances of an IS. Two types of mapping rules can be identified: Command_Rule and Object_Rule. Bieber[4] and Wan[5] implemented mapping rules (or bridge laws) using Prolog. However, for clarity, mapping rules are discussed here in terms of functional procedural calls.

**1. Command_Rule(System, Type).** This rule infers commands for operating on the selected object. The "System" parameter is used to discriminate among different information systems.

This rule should provide the following functions.

- Search the knowledge database for commands accessing various relationships on the selected IS object
- Map commands to links
- Form an HTML document that includes mapped links and send the document to the Web server

For example, Command_Rule ("FIS", "SHEET") will execute the aforementioned functions and create the HTML document displayed in Exhibit 3. To conserve space, only one command (showData) is listed here. In reality, the system would present all commands (or a filtered subset). Some available commands are listed in Exhibit 2.

**Exhibit 3.    Command_Rule ("FIS", "SHEET") HTML Page**

```
<HTML><BODY>
.  .  .  .  .
<A
href="http://127.0.0.1/fis/MasterHandler.asp?SYSTEM=FIS&ID=
FL,EBIT,Y1999 &TYPE=Sheet
&COMMAND=showData">showData</A>
.  .  .  .  .
</BODY></HTML>
```

In Exhibit 3, the following assumptions are made: (1) the "EBIT" workbook belongs to financial leverage (FL) subsystem and contains the "Y1999" worksheet; and (2) the IS handler is an ASP application called "MasterHandler." Note that the link anchor has a "Command" attribute whose value is "showData." This type of link anchor is called a "command link anchor."

**2. Object_Rule(Command, System, ID, Type).** This rule has four parameters. The object identifier (ID) is the key to determine which object of the given system the command should operate on. For example, the ID "FL,EBIT,Y1999" means the "Y1999" sheet of the "EBIT" workbook; FL means financial leverage subsystem.

This rule should provide the following functions.

- Map commands to actual IS commands
- Send actual commands and other parameters to the IS
- Receive display output from the IS
- Infer links from the output generated by the IS
- Create the HTML document with inferred links and send the document to the Web server

Here is an example in which the command accesses a structural relationship (from step 2). Object_Rule ("showData", "FIS", "FL,EBIT,Y1999", "SHEET") will execute the five aforementioned functions and send the HTML document shown in Exhibit 4 to the Web server. To conserve space, one can just list the cell called "EPS." Note that the link anchor has a "Command" attribute that value is "NO." This type of link anchor is called an "object link anchor."

Exhibit 5 shows the interface of the prototype. This system has three areas:

- System structure area
- Command area
- Content area

**Exhibit 4.** **Object_Rule("showData", "FIS", "FL,EBIT,Y1999", "SHEET") HTML Document**

```
<HTML><BODY>
. . . .
<A href="
http://127.0.0.1/fis/MasterHandler.asp?SYSTEM=FIS&ID=FL,EBI
T,Y1999,C3&TYPE=CELL
&COMMAND=NO">EPS</A>
. . . .
</BODY></HTML>
```

## IMPLEMENTATION

The mapping rule approach is a new technique, so it is not used in business today. Some organizations have made resources of information systems available to users through the Web. However, those implementations do not meet this definition of integration with IS because they do not infer useful links that give users more direct access to the system's primary functionality, give access to meta information about IS objects, and enable annotation and *ad hoc* links. The following are cases that do not meet this definition of integrating IS with the WWW.

- Most Web database applications handle queries and generate HTML documents from query results without mapping query results to useful links that allow users to view and manage DBMS knowledge, by navigating among items of interest and annotating with comments and relationships (links).
- WWW search engines use simple mapping rules to map the query result to a dynamically generated Web page with links based on the "URL address" and "page title" for each hit.

A proof-of-concept prototype (see Exhibit 5) has been created using a financial information system as the target IS. The financial information system was built using Microsoft Excel. The master handler is an ASP program (i.e., MasterHandler.asp). The IS handler has two parts: an ASP program (i.e., FISHandler.asp) and a DLL (i.e., FISHandler.DLL) built using Visual Basic. This section explains how to program Command_Rule and Object_Rule using program codes (ASP and Visual Basic codes) and flowcharts (see Exhibits 6 and 7).

### Command_Rule

This subsection uses a simple example (i.e., click on the "EPS" object) to explain how to program this rule. However, one skips codes about error handling, displaying data in specified window, etc.

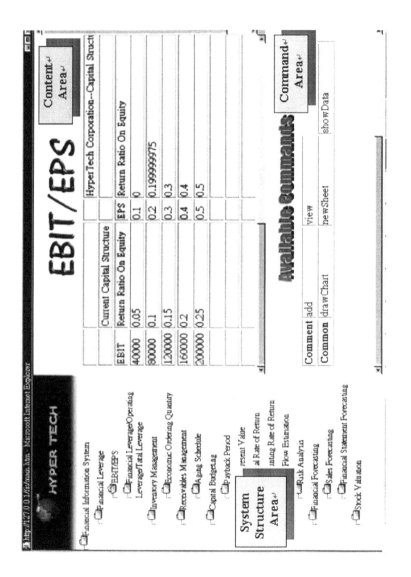

**Exhibit 5.   The Interface of the Prototype**

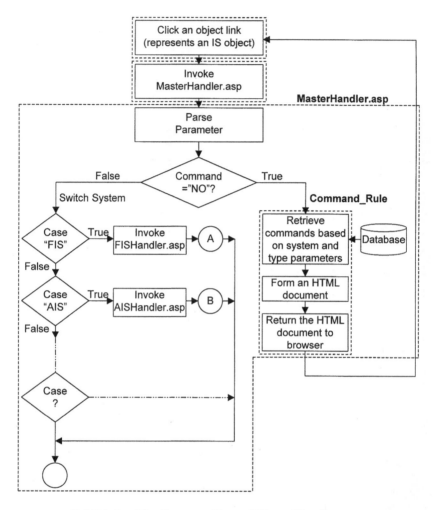

**Exhibit 6.   The Program Flow of MasterHandler.asp**

- Click the "EPS" object link: the link anchor underlines the "EPS" object (see Exhibit 5):

  ```
  <A href="http://127.0.0.1/fis/MasterHandler.asp?SYSTEM=FIS&
  ID=FL,EBIT, Y1999,C3&TYPE=CELL&COMMAND=NO">EPS</A>
  ```

- Parse parameters:

  ```
  system = request.querystring("SYSTEM")
  id = request.querystring("ID")
  objType = request.querystring("TYPE")
  command = request.querystring("COMMAND")
  ```

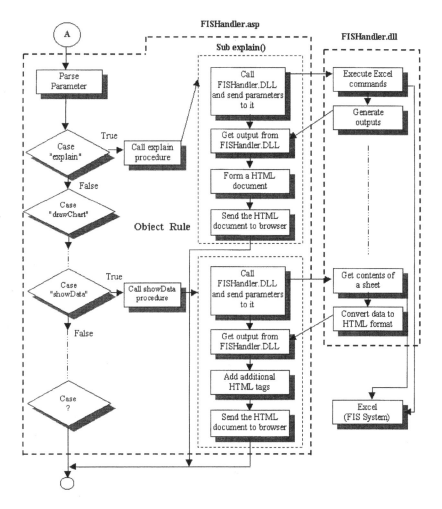

**Exhibit 7.   The Program Flow of FIS Handler (i.e., FISHandler.asp and FIS-Handler.dll)**

- To update the value of a cell, one needs this attribute to store the new value:

```
value = request.querystring("VALUE")
```

- Determine whether the command equals to "NO":

```
select case command
    case "NO"
        call Command_Rule()
```

```
        case else
            select case system
                case "FIS"
                    ' Invoke FISHandler.asp and send parameters to
                    to it
                    response.redirect "FISHandler.asp?ID=" & id &
                    "&TYPE=" & objType & "&COMMAND=" & command &
                    "&VALUE=" & V
            end select
    end select
```

- Command_Rule( ):

```
<% set conDB = server.createobject("adodb.connection")
conDB.open "DRIVER={SQL Server};SERVER=127.0.0.1;
DATABASE=TestDB", "testman", "testman"
set rsCommand = server.createobject("adodb.recordset")
' Retrieve commands based on system and type parameters
rsCommand.open "select * from Command where Type = '" &
objType & "' and System = '" & system & "'
order by Category", conDB, 1, 3
%>
' Form a HTML document and return it to browser
<html><body>
<table border>
<%
do until rsCommand.eof
  c = rsCommand("Category")
  response.write "<tr><th>" & c '    Return the HTML
                                     document to browser
  do until rsCommand("Category") <> c or rsCommand.eof
          cmd = rsCommand("Command")
%>                                 ' Return the HTML
                                     document to browser
  <td><a href="MasterHandler.asp?SYSTEM=FIS&ID=<=id%>&TYPE=
  <%=objType%>&
  COMMAND=<%=cmd" %><%=cmd%></a>
<%
          rsCommand.movenext
          if rsCommand.eof then
          response.write "</tr></table></body></html>"'
          Return the HTML document to browser
          exit do
      end if
  loop
loop                                                      %>
```

## Object_Rule

This subsection uses a flowchart to describe the structure of Object_Rule. A simple example (i.e., click on the "explain" command link) is used to explain how to program this rule. The Object_Rule is divided into sub-rules (i.e., procedures). Exhibit 8 shows the structure of the Object_Rule.

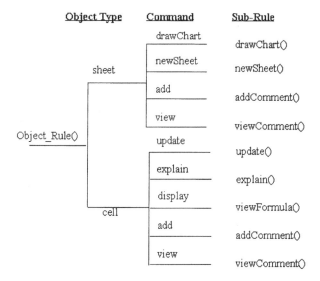

**Exhibit 8.   Object_Rule and Its Subrules**

- Click the "explain" command link of the "EPS" object. The link anchor that underlines the "explain" command is:

```
<A href="http://127.0.0.1/fis/MasterHandler.asp?SYSTEM=FIS&
ID=FL,EBIT,Y1999,E3& TYPE=CELL&
COMMAND=explain">explain</A>
```

- Parse parameters

```
objType = request.querystring("TYPE")
command = request.querystring("COMMAND")
value = request.querystring("VALUE")
id = request.querystring("ID")
temp = id
    dot = instr(temp, ",")
    category = left(temp, dot - 1)
    temp = right(temp, len(temp) - dot)
    dot = instr(temp, ",")
    subSystem = left(temp, dot - 1)
```

```
    select case objType
    case "SHEET"
    sheet = right(temp, len(temp) - dot)        'to get the name
                                                 of the selected
                                                 sheet

    case "CELL"
    temp = right(temp, len(temp) - dot)
    dot = instr(temp, ",")
    sheet = left(temp, dot - 1)          'to get the name of the
                                         sheet to which the
                                         elected cell belongs
    cell = right(temp, 2)                'to get the name of the
                                         selected cell
    end select
```

- Call explain procedure

```
select case command
    case " explain "
    call explain()
    case "drawChart"
    call drawChart()
    case " showData "
    call showData()
    ...
end select
```

- Send parameters to FISHandler.DLL and get output from FISHandler.DLL

```
sub explain()
    <html><body bgcolor=lightyellow>
    ' xlHandler is a FISHandler.DLL object variable
    <font color=blue><%=xlHandler.GetExplanation(Cell)
    %></font></body></html>
end sub
```

- Execute Excel commands: the following function is defined in FISHandler.DLL; xl is an Excel object variable

```
Public Function GetExplanation(ByVal strRange As Dtring) As
String
GetExplanation =
xl.ActiveSheet.Range(strRange).Comment.Text
End Function
```

The output of executing "explain" command is shown in Exhibit 9. Exhibits 10 through 13 show outputs of executing other commands.

**Exhibit 9. Output of Executing the "explain" Command**

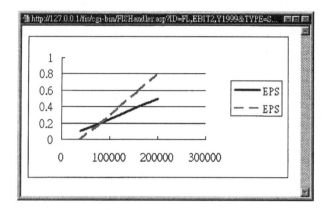

**Exhibit 10. Output of Executing the "draw chart" Command**

**Exhibit 11. Output of Executing the "view formula" Command**

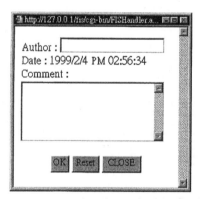

**Exhibit 12. A Form for Users to Add Comments**

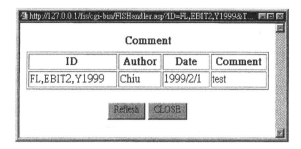

**Exhibit 13.    Output of Executing the "view comment" Command**

## CONCLUSION

The WWW presents a way to integrate hypermedia into information systems and information spaces. The authors believe that integrating the WWW with information systems in the business world should constitute a major thrust for WWW research. This will go a long way toward making applications more understandable. When reengineering applications for the WWW, dynamic relationship mapping may prove an effective way to add additional hypermedia links. This should help counteract the danger that new Web applications (especially Information systems) will have no hypertext in them.[3] The authors hope that this chapter will encourage people to think about mapping rules for better integrating the WWW and information systems.

**References**

1. Chiu, C.M. (1997). Fusing the World Wide Web and the Open Hypermedia system Technologies. Ph.D. Dissertation, Rutgers University, Newark NJ 07102.
2. Bieber, M. and Kacmar, C. (1995). Designing Hypertext Support for Computational Applications, *Communication of the ACM,* 38(8), 99–107.
3. Bieber, M. and Vitali, F. (1997). Toward Support for Hypermedia on the World Wide Web, *IEEE Computer,* 30(1), 62–70.
4. Bieber, M. (1992). Automating Hypermedia for Decision Support, *Hypermedia,* 4(2), 83–110.
5. Wan, J. (1996). Integrating Hypertext into Information Systems through Dynamic Linking, Ph.D. Dissertation, New Jersey Institute of Technology, Newark, NJ 07102.

# Chapter 21
# Integrating the Web and Enterprisewide Business Systems

*Chang-Yang Lin*

WITH THE REMARKABLE GROWTH OF THE WEB, USERS, BOTH CUSTOMERS AND EMPLOYEES, WILL INEVITABLY REQUEST THE ABILITY TO ACCESS ENTERPRISE DATA VIA THE WEB AS WELL AS TO RUN WEB-BASED ENTERPRISEWIDE APPLICATIONS. Systems development managers have many issues to consider before setting a plan in motion to satisfy these users' needs. In addition to providing background information on the Web and its capabilities, this chapter describes the four primary components of the Web. Key terms are examined, including HyperText Transfer Protocol (HTTP), HyperText Markup Language (HTML), and Uniform Resource Locator (URL). The chapter also discusses Web limitations and the "unanswered" business questions; the limitations of current technology are identified. Intranets and their use in corporate settings are examined. The chapter introduces approaches for tying the Web and enterprise systems into a coherent system. The development tools and products for the integration are also identified. Finally, the chapter presents planning issues useful in preparing for Web-based enterprisewide business applications.

## THE WEB AND ITS CAPABILITIES

The World Wide Web is a way of organizing the Internet that allows users to search for and retrieve information quickly and easily in a nonlinear way. This information is structured into small chunks, called pages, and it can be displayed page by page through electronic links. Pages may store information in a variety of formats, including numbers, text, graphic images, video, audio, and programs. Essentially, the Web is a collection of independent, yet interrelated, pages wired together by hypermedia links.

Technically, the Web is a kind of client/server networking technology for the purpose of requesting and providing services. The Web is composed of four components: clients, servers, publishing tools, and communication protocols.

### Web Clients

A Web client acts as a front-end browser for requesting service from the servers. Popular Web browsers include Netscape Navigator, Mosaic, and Microsoft's Internet Explorer. These browsers are generally equipped with graphical user interfaces (GUIs), which make Internet navigation relatively easy.

### Web Servers

A Web server is the back-end distributing system that processes and manages requests for service from the clients. Popular Web servers include Netscape's Commerce Server, Microsoft's Internet Information Server, Process Software's Purveyor, and O'Reilly and Associates' WebSite. These Web servers can be evaluated in terms of such factors as performance, security, and manageability.

### Publishing Tools

HTML is an open platform language used to define Web pages. This language includes a set of tags that must be embedded in the text to make up a hypertext document. Thus, creating an HTML page involves primarily the process of tagging documents; HTML encoding can be done by inserting the code into a standard ASCII text file, inserting tags into a word processing program, or using special software programs that build the code for the user. Such programs allow the user to select, through menu and interactive commands, the desired effects; the programs then build the appropriate HTML code.

Although word processors and other text editors can be used to create Web pages from scratch, tools specifically designed to publish Web pages are available to make working with HTML easier. Examples of these publishing products include Interleaf's Cyberleaf, SoftQuad's HotMetal Pro, InContext Systems' Spider, HTML Assistant Pro, HTMLed, and HotDog. All these products automate at least the tagging process by supporting intuitive what-you-see-is-what-you-get (WYSIWYG) screens, menu, toolbar, and drag-and-drop interfaces. In addition, some products such as Cyberleaf are equipped with utility programs able to convert Microsoft Word or WordPerfect documents into HTML pages. The capabilities of these Web publishing tools can be classified loosely into four groups:

- *HTML Editing.* These features are used to enforce HTML syntax rules and to manage the HTML tags for formatting text, designing forms, inserting URLs, and calling up photos, video clips, or sound files.

- *Fundamental Word Processing.* These features are used to create and edit the text.
- *Previewing and Testing.* These features invoke any Web browser to preview or test HTML pages in WYSIWYG form.
- *Document Conversion.* These features convert documents from plain ASCII text files or specific software-dependent files into HTML formats.

Whereas creating simple pages using these publishing tools requires no specific skills, rich and interactive online pages will require extensive knowledge and skills to integrate hyperlinks, multimedia, and embedded objects.

**Communications Protocols and URLs**

The Web depends on three protocols to facilitate communications. The Internet protocols include TCP/IP, HTTP, and URLs to communicate over the multiple networks. HTTP is the method that Web servers and Web clients use to exchange HTML pages. This method is built on the concept of hypertext/hypermedia that permits nonlinear accessing of the pages.

URLs define the unique location where a page or service can be found. An example of a URL would be http://home.netscape.com/comprod/index. html. This URL begins with the letters *http* as the transfer format, which indicates that the last portion of the address (i.e., index.html) is an HTML page. The section after ://, in this case, home.netscape.com, represents the host computer where the information is stored. This is also referred to as the "home" page or the Web site of the Netscape Communications Corporation because it can be used as the starting point to explore other pages in detail. Anyone can publish a home page or start at someone's home page. The rest of this URL is a path name to the file.

URLs do not always begin with the letters *http*. Other formats are also available, including ftp and News. Together, URLs and Internet protocols enable users to reach, in addition to the Web, other Internet resources, such as e-mail, ftp, gopher, telnet, and discussion groups via Web browsers.

**Search Engines**

In addition to the above four components, search engines are constantly being created that help users find the Web sites that store desirable information. WAIS (http://www.wais.com), InfoSeek (http://www.infoseek.com), Yahoo (http://www.yahoo.com), WebCrawler(http://www.webcrawler. com), Lycos (http://lycos.cs.cmu.edu) and SavvySearch (http://guaraldi. cs.colostate.edu:2000) are often used for Web searches. These search engines organize their own databases, start their own search mechanisms to support queries ranging from simple query statements to complex formations and even natural-language queries, and they return a list of URLs.

Without these searching machines, finding a list of desirable URLs from the vast, unstructured, uncoordinated Web resources is time-consuming and could take the users months of point-and-click navigation to assemble.

## WEB LIMITATIONS: UNANSWERED BUSINESS QUESTIONS

The Web is able to facilitate electronic business transactions. Product promotion, customer support, and electronic publishing are a few examples of functions in which Web technology has been successful. Nevertheless, from a business perspective, four fundamental questions, described below, remain unanswered. These questions have prevented many corporations from carrying out business on the Web.

- *Is the Web navigation mechanism effective*? The Web employs the hypertext mechanism for navigation. For a typical query, the user is often required to click the mouse several times to reach a desired Web site. Once arrived at the Web site, the user must do more clicking before information can be obtained. Although search engines have alleviated some of the difficulty in reaching Web sites, users are still required to do a lot of clicking and bouncing around from page to page following pre-designed links. Such a simple navigation mechanism is not flexible enough to give users more specific information and quicker responses to business queries.
- *Is the Web data structure adequate to support information reporting and query responses*? The Web employs a hypermedia data structure in which information is stored in small chunks, called pages. Text documents and other object-oriented data are fitted into these pages. However, traditional record-based business data and numerical data are not suitable for storage in pages, partly because business data, if stored in pages, cannot be easily accessible on a record-by-record basis. In addition, HTML is just not powerful enough to handle record-oriented business data, nor does it allow user-controlled queries to be easily formulated. Consequently, key information cannot be provided under present Web-based data structure.
- *Can enterprise data or legacy data be available on the Web?* To date, enterprise data—mostly transaction oriented—is stored mainly in mainframe computers. Security and performance concerns are two major reasons why enterprise data is mostly inaccessible from the Web. Methods and techniques are being developed to bring mainframe-based data into the Web. At present, these methods and techniques are not feasible and therefore transaction-related information on order status, invoice, bill of lading, and payment will remain mostly unanswered.
- *Is the Web suitable for mission-critical business applications?* The Web is not set up for online transaction processing and has failed to meet the standards of security, performance, backup, and user management.

For example, Web technology is inadequate to perform the five security-related tasks (i.e., authentication, certification, confirmation, non-repudiation, and encryption); therefore, an interactive transaction between trading partners is not reliable. Besides the security concern, other key factors have also contributed to a lack of Web-based mission-critical business applications. These factors include stateless conditions during transaction processing, questionable bandwidth to handle real interactive transactions, and lack of user preparedness for electronic commerce.

## INTRANETS

Despite a lack of legacy data on the Web and immature Web technology for effective transaction processing, an increasing number of corporations are now turning to the Web as their IS solution for addressing business problems within corporations. The key factors involved in adopting intranets are open platform standards (e.g., HTTP and HTML), ease of installing Web servers and using Web clients, and multimedia capabilities.

The range of intranet applications that can be developed is virtually unlimited. Currently, corporations are deploying intranets as a way to organize their internal communications. Examples of these intranets are

- Web-based internal e-mail systems
- Project planning, monitoring, and reporting
- Forums for brainstorming, collaborations, or problem solving
- Delivering marketing materials, training materials, or software products
- Online customer information queries
- Online human resource queries on employee benefits, company policies, personnel information, employee and telephone directories, job listings, and training and education workshops

One main concern of deploying intranet applications on the Web is security. Currently, several measures are being installed, including firewalls. Most firewall products focus on keeping external Internet users from getting into intranet applications. Others ensure that users are authorized to access the information they seek.

## INTEGRATING THE WEB AND ENTERPRISE SYSTEMS

The process of integrating the Web and enterprisewide systems or building some intranet applications can be approached from two directions. One involves converting enterprise data into hypermedia pages. The other involves building a link between these two systems. Regardless of which approach is used, the goal remains the same making enterprise data and the various business applications accessible through Web browsers. The use of Web browsers eliminates concerns about heterogeneous hardware and various operating systems over the Internet and intranets as well.

Building links to tie the Web and enterprise systems into a coherent system is much more feasible than converting to hypermedia pages. This is partly because the linkage programs will not interfere with the normal operations of enterprise systems for supporting day-to-day business activities and management decisions. Both researchers and vendors have been placing their emphasis on developing architectures and tools to support construction of the linkage programs.

## Converting to Hypermedia Pages

Enterprise systems are characterized by a variety of data structures, including traditional flat files, relational databases, IMS databases, object-oriented databases, and special package-related files (e.g., spreadsheet files, song clips, and photo images). Theoretically, this data can all be converted into hypermedia pages to support applications ranging from information inquiry to transaction processing over the Web.

Although current technology is not mature enough to support certain tasks effectively over the Web (e.g., complex interactive transaction processing), shifting key enterprise data to the Web will certainly give customers speedy query responses for such applications as marketing and electronic cataloging.

## Building Linkage Programs

Building the linkage programs to tie the Web and enterprise systems into a coherent system involves two similar approaches: augmenting HTML programs and augmenting enterprise programs.

**Augmenting HTML Programs.** The augmented HTML programs include a data-access subprogram. In addition to the data-access function, many augmented programs include programs to facilitate interactive input and to merge the enterprise data into pages for presentation. These subprograms may contain SQL statements or procedure codes, called scripts. Examples of these tools or products include DECOUX, SWOOP, OpenUI and OpenWeb, WebDBC, and Open Horizon's Connection for Java.

DECOUX supports an augmented form of HTML that includes embedded SQL statements. SWOOP supports the generation and maintenance of Web systems that store information in an ORACLE relational database. The development tools OpenUI and OpenWeb, WebDBC, and Open Horizon's Connection for Java are based on the function-call models that let developers integrate prebuilt, vendor-driven key components together using C++

or other nonprogramming tools. These tools are now being investigated for applications such as hotel reservations, payroll, and human resources.

**Augmenting Enterprise Programs with Embedded HTML Statements.** Advanced features of HTML, such as forms, are embedded into enterprise programs and are used to capture input transaction data from Web clients. The input data are then fed into enterprise programs for processing. For example, Visual Object COBOL 1.0 by Micro Focus uses CGI to link HTML forms to COBOL programs and let COBOL programs take input from HTML forms.

Besides using the above tools, Java, Sun's object-based open-system language, can be used to create the linkage programs to tie key components together. Furthermore, Java is said to be able to create Web-enabling interactive applications from scratch.

## CHALLENGES AND STRATEGY ISSUES

As commercial Web sites and users continue to grow at an incredible rate, corporations are faced with an opportunity: incorporating Web technology into enterprisewide applications to improve their competitiveness in the global market. The following is a list of questions and suggested solutions that address this opportunity:

- *How do corporations attract potential customers via the Internet and the Web*? They can build a presence on the Web, and then expand and enhance their Web pages.
- *How do corporations make enterprise data accessible via the Web to enhance service effectiveness for both employees and customers*? They can move enterprise data into a HTML format, use Web technology to connect legacy data, build search and index mechanisms to enterprise data, or develop intranet applications.
- *How do corporations deal with barriers that slow down the implementation of enterprisewide systems, such as multiplatforms, security, bandwidth, and multiple development tools*? Organizations can plan both external Web and internal Web as an ideal solution for multiplatforms or make intranets a solution for addressing internal communication concerns. They can also install security tools or firewalls to prevent unauthorized users from reaching vital legacy data or applications and implement systems to track appropriate technologies, such as Web development tools, Web servers, and security tools.
- *What strategies will corporations need to develop to remain competitive*? They can recognize the Web as one part of the IS solution, integrating traditional systems and Web-based systems. Systems development managers can support a new intranet development environment. Organizations can prepare for electronic commerce and provide staffing and training for Web technology.

Regardless of Web technology's effectiveness for certain tasks, the rapid growth of the Web and its impact in the global market should not be viewed lightly. Facing these challenges and thus effectively deploying the Web to empower users requires planning. The following sections expand on the previous suggestions, for better planning.

**Building a Presence on the Web.** Corporations should position themselves on the Internet's Web by building home pages without any delay. As competitor presence on the Web increase, one way to guarantee the failure of the above challenges is to adopt a "wait-and-see" approach.

**Expanding and Enhancing the Pages.** Simply shifting paper-based product catalogs to the pages and recording CEO's welcome messages is insufficient to attract potential customers to repeatedly visit the organization's Web sites. Corporations need to think of new ways to both enhance and expand the pages. These might include

- *Making key enterprise data accessible via Web browsers.* Enterprise data always serves as a foundation from which information can be derived. Both predesigned and ad hoc queries on key enterprise data must be considered to reflect friendliness and flexibility.
- *Providing additional services and facilities from the pages.* Examples of these services include customer and technical support; downloading reports, forms, policies and procedures, or software products; and on-line documentation. Examples of facilities include a registration form to collect user information and interests, a special form to allow users to comment on products, and a platform to facilitate interactive communications.

**Plan Intranet Applications.** How the Web is used within a corporation must be planned. Although many applications can be developed based on Web technology, those that involve communication, information sharing, and information distribution should be planned and built first.

**Preparing for Electronic Commerce.** As Web technology continues to mature, solutions designed to prevent security breaches, stateless transactions, and performance concerns will gradually become available. Thus, corporations must prepare for electronic commerce by making enterprise-wide applications—including mission-critical applications—Web-capable. This might include building Web-capable applications from scratch, linking the enterprise data to the Web, and building linkages between existing enterprise applications and the Web.

Corporations should identify and plan the projects for electronic commerce. Information reporting or inquiry projects should be built first, because linking SQL databases to the Web is easier to do. Designing special searching mechanisms on enterprise data is also necessary for fast inquiry response.

Building the linkages between existing enterprise applications and the Web can be performed next. The proven tools and techniques necessary for building such linkages should be evaluated and selected. Depending on the specific needs of the individual corporations, applications to be linked are ranked.

**Education and Training.** Both developers and users must undergo proper training for the emerging Web technology. Overall, developers and users should understand how the Internet and the Web can be accessed, used to gather information, and implemented to create business opportunities. The users who are responsible for publishing must learn HTML tools to create pages. Developers must learn the development tools to reengineer applications on the Web. Developers mastering the tools, including such programming languages as C++ and Java, will be essential for successful Web-enabled transformation.

## CONCLUSION

Web capabilities are extensive and are growing more complex and sophisticated at a rapid rate. To keep abreast of such changes, systems developers must consider such factors as security, transfer protocols and languages, and development tools and environments. All capabilities must be evaluated in the context of the enterprise—its goals as well as its propensity for risk taking. Only with a careful weighing of the advantages and disadvantages can an organization move into the technology of the World Wide Web.

# Chapter 22
# Proposed Reporting Architecture
*Wayne Thomas*

DATASOFT, INC., AN IT-CONSULTING COMPANY BASED IN MARKHAM, ONTARIO, HAS DEVELOPED A TECHNICAL APPROACH FOR CREATING REPORTING ARCHITECTURE-TYPE SYSTEMS, WHICH ARE CURRENTLY BEING USED WITH VARIOUS CLIENTS.

This methodology is used to build the three-tier reporting development and, to a lesser extent, a two-tier reporting development. We offer it to our clients, to our potential clients, and to other consulting firms to help improve the quality of systems development in today's market.

This document defines the architecture approach for implementing a report processing system that will

- Provide a flexible and productive development environment for creating, testing, and managing report definitions
- Provide flexible integration alternatives for embedding reporting capability into both client-server and Web-based applications
- Re-use complex calculations from the application middle tier and avoid duplication of calculations in the database environment
- Provide a security model that is effective for both client-server systems on a private network and Web-based applications on the public Internet
- Allow extensions to the security model to integrate custom data-driven authorization used by the main application components
- Provide a scalable *n*-tier platform that can "scale out" to support projected load profiles
- Provide a robust and easy-to-use systems management environment that can be integrated with Windows NT or Windows 2000 networks

## ARCHITECTURE OVERVIEW

Crystal Reports was selected for the Report Development environment, and XML Data Streams was used for the Data Source. (See Exhibit 1.)

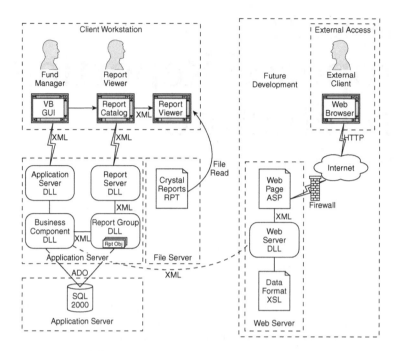

**Exhibit 1.  Reporting Architecture Overview**

## Report Development Environment: Crystal Reports 8.5

The report development environment is based on the Crystal Reports 8.5 toolset. Crystal Reports, the current industry standard for enterprise report development, provides

- Connectivity to a wide variety of data sources
- Rich features for building business logic
- Comprehensive report formatting and layout design
- High-fidelity output for the Web or print

## Data Source: ADO XML Data Streams

The architecture uses ADO XML data streams extracted from the core application business components as the data source for developing and running Crystal Reports.

In many cases, for example, where complex financial calculations are involved, DapaSoft has found that it is not practical to render reports directly from the SQL Server 2000 database. Instead, we reuse the core business components to produce XML documents to be used for formatting reports.

The primary data source for developing and running Crystal Reports is ADO recordset objects populated in the reporting middle tier, supplemented with calculated values from business components whenever necessary. We use the ADO Stream object to export the recordset contents as an XML document to be transmitted to the user's workstation. This approach enables optimal database access processing in the database server for collecting static database values, while utilizing business objects for calculated values.

In the case described in this document, we used the XML data source as a standard for *all* reports. There are no Crystal Report layouts accessing the SQL Server 2000 database directly (i.e., bypassing the middle-tier reporting architecture components).

## PROCESSING OVERVIEW

The steps described in this section refer to Exhibit 2. This diagram shows the step-by-step processing through the reporting architecture for an end user requesting a report.

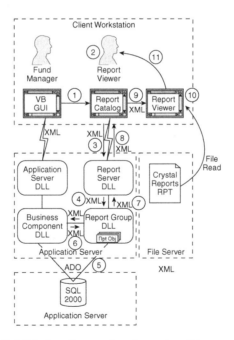

**Exhibit 2.    Processing Overview Diagram**

## Processing Overview Steps

This document section describes step-by-step processing through the reporting architecture.

1. User selects menu option, Reports, Catalog... from the main window of the application.
2. Report Catalog window appears for the user to select desired report. The list of report layouts is organized by Report Group headings. After the user selects a report layout, a pop-up window prompts the user to enter report parameters (e.g., select accounts, enter start/end dates, etc.).
3. Report Catalog submits request information to the Report Server to process the desired report with specified parameters. All request data is formatted into XML data for transmission across the network.
4. Report Server receives the report request and dispatches it to the appropriate Report Group component. Then, the Report Group component dispatches the request to the appropriate report object for processing. A single class module is created for each individual report in the system, and these class modules are packaged together within a Report Group component.
5. The Report Object loads an ActiveX Data Objects (ADO) recordset with the set of records to be included in the report. The recordset object must contain all fields that are required for the report layout. However, the recordset may contain dummy placeholder columns that will be overwritten with calculated values retrieved from the business components.
6. As needed, the Report Object interacts with business components to retrieve calculated values to overwrite dummy values in the recordset.
7. The Report Server component receives XML data from the Report Group component.
8. The Report Server component forwards the XML data to the client-side Report Catalog window.
9. Report Catalog window invokes the Report Viewer window and forwards the XML data returned from the Report Server.
10. Report Viewer loads the XML data into an ADO recordset object (i.e., with no database connection), loads the RPT file from a file server, and displays the report layout with the recordset object as a dynamic data source.
11. The end user may interact with the report content using the full functionality of the client-side Crystal Viewer control, including export processing, to a wide variety of file formats.

## CONTENT DELIVERY

Methods for content delivery include a report catalog, a report viewer, export formats, and ad hoc reporting.

### Report Catalog

The solution uses a custom report catalog application as the top-level user interface for accessing reports. This application provides a GUI for the end user to select a desired report layout and specify report parameters.

Report Catalog also controls client-server processing to send the report request to the application server and process the response dataset appropriately.

The Report Catalog application

1. Provides user interface for selecting desired report layout based on security credentials
2. Organizes report layouts by report groups
3. Provides user interface for selecting parameters from pick lists based on security credentials (e.g., manager can select accounts only from a list of related clients)
4. Transmits client-side report request to Application Server as XML data
5. Receives report dataset from Application Server as XML data
6. Launches report viewer to render report layout from XML data
7. Provides user interface for selecting desired report layout based on security credentials
8. Organizes report layouts by report groups
9. Provides user interface for selecting parameters from pick lists based on security credentials (e.g., manager can select accounts only from a list of related clients)
10. Transmits client-side report request to Application Server as XML data
11. Receives report dataset from Application Server as XML data
12. Launches report viewer to render report layout from XML data

### Report Viewer

The solution uses the client-side Crystal Viewer control to present formatted report content on the user's workstation. The report viewer control is a freely distributable client-side component that allows the user to interact with report data. The report viewer control ships with Crystal Reports and can be tightly integrated with a Visual Basic user interface application.

The report viewer enables the user to

- Navigate using a hierarchical data tree with report groups and report details
- Page forward, page back, go to end, go to beginning
- Zoom in, zoom out
- Find text

**Export Formats**

The report viewer provides built-in support for exporting high-fidelity output to a variety of popular file formats. Crystal Reports viewer control provides more than 20 different export types, as listed in Exhibit 3.

**Exhibit 3.  Export Types Available to Crystal Reports Viewer Control**

- Adobe Acrobat (PDF)
- Character-separated Values
- Comma-separated Values (CSV)
- Crystal Reports (RPT)
- Crystal Reports 7 (RPT)
- Data Interchange Format (DIF)
- Microsoft Excel
- HTML 3.2
- HTML 4.0 (DHTML)
- Lotus 1-2-3
- ODBC
- Paginated Text
- Record Style (columns of values)
- Report Definition
- Rich Text Format
- Tab-separated Text
- Tab-separated Values
- Text
- Word Format
- Word for Windows Document
- XML

**Ad Hoc Reporting**

The report catalog allows the flexible selection of report parameters based on predefined layouts. However, there are no ad hoc report creation tools in the application for end users to create custom layouts.

## REPORT DEVELOPMENT

This section outlines the stages in report development: from prototypes, through framework and standards, to templates.

### Prototypes

During the architecture phase, functional prototypes are developed for one or two reports based on the defined architecture. These technical prototypes

- Provide a technical "proof of concept" for the approach defined in this article
- Develop common application services for the reporting architecture
- Demonstrate proper interaction between software components

### Framework

Following the prototype phase, it is necessary to identify common services that will be developed and packaged as common application services. These application services provide the common "plumbing" for developing, testing, and deploying report modules.

The following framework components are required for this architecture:

- *Report Catalog*—client-side user interface for launching report requests
- *Common Windows*—for selecting report parameters (e.g., select client accounts, select high/low dates)
- *Report Viewer*—client-side window with embedded Crystal Viewer control for user interaction with report content
- *Report Server*—server-side component to receive report requests

### Standards

During the architecture phase, development standards are identified to ensure a consistent "look and feel" and a consistent implementation approach for all reporting modules. The development standards for reporting cover the following topics:

- Visual standards for "look and feel"
  — Report style options (using Report Expert in Crystal Reports)
  — Standard fonts
  — Page margins
  — Logo picture
  — Header/footer
- Data formatting standards
  — Number of decimals
  — Field alignment

- Report definition options
  - Data source configuration
  - File naming conventions
- Server-side development
  - Creating server-side module to produce reporting dataset
  - Aadding functionality to business components
  - Programming standards (e.g., error handling, dataset formatting)

## Templates

The technical prototype reports serve as "template modules" for developing reports for this project. The technical prototype provides template files demonstrating proper development of the necessary components for a report module. Components include

- Crystal Reports layout definition based on standard "look and feel" (RPT file)
- Sample stored procedure to load ADO recordset from database (SQL file)
- Sample "report object" class module to process report request (CLS file)
- Sample parameter window to capture user-specified report parameters (FRM file)

## SECURITY

The two primary responsibilities of any security architecture are user authentication and authorization. Authentication, or "logging onto the system," is the mechanism used to verify the identity of a user attempting to access the system. Authorization determines which resource(s) a particular user can access.

## Authentication

When users attempt to log on to the system, they specify their credentials (such as username and password), which the system attempts to verify. Upon successful verification of a user's credentials, the user is granted access to the system; otherwise, access is denied.

In this application architecture, the Windows 2000 or Windows NT operating system manages authentication. When the user logs into the corporate network, his or her username and password is verified against the NT user database at the domain server. Once the user has successfully logged into the domain, the application assumes that he or she is an "authenticated" system user. All application privileges are managed based on the user's authenticated network identity.

This integrated Windows 2000 authentication provides "single sign-on" capability for the application. Since the application relies on network log ins, there is no separate log in when starting the application. This avoids the user having to remember a new username and password combination.

Windows 2000 authentication eliminates the need for custom processing or administration to manage passwords. This architecture relies on the password authentication and management functions of the Windows 2000 operating system.

However, DapaSoft developed a custom application to manage usernames in the application database (i.e., without passwords). The custom application also manages user groups and the assignment of usernames into user groups.

**Authorization**

Authorization determines which actions a user can perform on a particular resource and prevents unauthorized access or actions from occurring on a resource.

This security architecture supports management of system privileges for user groups (a set of individual users) and for individual users. User groups provide a convenient mechanism for assigning system privileges to a predefined set of users. When setting access permissions for a privilege, the administrator can grant permission to a group of users rather than assigning them for each individual user.

This solution includes a custom common application service to support "data-driven" authorization for accessing system resources. This data-driven authorization component provides check-access privileges for application objects (forms, reports, and occasionally specific processing functions) and for specific client accounts based on a hierarchical organization of fund managers (i.e., users).

Within the reporting architecture, this custom authorization component allows the system to

- Display only authorized reports for selection in the report catalog window
- Display only authorized client accounts for report parameters in the pick-list windows
- Check authorization in the report server data definition language (DLL) as needed, to verify that users have access to client accounts
- Return a list of authorized client IDs in the business components for building database queries

A custom administration application was developed to manage the assignment of system privileges to user groups or individual usernames. However, this security administration application does not manage the assignment of client accounts to fund managers. Instead, assignment of client accounts to fund managers is managed by mainline application windows.

## INFRASTRUCTURE SERVICES

This reporting architecture is built on a sophisticated $n$-tier architecture that provides the scalability and uptime required for mission-critical applications. Infrastructure services provide a robust backbone for scalability and reliability.

### Multiserver

Multiserver support is a critical component of a scalable architecture. The ability to split server components and attach them to multiple physical machines allows an organization selectively and incrementally to add hardware resources where they will have maximum impact.

This application will be built on a distributed component architecture. This means that individual system components can be decoupled and spread across multiple machines in a single deployment.

### Load Balancing

Intelligent load balancing algorithms eliminate bottlenecks and maximize hardware efficiency. In a multiserver environment, balancing load efficiently across multiple machines greatly enhances scalability and end-user response time. Load balancing also ensures effective use of hardware and minimizes performance bottlenecks.

The distributed component architecture for this application enables load balancing to spread application processing across a server farm of cloned hardware.

### Caching

This reporting architecture approach does not support caching of report data. Most reporting requests require real-time portfolio data, and a caching implementation could result in stale report data.

Each report request is generated with fresh data from the business components and the SQL Server 2000 database.

## FUTURE CONSIDERATIONS

### Report Scheduling

In the future, report request scheduling may become a requirement for large client site installations. Report scheduling would allow report processing to be deferred to execute in an offline environment (e.g., overnight). A report scheduler that enables regular scheduled execution of standard reports and on-demand scheduling for specific reports can significantly reduce database contention during peak online periods.

Many standard reports could be scheduled to execute at regular recurring intervals. For example, each fund manager could set up a nightly scheduled report to summarize portfolio performance for all related clients as of the previous business day. This standard report could be configured to arrive in his/her email to be reviewed each morning or sent directly to a specified printer for hardcopy output.

In addition, users could request reports to run in an offline mode if the report would place a heavy load on the online environment. For on-demand report requests, users must be able to specify the following runtime parameters:

- Execution date/time
- Report layout
- Report parameters (e.g., client ID, high date, low date)
- Delivery mode (printer, e-mail, file export)

Report scheduling requires a mechanism for saving preprocessed reports and retrieving report results in a desired format. The storage system would likely be based on a file server directory structure containing XML dataset files. These dataset files could be accessed by user requests and rendered into the desired report format.

This storage and retrieval mechanism would require a nightly and weekly data maintenance application to purge expired report files from the directory structure, and possibly archive results to an inexpensive media.

## CONCLUSION

For large client site installations, it should be possible to move reporting requirements to a replicated reporting database. This would substantially reduce system load on the main application database.

A reporting database could be configured to receive replication packages from the main application database in "near real time" using SQL

Server transactional replication. The delay between data updates in the main database and the replication of updates to the reporting database would generally be less than one minute. However, there is no guarantee of replication delivery time.

We have built the reporting architecture to allow a configuration setting for report requests to use an alternate database connection for the reporting database. With this approach, a reporting database could be implemented in the future with minimal rework to the reporting architecture and reporting components.

# Chapter 23
# Publishing Host Data Using 3270-to-HTML Conversion

*Carlson Colomb*

THE INTERNET AGE HAS TRANSFORMED THE FACE OF BUSINESS. The explosion of the Internet has underlined the public's demand for 24/7 access to information. And it is this same technology and demand for information that now drives business-to-business transactions around the globe. With an estimated 70 percent of corporate data residing on legacy host systems, it only makes sense to leverage this valuable source of information to fulfill this demand. Now, corporations can use 3270-to-HTML conversion products to extend host-based information to their employees, partners, suppliers, and customers. By bringing host data right to users' Web browsers, corporations are realizing tremendous savings through efficiencies and new revenue opportunities. In fact, utilizing existing host applications and extending the reach of those applications provides an extremely high return on IS investments. By leveraging legacy systems, enterprises benefit from a new application portfolio without the high cost needed to design, develop, test, and roll out new applications. In addition, 3270-to-HTML conversion solutions can be implemented much faster than new host application development or rewrite.

Web-enabling SNA applications via 3270-to-HTML conversion is uncomplicated, flexible, highly cost-effective, and proven. Eicon's Aviva Web-to-Host Server, Novell's HostPublisher, and Attachmate's Host Publishing System are leading examples of this technology that permit SNA applications running on a mainframe to be readily accessed from within a standard Web browser. These products can essentially provide two levels of rejuvenation capability for Web-enabled host access, without having to change the original host application. First, they can provide an out-of-the-box, on-the-fly 3270-to-HTML conversion that provides a simple "default" rejuvenation of the dated "green-on-black" 3270 user interface used by most SNA applications, which

**Host Green Screen**

**"On-the-fly" Conversion**

**Complete Rejuvenation Example**

**Exhibit 1. Eicon's Aviva Web-to-Host Server**

may be useful for certain intranet users. Second, and where the *true strength* of 3270-to-HTML conversion lies, is enabling companies to develop completely custom rejuvenation of the "green-screen," into a more intuitive contemporary Web page interface within a Web browser. The end result is so remarkable and transparent that users are unable to distinguish that the data provided to them in the Web page resides on one or more legacy applications written a decade ago. That is the power of 3270-to-HTML conversion: SNA applications appear as custom and modern Web pages (Exhibit 1).

## FLEXIBLE TO SERVE MANY USES AND USERS

Diverse user groups each have differing needs for host data, and the application possibilities for 3270-to-HTML conversion are virtually limitless. 3270-to-HTML conversion is most often implemented for users external to the enterprise or for users who require occasional access to information. It is best suited for providing access to limited, select, and specific host data for an end-user base that is not familiar with navigating host applications and requires only quick transaction-based access to certain host data. Although such users are typically found in E-commerce scenarios (e.g., transacting with customers over the Internet), there are also numerous cases of such user requirements in E-business type scenarios with partners/suppliers, or internal uses such as mobile employees or smaller remote offices. And so, Web browser users can access data center resources across intranets, extranets, and the Internet.

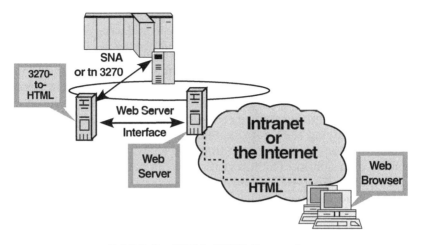

**Exhibit 2.   3270-to-HTML Conversion**

Another advantage of 3270-to-HTML conversion is that the end-user desktop does not have to meet any minimum requirements for, say, running Java or ActiveX. All that is required is that the end user have a browser; thus, virtually any operating environment is supported: DOS, 16- or 32-bit Windows, OS/2, UNIX, Linux, and even Mac. This is especially critical for E-commerce and some E-business applications where there is little or no control over the end-user computers. Thus, the customer/user base is not limited to those with a given browser or OS. And equally important in E-commerce and E-business is security. 3270-to-HTML conversion, due to its very nature, supports industry-standard SSL security through the connection between the Web server and the end user's Web browser. Further security is also realized thanks to the nature of the 3270-to-HTML conversion; since the technology only extracts certain host data and there is no "direct" connection with the host, users cannot access other confidential host data.

## SIMPLE YET POWERFUL ARCHITECTURE

3270-to-HTML conversion is a gateway function usually performed on a Web server (Exhibit 2). After the user submits data in a form on the Web browser, it is delivered to the gateway by a Web server in Internet-standard HyperText Markup Language (HTML). The gateway converts this HTML request into a 3270 data stream, over SNA or tn3270, to the host application, subject to the necessary authentication and security measures. The host application responds to the request by automatically navigating to one or more 3270 screens that contain the desired data. These data are extracted and communicated to the gateway, which formats it to HTML as desired and then passes it to the Web server for delivery to the browser user. Of course, 3270-to-HTML conversion implementation can be either unidirectional (read-only) or bidirectional (read and write) so that information that is accessed can be updated from the Web browser interface.

Web pages can be custom designed to include data from one or more data sources. 3270-to-HTML conversion offers a variety of data integration options. Thus, it can also integrate nearly any back-end data source without the need for application rewrite or new application development. Instead of modifying each data system for Web access, one can install a 3270-to-HTML conversion product that also allows interfaces to 5250, VT, and ODBC data access. The integration of the back-end systems is performed on the 3270-to-HTML conversion server, resulting in HTML being delivered to the Web server where the Web page is customized.

## ADVANTAGES OF 3270-TO-HTML CONVERSION

The advantages of 3270-to-HTML conversion includes

- Host applications residing on a mainframe are Web-enabled
- AutoGUI tools and scripting permit custom rejuvenation of the user interface without changing the host application
- The ability to consolidate data from multiple hosts, multiple host applications, and other data sources within a single Web page
- No client software required at the user workstation other than a standard Web browser (zero deployment)
- Browser and client operating system independence via pure HTML output (PCs, Macs, UNIX workstations, Windows CE, etc.)
- Works with standard Web server-based security and encryption schemes, such as SSL; permits persistent user sessions and user authentication; further security because the user never logs "directly" on to the host
- Configuration management centralized on the Web server and remotely accessible by administrator
- Reduced cost of ownership due to centralized installation; it is not necessary to update workstations, as they simply use their browsers
- No learning curve due to completely familiar data presentation through customizable intuitive Web page interface, resulting in decreased user-training costs
- Faster time to market through low-cost, simple, and virtually overnight "augmentation" of host applications, eliminating the need for time-consuming and costly rewriting of host applications
- Extends proven and established data center applications to the Web for E-commerce and E-business
- Replace existing private multi-protocol networks used to interconnect remote offices with corporate headquarters by Internet-based and cost-effective Web-to-host access

## 3270-TO-HTML CONVERSION APPLICATION SCENARIOS

Web-to-host integration technology can be profitably used to synergistically bring together proven data center applications and new Web-based users in a plethora of different scenarios ranging from purely in-house intranet-specific situations to E-commerce initiatives that straddle the globe. Some examples of high-return-on-investment uses for today's proven Web-to-host integration technology follow.

### Online Trust Management

Many banks provide a variety of trust management services for some clientele. Often, a trust fund will consist of underlying stocks, bonds, mutual funds, and real estate holdings. Understandably, fund owners require up-to-date status checks on the performances of their trust funds. Typically, banks use mainframe applications to manage these trust funds. Many banks require trust fund clients to either call or visit the bank and talk to a trust fund manager to gain the information they require. This approach is inconvenient for the clients and inefficient, disrupting the trust manager's schedule and tasks.

A more ideal solution is available through 3270-to-HTML conversion, which can be used very effectively to provide trust fund clients with easy, realtime access to trust fund information. It has all the necessary security features to guarantee that only authorized users can gain access to the data, and that all data being conveyed across the Internet is securely encrypted on an end-to-end basis. The user interface seen by the trust fund clients is presented as a contemporary Web page of a "point-and-click" nature. Finally, since the mainframe access is across the Internet, the trust fund clients will only require a standard Internet connection to reach the bank. This access will not require any special software — just a standard Web browser.

The result is a secure and easy-to-implement Web-based access to trust fund status that eliminates the need for trust fund holders to regularly call or visit the bank trust fund manager to obtain information on their trust funds. This improves trust fund client satisfaction by providing fast access to required data, and increases savings through better allocation of trust fund management time.

### Courier Parcel Tracking Service

Thanks, partially, to the Internet facilitating global business, there is a strong and growing demand around the world for freight and expedited package delivery services. Commercial airlines augment their passenger revenues by transporting freight and urgent packages. There are also traditional cargo-carrying van lines (e.g., National Van Lines, Atlas, etc.) and specialized expedited package delivery companies (e.g., FedEx, UPS, etc.).

Such companies usually rely on mainframe applications to track freight movement and delivery status. With enormous volumes of freight and packages being delivered to all corners of the globe, around the clock, there is constant demand for up-to-date information on shipment status. In the past, call centers were the only means these companies used to address queries for shipment status. Shippers or customers awaiting freight/packages would phone the call center, quote a parcel number, and then have a representative track the progress of that item using a mainframe application.

With today's popularity of the Internet, 3270-to-HTML conversion provides a more cost-effective means to provide parcel tracking. Customers are able to directly access the requisite information just by entering the parcel number(s) into a specified input field on an easy-to-use Web page incorporating 3270-to-HTML conversion technology. Rather than phoning a call center, customers are able to get all the information they want online, 24/7 across the Web — quickly, securely, and effortlessly — without having to wait patiently "on hold" until "the next available operator" can take the call. Thus, customer satisfaction is increased via self-serve access to delivery data, while freight companies realize significant cost savings by scaling back their call center operations.

### Government Agencies Publishing Public Information

Many local and state governments and their associated agencies maintain large and diverse databases of public domain information on IBM mainframes. For example, a particular State Department maintains its entire library of land zoning, property plot plans, and building layout maps on a central mainframe. This information, which one would expect to find in a "map room" at a local authority, is nonclassified, public domain information that is open to any member of the public. Providing the general public with direct access to such mainframe information, across the Internet via a standard Web browser, eliminates the need to visit or call the local authority. Given that U.S. public libraries now offer free Internet access, providing this type of host information via the Web is a complementary and logical approach. It ensures fast and efficient service, eliminating delays associated with trying to gain this type of data via the telephone, fax, or mail. Providing such data over the Web also satisfies the charter that most states have already instituted to make as much of their data Web-accessible, as soon as possible.

Governments can thus better serve their public by making public information more readily available. The public no longer needs to be constrained by the limited government "open hours" of operation, and can access information at any time. 3270-to-HTML conversion has provided an inexpensive, easy-to-implement, near-zero maintenance solution that enables the general public access to data to which they are entitled, over the Web, in a user-friendly interface, without the need for either any special software at the client end or any specialized hardware.

### Web-Enabling Automobile Dealer-to-Manufacturer Communications

Automobile manufacturers have chains of dealerships worldwide that sell and service the manufacturer's automobiles in addition to supplying customers with parts or accessories they might require. These dealerships require constant online access to the manufacturer's mainframe host systems to look up parts, order parts, order new automobiles, check on delivery schedules, and reconcile financial accounts. Typically, dealers need to purchase IBM-specific communications adapters and emulation software for multiple PCs and then use dial-up connections to realize host access. Some of the larger dealerships might have dumb terminals, 3270 control units, and even expensive leased lines, which are old, unreliable, slow, and very expensive to maintain.

3270-to-HTML conversion PC-to-mainframe access across the Internet will provide these dealerships with the host access they require without the complexity, cost, or unreliability of what they have today. Using 3270-to-HTML conversion, automobile manufacturers need not change host applications in any way. Dealers will require simple PCs with standard Web browsers and local Internet connections through an Internet service provider (ISP). Manufacturer host data can be accessed directly from the dealership user's Web browser, appearing as a user-friendly Web page. Increased user efficiency and reduced user training time are realized. But even greater benefits result from increased reliability and reduced complexity and maintenance costs of dealer-to-manufacturer communications.

### Web-Based Access to Host Data for Mobile Salesforce

Mobile salespeople in the field require online access to customer accounts, product pricing, and availability data. In many corporations, this data is stored on host systems. Many salespeople rely on printed materials or telephone communications in order to receive such information. However, printed documents can quickly become out of date and thus prevent giving a specific customer the most competitive price. Similarly, product managers or accounts receivable personnel may not be available when the salesperson calls for information, and cannot function as a "salesforce call center." Often, salespeople must make numerous sales visits to a given customer in order to deliver price quotes or delivery dates piecemeal. The result is poor salesforce efficiency due to longer sales cycles, increased cost of sales due to increased number of visits, increased risk of competitors stealing business, and lost opportunity costs.

3270-to-HTML conversion allows salespeople to benefit from having direct access to required host information in realtime over the Internet, while at the customer site. Easy-to-use Web page interfaces provided by 3270-to-HTML conversion allow salespeople to access the necessary host data by simply dialing a mobile ISP account (e.g., AT&T Business Internet Services) while at the customer location. In addition, because 3270-to-HTML conversion delivers pure HTML, this Web-to-host access is available through "thin" Web browsers, such as Microsoft's Pocket Internet Explorer for Windows CE portable computers. With 3270-to-HTML conversion, Web pages can be designed to fit the screen size of the palm-sized or hand-held devices running Windows CE that are popular with mobile salespeople.

Armed with direct access to current information, salespeople can react faster to customer questions and arguments and provide firm price quotes and delivery dates with confidence, while on site. A knowledgeable and confident sales representative often wins the business. Similarly, this sales representative knows when to walk away from a potentially money-losing sales agreement.

### Online Access to Student and Curriculum Information

Many academic institutions maintain much of their student information (e.g., grades, courses taken, requirements for graduation) plus their course curriculums on mainframe host computers. Since mainframe access, until now, has required special emulation software (or equipment), academic institutions did not provide students with direct access to the information maintained on the mainframes. Instead, students had to either visit or call an administrative center and talk to a representative to get information about their courses, performance, or academic requirements. Considering the number of students in the average college-level institution, this one-on-one type of administrative service is costly, requiring multiple representatives to handle student queries. In addition, in order to attract new students, including foreign students, these institutions need to publicize their curriculums with as much detail as possible.

3270-to-HTML conversion provides a very easy mechanism for existing and prospective students to gain authorized, secure, and monitored access to mainframe-based data. By enabling mainframe access across the Web, existing students can check and print their academic reports online, using their current Web browser. Prospective students from around the globe and existing students can also investigate curriculums and course details, across the Web, and even register to attend courses. This allows the academic institution the ability to significantly reduce administrative costs, provide better service to students, and easily extend the target market for the university/college to cover the world.

## CONCLUSION

3270-to-HTML products are a versatile, secure, and cost-effective means to publish host data to new user groups. They allow corporations to leverage and extend their existing host applications for uses that go far beyond their original design, without changing a line of code. A synergistic relationship results from melding the vast wealth of twentieth-century data center resources with twenty-first century Web technologies in order to deliver unprecedented access to information. 3270-to-HTML conversion can effortlessly serve various types of applications and user groups, from lucrative Internet-based E-commerce initiatives, to achieving partner efficiencies via E-business, or even internal users by slashing networking costs and making host information mobile. With 3270-to-HTML conversion solutions currently available and proven — from such notable vendors as Eicon Technology, Novell, and Attachmate — the time has come for corporations to realize the true potential of their data centers.

# Section V
# Internet Variations and Applications

This section explores some of the popular enhancements to the Internet and Web applications. Intranets, in particular, are powerful business enablers that provide the benefit of the Internet to organizations (e.g., a standard use of a Web browser as an application interface), while protecting against some of the common exposures (e.g., security threats). Intranets have the capacity to bring a lot of the core internal corporate applications under a single umbrella. This includes such processes as Human Resource (HR) systems, time and expenses (T&E), purchasing modules, invoicing, and employee benefit enrollment.

"Implementing and Supporting Extranets" discusses architecture, policy, and approaches that are necessary to securely handle extranets in organizations. An extranet connects two or more separate LAN/WANs from different business sources.

"Challenges of Intranet Implementation" examines four primary challenges to intranet implementation and describes methods of dealing with these.

"Application Servers: Next Wave in Corporate Intranets and Internet Access" shows how to seamlessly tie Web servers, host applications, and client/server solutions to produce corporate application servers that service internal and external users.

"Web Site Design and Performance for Intranets" offers guidelines for efficient and effective Web site design and operation to reduce overall costs.

"Managing Risk in an Intranet Environment" explains how to identify, analyze, and control risks while building, implementing, and operating intranets in the corporate environment.

# Chapter 24
# Implementing and Supporting Extranets
*Phillip Q. Maier*

EXTRANETS HAVE BEEN AROUND AS LONG AS THE FIRST RUDIMENTARY LAN-TO-LAN NET-WORKS BEGAN CONNECTING TWO DIFFERENT BUSINESS ENTITIES TOGETHER TO FORM WANS. In its basic form, an extranet is the interconnection of two previous separate LANs or WANs with origins from different business entities. This term emerged to differentiate between the previous definitions of external "Internet" connection and just a company's internal intranet. Exhibit 1 depicts an extranet as a Venn diagram, where the intersection of two (or more) nets form the extranet. The network in this intersection was previously part of the "intranet" and has now been made accessible to external parties.

Under this design, one of the simplest definitions comes from R.H. Baker: "An extranet is an intranet that is open to selective access by outside parties."[1] The critical security concept of the extranet is the new network area that was previously excluded from external access now being made available to some external party or group. The critical security issue evolves from the potential vulnerability of allowing more than the intended party, or allowing more access than was intended originally for the extranet. These critical areas will be addressed in this chapter, from basic extranet set-up to more complex methods and some of the ongoing support issues.

The rapid adoption of the extranet will change how a business looks at its security practices, as the old paradigm of a hard outer security shell for a business LAN environment has now been disassembled or breached with a hole to support the need for extranets. In many cases, the age-old firewall will remain in place, but it will have to be modified to allow this "hole" for the extranet to enable access to some degree for internal resources that have now been deemed part of the extranet.

Recognizing the growth of extranets as a common part of doing business today is important, and therefore the business enterprise must be ready with architectures, policy, and approaches to handle the introduction of

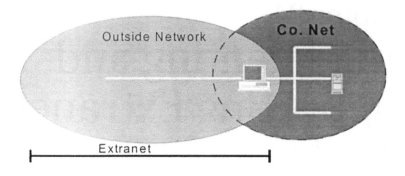

**Exhibit 1.    Extranet Venn Diagram**

extranets into its environment. A few of the considerations are the require-ments-versus-security balance, policy considerations, risk assessments, as well as implementation and maintenance costs.

From a requirements-versus-security balance standpoint, the issue is the initial claim by business that extranets are an immediate need and abso-lutely must be established "if we are to remain competitive." But from a secu-rity standpoint, such a drastic change to the environment, which may not have had any form of an extranet in place, may well be throwing its financial data assets out the door with the first implementation of an extranet. There-fore, care must be taken from a security perspective and put in balance with the claimed business need for an extranet implementation.

One of the first areas of review and (possibly) update is the inner com-pany's security policy. This policy most likely was not written with extra-nets in mind and thus may need modification if a common security philos-ophy is to be established regarding how a company can securely implement extranets. However, the policy review does not stop with one company's review of its own policy, but also includes connecting the company or com-panies on the outside. In the case of strategic business relationships that will be ongoing, it is important that both parties fully understand each other's responsibilities for the extranet, what traffic they will and will not pass over the joined link — what degree of access and by whom will occur over this link.

Part of any company's policy on extranets must include an initial requirement for a security risk assessment. The main question is: What additional levels of risk or network vulnerability will be introduced with the implementation of the proposed extranet? As well as vulnerability assessment, a performance assessment should be conducted to assist in the design of the extranet to ensure that the proposed architecture not only addresses the security risk but that it also will meet performance expectations. Some of the questions to be asked in a combined security and performance assessment should be:

- Data classification/value of data
- Data location(s) in the network
- Internal users access requirements to extranet components (internal access design)
- Data accessibility by time of day (for estimating support costs)
- Protocol, access services used to enter extranet (network design implications)
- Degree of exposure by transmission mechanism (Internet, private net, wireless transmission)
- End-user environment (dial-up, Internet)
- Number of users, total/expectation for concurrent users access (line sizing)
- Growth rate of user base (for estimating administrative costs)
- CONUS (continental U.S.), international access (encryption implications)

The risk and performance assessment would, of course, be followed by a risk mitigation plan, which comes in the form of selecting an acceptable extranet architecture and identifying the costs. The cost aspect of this plan is, of course, one of the critical drivers in the business decision to implement an extranet. Is the cost of implementing and maintaining the extranet (in a secure manner) less than the benefit gained by putting the extranet in place? This cost must include the costs associated with implementing it securely; otherwise, the full costs will not be realistically reflected.

Finally, the member company implementing the extranet must have a clear set of architectures that best mitigate the identified vulnerabilities, at the least cost, without introducing an unacceptable degree of risk into its computing environment. The following section reviews various extranet architectures, each with differing costs and degrees of risk to the environment.

## EXTRANET ARCHITECTURES

### Router-Based Extranet Architecture

The earliest extranet implementations were created with network routers that have the capability to be programmed with rudimentary "access control lists" or rules. These rules were implemented based solely on TCP/IP addresses. A rule could be written to allow external user A access to a given computer B, where B may have been previously unreachable due to some form of private enterprise network firewall (and in the early days, this firewall may have been a router also). Exhibit 2 depicts this very basic extranet. A more realistic rule can be written, where all computers in an

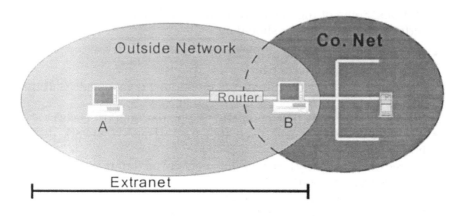

**Exhibit 2.    Basic Extranet with Router**

"outside network" are allowed to access computer B in a company network, thus forming an extranet. This is depicted in Exhibit 3.

As network security architectures matured, routers as the sole network access control device were replaced by more specific security mechanisms. Routers were originally intended as network devices — and not as security mechanisms — and lost functionality as more and more security rules were placed in them. Additionally, the security rules that were put into them were based on TCP/IP addresses, which were found to be subject to spoofing/masquerading and thus deemed ineffective in positively identifying the real external device being granted access. Therefore, routers alone do not provide an entirely secure extranet implementation, but when

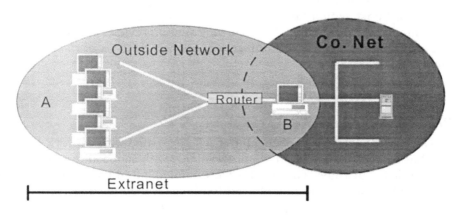

**Exhibit 3.    More Realistic Extranet**

used in conjunction with one of the following extranet architectures, routers can be a component to add some degree of security, but only when used in conjunction with other network security devices.

## Application Gateway Firewalls

As network security architectures matured, the introduction of application layer gateway firewalls, a software tool on a dedicated machine, usually dual homed (two network interfaces, one internal, one external), became the more accepted external protection tool. These software tools have the ability not only to perform router-type functions with access control rules, but also to provide user authentication services on a per-user basis. This user authentication can take the form of an internal user authentication list, or an external authentication call to token-based authentication services, such as the ACE SecureID™ system. Exhibit 4 depicts this type of architecture setup to support an extranet using an a application layer gateway firewall to enable authenticated users inward access to an enterprise in a controlled manner.

In addition to supporting access control by IP address and user, some gateways have the further capability to restrict access by specific TCP/IP service port, such as port 80, HTTP, so the extranet users can only access the internal resource on the specific application port, and not expose the internal machine to any greater vulnerability than necessary.

Follow-on application layer gateway implementations have since emerged to provide varying additional degrees of extranet connectivity and security. One such method is the implementation of a proxy mechanism from an outside network to a portion of an internal company network. Normally, a proxy

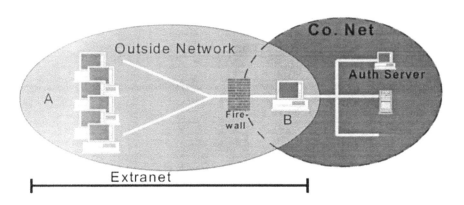

**Exhibit 4. Extranet Using an Application Layer Gateway Firewall**

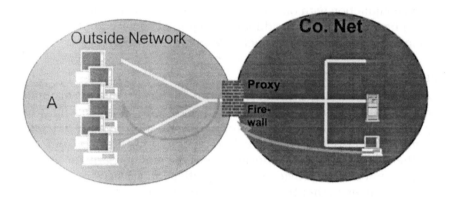

**Exhibit 5.   Outbound Proxy Architecture**

performs control and address translation for access from an intranet to the external Internet. These types of proxies normally reside on the firewall, and all user access to the Internet is directed through the proxy. The proxy has the ability to exert access control over who in the intranet is allowed external access, as well as where they can go on the Internet. The proxy also provides address translation, such that the access packet going to the Internet is stripped of the user's original internal address, and only the external gateway address of the enterprise is seen on the packet as it traverses the Internet. Exhibit 5 depicts these proxy functions.

The proxy provides both security and network address functional although the entire process can be used in its reverse to provide an extranet architecture, because of its ability to provide access rules over who can use the proxy and where these proxy users are allowed to go, or what resources they can access. Exhibit 6 depicts a *reverse proxy* extranet architecture.

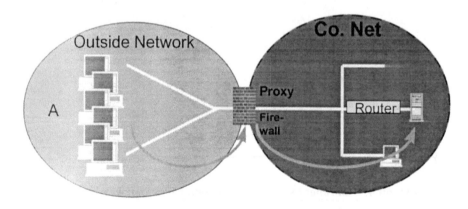

**Exhibit 6.   Reserve Proxy Extranet Architecture**

Today, most proxies are set up for HTTP or HTTP-S access, although application layer gateway proxies exist for most popular Internet access services (telnet, ftp, sql, etc.). One of the major issues with proxy servers, however, is the amount of cycle time or machine overhead it takes to manage many concurrent proxy sessions through a single gateway. With highly scalable hardware and optimized proxy software, it can be carried to potentially handle high user demands but the system architecture must be specifically designed for high loads to be able to meet user response expectations, while still providing the security of an authenticated proxy architecture. On the *inward* proxy depicted in Exhibit 6, the proxy can be configured to allow access to only a single internal resource on a given TCP/IP port. Further protection can be added to this reverse proxy architecture by putting the target internal resource behind a router with specific access control rules, limiting the portion on the company intranet that inbound proxies can reach, which can ensure limited access on the intranet; should the internal machine ever be compromised, it cannot be used as a 'jumping off point' into the rest of company intranet.

A somewhat *hybrid* architecture extranet, where some firewall controls are put in place but the external user is not granted direct inward access to an enterprise's internal domain, has been evolving and put in place as a more popular extranet implementation. In this architecture, the external user is granted access to an external resource (something outside of the enterprise firewall), but still on the property of the enterprise. Then, this external resource is granted access to one or more internal resources through the enterprise firewall. This architecture is based on minimizing the full external access to the intranet, but still makes intranet-based data available to external users. The most popular implementation is to place an authenticating Web server outside the firewall, and program it make the data queries to an internal resource on the enterprise intranet, over a specific port and via a specific firewall rule, allowing only that one external resource to have access to the one internal resource, thus reducing the external exposure of the intranet. Exhibit 7 depicts this type of extranet.

Issues with this type of architecture include reliance on a single user interface that can be safely placed outside the enterprise firewall, which makes it vulnerable to attack. Additionally, there is the issue of whether tight enough access rules can be placed on the access method between the external user interface resource (the Web server in this example) and the internal resources that it needs access to on the protected enterprise intranet. If these two issues can be safely addressed, then this form of extranet can be very useful for an enterprise extranet, with a high volume or varied user base, and a large intranet-based data repository.

The user front end has been deployed as a Web server, usually SSL enabled to ensure data integrity and protection by encrypting the data as

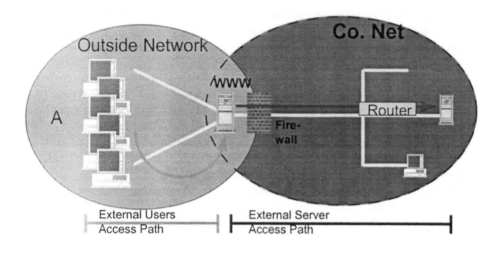

**Exhibit 7. Extranet with Athenticating Web Server**

it passes over an external SSL link. Access to this external server is also associated with some form of user authentication, either a static ID and password over the SSL link, and more recently with client digital certificates, where each individual accessing the SSL-enabled site is issued his own unique digital certificate from an acknowledged certificate authority, thereby validating his identity. Each client maintains its own digital certificate, with the Web server having some record of the public-key portion of the client's digital certificate, either directly in the Web server internally, or accessible from a standalone directory server (usually LDAP reachable).

The most recent entrant in the extranet architecture arena is the Virtual Private Network (VPN). This architecture is based on a *software tunnel* established between some external entity, either client or external network, and a gateway VPN server. Exhibit 8 depicts both types of VPN architectures. External network A has a VPN server at its boarder, which encrypts all traffic targeted for company network C, this would be a gateway-to-gateway VPN. Or, external client B may have client VPN software on his workstation which would enable him to establish a single VPN tunnel from his workstation over the external network to company C's VPN server.

Although both server-to-server VPN and client-to-server VPN architectures are offered in the industry today, it is this author's experience that the more popular extranet architect is the client-to-server VPN architecture, as it offers the most flexibility for the most diverse audience of external users. This flexibility does add to the complexity of the implementation, as it can potentially involve a large number of external desktops, all with differing configurations. The benefits of VPNs include the ability to safely traverse

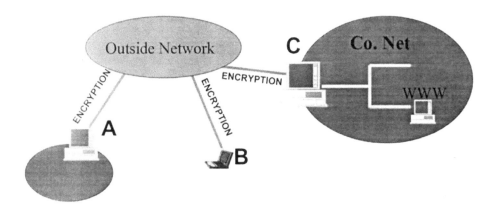

**Exhibit 8.    VPN Architectures**

external public networks, with some assurance of data integrity and authentication as part of the VPN implementation. This architecture shows the most promise to meet the needs of extranets, and cost savings for a world hungry for connectivity over public/external networks, although it still has some growing pains to go through to reach full product maturity.

An emerging standard for VPNs is coming out of the ITEF IPSec implementation, which draws a roadmap for the next-generation TCP/IP security protocol. Under this protocol, standards are being drafted that will enable differing devices to securely communicate under a pre-agreed upon security protocol, including key exchange for encryption and standardized authentication. Today, there are IPSec-compliant products on the market; however, the standard is still evolving and tests are being conducted to evaluate differing vendor compatibilities with each under the IPSec standards. One of the leading initiatives to evaluate this compliance is the Automotive Network Exchange (ANX) test, which is intended to establish a large extranet environment between the core automotive manufacturers and their vendors.

In the meantime, there is a wide variety of VPN product vendors on the market — some touting IPSec compliance and others with proprietary implementations, with IPSec in their future product roadmap, choosing to wait until the standard stabilizes. The recommendation is to either select a vendor offering IPSec if it has some degree of maturity within its own product line, or one that is planning on adopting the standard: IPSec appears to be a viable standard once it fully matures.

Regardless of whatever VPN solution is being considered for implementing secure extranets, a few technical considerations must be understood and planned for before selecting and implementing a VPN extranet architecture.

**Scalability.** Similar to proxy servers, VPN servers incur a fair amount of processing overhead that consumes processing resources as high levels of concurrent VPN sessions pass through a single server. It is important to attempt to estimate one's projected user base and current access to appropriately size a VPN server. Some servers are established on lower-level processors for smaller environments, and should not be implemented where high concurrent access rates are expected, although there is some benefit to physical load balancing, spreading the access among multiple servers. However, there is also concern about implementing too many servers to easily manage. A balance between installing a single large server and creating a single point of failure — versus implementing many smaller servers — creates an administrative nightmare.

**Multi-Homed Intranets and Address Translation.** In large intranet environments, many operate under a *split DNS* (domain naming structure), where intranet addresses are not "advertised" to the external networks, and external addresses are kept external, so as not to flood the internal network. Additionally, many larger intranet environments have multiple gateways to external networks. If one of the gateways is established with a VPN gateway and an external client makes a connection to the internal intranet, it is important that the tunnel comes in through the appropriate VPN gateway, but also that the return traffic goes back out through that same gateway so that it gets re-encrypted and properly returned to the external VPN client. Exhibit 9 depicts the correct traffic patterns for a multi-homed intranet with a single VPN gateway and an external VPN client.

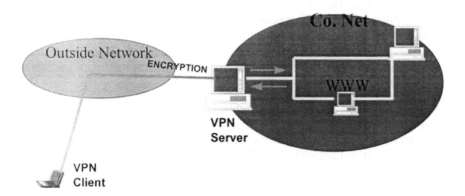

**Exhibit 9.   Traffic Patterns for Multi-Homed Intranet with a Single VPN Gateway and an External VPN Client**

**VPN-Based Access Control.** Many forms of gateway VPN servers offer the ability to restrict user access to a company intranet based on access groupings. This is especially important when intranets are being established for a diverse set of external users, and it is important to minimize user access to the intranet. This type of access control is, of course, critical in establishing secure extranets, which further highlights the importance of understanding VPN access control capabilities.

**User Authentication.** Multiple options exist for user authentication, although the recommended option is to select a high-level authentication method (e.g., one-time passwords) or a time-synchronized password method. Under the IPSec standard, client-side digital certificates are evolving as a standard for high-level authentication. Unfortunately, initial implementations of client-side digital certificates for user authentication are entirely software based, eliminating the second-factor authentication, the "something the user physically has" in his possession. The return to true two-factor authentication under digital certificates will not really occur until physical smart cards become part of the authentication architecture. (Smart cards are credit card-type tokens that have a physically embedded chip, which can be electronically read and written to, either with a portion of the client's digital certificate or the encryption algorithm used to unlock the digital certificate.)

**IPSec Interoperability.** Ultimately, the IPSec standard will stabilize, and all vendors following the established standard will allow different vendors' VPN products to interoperate. Under this environment, a company can implement a vendor's VPN server, and its acknowledged clients can purchase and use an IPSec-compliant client to gain access to the company intranet once they are authorized.

## SUMMARY

Secure extranets are becoming the external network of choice in today's business world. There are multiple implementation options, as depicted in this chapter, each with varying degrees of risk and implementation complexity. Each implementation must be evaluated against a business case, using the recommended risk and performance analysis outline. The basic router-controlled extranets are only recommended for the least valuable data environments, while the more sophisticated VPN extranet architectures appear to be the future for extranets, especially when the IPSec standard matures and gains industry adoption.

# Chapter 25
# Challenges of Intranet Implementation

*Nathan J. Muller*

AN INTRANET IS A PRIVATE TCP/IP NETWORK THAT USUALLY SUPPORTS THE SAME PROTO-
COLS AND SERVICES AS THE PUBLIC INTERNET, INCLUDING E-MAIL, NEWS, CHAT ROOMS, AND
WEB PAGES. Companies build intranets to improve internal communication,
distribute information, and enable more employees to access legacy data.
With links to the public Internet, intranets have allowed companies to reach
more potential customers, enter untapped markets, and engage in electronic
commerce. Coupled with such innovations as the Java development language and new zero-administration netcentric computers, intranets can
become the base around which businesses can reinvent themselves.

## IMPLEMENTATION ISSUES

The decision to implement an intranet is relatively easy for large companies because they typically have the necessary components already in
place. For example, they use TCP/IP (transmission control protocol/Inter-
net protocol) on the wide area network in support of e-mail, file transfers,
remote database access, and other routine communications needs. They
usually have the technical expertise to install and configure the necessary
components, including routers, switches, and gateways, and manage these
and other network elements through the simple network management protocol (SNMP). They also have people who implement and maintain cli-
ent/server technology over local area networks (LANs) that also provide
connectivity to legacy host systems. For these companies, it is relatively
simple to add a graphical front end to this environment in the form of easy-
to-use Web browsers and offer extra functionality from Web servers distributed on the TCP/IP network.

Even for companies that do not already have an existing TCP/IP-based
infrastructure, it does not take much to learn how to take advantage of

Internet technology and adapt it for internal use. These companies, as well as very small companies that lack any kind of technical expertise, can avail themselves of numerous vendors and service providers who are eager to educate potential customers on the benefits of corporate intranets and offer their own ideas concerning intranet implementation. If a company does not want to build and run its own intranet, there are service providers that handle this as well. In fact, every aspect of building and running a corporate intranet can be outsourced to third-party firms — from designing the intranet Web page, hosting one or more intranet Web sites, and procuring and managing the private IP network itself.

Achieving the benefits of an intranet necessitates proper implementation. First, resources must be available to establish the service, to establish or upgrade the TCP/IP network over which it runs, and to train users. Second, the impact on existing systems must be considered. This includes, for example, the capacity of the current network to support an intranet, the future usefulness of existing legacy systems, and the availability of hardware to properly run multimedia applications. More difficult to resolve is the issue of intranet content. It is necessary to decide what information will be presented, where it will come from, how its accuracy will be assured, and how often it will be updated.

Finally, appropriate security must be implemented — both to prevent external users from accessing corporate resources and to prevent employees, workgroups, departments from being able to access each others' sensitive information and applications. Not only must servers and databases must be structured to prevent unauthorized access, but appropriate tools must be available to easily administer passwords and log-on procedures, log all system activity, and trace the source of attempted break-ins.

These issues, particularly the problem of security, can be construed as disadvantages to implementing a corporate intranet. However, these are basically the same issues that confront users of any type of corporate network. From the perspective of security, for example, even corporate PBXs (private branch exchanges) are susceptible to the problem of toll-fraud by external hackers. And if the PBX supports data communication as well, tenacious hackers can find their way right onto the LAN or mainframe. It is important to understand that all of these potential disadvantages can be overcome by using the right tools, implementing the right procedures, or selecting a reputable third-party firm. In the final analysis, the advantages of implementing a corporate intranet far outweigh the potential disadvantages.

## RESOURCES

Costs are an important consideration when developing an intranet. Beyond the list prices for hardware and software components lie the less obvious costs of administration, maintenance, and additional applications development.

The skill sets that are required for developing an intranet are varied and quite specialized. They include technical people with knowledge of system and network architectures, an understanding of the Internet protocol (IP), and experience in developing applications with such tools as Java, ActiveX, and PERL. There is also a need for creative people, particularly graphic artists and HTML coders who excel at making the content visually compelling through the integration of images, text, and animation.

The cumulative efforts of many people can go into the initial development and implementation of a corporate intranet. However, many of these people may be only peripherally involved. For example, the same network managers and technical staff that keep the division's telecommunications network up and running, by default, keep the intranet up and running, since they both may share much of the same equipment and lines.

The daily maintenance of an intranet may require only the part-time efforts of a few people from the marketing and technical groups. The caliber of skills of the individuals involved in the task, not the number of people, is what makes all the difference. Though it takes people with specialized skills to develop an intranet, it takes a different set of skills to sustain it. Companies usually deal with this situation by recruiting multifunctional people — those who can apply what they normally do on the job to the medium of the intranet.

## INTRANET MANAGEMENT

Intranets bring together yet another set of technologies that need to be managed. Instead of using different management systems, organizations should strive to monitor and administer intranet applications from the same console used to manage their underlying operating system software and server hardware. This is a distinct advantage when it comes to ensuring end-to-end availability of intranet resources to users.

### Server Performance

Vendors are scrambling to meet this need. For example, the hierarchical storage management capabilities of the Unicenter platform from Computer Associates can be extended to HTML pages on a Web server. HTML pages that are not accessed from the server for a given period of time can be migrated to less costly near-line storage. If a user then tries to access such a page, storage management will direct the query to the appropriate location.

Some enterprise management vendors are turning to partnerships to provide users of their management platforms with data on intranet server performance. For example, Hewlett-Packard and Cabletron have joined with BMC Software Inc. to provide application management software that monitors Web server performance and use. The software forwards the data it collects to management consoles, such as HP's OpenView and Cabletron's Spectrum, in the platforms' native format or as basic SNMP (simple network management protocol) traps. Instead of looking at their internal Web sites in an isolated way, this integrated method permits full-fledged enterprisewide applications management.

### IP Administration

Managing the Web servers and firewalls is only one aspect of keeping an intranet up and running. IP administration also can become unwieldy as intranets lead to a proliferation of devices and addresses. Intranet-driven IP administration can be facilitated by dynamic host configuration protocol (DHCP) software, which streamlines the allocation and distribution of IP addresses. This insulates network operators from the complexity of assigning addresses across multiple subnetworks and platforms. Since intranets depend on the accurate assignment of IP addresses throughout a company, such tools are virtually essential for ensuring the availability of resources.

### OUTSOURCING

In addition to the several thousand small Internet service providers (ISPs) nationwide, the regional telephone companies and long distance carriers provide one or more pieces of the intranet. Some provide Web page design, system integration, and full-service private IP networks that offer a choice of access methods and are supported by high-speed backbones.

By tapping into CompuServe's private IP network, for example, mobile professionals and employees at branch office locations not only have remote access to corporate resources, but they can communicate with each other via e-mail, route documents, and share basic business information. In essence, the use of such services provides organizations with what amounts to a virtual private network (VPN).

When a sales rep at a branch office wants to access a corporate database to execute pricing calculations based on a specific product configuration, for example, he or she dials a local number to access the private CompuServe network, which connects to the company's enterprise hub or a regional communications server. Since all traffic traverses CompuServe's private IP network — which is separate from its public network used by its online subscribers — the privacy of corporate information is assured. This option is also cost-effective because users make a local call to one of the many private nodes managed by CompuServe.

Many other Internet service providers have their own flavor of private IP that can be used for remote access, such as IBM's Global Services Network.

Another is PSINet's Business Remote Access InterRamp service, which relies on PSINet's proprietary authentication technique to ensure privacy.

These IP-based virtual private networks are becoming increasingly popular for a variety of reasons. Organizations can rid themselves of costly leased lines and avoid long distance charges for dialup access. They also can save on modem banks. Since support is done by the service provider, there is no need for a round-the-clock support staff, which is almost always required for implementing private intranet solutions. Security is implemented by a combination of authentication and filtering techniques, the use of secure protocols, and firewalls — all of which can be difficult for many organizations to set up and maintain by themselves. By outsourcing its intranet, a company can save as much as 50% of its startup costs and free up IT staff to work on core business issues.

In addition to being a secure, cost-effective solution, other reasons to outsource the corporate intranet include:

- Faster intranet development
- Easier integration of new technologies and capabilities
- The availability of better equipment and higher-speed lines than a company can otherwise afford
- The availability of a wider range of expertise
- Quality-of-service guarantees
- Continuous network management and faster response to problems
- One-stop service and support

## IMPACT ON EXISTING SYSTEMS

### Network Performance and Standards

Intranets also have the potential to significantly increase traffic, causing bandwidth problems. This has some technology managers concerned that bandwidth for vital business applications is being consumed by less-than-vital intranet data. Users are now accessing files that may contain huge graphics, and this has created a tremendous bandwidth issue. As Web servers across an enterprise entice users with new content, intranets also can alter the distribution patterns of network traffic as users hop from one business unit's intranet server to another's, and as companies make it easier to access information and applications no matter where they may be located.

Of course, more servers and bandwidth can be added and the network itself can be partitioned into more subnets to help confine bandwidth-intensive applications to various communities of interest. But these are expensive solutions. A policy-based solution can be just as effective, if not more economical. To prevent these applications from wreaking too much havoc on the network infrastructure, companies can issue standards that establish limits to document size and the use of graphics so that bandwidth is not consumed unnecessarily. These policies can even be applied to e-mail servers, where the server can be instructed to reject messages that are too long or which contain attachments that exceed a given file size. An automated reply message can even be sent back to the originator, stating why the message or attachment was refused and inviting him or her to send it again provided that it meets the stated parameters.

The use of TCP/IP-based nets can also save on the cost of leased lines, or eliminate some of them entirely, particularly if they are used mostly for data communications. Most types of routine data — synchronous and asynchronous — are easily handled by TCP/IP. However, owing to its real-time delivery requirement, isochronous data over TCP/IP nets is still problematic.

In a video conference application, for example, the individual packets of voice and video may take different routes to their destinations which causes them to arrive at different times. Often, the network might be congested at various points, causing variable delay. Either way, the result is that the voice component is rarely synchronized properly with the video component, and the video itself looks jerky most of the time. Even if the TCP/IP network is used for an audio-only conference, the inherent delay can be disruptive and significant delay in packet delivery can cause voice to be clipped.

Although quality-of-service (QoS) protocols, such as the resource ReSerVation Protocol, are available that improve the ability of TCP/IP-based nets to handle isochronous data, they are not yet widely implemented on the wider Internet. If a company plans to implement an intranet that uses the Internet as a backbone between far-flung locations, it is best to leave voice and other real-time applications on scaled down leased-line networks or continue using the public switched telephone network (PSTN), where consistently high quality is assured.

However, if a company plans to rely exclusively on its own TCP/IP net, where it is possible to size the bandwidth to application needs, exercise more control over packet delay, and implement the protocols that improve the performance of isochronous applications, it is possible to move voice and video traffic off leased lines entirely and achieve acceptable quality for internal communications. The PSTN can continue to be used for off-net calls or as a backup when the intranet experiences a temporary outage.

## DATABASE ACCESS

Of course, giving outsiders limited access to internal databases raises security concerns. Initially, however, the principal challenge is providing a uniform view into a company's varied systems, which may even be scattered around the world. One solution is to implement a data warehouse with decision-support tools. The decision-support tools are the glue in the middle, a middleware layer that couples the warehouse to the desktop. The tools are run on a server dedicated to the task of querying the warehouse, building intermediate data sets, and then converting the results into reports that can be viewed in various ways.

Together, the tools represent an active middleware that basically moves the processing from the fat client desktop out onto a server. The desktop simply becomes a dumb device, and all the processing occurs out on the network. This makes it possible to pluck information from the warehouse and other resources and deliver it to different types of clients, be they Web browsers, Windows-based machines or even pagers. The use of intelligent agents to explore vast amounts of data means that users do not have to spend hours sifting through voluminous amounts of information. When the agent finds the desired item, it sends out a notification to the user. A user can send out any number of agents to explore the database. These agents can even go out onto the greater Internet to accomplish their mission.

## PERFORMANCE ENHANCEMENT

Intranets are becoming pervasive because they allow network users to easily access information through standard Web browsers and other World Wide Web technologies and tools to provide a simple, reliable, universal and low-cost way to exchange information among enterprise network users. However, the resulting changes in network traffic patterns may require upgrading the network infrastructure to improve performance and prevent user frustration due to slow intranet response times.

These changes include the graphical nature of Web-based information, which dramatically increases network traffic and demands greater network bandwidth; the integration of IP throughout the network; easier access to data across the campus or across the globe, leading to increased inter-subnet traffic which must be routed; and new, real-time multimedia feeds requiring intelligent multicast control.

LAN switches traditionally operate at Layer 2, or the data link layer, providing high performance segmentation for workgroup-based client/server networks. Routing operates at Layer 3, or the network layer, providing broadcast controls, WAN access, and bandwidth management vital to intranets. Most networks do not contain sufficient routing resources to handle the new inter-subnet traffic demands of enterprise intranets.

The optimal solution — intranet switching — is to add Layer 3 switching, the portion of routing functionality required to forward intranet information between subnets, to existing Layer 2 switches. This enables network managers to cost-effectively upgrade the Layer 3 performance in their networks. This is the approach being taken by new intranet switches and software upgrades to existing switches.

Intranets are increasingly being used to support real-time information, such as live audio and video feeds, over the network. These multimedia feeds are sent to all subscribers in a subnet, creating increased multicast traffic and impeding network performance by consuming ever greater amounts of bandwidth. Intelligent multicast control provided by intranet switches helps organizations conserve network bandwidth by eliminating the propagation of multicast traffic to all end stations in a subnet. The intranet switches monitor multicast requests and forward multicast frames only to the ports hosting members of a multicast group.

Most enterprise networks use multiple protocols. In contrast, intranets are IP-based, requiring IP on all intranet access systems throughout the network. To ease IP integration, intranet switching supports protocol-sensitive virtual local area network (VLANs). This allows the addition of IP without changing the logical network structure for other protocols.

Combining IP and ATM routing through integrated private network-to-network interface (I-PNNI) signaling, simplifies network management because only one protocol is managed rather than two. Providing this unified view of the network by implementing a single protocol leads to better path selection and improved network performance.

To accommodate intranet traffic demands, increased switching capabilities must be added to both the edge of the network and to the backbone network. Many organizations are using intranets for mission-critical applications, so the backbone technology must deliver superior performance, scalability, and a high degree of resiliency. For these reasons, ATM is the optimal technology for the core technology for intranet switches.

## ENSURING AN EFFECTIVE INTRANET HOME PAGE

Users access the corporate intranet by logging on to an internal Web server and entering their password. They typically download the company's home page with an ordinary Web browser and navigate the intranet using menus, directories, and hyperlinks — just as they would do if they were connected to the World Wide Web on the public Internet. Often, the look and feel of the company's internal Web page is indistinguishable from pages found on the public Internet. However, the layout of the company's home page can determine the success of the intranet. There are at least five areas that, if given careful consideration, can have a significant positive effect on the site's usability:

1. Graphics. While graphics can have high visual impact, they can also be overused. In addition to taking away valuable space from the more important content, they take time to download and consume an inordinate amount of bandwidth. This approach adds unnecessary costs to creating or updating pages. As a result, pages get updated less frequently and their information value decreases. Simple graphics and HTML-coded background colors can be just as effective in increasing the usability of information without incurring a performance penalty.

2. Navigation. The corporate site should be easy to navigate and require as few clicks as possible to find the desired information. Sometimes this is difficult to achieve, especially when there is no centralized control or funding, as when each business unit pays for the creation of its own home page out of its own budget. The result is a variety of looks and navigation paths. For example, if the corporate telephone directory is published on the intranet, it should be available on one page, instead of on multiple pages buried deep within the various business unit Web sites. Since some companies have tens of thousands of employees, a search engine should also be included on the directory page to enable users to find contact information quickly.

3. Information prominence. Static, or reference, information should not be positioned on the same page or given the same weight as frequently changing and time-sensitive information, especially when there is no indication as to what information has been updated recently and what information has not been changed. For example, it would not be advisable to put employment opportunities on the same page as the company history, which visitors might read once, if at all.

4. Links. Links to internal sections and external sites should not appear to be the same. An intranet user should always be aware of what information is company-sponsored and what information is publicly available. Links to the outside should be relevant to the business objectives of the intranet. While it may be relevant to link to another Web site to review information about a customer or supplier, it is not usually appropriate to provide links to Internet sites that are unrelated to the company's business. This might even encourage employees to waste time surfing the Web.

5. Prioritization. Care should be taken to avoid burying important content too deep within the site. For example, it is unwise to put detailed product information or a company directory within the FAQ (frequently asked questions) section, since visitors are not likely to look there for this kind of information.

For an intranet to be successful, it must be designed to encourage usage. It is not enough to update content regularly; the site must adequately convey that new features and information are added frequently. If employees get the impression that the site is changing, they will visit it regularly. The best way to give the site this kind of appeal is to create a dynamic front page. Instead of using unchanging, bit-intensive graphics to draw users into the site, the first page should include the latest company headlines with a tightly written paragraph that summarizes the content behind the links. In this way, employees can quickly visit the site to see what has changed, instead of following multiple links before discovering some new announcement. Even a Javascript-generated scrolling banner embedded somewhere in the home page can be used to indicate that the site contains new information. Many intranet sites even have the date of last revision posted at the bottom of the home page.

Because home page development takes talent and creativity that is not always readily available in house, many companies farm out this task to outside firms that specialize in Web page design. In fact, just about all aspects of intranet development can be outsourced to third-party vendors or service providers.

## SECURITY

Increasing the number of people who have access to important data or systems makes a company's information technology infrastructure vulnerable to attack if precautions are not taken to protect it. Integrating security mechanisms into an intranet minimizes exposure to misuse of corporate data and to overall system integrity. A secure intranet solution implies seamless and consistent security function integrated between desktop clients, application servers, and distributed networks. It should include policies and procedures, the ability to monitor and enforce them, as well as robust software security tools that work well together and do not leave any gaps in protection.

The following basic functions are necessary for broad security coverage:

- Access control software allowing varying degrees of access to applications and data
- Secure transmission mechanisms like encryption to impede outside parties from eavesdropping or changing data sent over a network
- Authentication software to validate that the information that appears to have been originated and sent by a particular individual was actually sent by that person
- Repudiation software to prevent people who have bought merchandise or services over the network from claiming they never ordered what they received
- Disaster recovery software and procedures to assist in recovering data from a server that experiences a major fault

- Anti-virus software to detect and remove viruses before they cause damage

Intranets that extend beyond organizational or company boundaries may require integration among various security systems. In addition, special firewall software may be required to prevent attacks from malicious hackers on the Internet.

### Firewalls

A firewall can be a dedicated device, or its functions can be added as software that runs on an existing server. In addition, there are routers available that implement the functions of firewalls and which are specifically designed for extranets.

Firewalls come in three types: packet filters, circuit-level gateways, and application gateways. Some firewall products combine all three into one firewall server, offering organizations more flexibility in meeting their security needs.

**Packet Filtering.** With packet filtering, all IP packets traveling between the internal network and the external network must pass through the firewall. User definable rules allow or disallow packets to be passed. The firewall's graphical user interface gives system administrators the ability to implement packet filter rules easily and accurately.

**Circuit-Level Gateway.** All of the firewall's incoming and outgoing connections are circuit-level connections that are made automatically and transparently. The firewall can be configured to enable a variety of outgoing connections such as Telnet, FTP, WWW, Gopher, America Online, and user-defined applications such as Mail and News. Incoming circuit level connections include Telnet and FTP. Incoming connections are only permitted with authenticated inbound access using one-time password tokens.

**Applications Servers.** Some firewalls include support for several standard application servers. These include Mail, News, WWW, FTP, and DNS (Domain Name Service). Security is enhanced by compartmentalizing these applications from other firewall software, so that if an individual server is under attack, other servers/functions are not affected.

To aid security, firewalls offer logging capabilities as well as alarms that are activated when probing is detected. Log files are kept for all connection requests and server activity. The files can be viewed from the management console, displaying the most recent entries first. The log scrolls in real time as new entries come in. The log files include a variety of information including connection requests, mail and news traffic, server activity, FTP session activity, and error conditions.

An alarm system watches for network probes. The alarm system can be configured to watch for TCP or UDP probes from either the external or internal networks. Alarms can be configured to trigger e-mail, pop-up windows, messages sent to a local printer, and/or halt the system upon detection of a security breach.

Another important function of firewalls is to remap and hide all internal IP addresses. The source IP addresses are written so that outgoing packets originate from the firewall. The result is that all of the organization's internal IP addresses are hidden from users on the greater Internet. This provides organizations with the important option of being able to use non-registered IP addresses on their internal network. In not having to assign every computer a unique IP address and not having to register them for use over the greater Internet, which would result in conflicts, administrators can save hundreds of hours of work.

## COSTS

The cost of developing a corporate intranet varies considerably on a case-by-case basis. Large companies can often build sophisticated intranets using existing TCP/IP networks, equipment, and management tools. In such cases, the intranet is treated as just another application that is added to meet business needs. For large companies, the startup cost for intranet development can be incremental.

### Staffing

For example, the creative aspects of intranet development, especially the design of the corporate home page and the pages of various business units, are often handled by employees temporarily assigned to the effort and others who are eager to demonstrate what they can do with HTML and graphics, even if they have to do the work on their own time. The same is often true of programming tasks involving Java. The programming language is so new and intriguing that many veteran C programmers jump at the chance to put what they have learned to practical use and push the envelope in the process.

However, the spirit of volunteerism that gets a pilot intranet project off to a good start can fade quickly as the work consumes more of an employee's time. Eventually the time comes when many employees will want to get paid for what they are doing, or they will opt out of the project. This results in a sudden increase in staffing costs for running the intranet, something most companies do not always plan for at the start and which can easily throw a budget off track.

Another hidden cost is for creating and updating content, designing Web presentations, building hyperlinks, and checking for error, duplication, and outdated information. A corporate intranet almost always requires continual tweaking, which consumes staff time. The result is that companies generally spend much more than they expect on managing and administering the site. Staff also must continually learn new technology, since Web products, applications, and development tools are evolving at a very rapid pace.

Of course, if the objectives and expectations of the intranet are such that they cannot be achieved by leveraging existing assets, the costs can add up quickly, depending on the number of corporate locations that must be tied together and the degree of sophistication desired. While the cost of staff is often difficult to quantify, the cost of hardware, software and services is relatively easy to figure out.

### Hardware, Software, and Services

Hardware, software, and services generally fall into the following categories:

- Web-specific hardware, such as servers and peripherals.
- Communications hardware, such as routers and modems, and a firewall.
- Carrier-provided facilities and services, such as leased lines and ISDN. Mobile professionals may require wireless connectivity options. If a private high-speed intranet backbone is required, T1 and T3 lines should be considered.
- Software, including Web browsers, database management, utilities, and development tools.

The startup cost for an intranet that supports 400 to 500 people can be as low as $25,000. This includes the Web browser client software, Web server software, development tools, and the communications hardware. The recurring cost of facilities and services can be obtained from the various carriers and compiled into an annual figure. Companies that do not have in-house technical expertise should also plan to spend 10% of the total startup cost for equipment and software on integration services.

Fortune 100 companies with worldwide locations that must be tied into the intranet can expect to pay quite a bit more, especially if they intend to offer a high level of interactivity, engage in electronic commerce, and Web-enable various office operations. Such companies should plan to spend at least $10 million.

### RETURN ON INVESTMENT

As companies put together budgets for intranet development and management, eventually they will have to address the issue of return on investment (ROI), as they typically do for any other major capital expenditure.

The extent to which this can be done with any degree of accuracy often depends on how the proposed intranet will be used.

For example, if the intranet will be used to publish staff handbooks, telephone directories, forms, office notices, and other administrative documentation, the annual cost of printing, distributing, updating, and storing these materials contributes to the ROI of the intranet. Although harder to quantify, there is also the significant cost of staff time for filing, updating, and referring to paper-based material that would also be eliminated. A publishing application can garner an annual ROI of as much as 30%. Other applications, such as database access and inventory management, may yield 70% and 50% annual returns, respectively.

Reliance on electronic publishing would improve overall productivity, which is a soft-dollar benefit that can be used to cost justify the intranet, especially when the intranet includes a search engine that allows users to key in on desired information quickly.

There are even ways to set up text-based customer help desks on the intranet that allow customers to quickly diagnose and solve problems with the products they have purchased from the company, further enhancing customer loyalty and reducing staff time. Companies like Cisco Systems and Cabletron Systems have Web pages that allow customers to custom configure such products as routers and hubs and submit orders via fill-in e-mail forms that are sent to the vendor. Customers are notified of errors during the configuration process and alternatives are given to correct the errors before the order is submitted. Many computer companies allow customers to custom configure systems and obtain pricing before submitting the order electronically.

If the company plans to use the intranet for transaction processing, ROI can be fairly easy to calculate. For example, the company can post all of its business forms on the intranet, including various health insurance forms, travel authorization and expense reimbursement forms, vacation schedule forms, worker's compensation forms, 401K plan forms, and purchase order forms — just to name a few. These and other forms can be called up on the intranet with a Web browser, filled in by the employee, and sent to the appropriate department via e-mail. Employees need not waste time tracking down the paper forms they need and, since the employee-supplied information is submitted in electronic form, departments can process it faster and readily integrate it into various databases. The savings in wasted time and improved forms processing constitute another element that can be factored into the intranet's return on investment.

Companies can also realize substantial savings on software development. This is due in large part to the universal nature of the Web browser. An MIS department, for example, does not have to spend thousands or hundreds of thousands of dollars to have software developed to access legacy systems when there are simple Java-based terminal emulators available that allow Web browsers to access legacy data through an intranet. Using Java-enabled Web browsers also saves on the cost of administering clients, since program code resides on a central server where it can be easily maintained and secured. Users automatically have access to the most updated versions of various programs, since the client machines do not retain copies of the programs themselves. Since Java is object oriented, programmers can reuse and extend existing code to develop new applications faster.

## THE BOTTOM LINE

Corporate intranets are becoming as significant to the telecommunications industry as the PC has become to the computer industry. They fundamentally change the way people in large organizations communicate with one another. In the process, intranets can improve employee productivity and customer response. Intranets are also being used to connect companies with their business partners, allowing them to collaborate in such vital areas as research and development, manufacturing, distribution, sales, and service. A variety of tools are used for these purposes, including interactive text, audio and video conferencing, file sharing, and whiteboarding. In fact, anything that can be done on the public Internet can also be done on a private intranet — easily, economically, and securely.

# Chapter 26
# Application Servers: The Next Wave in Corporate Intranets and Internet Access

*Lisa M. Lindgren*

A CORPORATION'S WEB PRESENCE TYPICALLY EVOLVES IN THREE STAGES. In the first stage, static information is published via Web pages. Information about the company, its products, and its services is made available to the general public via the Internet. In a more secure internal intranet, employees have access to company holiday schedules, personnel policies, company benefits, and employee directories.

While this first step is necessary, it is really only a substitute for other traditional forms of publishing information. The information can become dated, and there is no interaction with the user. Most organizations quickly evolve from the first step to the second — publishing dynamic information and dynamically interacting with the user via new scripts, applications, or applets that are written for the Web server or Web client. An example of this stage of Web presence is a newspaper that offers online news content and classified ad search capabilities. This stage offers realtime information, rather than static "brochure-ware," and presents the opportunity to carry out electronic commerce transactions. The second stage usually demonstrates to an organization the vast efficiencies and increased customer and employee satisfaction that can result from a well-designed and executed intranet and Internet presence. The challenge many organizations then face is how to rapidly deliver new services over their corporate intranets and the Internet.

In the third stage of Web evolution, the focus is on offering new transactional services that communicate directly with the core IT systems. This allows companies to maintain a competitive edge and meet the unslaked thirst for new and better ways to interact with an organization via the familiar Web interface. The transactional services are offered over the Internet for public use, over business-to-business extranets to allow business partners to more effectively do business, and over internal corporate intranets to offer employees new and better ways to do their jobs. Examples of this third stage of Web presence geared to the public over the Internet include home banking, package tracking, travel booking, stock trading, and the online purchase of consumer goods. Business-to-business examples include online policy sales and updates for insurance agents, manufacturing and delivery schedules for distributors, and direct order entry into suppliers. Intranet examples geared to employees include expense report submission, benefits calculation, and conference room scheduling.

The key emphasis of this third stage of Web presence is its transactional nature. This next level of services can only be achieved by tapping the vast and sophisticated systems and applications that have been built over a period of years. These mission-critical systems and applications represent the "crown jewels" of an IT organization, and include customer records, product availability and pricing, customer service databases, and the transactional applications that literally keep the business running. IT organizations must try to create a unified interface, leveraging a variety of existing systems. The problem is that the existing systems are usually very diverse. They differ in architecture (i.e., client/server versus hierarchical), operating system, programming language, networking protocol, interface (i.e., real-time, batch, programmatic), and access control. The application server is a new breed of product that unifies a variety of different systems and technologies in order to deliver new transactional services to a variety of clients.

## OVERVIEW OF A WEB SERVER

To fully understand what an application server does, it is first useful to review the functions of a Web server. A Web server's primary function is to "serve" Web pages to Web clients. The protocol used between the Web client and the Web server is HyperText Transfer Protocol (HTTP). HTTP defines the valid operations between the Web server and the browser. For example, the Get operation is how the browser requests the download of a particular Web page or file. Exhibit 1 illustrates the sequence of events when a Web client requests the download of a particular Web page.

HyperText Markup Language (HTML) defines the contents and structure of the Web page. It is the browser, not the server, that reads and interprets the tags within HTML to format and display a Web page. Extensible Markup Language (XML) is the next-generation Web page content language that allows programmers to define the tags in a page for better programmatic

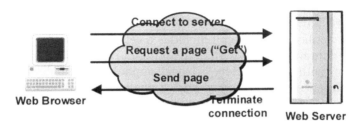

**Exhibit 1.   Sequence for Download of a Web Page**

access to the page content. XML separates the definition of content from the presentation of that content.

The Web page can contain text, images, video, and audio. The Web server serves up the files associated with these different types of content the same. It is the Web browser that must display or play the different data types. As long as the request from the Web browser is valid, the file type is known, and the file exists, the Web server simply downloads whatever is requested.[1] The server behaves differently, however, if the page that the Web browser requests is actually a script.

A script, quite simply, is a program. It can be written in any language and can be compiled or interpreted. A script can be used to access non-Web resources such as databases, to interact with the user via forms, and to construct documents dynamically that are specific to that user or that transaction. The Web server executes the script and the results are returned to the user in the form of a Web page. Scripts interface to the Web server using either a standard or a vendor-proprietary application programming interface, or API2. The base standard API is the Common Gateway Interface (CGI). Some Web server vendors offer proprietary APIs that extend the capability beyond what is possible with CGI. For example, Netscape and Microsoft both defined proprietary extensions in their products (NSAPI and ISAPI, respectively). Microsoft's Active Server Pages (ASP) technology is an alternative scripting technology for Microsoft Web servers.

A Web server, then, serves Web pages to users but also executes business logic in the form of scripts. The scripts can gather data from databases and applications on various systems. The result is returned to a single type of user, the Web browser user.

## OVERVIEW OF AN APPLICATION SERVER

An application server is an extension of a Web server running scripts. Like Web servers, application servers execute business logic. The scripts that execute on a Web server can be written to integrate data from other systems, but there are no special tools provided with the Web server to do so. In contrast, this integration of other systems is a key focus and integral part of the application server. It includes a set of "back-ends" that handle the job of communicating with, extracting data from, and carrying out transactions with a wide variety of legacy applications and databases. And while a Web server only accommodates a single type of user, an application server can deal with several types of end users, including Web browsers, traditional desktop applications, or new handheld devices.

Some application servers are sold bundled with a Web server. Others are sold independently of a Web server and will communicate with a variety of different Web servers running on the same physical server or across the network to a Web server on a different machine. However, most application servers can function without a Web server. An IT organization could implement an application server that only communicates with in-house PCs over an internal network without using Web servers or Web browsers at all. Nonetheless, the strength of the application server, compared to other types of middleware, is its ability to form a bridge between the existing legacy applications (including traditional client/server applications) and the new, Web-based applications driving what IBM calls "E-business." Exhibit 2 depicts the basic architecture of an application server.

At the core of the application server is the engine that ties all of the other pieces together and sets the stage for application integration. In many application servers, this engine is based on an object-oriented, component-based model like the Common Object Request Broker Architecture (CORBA), Enterprise Java Beans (EJB), or Microsoft's (Distributed) Component Object Model (COM/DCOM). Each of these architectures supports the development, deployment, execution, and management of new, distributed applications.

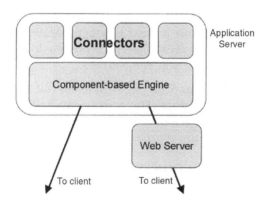

**Exhibit 2.   Basic Architecture of an Application Server**

- CORBA: Defined over a period of years by the Object Management Group (OMG), a vendor consortium of approximately 800 members, CORBA is a component framework that is language-neutral and supported on a wide variety of platforms. At the heart of the CORBA framework is the Object Request Broker (ORB). Communication between objects is achieved with the Internet Inter-ORB Protocol (IIOP).
- Enterprise Java Beans: EJB is a Java-based component framework defined by Sun Microsystems. Once potentially at conflict with CORBA, the two frameworks have begun to complement one another. The EJB specification defined the Remote Method Invocation (RMI) as the method for components to communicate across Java Virtual Machine (JVM) and machine boundaries. RMI-over-IIOP is becoming common as the two frameworks begin to more explicitly support one another.
- COM/DCOM: The vendor community positions COM/DCOM as yet another Microsoft proprietary architecture meant to lock customers in to Microsoft-specific solutions. Microsoft positions it as the most widely implemented component model because COM/DCOM has been an integral part of all Windows systems since the introduction of Windows 95. A number of UNIX system vendors have indicated they will support COM in the future.

The definition of standards and architecture for creating stand-alone components, or objects, allows application developers to combine previously developed components in new ways to create new applications. The developer is then able to focus on the business logic of the problem at hand rather than the details of the objects. With the combination of object technologies and the new visual development tools, new applications are more easily built and more stable than the monolithic, built-from-the-ground-up applications of the past. It is because of this flexibility that most application servers are based on a core component-based engine.

Application servers offer "back ends" that provide an interface into data and applications on other systems. These back ends are often called connectors, bridges, or integration modules by the vendors. These connectors can interact with an application or system in a variety of different ways and at a variety of different levels. The following connectors are available on some or all of the commercially available application servers:

- Web server interfaces
- Message queuing interfaces for Microsoft's MSMQ and IBM's MQSeries
- Transactional and API interfaces to the IBM CICS or the Microsoft Transaction Server (MTS)
- Structured query database interfaces (e.g., SQL, ODBC, DRDA)
- Component connectors to Java applets and servlets, ActiveX components, CORBA objects, Enterprise Java Beans, and others

- Terminal interfaces to legacy applications on mainframes and midrange systems (e.g., 3270, 5250, VT220, HP, Bull)
- Application-specific interfaces to Enterprise Resource Planning (ERP) applications, such as those from SAP, PeopleSoft, and BAAN
- Custom connectors for custom applications

Downstream from the application server to the client, the protocol can vary, depending on the type of client and the base technology of the application (i.e., CORBA, EJB, COM). A common and basic method of exchanging information with end users will be via standard Web pages using HTTP, HTML, and possibly XML. Another option that involves some local processing on the part of the client is to download Java or ActiveX applets to the client. This thin-client approach is desirable when some local processing is desired but the size of the client program is sufficiently small to make downloading over the network feasible. When a more traditional fat-client approach is required, in which the end user's PC takes on a larger piece of the overall distributed application, a client-side program written in Java, C, C++, or any other language is installed. In this case, the client and the application server will utilize some communication protocol, typically over TCP/IP. In the case of CORBA, the standard IIOP is used. In Java environments, the standard scheme is Remote Method Invocation (RMI). Microsoft's COM/DCOM specifies its own protocol and distributed processing scheme. Exhibit 3 illustrates an example of an enterprise that has application servers, multiple back ends, and multiple client types.

A final but important piece of the application server offering is the support for visual development tools and application programming interfaces (APIs). Because application servers are focused on building new applications that integrate various other systems, the ease with which these new applications are developed is key to the viability and success of the application server. Some application servers are packaged with their own integrated development environment (IDE), complete with a software development kit (SDK), that is modeled after the popular visual development tools. Other vendors simply choose to support the dominant visual development tools, such as the IBM VisualAge, Microsoft's InterDev, or Symantec's Visual Café.

The number of application servers available on the market grows each day. Vendors offering these products come from a wide variety of backgrounds. Some have a solid background in providing client/server integration middleware; others were early adopters of standards-based component technology like CORBA; and still others have evolved from the Web server space. Exhibit 4 lists some of the application servers available, along with some of the key points of each of the products.

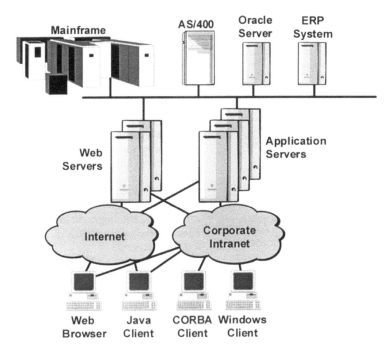

**Exhibit 3. Examples of an Enterprise with Application Servers**

## DEPLOYMENT IN THE ENTERPRISE

When deploying application servers in an enterprise environment, there are some very important and key capabilities of the application server that must be considered above and beyond its component architecture, protocols, and back ends. IT organizations that have made it through the first two steps of Web integration and Web presence and are now ready to embark on this third phase realize how quickly Web-based systems become mission critical. Once new services like online catalog ordering, home banking, Web-based trading, and others become available, new users rapidly adopt the services and become reliant on them. If the Web-based systems of a company fail, consumers are likely to go elsewhere and never return. Therefore, it is essential that the application servers be designed and implemented with ample security, scalability, load balancing, fault tolerance, and sophisticated management capabilities.

## SECURITY

Security is even more critical in an application server environment than in a stand-alone Web server environment. This is because an integral part of

**Exhibit 4.  Application Servers Available**

| Vendor | Product | Key Points |
|---|---|---|
| BEA | WebLogic | Family of products offering different levels; based on Java but CORBA support comes in at the high end; built on common base of the BEA TUXEDO transaction monitor; includes support for Microsoft's COM |
| Bluestone Software | Sapphire/Web | Java-based solution; includes integrated development environment for application development; large number of integration modules for back-end access to systems; state management and load balancing |
| IBM | WebSphere Application Server Enterprise Edition | Includes Web server; focused on high-volume transactions and high reliability; core technologies are CORBA, EJB, XML; common IIOP infrastructure |
| Inprise | Application Server | Built upon Inprise's VisiBroker, a dominant ORB in the CORBA market space; integrated solution with Web server, IDE (Jbuilder), and management (AppCenter) |
| Novera | Integrator | Integrator includes the component designer back ends with Novera's Integration Server, the runtime environment; Integration Server runs in a Java Virtual Machine; communication to objects and other servers is based on the CORBA IIOP |

the application server is the integration of existing data and applications. Often, these data and applications reside on mission-critical systems like IBM mainframes and midrange systems and high-end UNIX platforms. These are the systems that house the most important and sensitive information in an enterprise, including customer records, historical sales information, and other material that would be valuable to the competition or to the malicious hacker.

An overall security plan and architecture must accomplish three things. First, it must ensure that the data flowing in the network and on the wire is not legible to prying eyes. Second, it must ensure that the identity of the user is verified. Third, it must ensure that a particular user can only access the resources for which he or she is authorized.

A number of different technologies and products can be leveraged to accomplish these three goals. For example, Secure Sockets Layer (SSL) is a popular security protocol that accomplishes the first two goals by using encryption on the wire and digital certificates for user authentication. Secure HTTP (HTTPS) is also used to protect Web transactions. Application-specific user ID/password schemes as well as centralized servers, such as those based on the Lightweight Directory Access Protocol (LDAP) standard, provide user authorization.

Application servers must also take into account the notion of session persistence as a facet of security. There is a fundamental mismatch between the Web paradigm of user-to-server interaction when compared to client/server or traditional hierarchical applications. In the Web paradigm, each individual page interaction or request is a stand-alone transaction. The Web server does not maintain state information for each user. Session state information must be maintained by an application server to prevent the possibility of one user gaining access to an existing, active session. This is a security issue because, without session persistence, user authentication and user authorization security schemes are compromised.

## SCALABILITY, LOAD BALANCING, AND FAULT TOLERANCE

Scalability refers to the ability of a system to grow seamlessly to support an increasing number of users. Systems that are scalable are able to add users in such a way that the consumption of resources is linear. The system should not hit a bottleneck point or barrier beyond which the addition of another user dramatically impacts session resources or overall response time. Systems that are scalable can grow to accommodate a particular maximum number of concurrent users in such a way that the response time is roughly equivalent for all users. For many organizations, the design point for scalability will be thousands — or even tens of thousands — of concurrent users.

This level of scalability is usually only achieved by implementing multiple, load-balancing servers. In this design, there are multiple application servers, each supporting the same services and presenting a portion of the total pool of available servers. End users, either fat-client PCs or thin-client Web-based users, should all have a common view to the pool of application servers. That is, one should not have to configure each device or session to use a specific server in the pool. The load-balancing front end (which may be a separate unit or integrated into the application server) should load-balance sessions across all available servers in an intelligent manner based on system capacity, current load, and other metrics.

High availability is provided by the load-balancing front end through its awareness of the availability of the application servers. If a server fails, it obviously should be removed from the pool of servers to which new sessions are allocated. Existing sessions that are active at the time of the failure of an application server will usually be disrupted, although some systems, like the IBM mainframes with Parallel Sysplex, can avoid even session disruption.

## MANAGEMENT

Because an application server environment encompasses a variety of different types of users, back ends, and distributed processing technologies, it can be a very complex environment to manage. Most application server vendors provide tools that are supported using one or more of the common management platforms, including IBM TME 10/NetView, CA UniCenter, and HP OpenView.

The management tool should include the ability to manage the pool of application servers as a logical entity. The operator should be able to view and control all of the resources, objects, and sessions from an application viewpoint. A visual display of all elements with current status should be an integral capability. The management tool should be able to assist with the deployment and tracking of new applets and applications. The ability to specify actions based on certain events can help to automate some of the routine management functions. Additional information for capacity planning and modeling is helpful.

## CONCLUSION

Application servers allow organizations to evolve to the third phase of Web presence, in which the focus is on providing realtime transaction-based services to both internal and external users. The integration of the wealth of existing data processing systems, applications, and data is essential to the ability to deliver new transactional services quickly and efficiently. Application servers unify the existing systems with the Web-based infrastructure, allowing IT organizations to leverage their vast investment in systems and applications to deliver new services to their employees, business partners, and the public.

**Notes**

1. *Web Server Technology: The Advanced Guide for the World Wide Web Information Providers,* Nancy J. Yeager and Robert E. McGrath, Morgan Kaufmann Publishers, Inc., pp. 37–41.
2. *Ibid.,* pp. 58–59.

# Chapter 27
# Web Site Design and Performance for Intranets

*Ralph L. Kliem*

COMPANIES ARE QUICKLY SEEING THE ADVANTAGES OF PURSUING INTRANET APPLICATIONS, AND THE PREDOMINANT REASONS ARE INCREASING PRODUCTIVITY AND COMMUNICATIONS. The Business Research Group found that 75 percent of companies want to set up an intranet to increase effectiveness, and another 52 percent to save on communications costs.[1]

However, realizing these advantages of the intranet does not come easily. Logic dictates that the first step in increasing effectiveness and improving communications is to create Web pages that will do the job — but yet the evidence seems to be to the contrary. Many Web pages share a lot of characteristics of earlier interfaces and the content of immature mainframe and client/server systems, thereby defeating effective communications and productivity. Here are a few examples:

- A feeling of "Oh my gosh, where am I going?" after selecting an icon
- Cluttered screens, especially with graphics
- Cryptic messages
- Excessive navigation and hypertext links
- Large blocks of text
- Long processing speeds
- Poor grammar and spelling
- Too many frames
- Too many and too large icons and graphics
- Too much audio or animation
- Unsparing use of color

There is more. Many organizations release sites that are incomplete (e.g., the construction worker shoveling is a popular indicator of an incomplete site). Others release untested or poorly tested sites, exemplified by visitors finding themselves lost in a tangled web of links. Still others release sites with errors either in the content or with the links.

The impacts are real. Visitors no longer bother to visit the site because they find the design frustrating. The Web pages are no longer a valuable communications tool once the reliability and integrity of the information comes into question. In the end, the servers become burial grounds for unvisited Web sites.

## REASONS

There are four major reasons for why many Web sites that exist are ineffective and inefficient.

1. More is better. Put as much as possible on a Web page. "More" might be text or graphics, or both. Never mind the relevancy, just put everything remotely related to the subject on the Web page. "Keep them full" and visitors will never leave. After all, goes the reasoning, why not put ten pounds of groceries in a five-pound bag if one can do it?

2. Plenty of glitter. Many Web sites, thanks now to Java, are putting more glitter than substance on their pages, such as movable or flashing icons and graphics, for no other purpose than to draw attention. Yet, trying to find something simple like an address to contact someone is like walking blindfolded through a maze. Glitter like this raises the question, "Wow, but what is the message?"

3. Excessive linkage. Many sites add links to other sites which, in turn, provide navigational and hypertext links to other sites. After a while, the linkage gets so elaborate the visitor gets lost. The linkage turns into a chaotic sailing escapade similar to Minnow in *Gilligan's Island* getting lost in a storm and the crew never having any idea where they are at or how to return from where they came.

4. Get it out there first. It seems that everyone wants to have the first Web site, or at least be one of the first. By being in the forefront, recognition comes right away. Forget about the interface or content design of the Web pages. Just get that Web site up and running, even at the risk of sacrificing quality and the organization's image.

## BACK TO BASICS

The four reasons given above contribute to poor Web site design, indicating that designers failed to answer the following fundamental questions before writing the first line of HTML.

- *Who* is the customer? Who does one want to access the site?
- *What* is one trying to communicate to the customer? Is it to persuade them to action? To provide them data?

- *Why* should they visit your site as opposed to another site?
- *Where* can the customer go to get access to the site (e.g., through a search engine)?
- W*hen* should one modify or update the site? Frequently? Never?
- *How* is one going to get customers to visit? How is one going to lure them to the site?

A good approach to building a Web page is to borrow a technique used by designers of the past for earlier technologies: build a model of what the site should look like using a paper prototype. As in the past, a prototype can go a long way in helping to answer the six fundamental questions above.

Another excellent approach that has worked in the past is to hold a beta test. Select people who are not knowledgeable about Web design and have them access and navigate through the new Web pages. Record their insights, especially about the "look and feel," and then make any appropriate changes.

Of course, good Web design not only just makes Web site visitations a pleasure, there are also other advantages. For one, it helps to reduce or slow down the increasing need for bandwidth and storage requirements. It also makes content maintenance and path management easier because there is less to track.

A superb book that people can still learn from and is just as relevant today as it was 15 years ago is Paul Heckel's *The Elements of Friendly Software Design* (Warner Books). The principles described in the book, if applied to Web sites, would go a long way toward improving design and content of many internal sites. The emphasis in the book is on the user's intuition and perspective — and not on his ability to unravel complexity. In other words, it calls for designing systems from the "outside in" and not from the "inside out."

## REMEDIES

Naturally, bad design weeds out the good, and the potential for getting worse increases with each Web site going online. Here are some tips to ensure that Web sites in the future do not encourage bad design.

- Apply simplicity in word and image choice
- Ensure clarity of message
- Ensure contents and paths are active and relevant
- Have text and graphics support one another
- Keep consistent in layout and terminology
- Logically structure content
- Minimize excessive navigation
- Modularize layout

- Prefer the specific to the general
- Provide ease of access to data or information
- Provide straightforward navigation within the site
- Spell correctly
- Standardize page layout
- Use proper grammar
- Use graphics, video, and color selectively to emphasize a point
- Use meaningful messages and ease of recovery when an error arises
- Use plenty of white space to reduce clutter and increase readability
- Use a positive tone throughout all pages

Here also are some tips to improve intranet efficiency that will increase bandwidth and reduce download speed.

- Give visitors choices whether to download hypermedia like audio, video, and plug-in files
- Prepare a Web usage policy to control surfing during key production hours
- Provide a site map, accessible directly from the home page
- Provide options for viewing text only
- Restrict graphics to 30,000 bytes or less
- Set up standards for Web site design (e.g., common structure and organization)
- Store icons in GIF rather than JPEG format
- Use capacity planning and performance management tools and techniques to track and monitor bandwidth requirements
- Use frames sparingly
- Use Java applets only when necessary
- Use thumbs and interlaced GIFs for larger images

When developing a Web site, also consider the network infrastructure that supports the site by answering questions like, does the network

- Minimize response and queues through load balancing or other performance management approaches?
- Provide data on network performance and use that data to continuously optimize and configure the network?
- Support different operating systems and servers?
- Support existing and growing number of users on the network in general and the number of visitors to a site in particular?

On a client level, there are hardware options to improve performance on the client side. Two common improvements are increasing the amount of random access memory (RAM) and installing faster CPUs and controller cards.

On a companywide level, the options include increasing the number of servers, making more powerful servers available during peak periods, and providing higher speed lines to the servers.

On the same level, it makes good sense to put together something like a standards and guidelines manual for building Web pages. The manual might provide a recommended page layout; templates of different layouts of Web pages; guidelines for use of graphics, audio, and animation; instructions for dealing with copyright issues; maintenance of content and links; and how to handle errors and other difficult situations. The manual could go a long way in "weeding out" the bad and encouraging the good in Web page design.

## IT IS UP AND RUNNING. NOW WHAT?

Having new Web pages up and running is only half the battle. The other half is maintaining the site. One way to maintain a site is to conduct periodic reviews. These reviews should focus on the "staleness" of the content, its relevancy, and its appearance. Although the content may be current, visitors may grow tired of the appearance and cease visiting. Navigational maps (for detecting nonexistent links and seeing how all the links and pages relate to one another) and storyboards can ease the maintenance of Web pages. However, there is more that one can do.

On a solo basis, Web site maintenance is relatively easy. Some activities include monitoring to ensure that:

1. Content is accurate and current
2. Functionality and transactions are reliable
3. Links are active
4. Site accessibility is provided to all current browsers and hardware configurations

As the number and purposes of Web sites grow, however, management tools can play a very important role in site maintenance and management. These tools allow tracking and analyzing traffic to, from, and within a Web site. They also allow fine-tuning of one or more Web sites and, indeed, an entire network, if necessary.

For an individual site, a log tool collects information about access to a site via log files residing on a server. Typically, this file will provide a plethora of data on visitors to a site, such as IP address, date and time of access, pages visited, and any downloads. It also tracks any errors that users may encounter when accessing the site. The volume of data can become quite large, of course, so content analyzer software can prove quite useful.

A content analyzer tool can compile the data and convert it into information to answer questions like:

- What are the statistics for the average number of visitors per day? What are the most and least active days? What is the most and least popular browser used?
- What broken links exist?
- What are the most common errors that visitors experience? What is the source of those errors?
- What is the most frequent activity at the Web site (e.g., surfing or downloading)?
- What is the number of visitors to the site?
- What are the best, least, and average response times?
- What links lead visitors to the site?
- Which Web pages and files are the most popular during different time intervals?

Answers to the above questions can help fine-tune and maintain the Web site by eliminating or reducing the least frequently visited Web pages, shifting files to more frequently visited Web pages, developing more appealing content, and fixing problems that lead to errors.

A number of log file analysis tools exist on the market that provide either reporting or error corrections, or both. A graphical reporting capability is especially useful to track and monitor site visits over a period of time.

On a grander scale are Web-based performance management tools for a server or an entire network. These tools not only collect data about specific sites but also on an array of servers to track and monitor the performance of servers and networks. They can help provide data on individual sites but also the overall performance of the entire network. These tools specifically enable one to:

- Perform an analysis of traffic (e.g., most frequently visited sites and most active paths)
- Create and maintain individual sites (e.g., identify broken links and slow downloading files)
- Detect server failures and provide adequate recovery procedures
- Develop a more effective accounting practice for use of the servers
- Develop a more efficient allocation of bandwidth scheme
- Develop a more optimized configuration using load balancing techniques
- Filter access to certain files
- Identify "spikes" in bandwidth usage that cause traffic bottlenecks
- Identify event sequences
- Identify the most frequent problems dealing with the connections with communications devices (e.g., modems, routers)

- Manage bandwidth requirements and project future needs (e.g., during peak periods and simulating traffic)
- Map existing server configurations
- Provide "alerts" of existing or impending problems with the network
- Provide site update and replication services (e.g., for remote Web sites)
- Track server availability

## ONLY GOLD GLITTERS

If one likes to use the comparison of a Web page to a page in a book, then it is especially clear that few people are studying the past. The layout of a Web page is very much like the page of a book. The best practice, therefore, is to capitalize on what has worked best in the past to make the transition easier. It is amazing how even the fundamental questions get overlooked by the glitter of Web technology. Yet, answering and applying the fundamental questions can go a long way toward turning a site into an effective communications tool rather than just an electronic brochure that people toss after the first reading.

**Notes**

1. Surfing Down the Cost Curve, *CommuicationsWeek,* July 22, 1996, p. 12.

# Chapter 28
# Managing Risk in an Intranet Environment
*Ralph L. Kliem*

THE RUSH TO ADOPT INTRANET TECHNOLOGY KEEPS GROWING DAILY. IT IS NOT HARD TO UNDERSTAND THE ENTHUSIASTIC EMBRACE OF THIS NEW TECHNOLOGY. It is, quite frankly, quite inviting. It provides many advantages, especially when compared with the rigid, complex technology of the past. It builds on the existing client/server or distributed systems environment. It provides a convenient means to access and distribute information throughout an enterprise. Users find it easy to enter and navigate. It encourages a truly open computing environment. It enables easier distribution of applications. The advantages go on and on. It seems something akin to a perpetual motion machine. It is just too good to be true.

All these advantages can prove beguiling; many companies are finding that the intranet is too good to be true. As they embrace this technology, many companies are finding that they have more of a perpetual problem machine than one of perpetual motion. This is especially the case when they fail to prepare themselves in advance for the new technology. What is happening, of course, is that many companies are finding that they must deal with issues pertaining to organizational structuring, internal and external access to data, copyright protection, data ownership and maintenance, configuration of hardware and software, traffic management, and many others.

## GROWING RISK

Many intranets are like some mystic poltergeist, lacking any structure, purpose, or boundary. Yet, the positive and negative benefits of going the intranet route remain untested despite the history of its sister technology, the Internet.

As the intranet becomes more pervasive and complex, the opportunities for vulnerabilities increase. With these vulnerabilities comes risk. Many companies have implemented intranets, for example, without any thought about standards or policies on access, content, or use. Their oversight or deliberate neglect appears acceptable to them, reflecting a willingness to face the consequences if something goes awry.

Part of the problem is that many industries across the United States are willing to accept a certain level of risk as a tradeoff for realizing short- and long-term gains in productivity. Another contributor to the problem is that risk is often narrowly construed as being only security. In reality, a security risk — albeit important — is just one of the many types of risks facing an intranet. Many corporations find themselves facing a host of unanticipated risks related to transaction security, network capacity, configuration control, directory services, maintenance skills availability, upgrades to hardware, and backup procedures. Other intranet-related risks include performance, integration, scalability, and planning.

The risks tend to multiply as the size of, complexity of, and level of reliance on the intranet grows. Once an intranet gains momentum within an organization, it is very difficult to avoid fighting fires. The only mechanism to deal with such an environment is to perform risk management as early as possible, preferably before the intranet is up and running.

## RISK MANAGEMENT CONCEPTS

Before discussing the specific types of risks facing an intranet, however, it is important to understand some general concepts about risk management. Risk is the occurrence of an event that has consequences. A vulnerability, or exposure, is a weakness that enables a risk to have an impact. The idea is to institute controls that will prevent, detect, or correct impacts from risks.

Risk management is the entire process of managing risk. It consists of three closely related actions:

- Risk identification
- Risk analysis
- Risk control

Risk identification is identifying the risks confronting a system. Risk analysis is analyzing data collected using a particular technique. Risk control is identifying and verifying the existence of measures to lessen or avoid the impact of a risk. Risk control may involve avoiding, accepting, adopting, or transferring risk. The measures in place to prevent, detect, or correct are called controls.

Risk management for an intranet offers several advantages. It identifies the most likely and most important risks facing an intranet. It enables taking a proactive approach when managing the intranet, such as identifying assets that need augmentation or improvement. It provides an opportunity to define exactly what constitutes an intranet within a company. It enables building an infrastructure to support the overall business objectives that the intranet is to help achieve. It identifies where to focus energies. Finally, it provides the material to develop contingency plans to respond appropriately to certain risks, if and when they do arise.

Of course, it makes sense to do risk assessment as early as possible. It enables identifying control weaknesses before an intranet is implemented and, therefore, institutionalizes them. It allows incorporating better controls when it is cheaper to make the appropriate changes rather than when the intranet is up and running. Finally, it gives everyone a sense of confidence early on that they are using a secure, reliable, well-managed system.

## RISK IDENTIFICATION

For an intranet, the risks are innumerable, especially since the technology is new and has been adopted rapidly. Its growth has been so dramatic that a complete listing would be akin to trying to calculate the end of infinity. It impacts both functions and processes within an organization to such an extent that listing all the risks would prove futile. It is possible, however, to categorize the risks according to some arbitrary but generic criteria. Intranet risks can fall into four basic categories: personnel, operational, economic, and technological.

Personnel risks deal with the human side of an intranet. Some examples are:

- Inadequate training of users
- Lack of available skills for intranet development and maintenance
- Lack of available skills for intranet publishing and design
- Lack of available skills for systems administration
- Poor role definition for data content, usage, and maintenance
- Unclear responsibilities for dealing with traffic flow problems

Operational risks deal with business processes. A process transcends a functional entity (e.g., department) within an organization, receives input, and transforms it into output. Some examples are:

- Inadequate capability to find data
- Inadequate presentation of data
- Lack of backup and recovery procedures
- Not adequately controlling access to sensitive data
- Poor directory services
- Poor integration with legacy systems
- Poor online service support
- Poorly maintained links
- Transferring sensitive data over a network with poor security
- Uncontrolled access to unauthorized sites

- Unexpected rise in network traffic

Economic risks relate to the costs of an intranet — from development to ongoing operation. Some examples are excessive or out-of-the-ordinary costs related to:

- Internet service provider services
- Hardware upgrades
- Software upgrades
- Integration of components (e.g., desktops, server applications)
- Integration of applications with legacy systems and databases
- Labor for developing and maintaining the infrastructure (e.g., administering the site)

Technological risks deal with the hardware, software, and other media that form an intranet. Some examples are:

- Immaturity of the technology being employed
- Inadequate communications hardware and software
- Inadequate system hardware and software
- Insufficient availability of network bandwidth
- Poor availability of development and publishing tools
- Poor configuration control of clients
- Poor integration of components (e.g., local area networks, server applications)
- Poor retrieval tools and services
- Slow connection
- Unreliable server hardware and software

It would be a mistake, however, to think that these four categories are mutually exclusive.

Deciding what risks fall within each category is often a judgment call and is mainly academic. The key is to use the categories to identify the risks, determine their relative importance to one another, and recognize the controls that do or should exist.

### RISK ANALYSIS

After identifying the risks, the next action is to determine their relative importance to one another and their probability of occurrence. The ranking of importance depends largely on the purpose management has established for the intranet. In other words, what business value is the intranet supposed to provide? In what ways is the intranet supposed to serve the interests of its users?

There are multiple approaches to analyzing risk. Basically, the approaches fall into three categories:

- Quantitative
- Qualitative
- A combination of both

Qualitative risk analysis relies on mathematical calculations to determine a risk's relative importance to another and its probability of occurrence. The Monte Carlo simulation technique falls within this category.

Qualitative risk analysis relies less on mathematical calculations and more on judgmental considerations to determine a risk's relative importance to another and probability of occurrence. Heuristics, or rules of thumb, fall within this category.

A combination of the two, of course, uses both mathematical and qualitative considerations to determine a risk's relative importance to another and its probability of occurrence. The precedence diagramming method, which uses an ordinal approach to determine priorities according to some criterion, falls within this category. Regardless of the approach, a resulting rank order listing of risks is shown in Exhibit 1.

## RISK CONTROL

With the analysis complete, the next action is to identify controls that should exist to prevent, detect, or correct the impact of risks. Risk control involves a painstaking effort to understand the environment where the intranet finds itself. It means looking at a host of factors, such as:

- Applications at the client and server levels
- Architectural design of the network
- Availability of expertise
- Content and structure in databases (e.g., images, text)
- Current network capacity
- Degree of integration among system components
- Firewall protection
- Hardware components
- Importance of copyright issues
- Level of anticipated network traffic in the future

**Exhibit 1.    An Ordered Listing of Intranet Risks**

| Risk | Probability of Occurrence | Impact |
|---|---|---|
| Lack of available skills for system administration | High | Major |
| Uncontrollable access to unauthorized sites | High | Minor |
| Poor integration of components (e.g., local area networks, applications) | Low | Minor |
| Unexpected network utilization costs | High | Major |

- Level of financial resources available for ongoing maintenance
- Level of security requirements
- Number of mission-critical systems depending on the intranet
- Sensitivity of data being accessed and transported
- Software components

After identifying the controls that should be in place, the next action is to verify whether they are actually in place to prevent, detect, or correct. Preventive controls mitigate or stop an event that exploits the vulnerabilities of a system. Detective controls disclose the occurrence of an event that exploited a vulnerability. Corrective controls counteract the effects of an event and preclude similar exploitation in the future.

To determine the types of controls that are in place requires painstaking "leg work," often achieved through interviews, literature reviews, and a thorough knowledge of the major components of the intranet. The result is the identification of what controls do exist and which ones are lacking or need improvement.

There are many preventive, detective, and corrective controls to apply in an intranet environment. These include:

- Adequate backup and recovery to safeguard data
- Adequate, relevant, and timely training for users and developers
- Changing passwords
- Documented and followed policies and procedures
- Metrics to ensure goals and objectives are being achieved
- Monitoring of network utilization regarding traffic flow and data content
- Monitoring system performance
- Restricting user access to specific server applications and databases
- Restricting user privileges
- Security for sensitive data and transactions
- Segregation of duties, such as reviews and approvals
- Setting up a firewall
- Tracking of hardware and software
- Tracking user access
- Upgrading hardware and software

Armed with a good idea of the type and nature of the risks confronting an intranet, the next step is to make improvements. This involves strengthening or adding controls. It means deciding whether to accept, avoid, adopt, or transfer risk. To accept a risk means letting it occur and taking no action. An example is not doing anything about external breach to the intranet. To avoid a risk means taking action not to confront a risk. An example is continuing to expand bandwidth without considering the

**Exhibit 2.    Intranet Risks and Their Controls**

| Risk | Control |
|------|---------|
| Lack of available skills for system administration | • Cross-training<br>• Outsourcing |
| Uncontrolled access to sensitive databases | • Restrictive access policies<br>• Firewall |
| Poor integration of components (e.g., local area networks, server applications) | • Client and server configuration guidelines and standards |
| Unexpected network utilization costs | • Periodic network capacity planning<br>• Limiting nonessential access during high peak periods |

causes (such as surfing). Adopting means living with a risk and dealing with it by working "around it." An example is waiting until a later time to access the network when usage is less. Transfer means shifting a risk over to someone else or some other organization. An example is having the user assume responsibility for accessing and displaying proprietary data. Exhibit 2 presents some examples of controls that may be implemented for selected types of risks in an intranet environment.

## CONCLUSION

The advantages of performing risk management for an intranet are quite obvious. Yet, the lure of the technology is so inviting that even the thought of doing any risk assessment appears more like an administrative burden. The decision to manage risk depends on the answers to two key questions: Do the advantages of not bothering to identify, analyze, and control risks exceed not doing it? Are you willing to accept the consequences if a vulnerability is taken advantage of, either deliberately or by accident? In the end, the decision to manage risk is, ironically, one of risk.

# Section VI
# Wireless and Mobile Solutions: Expanding the Internet Infrastructure

Wireless and mobile solutions are a strong complement to the Internet and are likely to provide technology access to more users in more places than ever before. Although this technology has been around for over a decade in some form or other, the recent convergence of improved hardware, more sophisticated input devices such as handwriting and voice analysis, and growing international wireless standards such as wireless application protocol (WAP) and Bluetooth make the current environment ripe for a breakthrough in this space.

Wireless applications extend the notion of access anywhere and anytime. Personal device assistants (PDAs) have proven their value to a large portion of the consumer market. This suggests that increasing the capabilities of mobile devices even further is likely to be met with enthusiasm. The chapters in this section examine some of the possibilities in this space.

"Wireless Communications for Voice and Data" examines wireless technologies, including wireless private branch exchange, cellular digital packet data, enhanced special mobile radio, and satellite communications.

"Wireless Data Networking" discusses wireless technologies and compares wireless and wired networks as well.

"Wireless Technology Impacts the Enterprise Network" explores opportunities to reduce operating costs by operating a wireless solution within an organization and discusses some of the common standards and protocol wireless solutions.

"Mobile Database Interoperability: Architecture and Functionality" examines the architecture and functionality of interoperating mobile clients within a federated database application.

"Does WAP Fill in the Gap?" explains the wireless application protocol and reflects on some of the future opportunities that this standard will support.

# Chapter 29
# Wireless Communications for Voice and Data

*Andres Llana, Jr.*

WIRELESS TECHNOLOGY HAS BECOME ONE OF THE FASTEST-GROWING COMMUNICATIONS APPLICATIONS AROUND THE WORLD. Recent innovations have greatly increased the availability of the telephone in many parts of the world, yet wireless communications have been around since the early 1900s. Back then, radio served as the principal means of mass communication and, like TV, was the principal means of public entertainment. During World Wars I and II, wireless communications allowed combat forces to communicate. Today, law enforcement agencies, marine agencies, and transportation companies, among many others, use wireless communications to manage deployed resources.

In the 1950s, the Rural Electrification Administration considered wireless radio technology as a means of supplying telephone service to rural populations. This experimentation proceeded through many iterations but was largely abandoned during the mid-1980s as cellular technology emerged.

Today, radio communication is thought of as an innovation because of its growing ubiquity and its support for personal communications, data, and information collection. Lower costs have made it possible for users to enjoy cellular telephones, personal digital assistants (PDAs), and a host of other devices to simplify the conduct of commerce. Wireless technology has improved intra- and intercorporate communications, enabling more cost-effective control of such business resources as deployed sales forces and technical service personnel.

0-8493-1160-8/02/$0.00+$1.50
© 2002 by CRC Press LLC

## WIRELESS TECHNIQUES: A STRATEGY FOR WORLDWIDE VOICE COMMUNICATIONS

### Cellular Voice

Great strides have been made in the adaption of cellular radio as a means of supporting local telephone service. In many undeveloped countries there is little or no infrastructure to support telephone services. For this reason, it is not uncommon in some parts of South America, Asia, Russia, and eastern Europe for a subscriber to wait as long as one year to get local telephone service. Because of this situation, wireless subscriber penetration has grown at about 45 percent per year. For example, Motorola, Inc., recently reported that it had orders for 150 wireless systems for 21 provinces of China and the three municipalities of Beijing, Shanghai, and Tianjing—an area with a combined population of more than 1 billion people. As a result, wireless local loop (WLL) systems are being installed around the world at an accelerated rate to reduce the time to service.

### Wireless Radio

Wireless radio is being installed in place of traditional central office systems that require expensive extended copper wire external networks. Service providers are finding that wireless radio central office systems are convenient, fast, and less costly than traditional central office switching systems. Because there are no copper wires to string and no wire plant to maintain, subscribers can enjoy telephone service as soon as the radios are turned on.

Building a traditional central office system with a stationary copper landline network costs between $1,250 and $1,750 per subscriber, depending on terrain and labor. A Motorola WLL system can be installed for between $800 and $2,000 per subscriber. About 80 percent of these costs are in the construction of cell sites, which can also be used for other forms of wireless communications, such as personal communications services (PCS).

### Wireless PBX Systems

In companies where operations are widespread, such as chemical and heavy equipment manufacturing, it is often necessary for first-line supervisors and other key employees to cover a lot of terrain in a day. Often these personnel are in high demand, and maintaining contact with them is difficult. For these applications, PBX manufacturers have developed wireless radio frequency (RF) systems that can be integrated into the architecture of a PBX system.

AT&T, Ericsson Messaging Systems, Intercom Computer Systems, Inc., Northern Telecom, Inc., Mitel Corp., and Siemens-ROLM Corp. offer systems that integrate into their PBX architectures. These systems are integrated through the PBX line cards and support the same line appearances as any hard-wired single line or electronic station set. A base radio operating in the unlicensed frequency range together with a series of antennae spaced around the user's facility comprise the basic network. Low-powered mobile handsets are used with these systems to avoid interference with other frequencies operating in the same area.

**Wireless PBX Add-On Systems.** Motorola and Spectralink have developed wireless PBX add-on systems similar to those developed by the PBX manufacturers. The Motorola InReach design concept is slightly different because it was developed as an extension to a cellular operator's service offering. An InReach handset can be used either as a cellular terminal or a PBX station set.

For example, when a user enters an InReach-equipped building, the handset can function as an electronic desk telephone. The handset provides access to all the features on the PBX, including access to the corporate and public network. When the user leaves the building, the handset can then be used to access the cellular network, and functions as a mobile handset.

Wireless add-on PBX facilities are expensive because of the addition of a base radio module and antennae infrastructure to the established internal PBX network. A typical midrange (i.e., 75 * 450 line) PBX system, when configured with a wireless add-on system, can easily double the cost of the basic PBX system. However, as PCS and other handheld terminal-based services proliferate, the costs for PBX wireless systems will continue to decline.

### Satellite Voice Services

Satellites are playing an increasing role in establishing still another layer of worldwide voice communications. Two of the most widely heralded impending services are the Iridium and Teledesic low earth orbital (LEO) systems. These systems will offer worldwide telephone service through the use of a small handheld telephone similar to those now used for cellular systems. Iridium is owned by a consortium of international companies, one of which is Motorola, Inc. Teledesic is owned by McCaw Communications and Microsoft Corp.

Inmarsat now offers voice services through a worldwide consortium of 65 member nations. Special briefcase-size terminals are used to communicate with the satellite. Typical terminal costs range between $18,000 and $22,000, and connect-time costs are approximately $5.00 per minute. A new service that is planned, Inmarsat-P, will compete directly with the LEO systems. Although details of the Inmarsat-P service are still in the making, terminal and initiation costs are expected to be in the vicinity of $1,500, with connect costs of about $1.00 per minute.

These satellite-based voice systems provide the capability to support both voice and data communications in any remote area of the world.

## WIRELESS CONSIDERATIONS FOR A DATA COMMUNICATIONS STRATEGY

A variety of services are available to support wireless data communications. Wireless services such as Cellular Digital Packet Data (CDPD), enhanced specialized mobile radio (ESMR), Ardis Mobile Data, and RAM Mobile Data, Inc., support slightly different needs, although there is some overlap. For this reason, users should not look for a single vendor to supply an all-encompassing wireless service solution. In fact, it is less costly to consider a mix of voice, paging, and data services.

ESMR and CDPD offer competitive data communications services. For example, the Nextel interconnect option on the Motorola Integrated Radio System (MIRS)-based network costs $40 per month for the first 256 minutes plus $0.50 for each additional minute. This assumes that the subscriber also is a dispatch subscriber at about $25 per month for access.

A MIRS Motorola Lingo mobile handset is required to access service on a MIRS system and is priced around $1,000. In comparison, cellular telephones can cost up to $350. Cellular subscribers start out at $14.95 for monthly access plus about $0.45 or more per minute for airtime.

Although there are still many smaller specialized mobile radio (SMR) operators across the United States that will continue to offer dispatch and interconnect services in second-tier markets, major players such as Nextel, Dial Page, and other members of the MIRS-related roaming consortium are likely to maintain their interconnect rates in competition with cellular service providers.

### CDPD as a Wireless Option

Implementing CDPD networks often requires a number of systems applications modifications. For example, a special CDPD modem is required at either end for the transmission of data from one point to a host computer's communications port. This device must be established separately from the other host communications ports and should be installed by the cellular service provider. This task includes assigning the device with an IP address and configuring it for access to the cellular network.

**CDPD Costs.** Communicating over a wireless network is more costly than using the public network for a number of reasons, not the least of which is the cost of airtime. For example, regular transmission control protocol/internet protocol applications generate a lot of extraneous traffic that can drive up the cost of transmission on a network that is usage-sensitive. A hardware fix is available to alleviate this type of network condition. For example, products are available to monitor data flow as a means of reducing the number of acknowledgments being sent.

**Potential Performance Problems.** Another problem that must be taken into account is packet delay. This condition can result in dropped connections or unnecessary retransmissions and is caused by network congestion. Although cellular networks are still relatively lightly loaded, network congestion becomes a problem as greater penetration develops in the wireless market and CDPD networks become crowded. In addition, under some traffic circumstances, it is possible for packets to be dropped; therefore, delivery of packets cannot be guaranteed. Noisy lines and poor radio coverage can also present the same types of problems as a congested network.

Under some traffic conditions, duplicate packets can be introduced through retransmission facilities. If the packet acknowledgment is lost, the packet's source will time out and retransmit a second or duplicate packet. Packets can also be thrown out of order when the data path is subjected to delay from rerouting events. These are just a few of the transmission characteristics that must be countered when a CDPD network is used for data transmission. Users should carefully review their applications and develop the measures that may be required to safeguard their data transmissions.

**CDPD Test Areas.** CDPD is being tested by McCaw (in Las Vegas, Dallas, and Seattle), Ameritech Mobile (in Chicago), GTE Mobilnet, and AirTouch Cellular (PacTel Cellular), among others. Bell Atlantic Mobile, Inc., has announced pricing for CDPD services offered in its Baltimore/Washington, D.C. and Pittsburgh test markets. GTE PCS and McGraw Cellular have also initiated trial services in their franchise areas.

## Specialized Mobile Radio

SMR services began in 1970 when the FCC established frequencies in the 800–900 MHz range for use in land mobile communications. A typical application of specialized mobile radio is a radio dispatch for service fleets and taxicabs. SMR operators are assigned licenses for exclusive use of assigned channels in a given area. SMR operators can also provide interconnection to the public network.

Racotek is one provider of SMR wireless voice/data service. Racotek provides a vehicle fleet management service that is based on SMR or trunk radios. A Racotek communications gateway facility linked to a mobile communications controller in a customer's vehicle provides a data communications link between customers (e.g., truck drivers) and their dispatch control centers. A mobile radio collocated in the vehicle with the mobile communications controller unit completes the communications link. This system allows the dispatcher to send route information, messages, or other information that cannot be sent over the radio to customers while they are en route to or from a location.

### Commercial Mobile Data Communications Services

**RAM Mobile Data, Inc.** RAM Mobile Data, Inc., is a joint venture between Bell South and RAM Broadcasting and provides a two-way data communications service that is based on the Mobiltex network architecture. This service is used by many companies for management of their field sales and service operations. RAM Mobile Data provides mobile data communications service in 90 percent of the urban business areas in the United States, covering 6,000 cities and 210 metropolitan trading areas.

Access speeds of up to 9.6K bps can be supported in all areas; in select areas, it is possible to access the network at up to 19.2K bps. Common applications include e-mail and basic information access to the corporate data center for mobile travelers.

Some companies have greatly reduced their cellular telephone use by deploying the lower-cost RAM mobile network to send e-mail and messages to corporate personnel while traveling. A traveler equipped with a radio-enabled laptop or PDA can access the nearest RAM base station. The message is then routed over a leased land line to the corporate data center. Messages can be sent to a traveler over the RAM mobile network where it is routed to the RAM local switch nearest the traveling employee. Conrail uses RAM Mobile Data to transmit train loading information to train crews advising the disposition of freight and empty freight cars. Other user companies, such as TransNet and MasterCard, use RAM Mobile Data to provide access to their central hosts so that merchants in the field can validate credit card purchases.

**Ardis Mobile Services.** Ardis is a joint venture between IBM and Motorola and is composed of a formerly private corporate network that supported deployed field sales forces and service personnel. Ardis provides data communications services to 4,000 major metropolitan centers and 8,000 cities in the United States, Puerto Rico, and the Virgin Islands. The network was originally designed by Motorola to support IBM's 18,000 deployed field service personnel. Access to the network ranges from 4.8K to 19.2K bps and can be reached from within a building or from a moving vehicle. Laptops and PDAs equipped with an Ardis/Modacom modem can be used to access company host computers to retrieve e-mail, enter orders, access diagnostic information, or obtain product information. Salespeople equipped with laptop computers can access product files to provide customers with product specifications as well as check inventories, enter orders, and print on-the-spot order confirmations.

## Satellite Data

Satellite systems contain a transmission device that is capable of receiving a signal from a ground station. The signal is then amplified and rebroadcast to other earth stations capable of receiving its signal. User signals neither originate nor terminate on the satellite, although the satellite does receive and act on signals from the earth that are used to control the satellite once it is in space. A satellite transmission originates at a single earth station and then passes through the satellite and ends up at one or more earth stations.

The satellite itself acts as an active relay much the same as a microwave relay. A satellite communications system involves three basic elements: the space segment, the signal element, and the ground segment. The space segment consists of the satellite and its launch vehicle. The signal element consists of the frequency spectrum over which the satellite communicates, and the ground segment includes the earth station, antennae, multiplexer, and access element.

**Advantages of Satellite Systems.** The advantage of a satellite system can be seen in the transmission costs, which are not distance sensitive, and the costs of broadcasting, which are fixed whether there are 1 or 100 stations that receive the down signal. Another advantage is the high bandwidth that satellite signals are capable of supporting. Bit errors are random, making it possible to use statistical systems for more efficient error detection and correction. Some satellite service providers are described in the following sections.

**American Mobile Satellite Corp. (AMSC).** AMSC offers satellite-based mobile data services using its own L-band satellite. AMSC is owned by three major shareholders—McCaw/AT&T, MTEL, and Hughes—although its stock is publicly traded. In the United States, AMSC offers service through its Virginia hub. Downlink services may come through the Washington, D.C. international teleport for services sold through the Virginia hub. Pricing is competitive with terrestrial services. For example, a full-time, 64K-bps link between Washington, D.C. and Brussels, Belgium, would cost $1,350 per month.

**OmniTracs.** OmniTracs, a service of Qualcomm, Inc., uses excess capacity on Ku-band U.S. satellites to provide a data-only mobile tracking service for large trucking companies. The OmniTrac service now has more than 50,000 terminals deployed in trucks in North America. Qualcomm plans to expand its service into Europe, Japan, and South America using excess capacity on existing Ku- and C-band satellites.

**Globalstar.** Globalstar is the name of a low earth orbit system designed for mobile voice services by a joint venture of Loral and Qualcomm. Globalstar has recently extended its ownership to an entirely new set of investors who plan to use excess capacity on available satellites. A series of gateways around the globe will provide an integrated network into the public switched telephone network and the satellite links.

**Odyssey.** Odyssey, a system proposed by TRW, is composed of four satellites. The TRW system will use fewer satellites for nearly global coverage because the system will be higher in the sky. The Odyssey uses the TRW advanced bus (AB940) L-band dish for mobile-to-satellite links, an S-band dish for satellite-to-mobile links, and two small Ka-band antennae for satellite/ground station links. Each satellite will operate as a bent pipe system, with switching and processing performed at the ground stations using spread spectrum modulation.

**Ellipso.** Ellipso, proposed by Mobile Communications Holding, Inc., is a high elliptical orbiting system, consisting of 6 (although 24 are planned) small satellites deployed in three elliptical orbits. Two of these orbits, called Borealis, will be inclined at 116°. One orbit will be equatorial, which will provide dependable access to users in the northern and southern hemispheres. The Ellipso satellites will be small and use a simple bent-pipe design with L-band for uplink and S-band for downlink.

**Orion Atlantic.** Orion is an international partnership of eight companies that operates its own Ku-band satellite composed of 34 transponder. Orion's focus is European business-to-business communications arrangements, as well as transatlantic connectivity. Services include cable distribution, business television, news and network backhauls, feeds, and standard business communications requirements. The service can support a full range of multimedia requirements, including telecommuting and interactive desktop video.

A unique mesh network provides completely independent service for international firms with multiple locations. Uplink/downlink services for 64K-bps access is in the vicinity of $2,000 per month for an enterprisewide LAN. A dedicated 64K-bps full service point-to-point link can be provisioned for about $1,400 per month for a 36-month contract. This service includes all equipment for rooftop-to-rooftop access, which is configured to support a dynamically allocated bandwidth service supporting both voice and data requirements. Installation for such a service would be about $10,000. Such an international connection is priced below regular internal terrestrial services and completely bypasses all monthly recurring local loop costs. A second system is planned that would cover a large part of Russia, the Middle East, Africa, and South America.

## WIRELESS LANS

Wireless LANs are governed by the IEEE Wireless Local Area Networks Standard Working Group Project 802.11. The 802.11 standard establishes the components and interface requirements for a wireless LAN. The basic architecture established by the 802.11 committee organizes wireless LANS into basic service areas (BSAs) and access points (APs). Multiple BSAs can be interconnected at the APs into an extended service area (ESA). The protocols for this model are divided into two groups: the Media Access Control specification and physical specifications. There are different specifications for each RF supported: 915 MHz, 2.4 GHz, and 5.2 GHz.

## WIRELESS COMMUNICATION AS AN ALTERNATIVE TO FIXED MEDIA

Traditional fixed-media systems are based on coaxial cable, twisted-pair wiring, fiber optics, or a combination of all three. Over time, the documentation for fixed networks can become lost or rendered inaccurate because of unrecorded equipment moves and changes. As new functions are established or offices rearranged, segments with undocumented cables are often installed to support added network nodes. Some companies that experience a high degree of internal moves and changes find it necessary to abandon at least 30 percent of their original network media. For these companies, a wireless network strategy superimposed over a base network provides the flexibility to support many permanent and temporary moves. Under this plan, the user is required only to establish a base radio, transmitters for each terminal to be moved, and a series of line-of-sight antennas. Thereafter, relocating network users requires only that the new location has line-of-sight to a network antennae.

### The Wireless Cost Advantage

A wireless LAN solution at $750 to $1500 per node may be expensive when compared with a traditional wired solution (approximately $350 to $550). However, when the costs of lost productivity and rewiring are added, a wireless solution may be more cost effective for organizations that move or change equipment frequently. Wireless solutions find their best fit where there are large unwired manufacturing areas to support, campus buildings that must be interconnected, open office areas without access to wire facilities, or older buildings with concrete partitions and no wire access.

### Vendor Support for Wireless Solutions

There are several different vendor approaches for supporting wireless LANs. For example, Motorola's Altair systems use the 18–19 GHz frequency range to support a microcellular approach. A series of intelligent antennae is used to establish microcells within the user's building. These microcells are supported with low-powered, high-frequency radios designed to support frequency reuse. This process results in a very efficient network.

Other manufacturers often use two basic components: the radio hub and the transceiver. In some systems, a single hub can support up to 62 transceivers. The transceivers are attached to the terminals and communicate with the hub using a line-of-sight arrangement.

Wireless LAN bridges are used to connect LANs in neighboring buildings. These devices establish a point-to-point connection and may not be a complete system. Examples of wireless bridges can be seen in Motorola's Altair VistaPoint and the Cylink Airlink.

Infrared and laser technology can also be used to interconnect LANs in different buildings. This technique places information on a beam of light and can support very wide bandwidth over a short distance. In addition, this technology is immune to electrical interference and is much more secure than radio transmission. Although infrared and laser techniques do not require an FCC license, users are responsible for any radio interference that develops while they are operating in a densely occupied area. LCI has been developing laser systems for several years and has well over 750 mature systems installed.

## OUTLOOK FOR WIRELESS APPLICATIONS

Projections for wireless applications vary depending on the user and the interpretation of the technology. There is no doubt that there will be a tremendous penetration in the basic telephone service market. Wireless local loop (WLL) access will allow more users in developing nations to enjoy telephone service faster and at an affordable level.

The continued decline in the cost of PCMCIA cards for mobile radio will result in the continued rise in the number of laptops and PDAs used for basic communications functions such as e-mail and information access.

Satellite and radio-based service will continue to support vehicle management and tracking. Services such as Qualcomm's OmniTrac provide a cost-efficient method of tracking and establishing data communications connections with truck assets in the field.

Global positioning systems (GPSs) will allow users to track vehicles and provision driver information. Avis rental car agency is testing a system that tracks Avis cars and sends driver information to fleets of specially equipped rental cars.

Hertz, Alamo, and other rental car agencies are using RAM Mobile Data to allow their service personnel to directly process returned vehicles as they are driven onto company ramps. Using a handheld data entry terminal, the service person is able to enter the vehicle ID code and rental status. This process allows the rental car location to more efficiently manage its available pool of cars.

## CONCLUSION

Considering that many of the current wireless applications have come into being in only the last few years, new applications are certain to proliferate as users gain confidence in the available services. Mobile workers such as field sales representatives can spend more time with customers. New levels of productivity will emerge as telecommuting employees freed from expensive office space are able to focus more on the delivery of an end product.

AT&T Paradyne's Enhance Throughput Cellular (ETC) can greatly improve the process for sending data over the cellular network. This technology makes the cellular data user transparent to all other cellular traffic. Advancements such as this will allow wireless users to resolve many of their data transmission requirements that were previously difficult to resolve. There is no question that users are adopting wireless solutions. The important issue to consider is the rate at which this technology is absorbed by mobile workers and the extent to which the penetration of services exceeds the available capacity of the network to support these users' needs.

# Chapter 30
# Wireless Data Networking

*Nathan J. Muller*

WIRELESS TECHNOLOGIES FOR TWO-WAY MESSAGING HAVE BEEN AVAILABLE FOR MORE THAN A DECADE, BUT THE INCREASING MOBILITY OF COMPUTER USERS IS DRIVING THE MAINSTREAM ACCEPTANCE OF WIRELESS TECHNOLOGIES FOR LANs. Although wireless technologies are not yet ready to replace the wire-based networking infrastructure, they are serving niche markets effectively and expanding into new markets almost daily. Technology innovations continue at a furious pace to improve transmission range and throughput, as well as security and immunity to interference. Installation and manageability are also being improved. Although wired networks will doubtless stay ahead of wireless in most of these areas, the latter offers the unrivaled advantage of providing mobile computer users with the connectivity they need to be productive and the flexibility businesses need to stay competitive.

## WIRELESS TECHNOLOGIES

There are many wireless technologies in use today. Each offers cost-performance tradeoffs and is suited to specific applications.

### SMR Technology

Introduced in 1970, specialized mobile radio (SMR) was the first commercially successful wireless technology. The traditional SMR technology employs analog transmission and a single-site, high-powered transmitter configuration that precludes the use of any given RF by more than one caller at a time within a given service area. These constraints have caused traditional SMR operators to emphasize radio dispatch service, which involves limited-distance communications and places less demand on system capacity. Users of radio dispatch services include contractors, service companies, and delivery services that have significant field operations and need to provide their personnel with the ability to communicate directly with one another, either on a one-to-one or one-to-many basis.

0-8493-1160-8/02/$0.00+$1.50
© 2002 by CRC Press LLC

## Microwave Transmission

Microwave transmission was developed from the same principles that guided the development of radio. The first demonstration of microwave occurred in 1933 with a transmission across the English Channel. Microwave came into commercial use in the United States in 1947 to provide trunking in support of long distance telephone service. By the 1970s, not a single telephone call, television show, telegram, or data message crossed the country without spending some time on a microwave link.

Microwave generally has a line-of-sight path, high transmission towers, and antennae. Each relay station is positioned to maintain a direct transmission path with its two neighboring relay stations. This line-of-sight compensates for the earth's curvature. Under ideal conditions, the distance between these stations (towers) may span up to 30 miles. Signals are received, amplified, and then passed to the next relay station along the route.

The use of microwave requires a Federal Communications Commission (FCC) license. Private networks, which include most LAN-to-LAN interconnections, are regulated under FCC Rules Part 94. As part of the licensing process, the applicant must complete a microwave feasibility survey. This survey includes path performance calculations, link availability (up- and downtime), a physical survey, and interference studies for both radio frequency interference (RFI) and electromechanical interference (EMI). A number of engineering firms offer frequency coordination and FCC license application assistance.

The use of microwave technology continues to expand, supporting more applications, including LAN bridging (see Exhibit 1). As new technologies emerge, short-haul microwave is sure to find a niche as one of the most economical transmission options. Microwave is one of the most agile and adaptable media available, with the capability to handle data, voice, and video for personal communications services, disaster recovery, local access bypass, and cellular telephony.

Most of the microwave equipment sold in the United States operates at 18 GHz to 23 GHz. At these frequencies, the antenna diameters range from 3.28 feet (1 m) down to 12 inches (30 cm). There are about 23,000 microwave networks in the United States alone.

## Satellite Communications

Satellites are used to deliver a variety of broadcast services. A geosynchronous satellite circles in an orbit that keeps it above the same spot in relation to the earth at all times. Because such satellites never disappear from view, they can be used for continuous communications. This requires that the satellite be 22,300 miles above the earth and move at a velocity of 280,000 miles per hour.

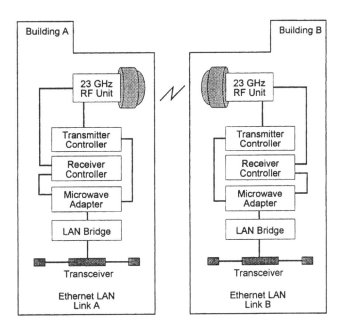

**Exhibit 1.    Microwave Transmission System Configured for LAN Bridging**

Among the frequency bands used for satellite communications, the two most popular are the C-band and Ku-band. The C-band uplink frequency range is 5.9 GHz to 6.4 GHz, and the downlink range is 3.7 GHz to 4.2GHz. The Ku-band uplink frequency range is 14 GHz to 14.5 GHz, with an 11.7 GHz to 12.2 GHz downlink range. The older of the two frequency ranges is the C-band, which is used by thousands of earth stations. It is highly immune to atmospheric disturbances. However, the C-band frequency operates within the same range as the domestic terrestrial microwave. Microwave signals can overwhelm weaker satellite signals. This means that RFI must be considered when designing a C-band satellite or terrestrial microwave system.

The Ku-band offers the advantages of higher power, minimal terrestrial interference from microwaves, flexibility, and the use of smaller, less expensive earth stations. The Ku-band is used exclusively for communications between satellites and stationary earth stations. Densely populated metropolitan areas, because of significant RFI, are more suited to Ku-band systems. However, there is a trade-off. Ku-band satellite transmissions are more susceptible to atmospheric disturbances than are C-band transmissions.

Most recently, the Ku-band spectrum has been opened up to U.S. satellite communications, which receives at 30 GHz and sends at 20 GHz. This part of the frequency spectrum is being used by NASA's advanced communications technology satellite (ACTS), launched in July 1993. ACTS offers data rates 20 times that offered by conventional satellites and is capable of

371

supporting a variety of applications on a demand basis. Among the other innovations of ACTS is its switching capability, which provides hopping spot beams rather than the single, wide-coverage footprint used by conventional satellites. ACTS also uses adaptive coding and power control techniques to overcome signal fade due to atmospheric conditions. This involves reassigning channel capacity to increase the signal, which combats the fade.

Exhibit 2 shows a private satellite link using very small aperture terminals (VSATs) to connect geographically separated LANs. A bridge filters packets based on Media Access Control addresses. Packets with recognized addresses stay on the local network, whereas packets with unrecognized addresses are assumed to be destined for another network and are allowed to pass the bridge. These packets are sent to the VSAT controller, or hub, where they become part of a composite transmission that is sent to the satellite and relayed to the receiving VSAT.

The satellite uses a transponder (a device that receives radio signals at one frequency and converts them to another for transmission) to transfer the composite signal from one VSAT to another. At the receiving VSAT, the data is transferred by a copper wire or fiber-optic connection (or microwave link) to the controller or hub where the composite signal is then separated into individual communications channels and sent to the appropriate destination. A management terminal is used to monitor VSAT performance and reconfigure bandwidth if necessary.

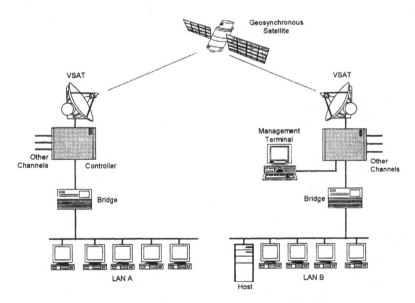

**Exhibit 2. Satellite System for Linking Geographically Separated LANs**

Although the expense of initiating a satellite circuit is dropping every year, it is still expensive because it includes the cost of earth stations, which serve office facilities, and the satellite channel itself. Once established, however, the price of a satellite connection between Washington, D.C. and Atlanta, GA is about the same as one between Washington, D.C. and Los Angeles, CA.

VSATs are customer premises equipment. Together with the controller, they integrate transmission and switching functions to implement preassigned and on-demand assigned links for point-to-point and broadcast networks. In contrast to terrestrial trunks, bandwidth can be added by simply requesting it from the satellite service provider rather than ordering new trunk lines. Thus, satellite services virtually eliminate user dependence on terrestrial communications links as well as local and public-switched networks, offering companies a rapid and cost-effective method of communicating with remote office locations.

## WIRELESS LANS

The technologies that are now being advocated for wireless LANs are infrared and two types of RF systems: narrowband radio and spread spectrum.

### Infrared

Briefly, infrared uses the same technology as a television remote control unit. Over limited distances, infrared offers the highest transmission speed and can potentially match the speed of most wire-based LANs, up to 100M bps over a distance of 1 km. Infrared also offers a high degree of immunity from interference and does not require an FCC license to operate.

However, infrared's line-of-sight requirement has its limitations in the business environment, because signals cannot pass through walls or floors. On the other hand, this limitation is what makes infrared more secure than RF systems. With signals confined to an enclosed area, there is little chance of interception. However, the line-of-sight limitation can be overcome with a technique known as "indirect infrared," in which signals are bounced off walls or ceilings to make the connection.

### Radio Frequency

At certain frequencies, radio frequency (RF) can penetrate walls, making it the technology of choice for networks that must breach walls and other unavoidable obstacles. The two most common RF technologies are narrowband radio, which concentrates significant RF energy at a single frequency, and spread spectrum, which uses a lower-level signal at several frequencies simultaneously.

Narrowband radio systems are relatively old technology. Radio stations (both AM and FM) are examples of narrowband communications. The encoded input signal is mixed with a constant frequency, known as the carrier. The resulting RF signal is broadcast through an antenna. At the other end, the receiver picks up the signal through its antenna and filters out the carrier frequency, leaving the original signal for further decoding.

A significant drawback of RF is that it is quite vulnerable to sources of interference. Consequently, each narrowband radio must be individually licensed by the FCC to operate at a certain frequency and in a particular location. Neither the frequency nor the location can be significantly altered without violating the terms of the license. Companies that manufacture RF components for computers and networks have an arrangement with the FCC in which they hold a primary license for narrowband transmissions over the entire country. They then offer their customers a sublicense for a particular area. The licensing procedure ensures that other nearby systems will not be allowed to operate in the same frequency band and cause interference.

Spread spectrum is a more recent innovation. It was originally developed by the military during World War II for use in secure communications. Because the information is spread over so broad a frequency range, the communication is far less vulnerable to casual eavesdropping and most sources of interference.

Spread spectrum systems send signals using either direct sequence coding or frequency-hopping. With direct sequence coding, data is broadcast across a range of frequencies according to a predetermined code. However, this presents a stationary target for interception or interference. In the frequency-hopping technique, a range of frequencies is also used for transmission, but with an added twist—a transmitter sends data on one frequency for a very short time, then jumps to another frequency. The receiver tunes to those frequencies in sequence to receive the data. This process is continuous for the life of the transmission, and intruders who try to tune in to one frequency will get only fragments of the information. Some vendors claim that frequency hopping provides up to 100,000 times more immunity to interference than direct-sequence coding.

Although frequency hopping produces a signal that is constantly moving, making the signal more immune to interference and interception, it does so with some sacrifice in speed. Though not suitable for LAN backbone use, frequency hopping works well for low-speed (9.6K bps) applications. In contrast, some spread spectrum LAN systems that use direct sequence coding now offer data rates of almost 6M bps.

## WIRED VERSUS WIRELESS LANS

While the wireless technologies for voice communication and data messaging continue to improve, the technologies for LAN extension and interconnection are experiencing the most innovation. The concerns being addressed include reliability, security, transmission speed, and connectivity range. And then there is the cost of implementation, which is still high compared with existing wired systems.

One way to put wireless technologies into proper perspective is to discuss them in terms of advantages and disadvantages. With regard to LANs, for example, wireless technology is widely appreciated because it is easier to install and reconfigure than cabled networks, consisting only of a central control unit (hub) and transceiver connected to each workstation and peripheral (see Exhibit 3). On the other hand, wireless LANs generally have slower throughput and work over shorter distances than their wired counterparts. This has relegated wireless technology to LAN extension rather than cable replacement, at least for the foreseeable future.

Although "wireless" LANs typically include wired components—a wire link between external wireless adapters and workstations, for example—there are still fewer wires to install and maintain. Consequently, the cost of setting up a wireless LAN is usually less than that for a cabled network. This is especially true for older buildings containing asbestos insulation, which must be removed prior to cable installation. Since the electrical wiring plans of many older buildings may not be available or up-to-date, there is always the risk of electrical shock when drilling through walls or

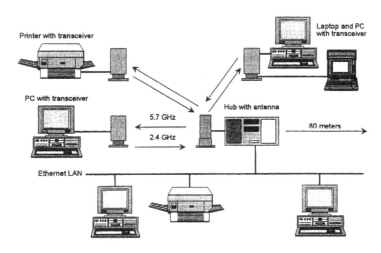

**Exhibit 3.    Typical Wireless LAN Configuration**

floors to install new cable. Although the use of wireless LANs can circumvent these problems, it is also true that the signals may not be strong enough to penetrate certain building materials.

Nevertheless, the choice of an appropriate wireless technology offers the means to quickly set up and break down LANs, as the needs of the workgroup, department, or organization change. Whereas it can take several days to get 25 nodes up and running on a conventional LAN, it can take as little as two hours to get the same number of nodes networking with a wireless system. There is a price associated with obtaining this degree of flexibility. The cost of wireless LAN cards and adapters for PCs and workstations is high today compared with the cost of components for wired LANs. Likewise, the cost of wireless modules for "intelligent" wiring hubs, switches, and other types of LAN interconnection equipment is comparably high.

The high initial cost of implementing a wireless LAN can be offset by its inherent reliability in some situations. Whereas wire-based LANs can experience six to eight hours of downtime a year due to cable-related problems, wireless LANs have been known to provide uninterrupted service for more than a year in environments that are relatively interference free.

Wireless networks are not without their share of performance problems. Whereas wired networks are highly reliable for data transmission, wireless networks can be disrupted by signal interference from adjacent equipment sharing the same frequency range on the electromagnetic spectrum.

Also, the farther a signal must travel, the weaker it becomes and the more susceptible it is to sources of interference. This can be overcome somewhat by spacing wireless transceivers closer together to maintain signal strength or by selecting an appropriate wireless technology that is more robust in a particular environment. Normally, optical fiber would be a good choice for the factory floor due to its inherent immunity from RFI and electromechanical interference. However, an optical fiber backbone can cost as much as 75 percent more to install than a wireless system.

Although eliminating wires is certainly the most attractive feature of wireless LAN technologies, there are legitimate security concerns associated with wireless technology. Because the signals travel through the air, they can be intercepted by network intruders and unauthorized users more easily than signals traveling over wire. Security concerns can be alleviated to a certain extent by the appropriate selection of wireless technology and to a greater extent by adding encryption.

Encryption offers virtually foolproof security. It can be implemented at each node or at the central control unit, and is typically available from the wireless LAN vendor or a third party as an add-on. Some vendors can support more than one encryption algorithm at the same time. As for wireline networks, however, the use of encryption adds to the overall cost of operating wireless networks.

## WIRELESS LAN INTERCONNECTION

Wireless technology is also being used to link together similar LANs—Ethernet or token ring—over bridges. These protocol-transparent interconnection devices are used to create wireless links between cabled LANs in different buildings across the street, or to span an interstate highway or airport (see Exhibit 4). A wireless bridge cannot only connect these offices, but it also offers performance similar to that of a wired bridge. And with additional hardware, the primary wired facilities can automatically switch over to the wireless bridge system to avoid loss of critical data when disaster occurs. The products of some vendors can be configured to work in parallel, allowing two wireless bridges to work together for greater throughput, traffic load balancing, and disaster recovery.

Packet size and protocols determine the performance of wireless bridges. The distance between wireless bridges is also a factor, with speed being inversely proportional to distance. A wireless bridge operating at 256K bps, for example, can have a range of up to 50 miles, whereas the same device operating between 1M bps and 3M bps can have a range of only 6 miles. Compared with the 10M bps for a local Ethernet connection, these throughput rates may seem slow. But when compared with alternative wide-area links such as a full T1/E1 offering 1.544/2.048M bps, the use

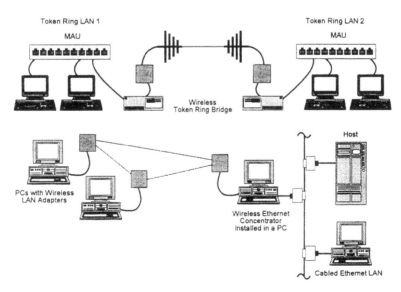

**Exhibit 4.   Wireless Bridging for Token Ring and Ethernet**

of wireless bridges can be very attractive. And whereas leased T1/E1 lines (or fractional T1/E1 lines) involve recurring monthly costs, there are no such charges associated with wireless bridges. Moreover, the use of wireless bridges installed indoors and aimed out office windows eliminates the connection delays typically involved with ordering new T1 lines from the telephone company.

Depending on the vendor, wireless bridges may include built-in network management agents so they can be managed using SNMP tools. These tools give network managers the means to enable and disable transceivers, provide notification of selected events, monitor performance and link status, and diagnose problems. Support for SNMP allows network managers to control wireless LAN resources as they would nodes on any other LAN.

## COMMUNICATION-ENABLED APPLICATIONS

A notable trend among application software vendors is to communication-enable their products, giving users instant connections to nationwide wireless messaging and cellular data network services for access to word processing, database, and spreadsheet files located on remote file servers or desktop machines. The setup includes a radio modem which connects to a laptop or a desktop computer via an RS-232 port. The modem usually comes equipped to support one of several leading e-mail applications and provides access to a nationwide service provider using the Hayes AT command set. The packet and radio protocols used by the service provider are also bundled with the modem.

The installation procedure is relatively simple. New users can get online by simply filling out an on-screen form included with the installation package, and messaging it back to the service provider, which will hook up the user to its cellular data network within a few hours.

Once the communication software establishes the connection, users have access to directories on the file server or desktop machine as if it were another logical drive. If a word processing file is accessed, for instance, the communication software brings the entire file to the mobile machine and allows the user to work locally. The software automatically synchronizes the updated files or directories whenever a connection is detected. In the case of database files, some programs include a Structured Query Language query function that transfers individual records to the wireless client and synchronizes them with those on the home machine.

Depending on the vendor, communication software may include compression and caching to reduce network traffic, and encryption for security. Another feature, called "filtering," blocks the transfer of frequently used information, such as repetitive screens, which can inflate transmission costs. If the connection is dropped, files are not necessarily lost. The program just waits for the connection to be reestablished and completes the file transfer. Response is not immediate. It can take several minutes to retrieve word-processing or spreadsheet files of 4K bytes, for example.

Wireless messaging has the potential to extend the reach of many applications, including scheduling software and network management tools. Changes made to electronic scheduling programs can be sent instantly to users on the road and displayed on an alphanumeric pager, or sent to a portable computer via an integral wireless receiver. In the area of network management, wireless messaging can enable network management programs to alert managers to problems when they are away from their desks through a pager, PDA, palmtop computer, or notebook. With a notebook computer equipped with remote control software, the network manager can view the management console's screen and initiate diagnostic or reconfiguration routines as if he or she were sitting in front of the console.

## WIRELESS SERVICE PROVIDERS

There are numerous providers of wireless data services. These services range from one-way radio, two-way paging, and e-mail, to interactive data networking. Wireless messaging services allow users to communicate with customers and colleagues and access all kinds of information without being tethered to their desks. This freedom allows personal schedules to be highly flexible and permits the user to stay informed of current developments regardless of location, both of which often translate into productivity gains. More important, two-way wireless messaging services empower users by allowing them to react to information instantly.

As messaging technologies develop and new capabilities are added, users are confronted with a range of choices in service selection. Many of these services support more than beepers and alphanumeric pagers. In addition to being able to send e-mail and retrieve files from corporate databases, users can access online services and have personalized news feeds sent directly to their pocket computer. Some services can even relay voice mail and provide connections to the Internet.

### Long Distance Carriers

The major long-distance carriers are also involved in the provision of cellular services. The carriers' support for wireless technology and mobile communications services could facilitate nationwide coverage, eventually leading to lower prices and new service options.

### CONCLUSION

The acceptance of wireless technology among mobile computer users has forced network managers to explore new ways of enabling professionals at all organizational levels to roam free, yet maintain links with essential corporate resources. Although wireless data networking already provides a partial solution to the cabling and logistical problems of large traditional networks, it has the potential to provide the much-needed infrastructure for the explosive growth of portable computing. But before it can live up to this potential, wireless data networking technologies must develop the same level of protocol standardization, reliability, and security as wired networks. Fortunately, progress is being made in all these areas.

# Chapter 31
# Wireless Technology Impacts the Enterprise Network

*Andres Llana, Jr.*

WIRELESS TECHNOLOGY HAS BEEN WITH US FOR MANY YEARS; HOWEVER, THE APPLICATION OF THIS TECHNOLOGY DID NOT BEGIN A VERY REAL ADVANCE UNTIL THE MID-1990s. Much of the success of this technology can be traced to the rapid deployment of wireless technology in European countries. In these areas, the deployment of wireless local loop (WLL) systems made it possible to provide an alternative to the lack of a dependable copper infrastructure. In some countries where subscribers waited years for a telephone, the availability of wireless technology reduced the wait time to weeks. Later, as GSM networks began to proliferate, the concept of greater mobility (i.e., mobile handsets) enabled many more subscribers to move onto the public network without the requirement for even a terminal in their homes — as was the case with the WLL systems.

Due to the growing penetration of cellular services, the ITU projects that by 2008 there will be more mobile than fix-line subscribers, perhaps as many as a billion cellular subscribers. The fast-paced growth in global wireless services has greatly impacted the expansion of wireless data communications. This is not to say that wireless systems in support of data communication requirements have not been around for some time; it just was not embraced as an enterprise network solution.

However, with the success of wireless technology in European countries and around the world, more viable wireless solutions have made their way into the marketplace. Broadly speaking, the driving forces for change can be seen in the growth of the Internet, increased user mobility, and pervasive computing, where computer chips now play a greater role in the monitoring and control of various service devices. Mobile telephones and pagers have accomplished a great deal in supporting the remote worker's requirement for maintaining a meaningful information exchange with corporate headquarters. Applications such as voice messaging, online fax, and online information access have driven wireless data transmission to the next tier. These applications have served to give the new-age "road warrior" a definite advantage as a remote worker.

## WIRELESS COMMUNICATIONS

Wireless communications in the United States extend back to the early 1950s when the Rural Electrification Administration (REA) sought ways to provide telephone service to remote farms and ranches. Early efforts bore little fruit and, as late as 1985, the REA was still trying to get a system into operation. However, by the mid-1990s, a rush of new products resulted following the successful deployment of global analog cellular mobile telephone service. The most common form of wireless telephones came with the application the CT-10 cordless telephone and later the CT-2 digital phone. Wireless internal telecommunications became fairly commonplace when AT&T, Ericsson, Nortel, NEC, and Rolm introduced wireless adjunct systems for installed PBX systems. These adjunct systems linked to a PBX via separate station line cards based on the standard 2500 nonelectronic desk telephone (see Exhibit 1). These add-on systems supported an RF controller that used the ISM (Industrial-Scientific-Medical) 900 MHz frequencies. Remote RF controllers were positioned around the user's premises to receive transmissions from roving users with mobile handsets.

Today Lucent (AT&T), Ericsson, NEC, and Rolm (Siemens) have all introduced an entirely new generation of wireless PBX products that allow the end user to establish a totally integrated wireless voice and data network. For example, Lucent has introduced their Definity Wireless Business Systems as well as their TransTalk 9000 system. This latter system can be either a dual-zone or single-zone system and can support up to 500,000 square feet. A similar two-zone system can be used to support a multi-level building or a combination of several closely coupled buildings (i.e., warehouse, manufacturing, etc.). The Definity Wireless DECT (Digital Enhanced Cordless Telecommunications) system, which operates in the 1880 to 1900 MHz range, has similar capabilities and is marketed outside the United States. The Nortel Companion system is another similar wireless system and works off of the Meridan I (Option 11 C) system. The Companion system supports all of the same station features as found on a standard electronic desk telephone.

These new wireless PBX systems can be integrated directly to the corporate LAN or WAN and function as centralized communications servers. For example, the Ericsson MD 110 system, when configured with an IP gateway unit, serves to interface the MD 110 PBX to an IP network, allowing voice traffic to share bandwidth with data over the IP network (see Exhibit 2).

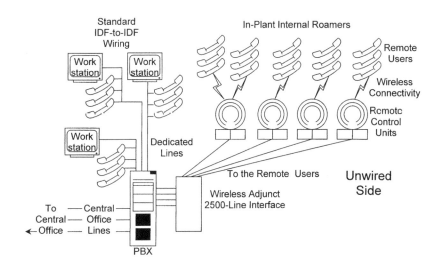

**Exhibit 1.  Wireless Internal Communications**

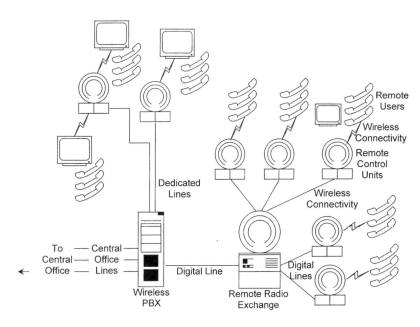

**Exhibit 2.  Wireless PBX System**

## WIRELESS OFFICE SERVICES (WOS)

Office complexes, manufacturing warehouses, and other facilities that are spread out and supported with disbursed population of employees are an ideal opportunity for the wireless service provider. Motorola, which introduced its M-Cell GSM access product at the 1998 GSM World Congress, was able to provide attendees with support for over 16,000 calls during the three-day conference. This system is essentially an internal telephone system that functions like any other PBX system except that it is supported by a localized GSM wireless network operator. In this environment, building distributed RF units linked to cluster controllers support internal interoffice calling. When a user leaves the office, his or her calls are then seamlessly linked via the local GSM wireless network. Once General Packet Radio Service (GPRS) support is added to the network, non-voice services can also be supported.

In the United States service providers are now pursuing wireless office services (WOS) as a new market niche. In this environment, the service provider establishes a distributed radio system (DRS) throughout the office or multi-tenant facility in much the same way that a PBX system or wireless LAN is configured. In this scenario, mini base stations (MBS) are interfaced to distributed antennas (DAS), forming the basic infrastructure. The MBS units are linked in much the same way as in building data network, which in turn are linked to a central radio. The advantage of these carrier-provided solutions is the transparent mobility of the end users in the system. While in the building or corporate facilities, the end users do not incur any per-minute billing; however, once they leave the premises, they are treated like regular mobile users and billed accordingly.

In this arrangement, the end user is never out of touch and always within reach, as one assigned telephone number follows the end user both on and off premises. Cellular One on the West Coast is currently offering this service in the San Francisco area.

Sprint has begun to offer wireless data service over its PCS network, which comprises over 11,000 base stations. This network exceeds the Bell-South Wireless Data service and ARIDS combined data networks. The Sprint data network will work through Sprint PCS smart phones, such as the Nokia, Motorola, or Qualcom, that support smart set displays. Further, these smart sets, when configured with microbrowsers, can be used to access the Internet for e-mail and other abridged services. This new data service also provides access to stock quotes and other time-critical information. Kits are available to provide Internet access for laptops or PDAs at 14.4 Kbps.

## MORE INTEGRATION

Wireless data communications using a packetized data standard called Cellular Digital Packet Data (CDPD) has been getting more use as more wireless applications are being deployed. However, this service is limited to low speeds of 19.2 Kbps or less, and has been implemented on D-AMPS IS-136 networks. CDPD technology serves to enhance the existing AMPS cellular infrastructure by detecting unused cellular channel space in which to transmit data. This allows the operator to maximize the use of the available physical cell site infrastructure.

While 19.2 Kbps may seem slow, it does answer a broad requirement for low-speed transactions aimed at one-way data collection for meter or device reading. This application of CDPD has made it possible to offer many new data collection type applications for electric, gas, and water meter reading.

To meet the growing demand for wireless data applications, newer CDPD modems have made their appearance. For example, Novatel has introduced the Minstrel modem for applications with Palm computing devices. These modems have their own IP address and can be used to access the Internet. The modems also support a built-in TCP/IP stack that can be used for custom software development using the Palm OS™. The Minstrel modem is configured with SmartCode software, HandMail™ and HandWeb™ software, and a modem management package. This new technology has resulted in a number of sales terminal applications, field technician applications, as well as mobile applications in transportation (e.g., fleet and vehicle management, public safety, and disaster recovery). Handheld terminal applications have also been aided by the introduction of Windows CE software configured with utilities such as Pocket Excel, Pocket Word, Internet Explorer, Scheduler, e-mail, Calendar, and Task Manager. All of these packages allow mobile workers to manage their time in transit more efficiently.

### Wireless Local Area Networks

Some of the earliest wireless LAN products were slow by comparison with today's products. For example, in the early 1990s Motorola introduced a product that was developed around a microcellular design using the 18 to 19 GHz frequency. The system used an intelligent six-sector antenna, which was used for both data reception and transmission. The antenna supported a scanning system that was used to select the best transmission path from its associated terminal to the next terminal in the network. A high-performance RF digital signal processor was used to handle the modulation and demodulation of the 18 GHz carrier using four-level frequency shift keying (FSK). This would ultimately support 10 Mbps Ethernet, which was considered fast in the early 1990s.

Wireless LAN technology in the early 1990s was slow to catch on as many networks were hard-wired; it was not until changes were made in office and facility arrangements that wireless technology gained acceptance. Because the early products were unlicensed, they could be used to cover short distances (several hundred feet) within buildings and under a mile between buildings. A good example of such a wireless network can be seen in the Jacob Javits Convention Center in New York. In this application, a wireless LAN was tailored to cover 1.5 million square feet of convention center floorspace. Distributed smart antennas, which act like mini base stations, are spread around the facility and allow transmission of voice and data throughout the facility.

## A NEW STANDARD

In 1997, the IEEE standard for wireless networking was finally ratified, establishing an interoperability standard for all vendor products. Essentially, the 802.11 standard made it possible for companies to introduce a higher performing wireless LAN product that offers a degree of interoperability. These new products provide wireless connectivity starting at the mobile PC level and include products to interface a wired LAN with wireless desktop PCs, and peripherals. Also new to wireless LANs are firewalls that protect against unauthorized access into the corporate LAN. These wireless LAN security devices are based on an IP network layer encryption using the IPSec (IP Security) standards. Also incorporated as part of these systems are a range of authorization keys, authentication policies, and automatic security procedures.

As a group, 802.11 products operate in the 2.4 GHz ISM band with a bit rate of up to 2 Mbps and a fall-back rate of 1 Mbps. Many vendor products can go higher; for example, Ericsson introduced a 802.11 product line in 1998 that provides a data rate of 3 Mbps.

The Wireless Ethernet Compatibility Alliance (WECA) is developing a series of interoperability tests that will allow vendors to test their products to determine if they are interoperable. This is seen as a vital step toward ensuring that when the new 802 High Rate Direct Sequence (HRDS) standard (2.4 GHz @ 11 Mbps) is agreed upon, the WECA will be able certify products for enterprise deployment. HRDS products have been announced by several vendors; for example, Cabletron has announced an 11 Mbps product for its RoamABOUT wireless LAN product line.

In some sectors, work is in progress on a HyperLAN/2 standard product that will support data rates of up to 54 Mbps. These devices will operate in the 5 GHz ISM band. Ericsson plans to offer a HyperLAN/2 product that will support an end-user data rate of 20 to 25 Mbps.

Many vendors now offer wireless bridges that provide the capability to link wireless LAN islands into a contiguous wireless/wired LAN network. Many of these devices operate in the ISM band and offer the network administrator a cost-effective means of linking remote "line-of-sight" locations for up to 20 km. A good example of such a class of terminals can be seen in Wireless, Inc.'s MicroLink microwave radio terminal. This device operates in the 2.4 GHz ISM band and supports two models: a low-end model at 64 to 256 Kbps and a high-end model at 512 and 1024 Kbps. The terminal can operate at distances of up to 20 km and integrates both voice and data traffic between locations (see Exhibit 3).

Other vendors with similar terminal products include ADTRAN, which recently introduced its Tracer terminal that will go up to 30 miles and support dual T1s. IOWAVE also provides a similar terminal that supports links of up to 20 miles for about $12,000 per link.

## WIRELESS INTERNET ACCESS

In some areas, broadband access to the Internet is gradually getting away from the ISDN or dial-up access model. This can be attributed in part to the FCC, which released 300 MHz of spectrum for the Unlicensed National Information Infrastructure (U-NII). The U-NII band is broken down into three bands: 5.15–5.25 GHz for indoor application, 5.25–5.35 GHz for

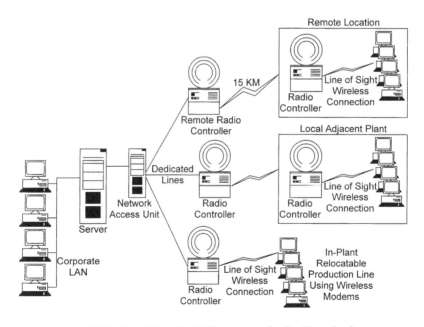

**Exhibit 3. MicroLink Microwave Radio Terminal**

campus application, and 5.75–5.85 GHz for local access of up to ten miles. This new spectrum has resulted in the introduction of a new generation of wireless Internet routers, also referred to Internet radios. Internet radios can be set up on rooftops by an ISP to provide direct Internet access via the ISP Internet hub. These terminals can be configured in a point-to-point configuration or a point-to-multipoint configuration. A good example of such terminals can be seen in Wireless Inc.'s WaveNet IP series, which can be used by an ISP to set up a point-to-multipoint Internet access arrangement completely outside of the public utility. By controlling the cost of local loop access, the ISP can offer better rates and higher speed access. The WaveNet IP arrangement is sometimes referred to as W-DSL because a network can support DSL-like access with speeds of up to 512 Kbps of symmetrical bandwidth.

## BROADBAND INTERNET ACCESS

Broadband Internet access is now being offered via licensed 38 GHz Local Multi-Point Distribution Services (LMDS) and Local Multi-point Communications Systems (LMCS) license holders. These fixed wireless service providers are able to support fiber optic network bandwidth without the physical fiber being in place. A good example of a broadband wireless (LMDS) system can be seen in the TRITON Invisible Fiber product line used to deploy a network of rooftop terminals in a consecutive point network.

These networks are capable of supporting a 20 to 40 square mile geographic area, providing local broadband service for an entire metropolitan area. MaxLink Communications of Ontario, Canada, has launched an LMDS service in Canada using a Newbridge LMDS system to offer IP over ATM. Home Telephone, a successful bidder in the 1998 FCC LMDS spectrum auction, is offering LMDS service in the Charleston, South Carolina, basic trading area (BTA), using the Newbridge LMDS system. A similar service is being trialed in San Jose using the TRITON Invisible Fiber product. Initially, this service is limited to a select user group within an office park and will be expanded from there.

LMDS broadband services provide the enterprise network designer with a potentially more cost-effective option where broadband services are required to support multimedia, video, and IP data transport requirements.

## WHO USES WIRELESS TECHNOLOGY?

Some of the largest users of wireless technology can be seen in the transportation and shipping industry. Federal Express and United Parcel are good examples of perhaps the largest users of wireless technology. Another area is that of automated vehicle location systems that are supported through a combination of satellite and land line systems coupled with the Internet.

## CONSUMER APPLICATIONS

A good example of a consumer-level system can be seen in the OnStar system being offered as an option with some high-end General Motors products, such as its Cadillac automobile product line. The OnStar system is combined with a cellular service and the GPS tracking system. The system provides a series of end-user services that includes travel directions, emergency road services, automobile enabling services, personal notification, and theft notification.

The OnStar system uses a GPS tracking device that is installed on the vehicle and allows the OnStar control center to locate a subscriber's vehicle. Through a cellular link with an on-board computer, the control center can detect if the car's airbags have been deployed. If so, the control center detects a change, and a call to the subscriber is made to determine if there is a need for assistance. The control center can also remotely open the car doors if the subscriber has locked himself out of the car.

## TRANSPORTATION

Qualcom offers a multi-level vehicle location and monitoring service for large trucking and transport companies. This service is supported through a combination of satellite, cellular, and land line services. Trucks with special roof-mounted units can be tracked and monitored anyplace within the United States and Canada. Monitoring includes truck system performance, loading and unloading events, as well as redirection of vehicles for new load pickups. Drivers are able to communicate with the control center via messaging or cellular wireless contact. Dispatchers are able to, through land line contact with the Qualcom control center, dispatch and manage all company assets deployed on the nation's highway network.

### Health Care

A surprisingly large number of health care service providers have taken advantage of wireless technology. Good examples of the application of wireless technology can be seen at Austin Regional Clinic, Indiana Methodist Hospital, St. Joseph Hospital, Wausau Hospital, and Winthrop-University Hospital, to name a few. All of these facilities have essentially the same problem — getting to patient information, where and when needed. Many found that they had to take handwritten notes to the nearest nurse station and enter the information manually into a computer terminal. As a result, administrators had to come up with a more efficient way to operate.

Austin Regional Clinic elected to supply its medical professionals with mobile handheld computers to record and retrieve patient information in real time. These terminals were linked to the clinic's Novell Netware LAN using PCMCIA modem cards. A series of wireless distributed access points located throughout the clinic provided a direct link to the LAN via a corresponding link in the clinic's communication server. The portable computers used were grid pad, pen-based portables configured with application screens, and allowed medical professionals simplified data entry and retrieval. This system eliminated large amounts of paperwork, thus allowing the professionals to function in a paperless environment.

## Manufacturing

In some manufacturing plants, sensors and programmable logic controllers (PLCs) are used to control many of the processes related to product manufacturing. In many places, these devices are hard-wired into high-maintenance networks that need frequent attention. In many plants, these networks have been fitted with Ethernet interfaces as part of a plantwide LAN. However, many plant managers have found that they can refit with wireless adapter cards that provide an RF link to wireless access points located around the plant. These arrangements link the PLCs directly into the wired LAN and the server, ensuring timely monitoring of all devices.

Avon Products, Inc., faced an expensive problem in extending the LAN in a Chicago area plant's factory floor. In this facility, production lines were not static and subject to regular reconfiguration. Further, operator mobility required to support 50 production lines along 500 linear feet confounded the problem of rewiring print stations to support the operators with barcode labels. Instead of rewiring, a series of printers configured with wireless modems were set up to receive barcode label files from print servers. The plant has a series of distributed base stations (terminal servers) that are linked to the LAN and a host system that supports the wireless link between the wireless printers and the LAN. The print servers, which are linked to the LAN Ethernet, receive barcode files from a VAX computer. As product is being manufactured, barcode information can be sent to the appropriate print server, where it can then be routed to the proper remote wireless printer.

## Financial

The Pacific Exchange (on the West Coast) and Hull Trading (headquartered in Chicago) both opted to deploy wireless terminals on the trading floor to simplify the trading process. Instead of walking to a static terminal to enter trade information, traders can now do that from their handheld terminals. This innovation permits much faster trades, while eliminating many manual steps as well as the reliance on handwritten notes.

## SEARCHING FOR A WIRELESS SOLUTION

In planning for the migration to a wireless network arrangement, the planner must be certain of his or her plan. Wireless applications require antennas and base stations to receive and transmit wireless signals between a mobile terminal and a mini base station. That said, the planner must be certain that antenna coverage can be established throughout the area(s) to be served by the wireless terminals.

While most wireless modems and RF base stations work, many may not be interoperable between vendor equipment. Because there are so many vendors offering products, the planner needs to be certain of the vendor's commitment to the market. Now that the 802.11 standard has been accepted, the planner should not consider proprietary systems to avoid early obsolescence; many products and vendors of the early 1990s that had great products are no longer with us.

Wireless network arrangements provide a great deal of flexibility, but the planner should limit the migration to a wireless network arrangement to those applications that will produce a reasonable savings in terms of reduced manpower.

Application software requires careful review because much of the software designed to function over a LAN with standard PCs may not work the same way with a laptop PC. Further, because many mobile terminals are configured with Windows CE software, one needs to be aware of the differences and their interface to the LAN operating system. Where the opportunity for the application of wireless technology is limited, the planner may find opportunities for direct linking of facilities to avoid central office (CO) dedicated circuit costs for voice and data transport. With many of the newer systems on the market, the planner can gain greater reach than before to link company facilities. Further, by working with an ISP provider, many times the planner can arrange for a rooftop Internet radio to link the ISP hub directly with the corporate network hub, thus providing much higher speed access to the Internet for the corporate network users.

## SUMMARY

Wireless technology has opened up a new range of possibilities for linking the enterprise network than previously available to the network planner. The keys to success are proper preplanning and selection of equipment; adherence to established standards with an eye toward the future; and the availability of future systems with higher throughput options. Careful alignment of applications software is another important issue as some tailor made soft
ware may be necessary to link legacy applications.

Enhancing the corporate network to bring it into line with the state-of-the-art should not be the end-all, but rather an opportunity to reduce operating costs and improve overall corporate productivity.

# Chapter 32
# Mobile Database Interoperability: Architecture and Functionality

*Antonio Si*

WIRELESS NETWORKS AND MOBILE COMPUTING HAVE OPENED UP NEW POSSIBILITIES FOR INFORMATION ACCESS AND SHARING. The need to interoperate multiple heterogeneous, autonomous databases is no longer confined to a conventional federated environment.

A mobile environment is usually composed of a collection of static servers and a collection of mobile clients. Each server is responsible for disseminating information over one or more wireless channels to a collection of mobile clients. The geographical area within which all mobile clients could be serviced by a particular server is called a cell of that server.

In this mobile environment, databases managed by database servers of different cells might be autonomous. Information maintained in a database will usually be most useful to clients within its geographical cell. In this respect, information maintained by databases of different cells might be disjoint or might be related. A mobile client, when migrating from one wireless cell to another, might want to access information maintained in the database server and relate it to the information maintained in its own database. Such an environment is termed a mobile federation, to distinguish it from a conventional federated environment. The database managed by a mobile client is termed a mobile database, while the database managed by the server is a server database. Using similar terminology, the database system managed by a mobile client is referred to as a mobile component and the database system managed by a server is referred to as a server component.

0-8493-1160-8/02/$0.00+$1.50

It is not clear if existing techniques can address interoperability in this newly evolved computing environment. This article presents a reference architecture for a conventional federated environment, proposes a set of functional requirements that a federated environment should support, and examines existing techniques for a federated environment with respect to each functional requirement in the context of the newly evolved mobile federation.

## A WORKING SCENARIO

A tourist would like to discover information about attractions and accommodations within a certain area. With a portable computer equipped with a wireless communication interface, each mobile client (tourist) can receive travel information from the server over a wireless channel. Such an application might be called an Advanced Traveler Information System (ATIS).

In practice, each server database would maintain traveler information restricted to its own cell. For example, a server database serving the city of Los Angeles might provide vacancy information in all hotels within the Los Angeles area, such as the Holiday Inn near the Hollywood freeway. A user might query the server database to obtain the names of all hotels that have vacancies. Information maintained by different server databases might, to a large extent, be disjoint in this application domain, but there might still be some information overlap among different server databases.

For example, a Holiday Inn within the Los Angeles region might decide to maintain partial information on Holiday Inns in other regions, such as Pasadena. It is also important to note that each different server database will, in general, be autonomous, employing different database management tools and even different data models to manage its own information. Exhibit 1 illustrates a snapshot of the information maintained in different server databases and a mobile client who accesses information via a wireless channel.

It would be useful to have a high-level capability that allows structured units of information to be identified from a server database and incorporated into a local database managed by a mobile client. For example, a client might want to maintain information on all hotels in cell 1 and cell 2, since it travels to these two areas the most. A client visiting cell 1 (as shown in Exhibit 1) might issue a query to obtain all hotel information. When the client visits cell 2, the hotel information incorporated into his or her database will have to be interoperated with the existing information that the client previously incorporated from the server database in cell 1. This allows a mobile client to query the information using its own familiar database management tools. These various server databases, together with the local database of the mobile client, form a mobile federation. It is

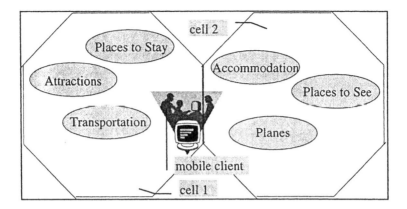

**Exhibit 1.  Snapshot of ATIS Databases**

interesting to note that the local database maintained in a mobile client is, in effect, a data warehouse since its data is constructed by integrating data from various data sources.

The objective of a mobile federation is similar to a conventional federated database environment. Both environments are trying to share information among multiple autonomous databases. In a mobile federation, the sharing of information is implicit; the information is shared within the context of a mobile client. In a conventional federated system, the information is shared among the databases themselves. Obviously, the server databases of various cells could also share information among themselves, in which case the server databases form a conventional federated environment as well.

## FEDERATED ENVIRONMENT ARCHITECTURE

Exhibit 2 illustrates a typical federated environment. As the exhibit shows, a collection of independent database components is interconnected via a communication network. Each component consists of a database and a schema. A database is a repository of data structured or modeled according to the definition of the schema, which can be regarded as a collection of conceptual entity types. (The implementation of an entity type, of course, depends on the database model employed by the component; it may be a relation in a relational model, or it can be an object class, if an object-oriented model is employed.)

### Information Sharing Techniques

Sharing of database information in this federated environment could be achieved at three different levels of granularity and abstraction:

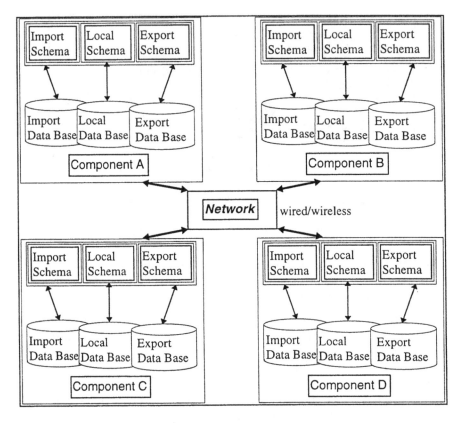

**Exhibit 2: Reference Architecture for a Federated Environment**

- Entity types belonging to the schema of individual components could be shared such that modeled real-world concepts could be reused.
- Data instances stored in individual components' databases (the implementation of which also depends on the database model employed) could be shared such that information of modeled real-world entities could be reused.
- Applications developed on a component's database could be shared among any other components. For example, if the server database in cell 1 in Exhibit 1 develops a pathfinder application that allows a mobile client to search for the shortest route to a destination, it could be reused by a mobile client in searching paths within cell 2 as well.

The simplest way to achieve information sharing in a database federation is for a component to simply browse through the content of a nonlocal (i.e., remote) component's database. In this respect, an explorer should be provided. Alternatively, a component could integrate remote information into its local database. The newly integrated information could be reused by the component in the future. To support such reuse of information, the database of a component, say X, is logically partitioned into three different subsets, as shown in Exhibit 2:

- *Local database.* The local database (LD) refers to the set of data instances originally created by X.
- *Import database.* The import database (ID) refers to the set of remote data instances that X retrieves from the export databases of remote components.
- *Export database.* The export database (ED) is a subset of the union of the local database and import database, which represents the set of data instances the component is willing to share with other components. In other words, a component should be able to export its imported data instances if the access privilege constraints specified on the imported instances are not violated.

Similarly, from the reference architecture in Exhibit 1, the schema of a component X is also partitioned into three different subsets. The local schema (LS) refers to the entity types originally created by X and is used to model the local database. The import schema (IS), which refers to the entity types X retrieves from the export schema of remote components, is used to model the import database. Finally, the export schema (ES), which is the subset of the union of LS and IS, is used to model the export database.

Integrating a remote application belonging to a remote component, say Y, into X's local system is difficult because X's local computer system might be different from that of Y. One possibility (proposed by D. Fang, et al.) is to integrate the signature of the remote application into X's local system. To execute the application, X's local data is passed to component Y; the application is run on the remote component using X's data and the results are returned back to X. The Java virtual machine could make application sharing easier.

## CHARACTERISTICS OF A FEDERATED DATABASE ENVIRONMENT

Each component within a federation is usually heterogeneous and autonomous in nature. Heterogeneity is a natural consequence of the independent creation and evolution of autonomous databases; it refers to the variations in which information is specified and structured in different components. Autonomy means each component is under separate and independent control.

### Heterogeneity

In general, a spectrum of heterogeneities of different levels of abstraction could be classified.

**Database model heterogeneity.** Each component may use different database models to describe the structure and constraints of its data.

**Conceptual schema heterogeneity.** Each component may model similar real-world concepts in different ways, such as the different schema used by the different database components of the multiple ATIS databases depicted in Exhibit 1. This is also referred to as semantic heterogeneity. This conceptual schema heterogeneity could be further divided into three discrepancies, each of which can be explained as follows:

- *Naming mismatch.* Two entity types from different components modeling the same real-world concept might use different naming conventions in representing the attributes. In the ATIS database in Exhibit 1, the ranking of a hotel might be modeled by an attribute called "rank" of Places to Stay in component A, while the same information might be modeled by an attribute called "number of stars" of Accommodation in component B.
- *Domain mismatch.* The same attribute of two entity types from different components might be represented in different domains. For example, both Attractions and Places to See of components A and B, respectively, in Exhibit 1 might have an attribute "zip code." However, component A might represent the attribute as an integer, while component B might represent it as a string.
- *Schematic discrepancy.* Data in one database might be represented as entity types in another database. In Exhibit 1, entity type Planes of component B might be represented as an attribute of Attractions in component A.
- *Data specification heterogeneity.* Each component may model similar real-world entities in different units of measure. One component might represent the distance of an attraction in meters, while another component might represent it in miles.
- *Update heterogeneity.* Since each component is under separate and independent control, data instances modeling the same real-world entity in different databases might be updated asynchronously. When the daily rate of a hotel is updated, databases A and B in Exhibit 1 might be updated at different times.
- *Database tools heterogeneity.* Each component may use different tools to manipulate its own database. For example, different components might use different query languages.

## Types of Autonomy

Orthogonally, each component can exhibit several different types of autonomy.

**Design autonomy.** This refers to the ability of a component to choose its own design on the data being managed, the representation of the data instances, the constraints of the data, and the implementation of the component's database system.

**Association autonomy.** This refers to the ability of a component to decide to what extent the component would like to participate in the interoperability activity. A component is free to share its schema, data, or applications with other components; a component can even decide not to participate in the sharing activity at all.

**Control autonomy.** This refers to the ability of a component to control the access privileges of any remote component on each of its exported information units (entity types or instances). In general, four types of access control privilege could be granted by a component to a remote component on each of its exported information units:

- Read (R) access to the database instances
- Read definition (RD) access to entity types
- Write (W) access to database instances
- Generate (G) access for creating database instances

These four access privileges form a partial order such that $W > G > RD$ and $W > R > RD$. Neither G nor R dominates the other. For instance, if component X grants W access privilege to remote component Y on one of its exported entity types, component Y is allowed to read the instances of the entity type as well. By contrast, if X only grants R access privilege to Y on the entity type, Y is not allowed to modify any instances of the entity type.

If an exported unit of a component, say X, is imported from another component, Y, the capability of X to control the access privileges on the exported unit will depend on whether the unit is imported by copy or imported by reference from Y.

**Execution autonomy.** This refers to the ability of a component to execute local operations without interference from external components. If, for example, component X might run an application on behalf of remote component Y. This autonomy implies that X can run the application as if it is a local execution (i.e., X can schedule, commit, or abort the application freely).

## FUNCTIONAL REQUIREMENTS OF A FEDERATED DATABASE ENVIRONMENT

From the perspective of a component, X, several functional capabilities need to be supported in order to be able to participate in the interoperability activity with other components.

## Information Exportation

Component X must be able to specify the information it is willing to share with other components. Such a facility should allow the component to specify the export schema, the export database, or any application that the component would like to be sharable. Furthermore, X should be able to specify the access privileges of each remote component on each of its exported information units.

A mobile federation is comparatively more dynamic than a database federation, connecting and disconnecting from the wireless network frequently. A mobile component also enters and leaves a cell frequently. It is difficult for a server component to keep track of which mobile components are currently residing within the cell under its management. Furthermore, a cell can potentially have many components visiting at any moment. Therefore, it is not possible for a server component to indicate the access privileges of each mobile component. An access control mechanism that is scalable with respect to the number of mobile components is necessary. Due to the dynamic nature of a mobile component, it is not always possible to incorporate information from a mobile component.

## Information Discovery

Before component X can access or use any remote information, X must be aware of the existence and availability of the information in which it is interested. A facility must be provided to allow X to discover any remote information of interest at various granularity or abstraction, including schema, data, or applications.

In general, there are two ways information could be discovered by component X. One possibility is that X can formulate a discovery request for its interested information, in which case a facility must be provided to identify the components containing information units that are relevant to the request. Another possibility is for component X to navigate or explore the exported information space of each remote component and look for the interested information. An explorer must then be provided for such a navigation purpose.

## Information Importation

Once interested information units from remote components are discovered, component X can import the information units into its local database. Through importation, component X can reuse the discovered information in the future. In general, three importation capabilities are required: schema importation, data importation, and application importation.

**Schema importation.** This refers to the process of importing remote export schema into X's local schema. This process is further composed of two activities — heterogeneity resolution and schema integration. Heterogeneity resolution is the process of resolving any conflict that exists between X's local schema and the remote schema.

Since different components might use different database models to specify the data, a facility must be provided to translate the remote schema from the remote database model to the one used in X's local system. Furthermore, since different components might model similar real-world concepts differently, another heterogeneity that must be resolved is to identify the relationship between X's local schema and the remote schema.

Referring back to the ATIS federation in Exhibit 1, two entity types belonging to two different schema might model the same real-world concept, such as the Attractions information of component A and the Places to See information of component B. Alternatively, two entity types might model related information, such as the Transportation information of component A and the Planes information of component B. Finally, two entity types might model different concepts, such as the Attractions information of component A and the Planes information of component B.

**Data importation.** Similarly, data importation refers to the process of importing remote export database information into X's local database. This process is composed of two activities — instance identification and data integration.

Instance identification refers to the process of identifying the relationship between the remote database and the local database. Two data instances from different databases might model the same, related, or different real-world entities. This process is complicated because, on the one hand, instances from different databases cannot be expected to bear the same key attributes; on the other hand, merely matching non-key attributes may lead to unsatisfactory results because data instances modeling different entities may possess the same attribute values. This process is further complicated by possible update heterogeneity that might exist between the two instances.

Once the relationship between the remote database and X's local database is identified, the remote database can be integrated into the local database. Again, the remote database should be integrated such that its relationship with the local database is reflected.

There are two different paradigms for integrating a remote data instance from a remote component, Y, into X's local database: imported by copy and imported by reference.

When a remote instance is imported by copy, the data instance is copied into the local database. The copied data instance becomes part of the local database. Any access to the imported instance is referred to its local copy.

When a remote instance is imported by reference, a reference to the remote instance is maintained in the local database. Any access to the imported data instance requires a network request to Y for up-to-date data value. When a remote data instance is imported by copy, the local component, X, has complete control on the local copy of the imported instance and is allowed to specify the access privileges of other remote components on the local copy of the imported instance. However, when a remote data instance is imported by reference from component Y, Y still maintains its control over the imported instance. Component X is still free to export the imported instance; however, X cannot modify the access privileges specified by Y on this imported data instance.

Application importation can only be achieved to a very limited extent due to the possible differences in the computer systems of the different components. However, with the advent of Java mobility code, this could soon become a reality.

In a mobile federation, communication between a mobile component and a server database is usually over an unreliable wireless channel. It is more efficient for a mobile federation to import an instance by copying since a component does not need to rely on the network to obtain the data value of the instance. A mobile component, in general, has less storage space than a federated component. A mobile component, therefore, might not be able to import all data instances and will have to maintain only those instances that it accesses most frequently.

**Information querying and transaction processing.** Component X should be able to operate its imported information in its local system. The operation on the imported information should be transparent in the following manner:

- *Functional transparency.* All existing local tools of component X, such as its query language and DBMS software, should be operational on the imported information units in the same manner as they operate on the local information units.
- *Location transparency.* Users and tools operating on the imported information units should not be aware of their original locations and remote nature.

Very often, there is a conflict between supporting the described functional capabilities in a component and preserving the autonomy of the component. To preserve the autonomy of a component, modifying any component of the DBMS software is not recommended.

## TECHNIQUES FOR DATABASE SHARING

To support database sharing functional capabilities, data model heterogeneity must be resolved. This is usually addressed by employing a common canonical model, which provides a communication forum among various components. Schema and instances represented in the local data model are required to convert to the canonical model. Most research prototypes use an object model as the canonical model because of its expressive power. Most corporations, however, use relational models. ODBC from Microsoft and JDBC from Sun Microsystems are generally considered the industry standards.

**Information Exportation**

Information exportation can be easily achieved using database view mechanisms. Exhibit 3 illustrates the management of exported information. A sub-hierarchy rooted at class Exported-Classes is created under the root of the class hierarchy (i.e., OBJECTS). To export a class, O, a class name E_O is created as a subclass of Exported-Classes. To export an attribute of O, the same named attribute is created for E_O; this allows a component to specify exported information at the granularity of a single attribute.

Each exported instance is handled by a multiple-membership modeling construct of the object model, relating the original class to which the instance belongs to the E_ counterpart. In effect, classes belonging to the sub-hierarchy rooted at Exported-Classes represent the export schema, and the instances belonging to the sub-hierarchy represent the export database (depicted by the shaded region in Exhibit 3).

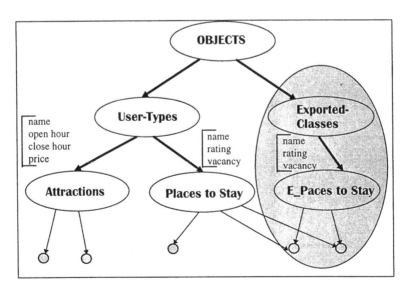

**Exhibit 3.   Information Exportation via Object View**

In Exhibit 3, only class Places to Stay is exported because only Places to Stay has a corresponding E_Places to Stay class. All attributes of Places to Stay have the corresponding ones defined on E_Places to Stay. Furthermore, two instances of Places to Stay are exported, relating via a multiple membership construct to E_Places to Stay. A component employing a relational data model could use a similar technique to specify its exporting information units since the export schema and database are, in effect, a view of the database.

Access control mechanisms for exported information are limited and especially difficult to achieve in a mobile federation. It is difficult for a server component to keep track of which mobile components are within the cell under its management and specify their individual access privileges. A multilevel access control mechanism is more applicable in this domain.

In a multilevel system, database information units are classified into privilege levels. The privilege levels are arranged in an order such that possessing a privilege level implies possessing all its subordinate levels. For example, a typical multilevel system contains four privilege levels: top secret (TS), secret (S), confidential (C), and unclassified (U). A typical database system could have arbitrary number of privilege levels. To access an information unit, the user needs to obtain a clearance at least equal to the privilege level of the unit. In a mobile federation, a mobile component could join a privilege level that will inherit the database information units that it could access from the server database.

## Information Discovery

Information discovery can be achieved by exploring the exported information of a database component. A typical device that explores the content of several databases is depicted in Exhibit 4. This explorer is implemented on the Netscape Navigator, providing a platform-independent browsing capability because of the availability of Netscape in UNIX workstations, Macintosh computers, and PCs.

The explorer in Exhibit 4 allows a component to explore multiple databases at the same time. It employs a relational model as the canonical model. Exported information units are viewed as relations. The explorer has windows to browse four separate databases of remote components and a window to the local database of a component.

An alternate approach to discovering remote information units that are interesting to a particular component is to specify the requirements of the interested information units. Remote information units that are relevant to the discovery specification will be identified. Specification could be initiated in an ad hoc manner. Following are three different types of discovery requests:

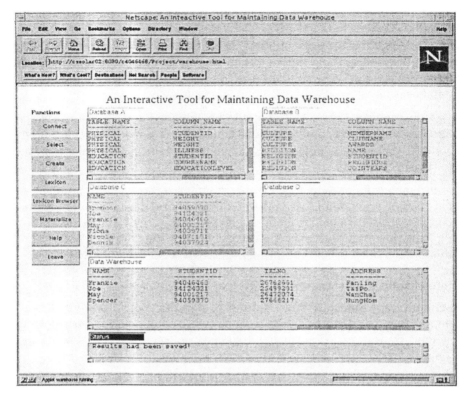

**Exhibit 4.   A Sample Information Discovery Explorer**

- A component can request remote entity types (instances) that model the same real-world concept (entity) as a local entity type (instance).
- A component can request remote entity types (instances) that model a complementary view of a local entity type (instance).
- A component can request remote entity types (instances) that model an overlapping view of a local entity type (instance).

To support these three types of discovery requests, one approach is to use a probability model to determine the extent to which two entity types (instances) from different databases modeled the same real-world concept. The probability model is based on two heuristics derived from the common attributes of the two entity types: intra-concept similarity indicator and inter-concept dissimilarity indicator.

Intuitively, an intra-concept similarity indicator refers to the probability that the common attributes will be modeled in related entity types. Inter-concept dissimilarity indicator refers to the probability that the attributes will be modeled in unrelated entity types. Two entity types from different databases will have a high probability of similarity if their overlapped attributes have a high intra-concept similarity indicator as well as a high inter-concept dissimilarity indicator. The use of these heuristics is based on the observation that different databases might model complementary or even disjointed views of the same concept; on the other hand, different databases might model different concepts similarly.

A more general specification could be achieved using first-order logic like language. Each component will thus require a mediator that understands the specification language and identifies information units relevant to the specification.

In a mobile federation, it is not important if a server database returns all information relevant to a discovery request; rather, it is much more important that the returned information units are indeed relevant because of the typically low bandwidth on a wireless channel. One approach to ensure this is to create a profile capturing the interests of each component.

### Information Importation

**Schema importation.** As mentioned previously, a component, X, can import (partial) remote schema from a remote component, Y, into its local schema by first resolving any heterogeneity between X's local schema and Y's schema.

One common approach to resolve schema heterogeneity between X's local schema and Y's remote schema is through a common knowledge base that contains various real-world concepts. Entity types from different databases are required to match with the concepts in the knowledge base. If both entity types map to the same concept in the knowledge base, they are regarded as modeling the same real-world concept. The knowledge base also provides instructions that define how a remote entity type could be integrated into the schema of a component's local database. The instructions could be specified in the form of rules or in a logic-like syntax. The former is easier to understand, but is less flexible. The latter is more flexible, but is less user-friendly.

In a mobile federation, it is difficult to specify a knowledge base that is applicable to all mobile components because there is a potentially unlimited number of mobile components visiting a wireless cell. It is perhaps more appropriate for a mobile component to provide its own knowledge or its personal profile, containing its own view for integrating remote schema into its own local schema.

**Instance importation.** To identify the relationship between instances from two databases, one needs to address the data specification heterogeneity and the update heterogeneity problems. Data specification heterogeneity is usually resolved, again, via a knowledge base, indicating how the representation of a remote instance could be converted into the representation of the local database.

Exhibit 5 illustrates the importance of update heterogeneity in identifying the relationship between instances from various databases. In Exhibit 5, valid time denotes the time in which a fact was true in reality, while the transaction time denotes the time in which a fact was captured in a database.

One approach to addressing update heterogeneity is to use historical update information on the instances to determine their degree of similarity. The historical update patterns of each instance represent the changes of states of the instance since its creation, inherently capturing its behavioral properties. This allows the instance identification to be performed based on behavioral property in addition to their structural property, as is done traditionally. The historical update information of an instance could be easily obtained through a transaction log.

As mentioned previously, instance integration could be performed via import by copy or import by reference. Using an object model as a canonical model, it is quite easy to support these two integration paradigms within one general framework. Exhibit 5 illustrates the partial conceptual schema of two components, A and B, of the ATIS databases from Exhibit 1.

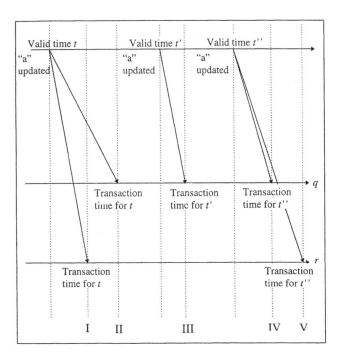

**Exhibit 5.    Update Heterogeneity in a Database Federation**

Instances x and y of component B are imported from class Accommodation of component A. The class Remote-Classes is created in component B to hold the object instance of definitions (OIDS) of the imported instances and the address of components from which the instances are imported (i.e., address of component A in the example). These two types of information are placed in the attributes r_oid and r_host, respectively. A class called R_Accommodation is created in component B as subclass of Remote-Classes to model the imported instances.

In effect, the sub-hierarchy rooted at Remote-Classes represents the import schema and the instances belonging to the sub-hierarchy represent the import database; this is depicted by the shaded region in Exhibit 6. Notice that the import sub-hierarchy has a mirror structure as the export sub-hierarchy mentioned previously.

Attributes of classes belonging to the Remote-Classes sub-hierarchy are user-defined methods. To obtain the attribute value for attribute "a" of an imported instance, x, the method "a" will obtain the "r_oid" of x and initiate a remote request to the remote component, whose address is specified in "r_host" of x, to obtain the attribute value for the instance. This achieves the effect of imported by reference. To support import by copy, the imported instances are added to a local class via multiple-membership construct. The additional inherited attributes could be used as placeholders for the copied attribute values of the imported instance. This is illustrated in Exhibit 6. The obtained value of an attribute of an instance returned from the corresponding method could be stored in the additional attributes inherited.

In a mobile federation, the connection between a mobile component and the server component could be disconnected at any moment, either due to the unreliability of a wireless channel or due to the movement of a mobile component to another cell. It is, thus, more appropriate for a component to import an instance by copy rather than by reference. This also has an effect of caching the instance into the local database of a mobile component. In this respect, one could regard the local database of a mobile component as a data warehouse since the local database is derived from multiple database sources.

Information discovery and importation could be provided within a uniform framework or interface. This allows discovered remote information units to be imported into the local database of a component. The explorer in Exhibit 4 also provides functions for information importation as well. In this particular system, a relational model is employed as a canonical model. The integration of information units from several databases is basically achieved via the "join" operation in this explorer. A component could also create a lexicon containing relationships among attributes of different databases. This resolves the conceptual heterogeneity. This lexicon acts as

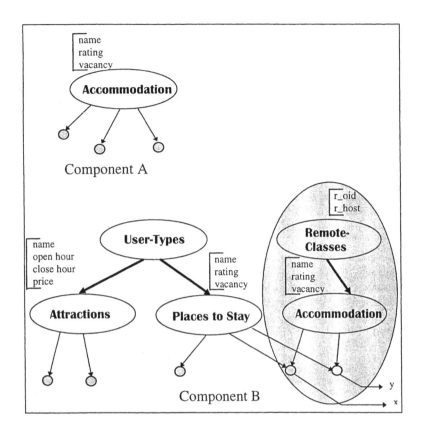

**Exhibit 6.   Data Integration**

a localized profile of the component, capturing the perspectives of the component on the relationships among information units from different databases.

### Information Querying and Transaction Processing

The notion of transaction is supported weakly in existing database federation prototypes. The reason stems from the fact that it is very difficult to support all the properties of transaction processing in a federated database system without seriously violating the autonomy of individual components and without rewriting the DBMS software of individual components.

Consider a situation in which a component X submits a transaction T to a remote component Y. The transaction T, when executed in component Y, is simply a local transaction of component Y. Component Y is free to abort the transaction without notifying component X. Component X, thus, might obtain inconsistent data.

## CONCLUSION

This article has presented a reference architecture and functional requirements for a federated database environment. Techniques for addressing each functional requirement have been presented. Limitations of existing techniques in the domain of a mobile federation have been discussed, and proposed solutions have also been briefly illustrated. Experiences with real applications in a mobile federation are necessary to further pinpoint additional problems that require research.

### ACKNOWLEDGMENTS

This work was supported in part by the Hong Kong Polytechnic University Central Research Grant Number 351/217. Part of the materials in this chapter are the results of the Remote-Exchange project at the University of Southern California.

# Chapter 33
# Does WAP Fill the Gap?

*Carlson Colomb*

## "THE INTERNET IS JUST A PASSING FAD"

DO YOU REMEMBER HEARING THESE WORDS NOT-SO-MANY MOONS AGO?

Did you speak them yourself?

Want to know the next "passing fad"?

The *wireless* Web.

Analysts predict a near-exponential wireless Internet market growth to be seen over the next three years. And it is easy to see why, with estimates that in the United States alone, there are currently more than 40 million households online; but there more than 75 million mobile phone subscribers and over 40 million paging subscribers. IDC has forecast that by mid-2001, all digital mobile phones shipped in the world will be Internet capable. With average wireless subscribers changing their mobile phones once a year, this means that by the end of 2002, there will be more wireless subscribers capable of Internet access than wired Internet users.

IDC is not alone in its crystal-ball reading of the wireless market. According to The Strategis Group, 291 million handsets were sold worldwide last year. The United States forms the lion's share of the market, followed by Japan, China, Italy, and the United Kingdom. The Yankee Group also predicts wireless commerce to account for as much as 25 percent of E-commerce by 2005.

But through what technology will this immense market be satisfied? With some areas in Europe already struggling to deliver quality audio or even network availability at peak times, how does one tackle the supplementary bandwidth issues associated with delivery of Internet data to the masses? And how will the vast content- and multimedia-rich Web fit onto a typical mobile phone screen? The answer is to kill two birds with one stone. Strip bandwidth-hungry images and deliver simplified information to the handset screen, formatted for the smaller interface. The answer is WAP.

0-8493-1160-8/02/$0.00+$1.50
© 2002 by CRC Press LLC

WAP (Wireless Application Protocol) is now the *de facto* worldwide standard for wireless information and telephony services on digital mobile phones and wireless devices such as PDAs (Personal Digital Assistants) that often run 3Com's Palm OS or Microsoft's Windows CE. The idea comes from the wireless industry, from companies such as Nokia, Motorola, Ericsson, and Unwired Planet, founding members of the WAP forum (www.wapforum.org) that is dedicated to the development of the standard.

The WAP Forum was formed after Omnipoint, a U.S. network operator, issued a tender for the supply of mobile information service. This resulted in responses from different vendors using proprietary technology to deliver the information, including HDML from Unwired Planet (now Phone.com). Vendors responding to the tender were informed that a common standard was desired and not proprietary technology. Because of the similarity of the vendors' approach, it made sense for them to cooperate to define such a standard.

WAP bridges the gap between the mobile world and the Internet and corporate intranets. An unlimited range of mobile value-added services can now be delivered to mobile users, independent of their network, mobile provider, and terminal. Using a pocket-sized or hand-held device, mobile subscribers can access the same wealth of information from a mobile handset device as they can from the desktop.

## WHY WAP?

In the past, wireless extranet access has been available through proprietary protocols that were designed for strict business applications, and never the consumer market. Examples of such are the portable shoebox-sized data collection terminals, such as those FedEX delivery people carry about on their route, logging customer signatures and delivery status wirelessly to the head office.

WAP optimizes the content of products that employ standard Internet technology to fit the small screen interfaces and bandwidth limitations of wireless devices and networks. Borrowing from the client/server model of the Internet, WAP uses a relatively simple microbrowser in the mobile phone, which requires only limited resources on the device. Thus, the services and applications reside on WAP servers, not in phones. A board member of the WAP Forum commented, "The philosophy behind WAP's approach is to utilize as few resources as possible on the hand-held device and compensate for the constraints of the device by enriching the functionality of the network."

WAP defines application, session, security, transaction, and transport layer protocols. The language in which pages are rendered to be delivered over WAP is WML (Wireless Markup Language). Thus, WML is to WAP what HTML is to HTTP. WML, although similar to HTML, is actually an XML application. The W3C defined XML as a meta-language, or a series of rules on creating other languages for specific applications. WML is such a language for wireless applications, which complies with XML rules.

The advantages of WAP include:

- Open vendor independent standard
- Carrier network independent
- Optimum for small screen size and low power consumption
- Multi-device support
- Transport mechanism is optimized for wireless data carriers

Everyone listens to radio station WIFM ("What's in it for me?"). So what are the underlying benefits for everyone concerned?

The benefit for wireless telecommunications carriers is simple. During WAP's infancy, WAP-capable carriers will attract customers from their competitors who are slower to move on the technology. Also, current wireless fence-sitters who have long held out will suddenly jump on the bandwagon due to the increased value-added WAP services. And, of course, there is all that additional "surfing" airtime usage that the wireless carriers get to bill their subscribers, perhaps via online billing using WAP, thereby cutting snail-mail billing costs and drawing another dime of airtime out of their customers. Wireless carriers will certainly be among the first to implement such applications, including wireless activation, call management, viewing of billing history information and payment options, push news on new services or promotions, voice message management, and more.

Content providers and application developers, familiar with the Internet model on which WAP relies, will soon be able to use WAP tools to quickly create a plethora of new online wireless services. These services will be sold by content providers to a variety of customers, such as WAP search engines or portals, ISPs, etc., that will seek to add value to their own service offerings for their subscriber base. These turnkey service or content solutions will help attract new subscribers, build loyalty, and increase revenues.

And, naturally, end users will benefit from secure access to Internet information and services such as instant messaging, banking, stock quotes, and more, through their mobile devices. Even intranet information such as corporate databases or legacy host systems can be accessed via WAP technology. One study conducted on the adoption rate of WAP devices concluded that most respondents who expected to get a WAP phone within the year did so because their employers would pay for it.

## APPLICATIONS FOR WAP

There are a wide variety of mobile applications that can exploit the mobile devices' unrivaled one-to-one interactive capabilities. As discussed, content providers and application developers will provide many services for ISPs, portals, and online businesses to add value to wireless subscribers. Such services and applications are virtually endless: e-mail, instant messaging, weather and traffic alerts, online directory services, maps, location triangulation and listing of nearby services, customer service, news, sports scores, travel booking, flight schedule tracking, E-commerce transactions, banking, billing, payment, stock brokering, online ticket purchasing, personalized location-based mobile shopping services, and more. WAP's push capability affords a distinct advantage over the WWW and represents tremendous potential.

But business applications will initially drive wireless Web adoption. Enterprises will deploy applications to leverage mobile technology's ability to deliver real-time corporate information to employees and partners on demand. For example, wireless E-business applications that allow mobile personnel such as sales people to access sales account information, inventory status, or order tracking from their WAP enabled mobile phones or PDAs will be immensely popular.

Whether wireless E-commerce or E-business-type applications or services, it seems clear that back-end connections will be required to existing big-iron legacy host systems such as IBM mainframes or AS/400s, which drive most of the required business logic. Whether it is banking or flight booking, inventory or order tracking, there will be an undoubtedly large demand for a means to access core business applications residing on legacy host systems. Hand-to-host access software solutions will therefore become an important underlying platform of many of the new WAP applications that will be created for both consumer and business markets.

Some traditional host access vendors, like Eicon Technology with its Aviva products, have been quick on the ball and are seeking this growing hand-to-host market. These solutions enable rapid development of wireless front ends, without having to modify existing core host applications that are tried and tested. Often, such legacy applications have millions of lines of code and any alteration of the actual business logic is a major undertaking. Thus, hand-to-host is easily achieved by developers writing a WAP application on top of products, such as Aviva, that do the back-end upstream connection to the host computer, sometimes over legacy protocols such as SNA, and automatically navigate through one or more host applications to retrieve the desired data. This is then securely returned to the mobile user via WAP to complete the transaction request.

## WAP TOPOLOGY

Current Internet technologies like HTML are not practical for wireless networks, having been designed for more powerful computers with generally reliable data networks and decent bandwidth. WAP utilizes Internet standards such as XML and TCP/IP but is optimized for the unique constraints of wireless technology, including bandwidth restrictions, higher latency, unreliable connection stability or predictability, less powerful CPUs, and less memory, power consumption, and interface constraints. Binary transmission allows greater data compression and optimization for long latency/low bandwidth wireless networks.

As depicted in Exhibit 1, there are two possible scenarios in a WAP topology. The URL request from the mobile device (WAP client) is sent to the WAP gateway, which lies between the carriers' network and the Internet. If the Web server provides content in WML, the WAP gateway transmits it directly to the WAP client. But if the Web server delivers a response in HTML, the WAP gateway converts the HTML into WML before passing it on. In both instances, the WAP gateway encodes the data from the Web server into compact binary form.

## WAP PREDICTIONS

Through the WAP Forum, worldwide mobile carriers, terminal manufacturers, and content developers are collaborating do deliver a wireless data solution based on a single standard. Timing, as they say, is everything. The current wired Internet has proven highly successful in reaching the home consumer market worldwide, with over a hundred million users online. It is foreseeable that the equally astounding mobile telephone adoption rate will lead the already Internet-initiated consumers to readily adopt wireless data services and applications with ease. They are already familiar and comfortable with both the Internet and their mobile phones. By mixing the Web's chocolate with mobile phone's peanut butter, a new taste sensation has been created that will revolutionize communications. The adoption of

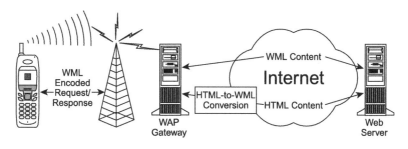

**Exhibit 1. WAP Network Topology**

the wireless Internet is virtually ensured. But will WAP be adopted as the way to get there?

As support by vendors for WAP grows, so do mounting claims that WAP is simply an intermediary technology and perhaps even a mistake. Sometimes these criticisms come from the WAP Forum's own members. One major criticism is that WAP is creating the necessity for rewriting Web sites in WML, in essence creating a parallel Internet limiting content available to users who have been accustomed to being able to access all the content they want. Redesigning and maintaining two Web sites is an expensive proposition. And although all WAP gateways currently provide a simplistic on-the-fly HTML-to-WML conversion, this is insufficient for some sites that are complex in their HTML design and navigation. Essentially, this on-the-fly HTML-to-WML conversion is not robust enough to make every HTML Web site navigable or accessible through WAP.

In the past, Microsoft has been one of the most vocal WAP critics, often making the "parallel Web" argument that there should be only one Internet standard for both wired and wireless Webs. The technology seemed to gain a lot of early support however, convincing even Goliath to assume the "if you can't beat 'em, join 'em" strategy. Thus, Microsoft has joined the WAP Forum in hopes of influencing WAP's direction and definition. Microsoft's original mobile phone browser did not support WAP. Microsoft is now in cooperation with the WAP Forum to drive the next version of WAP technology to a convergence with the original Web, which will help it migrate its current consumer and business products into the wireless Web more easily. Phone.com feels that although convergence is the utopian goal, a separate technology will always be necessary because phones will continue to lag behind standard PCs.

Other companies are taking a wait-and-see strategy. Japan's largest phone carrier, NTT DoCoMo, has 10 million subscribers to its iMode wireless data service, which already offers color and video over many phones through a simplified version of HTML — not WAP. iMode has been so popular that NTT DoCoMo announced it would have to limit sales because the demand has caused it to suffer 16 service outages. NTT DoCoMo, being careful, has said it will also support WAP in the future.

Another criticism is that WAP will be unnecessary with 3G network technology, Universal Mobile Telephone Service (UMTS), offering up to 2 Mbps expected to be delivered within two years. Current wireless data transfer speed is only 9.6 Kbps. The WAP Forum's argument for WAP's existence lies in the fact that the cost of bandwidth will never reach zero, and that many of the original constraints for which WAP was designed would still be valid after UMTS is available. These include intermittent coverage, screen size, low power consumption, carrier independence, multi-device support, and one-handed operation. In addition, the Forum argues that the bandwidth required by applications users want to use will also steadily increase, using up any headway gained. WAP, like any standard, will continue to evolve and be optimized. This is especially the case in terms of carrying multimedia over WAP. In defining WAP's evolution, support of streaming multimedia mobile services is the current WAP Forum brain tickler. Other outstanding interests include security, smart-card interfaces, persistent storage, billing interfaces, privacy, and push technology.

Yet another hurdle WAP must face is the fact that many members of the Forum, including NEC, Nokia, Phone.com, Geoworks, and others, are claiming that portions of the standard infringe on their intellectual property. Most of such claims, typical in developing any standard, can be settled through licensing fees. Any unrealistic or prohibitive fees will result in the Forum finding a workaround for the technology in question. However, even technologies that have to do with applications or services and not necessarily WAP technology seem to be up for patent-grabbers. The U.S. Patent Office has conditionally allowed Calgary-based Cell-Loc to claim the delivery of handset-based wireless location content and services over the Internet as its property, regardless of the technological method employed.

Whatever the criticism or difficulties, WAP seems to have critical mass with more than 300 companies, many of them industry giants, developing it. Over 75 percent of the world's major mobile terminal manufacturers are members of the WAP Forum and are announcing the release of WAP-capable handsets. It is fair to say that WAP, although having its share of naysayers, is well positioned for success.

The problems of size, due to usability of input and output interfaces, does not go away. One-handed typing is a desired feature of mobile devices, although some argue that using numeric keypads is impossible. It is doubtful that anyone will expect to type essays via a wireless hand-held device, even with a full QWRTY keypad shrunk to phone-size à la Nokia Communicator, an early version of 3G mobile phones. This also, because the output display will be limited in size on portable devices (although refractory computer screen sunglasses à la Mission Impossible may not be far away). Thus, the overall argument is that whatever the underlying protocol, certain things about wireless data access from mobile devices will remain unchanged for a long time — things that can be overcome using WAP.

Producers of Palm and Windows CE hand-held devices are already announcing WAP support. Through a survey taken on Yahoo mobile, about two thirds of the respondents said that they would prefer to have a hybrid device combining mobile phone and PDA functionality. Few would like to carry multiple devices around, or pay for more than one device. Users will want a James Bond-like gadget, capable of multiple functionality. Mitsubishi has already announced a hybrid device, the Mondo, a WAP-capable mobile phone with color display running Windows CE and featuring a slightly smaller touch-screen than a standard WinCE Palm-size device. Will the next big-money acquisitions be taking place between PC and cellular phone manufacturers? Will Dell and Nokia merge? This is not unthinkable.

WAP is indeed an intermediary technology. Are not all technologies? There are only two certainties after all: obsolescence and taxes. Moore's law is nothing new, so those who state that WAP is merely an intermediary technology will certainly be able to pat themselves on the backs for their astute predictions. Thus, such observations seem to be much ado about nothing. The fact is that WAP answers the needs currently required to make worldwide adoption of the wireless Web a reality in a short period of time. It is *the* standard that has the vast majority of supporting vendors, developers, and content providers; and as learned from the history of the VHS vs. Beta, or Microsoft vs. Apple, critical mass and standardization are all it takes, not technical superiority. Customers do not buy technology for technology's sake; they buy services and applications, and it would be foolish to expect that initial services will provide the perfect user experience. As users choose what types of services and applications they want to use, WAP will evolve. WAP and the current Web will converge, and thus, WAP is the means and not the end. One thing is certain: those late to jump on the bandwagon might not find a seat.

# Section VII
# Web Site Management

This section examines how to manage Web content using a variety of tools and techniques. The following chapters are included in this section:

"Web Site Design for Managers" examines design issues pertaining to Web site development. It focuses on management issues, including standards of good design. A useful checklist is provided for managers to get a head start on their projects.

"Web Content Management" explains methods of managing Web content, including concepts such as static or dynamic content.

"Internet Site Development in a Bandwidth-Hungry World: An Enterprise Dilemna" provides suggestions for improving an organization's image and productivity through a Web site. Techniques such as vector graphics and XML are examined.

"Selecting a Web Server Connection Rate" shows how to determine optimal connection rates between a WAN and an Internet connection.

# Chapter 34
# Web Site Design for Managers

*Louise L. Soe*

THE INTERNET, AND ITS INTRANET AND EXTRANET COUSINS, HAVE GROWN EXPONENTIALLY SINCE 1994. The Internet presents an abundance of opportunities for organizations to publish information relatively cheaply. It provides an inexpensive platform for performing transactions and carrying out exchange of information, both within and across organizations. Little wonder that managers have high expectations for the Internet and want to "hop on the bandwagon" to use it to corporate advantage. Web site development appears to be relatively simple, and much of the HTML and scripting code underlying Web pages is accessible, easy to view, "borrow," and reuse. Why then are there so many poorly designed Web sites?

The purpose of this chapter is to explain in simple, understandable terms, the elements of good Web site design to help managers recognize a well-designed Web site when they see it. An understanding of Web site design principles is important because any corporate material published on the Internet or on internal corporate intranets represents the company.

This chapter examines specific GUI (graphical user interface) design principles that apply to all corporate applications, and emphasizes the issues that are unique to Web publication. It includes an example of poor design and demonstrates how the example might be improved through application of these design principles. A Web design checklist at the end of the chapter lists questions managers can answer during a Web site design review. After managers read this chapter, they will recognize "good" Web site design when they see it.

## DESIGN PRINCIPLES

Similar design principles apply to many different types of publications and products — in many ways, they are the same principles everyone picked up in English 101 when they learned to write an essay, or in Systems Analysis and Design 101 when they learned to design computer applications. First, one must clearly understand the problem to be solved, so that

0-8493-1160-8/02/$0.00+$1.50
© 2002 by CRC Press LLC

one can determine the purpose of the product. Next, one must define the target audience so that one designs a product that clearly presents the intended message and appeals to the target people. One must also consider issues of content, clarity, ease of use, and organization so that the audience can easily find and understand the message. Finally, the layout, color, and graphic design should convey this message in a way that represents one's corporate image.

## PURPOSE OF THE WEB SITE

First and foremost, decide the purpose of the Web site. What is one trying to do? For example, the purpose of a Web site such as Amazon.com (http://www.amazon.com) is to sell books to the public over the Internet. However, the purpose of a Web site on an intranet might be to inform employees about the value of their corporate stock. In both cases, the Web site presents information. The purpose of the online bookstore is to market and sell books and other publications (e.g., videos and CDs). It invites customers and authors to review books, and provides order forms that the customers fill out and submit to order books.

The purposes of these two Web sites are different, and their audiences are different. Thus, the designs of these two sites will probably be very different — one is selling consumer goods to a mass audience and the other is presenting important financial information to a limited audience. The purpose of the Web site is a key decision because it determines the content of the Web site, as well as many other design decisions. Everything on the Web site should support its purpose. When managers review Web sites, there should be no questions about the purpose of the Web site.

## THE AUDIENCE

Once the purpose and theme of the project have been determined, one needs to consider the nature of the audience for the Web site. There are two important sets of information about the audience that are necessary; the first concerns demographics and the second concerns the technological capabilities of the intended audience.

### Audience Demographics

Audience demographics provide information about age, gender, educational level, income, skills, interests, and capabilities. Companies that jumped early into Internet retailing, such as Amazon.com, understood that most of their potential customers are younger (late teens to mid-30s in age), male, college educated, skilled at using computers, and interested in certain topics (e.g., computers, cars, sports, and entertainment). These potential customers also had higher-than-average disposable income. Amazon.com asks its customers to review the books it sells, an exercise that indicates to the customers that Amazon considers them to be educated, skilled, and knowledgeable. The reviews not only enhance the self-image of the reviewers, but they in turn attract customers who are in the market for a book on a topic, but are unsure which book to choose. In addition, the reviews also provide Amazon and the book publishers with important information about their potential customers and what they value in books. Although Amazon's audience has now broadened and expanded, Amazon continues its practice of making the customers feel as though they are "experts."

When designing a publication or product of any kind, one needs to consider the audience just as Amazon.com did — and does. The product must appeal to the tastes of that intended audience as well as make sense to them. The audience decision has far-reaching effects on the content, the type of language to be used, as well as graphical design (e.g., layout, colors, graphics, style, etc.).

## Audience Technological Capabilities

Another important audience question is whether the developer of the Web site has considered the level of computer and telecommunications equipment of the target audience for the Web site. In the case of intranet applications, it is probably fairly easy to find out the bandwidth of the networks, the types of computer equipment and the Internet browsers that the audience is likely to use to view the site. Corporations often define internal networks, standard computer technology, and default browsers. However, if the Web site is offered over the Internet, the Web site developer must consider a much broader range of possibilities in client technology.

The manager should check that the site developer has considered the audience and has consciously designed a site that the intended audience can view. For example, if the site is intended for the corporate intranet, which connects employees with Pentium-class computers and current versions of Web browsers (that handle certain types of multimedia files), the designer can include larger graphics files, dynamic HTML, and more interactive elements. However, if the intended viewers are on the Internet, they may use older computers and earlier versions of browsers, and connect to the site via low-bandwidth modems. The Internet audience might benefit from alternate versions of the Web site — one for viewers with more advanced technologies and the other for those without. The developer probably will use fewer multimedia elements and ensure that viewers who turn off the graphics capability of their browsers can still grasp the meaning of the Web site. Some corporations have established testing procedures for Web sites, and routinely view their sites on different platforms and via connections with different bandwidths.

## CONTENT

In English 101, everyone learned that the contents of communication should clearly present the intended message; the main idea should be stated early in the essay; and then every paragraph should support that main idea. Web sites convey meaning through images and other types of multimedia elements, as well as written text. Thus, all of the content of the Web site (e.g., images, videos, audio, graphics, and text) should clearly convey the message that is the purpose of the Web site.

Graphical symbols can provide important meaning to the Web site and reduce the need for textual content. Graphics convey content, style, and information. Graphical symbols can make the Web site much more attractive to the audience. Used in excess, they can also increase the amount of clutter on the Web site and the download time, and draw attention away from the meaning of the site. In general, question any graphical symbols that detract from the purpose of the Web site or that do not support the purpose of the Web site.

Employees and customers are too busy to spend time deciphering a confusing message; there is one chance to present the idea clearly. It is very important to have multiple people from different constituencies view the Web site to see whether it clearly conveys the message. Managerial oversight is very important here; managerial review of external publications is often a corporate requirement — an important reason why managers should have some knowledge of Web site design. In any information systems application, it is valuable to have the people who will use the application try it out to see whether it makes sense to them.

If the Web site is interactive, and part of the Web site content comes from the customers (e.g., Amazon's book reviews), then the site design must take into account whether the customers' contributions will be reviewed before they are posted to the site. Process and organizational policies may be necessary to govern this type of interactivity.

## NAVIGATION AND EASE OF USE

One of the critical success factors for information systems applications is ease of use. There are many examples of failed information systems and applications that were too difficult to learn or did not perform the functions required by the customers. The same ease-of-use goal applies to Web site design. The goal is to have the viewers of the Web site be able to understand what they view and interact with the Web site effectively and efficiently.

In Web site design, navigation is an important issue. Web sites use the Hypertext Transfer Protocol (HTTP), which means that hyperlinks can be set up on any Web page to link "hot spots" (text or images) on one page to a second page, or to specific areas on any page. The hyperlinked page can be resident on the same Web site or Web server, or it can be housed on a Web server anywhere on the globe.

Fortunately, there is a standard hyperlink for text. When there is a string of text that is underlined and blue, one assumes that it is a hyperlink and that it will take us somewhere else. Images can also be used as hyperlinks. Many hyperlink images have taken on standardized meanings. For example, an arrow pointing upward takes one to the top of the page, and an icon showing a house usually takes one to the "home" or core page of the Web site.

Web sites often use frames or menus for navigation. A frame is a formatting device that divides the Web site screen into different areas, each of which can hold a different document. Frames are commonly used to provide one area of the screen for a menu of document choices. The document that the viewer chooses from the menu is then displayed within another frame. The menu frame can remain constant throughout the entire Web site so that the same set of hyperlinks will appear inside the menu frame. While menu frames consume space on Web pages, they can be very useful for consistent navigation throughout the Web site.

The structure of the site (which may be accomplished with frames, menus, and tables) should be relatively consistent across the site and easily traversed by the viewer. The purpose of navigational tools is to help viewers get the information they need and want.

## PAGE LAYOUT

When large corporations design publications for print media (such as annual reports), they give careful consideration to graphical design issues such as layout, color, text style and size, graphical images, etc. Graphical designers use different types of layout to break up the published page. For example, they may have headings across the top and multiple columns of typed information below. A corporate publication, such as an annual report, will often include charts and tables to convey financial information. The important thing to understand about layout is that there are certain standard layout formats (e.g., three columns, two columns) with different proportions that graphical designers use. The layout will partly determine the direction the eye will travel. For example, if a page has three columns, one is likely to start reading the material starting at the top of the left-hand column. This is a cultural convention because, in Western cultures, one learns to read from top to bottom, left to right. The "eye-path direction" becomes especially important when using graphics because the page should be designed so that the eye travels to the most important object on the page, its focal point. The eye should be able to stay there long enough to comprehend the main message of the page.

How can one easily determine the "eye-path direction" of a Web page? One has to fool the eye, so that one pays attention to the abstract black-white-gray patterns rather than the content of the page. It is easy to accomplish by squinting at the page. Squint your eyes, and then notice how your eye moves around the page. Particularly notice when, where, and if it comes to rest on some object on the page. This resting point should be the focal point of the page. There are some very easy ways to lead the eye to the focal point. Text, lines, arrows, colors, layout, images with cultural meaning, and strong images with high contrast will all lead the eye on a particular path. (See Exhibit 1.)

It is almost impossible to keep one's eyes away from the recycling symbol — whether one squints at it or tries to focus on the text in the left-hand column. The image has a number of qualities that attract the eye. The arrows in the image are designed to direct the eye around and around the symbol — the point of one arrow brings the eye to the tail of the next arrow. They do that not only because of their curved arrow shapes (which also create an enclosure), but also because of a cultural convention that arrows point in the direction one should follow. Notice how frequently arrows are used on Web sites and in other technologies (such as VCR controls) to indicate direction. In addition, the recycling image is large, thick, and completely black, in contrast with the rest of the page. All of these characteristics of the image make it difficult to pull one's eyes away and read the message in the left-hand column. If there was an important message to convey on this page, the obvious place for it would be in the middle of the recycling symbol.

An important principle for good Web site design is "less is more." When designing a page for the human eye to view in printed format or on a computer screen, one wants to enable the viewer to comprehend the

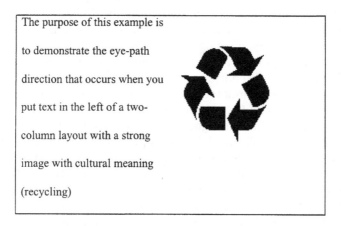

**Exhibit 1.   Two-Column Layout Example**

content and its meaning. The human eye requires space around this content in order to be able to look at it long enough to take it in. Blank space becomes very important. Look at an ordinary book, and consider all of the space on the page that is blank. The book could be printed using much less paper if there were no margins or spaces between headers, titles, page number, etc. Compare the amount of unused space in the example in Exhibit 2 with that in Exhibit 1. Notice how difficult it is to read text that hangs on the edge of the page or on a line. The graphics fight for the eyes' attention. The recycling image, which is larger, tends to win the war for attention, but the image war makes it even more difficult for the eyes to rest on the text and read the printed message.

## PAGE SIZE AND DIFFERENT SIZED MONITORS AND BROWSERS

The size of the optimal Web page is a matter of controversy. Some people insist that a page should be visible within a computer monitor screen. Others insist that pages should be as long as necessary. The page size decision also depends on the purpose of the site. If the site is to be viewed on a screen, then several smaller, hyperlinked pages may be preferable to one long page. If the page is to be printed on paper, perhaps because it contains important textual information or a form that is to be printed and faxed, then a longer page with scroll bars may be more appropriate.

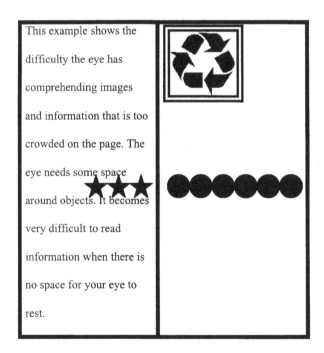

**Exhibit 2.    Cluttered Two-Column Layout Example**

## COLORS

Colors have several characteristics that are important to the design of publications. Color value refers to the degree of lightness and darkness. Graphics designers traditionally design pages in patterns of achromatic values: for example, blacks, whites, and grays. There are a number of reasons for doing this. Approximately 8 percent of the population is colorblind, a condition that may make it difficult to discern between two or more colors, such as orange and green. Thus, if there are two images with the same value (lightness) that are orange and green, a colorblind person might see them as a single image. In addition, many items that are published in color are printed or photocopied by machines that do not reproduce colors.

In Exhibit 3, an image of a house is inserted in the center column on a three-column page. The center column is twice as wide as the two side columns, and the photo in the center column is also divided almost directly in the middle. The path in the front of the house leads right up to the front door. The front door is centered in the photo; it has a pitched roof above it, with two chimneys balancing one another on either side of the roof. Although the original of this photo is quite colorful — with a red house and lots of green foliage — the pattern or graphical design of the page is contained in the achromatic image observed in Exhibit 3. One does not need to see the colors to make out the photo's meaning or to see the graphical design of the page.

Color can be used to enliven a publication, or to represent the corporate image, for example, subdued colors for calm, serious material, and bright colors for lively, exciting material. Colors provide signals that may convey meaning in and of themselves, whether from cultural or common usage. For example, red represents heat, anger, or negative numbers. Blue

**Exhibit 3.   Achromatic Patterns Define an Image**

represents coolness, calm, or water. Green is often associated with nature. Red images tend to pop out from the background because red color wavelengths come into focus a little behind the retina. Thus, red is a good color for an object that is the focal point of a page. Blue tends to recede into the background because blue color wavelengths come into focus in front of the retina. Thus, blue is a good background color, but not a good foreground color. Green and yellow come into focus at the retina. They require little accommodation and are just as visible at the periphery as they are at the center of the visual field. They are easy to look at for long periods of time. (Remember the faded green color of the early monochromatic computer terminals and monitors?)

Everyone remembers learning about complementary colors in elementary school: orange and blue are opposite each other on the color wheel, for example. Complementary colors are very difficult to use next to one another because they flicker. The eyes are drawn to the intense edges where the complementary colors meet and one cannot pay attention to the rest of the page. Complementary colors can be very distracting if they are not used carefully.

### Colors on the Internet

A computer stores images as bitmaps, pixels, or dots of color information. The image itself is put together from the contents of all of these pixels. The pixels contain information about the color of the pixel, including its value (lightness or darkness), hue (red, green, or blue), and the color saturation (intensity). The Internet has a limit of 216 Web-safe colors that it will display at a maximum of 72 dots-per-inch (dpi). An Internet browser will do the best it can (given the video capabilities of the client machine) to reproduce any image that is downloaded from the Internet. The number of colors may sound like a lot, but when some of the non-Web-safe colors are lost from an image, the images become distorted. There are books that discuss Web-safe colors to help the Web site developer (e.g., *Coloring Web Graphics* by Weinman and Heavin, New Riders Publishing, 1996).

There are two types of image compression commonly used on the Internet. It is possible to lower the amount of information contained in each pixel of the image by selecting different levels of compression. Higher levels of compression result in less information in a pixel and smaller memory size for the image. High compression of images (especially those with a wide range of colors) or displaying images at less than 72 dpi (e.g., by stretching a 1-inch square image to occupy a 4-inch-square space on a Web site) will result in a type of distortion called pixelation. If as a manager, one sees distorted images with dots of color (i.e., pixelation), make sure that the Web site developer is aware of ways in which to compress graphical images without losing quality. The two versions of a landscape photo below demonstrate the effects of pixelation. The pixelated version has visible dots of color. Compressing a photo with a wide spectrum of colors leads to pixelation because the compression algorithm tries to preserve the colors and lets go of the definition of the image, which is contained in the black-and-white layer of information. (See Exhibit 4.)

If the Web site developer uses any elements (e.g., text fonts, colors, HTML tags) that the browser or client machine is not configured to handle, the browser either will display what it considers an acceptable substitute or it will display nothing at all. Browsers and versions of browsers vary in their ability to handle unusual elements and HTML and scripting errors. Here, the technological capabilities of the audience become very important. If the Web site audience includes only viewers with very advanced technology, then their advanced browsers may handle a wider range of elements, such as colors, text fonts, and videos. However, if the audience will have a very wide range of technological capabilities, including slow modem connections and low-end computers or Web appliances, then the Web site should be designed with Web-safe colors, standard fonts, and a smaller set of capabilities. Of course, it is also possible to offer two alternative versions: one for the high-end viewer and one for the low-end viewer. The alternative versions should be offered on the entry page to the Web site, where it is also possible to indicate the browser version that is best suited for viewing the Web site.

## MEMORY REQUIREMENTS AND COMPRESSION

One of the most important issues that all Web site developers face is the question of the size of multimedia files published on a Web site. There are many ways to reduce the size of graphical images so that the site will load quickly and the viewer will not get tired of waiting and leave.

**Exhibit 4.   Normal Landscape Photo and Pixelated Landscape Photo**

## Graphical images

There are two widely used file formats for graphical images on the Internet, provided by two different compression algorithms. GIF compression is best suited for flat images, letters, and drawn images. JPEG compression works best with photographic images. There are a number of ways to alter an image before compressing it for the Internet, so that the manager checking a Web site should question the use of images that take a long time to load. For example, drastically reducing the range of colors within the photograph (e.g., from yellow, green, red, and blue, to a range of red-blue colors) will allow the developer to compress the image without losing much image quality. A good rule of thumb is to try different levels and types of compression and choose the level that provides adequate image quality.

The physical size of the image also affects its memory size. Images should be resized in an image editor to their display size on the Web page. Inserting a 4-inch square photo that takes 60KB of memory size into a cell that is 1-inch square on a Web site, will display a 1-inch square photo that still requires 60KB of memory and that requires the download time of a 60-KB file. A manager who is reviewing a Web site on a high-end machine should ensure that it has been tested under less optimal conditions (e.g., over a slower modem on a slower computer with a smaller monitor size). If the graphics take a long time to load on the page, question the developer about image size and suggest that the developer experiment with reducing image memory requirements, image physical size, or the number of images on a page.

## Video, Audio, and Animation

Multimedia involving video, audio, and animation can be very engaging on the Internet, but it generally requires large amounts of memory unless it is compressed. There are a number of compression programs for these media. Audio usually suffers much more from file compression because it is more difficult for one's ears to fill in lost sounds than for one's eyes to fill in lost images. The compression programs let the developer vary the audio and video compression independently. Again, the developer needs to experiment with determining a compression level that provides an acceptable quality as well as an acceptable file size.

Animation, even with sound, usually requires smaller amounts of memory and less download time. Vector-based animation programs (such as Macromedia Flash) enable the development of high-quality animation that can be compressed into relatively small media files that download quickly. (Visit the Macromedia Web site at www.macromedia.com to view examples of flash-enabled animations.) At this point in technological development, there are also many programs that will generate Java-based animation. If viewers set their browser security levels to refuse Java applets, then the animation will not work.

Again, one sees that the intended audience is an important consideration for video, audio, and animation. Some file formats require additional software for the browser (called plug-ins), and others may require downloading unwanted file formats. Plug-ins are freely available, but can be inconvenient for an audience with low-end technology because they may require more advanced hardware or a faster connection. Alternative versions of the Web site for low-end viewers will help convey the message to a wider audience.

## HYPERMEDIA: HOW DO YOU KEEP THEM ON YOUR SITE?

The fact that a Web site is hypertext means that another page or Web site is just a click away. If the Web site is an intranet site with valuable information for employees, there may be no problem keeping them on the site. However, if it is an Internet site available to the general public, the question of keeping the viewer on one's site becomes more problematical. One approach, adopted by some large commercial Web sites, is to provide no external links to any other site. Another approach, advocated by the popular third-generation or "killer Web site" model of site design (David Siegel, *Creating Killer Web Sites, 2nd edition,* 1997), is to provide the viewer with continually updated "fish food" that not only keeps the viewer on the Web site, but also brings the viewer back again. Examples of fish food might be entertainment, information, jokes, riddles, games, and free copies of trial software to download.

Ensuring that the Web site is maintained and kept up to date is essential to secure return visits from viewers. A "last updated" message lets viewers know that the site contains new information. Publicity for Web site addresses has also become an important way to draw viewers to Web sites, but that is outside the realm of this chapter.

## DESIGN EXAMPLE

An example of poor Web page design shown in Exhibit 5 tries to convey the design message "less is more." Review this example using the Web site checklist in Exhibit 7. Try to figure out exactly what is wrong with the Web site design. What is the purpose of this Web page? There is a written message, but it is difficult to pay attention to it. What audience would be attracted to this Web page? Next, look at the "better" Web site and see whether it ranks higher in the review.

### What Is Wrong with the Poor Design

This page is difficult to comprehend, even in its static blacks, whites, and grays. There are several strong images on the page that vie for one's

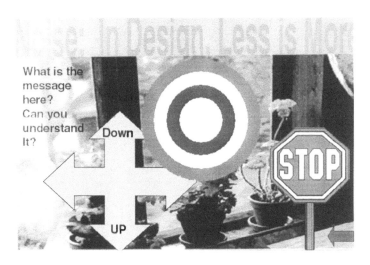

**Exhibit 5. A Poorly Designed Web Site**

attention. The sure-fire focal point, the bull's-eye in the middle of the page, keeps pulling the eyes back to it. Its round shape, its color value (which is lighter than everything on the page except the stop sign), and its meaning as a focal point are attractive. However, the stop sign that has white letters and is a highly meaningful symbol also attracts attention. Meanwhile, the message of the page ("Noise: In Design, Less is More") cannot hold one's attention. The text is middle gray in value — very similar to its background. The other textual message is also difficult to comprehend, although its dark value contrasts with the background. There is too much happening on this page, and one's eyes are drawn to extraneous content. Imagine this page with its bright colors (bright red, hot pink, green, and blue) and some flashing animation (see Exhibit 6).

**Improved Web Site**

What improved this Web site design? Much of the clutter is gone — the extra symbols and the distracting background wallpaper. The main message "Noise: In Design, Less is More" is now highly visible. It is larger, and its white value contrasts with the medium-gray background that makes it more legible. It occupies the right-hand column of the page. The stop sign draws one's attention right into the page, and adds meaning to the main message by suggesting that one stop and think. The secondary textual message in the upper left-hand quadrant of the page is smaller and less demanding above the dominant stop sign. It is also visible because it is not fighting the background wallpaper and the double arrow for attention. There is now space around the elements on the page. One can read the words and understand what they

**Exhibit 6.    An Improved Web Design**

mean without being distracted. The graphic makes sense and is not fighting with other graphics for one's attention.

## CONCLUSION

Managers who understand these simple principles about Web site design should be able to review Web sites developed for their organizations. Exhibit 7 is a list of questions to consider when reviewing Web sites. Be sure that the Web site developer understands the purpose of the site, and then ensure that everything on the site makes sense and supports that purpose.

**Exhibit 7.    Web Site Checklist**

1. What is the purpose of the Web site?
   a. Can you clearly figure out the purpose by looking at it?
   b. Do all of the pages on the site support that purpose?
2. Who is the audience for the Web site?
   a. Describe the potential audience for the Web site in demographic terms (e.g., age, gender, educational level, income level, and computer skills).
   b. Describe the technological capabilities of the audience (types of computers, bandwidth of their connections, browsers).
3. Content
   a. Does all of the content (text, images, audio, video, animation) contribute to the purpose of the Web site?
   b. If customer contributions are to be displayed on the Web site, what is the policy or process governing the display of their contributions?
4. Navigation and ease of use
   a. Is the Web site easy to understand and easy to navigate from one page or one element on a page to another?
   b. Does the Web site use consistent navigation aids?
5. Page layout
   a. Does the page layout reinforce your purpose?
   b. Does the page layout lead your eye to a focal point that contains the most important information on the page?
   c. Is the page cluttered or easy to comprehend?
6. Page size sense
   a. Pages that are to be printed may be long.
   b. Shorter, hyperlinked pages to be viewed on the screen.
7. Color
   a. Has the page been designed in patterns of achromatic color values (black-white-grays), so that it will be visible on different types of browsers and printers?
   b. Does the color match the purpose, style, and content of the site?
   c. Will the colors appeal to the target audience?
   d. Is the use of complementary colors done carefully?
   e. Are Web-safe colors used?
   f. Has compression distorted the image (e.g., via pixelation)?
8. Image compression
   a. Are the images of high enough quality?
   b. Is the memory size of the images small enough to accommodate a minimal download time for the expected audience?
9. Video, audio, animation
   a. Is the quality acceptable?
   b. Is the memory size of the elements small enough to accommodate a minimal download time for the expected audience?
   c. Is there an alternative version of the site for low-end customers?
10. Keeping viewers on the site
    a. Does the site have "fish food" that will attract an audience and bring it back?

**Is the Web site current?**

# Chapter 35
# Web Content Management

*Charles Banyay*

INFORMATION TECHNOLOGY (IT) HAS BEEN APPLIED TO THE SOLUTION OF BUSINESS PROBLEMS FOR THE PAST HALF CENTURY. Although studies have shown that most information in an enterprise is contained in unstructured data (i.e., content, documents, and tacit knowledge in the heads of the employees), traditional IT has done little to apply automation to any of these areas. During the second half of the 20th century, the overwhelming proportion of IT attention, initiatives, and dollars has focused on the management and processing of structured data.

With the advent of doing business over the Internet, or E-business, and the associated collaboration over wide geographic expanses and extensive publishing to the Web, the automation of content and documents and those processes that depend on them may be a critical requirement for most organizations. Those businesses that have not addressed content and document management issues may find their transitions to the digital economy significantly slower and more challenging than originally imagined.

## STRUCTURED DATA

Structured data is data that can be easily stored in a computer repository such as a relational database. Most of this data comprises numbers or simple text. Structured data is usually fixed in length or at least has an upper limit. It is easily encoded using some simple transformation to and from the binary code and is usually stored in a coded format.

The encoding format depends on the operating system and the chip set of the particular computer being used. The encoding is usually a base operation of either the operating system or the computer hardware, and in most instances is transparent to the application systems developers. It is totally transparent to the user. Some common examples of code formats are ASCII and EBCDIC. Because each character of structured data is encoded by the computer, it can be interpreted by the computer. Structured data, therefore, is sometimes referred to as content addressable data.

0-8493-1160-8/02/$0.00+$1.50
© 2002 by CRC Press LLC

## UNSTRUCTURED DATA (CONTENT AND DOCUMENTS)

There exists, however, another type of data that is far less structured. Unstructured data is neither encoded by the operating system nor the hardware. The encoding occurs at the higher level of application system software. The code is usually complex and is often proprietary to the specific application software used. For example, Microsoft Word and Corel WordPerfect are both popular word processing packages but they store their data in very different formats.

One consequence of this is that unstructured data is not directly understandable by most computers at the hardware or operating system software level. A developer cannot simply depend on access methods or services provided by the operating system to read unstructured data in a directly interpretable way. A further level of software — application software — is required. Another consequence of the application system level encoding is that there are sometimes as many formats as applications.

In addition to text such as that in most popular word processors, numbers and text in spreadsheets, presentation slides, images, video, or voice recordings are all examples of unstructured data. Most of this data is stored in some complex format that is proprietary to the application used to create it. Usually, one requires the application or a subset of it so that the data can be presented in some medium such as a computer display, or in print on paper, to enable interpretation by human beings.

Most documents comprise unstructured data. More precisely, documents are made up of multiple components. The components can be text, a picture, a drawing, or any of the other entities mentioned above. Each of these components is generally referred to as content. It is the content that is unstructured to begin with. Content is usually stored with limited presentation-level formatting. It saves space and processing time, and facilitates reuse.

Content components by themselves usually represent a single idea or concept. For example, content could be a single slide within a presentation, a single quote, or a picture. The primary objective of componentization is to facilitate easy content reuse. When content is stored together with other components as within a document, it is much more difficult to find and takes more effort to extract for reuse. There are no absolute rules defining what is content and what is a document. There are, however, some general rules-of-thumb. Documents are usually collections of multiple pieces of content. Some type of presentation formatting is applied to the aggregated content to provide an appropriate look-and-feel congruent with the intended message embedded within the document. The collective whole, aggregated content, formatted for presentation, is generally referred to as a document.

## CONTENT VERSUS DOCUMENT MANAGEMENT

The tools and approaches for managing content are somewhat different from those used for documents. Document management is one of those tool sets for managing unstructured data that have been around for some time. Document management is generally considered arcane and is associated with library functions and records management. For this reason and for some of the reasons discussed later, document management has been difficult to get into the mainstream of business IT. The base functional components generally associated with document management systems are:

- A conceptually centralized repository
- Secured access
- Search capability
- Versioning capability
- Check-in/check-out capability for editing

Some of the more sophisticated document management tool sets may offer additional functionality such as workflow for review, approve, and publish type document lifecycles, and integration to some of the desktop authoring tools. Some very high-end products may even offer integration with structured data management systems such as ERP applications.

Content management requires more sophisticated tools than document management. A content management system manages components of documents, so it requires all of the functionality of a document management system with some additions. The additions fall into three broad categories of functionality. The first is the ability to aggregate the components into documents and manage them in this aggregated form without keeping multiple copies. Some in the industry refer to this capability as virtual or compound document management. A compound document must be managed as any other document from the perspective of versioning and workflow. In addition, a compound document must be actively linked bi-directionally to each of its constituent content component parts. Compound document management can become very complex.

The second category of functionality is integration with the authoring tools used to create content. With the possible exception of some Web authoring tools, most tools in current use today were designed to create entire documents and not just content components. These authoring tools generally apply considerable presentation formatting to the unstructured data within the content. Most of this formatting must be stripped from the data before it is stored. The ability to create entire documents sometimes creates the requirement for disaggregation services, that is, the ability to componentize a document and store it as a collection of its constituent component content. This entire category of functionality should diminish in importance as the tools for creating content, especially those that will store the content in XML format, become more sophisticated.

The third category of functionality is publishing. This could cover publishing to any medium, including paper, personal devices, or the Web. Simple content is rarely published by itself. Usually, a document is published. Therefore, one of the first steps in publishing involves assembling the constituent components of the document. Assembly is different from the management of the aggregated components because management involves managing a set of pointers, whereas publishing involves assembling copies of the content into a unified whole. The next step after assembly is applying presentation formatting. This is done through the use of a template. The publishing system must be able to understand the unstructured data within each type of content component to some degree, to be able to apply the formatting and to be able to reproduce the formatted content in a meaningful way. As discussed previously, understanding the unstructured data can be complicated.

Publishing to the Web could almost be a category unto itself. In addition to the functionality for general publishing, publishing to the Web can require special hardware and software for Internet scalability. Special software may be required for the synchronization of multiple Web servers if more than one Web server is involved. Depending on the objective of providing the content over the Web, there may also be various application servers involved. For example, there may be commerce servers for buying and selling, or personalization servers to enable individuals to have a unique personal experience on a particular Web site. These application servers will require some integration with their indexing schemas.

As demonstrated, both content and documents comprise unstructured data. Unstructured data usually requires special tools, algorithms, and methodologies to effectively manage it. Standard IT tools such as relational databases by themselves are not effective.

All database management systems need to understand the content of the data in order to generate the indices that are used to store and retrieve the data. Because the computer cannot understand the content of unstructured data at the operating system level, it cannot generate the indices. Other tools, in addition to those provided in the standard IT toolkit, are required. One of the most common tools is the use of metadata or data describing the data (content). Metadata, however, needs to be generated by some intelligence that has at least a partial understanding of the meaning of the content. Metadata is stored externally as structured data in a relational database management system. The computer then uses this structured data and pointers to the content in the form of access paths provided by the operating system file access method, to manage information stored in the unstructured portion.

## WHY HAS IT NOT DONE MORE TO AUTOMATE CONTENT AND DOCUMENTS?

Proprietary formats, the variety of formats, and their complexity are not the only challenges one faces when working with unstructured data or content. Until recently — and even to some extent continuing to this very day — special equipment was or is required to capture, store, present, and manipulate information stored as unstructured data. In addition, the endeavors to bring automation to the world of unstructured data or content found that, in most instances, the mastering of the technical issues was the easy part. The painful redesign of processes and changing the way in which people did their everyday work was far more of a challenge. Documents are pervasive in most businesses. Studies have shown that knowledge workers spend most of their time working with content and documents. Anything that affects content and documents generally has a major impact on knowledge workers, as shown in Exhibit 1.

To deal with complex data structures requires special training and, at times, significant effort. The process redesign requires special talents and skill sets usually not found in most IT organizations. The special software and hardware requirements can be costly. Taken collectively, this all strengthens the perception that IT endeavors around the management of documents and content are expensive and difficult to cost-justify in all but the largest of enterprises.

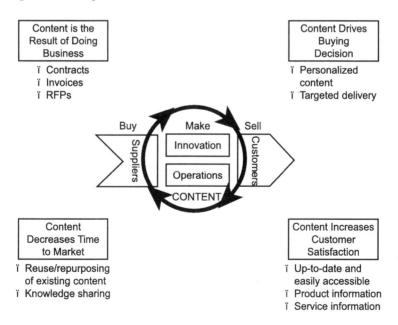

**Exhibit 1. Things That Affect Content**

One result of this perception is that most IT organizations do not find the managing of documents and content an attractive area in which to build their competencies. Most IT organizations find much more success in focusing their efforts only on managing information stored as structured data. Most IT methodologies and tools, such as structured analysis, design, and data modeling, were specifically created to handle only structured data. The applicability and utility of these structured methodologies and tools in the content world are questionable. As a result, IT skills and methodologies that were developed to address the complexities of managing information stored as documents or content are often perceived as arcane and not within the realm of mainstream IT.

The collective end result is that currently most IT professionals with standard IT backgrounds and skills often do not possess the additional skill sets to work effectively with unstructured data. In particular, they lack the in-depth understanding required to be able to effectively explain in business terms, the complexities around unstructured data to both colleagues and non-IT business professionals. More importantly, they lack the ability to recognize opportunities and to create effective business cases for addressing such IT endeavors.

## HOW DID THE LACK OF AUTOMATION IN CONTENT AND DOCUMENT MANAGEMENT CONTRIBUTE TO TODAY'S BUSINESS DILEMMA?

Without IT support and the benefits of automation, most business people dealing with documents and content have been left to their own devices. They attempted many different non-IT solutions to minimize the inefficiencies that were left as a result of a 19th-century approach to unstructured data in the office. Some examples of the attempts at a solution were:

- Optimizing antiquated local filing systems
- Retaining large numbers of administrative staff
- Engraining the old processes in the culture and the organization structure in the name of efficiency
- Expending considerable explicit and implicit effort on training people in the use of these antiquated filing systems
- Retaining otherwise unproductive individuals who were the old-time gurus of these processes and filing systems
- Optimizing paper processing, storage, and distribution
- Implementing departmental imaging applications
- Utilizing ever-increasing volumes of office space to enable the local presence of teams that needed to collaborate and access local files
- Creating more huge LAN server farms with complex directory structures and folder hierarchies where people could store and sometimes find their unstructured information

These attempts at solutions sometimes worked (an example is shown in Exhibit 2). The primary reason that they actually worked is that the problems were internally focused and so were the solutions. Most of the attempts at solutions were characterized by intimate familiarity with the internal processes and the physical knowledge repositories, and close geographic proximity to enable access to and sharing of knowledge content.

## INTERNAL FOCUS EXACERBATES THE LACK OF AUTOMATION

In parallel with the focus on structured data by business leaders and their respective IT organizations was an absolute focus on internal process improvements — internal processes, as opposed to external processes such as those between an enterprise, its partners, suppliers, and customers. Nothing exemplifies this internal focus more than the tremendous success enjoyed by most ERP (enterprise resource planning) applications during the past decade. ERP applications are almost exclusively focused on internal productivity and effectiveness. It is not surprising that the overriding justification of most IT-related efforts during the past half century has been cost reduction.

This propensity to focus IT efforts internally allowed, and at times encouraged, a single-dimensional approach to information or knowledge management focused on only the structured parts of data. The internal focus allowed IT to turn a blind eye to the unstructured world. IT could do what it knew best: manage structured data. The single-dimensional approach fed on itself as there was perceived success. Had there been a compelling requirement to address external processes as well, there could possibly have been an earlier recognition that geographical proximity and intimate familiarity with internal norms and processes are not sound bases upon which to build business solutions.

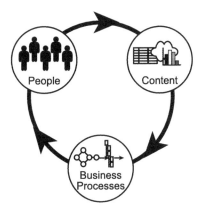

**Exhibit 2.    Departmental Solution**

445

The single-dimensional approach to IT has prevailed for over half a century, despite disturbing statistics such as the one compiled by the *Harvard Business Review*, which seemed to indicate that office productivity had increased by only 1 percent since the application of modern information technology to business problems. Another statistic with similar disturbing implications was from a recent study done by PricewaterhouseCoopers, indicating that most information in an enterprise, upward of 80 to 90 percent, is stored as unstructured data. The study also confirmed that the large majority of this data was not automated (see Exhibit 3).

One of the unforeseen consequences of the internal business focus has been the formation of large conglomerates. These conglomerates have formed through numerous upstream and downstream integration along the value chain. One of the perceived advantages seen in these integrations has been the synergies or efficiency gained through internalizing and possibly sharing common business processes, especially administrative processes and those dealing with documents and content.

The lack of automated document and content management, however, has produced the opposite effects. Those entities within an enterprise dealing with documents and content have become dependent on intimate familiarity with the document-based processes and the physical knowledge repositories, and close geographic proximity. This has made it difficult for large conglomerates to outsource many of the internal business processes. Within the conglomerates, it has become exceedingly difficult to determine where value is added and where it is not. Many business processes have become inefficient because the internalization has protected them from external market forces, which could mandate efficiencies on them.

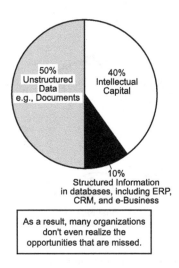

Exhibit 3.  Where Data Lies

## E-BUSINESS AND DISAGGREGATION

With the advent of transacting business over the Internet — a.k.a. B2B e-Business — the internal focus of many enterprises is quickly shifting. The ability to communicate and collaborate over the Internet, irrespective of geographic proximity, has been recognized by many early adopters of technology. They are using this aggressively for competitive advantage. This is forcing most organizations to shift their attention externally. They must address the external processes involving suppliers, partners, and possibly the customers.

The Internet is enabling many organizations to disaggregate along the value chain. The walls are coming down. Those internal components of large conglomerates that are primarily dealing with structured data and have the necessary IT tools to support their particular function are able to divorce the inefficient conglomerates and create a value proposition of their own. It is possible that during the next few years one could see the disaggregation of most high value-added functional units from the large conglomerates, leaving them with only the low value-added components. Another possible scenario is that all of the low value-added components or business processes will be outsourced to external business process providers.

There is an abundance of newly created organizations, offering a plethora of new services — in particular, business process outsourcing services. An example of this is the E-procurement enterprise announced by Chase Manhattan and Deloitte Consulting. Most early adopting organizations of the disaggregated enterprise model are ones that deal primarily with structured data. They are supported by the required IT systems and infrastructure. These organizations will be subject to external market forces and therefore, in all probability, will offer far more efficient and effective service than an internal business process provider. The disaggregated component entities will be able to team with other providers of the most effective and efficient business processes, thereby collectively creating higher value for customers.

These early adopters should not be confused with some of the more careless players in this new market. There are other newly created entities taking up positions on the value chain. These entities may also deal primarily with structured data; however, they have not made the requisite investment in the necessary IT applications and infrastructure. These are some of the pure play.coms that have never earned a cent of profit, and will either learn or be obliterated by the natural market forces.

The more responsible component organizations mentioned above — the quick movers — are the entities that deal primarily with structured data and are already supported by the necessary IT systems and infrastructure. Because of the speed with which these entities have been able to move into the new digital economic environment, they have created the expectation that this disaggregation will occur throughout the large conglomerates at the same speed. This may not be the case.

## E-BUSINESS AND E-COMMERCE

If one rolls back the clock just one or two years, one might remember that these early adopters of the Internet or the digital economy were referred to as players within the realm of E-commerce. The label here is quite important. Labeling them as E-commerce players as opposed to e-Business players is quite appropriate. Most of these new organizations were involved in one way or another with selling and marketing (see Exhibit 4). Selling and marketing over the Internet is most appropriately referred to as E-commerce. Central to this type of activity are secured financial transactions, and the backend integration to ERP applications for accounting and fulfillment. There may also be some limited customer relationship management (CRM) activity at the front end. The important point from the perspective of this discussion is that most E-commerce activities, such as order transactions, billing, accounting, and interfaces to ERP and CRM applications, primarily involve structured data.

E-business is far more than just E-commerce (see Exhibit 5). This is not to underestimate or belittle the transformation from the old brick-and-mortar selling and marketing to that of E-commerce. There are tremendous challenges involved in just this single transformation. Transforming from a brick-and-mortar enterprise to E-business, however, involves much more. E-Business incorporates E-commerce. In addition, it also refers to activities involving online customer service, support, and possibly front-end collaboration. It involves innovation, design, and other supply-chain collaboration. Finally, it may involve online procurement.

Most of these activities involve business processes that are dependent on documents and content. By all estimates, these represent the majority of the business processes within an enterprise. This is corroborated by the fact that between 80 and 90 percent of information within an enterprise is in unstructured data. For many of these functional units, B2B interactions generally involve protracted negotiations or collaboration using content. These interactions can involve partners, suppliers, and possibly customers. This occurs throughout the value chain, generally involving the sharing and re-purposing of information and knowledge (i.e., content).

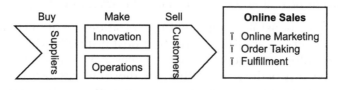

**Exhibit 4.   E-commerce**

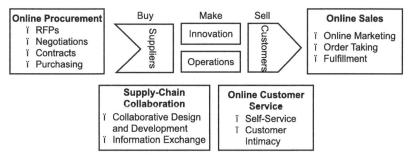

**Exhibit 5. E-business**

## CONTENT AND BUSINESS-TO-BUSINESS E-BUSINESS

Most organizations have had to develop an external focus. Competitive forces are mandating that the walls have to come down. However, for those entities owning processes within enterprises that depend on unstructured data, this may not be an easy process. There may be significant challenges. It has been found that in order to capture many of the benefits offered by E-business, they cannot be encumbered by business solutions designed with the assumption of:

- Intimate familiarity with the processes
- Intimate familiarity with the physical knowledge repositories
- Geographic proximity to enable collaboration, access to, and the sharing of knowledge content

Processes that were designed to operate with content management on a manual basis are proving to be grossly ineffective and in most cases just do not work in the B2B environment.

B2B interaction cannot suppose geographic proximity nor intimate familiarity with either the internal processes or the internal knowledge repositories. This mandates a focus on managing content in a way that IT has managed structured data during the past half century. The incentive for IT is that in the coming years, investment in content management could yield far greater returns than investments in standard IT. One reason simply may be due to the law of diminishing returns. Most of the structured data within organizations is computerized to a large degree, while the cherries in the content management orchard are yet to be picked.

To reduce risk and enhance efficiency and effectiveness, it is imperative that the content powering B2B interactions is trusted and is available through simple searches: (1) trusted because external entities cannot be expected to have intimate familiarity with the internal realities of other organizations against which they can compare content for validity; and (2) available through simple searches because they are not intimately familiar with the internal knowledge repositories in order to find content they require. Content must be managed. This managed environment at a minimum must ensure that:

- It can be scaled to an enterprise wide infrastructure (i.e., beyond just a few silos).
- Content goes through the necessary review and approval life cycle before it is available for consumption (i.e., published).
- There is an audit trail of each review and approval process.
- Content has integrity, that is, each instance of a particular content is the same in every physical repository.
- Content is versioned.
- Only published content is available for general consumption.
- Content is easily found through various metadata models such as attribute indexing, full text indexing, cabinet folder hierarchy indexing, and organizational ownership indexing.
- Only those with the appropriate authorization have access.
- Secured access is available at multiple levels for each content element, from no access at all through to full edit and deletion rights.
- Content can be aggregated and assembled without creating multiple copies.
- Aggregated content can be published in multiple formats.

Within this B2B environment, there must also exist the capability to collaborate. This requires spaces where shared content is readily available either through organizational ownership or cabinet folder hierarchy, metadata models, and where threaded discussions can occur. These collaboration spaces in essence are the electronic equivalents of bringing individuals who need to collaborate, be they departments or project teams, into the same physical location. Within this virtual physical location, they have the shared content that they require and have the ability to facilitate discussions and share ideas.

## SUMMARY

In summary, since the inception of the industrial revolution, most businesses have been almost exclusively focused internally. For a number of reasons during the past half century, IT has done very little to address the business problems and issues around the management of unstructured data. Not the least of the reasons is that unstructured data is complex and the solutions of the problems around its management are not limited to just technical solutions. Most IT professionals with standard IT backgrounds and skills often do not possess the additional skill sets to work effectively with unstructured data. In particular, they lack the in-depth understanding required to be able to effectively explain in business terms, the complexities around unstructured data to both colleagues and non-IT business professionals. More importantly, they lack the ability to recognize opportunities and to create effective business cases for addressing such IT endeavors.

The internal focus of business leaders has allowed IT to limit its endeavors primarily to the automation of structured data. This has left business people dependent on unstructured data or content to their own devices. Without content automation, most of the attempts at a solution were characterized by intimate familiarity with the internal processes and the physical knowledge repositories, and close geographic proximity to enable access to and the sharing of knowledge content.

In the new digital economy, processes that were designed to operate with content management on a manual basis are proving to be grossly ineffective and in most cases just do not work. B2B interaction cannot suppose geographic proximity nor intimate familiarity with either the internal processes or the internal knowledge repositories. To reduce risk and to enhance efficiency and effectiveness, it is imperative that the content powering B2B interactions is trusted and available through simple searches. Content management can make a major difference. Trusted content provided through automation can truly power E-business. Content managed through manual means can be the Achilles heel of many organizations looking to make the rapid transition into the digital economy.

# Chapter 36

# Internet Site Development in a Bandwidth-Hungry World: An Enterprise Dilemma

*Daniel Gonneau*

EVERYONE LIKES TO SEE WEB SITES WITH LOTS OF MULTIMEDIA CONTENT — VIDEO CLIPS, ANIMATIONS, AUDIO, ETC. — TO MAKE THE ONLINE EXPERIENCE RICHER, MORE INTEREST-ING, AND MORE INFORMATIVE. Unfortunately, many users use modems to access the Internet, and such content — even with the latest streaming media technologies — can be excruciatingly slow. Even enterprise intranets can have these bandwidth problems, particularly with so many people using modems to dial into the network while telecommuting or on sales calls. The addition of megabyte video files to an overtaxed network can be a seri-ous problem. Not all companies have the technological or financial where-withal to upgrade their networks to meet these challenges.

Unfortunately, this situation is unlikely to change any time soon. Few regular consumers have shown a willingness to spend real money on high-speed access, and even many Internet-savvy users have stayed with their 33.6 or 56KB/s modems. This is the case even though high-speed services are currently available in many of the largest markets, generally at $50 or more per month. Yes, everyone will all have inexpensive high-speed home access (cable modems, DSL, etc.) at some point in the future. But the ques-tion is: Will these services be in wide enough use in the near future to affect the many site design and development decisions one needs to make today? For most sites, the appropriate answer is "no."

0-8493-1160-8/02/$0.00+$1.50
© 2002 by CRC Press LLC

The situation at enterprises (both large and small) is different — but perhaps not as different as it might first appear. Networks are not free, after all, and network managers are under constant pressure to justify their budgets. The addition of multi-megabyte multimedia content to an intranet will probably not be received with open arms. And, as mentioned above, what happens to the telecommuters and sales personnel who are dialing into the network using slow-poke modems? For these reasons, bandwidth will continue to be a major factor in site development for most enterprises.

## LOW-BANDWIDTH, CONTENT-RICH INTERNET SITES

What then can be done to improve the functionality and attractiveness of our sites without imposing unrealistic bandwidth burdens on users and networks? This article reviews some of the techniques and technologies for adding brandwidth-friendly multimedia content to a site. It also looks at community and personalization technologies that add real interactivity to a site, as well as some of the browser compatibility issues that surround the use of these technologies. Whether one is responsible for an enterprise intranet, E-commerce effort, or any other type of Web site, one will want to know more about these technologies.

### Dynamic HTML

DHTML is a loosely knit group of Web technologies that allows "dynamic" features without using applets or plug-ins. It is an extension to HTML that lets browsers refresh Web pages without going back to the server for updates. This dynamic updating can take many forms, from purely graphical features like rollover buttons, to tables and forms that update themselves based on user input. DHTML-compliant browsers can do a surprising amount of processing without going back to the server for updates.

To implement DHTML, a few interlocking technologies are used:

**Dynamic Positioning.** DHTML allows unprecedented control over the positioning of elements on a Web page. This positioning can be dynamically changed based on user input or other events.

**Cascading Style Sheets (CSS).** Style sheets can control many features of the text on a Web page, from font size to indenting to font style. In addition, these features can be dynamically updated based on user inputs or other events.

**Dynamic Fonts.** Many headings, titles, and other text features on the Net are actually graphics, since browsers can only use the fonts found on users' computers. Thus, Helvetica, Times Roman, and Arial are extensively (excessively?) used on the Net. With dynamic fonts, designers can specify custom fonts that download with the page.

**Interactive Content.** DHTML pages can capture user mouse and keyboard clicks and process the Web page without going back to the server. A good example of this is a multicolumn table that lists, say, product manufacturer, price, and shipping cost. Without DHTML, the server would have to be contacted each time the user wanted to change the sorting of the table from, for example, price to manufacturer. With DHTML, the mouse click is captured and the table resorted without going back to the server. Another interesting capability is the ability to drag-and-drop elements on a Web page. With DHTML, one can imagine a user dragging a product photo to a Shopping Cart rather than clicking a static button that says "Click here to add to Shopping Cart."

**Layers.** Features can be layered, with only one layer visible at a time. The visible layer can be dynamically changed based on user input.

Using these technologies, simple animations, rollover graphics, and other graphical features — as well as interactive content — can be incorporated into Web pages without relying on plug-ins or applets.

To get a flavor of the possibilities, take a look at http://www.dhtml-zone.com. This site is a DHTML demonstrator, so it probably includes more DHTML than anyone needs at a particular site, but it will give a good idea of the possibilities.

### Vector Graphics

Regular bitmap graphics (.gifs, .jpgs, etc.) store graphical information as a series of pixels. Vector graphics, on the other hand, store a mathematical description of the graphic. This mathematical description is thus available for processing by the browser. Why is this important? One of the more dramatic capabilities of vector graphics is the ability to dynamically resize to the size of the user's browser window. Put another way, a large vector graphic is the same size as a smaller version; vector graphics are resolution independent. This is because vector graphics separate the mathematical description of the graphic from the rendering of the graphic. Thus, the size of the file is the same whether the browser renders it large or small. This capability thus eliminates the need for thumbnail graphics, and coding, extra page sets, etc., for handling multiple resolutions.

A good example of vector graphics can be found at the home page of Macromedia, the developer of the Flash vector graphics standard. The Flash plug-in is one of the most popular on the Internet — and, as of this writing, it should be built into Netscape Communicator 5. Once the plug-in is downloaded — quite small, at about 125K — one sees that the page automatically resizes whenever the size of the browser window is changed. While this is a neat trick, the real advantage is that developers only need to create one file, which will be automatically resized for all users, regardless of monitor size and resolution. This takes care of one of the nagging problems of developing for users with widely varying monitor resolutions. A monitor set at $1280 \times 1024$ — typical for most 19" and many 17" monitors — has fully four times the area of a monitor at $640 \times 480$. This can be a real problem for developing an interesting interface for all users.

However, the ability to dynamically resize graphics is just the beginning. Vector graphics can also be used for low-bandwidth animations, as one can see on the Macromedia home page. Click on one of the left-hand links, hear a "click" sound, and the appropriate links will appear. Unlike animated gifs (or any animation scheme based on bitmap graphics), these animations can be full-screen with no increase in file size. Flash files can include rollovers, sounds, and other features. All these animations, sounds, site navigation features, text, rollovers, etc. are included in a single 50K file that automatically resizes to the user's screen. This is indeed an impressive technology.

Flash is by no means the only vector graphics technology available. While Macromedia has made the Flash standard available to the Internet community, there are others and it remains to be seen which one will "win." Among them are Adobe's Precision Graphics Markup Language (PGML) and Microsoft's Vector Markup Language (VML). PGML is an interesting standard because:

- All text is searchable (not so with Flash)
- It is built on Postscript and PDF (Adobe's Acrobat document model)
- It is ASCII-based (Flash is binary)

For more information, see the online resources on vector graphics listed in Exhibit 1.

## XML

Both the familiar HTML and the not-so-familiar XML (eXtensible Markup Language) have their roots in SGML (Standard Generalized Markup Language), but they have very different purposes: HTML is the display language for the Web while XML works behind the scenes to link Web pages to data. While today's Web servers can certainly handle huge volumes of static page hits, database access can be awkward and slow. The same is true of searches, which can generate lots of unnecessary hits (false positives) and take a long time to process. Thus, technologies that streamline and speed up how Web pages link to databases are crucial to the further development of the Web as a medium for doing business.

XML allows developers to specify types of information. This can make connections to back-end databases much more efficient — and, thus, faster — as well as making searches much more precise.

**Exhibit 1.    Online Resources**

DHTML
    Netscape DHTML information (http://developer.netscape.com)
    Microsoft DHTML information (http://www.microsoft.com/workshop/author/)
    Inside DHTML (http://www.insidedhtml.com)
    Cross-browser DHTML (http://www.dansteinman.com/dynduo/)
    ZDNet HTMLUser (http://www.zdnet.com/products/htmluscr.html)
XML
    XML.com (http://www.xml.com)
    w3.org's XML information (http://www.w3.org/XML/)
Vector Graphics
    Flash (http://www.macromedia.com/software/flash/)
    Quick Start Guide to Flash 3 (http://webreview.com/wr/pub/98/07/31/
    feature/index.html)
    PGML (http://www.w3.org/TR/1998/NOTE-PGML)
    VML (http://www.w3.org/TR/NOTE-VML)
    Vector Graphics and XML (http://www.xml.com/xml/pub/98/06/vector/intro.html)
Browsers
    Microsoft Internet Explorer (http://www.microsoft.com/windows/ie/)
    Netscape Communicator (http://www.netscape.com)

To implement these features, XML allows the creation of custom tags. This is both a blessing and a curse. It is a blessing since, for example, developers will finally be able to identify <PRODUCT_NAME> or <PRODUCT_PRICE> or any other type of information. It can be a curse because the meanings of these terms vary from company to company and from industry to industry. Anyone who has worked on EDI (electronic data interchange) is familiar with this problem. For example, the word "purchase order" has widely varying meanings in different industries.

This may not be a problem within an individual enterprise, but it seems that cross-enterprise exploitation of XML will rely on creating standard XML tags — even more importantly, standard meanings for XML tags — for different industries. An example of this type of effort is the Open Financial Exchange (http://www.ofx.net). While not an XML effort, OFX allows customers using Microsoft Money and Intuit Quicken to connect to financial institutions to pay bills, check account balances, etc. The cost savings are considerable because the institutions do not need to develop separate interfaces for every financial package. A similar process will happen with XML, with similar benefits: much better and faster Web-based access to data and cost savings as standardized ways of interacting with that data are developed.

XML makes extensive use of style sheets, also used with Dynamic HTML. Fortunately, there are both free and commercial tools available to help with XML development (see Exhibit 2).

**Exhibit 2.    Site Development and Maintenance Tools**

Site Management/Database Access
  FrontPage (http://www.microsoft.com/frontpage/)
  Cold Fusion (http://www.allaire.com/products/ColdFusion/)
Graphics
  Photoshop (http://www.adobe.com/prodindex/photoshop/)
  Fireworks (http://www.macromedia.com/software/fireworks/)
  Paint Shop Pro (http://www.jasc.com)
  ColorWorks (http://www.spg-net.com)
HTML/DHTML Editors
  Allaire HomeSite (http://www.allaire.com)
  BBEdit (Macintosh) (http://www.barebones.com/)
  Dreamweaver (http://www.macromedia.com)
  FrontPage (http://www.microsoft.com/frontpage/)
Java Development
  Visual Cafe (http://www.symantec.com/domain/cafe/vc4java.html)
Streaming Media
  NetShow (http://www.microsoft.com/NTServer/Basics/NetShowServices/)
  RealPlayer (http://www.real.com)
Chat/Mailing Lists
  iChat (http://www.ichat.com)
  ICQ (http:/www.icq.com)
  Microsoft Chat (http://www.microsoft.com/windows/ie/chat/)
Portable Documents
  Acrobat (http://www.adobe.com/prodindex/acrobat/)
XML
  XML Pro (http://www.vervet.com)
  List of free tools (http://www.stud.ifi.uio.no/~larsga/linker/XMLtools.html)

## Streaming Media

Using various compression schemes, streaming video technology has made enormous strides in recent years. Compressed video is possible over 14.4Kbps modem links, albeit in a very jerky, low-resolution format. However, it looks like high-resolution Internet video will have to wait for true high-speed connections.

However, there are definitely applications — like Internet news broadcasts and customer-service applications — where low-resolution video can make a lot of sense. The two leading streaming media technologies are both proprietary:

- RealPlayer is an integrated environment, available as a multi-megabyte plug-in, for video and audio over the Net. As the early leader, many companies use RealPlayer to deliver news clips (both video and audio), music clips for selling CDs, and other multimedia features.
- NetShow is a collection of technologies that perform many of the same functions as RealPlayer. Unlike RealPlayer, the NetShow server is free with Window NT Server, while RealNetworks' server is not.

Audio streaming technology is often excellent, even over modems. There are numerous potential applications here, from music clips for E-commerce music sites to audio customer service to audio instruction manuals for the visually impaired.

The TIME proposal from Microsoft, Macromedia, and Compaq offers some interesting possibilities. TIME (Timed Interactive Multimedia Extensions) is a submission to the World Wide Web Consortium to cover the delivery of time-based media (e.g., animations) in Web browsers. Coming from Microsoft, one can only assume that it will be implemented in the next version of Internet Explorer. As of this writing, Netscape's participation in TIME is unknown.

## Community Technologies

A low-bandwidth way to add considerable interest to a site is the addition of community technologies; that is, any technology that helps to make the user feel as if they are participating in a community of people with like interests rather than simply visiting a static Web page. This can apply to both enterprise intranets — where "customers" might be users of a human resources site — and Internet sites for E-commerce or information delivery. There are two general types of community technologies (see Exhibit 3):

- Synchronous technologies allow realtime interaction between users and the owner of the Web site or between users. Examples are chat rooms, instant messaging, and Internet telephony.
- Asynchronous technologies allow non-realtime interaction between users. Examples include text-based chat rooms, e-mail, and newsgroups.

Community technologies can be further divided into two types:

- Public interactions are available for all to see; an example is a public newsgroup.
- Private interactions are user-to-user; an example is e-mail.

**Exhibit 3.  Technologies for Enterprise Community Development**

| Private | Public |
|---|---|
| Asynchronous | |
| E-mail | Mailing lists |
| Newsgroups | |
| Synchronous | |
| Chat (private) | Chat (public) |
| Internet telephony | Videoconferencing |
| Instant messaging | |

These distinctions can help one organize what types of technologies to consider for the various objectives of a site. For example, the customer-service pages of a commercial site might offer all these types of technologies because they tend to be used in different ways. Chat rooms and newsgroups tend to be used by people who have very specific questions. For more complex questions, there might never be a better solution than a customer-service rep at the end of a phone line. But today's Internet telephony solutions allow this "phone line" to be integrated right into the online environment. A user struggling with a piece of software might thus be able to reach a customer-service rep with one click on the screen, rather than looking up and calling a separate toll-free number. Even without Internet telephony, the ability to help customers with simple questions in an inexpensive, automated fashion can generate big cost savings. Cisco Systems estimates its annual savings in answering these types of questions without talking to a rep at $200,000.

Typically, community technologies are relatively inexpensive. For example, newsgroup servers are quite cheap to configure and operate. Newsgroup technology can help users help themselves. A good example is Macromedia's support newsgroup for its Dreamweaver Internet development product. This newsgroup, located at news://forums.macromedia.com, lets Dreamweaver users post questions about the product and how to use it. While it is monitored by Macromedia personnel, questions often are quickly resolved by the users themselves. This author has used it to post esoteric questions about site development, and been very satisfied with the responses. This contrasts markedly with many public newsgroups, which are sometimes dominated by spam and flames (in plain English, junk mail and offensive messages). Admittedly, this example involves Internet-savvy users, but the same principle can be applied to other businesses.

Efforts to personalize a site can also greatly help make it as useful as possible. Typical examples are news and search services such as http://my.yahoo.com or http://my.excite.com. The advantage of building local news, weather, and sports right into one's own personalized home page is an obvious benefit for these sites. But these technologies may signal a permanent move toward one-on-one marketing over the Internet. For example, Office Depot offers personalized online catalogs to small-business buyers. And intranets, that give users the ability to self-configure Web services can only help them be more efficient — with obvious benefits to the enterprise.

Like DHTML, personalization technology is really a cluster of interconnected technologies:

- Fast database access is a key technical issue because the server maintains information on each user.

- Collaborative filtering compares customers' purchase history, preferences, and other information to try to guess their overall product preferences, interests, etc.
- Dynamic page generation using systems like Microsoft's Active Server Pages (ASP) is also a key requirement, because some or all pages will be personalized for individual users.
- Secure transactions become even more important as potentially large amounts of information about individual consumers is processed.

Ultimately, these personalization technologies may lead to the mass customization of products and services, where users tell manufacturers exactly what they want before it is manufactured.

### Some Basics for Speeding up Your Site

The above-mentioned technologies allow the development of vibrant low-bandwidth sites, but there are also some decidedly low-tech techniques for simply reducing bandwidth load:

- Specify height/width for all graphics. A classic, it allows the page to be presented to the user before all the graphics are downloaded.
- Do not put the whole page in a single table. If this is done, the whole page has to download before anything is presented to the user. To get around this, a common technique is to put the top banner in one table and the rest of the page in a second table. That way, the banner downloads quickly, giving the user at least something to look at while the rest of the page downloads. One needs to be careful with WYSIWYG HTML editors, which often generate single-table pages.
- Use advanced graphics tools to reduce graphics size. See Exhibit 2 for a listing of tools. Just about all modern Web-centric graphics tools provide sophisticated ways of reducing the size of bitmap graphics. Some will even provide the download times with different download speeds (14.4, 28.8, etc.).
- Reduce the amount of copy. The amount of unnecessary copy on the Web can be astounding. Successful E-commerce sites such as amazon.com reduce the amount of extraneous copy to a minimum. Simply reusing copy from print sources often generates a site with far too much copy for the way people actually use the Internet. Many users read very little of the introductory material on, for example, a company home page before trying to find the specific information they are seeking. Try to get users as quickly as possible to what they are looking for, putting in-depth editorial coverage into the product pages and other "meaty" pages of the site. One consequence of this strategy is smaller Web pages and, thus, faster download times.

## Browser Incompatibilities

No discussion of these techniques and technologies would be complete without some discussion of the serious problem of browser incompatibility. If one is fortunate enough to be developing an intranet, this may not be a problem. But anyone who develops for the wilds of the Internet needs to address the problem.

The two most popular browsers are, of course, Microsoft's Internet Explorer and Netscape's Navigator/Communicator. Each includes many industry-standard features (see the World Wide Web Consortium at http://www.w3.org) but also includes proprietary features to enhance their products. See Exhibit 4 for some of these differences. Each browser is a "stew" of technologies that often conflict. As for the technologies discussed in this article:

- Dynamic HTML. The versions in MSIE4 and NS4 are basically incompatible. While tools exist for cross-browser DHTML development (see Exhibit 2), this process can nonetheless be complex and time-consuming — and, thus, expensive.
- Vector graphics. Microsoft has proposed its own standard, VML, while, at this writing, Netscape had chosen to integrate Macromedia's Flash into Version 5 of its browser.

**Exhibit 4.    Internet Technologies: Microsoft Internet Explorer 4 versus Netscape Navigator/ Communicator 4**

|  | MSIE4 | Netscape4 |
|---|---|---|
| HTML 4 | Yes* | Yes* |
| DHTML | Yes* | Yes* |
| CSS1 | Yes* | Yes* |
| XML | Yes | No |
| VB/Jscript | Yes | No |
| JavaScript | No** | Yes |
| Java | Yes* | Yes* |
| ActiveX | Yes | Plug-in |
| Flash3 | Plug-in | Plug-in |
| RealPlayer | Plug-in | Plug-in |
| Acrobat3 | Plug-in | Plug-in |
| iChat | Plug-in | Plug-in |

\* The Microsoft and Netscape implementations are often incompatible.

\*\* Microsoft's version of JavaScript is Jscript. The two versions are somewhat compatible. Fortunately, the development of ECMAscript may mean the end of the "script wars."

- Personalization/community technologies. These technologies are typically server based or rely on plug-ins. Thus, browser incompatibilities are less of an issue here.
- Streaming media. As of this writing, it is unclear which streaming media technology will dominate the market, or if a third standard will emerge. Microsoft's NetShow is built into their browser, but plug-ins like RealPlayer and QuickTime have large installed bases.

Developers who want to do anything beyond the basics are left with basically three choices:

1. Selectively develop for one browser
2. Develop advanced features for one browser, leaving people with the "other" browser to see basic features
3. Develop multiple features/pages to handle both browsers

The frustration of developing advanced features for both browsers has forced many developers to select one of the first two options, but surely this is not an ideal solution. For example, the versions of DHTML implemented in the two browsers are almost entirely incompatible, so the choice is particularly stark in this case. One can only hope that the two browser giants, working in collaboration with standards bodies, will develop standardized feature sets.

## CONCLUSION

With so many choices available, the world of Internet site development is certainly not getting any easier. The judicious use of Dynamic HTML, vector graphics, XML, community/personalization technologies, and streaming media should help in developing compelling, valuable content for a site *without* overwhelming the bandwidth of the enterprise network or user access speed.

# Chapter 37
# Selecting a Web Server Connection Rate

*Gilbert Held*

IF THE OPERATING RATE OF THE INTERNET CONNECTION IS TOO SLOW, ANYONE TRYING TO ACCESS AN ORGANIZATION'S SERVER FROM THE INTERNET MAY GET FRUSTRATED AND TERMINATE ACCESS OF INFORMATION FROM THE CORPORATE WEB SERVER SITE. At the opposite extreme, if an organization's Internet access connection operating rate exceeds the bandwidth required to support an acceptable level of access, you may be wasting corporate funds for an unnecessary level of transmission capacity.

As this chapter shows, with knowledge of the ways in which a Web server can be connected to the Internet, as well as knowledge about some of the transmission constraints associated with a Web server connection, it is possible to determine an appropriate Web server connection rate.

## BASICS OF CONNECTING TO THE INTERNET

Exhibit 1 illustrates the typical method by which Web servers are normally connected to the Internet. A Web server resides on a local area network (LAN), with the LAN connected via a router to an Internet access provider. The Internet access provider has a direct connection to a backbone network node on the Internet, commonly using a full T3 or switched multimegabit data service connection to provide Internet access for a large group of organizations that obtain Internet access through its connection facilities.

Although an Ethernet bus-based LAN is shown in Exhibit 1, in actuality any type of local area network that can be connected to a router (and for which TCP/IP drivers are available) can be used by the Web server. Thus, other common LANs used by Web servers include Token Ring and FDDI, as well as the numerous "flavors" of Ethernet, such as 10Base-T, 100Base-T, and 100VG-AnyLAN.

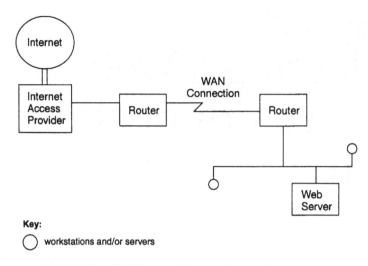

**Exhibit 1.  Web Server Connection to the Internet**

## Analog Versus Digital Leased Lines

The actual WAN connection between the Internet access provider and the customer can range in scope from low-speed analog leased lines to a variety of digital leased lines. Only a few access providers offer analog leased line connection options. When offered, the actual operating rate of the WAN connection is commonly limited to 19.2K bps or 24.4K bps, based on bandwidth constraints of a voice-grade analog leased line that limits modem operating rates. Concerning digital leased line operating rates, most Internet access providers recommend and offer 56K-bps, Fractional T1 in increments of 56K- or 64K-bps, full T1, fractional T3, and full T3 connectivity.

## Connection Constraints

Although the WAN operating rate can constrain users from accessing information from an organization's Web server, another less recognized but equally important constraint exists—the traffic on the local area network on which the Web server resides. Although the focus of this chapter is on determining an appropriate WAN operating rate to connect a Web server to the Internet, it also examines the constraints associated with LAN traffic that affect the ability of the server to respond to information requests received from the Internet.

## WAN CONNECTIVITY FACTORS

Three key factors govern the selection of an appropriate operating rate to connect a Web server to the Internet through a wide area network transmission facility. Those factors are

- The composition of the Web pages residing on a server
- The types of pages retrieved by a person accessing the Web server
- The number of "hits" expected to occur during the busy hour

A typical Web page consists of a mixture of graphics and text. For example, a university might include a picture of "Old Main" on the home page in the form of a graphics interchange format (GIF) file consisting of 75,000 bytes of storage supplemented by 500 characters of text that welcomes Internet surfers to the university home page. Thus, this university home page would contain 75,500 bytes that must be transmitted each time a member of the Internet community accesses the home page of the university.

By computing the data storage requirements of each page stored on the Web server and estimating the access distribution of each page, it is possible to compute the average number of bytes transmitted in response to each Internet access to the organization's Web server.

For example, assume an organization plans to develop a Web server that stores four distinct Web pages as well as a home page, providing Internet users with the ability to access two types of data from the home page. The construction of a two-tier page relationship under the home page is illustrated in Exhibit 2.

This example used to compute an appropriate WAN operating rate is for illustrative purposes only. Although the Web home page is always initially accessed, from the home page users typically access other server pages using hypertext links coded on the home page. Similarly, upon accessing different server pages, a user who wants to jump to other pages on the server is constrained by the links programmed on each page. Thus, the data transmitted in response to each page an Internet user accesses, as well as the sequence of pages accessed, will more than likely differ from organization to organization.

## PERFORMING THE REQUIRED COMPUTATIONS

Assume that an organization has already determined that when Web pages are arranged in a tier structure, access to a home page at the top of the tier represents 40 percent of all accesses, while the remaining 60 percent is subdivided by remaining tiers. Furthermore, the organization's Web page structure is to be constructed in two tiers below the home page, with the data storage associated with each page to include text and graphics as well as the access percentage of each page, as listed at the bottom of Exhibit 2.

After determining the data storage required for each Web page and the distribution of Internet access by page, it is possible to compute the average number of bytes that will be transmitted from the Web server in response to each "hit" on the organization's server. Here the term hit refers

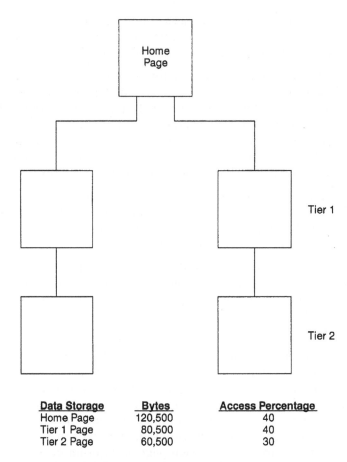

| Data Storage | Bytes | Access Percentage |
|---|---|---|
| Home Page | 120,500 | 40 |
| Tier 1 Page | 80,500 | 40 |
| Tier 2 Page | 60,500 | 30 |

**Exhibit 2.   Web Page Relationship**

to an access request to a Web page on the server via the HTTP using a URL that represents a file stored on the server, which equates to the contents of a Web page.

Using the information from Exhibit 2, the average data transmission rate resulting from a hit on the organization's server is computed as follows:

$$120,500 \times .40 + 80,500 \times .30 + 60,500 \times .30 = 90,500$$

Thus, each hit on the organization's Web server results in a requirement to transmit 90,500 bytes of data from the server to the Internet via the WAN connection to the Internet access provider.

**Hit Estimation**

Perhaps the most difficult estimate to make is the number of hits that are expected to occur during the busiest hour of the business day. Access to an organization's Web server depends on a large number of variables, many of which are beyond the control of the organization.

For example, although a company can control advertising of its Web's URL in trade publications, it may be difficult (if not impossible) to inhibit robot search engines from visiting the site, retrieving each page available for public access on the company's server, and indexing the contents of the server's Web pages. Once this index is placed onto the database of a search engine, access to the company's Web server can result from persons' invoking a Web search using Lycos, Alta Vista, or a similar search engine.

Unfortunately, because of limitations associated with many search engines, forward references to an organization's Web server may not be relevant and can alter the distribution of page hits as many persons, upon viewing your home page, may click on the Back button to return to the list of search matches provided by a search engine query and select a different match. If the organization is a tire distributor named Roosevelt Tires, for example, many Web search engines would return the home page URL in response to a search for the word "Roosevelt," even though the person is searching for references to one of the two U.S. presidents and not for a tire distributor.

Many Internet access providers can furnish statistics that may be applicable for use by an organization. A major exception to using such average statistics is if an organization is placing highly desirable information on the Web server, such as the results of major sports events (e.g., Super Bowl or World Series) as they occur. Otherwise, the information concerning busy-hour hits the company's Internet access provider supplies can be considered to represent a reasonable level of activity that will materialize.

Returning to the estimation process, assume the organization can expect 660 hits during the busy hour. Although this hit activity may appear to be low in comparison with millions of hits reported by well-known URL representing popular Web server sites, during a 24-hour period you are configuring the operating rate of the WAN connection to support $24 \times 660$ or 15,840 hits, based on a busy-hour hit rate of 660.

According to statistics published by several Internet access providers, several years ago the average number of hits per Web site when the top 100 sites were excluded was under 5,000 per day. Thus, if an organization is the typical business, college, or government agency, it may be able to use a lower WAN operating rate than determined by this example.

After determining the number of hits the Web site will support during the busy hour and the average number of bytes that will be transmitted in response to a hit, it is possible to compute other WAN operating rates. For this example, each hit results in the transmission of 90,500 bytes, and the

WAN operating rate is sized to support 660 hits during the busy hour. Thus, the results obtained are

660 hits per hour × 90,500 bytes per hit × 8 bits × 60 minutes per hour ×

60 seconds per minute = 132,733 bps

## LAN BANDWIDTH CONSTRAINTS

Based on the preceding computations, it would be tempting to order a 192K-bps Fractional T1 as the WAN connection to the Internet access provider, because the next lower fraction of service, 128K bps, would not provide a sufficient operating rate to accommodate the computed busy hour transmission requirement for 132,733 bps. However, before ordering the fractional T1 line, the business needs to consider the average bandwidth the Web server can obtain on the LAN to which it is connected.

If the average bandwidth exceeds the computed WAN operating rate, the LAN will not be a bottleneck that should be modified. If the average LAN bandwidth obtainable by the Web server is less than the computed WAN operating rate, the local area network will function as a bottleneck, impeding access via the WAN to the Web server. This means that regardless of any increase in the operating rate of the wide area network connection, users' ability to access the organization's Web server will be restricted by local traffic on the LAN.

If this situation should occur, possible solutions would be segmenting the LAN, creating a separate LAN for the Web server, migrating to a higher-speed technology, or performing a network adjustment to remove the effect of a portion of local LAN traffic functioning as a bottleneck to the Web server.

### Determining the Effect on Local Traffic

To illustrate the computations involved in analyzing the effect of local traffic, assume the LAN shown in Exhibit 1 is a 10M-bps 10Base-T network that supports 23 workstations and one file server in addition to the Web server, resulting in a total of 25 stations on the network. This means that, on the average, each network device will obtain access to 1/25 of the bandwidth of the LAN, or 400,000 bps (10M bps/25).

However, the bandwidth of the LAN does not represent the actual data transfer a network station can obtain. This is because the access protocol of the network will limit the achievable bandwidth to a percentage of the statistical average.

For example, on an Ethernet LAN that uses the carrier-sense multiple-access collision-detection (CSMA/CD) protocol, collisions will occur when two stations listen to the network and, noting an absence of transmission, attempt to transmit a frame at or near the same time. When a collision occurs, a jam signal is transmitted by the first station that detects the high voltage resulting from the collision, causing each station with data to transmit to invoke a random exponential back-off algorithm.

This algorithm generates a period of time the network station delays attempting a retransmission; however, the frequency of collisions, jams, and the invocation of back-off algorithms increases as network utilization increases. For an Ethernet LAN, network utilization beyond a 60 percent level can result in significant degradation of performance, which can serve as a cap on achievable transmission throughput. Thus, the average bandwidth of 400,000 bps previously computed should be multiplied by 60 percent to obtain a more realistic level of average available bandwidth obtainable by each station on the LAN to include the Web server.

In this example, the Web server will obtain on the average 240,000 bps of LAN bandwidth (i.e., 400,000 bps × 0.6). Since the average LAN bandwidth obtainable by the Web server exceeds the computed WAN operating rate, no adjustment is required to the LAN. If the Web server is connected to a Token Ring LAN, the average bandwidth of 400,000 bps should be multiplied by 75 percent, since a Token Ring LAN does not have its performance seriously degraded until network utilization exceeds 75 percent.

## MAKING WEB PAGE ADJUSTMENTS

As described thus far, network managers need to consider the LAN bandwidth obtained by the Web server as well as the WAN operating rate to effectively select a wide area network connection method to an Internet access provider. When computing the WAN operating rate, it is important to note that the rate depends on

- The number of hits expected to occur during the busy hour
- The storage in bytes required to hold each page (which represents data that has to be transmitted in response to a page hit)
- The distribution of hits on the pages that are placed on the company's Web server

The first and third factors are obtained by an estimation process. However, a company has a high degree of control over the composition of its server's Web pages, and this fact can be used as an effective tool in adjusting the WAN connection's ability to support the estimated number of hits expected during the busy hour.

Because initial access to a company's Web server is through its home page, that page will have the highest distribution of hits on the company server. Thus, if the estimate of busy hour traffic is low, it is possible to increase the selected WAN operating rate to support additional hits by reducing the transmission associated with each home page hit. Methods include replacing GIF images with their equivalent Joint Photographic Experts Group images that require less storage, cropping images to reduce their data storage requirements, and eliminating all or some images on the home page.

## RECOMMENDED COURSE OF ACTION

The selection of an appropriate wide area network operating rate to connect a corporate Web server to the Internet depends on three key factors, of which two—the expected number of hits during the busiest hour and the distribution of hits per server page—can only be estimated. This means that the WAN operating rate's ability to service expected traffic will be only as good as two traffic-related estimates.

However, by planning ahead the organization can adjust the third factor—the data storage on the server's home page—and obtain the flexibility to alter the selected WAN operating rate to support additional hits during the busy hour.

By following the methodology presented in this chapter, network managers and others involved in corporate Web page creation will be able to remove a large degree of the guesswork associated with connecting a Web server to the Internet. In addition, they should be able to rapidly adjust the capacity of a wide area network connection to support additional Web server hits if such an adjustment should become necessary.

# Section VIII
# Managing Information on the Internet

Data and information management have been the core of the information technology industry since the inception of computers. Data is stored in stand-alone databases connected to the Web, data warehouses, and legacy applications. This section examines some of the strategies and tools for leveraging these disparate data sources through the Internet.

"Creating Internet Server Documents with HTML" uses HTML to create Internet server documents.

"Java-Enabled Data Warehousing" explains how Java technology can be used to build a flexible, open architecture that supports users on a diverse set of devices, including browsers, palm pilots, and mobile phones.

"A Guide to Web-Enabled Data Warehouses" describes the strategy, architecture, infrastructure, and implementation of these solutions and also how to manage security, performance, and costs issues that result from an expanded user population.

"Bridging Legacy Data with XML" provides a straightforward process for transforming legacy data for the Extensible Markup Language (XML). XML is a popular standard for application communication over the Internet.

"Publishing Database Information on the World Wide Web" empowers organizations to publish their corporate data on Web sites for their employees to securely access information using a browser. This chapter focuses on publishing and accessing database information from a Web site.

"Web-Enabling Image and Sound Objects in Database Tables" examines software tools, Web-enabling tools, and database design for enabling manipulation of images and sounds in databases that are themselves Web enabled.

"Database Management and the Internet: Developments and Challenges" explores techniques for providing access, security, and reliability to databases on the Internet.

# Chapter 38
# Creating Internet Server Documents with HTML

*Gilbert Held*

THE HYPERTEXT MARKUP LANGUAGE (HTML) PROVIDES A STANDARDIZED MECHANISM FOR CREATING A WIDE RANGE OF DOCUMENTS. Users can create menus as well as generate database query results or online documentation. Because the HTML standard also provides a simple format for representing linked information, users can then view these links and skip around in the document to retrieve related information.

Because HTML gives developers a standardized mechanism for creating linked-list information displays, it also simplifies program maintenance. Anyone familiar with the structure of the language can easily modify the efforts of other employees when organizational requirements change. Consequently, the use of HTML can potentially lower program maintenance costs as well as make it relatively easy to shift personnel resources between projects when required.

HTML is a subset of Standard Generalized Markup Language, or SGML, which is an International Standards Organization (ISO) standard for formatting a text document in which the actual formatting commands are embedded in the text. Although the development of HTML coincided with the development of World Wide Web (WWW) servers on the Internet, HTML-created linked-list queries and database retrieval connections can also operate on individual workstations or on local area network client/server connections. Organizations may wish to consider using HTML for generating linked-list information not only for WWW servers but also for applications such as computer-based training.

## HTML DOCUMENTS IN OVERVIEW

An HTML document is similar to a text file and can be created using any text editor or word processor with an unformatted American Standard

Code for Information Interchange file output. Each HTML document consists of three parts:

- A declaration
- A prologue
- An instance

The declaration binds processing quantities and syntax token names to specific values. For example, a declaration might set the maximum length of a name to 50 characters.

A prologue specifies element types, element relationships and attributes, and references that can be represented by a markup. An example of an HTML prologue is the head element that contains at most one title element.

The instance contains the actual document data (i.e.,the text) and the markup of the document that controls its display.

Once an HTML document is created, a viewer is required for a person to actually look at it. The viewer examines the document, displays a page at a time, and interprets its structure, which is based on the markups in the text.

**HTML Text Structure**

The actual text of the HTML document, more formally referred to as the instance, represents a hierarchy of elements. The instance is the key part of an HTML document and can be used to illustrate how to use the language to create HTML documents.

Each element in the hierarchy has a name and may have one or more attributes or contents. Exhibit 1 illustrates an example of the structure of an HTML instance.

In the HTML instance structure in Exhibit 1, the indentations were established to illustrate the relationships of document markups. When creating an actual HTML document, indentations are irrelevant. In fact, the user does not have to place markup identifiers on separate lines and can string them together or alternate their placement. For example, the developer can end the text of a paragraph using the markup tag <P> instead of placing it on a separate line.

**Markup Tags**

A markup tag is an identifier that informs a viewer how to display text. HTML tags consist of a left angular bracket (<), which is the less-than symbol, followed by a keyword or mnemonic known as a directive and closed by a right angular bracket (>),which is the greater-than symbol on the keyboard.

**Exhibit 1.  HTML Instance (Text) Example**

| HTML Markup Tags | Meaning |
|---|---|
| `<HTML>` | Beginning of the HTML file (initiator) |
| `<TITLE>` | Title identifier |
| `Creating Internet Server Documents with HTML` | Title text |
| `</TITLE>` | End of title (terminator) |
| `<H1>` | Heading 1 identifier |
| `One of up to six headings` | Heading 1 text |
| `</H1>` | Terminator (end of heading 1) |
| `This is a paragraph.` | Paragraph text |
| `</P>` | End-of-paragraph marker |
| `<UL>` | Unnumbered list marker |
| `<LI>First item in unnumbered list` | List item marker |
| `<A NAME="anchor">anchor` | List item detail A marker (initiator) |
| `</A>` | End of list item detail A (terminator) |
| `<LI>Second item in unnumbered list` | List item marker |
| `</UL>` | End of unnumbered list marker (terminator) |
| `</HTML>` | End of HTML file (terminator) |

As in Exhibit 1, most markup tags are paired, with the terminator markup tag identical to the initiator tag with the exception of a prefix forward slash (/), which precedes the text or mnemonic enclosed in the brackets. The forward slash tells the viewer that the viewing operation established by a preceding markup tag is terminated. The primary exception to the pairing of markup tags is the <P> or end-of-paragraph tag. There is no such markup tag as </P>.

Text and mnemonic entries in markup tags are case insensitive. Thus, <TITLE>, <title>, and <Title> are completely equivalent to one another.

### Viewing an HTML Document

The primary method used to view a HTML document is a browser. Probably the most familiar browser is Mosaic, developed at the National Center for Supercomputing at the University of Illinois at Urbana-Champaign. Another browser in wide use is Cello, developed at the Cornell University School of Law. Both software programs, as well as other browsers, include coding that acts on HTML markup tags.

Because the HTML standard is still evolving, not all tags are supported by all browsers. If a browser does not support a specific markup tag it ignores the tag. However, some versions of browsers that ignore unknown markup tags also omit the display of information within pairs of unknown tag entries, so gaps will appear in the display of information. Most newer browsers support all HTML markup tags. Users should check the browser's release date; if it was released after late 1994, it should support the complete HTML markup tag standard.

### Function and Uses of Key Markup Tags

**Titles.** The directive for the title tag is <TITLE>. Usually the title is positioned on the first line of a document and the text of the title is used to identify the contents or purpose of the document.

Exhibit 2 shows two examples of the use of the HTML title tag. The first example includes the title terminator tag on the same line; the second example uses separate lines for each markup tag and the text of the title to be displayed. Both methods are acceptable, though the second method may be preferable because of its clarity when contained in an extensive document.

**Exhibit 2.   Title Tag Examples**

```
    <TITLE>Personnel Database Query </TITLE>
or  <TITLE>
    Personnel Database Query
    </TITLE>
```

*Note*: Text can be positioned with beginning and ending tags on one line or on separate lines.

**Headings.** Six levels of headings, numbered 1 through 6, are supported by HTML. Heading 1 is the most prominent; succeeding numbers represent subheadings. The first heading in a document is usually tagged <H1>, although any heading level can be used.

In constructing an HTML document, users can use a level 1 heading to identify a chapter, for example, while level 2 headings could be used to identify major sections within the chapter. Heading levels 3 through 6 could be used to identify different areas within a section or to visually highlight specific information for the user.The text within the beginning and ending heading markup tags is displayed by the browser in either a larger or bolder font than the normal body text.

The format of the heading tag is as follows:

```
<Hn>Text of heading</Hn>
```

where *n* is a number between 1 and 6, designating the level of the heading. For example, to display the string "Retrieve data by Social Security

Number" as a level 2 heading, the user would enter the following HTML statement:

```
<H2>Retrieve data by Social Security Number</H2>
```

**Paragraphs.** A paragraph in HTML is similar to a paragraph in a book or article, consisting of sentences of related information. Carriage returns and white spaces in HTML files are not significant when the user is creating a paragraph. In addition, word wrapping can occur at any point in the source file that has been created.

When creating a paragraph, the user should separate each paragraph from a succeeding paragraph by the <P> tag. Otherwise, the viewer will interpret separately entered paragraphs as one large paragraph and produce a visually unappealing display. The following example illustrates the use of title, heading, and paragraph tags within an HTML document:

```
<TITLE>Personnel Database Query</TITLE>

<H1>Retrieve data by Social Security Number</H1>

To retrieve personnel databased on the social security
number of an employee click on the number icon.<P>
```

## Creating Hypertext Links

**Uniform Resource Locators (URLs).** Hypertext documents are versatile because they let the user jump to a different section within the document or to specific sections in other documents. Hypertext lets the user link to other documents of significance.

The most important part of the function of HTML is creating hypertext links. This ability to create links is accomplished as a result of the development of a standardized mechanism for addressing documents. That mechanism is known as the URL.

The format of an URL is as follows:

```
scheme://host.domain<:port>/path/filename
```

The scheme can have a variety of values. For example, the scheme can be coded as `file` to denote a file on a local computer or on an anonymous FTP (file transfer protocol) server, as HTTP (hypertext transfer protocol) to access a file on a WWW server, as `gopher` to access a file on a Gopher server, or as `WAIS` to access a file on a wide area information server.

Exhibit 3 lists the scheme entries currently supported by URL. The port number is usually not required, but it should be used if the manager of the destination address changes port addresses from their default values as a means to obtain an additional degree of security.

**Exhibit 3.**     **URL Schemes**

| Scheme Entry | Scheme Access |
|---|---|
| ftp | File Transfer Protocol |
| gopher | Gopher protocol |
| mailto | Electronic mail address |
| mid | Message identifiers for electronic mail |
| cid | Content identifiers for MIME body part |
| news | Usenet news |
| nntp | Usenet news for local NNTP access |
| prospero | Access using Prospero protocol |
| telnet | Interactive Telnet session |
| tn3270 | Interactive Telnet 3270 session |
| WAIS | Wide area information servers |
| http | Hypertext transfer protocol |

As an example of the use of an URL, assume the user wishes to access the file `personnel.jan` on the FTP server whose address is `opm.macon.gov`. If the file is located in the PERSONNEL directory, the user would use the following URL:

```
ftp://opm.macon.gov/PERSONNEL/personnel.jan
```

**Anchors.** Anchor tags are used to establish links to a section in the same or a different document. To illustrate the creation and use of anchors, assume a user wishes to establish a link from document 1 to a specific section in document 2. The user must first establish a named anchor in document 2 and then create the link in document 1 that references the previously named anchor. For example, to add an anchor named SSN to document 2, the user must insert text similar to the following example:

```
<A NAME="SSN">Retrieval based on Social Security
Number</A>
```

In this example, text can be inserted before and after the beginning and ending anchor brackets.

To reference the location in document 2, the user must include its filename as well as the named anchor in document 1. In doing so, the URL for document 2 is separated by a hash mark (#). Thus, one possible entry in document 1 to establish a link to document 2 would be as follows:

```
To access the databased on the employee <A
HREF="URL#SSN">SSN</a>
```

In the previous example, URL would be replaced by the actual universal resource locator to denote the location of document 2. Then, clicking on the mnemonic SSN in document 1 would send the reader directly to the words "Retrieval based on Social Security Number" in document 2.

When establishing anchors within the same document, a user would follow the same method; however, it is also possible to replace the URL with the mnemonic HTML, since a hypertext jump is being requested within the same document.

**Lists.** HTML supports three types of lists:

- Unnumbered lists, representing unordered information
- Numbered lists, displaying ordered information
- Descriptive lists, displaying alternative descriptive titles

Each type of list is created using an appropriate set of markup tags. For example, an unnumbered list commences with an opening list <ul> tag. Next, each individual item in the list is prefixed with the list identifier <li> tag; however, no closing list identifier tag is required. Instead, the unnumbered list is completed with a closing list </ul> tag. The following example illustrates the creation of a four-item unnumbered list:

```
<UL>
<LI>1960-1970
<LI>1971-1980
<LI>1981-1990
<LI>1991-1995
</UL>
```

When a browser displays the entries in an unnumbered list, it prefixes each entry with a bullet. Thus, the output would be visually displayed as a bulleted list. Numbered and descriptive lists follow a similar creation process.

### Formatting Text and Adding Images to the Document

HTML supports a number of different text formats. Its preformatted <PRE> tag is used to identify a block of text that should be displayed with spaces, lines, and tabs functioning in their normal manner. Other text formats supported by HTML include block quotations and character formatting.

Character formatting lets users see individual words or sentences in italics or boldface, fixed with font or as the result of a specially defined tag. By using block quotes and character formatting, a user can customize the display to ensure it is both pleasing to look at and easy to read and follow.

In-line images can enhance the appearance of ordinary documents. Through HTML, a user of a human resources application can, for example, display the photograph of an employee while displaying database information and similar integrated image and text displays.

Embedded images can be inserted into a document display through the use of an image (IMG) element containing two possible attributes—SRC and ALIGN. The SRC attribute is used as the URL of the document to be embedded. ALIGN takes values of TOP, MIDDLE, or BOTTOM and defines the location where graphics and text should be aligned vertically.

To illustrate the use of graphics within a display, assume a user wishes to display the contents of the GIF file named SSCARD.GIF, which contains an image of a Social Security card. The user must enter the following HTML statement in which the text outside the brackets simply displays information around the image:

```
An Employee's Social Security Card <IMG SRC="SSCARD.GIF">
must be examined at time of employment.
```

## CONCLUSION

Anyone who wants to write or create a Web page needs a working knowledge of HTML. This chapter explains the basics for creating a simple HTML document that integrates text and graphics and provides links within or between it and other documents. Because HTML is standardized, documents created in HTML are easy to maintain. Thus, organizations should consider using HTML not only to create Web pages but also for other documents delivered over local client/server networks.

# Chapter 39
# Java-Enabled Data Warehousing

*Fred Neufeld*

TODAY'S BUSINESS CLIMATE IS MORE COMPETITIVE AND VOLATILE THAN EVER BEFORE. Increased competition, evolving global markets, mergers, and acquisitions: these factors and many more have forced enterprises to unlock their collections of market data and use the information to make better decisions faster. Now more than ever, decision support systems, data marts, and data warehouses are not only a component of a competitive advantage, but they are a requirement. They must be easily implemented and able to adapt and scale as the business climate changes.

Sun's Java computing architecture is an implementation framework that uses standard, currently available network protocols and services to deliver the power of Java application to the widest possible base of Java platform-enable devices and users. With this architecture, transactions can be moved transparently to the most cost-effective, appropriate support channel within a network owing to the portable nature of Java application.

There are many areas to consider when Web-enabling a data warehouse. Two of the key areas to address are as follows: hardware (system architecture) and software (tools). There are many hardware considerations to make, including performance, scalability, high availability, data security, and system and network management. This chapter focuses on the software required for a data warehouse and also answers the following essential question: "How does Java technology enable data warehouses to provide easier access and a more efficient, flexible architecture to meet the end-user requirements of today, tomorrow, and for the unknown requirements of the future?"

## BENEFITS OF A WEB-ENABLED DATA WAREHOUSE

With the evolution of the World Wide Web, the end user is becoming more Web-informed and therefore more sophisticated in its use. More and more corporate officers are becoming the end users of data warehouses. Learning complicated online analytical processing (OLAP) tools is no longer acceptable. A "Web-like" access tool requires little or no training and therefore becomes time-effective and cost-efficient.

The end users of the data warehouses are also more mobile. The standard, local area networks are not as effective in supporting a mobile workforce. The World Wide Web — the Internet — is becoming an inexpensive, effective model for deploying information to thousands of end users.

Maintaining a Web-enabled data warehouse has become easier and more cost-effective, because the application software and the data warehouse data structure can be transmitted over the Web. When the end user accesses the data warehouse, the application can determine if either a software or a data structure update is required and automatically update the application through the Web. This takes the whole maintenance cycle away from the end users — thus resulting in zero-client administration.

Using the Web standard protocols as the data warehouse infrastructure allows for greater end-user collaboration. The end user views and manipulates the data and then forwards the information (via e-mail) to other colleagues. The information can simply be viewed using a Java client — a Web browser; no specific application is required to be loaded on to their machines.

## WHY JAVA TECHNOLOGY IS IMPORTANT

There are many features or benefits that make Java technology important to application development and these benefits are extended to data warehouse development. They include:

- The Java language is an object-oriented language that enables faster application development.
- Java applications can be multi-threaded, which will enable them to scale across the enterprise.
- Java virtual machines (JVMs) are now available on all major platforms, allowing applications to be portable across all environments, platform-independent — Write-Once, Run Anywhere.
- Java technology was designed and built using industry standards (e.g., CORBA).
- Java applets are delivered on an as-needed basis, thus reducing the administration cost of upgrading client machines. Security has always been a key factor in developing the Java technology.
- Java applets run in a "sandbox" environment, shielding the end user's machine from unwanted security breaches. Better performance is also available by using the multi-threaded ability of the Java programming language and the just-in-time compilers.

## LAYERS OF THE DATA WAREHOUSE

At its most fundamental level, a data warehouse is a staging area for decision-support information. The data warehouse can be divided into five logical layers, as shown in Exhibit 1. These layers are:

1. Source layer: the operational data that needs to be extracted, including external sources
2. Extraction, transformation, and loading (ETL) layer
3. Target layer: enterprise data warehouse, operational data stores, and data marts
4. End-user layer: reports, *ad hoc* queries, OLAP, and data mining
5. Metadata layer: data about data, collected during each stage of the data warehouse process

### Sources

The sources are the starting point for the data warehouse. The sources consist of operational systems, current applications, new applications (e.g., ERP), and external data feeds. The data warehouse helps to bridge the data disparity from all operational systems and merges the information from various data types into a consistent format.

Most of the source systems used to feed the data warehouse are legacy systems. During the data warehouse project, there is no need to re-host the sources. Therefore, Java technology has not played a major role in this area of the data warehouse. However, there are significant enhancements to relational database management systems (RDBMS), and these will be highlighted in the Target section of this chapter because most enhancements are related to retrieving data for the end users.

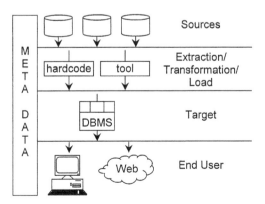

**Exhibit 1.   Five Logical Layers of a Data Warehouse**

### Extraction/Transformation/Load (ETL)

This layer takes the information from the source operational systems and transforms, merges, and loads the data into the target database. The purpose of this stage is to ensure that the data loaded into the data warehouse is consistent, standardized, and cleansed. The transformation is the process of filtering, selecting, conversion/translation, derivation/summarization, and cleansing of the data from disparate operational systems and external sources. The merged and cleansed data is then loaded into the target data warehouse.

### ETL Tools Written in Java

ETL tools developed using Java technology benefit from the object-oriented, fast development, and Write-Once, Run Anywhere. Tool vendors benefit because they incur lower development and maintenance costs since only one source code base is required. The benefit for the customers is the ability to have one ETL tool deployed throughout the organization on multiple platforms. The one tool reduces the training time of the IT staff and the time required to deploy different tools throughout the organization.

### ETL Tools Generating Java Programs

ETL Tools that generate Java code enable the system administrator to optimize system usage. Once the extraction processes are generated, in Java, the processes are portable. This flexibility allows the system administrator to select the best platform to optimize the ETL process. Over a period of time as the requirements for the ETL process evolve and the computing environment changes, the ETL process can be deployed to another platform or even be divided into pieces, which then can be executed on different platforms. The ETL processes do not have to be recompiled or retested, thus saving both time and resources.

Since the ETL processes are portable, the system administrator has control of the platform where the ETL process executes. The system administrator can optimize the source-to-target workflow and reduce network traffic by moving the ETL process closer to the source data.

By expanding the Java infrastructure with Enterprise Java Beans™ (EJB) technology, the corporation can purchase transformation components (e.g., address verification programs). These components then can be plugged into the current ETL process. This enables the ETL process to grow and expand quickly and easily as the requirements evolve.

### Targets

The target layer is where the enterprise data warehouse, operational data store, and data marts are defined and accessed. The information is compiled into a standard, consistent framework for access by the end user. Java technology incorporated into the database engines has many significant benefits for the data warehouse.

One of the key benefits is to add Java technology into the inline procedures. The inline procedures extend the standard SQL, allowing for specialized data types (e.g., voice, video, large binary objects) to be incorporated into the data warehouse.

The inline procedures can also be used for database triggers. These triggers written in Java, rather than a database-specific language, are easier to maintain by a development team. The database triggers are then transferable to other Java-enabled databases. Stored procedures become associated with the application and not with the RDBMS.

The object-oriented approach of Java technology enables the business logic to be separated from the database logic, making the data warehouse application easier to maintain. Besides being more maintainable, separating the business and database logic also makes the application more scalable. The more complex procedures can be executed on the database server rather than on the potentially smaller Java client — the Web browser. Performing the majority of the processing on the database server also reduces network traffic. The client machine formulates the query and passes it to the database server. The server processes the information and returns only the results back to the client, through the network.

Using Java to access the databases (JDBC) also enables the user's application to have a standard interface into the database engines. This builds flexibility into the application, allowing the database engine to be changed without affecting the application code.

The next step is to incorporate Enterprise Java Beans (EJB), Entity Beans, into the data warehouse structure. This enables the data warehouse application to access the contents of a database without any knowledge of the underlying database engine. The EJB structure allows the database to be substituted without affecting the application, thereby adding more flexibility to the data warehouse application.

## End-User Tools

The end-user layer is the layer that defines the end-user environment. There are many different categories of end-user tools: batch reporting, *ad hoc* queries, multi-dimensional analysis, and data mining. All categories of tools can benefit from Java technology with multi-platform support and lower maintenance costs. However, the largest benefits are gained when the end-user tools are deployed on the Web. Standard HTML is expanded, using Java technology enabling data-driven reports and graphics to be created and integrated on the fly.

## WEB INTERFACE

The Web allows end users to access the data warehouse information through *ad hoc* queries, or multi-dimensional fashion through their Web browsers. Traditionally, this functionality was only available by loading and maintaining the decision support application on every workstation (fat clients). Java technology removes the requirement for fat clients in the data warehouse architecture. The end users' machines become a zero-client administration, allowing application updates to be distributed through the Web.

Web-based tools created using the Web-like interfaces are easier to understand. The end user does not need to attend a training session or read a complex training manual to understand how to use the tool.

Java technology is based on a distributed computer model. The application logic is passed through the Web and the processing occurs on the end user's machine. Therefore, as end users access the data warehouse, the work is distributed to the client's machines, making the data warehouse more scalable.

### Metadata

Metadata is data about data. The metadata repository is a central repository to collect information during the data warehouse process. The end user accesses this information to understand the business rules applied to the data in order to build the data warehouse. All stages of the data warehouse should feed information into the metadata repository. Currently, there are not very many tools in this complex area of data warehousing; however, a number of standards groups are emerging.

Using Java technology in the metadata repository enables the other tools in the data warehouse architecture to write the appropriate information to the repository using open standards. The metadata repository uses Java inline procedures to validate the information being entered.

A metadata tool, developed using Java technology, benefits the end users by enabling them to use their browsers, over the Web, to access the metadata information. Ideally, the same Java-based tool used to access the data warehouse information should be used to access the metadata repository.

## CONCLUSION

A data warehouse is an important application that provides better access to the corporation's information. The structure of the data warehouse is complicated by the fact that information must be extracted from a number of disparate systems and merged into a uniform structure, for access by the end users. The data warehouse structure must be flexible so that it can evolve as the business requirements change.

In the data warehouse infrastructure, the use of Java technology — with its open standards, multi-platform support and portability — enables data warehouse processes to be easily moved to different platforms when required. Java technology also extends the standard SQL and creates flexible inline procedures and enables a more scalable data warehouse architecture. From a tools perspective, Java technology allows for a "thin client," easier distribution of software updates, and a browser-like interface that requires less end-user training. Extending the Java architecture to include Enterprise Java Beans allows new or improved data warehouse components to be easily added to the current data warehousing processes.

Leveraging the Java technology enables the IT organization to build and deploy data warehouses using an open-standard, portable architecture that is easily modified as business requirements change.

# Chapter 40
# A Guide to Web-Enabled Data Warehouses

*Mary Ayala-Bush*
*Walter Kuketz*

DELIVERING DATA WAREHOUSE ACCESS THROUGH WEB BROWSERS HAS A VARIETY OF BENE-FITS. Inside a corporate intranet, Web-enabled data warehouses can increase ease of use, decrease some aspects of training time, and cut costs by reducing the number of proprietary clients. Upgrades can also be accelerated given a standard client, and data warehouses can more easily integrate with other applications across a common platform. When extended to corporate trading partners through an extranet (a secure extension of an intranet outside a firewall), the information contained within a data warehouse may become a revenue source.

Although the internal and external benefits of Web-enabled data warehouses are appealing, they do not come without complicating issues. In traditional implementations, data warehouses have been used by a small population of either highly trained or high-ranking employees for decision support. With such a small number of users having the warehouse application on their desktop, access control was straightforward: either users could access a given table or they could not. Once the warehouse is to be entered by more people — possibly including some outside of the company — access may need to be restricted based on content. Security concerns also change as the user population increases, with encryption over the public Internet becoming one likely requirement.

Because Web-based access to a data warehouse means expanding the community of people who access the data, the types of queries are likely to be more varied. Better business intelligence may thereby be derived, but once again not without complications. In addition to security, performance (and therefore cost) issues become immediately relevant, dictating reconsideration of everything from replication patterns to log-in requirements.

This chapter discusses how Web-enabled data warehouses change the strategy, architecture, infrastructure, and implementation of traditional versions of warehouse applications.

## STRATEGY

### Business Relationships

The strategy for a Web-based data warehouse should answer at least the following two questions:

1. Who is being granted access?
2. Why are they being granted access through the Web model?

Answering these two questions supplies important information for the cost justification of broader access. Possible justifications might include getting better service from vendors, facilitating better relationships with customers, shortening time of products in the supply chain, and receiving revenues from an internal application. The implications of broader access include having to design an architecture flexible enough to allow for new audiences with needs and requirements that may not be well identified. In addition, going into the information business can distract a company from its core focus by raising the following questions:

- How are pricing levels determined?
- How does revenue derived from a potentially unexpected external source change payback and ROI models?
- What are the service-level agreements and how are they determined?
- Who becomes the customer service liaison, especially if the IS organization is already running at full capacity for internal constituencies?

### Access Control and Security

Security is a primary consideration when Web access to sensitive corporate information is under consideration. Authentication can be required at three separate stages, allowing administrators to fine tune who sees what when, whereas encryption (typically through the use of the secure socket layer or SSL) protects both queries and responses from being compromised in transit. Initially, the Web server can require either name and password log-in or the presence of a certificate issued by the data warehouse administrator. This grants access to the site and triggers the SSL encryption if it is implemented.

Once inside the data warehouse, the user might also be required to authenticate him- or herself at the query server, which allows access to the appropriate databases. This might be a dedicated data mart for a vendor, for example, that precludes vendor A from seeing anything pertaining to vendor B, whose information is held in a logically (and possibly physically) separate data mart. Finally, authentication may be required by the database to limit access within a given body of data: a clerk at vendor A can see only a selected portion of the A data mart, whereas A's president can see that company's entire data mart.

The logistics of security are extensive. Maintaining certificates requires dedicated resources, and planning for and executing multitiered log-ins are nontrivial tasks. At the same time, limiting access could limit the value of the data warehouse. For this reason, security must be designed to be flexible and as friendly to legitimate users as possible.

## New Components

Broader access to a data warehouse introduces several new elements into the traditional application model, such as what happens to the query engine vendor's pricing model as its proprietary desktop clients are no longer required? Where are the skill sets and hardware to implement Web servers and connect them to the query engine? How much will data be transformed (and by whom) if it is moved out of a central data warehouse into data marts for security, performance, or other reasons?

## ARCHITECTURE

If strategy is concerned with goals and objectives, architecture is the unifying conceptual design or structure. It defines a system's component parts and relationships. Effective architectures ensure that the component hardware and software pieces fit together as an integrated whole.

A Web-enabled data warehouse introduces additional components within a system architecture, which must be expanded to include:

- The Web server component
- The components that connect the Web server to the query engine
- The component that formats the results such that they are viewable by a Web browser

The system architecture may also need a component for integrating data marts.

Even with these elements, the architecture must be flexible enough to change rapidly to match the pace of innovation in the Internet arena and the evolving place of data warehouses in contemporary business. The warehouse components may change as a result of the increasing numbers of people using the warehouse, changing aggregations based on security or performance requirements, new access paths required by technological or organizational evolution, and so forth.

New design considerations are introduced by each of the components listed. Web servers introduce new complications, particularly regarding scalability issues. Secure transactions over a dial-up connection can be painfully slow, but detuning the security at either the firewall or the Web server can expose the corporate network to risk. Middleware between the Web server and the query server can dramatically affect performance, particularly if common gateway interface (CGI) scripts are used in place of APIs. Database publishing to hypertext markup language (HTML) is reasonably well advanced, but even here some of the newest tools introduce Java programming into the mix, which may cause implementation problems unless the skills are readily available. Java also presents the architect with new ways to partition the presentation layer and the application logic, with implications (for the network and desktop machines in particular) that are only beginning to be experienced in enterprise computing.

The system architecture must support competing enterprises accessing the data sources. One challenge is to support competing vendors where access control is data dependent. Both vendors can query the same tables — for example, product, by region, by week. If a given retail outlet sells both vendors' products, and people from the sales outlet are allowed to query the data warehouse, they will need to access to both vendors' histories.

An effective system architecture must include the facility for access control across the entire Web site, from Web server through to the database. If a mobile sales force is given access while on the road, the architecture must have a component to address the types of connections that will be used, whether they are an 800 dial-up service, local Internet service providers (ISPs), or national ISPs such as CompuServe or America Online.

## INFRASTRUCTURE

The infrastructure required to support the Web-enabled data warehouse expands to include the Web site hardware and software, the hardware and software required to interface the Web server to the query server, and the software that allows the query server to supply results in HTML. The corporate network may have to be altered to accommodate the additional traffic of the new warehouse users. This expansion increases the potential complexity of the system, introduces new performance issues, and adds to the costs that must be justified.

The Web-enabled warehouse's supporting infrastructure also introduces new system administration skills. Because the warehouse's database administrator should not be responsible for the care and feeding of the Web site, a new role is required: the Web site administrator, often called the Web master. This term can mean different things to different people, so clarity is needed as the position is defined. Depending on the context, corporate Web masters may or may not be responsible for the following activities:

- Designing the site's content architecture

- Writing and editing the material
- Designing the site's look and feel
- Monitoring traffic
- Configuring and monitoring security
- Writing scripts from the Web server to back-end application or database servers
- Project management
- Extracting content from functional departments

The amount of work that may have to be done to prepare for Internet or intranet implementation varies greatly by company. For example, if the warehouse is going to be accessible from the public Internet, then a firewall must be put in place. Knowing the current state of Web-based applications development is essential: if organizational factors, skills, and infrastructure are not in place and aligned, the data warehouse team may either get pulled from its core technology base into competition for scarce resources or be forced to develop skills that greatly differ from those traditionally associated with database expertise.

**Web Site**

Web site components include the computer to run the Web server on and the Web server software, which may include not only the Web listener but also a document manager for the reports generated from the warehouse. The common gateway interface (CGI), one of the Web protocols, allows the Web browser to access objects and data that are not on the Web server; in this way the Web server accesses the data warehouse. The interface used does not access the warehouse directly but accesses the query engine to formulate the queries; the query engine still accesses the warehouse.

The CGI has been identified as a bottleneck in many Web site implementations. Because the CGI program must incur the overhead of starting up and stopping with every request to it, high-volume systems lead to a situation of pronounced overhead and noticeably slow response time. API access tends to be faster, but it depends on the availability of such interfaces from or in support of different vendors.

**Application Query Engine**

The infrastructure must support the application query engine, which may run on the same computer as the data warehouse or on a separate computer networked to the data warehouse computer. This component must be able to translate the query results into HTML for the server to supply to the browser. Some of the query engines present the results in graphic form as well as in tabular form. Where such quantitative information is rendered into image form, the images will change as Java redefines the relationships between clients, servers, and networks. Traditional warehouses have supported relatively small user communities, so existing query engines have to be monitored to see how their performance changes when the number of users doubles, triples, or increases by even larger multiples. In addition, the type and complexity of the queries also have performance implications that must be addressed based on experience.

### Data Warehouse

The infrastructure for the data warehouse is not altered simply because Web browsers are being used; instead, the expanded number of users and new types of queries that may need to be executed forces changes to be made. When a data mart architecture is introduced for performance or security reasons, a change may be necessary as to where the mart is located: on the same machine as the warehouse, or on a separate machine. The infrastructure has to support both the method of replication originally specified and new patterns of replication based on DASD cost considerations, performance factors, or security precautions.

### SECURITY

Security should be addressed in the following four categories:

1. Web server access
2. Communication transport security
3. Query server application
4. Database access

### Web Server Access

Access to the Web server can be controlled through the following:

1. Requiring the user to log into the Web site by supplying a user name and password.
2. Installing client certificates into the browsers of the clients to whom access is granted.
3. Specifying only the IP (Internet Protocol) addresses allowed to access the Web site.

The client certificate requires less interaction on the users' parts because they do not have to supply a user name and password to access the system. The client's certificate is sent to the Web server, which validates the certificate and grants the user access to the system. (Part of the process of enabling a secure Web site is to install a server certificate. This must be requested from a third party, called a certificate authority, that allows you to transmit certificates authenticating that you are who you say you are.) A less secure strategy is to configure the Web server to allow connection from a selected number of computers, with all others being categorically denied access. This scheme lets anyone from an authorized computer — as opposed to authorized persons — access the Web site. Because this method is based on an IP address, DHCP (dynamic host configuration protocol) systems can present difficulties in specifying particular machines as opposed to machines in a particular subnet.

### Communication Transport Security

Both the query and especially the information that is sent back to the browser can be of a sensitive nature. To prevent others along the route back to the browser from viewing it, the data must be encrypted, particularly if it leaves the firewall. Encryption is turned on when the Web server is configured, typically through the secure socket layer (SSL) protocol.

### Query Server Application

To access the query server, the user may be asked to supply a user name and password. The information supplied by the certificate could be carried forward but not without some custom code. Various approaches are used to develop the user names and passwords: one can create a unique user name for each of the third parties that will access the system (allowing the log-in to be performed on any machine) or for each person who will access the warehouse. Each approach has implications for systems administration.

### Database Access

Database access is controlled by limiting the tables users and user groups can access. A difficulty arises when there are two competing users who must access a subset of the data within the same table. This security difficulty is solved by introducing data marts for those users, each of which contains only the information a particular user is entitled to see. Data marts introduce an entirely new set of administrative and procedural issues, particularly concerning the replication scheme to move the data from the warehouse into the data mart. Is data scrubbed, summarized, or otherwise altered in this move, or is replication exact and straightforward? Each approach has advantages and drawbacks.

### IMPLEMENTATION

The scope of implementing a Web-enabled data warehouse increases because of the additional users and the increased number of system components. The IS organization must be prepared to confront the implications, both of the additional hardware and software and of potentially new kinds of users, some of whom may not even work for the company that owns the data in the warehouse.

### Intranet

Training should cover the mechanics of how to use the query tool, provide the user with an awareness of the levels (and system implications) of different queries, and show how the results set expands or contracts based on what is being asked for. The user community for the intranet is some subset of the employees of the corporation. The logistics involved with training the users are largely under the company's control: even with broader access, data warehouses are typically decision support systems and not within the operational purview of most employees.

Implementing security for the intranet site involves sensitizing users to the basics of information security, issuing and tracking authentication information (whether through certificates, passwords, or a combination of the two), and configuring servers and firewalls to balance performance and security. One part of the process for enabling a secure Web server is to request a server certificate from a certificate authority. Administratively, a corporation must understand the components — for instance, proof of the legal right to use the corporate name — required to satisfy the inquiries from the certificate authority and put in place the procedures for yearly certificate renewal.

Monitoring a Web-based data warehouse is a high priority because of the number of variables that need tuning. In addition, broader access changes both the volume and the character of the query base in unpredictable ways.

### Intra/Extranet

In addition to the training required for internal users, training is extended to the third parties that will access the warehouse. Coordination of training among the third parties is usually more difficult: competing third parties do not want to be trained at the same time, and paying customers have different expectations compared to captive internal users. In addition, a public, purchased service may necessitate more thorough user interface testing of the look and feel within the application.

Security gets more complex in extranet implementations simply because of the public nature of the Internet. It is important to keep in mind the human and cultural factors that affect information security and not only focus on the technologies of firewalls, certificates, and the like. Different organizations embody different attitudes, and these differences can cause significant misunderstandings when sensitive information, and possibly significant expenditures, are involved.

Monitoring and tuning are largely the same as in an intranet implementation, depending on the profiles of remote users, trading partner access patterns, and the type and volume of queries. In addition, a serious extranet implementation may introduce the need for a help desk. It must be prepared to handle calls for support from the third parties and combine customer service readiness with strict screening to keep the focus on questions related to the data warehouse. It is not impossible to imagine a scenario in which third-party employees call for help on topics other than the warehouse.

## CONCLUSION

Because Web browsers have the ability to save whatever appears in them, information that appears in the browser of a Web-enabled data warehouse application can be saved to the desktop. Protecting information from transmission into the wrong hands involves a balancing act between allowing for flexibility of queries and restricting the information that can potentially move outside corporate control. Legal agreements regarding the use of information may need to be implemented, for example, and these tend not to be a specialty of the IS organization. Pricing the information is another tricky area, along with managing expectations on the part of both internal and third-party users.

By their very nature, however, data warehouses have always been more subject to unintended consequences than their operational siblings. With changing ideas about the place and power of information, new organizational shapes and strategies, and tougher customers demanding more while paying less, the data warehouse potential for business benefit is increased by extending its reach while making it easier to use. The consequences of more people using data warehouses for new kinds of queries, although sometimes taxing for IS professionals, may well be breakthroughs in business performance. As with any other emerging technology, the results bear watching.

# Chapter 41
# Bridging Legacy Data with XML

*Frank Cullen*

EXTENSIBLE MARKUP LANGUAGE (XML) IS CURRENTLY BEING CHAMPIONED AS THE LANGUAGE OF THE FUTURE FOR GREASING THE WHEELS OF THE DRIVE TOWARD E-COMMERCE OVER THE "NET." Already, thousands of new "dot.coms" have started from scratch to specifically take advantage of the booming Web-based business world. Light on their feet and already relying on modern relational database management systems (RDBMS), they are readily equipped to switch over to XML.

However, what about the long-established businesses whose database systems harken back to the days of "big iron"? These behemoths also recognize the need to migrate toward a Web-based commerce, and their long track records often endow them with the financial means to make the leap past HTML-prepared data, directly to XML. However, this feat is much easier said than done.

The necessary tagging — or assigning of a data type definition (DTD) — to pre-relational legacy database systems is fraught with unexpected pitfalls for the unwary. Quick solutions are hard to come by. Yet, understanding how to use data-cleansing tools to first untangle, and then migrate, data from older data structures can help immeasurably.

But first, a review of some of the common structures found in legacy databases will help uncover some of the problems often encountered in "untangling" or porting this data to more modern XML.

## DIFFICULTIES ENCOUNTERED WITH LEGACY DATA

The major areas of problems/challenges in legacy data management stem from five main categories:

1. Character sets and translations
2. Poor data typing
3. Hierarchical structures: header/trailer record systems

0-8493-1160-8/02/$0.00+$1.50
© 2002 by CRC Press LLC

    4. Embedded sub-table structures

    5. Departed "legacy programmers"

This chapter briefly discusses each of these areas and examines the problems, challenges, and solutions that arise as the migration to XML is performed.

**Character Sets and Translations.** The translation and movement of data between IBM midrange and mainframe systems, for example, introduce a huge potential for faulty translation and data corruption. That is because data stored on computer systems has two main forms: full-character (display) form and packed forms (including signed numeric, packed-decimal, computational, and binary).

Full-character forms are used extensively whenever alphanumeric data is present — in descriptions, names, etc. Conversion here is almost never a problem. However, packed data forms are an entirely different matter. These are reliant not on the 8-bit character as a whole, but rather on the parts (sometimes even the bit configuration) of each character. Translating computational and binary items almost never works and provides a host of examples why character-for-character translations corrupt data irretrievably.

**Poor Data Typing.** One of the principal contributors to data migration problems in mainframe applications is the lack of strong data typing (and enforcement). Calendar dates are an excellent example of items that are hybrids of data types, but there are countless others.

Fortunately, the development and popularization RDBMSs, such as SQL, has had the wonderful effect of formalizing the idea of rich data types and strict enforcement of data domain rules.

**Hierarchical Data Structures.** A hierarchical data structure has more than one record type. When a record can belong to at most one other record type, the relationship is said to be a "proper hierarchy." Data hierarchies play a crucial role in the philosophy and implementation of XML.

Adding records to the end of a hierarchical data file usually will not cause problems. But when records are added to the middle of the file, all the relative record numbers of the records beyond the point of insertion are bumped down. The idea of using relative record position as an ID generator is only valid for a "one-time" or "cut-and-run" conversion.

**Embedded Sub-Table Structures.** The popularization of variable-length record techniques brought with it a tremendous savings in mass storage space at a reasonably small price. However, a maximum allowable number of additional fields must be set. Unfortunately, overestimating the number wastes valuable space, while underestimating causes program failure.

**Departed Legacy Programmers.** Most companies have a "super programmer," who in times of trouble can be the only hope. But super programmers can define hideously complex records with bizarre relationships collapsed into variable length and self-describing attributes. When they leave the organization, their work can be one's worst nightmare. It becomes extremely difficult to clean up after their "legacy."

## THE DATA MIGRATION/TRANSFORMATION PROCESS

Preparing flat-plane databases for XML tagging requires a three-step process. Not a single step can be omitted, or the conversion is destined to create more problems that it solves.

1. Analyze current data
2. Clean up current data
3. Transform the data

### Analyze Current Data

Having decided to migrate data from one structure to another, the first step is to thoroughly analyze the existing data. This process should especially focus on domain analysis because it will help set the stage for data type identification.

If the data was analyzed during the Y2K compliance effort, the results of that analysis can be used again for the data transformation effort. This process already should have included the thorough testing of the output.

### Clean Up Current Data

The next step is to clean up any bad data revealed during analysis and testing. In many cases, this involves straightforward corrections to field values. What may sound easy at first, is complicated by values that intentionally do not fit the format. Some of these exceptional values carry specific meaning and are commonly referred to as embedded business rules. An example might be XXXX or 9999 to indicate "date unknown" in a field using YYMM format. One may wish to preserve these special rules or replace them with new ones. This can be done with such tools as Data Commander, which analyzes, cleanses, and transforms pre-relational legacy mainframe data, and is available from Blackstone & Cullen of Atlanta, Georgia. Its EXCEPTION statements allow one to exempt specified fields from the general conversion (or migration or transformation) process or to convert them in a manner different from the rest of the data fields. Exhibit 1 illustrates some of the processes that are a part of the entire migration effort.

The actual preparation and migration of legacy data from a pre-relational mainframe environment to a clean, consistent relational data store happens in two major places: (1) the host (or mainframe) location, where

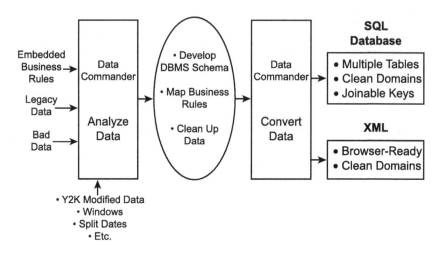

**Exhibit 1.    Pre-Relational Data Analysis and Migration Processes**

the main "untangling" takes place and the data is cleaned, reformatted, and scripted; and (2) the server, where the Web client resides. The data untangling is best done on the host, as moving the data *en masse* to a server first might corrupt the packed, binary, and signed data during the conversion of the characters from the host to the server.

**Denormalizing Data for XML Output.** One of the most important steps of the cleansing process is the denormalization (to 1st Normal Form) of the data. There are two main reasons for this: to avoid making multiple passes through the source data, and to provide data in a single-level hierarchy for an XML table for easier manipulation/access.

This process is also called "flattening" or "spreading" the hierarchy of the data. Exhibit 2 illustrates the general scheme used to both flatten and spread a hierarchy and generate XML output.

### Transform the Data

Once the cleansing processes are complete, the output data can then be converted directly as XML 1.0 tagged, or even as field-sensitive formats and SQL INSERT syntax (for RDBMS population).

The main benefit of direct output to XML rather than the movement to an intermediate data store (such as a SQL-based Transformation Data Store) is that there is no requirement for having a SQL engine or other RDBMS processor to receive the data and to pass it on; the transfer is direct. Downsides of using XML are similar to those for SQL scripts — mainly that of amazing verbosity. The number of characters it takes to

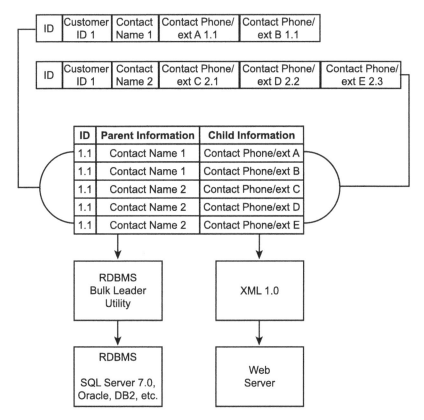

| ID | Customer ID 1 | Contact Name 1 | Contact Phone/ ext A 1.1 | Contact Phone/ ext B 1.1 | |
|---|---|---|---|---|---|

| ID | Customer ID 1 | Contact Name 2 | Contact Phone/ ext C 2.1 | Contact Phone/ ext D 2.2 | Contact Phone/ ext E 2.3 |
|---|---|---|---|---|---|

| ID | Parent Information | Child Information |
|---|---|---|
| 1.1 | Contact Name 1 | Contact Phone/ext A |
| 1.1 | Contact Name 1 | Contact Phone/ext B |
| 1.1 | Contact Name 2 | Contact Phone/ext C |
| 1.1 | Contact Name 2 | Contact Phone/ext D |
| 1.1 | Contact Name 2 | Contact Phone/ext E |

RDBMS
Bulk Leader
Utility

XML 1.0

RDBMS

SQL Server 7.0,
Oracle, DB2, etc.

Web
Server

**Exhibit 2. Flattening and Spreading Hierarchy Denormalizing for Data Warehouse Bulk Loading and XML Generation**

represent (and transmit) data originally in packed and/or binary form on a mainframe may blow up to 10 to 20 times that amount when all the unpacking and XML field tag insertion is done.

Nevertheless, there are an increasing number of options for receiving and processing XML-encoded data currently available. The ability to publish the legacy as XML data (either spread or not) directly to a Web browser using Data Commander is illustrated in Exhibit 3.

Instead of SQL output, Data Commander can generate XML DTD (data type definition) syntax. This generation is turned on or off in an OPTION statement, so Data Commander can be used to construct DTD-less XML data islands. The combination of the flattening/spreading with the suppression of header record XML syntax and DTD generation provide an easy method to generate XML strings immediately usable for IE5 data islands in live Web pages.

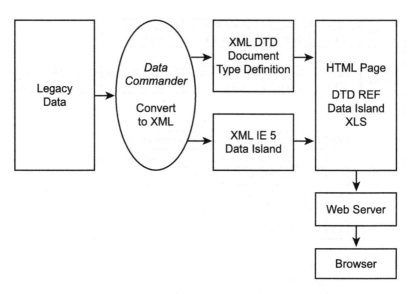

**Exhibit 3.    Legacy Data to XML with Data Commander**

## SUMMARY

Legacy data may represent a "Fort Knox" of wealth, but often this data is abandoned solely because it is difficult to access and get into a usable form. But cross-platform tools can extract valuable data from these complex structures, clean it, and generate XML syntax. Established organizations of any size can then take advantage of the golden opportunities afforded by Web commerce.

# Chapter 42
# Publishing Database Information on the World Wide Web

*James A. Larson*
*Carol L. Larson*

IN TODAY'S BUSINESS ENVIRONMENT, USERS MAY BE SCATTERED ACROSS THE GLOBE AND STILL NEED TO ACCESS DATABASE INFORMATION AT THEIR HOME ENTERPRISE OR HEADQUARTERS. How can users access database information from wherever they happen to be?

Typically, users access database information from a variety of computing platforms, including Windows, Macintosh, and UNIX. It is important that users are able to access database information from their chosen platform in a consistent fashion. This chapter discusses how to publish database information on the World Wide Web and the methods by which users can access it.

## THE WORLD WIDE WEB: AN EXPLOSION

The World Wide Web phenomenon has exploded onto the computing scene. In addition to e-mail and file transfer, the World Wide Web (or Web) supports document browsing. Users access a wide range of information available on the Web in the form of documents formatted using the hypertext markup language (HTML).

### HTML Documents

HTML documents consist of three components:

- Content (the database information)
- Annotation (the format and layout of the document)
- Links (connections that chain documents together)

0-8493-1160-8/02/$0.00+$1.50
© 2002 by CRC Press LLC

**A**

| Name | Amount | Department |
|---|---|---|
| Able | 400.00 | Toy |
| Baker | 350.00 | Car |
| Carson | 425.00 | Toy |

**B**

```
<TABLE BORDER=1>
<TR> <TH> Name   <TH> Amount <TH> Department                                        <TH> </TR>
<TR> <TD> Able   <TD> 400.00 <TD> <A href=URL of Toy Department's Homepage> Toy </A> <TD> </TR>
<TR> <TD> Baker  <TD> 350.00 <TD> <A href=URL of Car Department's Homepage> Car </A> <TD> </TR>
<TR> <TD> Carson <TD> 425.00 <TD> <A href=URL of Toy Department's Homepage> Toy </A> <TD> </TR>
</TABLE>
```

**C**

| | |
|---|---|
| <TABLE>, </TABLE> | Begin, End Table |
| <TH>, </TH> | Begin, End Table Heading |
| <TR>, </TR> | Begin, End Table Row |
| <TD>, </TD> | Begin, End Table Data Element |
| <A>, </A> | Begin, End Anchor |

**Exhibit 1. A Database Table and Its HTML Description**

Exhibit 1 illustrates a database table and its corresponding HTML document. HTML is used to annotate the document's content with tags (in Exhibit 1, tags are denoted by brackets). The tags specify how to format the content of the document when it is displayed to the user. Any platform can be used to display the document's contents because software on each platform interprets the tags in a manner appropriate for that computer. Thus, HTML provides "platform independence."

Once the publisher adds HTML tags to a document, the document can be presented to users. Not only does HTML describe the layout of text, it also integrates images, audio, and small applications (applets) for presentation to the user.

**Uniform Resource Locators.** A universal resource locator (URL) is a pointer to a document located in an HTML server connected to the Web. Documents may be linked explicitly by embedding an URL within an anchor tag of one document to provide the location on the Web of a related document. In Exhibit 1, URLs are used to link each employee with the home page of the employee's department and enable the employee to browse through sequences of related documents.

**Common Gateway Interface Scripts.** An HTML document is not limited to content containing static information; dynamic information may also be included. The common gateway interface (CGI) gives programmers a language for specifying how to derive data for presentation to the user.

For example, a CGI script might invoke a hardware thermometer to measure the current temperature and record it in the document's content. CGI scripts can also be used to solicit a database query from the user and insert HTML tags into the query results. Programmers implement CGI scripts using Visual Basic, C, C++, TCL, Perl, or other languages executable on a Web server.

## STATIC PUBLISHING: DISPLAYING DATABASE INFORMATION USING THE WEB

Exhibit 2 illustrates how database information is published on a Web server by extracting data and inserting HTML tags into the query results.

First, a database administrator (DBA) extracts the data to be published by submitting an structured query language (SQL) query to the database management system (DBMS). Programmers can insert HTML tags to control the appearance of the final HTML document. The resulting document is then placed on an HTML server that manages and accesses documents much like a DBMS manages database records. The HTML server responds to requests for documents by sending them to the requesting client browsers, which could be Netscape Navigator or Microsoft Internet Explorer.

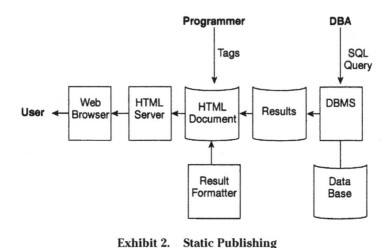

**Exhibit 2. Static Publishing**

Alternatively, software can automatically insert HTML tags to generate default layouts. For example, Corel's Web.Data uses a step-by-step process to create a database table to be inserted into an HTML document and guides the DBA through the required steps for formatting. The result is a "recipe file," which is a template describing how to process the results of a database query by inserting the appropriate HTML tags into the query's results. Corel's Web.Data can optimize the HTML document for Netscape Navigator or Microsoft Explorer.

BestWeb Pro Version 1.0 is another example of software that inserts HTML tags into ASCII files created by a database query. BestWeb allows the programmer to select specific properties and formatting options for each table field by indicating which fields should be indexed and customizing the HTML document with background images and corporate logos.

Static generation of HTML documents has its pros and cons. The primary advantage is that the process is straightforward because it is subject to automation. The resulting HTML documents are easy for users to browse, and no programming is required. However, the HTML documents are not linked to the source data in real time. The HTML document is not changed automatically when the user changes the source data in the DBMS. Users cannot change the data in the HTML document and may only change the underlying database directly by using traditional DBMS access facilities.

## DYNAMIC PUBLISHING: INTERACTING WITH A DATABASE USING THE WEB

Although static publishing is sufficient for many applications — even desirable from a security point of view because users cannot change the underlying database when they access the corresponding HTML document — many applications require the user to submit a query to retrieve specific data.

### Formulating a Query

To formulate a query, the user enters the query parameters into an HTML form consisting of input boxes or other user interface controls. A CGI script, which resides and executes on an HTML server, then takes the parameters and formulates an SQL query to the underlying DBMS, as illustrated in Exhibit 3. After the DBMS processes the query, it returns the extracted data to the CGI script, which reformats the response and inserts HTML tags. Finally, the reformatted response is sent to the user's browser and displayed.

Not only do special controls and CGI scripts allow users to specify parameters for a database query, but users may also specify a database update. Dynamic publishing enables users to obtain and modify up-to-the-minute database information.

### Java Applets

CGI scripts reside and execute on HTML servers. Java applets reside on HTML servers, but are downloaded to and executed on the user's Web browser.

Java applets are special types of applications written in the Java programming language. Applets cannot perform actions that may be harmful to the user's environment, such as accessing local disks and printers, accessing the user's identity, or accessing any server other than the one that provided the applet. These limits on what the applet can do ensure, to a degree, that it will not harm the user's computing environment.

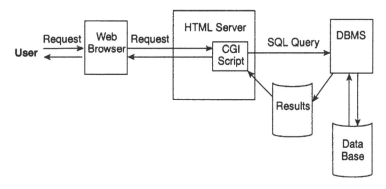

**Exhibit 3.   Dynamic Publishing with a CGI Script**

Applets can be embedded within an HTML document as shown in Exhibit 4. When executed, a Java applet can produce animation, perform calculations, and dynamically determine the layout and format of information to be presented to the user.

The Java database connectivity (JDBC) standard describes the Java application programming interface (API) for accessing relational databases. Most DBMS vendors support JDBC. Java applets use JDBC to directly access a DBMS to perform database queries and modifications.

**User Interface Controls.** Java applets can present user interface controls, such as data boxes, pull-down menus, and other user interface widgets, which allow users to enter database queries and update parameters. Applet Window Technology (AWT) is a series of Java classes that provide a collection of user interface controls. AWT is standard on all Java-enabled platforms, including Macintosh, Windows, and UNIX, among others.

Alternatively, programmers also may create or reuse customized user interface controls. CGI scripts execute in the HTML server, whereas Java applets are downloaded from the HTML server and executed within the user's browser. This division of labor minimizes data transmissions between the HTML server and the user's platform.

**Limiting Data Transmissions.** Generally, database administrators prefer that data element translations and reformatting are done in the HTML server.

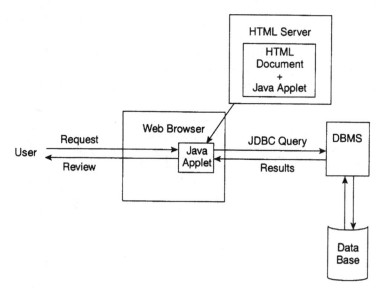

**Exhibit 4. Dynamic Publishing with a Java Applet**

Thus, a user's request can be satisfied by two data transmissions — one containing the request from the user's computing platform to the server and the second containing the translated, reformatted results from the server to the user's platform. DBAs write CGI scripts to perform the data element translations and data reformatting for execution on the HTML server.

User interface experts may write Java applets to accept data results from the HTML server and generate sophisticated user interfaces, which may involve graphics or animation. For example, Java applets may convert database data to graphs, bar charts, or even animated objects such as fluctuating temperature gauges, nodding heads, or moving clock hands. Java applets execute within the user's browser on the user's computing platform. By executing Java applets at the user's platform, no additional data transmissions are necessary between the user and the HTML server.

## SECURITY MECHANISMS

HTML forms provide limited control over database access. Like a relational database view, a form restricts the database elements users may access. For example, the CGI script can provide additional security by requesting that the user supply passwords and by asking questions to authenticate identity. The hypertext transfer protocol (HTTP) can also be used to restrict access to users listed in a file or cause the browser to prompt the user for a password.

Researchers and practitioners have proposed other security mechanisms, such as encryption, watermarks, seals against modification, and certificates of authentication. Many of these advanced security techniques will soon be available, if they are not already.

## CONCLUSION

Web publication allows users anywhere in the world with a Web browser to access specific databases subject to specified security constraints. Accessing database information over the Web requires an HTML server to manage documents.

Systems analysts determine whether users need to access static or dynamic data. If users can tolerate static data, software should be used to generate HTML documents automatically. If users require up-to-the-minute data, then programmers must write CGI scripts or Java applets to allow them to request needed information. CGI scripts should be used to perform data transformation and formatting, and Java applets should be used for sophisticated user interfaces.

# Chapter 43
# Web-Enabling Image and Sound Objects in Database Tables

*Judith M. Myerson*

OBJECT LINKING AND EMBEDDING (OLE) MEANS THAT AN OBJECT (DATA OR FILE) CAN BE EMBEDDED OR LINKED TO ANOTHER APPLICATION THAT DOES NOT DIRECTLY SUPPORT THE OBJECT FORMAT. The application that supports the object format is called the OLE server; examples include Acrobat document, RealPlayer G2 control, MIDI sequence, video clips and other image files, sound files, and video files. The application that can embed or link to OLE objects is called an OLE client or OLE container; two examples are Microsoft Access or SQL Server.

Linking requires a file, which can reside in any subdirectory or any disk drive. On the other hand, embedding does not require a file. An object can be created at insertion time or loaded from an existing file. The embedded object becomes part of the master form file and the data can only be changed through the OLE server application.

There are two ways of creating an OLE object in a Microsoft Access application. To include OLE objects on a form or report, put them in either bound object frame controls or unbound object frame controls. The type of control one chooses depends on what one wants to do with the OLE object. A bound object frame displays an OLE object that is stored as data in a table. An unbound object frame displays an OLE object that is not associated with data in a table.

When creating an OLE object, keep the file size small. The amount of information used to render the object is often greater than the object itself. Adding OLE objects can significantly increase the size of a database table. To minimize size increases caused by adding OLE objects to the table, display the object as an icon, or make the object easier to render by lowering the resolution of the object or decreasing the physical size.

0-8493-1160-8/02/$0.00+$1.50
© 2002 by CRC Press LLC

Storing an object as an icon causes the OLE server to send the object with rendering information consisting of only the icon rather than the complete object, using less storage space in the database table. Double-clicking the icon causes the OLE server to launch with the native data that the icon represents.

Present technology, however, only allows an OLE object to be stored as a data item in the table. It cannot do so with an icon that can only be embedded or linked on the forms or reports.

## BENEFITS OF WEB-ENABLING IMAGE AND SOUND OBJECTS

Database tools give users a choice of simple actions (embedding, Web-enabling, retrieving, updating, and other record operations). With additional training, these users can learn more complex actions, such as data analysis and image analysis, that would help them predict problems with network performance and recommend resolutions.

Another benefit is that telecommuters can use browsers on their laptops to retrieve table records embedded with images and sounds from a centralized server and send them to that server. They can employ a variety of remote access technologies to do any of the following:

1. Create and save files containing scanned images and recorded or synthesized voices/sounds, as well as the objects
2. Embed images and sounds in an existing database table on a local disk
3. Analyze the images, listen to voices/sounds, manipulate the data, and store the results on local disks
4. Export database tables to a centralized Web database server
5. Web-enable the table on a local disk
6. Export the resulting Web pages to the server
7. View these pages with a browser
8. Electronically forward the results to colleagues
9. Collaborate with colleagues via Web-based asynchronous services such as videoconferencing, fax to e-mail, or Voice-over-IP to e-mail

## LAYERS OF THE WEB-ENABLED DATABASE SERVER

An effective approach for Web-enabling image and sound objects in databases is to build a new model consisting of five layers and identifying what each layer is, as follows:

1. *Source layer:* the objects that need to be extracted and edited, including those from disparate sources
2. *IETL tools:* integration, extraction, transformation, embedding, and loading of (IETL) tools
3. *Target layer:* Web-enabled database tables

4. *End-user layer:* reports, queries, analytical tools
5. *Metadata layer:* data about data

The examples in this section draw heavily on Microsoft Access and SQL Server technologies. Microsoft Access 2000's Access Projects allows a user to create a database application with Access on the front end and a native connection to SQL Server via OLE DB on the back end.

### Source Layer

The source layer consists of operational systems, current applications, new applications, external data feeds from the legacy systems (concurrent or archived), as well as repositories of still photos, scanned images, recorded voices, synthesized sounds, image objects, and sound objects. Also covered are international database management systems, particularly the ones that support the relational data model. The Web database servers bridge the data from diverse operational systems, transform this data in a consistent standard format, and eliminate data redundancy via a data model normalization process.

In this aspect of a life cycle, there is no need to rehost the services, as Web-enabling the objects has not yet played a major role. Information can be obtained from documentation. However, there are significant enhancements to RDBMs and these will be highlighted in the Target Layer section of this chapter because most enhancements are related to inserting objects as well as retrieving, searching, adding, updating, and other record options on the database.

### IETL Tools Layer: Datasheet Publishing and Data Access Pages

Consider a **Network Topology** table that contains an OLE object field for an Acrobat document of several images and sound clips (see Exhibit 1). When a user first opens this table, Access will not actually display the Acrobat documents. It makes them available when the user double-clicks on a

| ⊞ Network Topology : Table | | | _ □ ✕ |
|---|---|---|---|
| **Title** | **Date Created** | **Location** | **Drawings** |
| Linear Bus Topology A12 | 11/12/00 | Site A12 | Adobe Acrobat Documer |
| StarTopology A567 | 4/24/99 | Site A567 | Adobe Acrobat Documer |
| Linear BusTopology B40 | 5/6/99 | Site B40 | Adobe Acrobat Documer |
| Star-WiredTopology C2908 | 12/22/98 | Site C2908 | Adobe Acrobat Documer |
| Star-Wired Topology C291 | 2/28/00 | Site C2910 | Adobe Acrobat Documer |
| TreeTopology C2912 | 11/6/00 | Site C2912 | Adobe Acrobat Documer |
| Star Topology D789 | 9/19/00 | Site D789 | Adobe Acrobat Documer |
| Record: I◀ ◀ ║ 1 ▶ ▶I ▶* of 7 | | | |

**Exhibit 1.   Network Topology Table**

link in the **Drawings** column. Windows responds by opening the corresponding Acrobat document in its default Adobe Acrobat application.

The FrontPage, in its present form, is unable to capture any OLE objects from either the Access or SQL Server databases. When the **Network Topology** table is published, the **Drawings** column appears blank (see Exhibit 2).

Two steps are involved to partially get around this problem. First, the user can declare the **Drawings** column as a Hyperlink field (see Exhibit 3). Second, the user can insert links into the **Drawings** column that points to the location of the Acrobat document files or can insert these files into the table.

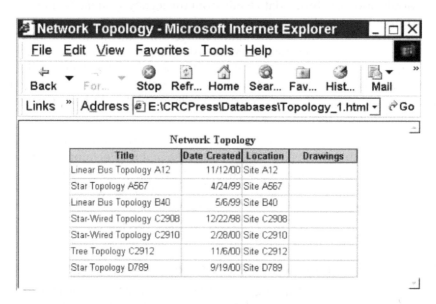

**Exhibit 2.  The Published Table with the Drawings Column Blank**

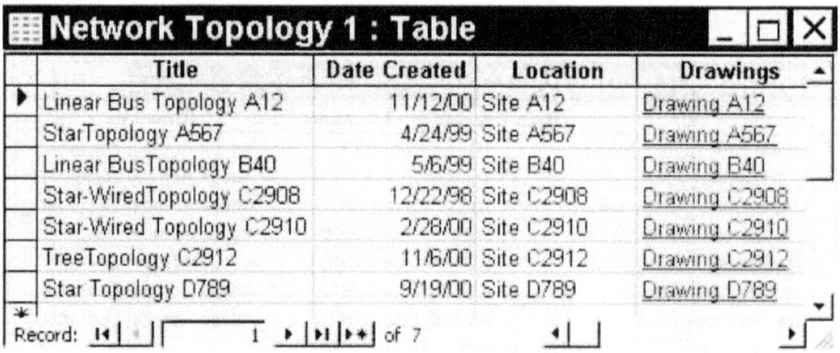

**Exhibit 3.  Inserting Links into the Drawings Column**

When **Network Topology 1** is published, the **Drawings** column shows up (see Exhibit 4).

The document, however, may take up the entire screen even after the user double-clicks a hyperlinked file. To return to the table in a previous screen, the user clicks the Back button on a browser. For those who would rather see part of the table while looking at the Acrobat document in a smaller window, they should insert links to JavaScript files to pop up windows of specified sizes.

Another method is to employ a data access page (DAP), a Web page with a special Microsoft Office Web Component to facilitate working with data sources. This component is one of the four Office Web Components and uses the Data Source control to manage data. DAPs delivers graphs and reports to Web applications using this control.

DAPs will not work for general Web publishing, as not all users have Internet Explorer 5 and Office 2000. If a client workstation within a corporation has the necessary software for a corporate intranet, it will properly run the DAPs.

One can use a Layout Wizard to create a DAP based on a table and edit the navigation bars. One can also include images and sounds on the DAP. The problem here is that one needs to add the address of each image and sound.

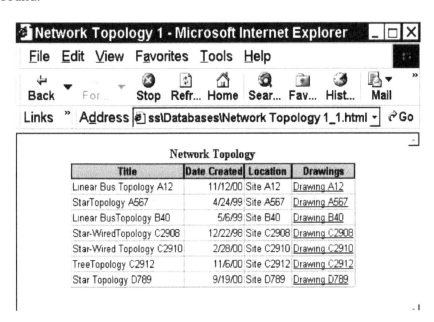

**Exhibit 4.   The Published Table with the Drawings Column Filled**

If one is thinking about inserting in a table links to an HTML file containing the <EMBED> tags, keep in mind that there are two kinds of video on the Web. One is non-streaming video (QuickTime) — the kind that must be completely downloaded before it can be viewed. The other is streaming video (Real Video or Shockware), which is run as it downloads. The file sizes are smaller because the information can be highly compressed before it is streamed. The downside to streaming video is that it may not be very clear due to slower connectivities, packet jitters, or other network problems. This is also true for sound clips. The <EMBED> tags work for internal video for Netscape and Internet Explorer browsers, and for internal sound only for Netscape. Internet Explorer has its own <BGSOUND> tags to run background sound.

**Target Layer**

The target layer is where the enterprise database is defined and accessed. The information is compiled into a standard consistent framework for access by the end user.

ASP technology is well suited for frequent updates and maintaining database tables with embedded and linked objects on a server. It enables the user's applications to interface with the database engines in a standard, consistent manner.

Like the object-oriented approach of Java technology, ASP technology allows the more complex procedures to be executed on the database server rather than on a Web browser client. Performing the majority of the processing on the database server also reduces network traffic, provided that:

- The effects of packet jitters are minimized
- The bandwidth is sufficiently managed at peak times
- Quality of service is maintained at acceptable levels
- Caching hits are good
- Traffic-shaper tools are utilized

With simple ASP applications, deployment is not much of an issue, but can be a problem when run in n-tier architectures that utilize reuse components. Existing versions of ASP are "interpreters" and are based on scripting languages like VBScript and JScript. They run slower than the compiled languages.

Active Server Pages+ (ASP+) allows developers to use compiled languages for complex applications. It outshines JavaServer Pages in scalability, reliability, deployment, and security. ASP+ also provides better support for different browsers. Also new to this Microsoft .NET Platform offering are page events, Web controls, and caching, as well as controls for data binding, development of Web services, and functionality modularization.

## End-User Layer

End users need timely reports to make critical decisions. They must be able to quickly query the database on a Web showing image and sound objects — with no or little knowledge of SQL statements. The images and sound panels that the users open from the objects must be simple to view and listen to, so that these users can make proper analyses. The time factor in getting the information from the objects is a critical process, especially when network performance is approaching levels above or below the established thresholds.

End users need some type of Web tools to allow them to enter information on the report screens. Another approach is to permit them to select from a list of "standard queries" to produce forms or reports. Those who desire one-time reports could enter SQL statements to query the database, but only when they are permitted to do so by system administrators. It is a good idea to create a help file to assist end users in formulating queries with examples not in the standard list. As a last resort, they can go to a database expert in formulating queries in special situations.

Whatever the methods chosen, the user should allow colleagues, especially at a conference, to do the following before all reach an agreement:

- Click the objects to bring up sound panels and map pictures
- Enter the results on their laptops
- Discuss them and collaborate on a whiteboard

Presenting results in a consistent, standardized format on the server-based Web pages is much easier and less time-consuming than writing notes on the results stored on the laptop's local disk and comparing one's own notes with others.

## Metadata Layer

Metadata is data about when a particular set of data was retrieved, how it was formatted, how it was collected from what source and by whom, and other useful information. There are, however, several metadata types, depending on which viewpoint the end user is taking: business user, system administrator, DSS developer, DDS user, Web master, Web content provider, or corporate manager.

For business users, metadata is data showing where information can be found using site maps, search engine data collection (Web crawling), and other metadata types. The database administrator needs metadata on what methods were used to populate image and sound data as objects, how often the database tables have been maintained, how the software versions are controlled, and when image and sound files were not or will not be available.

**Exhibit 5.     Title, Author, Description, and Keywords Metadata Items**

```
<head>

<title>Web-enabling Image and Sound Objects</title>

<meta name="author" content="Judith M. Myerson">

<meta name="description" content="This website focuses on
  tools to web enable image and sound objects.">

<meta name="keywords" content="HTML, embedding, embed, form,
  network traffic, CRC Press, Auerbach Publishers, web data-
  base, images, sounds, voices, objects, servers, servers man-
  agement, application management, Microsoft Access, MS
  Access, Microsoft SQL Server, FrontPage2000">

</head>
```

The metadata of an organization can become the starting point for the person responsible for analyzing the requirements and designing or enhancing data warehousing systems for DSS users. At the corporate level, metadata is a logical collection of data about data from various disparate, enterprisewide sources.

For the purposes here, Exhibit 5 displays a simple example of how a Web master would place at least four metadata items inside HTML documents to help improve their rankings on search engines. Doing so increases the chances of assisting end users in locating the sites they want.

## CONCLUSION

Microsoft Access 2000 currently leaves the OLE object fields blank when publishing the datasheets in either Microsoft Access or SQL Server databases. While more suitable for a corporate intranet, DAPs require a separate address for each image or sound file. It is only a matter of time until Microsoft will roll out a new version that allows users to directly Web-enable embedded objects.

# Chapter 44
# Database Management and the Internet: Developments and Challenges

*Bhavani Thuraisingham*

THERE IS AN EVER-INCREASING DEMAND TO ACCESS THE DATA STORED IN DIFFERENT DATA-BASES THROUGH THE INTERNET. The databases may be relational databases, object-oriented databases, or multimedia databases containing unstructured and semistructured data such as text, voice, video, and images. These databases are often heterogeneous in nature. Heterogeneity exists with respect to data structures, data types, semantic meanings, data models, architectures, query processing strategies, and transaction management techniques.

Many vendors of database management systems (DBMSs) are enhancing their products with capabilities for Internet access. Exhibit 1 illustrates how clients access multiple databases through the Internet. Special Internet protocols are needed for such access. The goal is to provide seamless access to the heterogeneous databases.

Although much progress has been made with respect to Internet database access, there is still room for improvement. For example, DBMS functions such as data modeling, query processing, and transaction management are impacted by the Internet. The algorithms for query processing and transactions management may have to be modified to reflect database access through the Internet. For example, the cost models for the query algorithms may have to include the price of accessing servers on the Internet.

0-8493-1160-8/02/$0.00+$1.50
© 2002 by CRC Press LLC

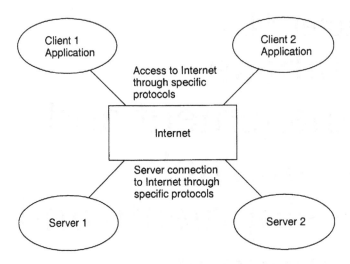

**Exhibit 1.    Internet-Based Client/Server Communication**

Furthermore, distributed object management technologies need to be examined for heterogeneous database integration through the Internet. This chapter discusses the impact of the Internet on various DBMS functions.

## DBMS FUNCTIONS

Key DBMS functions include data representation, query management, transaction management, storage management, security management, integrity management, and metadata management. For an Internet database, functions such as browsing and filtering also have to be managed.

### Data Representation

Various data representation schemes have been proposed for text databases, including Standard Generalized Markup Language (SGML), Hypertext Markup Language (HTML), and office document architecture (ODA). However, a considerable amount of data will also be stored in structured (i.e., relational and object-oriented) databases. Appropriate data models for representing structured as well as unstructured databases include integrated object-oriented, relational, and hypertext-based data models for Internet database management. Currently there are no agreed-on standard data models; appropriate mappings between the standards and the heterogeneous data models used by the databases must also be developed.

## Query Management

Query management involves developing language and processing techniques. The query language depends to a great extent on the data model used.

Languages based on Structured Query Language (SQL) are popular for relational as well as nonrelational database systems. For example, object-oriented DBMSs use variations of SQL for database access. An appropriate SQL-based language needs to be developed for accessing structured and unstructured databases. SQL extensions are being examined to handle different data types. Once a standard language has been developed, mappings between the standard language and the languages used by the individual databases must be examined.

For efficient query processing, modifications to current algorithms for distributed and heterogeneous databases should be considered. For example, current cost models focus mainly on the amount of data transferred between the different sites. Database administrators have many issues to consider, such as:

- Are such cost models still valid for Internet databases? Are there other factors that need to be considered in query processing?
- Will the cost of accessing remote database servers over the Internet have an impact on the query algorithms?
- What are the relationships between global and local optimization strategies? What parameters are common to both the global and local cost models?

Because of the information explosion caused by the Internet, various technologies such as agents and mediators are being considered for locating the data sources, mediating between the different data sources, fusing the data, and giving responses to the user.

## Browsing and Filtering

Although many traditional DBMSs do not support browsing, such systems on the Internet need to provide this capability. One of the main uses of the Internet is browsing through and accessing large amounts of information in a short time. Therefore, to efficiently access the database, the DBMS must be augmented by a browser. Numerous browsing tools are available for the Internet; however, they must be integrated with the DBMS.

Closely related to browsing is the filtering technique. With the Internet, the user can become overloaded with information. This means various filters have to be integrated with the browsers and the DBMSs so that unnecessary information is filtered out and users get only the information they want.

## Transaction Management

Transaction management, an integral part of DBMSs, involves concurrency control and recovery. New kinds of transactions are taking place on the Internet, such as making a purchase. In some cases, multiple users may want to purchase the same item and may bid on it. In such a situation, there should be a waiting period before the item is locked. The item is then sold to the highest bidder.

The previous example illustrates the need for flexible transaction models. The ability to perform long-duration transactions and transaction models for workflow management may also be valuable. Serializability conditions may be helpful for concurrency control. Otherwise, it may not be possible to ensure that all the data items accurately reflect the real-world values.

Transaction management also requires consideration of recovery management, as well as fine-grained versus coarse-grained locking issues.

## Storage Management

For appropriate representation strategies for storing multimedia data, efficient access methods and index strategies are critical. A user should be able to index based on content and context. Research on extensions to various strategies such as B-trees is one possible solution. Internet database management is such a challenge because of the large amount of information and user requirements for quick access. This is why development of methods for integrating database systems with mass storage systems is so critical.

## Security Management

Security is vital to Internet database management; however, the policies must be flexible. With the increasing number of databases, negotiations between the different administrators becomes important. The developers of security for Internet applications are faced with many questions, such as:

- Is there a need for one or more global Internet security administrators? That is, is there a group of one or more individuals responsible for overall database security on the Internet?
- Is it at all possible to designate a group of individuals to be in charge of global security when there may be many different systems on the Internet?
- If there are such global administrators, what are their roles? What are the security features that they enforce?
- What are the relationships between global administrators and local database administrators? That is, should the global and local administrators negotiate to determine their functions, or is there someone overseeing their actions?

If there is someone overseeing the local and global administrators' actions, then there must be a "supergroup" that has ultimate authority for security. If there are no global administrators, which may be the case because it would be very difficult to enforce security policies across different systems, then a type of negotiation needs to be established between the systems administrators of the individual systems on the Internet.

Other security issues include enforcing appropriate authorization and access control mechanisms. The implementation of these mechanisms depends on the standard data models and languages used. Extensions to the query language are necessary for enforcement of security constraints, including:

- Mechanisms for identifying and authenticating users
- Laws on electronic copyright protection
- Methods for detecting plagiarism

There are several additional concerns if multilevel security is needed. For example, the trusted computing base must be determined, as well as how much of the Internet software should be trusted.

## Integrity Management

Concurrency control and recovery techniques maintain the integrity of the data in the databases. Integrity issues revolve around data quality. With Internet database access, data could come from many different sources. Users need information concerning the accuracy of the source. Appropriate tagging techniques can be enforced, and integrity constraint checking techniques can be used for Internet database access.

## Metadata Management

Metadata describes the data in the database, including schema information. Metadata management is critical to other database functions. Metadata may include not only information about the data in the databases, but also information about the tools, resources, and policies and procedures. Metadata can be used to navigate through the Internet. In addition, information such as transactions history, access patterns, and access control may be part of the metadata. Standards and models are key, in addition to techniques for querying and updating.

## Interoperability

The heterogeneous databases on the Internet must be able to interoperate. Distributed object technology can be used for interoperability.

For example, an object request broker (ORB) based on the Object Management Group's (OMG) specifications can be implemented for interoperation through the Internet (see Exhibit 2). The major challenge is to

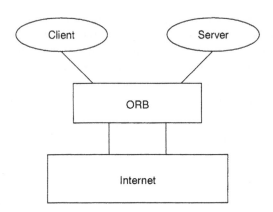

**Exhibit 2.    Internet-ORB Interoperability**

develop appropriate interfaces between the ORB and the Internet. The OMG's Internet Special Interest Group is focusing on these issues. Work is also being done on integrating OMG's CORBA, Internet, and Javasoft's Java technologies.

**Java.** As a programming language that can be used to develop systems as well as applications for the Internet, Java is showing a lot of promise for Internet database access. One of the major developments for data access is the standard called Java database connectivity (JDBC). Simply stated, database calls could be embedded in a Java application program so that databases can be accessed through these calls. JDBC may be built on other standard protocols. Many DBMS vendors are providing support for JDBC.

## CONCLUSION

This chapter has examined database management functions and discussed the possible impact of the Internet. There is a need for integrating structured and unstructured databases. Special query optimization techniques also must be investigated and DBMSs have to be integrated with browsers.

Information must be filtered so that users get only the relevant information—for this reason flexible transaction models are needed for Internet database management. Content and context-based indexing and special access methods for multimedia data should be examined. Integrating database systems with mass storage systems will become important to handling petabyte-size data stores. Support for flexible security policies and techniques for copyright protection and detecting plagiarism are also important.

Data quality issues require further investigation. There are many issues related to metadata. For example, database administrators are still trying to determine exactly what it is, who owns it, and whether it is realistic to have global managers responsible for the metadata that is not specific to any system or server.

Interoperability based on distributed object technology and Java is becoming increasingly popular. However, there is still a lot of work to be done in these areas to provide successful Internet database access. DBMS vendors are moving in the right direction, and the research community is also becoming very active. Once solutions are found to address some of the issues discussed here, users can expect efficient and secure access to the multitude of databases scattered across the various sites around the world.

**Bibliography**

1. *Java White Paper,* Javasoft 1996. URL: http://java.sun.com:80/doc/language_environment/
2. Proceedings of the First IEEE Metadata Conference Silver Spring, MD, April 1996.
3. Thuraisingham, B. Database Management and the Internet, *Object Management Group's Internet Special Interest Group Meeting Proceedings,* Washington, D.C.: June 1996.
4. Thuraisingham, B. *Data Management Systems Evolution and Interoperation* (Boca Raton FL: CRC Press, 1997.)

# Section IX
# Internet Security

For the Internet's success to continue in the mainstream, two conditions must be met. The first is to persuade the members of the public that their personal information is secure and protected in Internet applications. The other is to persuade them that monetary transactions will at least have the same degree of security as ATM and paper-based transactions. This section examines strategies for defining and rolling out a security strategy as well as tools for broadly implementing it.

"Security and the Internet" offers approaches for connecting to the Internet, router filtering, filtering oversights, firewalls, proxy services, address hiding, authentication, encryption, and alerts.

"Internet Security Architecture" explores why an overall architecture is important to security on the Internet. Methods for defining and building architecture are covered. This chapter also discusses a concept of a demilitarized Zone (DMZ), why it is important, and how one is created. Other topics include how to build and sell an architecture within an organization.

"Mitigating E-Business Security Risks: Public Key Infrastructures in the Real World" focuses on the PKI technology. This chapter describes on nontechnical aspects that are also important to the implementation of a PKI solution.

"Getting Started with PKI" examines the changing world of networked systems, the disintegration and reintegration of security mechanisms, the digital certificate and certificate authorities, registration authorities, certificate revocation list, and CA pilot considerations.

"Digital Signatures in Relational Database Applications" discusses the issues associated with integrating digital signature functionality into relational database applications. This includes a discussion of basic digital signature roles and strategies. Pitfalls unique to relational databases are also covered. A generic application is defined for storing digitally signed data in relational databases.

"A Primer on Cracking: Part 1" and "A Primer on Cracking: Part 2" explains some of the tools in widespread use for compromising computer and network security. Some defensive precautions are provided for the tools and techniques that are described.

"Protecting Data and Systems from Internet Viruses" examines how DBAs can analyze and understand virus attacks so as to prepare adequate defenses against them.

"Types of Firewalls" describes different firewall components and strategies for protecting corporate networks from intruders. A variety of functionality and features, such as strong authentication and easy-to-use interfaces, are also discussed in this article.

"Assessing and Combating the Sniffer Threat" explains how sniffers work, different types of sniffers, and countermeasures to these threats.

# Chapter 45
# Security and the Internet

*Gilbert Held*

ALTHOUGH MILLIONS OF INDIVIDUALS HAVE THEIR OWN INTERNET ACCESS ACCOUNTS THROUGH AMERICA ONLINE, COMPUSERVE, PRODIGY, AND INDEPENDENT INTERNET SERVICE PROVIDERS (ISPS), THE MOST COMMON METHOD USED TO CONNECT ORGANIZATIONS IS THROUGH THE USE OF A LEASED LINE, WHICH TERMINATES INTO THE CORPORATE LOCAL AREA NETWORK. Although this method of connection permits tens to hundreds or even thousands of employees to share the use of a common Internet connection, it also represents a security risk to the organization. That risk results from the fact that an organization has no control over the tens of millions of persons using the Internet. Thus, it becomes possible for one or more unscrupulous persons to attempt to gain access to any computational facilities connected to the private network once that network is connected to the Internet. This means that the data center operations manager carefully must consider the use of a number of security methods to protect the integrity of the organization's private network to include the computational facilities connected to that network. By understanding the role of routers and firewalls in providing different levels of security, the data center operations manager can select an appropriate method to secure the computational facilities of the organization from attack. In addition, the information presented in this chapter concerning the general security features associated with the use of routers and firewalls will provide readers with the ability to compare vendor products against their specific security requirements. Thus, this chapter also can be used as a mechanism to become familiar with the various security features incorporated into several types of communications products designed to bar intruders from private networks connected to the Internet.

## CONNECTING TO THE INTERNET

Because the opening of a private network to potential intrusion via the Internet results from the connection of that network to the Internet, the most appropriate point to begin an examination of security methods is by

0-8493-1160-8/02/$0.00+$1.50
© 2002 by CRC Press LLC

focusing upon that connection. Exhibit 1 illustrates the most common method used to connect a private network to the public Internet.

In examining the interconnection of the private network to the public Internet shown in Exhibit 1, note that a leased line is used to connect a router port located at an Internet service provider (ISP) location to the customer site. At the customer site the leased line is terminated into a router, which in turn is connected as a participant on a local area network. Although only one server is shown connected to the private LAN, in actuality there can be a large number of servers directly connected to that network or connected to other LAN segments that are connected by bridges or routers to the LAN shown. Those servers can range in scope from e-mail servers operating on Intel 486-based computers to Windows NT servers operating on Pentium Pro processor-based computers, IBM AS/400 minicomputers, and even IBM S/390 mainframes. Thus, any unauthorized access onto the private LAN from the Internet has the potential to result in at best unanticipated traffic and at worst attempts, perhaps successful, to gain access illegally to the computational facilities of the organization. Recognizing the necessity to bar unauthorized access to private networks, router manufacturers added a packet-filtering capability to their equipment. Thus, the first area in which to begin

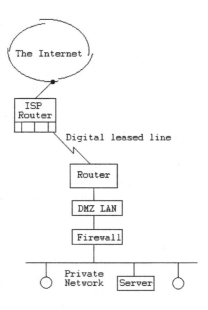

**Exhibit 1. Connecting a Private Network to the Internet**

an examination of security measures that the data center operations manager can consider is the packet-filtering capability of routers.

## ROUTER FILTERING

Recognizing the requirement of organizations to obtain a mechanism to bar certain types of data packets from flowing between networks, router manufacturers added a packet filtering capability to their products. Although different router manufacturers use different packet filtering methods, in a TCP/IP protocol environment all routers are designed to filter packets based upon three metrics. These metrics include the source and destination address of the packet and its well-known port.

The source address represents the originator of the packet. Through filtering on the source address the router can be programmed to allow or deny access based upon the computer originating the packet. Similarly, the destination address can be filtered to enable or deny access through the router to predefined computers on a private network. The third metric, the well known port, represents a numeric that identifies the type of traffic transported in a packet. For example, packets transporting Simple Mail Transport Protocol (SMTP) information, such as electronic mail messages, use port 25. Thus, enabling or disabling traffic on port 25 provides a network manager or router administrator with the ability to enable or disable the flow of electronic mail messages between the Internet and an organization's private network.

Although all router manufacturers support the previously described TCP/IP metrics, the manner by which they do so can differ between vendor products. For example, some routers are designed on the basis that all packet flows are denied unless specifically enabled. In comparison, other routers are designed on the basis that all packet flows are enabled unless specifically denied. Thus, it is important to understand the basic structure of a router's packet-filtering capability prior to creating packet filters to satisfy an organization's data security requirements.

To illustrate the use of router packet filtering, assume that the router denies all packet flows unless they specifically are enabled. Further assuming an organization has an e-mail server whose network address is 192.27.15.7 and wants to restrict access via the organization's Internet connection to e-mail messages routed to your e-mail server, enter the following router packet filter:

Enable *.*.*.* 192.27.15.7 port 25

In the preceding example the network address *.*.*.* represents a do not care condition for the from address. Thus, the preceding packet filter enables or allows all incoming packets regardless of source as long as they are destined to network address 192.27.15.7 and transport SMTP traffic, which is carried on port number 25.

## FILTERING OVERSIGHTS

Although packet filtering provides a mechanism for controlling the source of packets, their destination and the type of packets allowed to flow to a predefined destination, this security technique includes several major loopholes. These loopholes include the inability to monitor traffic to determine if an illegal sequence of operations is in progress or if the actual data transported in a packet could be harmful, such as a virus carried in an E-mail message. In addition, by itself, packet filtering cannot determine if the originator of a packet is at the source location contained in the packet, nor does packet filtering preclude the ability of a person connected to the Internet from observing the contents of packets. Recognizing these limitations, manufacturers of communications products developed a new device known as a firewall to plug the previously mentioned loopholes in packet filtering. However, it should be noted that the features and capabilities of different firewall products can vary significantly between vendors. Focus on this product to obtain an understanding of the scope and depth of the features supported by firewalls as well as their basic operation.

## THE FIREWALL

A firewall is a stand-alone communications product designed as a programmable barrier between two networks. When used as a mechanism to protect a private network from threats emanating via an Internet connection to the private network, the firewall typically is installed between the router and the private network. In doing so a hub without any workstation and server connections is used as a mechanism to interconnect the router to one interface on the firewall. The second firewall interface is then connected to the private network, as illustrated in Exhibit 2.

In examining the topology of the firewall installation shown in Exhibit 2, it should be noted that the hub without any workstation or server connections commonly is referred to as a demilitarized (DMZ) LAN. By connecting the router and firewall via a hub without any workstations and server connections, all inbound packets from the Internet must be examined by the firewall before they are received by any computational device on the private network. Thus, this installation method ensures that all packets are examined prior to being received by any computer on the private network.

When considering the capability of a firewall there are several key features to evaluate. These features include the services the firewall supports to include proxy services, addressing hiding, authentication, encryption, and alert generation. Because each of these features is beyond the capability

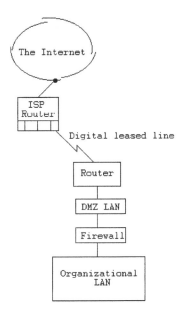

Legend:     ISP Internet Service Provider
            DMZ Demilitarized

**Exhibit 2.    Installing a Firewall to Protect a Private Network**

of a router, by itself a requirement for just one feature can justify the acquisition of a firewall to obtain an additional level of security for a private network connected to the Internet. Thus, examining each of these features will
provide an appreciation for how they add a level of protection to a private
network.

### SERVICES SUPPORTED

In a TCP/IP environment a service references the ability of a firewall to
recognize and control a specific type of packet based upon the numeric
value used for the packet's well-known port. Exhibit 3 illustrates a portion
of the Technologic Interceptor firewall Network Services configuration
screen display. Technologic is an Atlanta-based vendor that specializes in
the development of firewall software.

In examining Exhibit 3 note that the service http was selected by clicking
the cursor on the circle to the left of the entry. Once this is accomplished,
the firewall administrator can scroll down to the bottom of the window
shown in Exhibit 3 and click on a button labeled Edit to edit the selected
network service. Exhibit 4 illustrates the result obtained from clicking on
the Edit button.

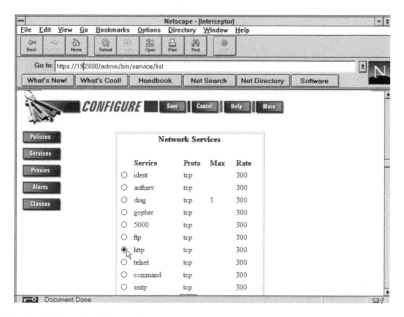

**Exhibit 3.   Using the Technologic Interceptor Network Services Configuration Display to Edit a Selected Service**

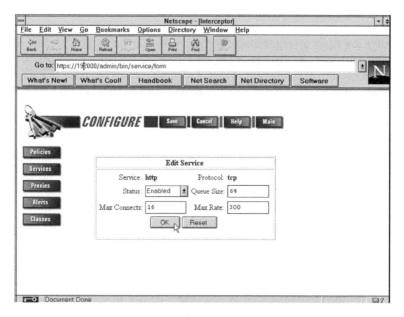

**Exhibit 4.   Editing the HTTP Service Using a Technologic Interceptor Firewall**

The edit service dialog box displayed in Exhibit 4 illustrates how a firewall administrator can control the use of http through a technologic interceptor firewall. In examining Exhibit 4 note that the status of the service is shown as enabled, allowing http packets to flow through the firewall. Also note the queue size is shown set to 64. This metric governs the length of the TCP queue of pending connections, as the value of 16 for Max connects devices governs the maximum number of simultaneous http connections to the service. The max rate entry defines the maximum rate of new connections on a per minute basis and uses a default value of 300. By adjusting values for the queue size, maximum number of connections, and maximum rate of new connections, this firewall can be used to balance loads of heavily used services so their effect upon other services is minimized. In addition, the effect of an http denial of service attack can be precluded from shutting down all Internet services to an organization. Thus, the ability to enable and disable a service as well as to control its rate of connections and other metrics can be a valuable tool for both security and performance.

## PROXY SERVICES

A proxy represents an intermediary process that intercepts user requests and sets up a second connection to the desired location. However, prior to passing packets the firewall may perform one or more operations on the contents of the packet. These operations can include conventional packet filtering as well as virus checking and what is known as stateful inspection. Concerning the latter, stateful inspection represents a term coined by Checkpoint Software, a firewall manufacturer, that references the examination of the contents of a current packet against previous packets that have the same destination. Thus a stateful inspection process can be used to determine if a remote user is attempting a repetitive operation that could be illegal, such as continuously attempting to log onto a computer on the private network by using different passwords. In fact, until the development of a stateful inspection process, a favorite activity of hackers was to obtain a computer network address and then write a program to use every entry in an electronic dictionary as a mechanism to gain access illegally to a computer.

## ADDRESS HIDING

Most firewalls include an address-hiding capability, which results in the translation of real computer addresses on the private network to public addresses used on the Internet side of the firewall. Although address hiding originally was developed as a mechanism to hide private network computers from a direct attack via the Internet, this feature also allows an organization with a limited number of valid IP addresses to support a larger number of computers than there are available addresses. To accomplish this, a network administrator would use the Internet-assigned addresses on the Internet side of the firewall and assign locally administered addresses that are virtually unlimited to computers on the private network. Then, as long as the number of computers on the private network requiring Internet access at any point in time does not exceed the number of assigned IP addresses, the translation process allows each computer to transmit and receive information via the Internet.

## AUTHENTICATION

One of the problems associated with connecting a public network with the Internet is that many knowledgeable hackers can learn the conventional user ID-password combinations used to access computers by monitoring Internet traffic. Then they can use this information to gain illegal access to a computer on the private network. Recognizing this problem, several firewall vendors now include an optional authentication feature that can be used to verify the identity of the person seeking access.

Authentication is based upon the use of an algorithm to generate a one-time password. That password can be generated by software on a client computer or through the use of a credit card-size device that contains circuitry that displays a new pseudo-random generated sequence of digits every minute. For both methods a server program is installed on the firewall that uses the same algorithm as the client. Each client computer user transmits his or her PIN as well as the one-time password. The PIN is used by the firewall to generate a new password, which is compared to the transmitted password, and the identity of the user is verified if the passwords match. Because the password is only valid for the current session, any illicit monitoring results in a hacker obtaining an invalid password. Thus, authentication provides an additional level of security that can bar the use of illicitly gained user ID-password combinations.

## ENCRYPTION

Although authentication verifies the identity of a person accessing the facilities of a network through a firewall, it does not protect the contents of information being transmitted from illicit monitoring. To do so requires the use of encryption, which represents another option supported by some firewalls. Thus, examine the encryption capability of a firewall if the protection of the contents of messages routed via the Internet to the organization's private network is a requirement.

## ALERTING APPROPRIATE EMPLOYEES

When a possible illegal activity is determined to be occurring, it is important that appropriate employees are alerted to this fact. This is the function of an alert capability, which is a feature included in most firewalls.

Exhibit 5 illustrates the Add Alert screen of the Technologic Interceptor firewall. Note that the pull-down pattern menu was activated with the highlighted bar over the Failed_Authentication entry. Thus, the alert being added will alert an employee when the number of failed authentication attempts reaches a certain level. That level is defined by entering a value to a box labeled Frequency, which is hidden from view by the pull-down menu. Once one selects a pattern, he or she can set both a frequency of occurrence and a time period of occurrence for which an alert will be generated. Then he or she can have the alert generate an E-mail message as well as a pager message to alert an appropriate employee to the occurrence of a suspicious type of activity.

When configuring an alert it is important to recognize that many activities that match an alert pattern can be caused by an innocent mistake instead of an attempt to penetrate your organization's network. Rather than being beeped at 3:00 A.M. on a Sunday morning by a traveling executive in Europe who entered his or her authentication sequence incorrectly, this situation can be precluded from occurring by setting an appropriate frequency value. For example, a frequency of four or five is high enough to allow an employee to make several incorrect entries prior to an alert being generated. In comparison, a frequency of one or two leaves little margin for error.

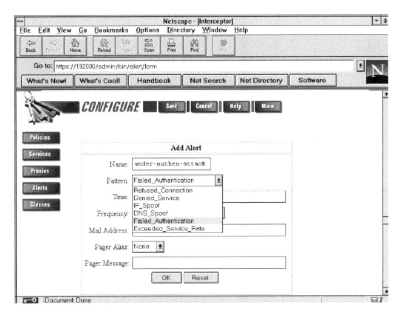

**Exhibit 5.  Through the Add Alert Dialog Box, One Can Define the Frequency of Occurence of a Pattern as a Trigger to Generate an Alert Message.**

## RECOMMENDED COURSE OF ACTION

By carefully examining an organization's security requirements against the operational capabilities of routers and firewalls, one can determine if a firewall is needed to supplement the packet filtering capability of a router. If so, the features of different firewall products should be carefully examined to ensure that the equipment selected can satisfy fully the security requirements of the organization.

# Chapter 46
# Internet Security Architecture

*Carol A. Siegel*

ARCHITECTURE IS THE ART OR SCIENCE OF BUILDING, INCLUDING PLAN, DESIGN, AND CON-STRUCTION. Architecture as it relates to physical structures has perhaps been best illustrated by such ancient marvels as Stonehenge or the Pyramids; however, architecture as it relates to technology is still an extremely young field. With the proliferation of computers and the advent of distributed computing, technology architecture started to gain recognition as a discipline within corporate America in the 1980s. As the computer industry matured — mainframes giving birth to minis and micros, and network interconnectivity starting to play a more significant role — choices in technology were not so simple. It became more challenging for a large company to remain true to one vendor, whether for hardware, software, or telecommunications. As computing infrastructures in medium- to large-size companies became increasingly diverse, interoperability problems were the first to surface. Often, when two vendors' products were used, they did not work. Sometimes vendors wanted to constrain customers to their products (in certain cases this might have been true), or it was a situation of products not operating by the same standards.

Good architecture becomes the first means by which technologists ensure compatibility between technology platforms. This leads to the inevitable question: Why is architecture important? To illustrate its importance, consider a large company: What might happen if each business unit wanted to make its own technology choices, independent of all others? Under this scenario, each unit does its own R&D, implements, administers, and supports its own specific solution. What may result is different platforms, technologies, and industry standards. Costs may be significantly more than if the whole organization provided a standard solution. With individual solutions, there may be compatibility and interoperability issues, not to mention eventual replacement and unwind costs.

0-8493-1160-8/02/$0.00+$1.50
© 2002 by CRC Press LLC

The kinds of security issues that are being resolved today involve solutions that affect the entire enterprise. For example, take the use of a Public Key Infrastructure (PKI), which is used to provide digital certificates to entities to ensure strong authentication. This type of a solution will only work if all businesses in the organization participate. Other reasons involve risks associated with making a bad choice — one that might expose a vulnerability from inadequate security — going to a technology that is based on proprietary not "open" standards, using a vendor that cannot provide adequate support or just goes out of business. For example, by standardizing on APIs, application portability is achieved; by standardizing on protocols or tokens (X.509 Certificates, Kerberos Tickets, any defined data structure) one achieves implementation interoperability; by standardizing on all of the above, one achieves implementation replaceability of products. In fact, in terms of bang for the buck for information risk management, architecture will always be the best choice, as illustrated in Exhibit 1.

## WHAT IS ARCHITECTURE AND HOW IS IT CREATED?

In general, the objective of architecture is to provide a framework that allows products to be assembled quickly and seamlessly, permitting the old and the new to interoperate. Client/server, legacy, and distributed systems must bond into a uniform processing machine on a network that enables ubiquitous communications. The enterprise architecture should provide a vehicle for information sharing and promote component reuse. The enterprise architecture can be discussed on four different levels:

- The cost of security is rising exponentially as technology becomes more sophisticated and ubiquitous
- Allocation of risk dollars must be carefully targeted where they yield the most benefit
- Businesses must decide where they are prepared to accept risk

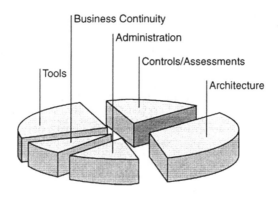

**Exhibit 1. Where the Risk Dollar Should Be Spent**

business, information, application, and technical architectures. These are considered to be horizontal architectures, while security architecture is a vertical architecture contributing to each of these efforts. Security in the business architecture concerns system ownership, business risks, correct deployment of security services in accordance with business risks, and separation of duties. Security in the information architecture concerns information risk management and data risk assessment. Information risk assessments should be conducted on all data, which should be classified according to sensitivity or business confidentiality. Any inherent risk in the technology, as well as operation risk, should also be assessed. Security in the application architecture includes placement of mechanisms such as identification and authentication, access control, audit, cryptographic, nonrepudiation, and administration. It is at the application layer we talk about APIs. This chapter focuses on the technical architecture.

An enterprise architecture should be based on a company's information risk and security policies, but should be tempered by business requirements. The security and risk policies are normally determined by policy committees and can have input from other corporate entities such as audit, compliance, and a corporate communications function. The policies should be technology independent and high level in nature. Based on the policies, more specific technical standards can be written to guide the implementation of the policies. The technical standards should address key technologies and industry standards, but still attempt to be product independent. Both the policies and standards provide input into the architecture. From the architecture, specific products can be determined. Exhibit 2 illustrates the architecture creation process.

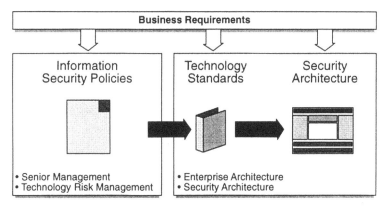

**Exhibit 2. Architecture Creation Process**

## THE IMPORTANCE OF BUSINESS REQUIREMENTS

All architectures must be based on business requirements, which can be different for each organization. They can also vary tremendously from unit to unit within the same organization. The first step in designing any architecture is to collect business requirements. This may seem simple, but it can be the most challenging step. Either by interview or by asking units to submit requirements immediately raises questions about how the requirements should be articulated. Simply put, business people talk about requirements in business terms and security professionals talk about requirements in terms of security services. The seven security services are defined in Exhibit 3.

In general, the two perspectives of business requirements are quite different. Businesspeople want to know what products meet their business needs while satisfying the "policy" people. Their concerns often do not involve (nor do they care particularly) about the information risk level of the data or how each security service is provided.

These two perspectives are illustrated in Exhibit 4.

When talking to businesspeople, one might hear requirements such as the following:

- We need to exchange documents/files with our clients, prospective clients, our business partners and suppliers in a secure way.
- We need to be able to give our clients the ability to place orders and receive confirmations remotely over the Internet.
- We need to enable our portfolio managers to remotely manage their clients' portfolios.
- We would like to be required to login only once to our company's systems via the Web and able to access all of our company's internal databases without having to login a second time.

**Exhibit 3.    Security Services**

1. Access control. The prevention of unauthorized use of a resource.
2. Authentication. Verifying the identity of an individual or entity in order to determine the right to access specific categories of information or services.
3. Confidentiality. The prevention of unauthorized disclosure of information.
4. Integrity. The prevention of unauthorized modification or destruction of information.
5. Nonrepudiation. The process that prevents someone from denying initiation and/or receipt of a message/transaction.
6. Audit. The performance of monitoring and independent review of system records, operational procedures and system activities to test for the adequacy of controls, and compliance with policy.
7. Availability. Ensuring that information resources and/or computing services are usable by authorized persons or programs when needed.

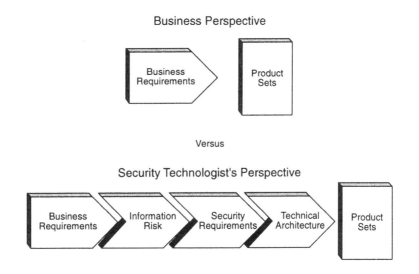

**Exhibit 4. Perspectives: Business versus Security Technologist**

- We would like to provide for end-to-end security (from client to back-end data) when performing financial transactions over the Internet.

Both business and security professionals agree, however, that there are fundamental technology business drivers. A framework of solid business controls will help minimize financial losses and damage to reputation. Facilitating secure communications between clients and the enterprise will enable new business and permit business to be conducted independent of location. An architectural strategy will aid the building of global business, increase market share, and reduce technology cost, while improving availability of information. At the same time, confidentiality and the integrity of client data can be maintained.

The business requirements must be translated into security requirements before the architecture is built. Solutions for classes of requirements can be found, which can be categorized on a high, medium, or low information risk level of data. Examples of each of the risk levels of data are given in Exhibit 5.

The security technologist goes through more steps to arrive at the desired product solution. He starts with the business requirements and does an information risk assessment of the business data. This determines whether the data is high-, medium-, or low-risk and which security services are required (e.g., strong authentication, nonrepudiation). The risk assessment then translates into security requirements that define the technical architecture. Out of the technical architecture comes the product set solutions.

**Exhibit 5.   Business Requirements: Relative Risk Level and Security Service Provided**

| | Business Requirement | Risk Level of Data | Access Control | Authentication | Confidentiality | Integrity | Non-Repudiation | Audit | Availability |
|---|---|---|---|---|---|---|---|---|---|
| | | | Security Service Required | | | | | | |
| 1 | View/Query non-sensitive, non-client information | L | Y | Y | | Y | | | |
| 2 | Sales/Marketing information | L | Y | Y | | Y | | | |
| 3 | Client query of research data | M | Y | Y | Y | Y | | | Y |
| 4 | Client use of analytical tools | M | Y | Y | Y | Y | | | Y |
| 5 | View/Query client information | H | Y | Y | Y | Y | | Y | Y |
| 6 | Update client information | H | Y | Y | Y | Y | Y | Y | Y |

## THE PURPOSE OF A DEMILITARIZED ZONE (DMZ)

Adopting a term from the military, a demilitarized zone or DMZ is used to refer to any kind of screened subnetwork placed between an internal network (i.e., a corporate network) and the Internet. The screening of the subnet is generally achieved by a dual firewall architecture, which can include elements such as bastion hosts and choke routers as well as commercial firewall boxes. The purpose of the firewalls is to provide controlled access to/from the DMZ from both the Internet as well as the corporate or trusted network. A DMZ architecture creates three distinct areas to which access is controlled by the rules set by the firewalls. A typical firewall architecture for a DMZ is illustrated in Exhibit 6.

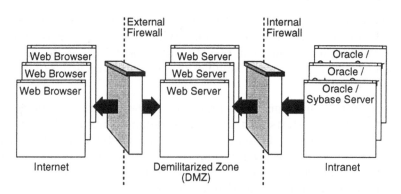

**Exhibit 6.   A Firewall Architecture for a DMZ**

The left area labeled "Internet" provides no protection to systems located in it. This area is defined as accessible to and by the general public. All systems and data located in the Internet area are assumed to be insecure and potentially compromised. Any information placed on systems in the Internet area must be low risk, that is, not be sensitive, critical, confidential, or proprietary in nature. The Internet area is typically used for public Web services or any type of public application services a company may want to provide to the Internet community. The middle area, labeled "DMZ," is used to house systems that can provide data and application services to clients of the company via the Internet. Any client application placed in the DMZ affects other systems that reside in the DMZ in terms of overall risk. If one application is compromised in the DMZ, others are exposed to increased risk. These considerations must be taken into account when designing DMZ systems and determining the viability and potential liability of client data that reside there. However, in general, both the Internet and DMZ areas are to be considered part of the Internet; only low risk data may be transmitted through or stored in these areas without additional security controls. The right area, labeled "Internal," represents the corporate or trusted network. All systems and hosts in this area are considered to be fully protected and secured according to company security policies and standards.

The three areas are controlled by the external and internal firewalls, which protect and restrict access to/from the DMZ. The primary role for the external firewall is to provide controlled access by providing packet filtering rules as well as additional authentication to systems located in the DMZ. This firewall is configured to allow only those systems and services that reside in the DMZ to pass into company network. The internal firewall has a dual function. The first is to protect the internal network from any unauthorized external access. The second is to protect those hosts and applications residing in the DMZ from any unauthorized access by internal company users. To meet additional future needs, the DMZ can be divided into several segments to provide additional segregation between applications and areas pertaining to different clients.

Some general rules for configuring a firewall are:

- "That which is not explicitly allowed is denied." All services that pass through a company's firewall systems must be specifically allowed.
- No network packet is allowed to enter or leave the company network without first being inspected by the firewall.
- Only those services that can be secured will be allowed to traverse the firewall.
- All inbound and outbound traffic from the corporate network must be explicitly allowed and defined by source and destination addresses, protocol, port, and service type. All other undefined traffic is denied.

- All inbound network traffic from an external source first must be initiated by a host from within the internal network before the network packet is allowed to traverse the firewall. All inbound traffic that has not been initiated from within the Internal network is denied.

## AN EXAMPLE OF A DEMILITARIZED ZONE ARCHITECTURE

So what does an architecture really look like? It will have an implementation model that shows technical components (such as browsers, servers, and certification authorities), how these components talk to one another, and where they physically reside, whether on an internal network, a DMZ, or the Internet. It will contain the characteristics of the model and discuss the flow of a typical message through the architecture. It also should include what level of information risk the data flowing through it can have and how the model addresses the information security services. An example of a security architecture for a DMZ configuration is shown in Exhibit 7.

Exhibit 7 represents a three-tier architecture that can support high risk data. The heart of the architecture is end-to-end security, achieved between Tiers 1 and 3. Additionally, transport layer security is achieved between Tiers 1 and 2 and between Tiers 2 and 3. The path of a request through the architecture is as follows:

1. A secure transport layer is established between Tiers 1 and 2 using Transport Layer Security (SSL). This establishes mutual identification and authentication as well as data confidentiality and integrity.
2. The browser sends a request to the Web server in the DMZ.
3. The request is digitally signed and enciphered by the user.

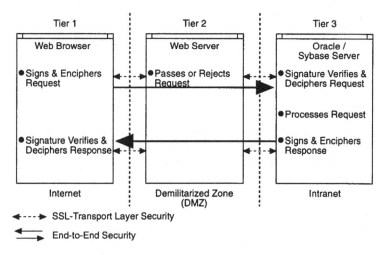

**Exhibit 7.  Security Architecture for a DMZ**

4. The Web server passes or rejects the request based on the identity established by the transport layer security.
5. If accepted, another secure transport layer is established between Tiers 2 and 3, also using SSL (or some other transport layer security protocol).
6. The request is passed to an application server (Oracle or Sybase), which signature verifies and deciphers the request. Note that there may be other required steps for processing not indicated on this diagram.
7. The application server processes the request and signs and enciphers the response.
8. The response is passed back to the Tier 2 Web server and then to the Web browser, both over a secure transport layer links.
9. The Web browser signature verifies and deciphers the response, thereby achieving end-to-end security.

With this model, mutual authentication, confidentially, integrity, and access control are achieved from end to end. As this model represents a security architecture view, products must be found or developed that provide these functionalities. The marketplace is quite close to providing commercial off-the-shelf (COTS) products to fit this model, but in some cases, some custom development must be undertaken. In general, implementing a COTS products will ready the architecture more quickly, but building custom components will give an organization some competitive advantage.

## HOW TO MAKE AN ARCHITECTURE SUCCESSFUL

Creating a master project plan is always advisable when undertaking such a monumental task as developing and implementing a security architecture. There are tasks that need to happen serially and those that need to happen in tandem. High-level tasks of such a project plan would most likely include the following:

1. Assemble a team of cross-business representatives.
   - The team must include both technologists and business people, which gives a more complete perspective.
   - This group should make all the major decisions, thereby inherently giving buy-in to any conclusions.
   - Funding should come in part from each business unit and in part from the central infrastructure group.
2. Determine the scope of the project.
   - Decide if the architecture will be for the Internet, an intranet, or an extranet, or all of the above.
   - Decide if the architecture is to last one or five years.

- Decide if the architecture is to be based on any given infrastructural choices on which the organization has already made a sizable investment.
3. Gather the cross-business requirements.
    - Gather the requirements in business terms, helping the team to focus on like categories of requirements.
    - Translate the business requirements into security terms, because the products must meet the security requirements.
4. Design a security architecture that meets the security requirements.
    - Base solutions on open standards: Internet Engineering Task Force (IETF), Object Management Group (OMG), the OpenGroup, and other standards that are on a standards track to ensure that the architecture is interoperable and compatible with other technologies and products.
    - Base solutions on official corporate technology policies and standards.
    - Choose one or two businesses with a current and pressing need for the architecture and work with them to develop a solution that will fit their needs.
5. Develop an implementation plan for the architecture.
    - Develop two or three business-specific implementation architectures that map to the general architecture.
    - Identify all common components and services to be reused. These components and services may already be in existence or may have to be built.
    - Evaluate and select the actual products to implement the architecture and custom build any components that are not COT products.
    - Discuss the implications of deploying a technology that is not one of the core infrastructural choices. Discuss any unwind costs or technical transition/migration issues.
    - Develop specific implementation road maps (timelines to implement specific technologies) for any infrastructure service or reusable component.
    - Develop critical path diagrams (Gantt Charts) to show which tasks must occur in tandem, and which serially. Include all start dates and end dates to determine windows of availability for products and components.

The final document should also include a discussion of the legalities of privacy as well as the export of encryption (international vs. domestic). Products that use encryption are subject to specific export controls by the U.S. Department of Commerce (DOC). The controls center around the length of the encryption key and who is the designated user of the encryption (such as name and country). These names must be registered/verified with the DOC twice per year. Export controls also vary depending on requesting institution. In the past, financial institutions have been given more flexibility. In general, these laws may change quickly because financial services organizations are being redefined.

There also may be issues with data privacy laws covering the monitoring of individuals in Germany, Scandinavia, Singapore, and some other countries. Other issues will likely surface with the European Privacy Directive. For example, France does not permit the use of any encryption unless it is with permission. There may be restrictions from the People's Republic of China and Russia as well as some type of "process" requirement from Singapore. These restrictions/laws need to be investigated, and if possible, attorneys should determine the most current laws and regulations.

## "SELLING" THE ARCHITECTURE

Measurable benefits must be identified to cost justify the architecture. Show dollar values where at all possible. Generally, the benefits fall into three categories:

1. Business enablements. Typical business enablements that may result from a security architecture might be:
   - Secure financial transactions over the Internet
   - Single sign-on to multiple Web servers
   - Secure communications with clients via e-mail or FTP
   - Strong authentication of clients from any location or any machine
   - Secure remote client portfolio management by salesforce
2. Cost savings. Typical cost savings might be:
   - Electronic delivery of services (sales, fulfillment, and support)
   - Reuse of infrastructure services
   - Reuse of software components
3. Cost avoidance: This category is the hardest to quantify, but include:
   - Elimination of redundant architectural efforts
     - R&D and tools evaluation
     - Analysis of security risks and countermeasures performed by information risk and security professionals
   - Risk reduction resulting from single architectural effort
     - Information risk
     - Audit findings
   - Centralization of resources (architectural implementation, required infrastructure, security administration, security monitoring, standards research and analysis)
   - Unwind costs of bad technology choices: nonstandard, noninteroperable, etc.

The final architecture document should include a matrix that maps the solutions back to the original business requirements to close the loop. This is critical: it shows how the architecture meets the requirements on a one-by-one basis. Now, to really sell the architecture, put on a roadshow with a fancy presentation illustrating all the key benefits; getting buy-in from key senior players. Nothing sells like how to save money!!

# Chapter 47
# Mitigating E-Business Security Risks: Public Key Infrastructures in the Real World

*Douglas C. Merrill*
*Eran Feigenbaum*

MANY ORGANIZATIONS WANT TO GET INVOLVED WITH ELECTRONIC COMMERCE — OR ARE BEING FORCED TO BECOME AN E-BUSINESS BY THEIR COMPETITORS. The goal of this business decision is to realize bottom-line benefits from their information technology investment, such as more efficient vendor interactions and improved asset management. Such benefits have indeed been realized by organizations, but so have the associated risks, especially those related to information security. Managed risk is a good thing, but risk for its own sake, without proper management, can drive a company out of existence. More and more corporate management teams — even up to the board of directors' level — are requiring evidence that security risks are being managed. In fact, when asked about the major stumbling blocks to widespread adoption of electronic business, upper management pointed to a lack of security as a primary source of hesitation.

An enterprisewide security architecture, including technology, appropriate security policies, and audit trails, can provide reasonable measures of risk management to address senior management concerns about E-business opportunities. One technology involved in enterprisewide security architectures is public key cryptography, often implemented in the form of a public key infrastructure (PKI). This article describes several hands-on examples of PKI, including business cases and implementation plans. The authors attempt to present detail from a very practical, hands-on approach, based on their experience implementing PKI and providing large-scale systems integration services. Several shortcuts are taken in the technical discussions to simplify or clarify points, while endeavoring to ensure that these did not detract from the overall message.

Although this chapter focuses on a technology — PKI — it is important to realize that large implementations involve organizational transformation. Many nontechnical aspects are integral to the success of a PKI implementation, including organizational governance, performance monitoring, stakeholder management, and process adjustment. Failing to consider these aspects greatly increases the risk of project failure, although many of these factors are outside the domain of information security. In the authors' experience, successful PKI implementations involve not only information security personnel, but also business unit leaders and senior executives to ensure that these nontechnical aspects are handled appropriately.

## NETWORK SECURITY: THE PROBLEM

As more and more data is made network-accessible, security mechanisms must be put in place to ensure only authorized users access the data. An organization does not want its competitor to read, for example, its internal pricing and availability information. Security breaches often arise through failures in authentication. Authentication is the process of identifying an individual so that one can determine the individual's access privileges. To start my car, I must authenticate myself to my car. When I start my car, I have to "prove" that I have the required token — the car key — before my car will start. Without a key, it is difficult to start my car. However, a car key is a poor authentication mechanism — it is not that difficult to gain access to my car keys, and hence be me, at least as far as my car is concerned. In the everyday world, there are several stronger authentication mechanisms, such as presenting one's driver's license with a picture. People are asked to present their driver's licenses at events ranging from getting on a plane to withdrawing large amounts of money from a bank. Each of these uses involves comparing the image on the license to the appearance of the individual presenting the license. This strengthens the authentication process by requiring two-factor authentication — an attacker must not only have my license, but he must also resemble me. In the electronic world, it is far more difficult to get strong authentication: a computer cannot, in general, check to ensure that a person looks like the picture on his or her driver's license. Typically, a user is required to memorize a username and password. These username and password pairs must be stored in operating system-specific files, application tables, and the user's head (or desk). Any individual sitting at a keyboard that can produce a user's password is assumed to be that user.

Traditional implementations of this model, although useful, have several significant problems. When a new user is added, a new username must be generated and a new password stored on each of the relevant machines. This can be a significant effort. Additionally, when a user leaves the company, that user's access must be terminated. Ensuring that users are completely removed is not easy if there are several machines and databases. The authors' experience with PricewaterhouseCoopers LLP (PricewaterhouseCoopers) in assessing security of large corporations suggests that users are often not removed when they leave, creating significant security vulnerabilities.

Many studies have shown that users pick amazingly poor passwords, especially when constrained to use a maximum of eight characters, as is often the case in operating system authentication. For example, a recent assessment of a FORTUNE 50 company found that almost 10 percent of users chose a variant of the company's logo as their password. Such practices often make it possible for an intruder to simply guess a valid password for a user and hence obtain access to all the data that user could (legitimately) view or alter.

Finally, even if a strong password is selected, the mechanics of network transmission make the password vulnerable. When the user enters a username and password, there must be some mechanism for getting the identification materials to the server itself. This can be done in a variety of ways. The most common method is to simply transmit the username and password across the network. However, this information can be intercepted during transmission using commonly available tools called "sniffers." A sniffer reads data as it passes across a network — data such as one's username and password. After reading the information, the culprit could use the stolen credentials to masquerade as the legitimate user, attaining access to any information that the legitimate user could access. To prevent sniffing of passwords, many systems use cryptography to hide the plaintext of the password before sending it across the network. In this event, an attacker can still sniff the password off the network, but cannot simply read its plaintext; rather, the attacker sees only the encrypted version. The attacker is not entirely blocked, however. There are publicly available tools to attack the encrypted passwords using dictionary words or brute-force guessing to get the plaintext password from the encrypted password. These attacks exploit the use of unchanging passwords and functions. Although this requires substantial effort, many demonstrated examples of accounts being compromised through this sort of attack are known.

These concerns — lack of updates after users leave, poor password selection, and the capability to sniff passwords off networks — make reliance on username and password pairs for remote identification to business-critical information unsatisfactory.

## WHY CRYPTOGRAPHY IS USEFUL

Cryptography (from the Greek for "secret writing") provides techniques for ensuring data integrity and confidentiality during transport and for lessening the threat associated with traditional passwords. These techniques include codes, ciphers, and steganography. This chapter addresses only ciphers; for information on other types of cryptography, see Bruce Schneier's *Applied Cryptography* or David Kahn's *The Codebreakers*. Ciphers use mathematics to transform plaintext into "ciphertext." It is very difficult to transform ciphertext back into plaintext without a special key. The key is distributed only to select individuals. Anyone who does not have the key cannot read or alter the data without significant effort. Hence, authentication becomes the question, "Does this person have the expected key?" Additionally, the property that only a certain person (or set of people) has access to a key implies that only those individuals could have done anything to an object encrypted with that key. This so-called "non-repudiation" provides assurance about an action that was performed, such as that the action was performed by John Doe, or at a certain time, etc.

There are two types of ciphers. The first method is called secret key cryptography. In secret key cryptography, a secret — a password — must be shared between sender and recipient in order for the recipient to decrypt the object. The best-known secret key cryptographic algorithm is the Data Encryption Standard (DES). Other methods include IDEA, RC4, Blowfish, and CAST. Secret key cryptography methods are, in general, very fast, because they use fairly simple mathematics, such as binary additions, bit shifts, and table lookups.

However, transporting the secret key from sender to recipient — or recipients — is very difficult. If four people must all have access to a particular encrypted object, the creator of the object must get the same key to each person in a safe manner. This is difficult enough. However, an even more difficult situation occurs when each of the four people must be able to communicate with each of the others without the remaining individuals being able to read the communication (see Exhibit 1). In this event, each pair of people must share a secret key known only to those two individuals. To accomplish this with four people requires that six keys be created and distributed. With ten people, the situation requires 45 key exchanges (see Exhibit 2). Also, if keys were compromised — such as would happen when a previously authorized person leaves the company — all the keys known to the departing employee must be changed. Again, in the four-person case, the departure requires three new key exchanges; nine are required in the ten-person case. Clearly, this will not work for large organizations with hundreds or thousands of employees.

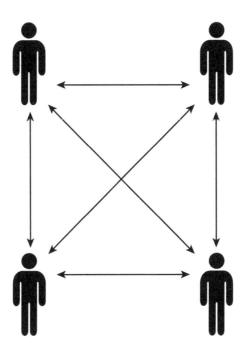

**Exhibit 1.   Four People Require Six Keys**

In short, secret key cryptography has great power, employs fairly simple mathematics, and can quickly encrypt large volumes of data. However, its Achilles heel is the problem of key distribution and maintenance.

This Achilles heel led a group of mathematicians to develop a new paradigm for cryptography — asymmetric cryptography, also known as public key cryptography. Public key cryptography lessens the key distribution problem by splitting the encryption key into a public portion — which is given out to anyone — and a secret component that must be controlled by the user. The public and private keys, which jointly are called a key pair, are generated together and are related through complex mathematics. In the public key model, a sender looks up the recipient's public keys, typically stored in certificates, and encrypts the document using those public keys. No previous connection between sender and recipient is required, because only the recipient's public key is needed for secure transmission, and the certificates are stored in public databases. Only the private key that is associated with the public key can decrypt the document. The public and private keys can be stored as files, as entries in a database, or on a piece of hardware called a token. These tokens are often smart cards that look like credit cards but store user keys and are able to perform cryptographic computations far more quickly than general-purpose CPUs.

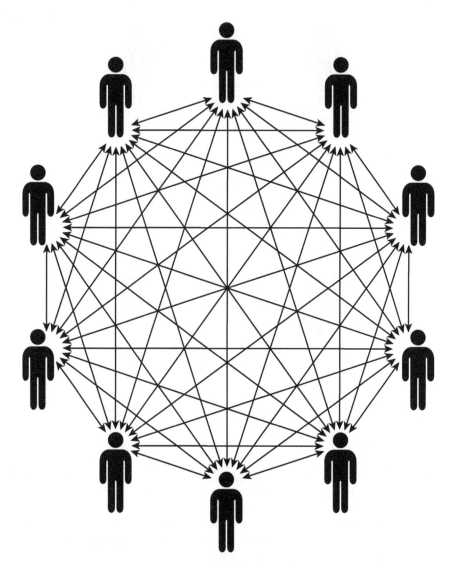

**Exhibit 2.  Ten People Require 45 Keys**

There are several public key cryptographic algorithms, including RSA, Diffie-Hellman, and Elliptic Curve cryptography. These algorithms relay on the assumption that there are mathematical problems that are easy to perform but difficult to do in reverse. To demonstrate this to yourself, calculate 11 squared ($11^2$). Now calculate the square root of 160. The square root is a bit more difficult, right? This is the extremely simplified idea behind public key cryptography. Encrypting a document to someone is akin to squaring a number, while decrypting it without the private key is somewhat like taking the square root. Each of the public key algorithms uses a different type of problem, but all rely on the assumption that the particular problem chosen is difficult to perform in reverse without the key.

Most public key algorithms have associated "signature" algorithms that can be used to ensure that a piece of data was sent by the owner of a private key and was unchanged in transit. These digital signature algorithms are commonly employed to ensure data integrity, but do not, in and of themselves, keep data confidential.

Public key cryptography can be employed to protect data confidentiality and integrity while it is being transported across the network. In fact, Secure Sockets Layer (SSL) is just that: a server's public key is used to create an encrypted tunnel across which World Wide Web (WWW) data is sent. SSL is commonly used for WWW sites that accept credit card information; in fact, the major browsers support SSL natively, as do most Web servers. Unfortunately, SSL does not address all the issues facing an organization that wants to open up its data to network access. By default, SSL authenticates only the server, not the client. However, an organization would want to provide its data only to the correct person; in other words, the whole point of this exercise is to ensure that the client is authenticated.

The SSL standards provide methods to authenticate not only the server, but also the client. Doing this requires having the client side generate a key pair and having the server check the client keys. However, how can the server know that the supposed client is not an imposter even if the client has a key pair? Even if a key does belong to a valid user, what happens when that user leaves the company, or when the user's key is compromised? Dealing with these situations requires a process called key revocation. Finally, if a user generates a key pair, and then uses that key pair to, for example, encrypt attachments to business-related electronic mail, the user's employer may be required by law to provide access to user data when served with a warrant. For an organization to be able to answer such a warrant, it must have "escrowed" a copy of the users' private keys — but how could the organization get a copy of the private key, since the user generated the pair?

Public key cryptography has a major advantage over secret key cryptography. Recall that secret key cryptography required that the sender and recipient share a secret key in advance. Public key cryptography does not require the sharing of a secret between sender and recipients, but is far slower than secret key cryptography, because the mathematics involved is far more difficult.

Although this simplifies key distribution, it does not solve the problem. Public key cryptography requires a way to ensure that John Doe's public key in fact belongs to him, not to an imposter. In other words, anyone could generate a key pair and assert that the public key belongs to the President of the United States. However, if one were to want to communicate with the President securely, one would need to ensure that the key was in fact his. This assurance requires that a trusted third party assert a particular public key does, in fact, belong to the supposed user. Providing this assurance requires additional elements that together make up a public key infrastructure (PKI).

The next section describes a complete solution that can provide data confidentiality and integrity protection for remote access to applications. Subsequent sections point out other advantages yielded by the development of a full-fledged infrastructure.

## USING A PKI TO AUTHENTICATE TO AN APPLICATION

Let us first describe, at a high level, how a WWW-based application might employ a PKI to authenticate its users (see Exhibit 3). The user directs her WWW browser to the (secured) WWW server that connects to the application. The WWW page uses the form of SSL that requires both server and client authentication. The user must unlock her private key; this is done by entering a password that decrypts the private key. The server asks for the identity of the user, and looks up her public key in a database. After retrieving her public key, the server ensures that the user is still authorized to access the application system by checking that the user's key has not been revoked. Meanwhile, the client accesses the key database to get the public key for the server and checks to ensure it has not been revoked. Assuming that the keys are still valid, the server and client engage in mutual authentication.

There are several methods for mutual authentication. Regardless of approach, mutual authentication requires several steps; the major difference between methods is the order in which the steps occur. Exhibit 4 presents a simple method for clarity. First, the server generates a piece of random data, encrypts it with the client's public key, and signs it with its own private key. This encrypted and signed data is sent to the client, who checks the signature using the server's public key and decrypts the data. Only the client could have decrypted the data, because only the client has access to the user's private key; and only the server could have signed the data, because to sign the encrypted data, the server requires access to the server's private key. Hence, if the client can produce the decrypted data, the server can believe that the client has access to the user's private key. Similarly, if the client verifies the signature using the server's public key, the client is assured that the server signed the data. After decrypting the data, the client takes it, along with another piece of unique data, and encrypts both with the server's public key. The client then signs this piece

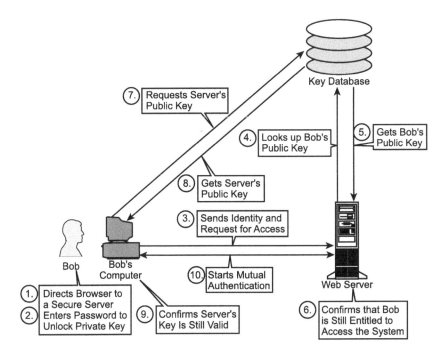

**Exhibit 3. Using a PKI to Authenticate Users**

of encrypted data and sends it off to the server. The server checks the signature, decrypts the data, checks to be sure the first piece of data is the same as what the server sent off before, and gathers the new piece of data. The server generates another random number, takes this new number along with the decrypted data received from the client, and encrypts both together. After signing this new piece of data, the resulting data is sent off to the client. Only the client can decrypt this data, and only the server could have signed it. This series of steps guarantees the identity of each party. After mutual authentication, the server sends a notice to the log server, including information such as the identity of the user, client location, and time.

Recall that public key cryptography is relatively slow; the time required to encrypt and decrypt data could interfere with the user experience. However, if the application used a secret key algorithm to encrypt the data passing over the connection, after the initial public key authentication, the data would be kept confidential to the two participants, but with a lower overhead. This is the purpose of the additional piece of random data in the second message sent by the server. This additional piece of random data will be used as a session key — a secret shared by client and server. Both client and server will use the session key to encrypt all network transactions in the current network connection using a secret key algorithm such

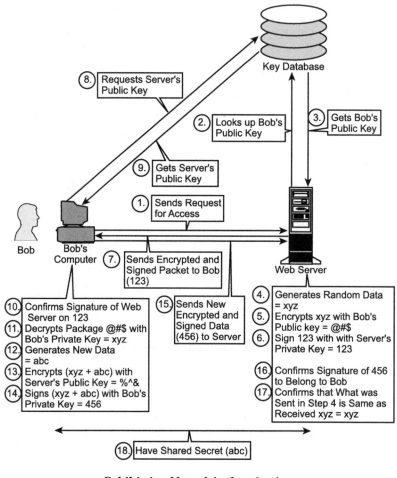

**Exhibit 4.  Mutual Authentication**

as DES, IDEA, or RC4. The secret key algorithm provides confidentiality and integrity assurance for all data and queries as they traverse the network without the delay required by a public key algorithm. The public key algorithm handles key exchange and authentication. This combination of both public and private key algorithms offers the benefits of each.

How did these steps ensure that both client and server were authenticated? The client, after decrypting the data sent by the server, knows that the server was able to decrypt what the client sent, and hence knows that the server can access the server's private key. The server knows that the client has decrypted what it sent in the first step, and thus knows that the client has access to the user's private key. Both parties have authenticated the other, but no passwords have traversed the network, and no information that could be useful to an attacker has left the client or server machines.

Additionally, the server can pass the authentication through to the various application servers without resorting to insecure operating system-level trust relationships, as is often done in multi-system installations. In other words, a user might be able to leverage the public key authentication not only to the WWW-based application, but also to other business applications. More details on this reduced sign-on functionality are provided in a later section.

## COMPONENTS OF A PKI

The behavior described in the example above seemed very simple, but actually involved several different entities behind the scenes. As is so often the case, a lot of work must be done to make something seem simple. The entities involved here include a certificate authority, registration authorities, directory servers, various application programming interfaces and semi-custom development, third-party applications, and hardware. Some of these entities would be provided by a PKI vendor, such as the CA, RA, and a directory server, but other components would be acquired from other sources. Additionally, the policies that define the overall infrastructure and how the pieces interact with one another and the users are central components. This section describes each component and tells why it is important to the overall desired behavior.

The basic element of a PKI is the certificate authority. One of the problems facing public key solutions is that anyone can generate a public key and claim to be anyone. For example, using publicly available tools, one can generate a public key belonging, supposedly, to the President of the United States. The public key will say that it belongs to the President, but it actually would belong to an imposter. It is important for a PKI to provide assurance that public keys actually belong to the person who is named in the public key. This is done via an external assurance link; to get a key pair, one demonstrates to a human that they are who they claim to be. For example, the user could, as part of the routine on the first day of employment, show his driver's license to the appropriate individual, known as a registration authority. The registration authority (RA) generates a key pair for the individual and tells the certificate authority (CA) to attest that the public key belongs to the individual. The CA does this attestation by signing the public key with the CA's private key. All users trust the CA. Because only the CA could access the CA's private key, and the private key is used to attest to the identity, all will believe that the user is in fact who the user claims to be. Thus, the CA (and associated RA) is required in order for the PKI to be useful, and any compromise of the CA's key is fatal for the entire PKI. CAs and RAs are usually part of the basic package bought from a PKI vendor. An abridged list of PKI vendors (in alphabetical order) includes Baltimore, Entrust Technologies, RSA Security, and Verisign.

When one user (or server) wants to send an encrypted object to another, the sender must get the recipient's public key. For large organizations, there can be thousands of public keys, stored as certificates signed by the CA. It does not make sense for every user to store all other certificates, due to storage constraints. Hence, a centralized storage site (or sites) must store the certificates. These sites are databases, usually accessed via the Lightweight Directory Access Protocol (LDAP), and normally called directory servers. A directory server will provide access throughout the enterprise to the certificates when an entity requires one. There are several vendors for LDAP directories, including Netscape, ICL, Novell, and Microsoft.

There are other roles for directory servers, including escrow of users' private keys. There are several reasons why an organization might need access to users' private keys. If an organization is served by a warrant, it may be required to provide access to encrypted objects. Achieving this usually involves having a separate copy of users' private keys; this copy is called an "escrowed" key. LDAP directories are usually used for escrow purposes. Obviously, these escrow databases must be extremely tightly secured, because access to a user's private key compromises all that user's correspondence and actions. Other reasons to store users' private keys include business continuity planning and compliance monitoring.

When a sender gets a recipient's public key, the sender cannot be sure that the recipient still works for the organization, and does not know if someone has somehow compromised that key pair. Human resources, however, will know that the recipient has left the organization and the user may know that the private key has been compromised. In either case, the certificate signed by the CA — and the associated private key — must be revoked. Key revocation is the process through which a key is declared invalid. Much as it makes little sense for clients to store all certificates, it is not sensible for clients to store all revoked certificates. Rather, a centralized database — called a certificate revocation list (CRL) — should be used to store revoked certificates. The CRL holds identifiers for all revoked certificates. Whenever an entity tries to use a certificate, it must check the CRL in order to ensure that the certificate is still valid; if an entity is presented a revoked certificate, it should log the event as a possible attack on the infrastructure. CRLs are often stored in LDAP databases, in data structures accessible through Online Certificate Status Processing (OCSP), or on centralized revocation servers, as in Valicert's Certificate Revocation Tree service. Some PKIs have ability to check CRLs, such as Entrust's Entelligence client, but most rely on custom software development to handle CRL checking. Additionally, even for PKIs supporting CRL checking, the capabilities do not provide access to other organization's CRLs — only a custom LDAP solution or a service such as, for example, Valicert's, can provide this inter-organization (or inter-PKI) capability.

Off-the-shelf PKI tools are often insufficient to provide complete auditing, dual authentication, CRL checking, operating system integration, and application integration. To provide these services, custom development must be performed. Such development requires that the application and PKI both support application programming interfaces (APIs). The API is the language that the application talks and through which the application is extended. There are public APIs for directory servers, operating system authentication, CRL checking, and many more functions. It is very common for applications to support one or more APIs. Many PKI vendors have invested heavily in the creation of toolkits — notably RSA Security, Entrust Technologies, and Baltimore.

For both performance and security reasons, hardware cryptographic support can be used as part of a PKI. The hardware support is used to generate and store keys and also to speed cryptographic operations. The CA and RAs will almost always require some sort of hardware support to generate and store keys. Potential devices include smart cards, PCMCIA cards, or external devices. An abridged list of manufacturers includes Spyrus, BBN, Atalla, Schlumberger, and Rainbow. These devices can cost anywhere from a few dollars up to $5000, depending on model and functionality. They serve not only to increase the performance of CA encryption, but also to provide additional security for the CA private key, because it is difficult to extract the private key from a hardware device.

Normally, one would not employ a smart card on a CA but, if desired, user private keys can be stored on smart cards. Such smart cards may provide additional functionality, such as physical access to company premises. Employing a smart card provides higher security for the user's private key because there is (virtually) no way for the user's private key to be removed from the card, and all computations are performed on the card itself. The downside of smart cards is that each card user must be given both a card and a card reader. Note that additional readers are required anywhere a user wishes to employ the card. There are several card manufacturers, but only some cards work with some PKI selections. The card manufacturers include Spyrus, Litronic, Datakey, and GemPlus. In general, the cards cost approximately $100 per user, including both card and reader.

However, the most important element of a PKI is not a physical element at all, but rather the policies that guide design, implementation, and operation of the PKI. These policies are critical to the success of a PKI, yet are often given short shrift during implementation. The policies are called a "Certificate Practice Statement" (CPS). A CPS includes, among other things, direction about how users are to identify themselves to an RA in order to get their key pair; what the RA should do when a user loses his password (and hence cannot unlock his private key); and how keys should be escrowed, if at all. Additionally, the CPS covers areas such as backup policies for the directory servers, CA, and RA machines. There are several good CPS examples that serve as the starting point for an implementation. A critical element of the security of the entire system is the sanctity of the CA itself — the root key material, the software that signs certificate requests, and the OS security itself. Extremely serious attention must be paid to the operational policies — how the system is administered, background checks on the administrators, multiple-person control, etc. — of the CA server.

The technology that underpins a PKI is little different from that of other enterprisewide systems. The same concerns that would apply to, for example, a mission-critical database system should be applied to the PKI components. These concerns include business continuity planning, stress and load modeling, service-level agreements with any outsourced providers or contract support, etc. The CA software often runs either on Windows NT or one of the UNIX variants, depending on the CA vendor. The RA software is often a Windows 9x client. There are different architectures for a PKI. These architectures vary, depending on, among other factors, the number and location of CA and RA servers, the location, hierarchy, and replication settings of directory servers, and the "chain of trust" that carries from sub-CA servers (if any) back to the root CA server. Latency, load requirements, and the overall security policy should dictate the particular architecture employed by the PKI.

## OTHER PKI BENEFITS: REDUCED SIGN-ON

There are other benefits of a PKI implementation — especially the promise of reduced sign-on for users. Many applications require several authentication steps. For example, a user may employ one username and password pair to log on to his local desktop, others to log on to the servers, and yet more to access the application and data itself. This creates a user interaction nightmare; how many usernames and passwords can a user remember? A common solution to this problem is to employ "trust" relationships between the servers supporting an application. This reduces the number of logins a user must perform, because logging into one trusted host provides access to all others. However, it also creates a significant security vulnerability; if an attacker can access one trusted machine, the attacker has full access to all of them. This point has been exploited many times during Pricewaterhouse-Coopers attack and penetration exercises. The "attackers" find a development machine, because development machines typically are less secure than production machines, and attack it. After compromising the development machine, the trust relationships allow access to the production machines. Hence, the trust relationships mean that the security of the entire system is dependent not on the most secure systems — the production servers — but rather on the least secure ones.

Even using a trust relationship does not entirely solve the user interaction problem; the user still has at least one operating system username and password pair to remember and another application username and password. PKI systems offer a promising solution to this problem. The major PKI vendors have produced connecting software that replaces most operating system authentication processes with a process that is close to the PKI authentication system described above.

The operating system authentication uses access to the user's private key, which is unlocked with a password. After unlocking the private key, it can be used in the PKI authentication process described above. Once the private key is unlocked, it remains unlocked for a configurable period of time. The user would unlock the private key when first used, which would typically be when logging in to the user's desktop system. Hence, if the servers and applications use the PKI authentication mechanism, the users will not need to reenter a password — they need unlock the private key only once. Each system or application can, if desired, engage in authentication with the user's machine, but the user need not interact, because the private key is already unlocked. From the user's perspective, this is single sign-on, but without the loss of security provided by other partial solutions (such as trust relationships).

There are other authentications involved in day-to-day business operations. For example, many of us deal with legacy systems. These legacy systems have their own, often proprietary, authentication mechanisms. Third-party products provide connections between a PKI and these legacy applications. A username and password pair is stored in a protected database. When the user attempts to access the legacy application, a "proxy" application requests PKI-based authentication. After successfully authenticating the user — which may not require reentry of the user's PKI password — the server passes the legacy application the appropriate username and password and connects the client to the legacy application. The users need not remember the username and password for the legacy application because they are stored in the database. Because the users need not remember the password, the password can be as complicated as the legacy application will accept, thus making security compromise of the legacy application more difficult while still minimizing user interaction headaches.

Finally, user keys, as mentioned above, can be stored as files or on tokens, often called smart cards. The user inserts the smart card into a reader attached to the desktop and authenticates to the card, which unlocks the private key. From then on, the card will answer challenges sent to it and issue them in turn, taking the part of the client machine in the example above. Smart cards can contain more than simply the user keys, although this is their main function. For example, a person's picture can be printed onto the smart card, thus providing a corporate identification badge. Magnetic stripes can be put on the back of the smart card and encoded with normal magnetic information. Smart card manufacturers can build proximity transmitters into their smart cards. These techniques allow the same card that authenticates the user to the systems to allow the user access to the physical premises of the office. In this model, the PKI provides not only secure access to the entity's systems and applications with single sign-on, but also to physically secured areas of the entity. Such benefits are driving the increase in the use of smart cards for cryptographic security.

## PKI IN OPERATION

With the background of how a PKI works and descriptions of its components, one can now walk through an end-to-end example of how a hypothetical organization might operate its PKI.

Imagine a company, DCMEF, Inc., which has a few thousand employees located primarily in southern California. DCMEF, Inc. makes widgets used in the manufacture of automobile air bags. DCMEF uses an ERP system for manufacturing planning and scheduling as well as for its general ledger and payables. It uses a shop-floor data management system to track the manufacturing process, and has a legacy system to maintain human resource-related information. Employees are required to wear badges at all times when in the facility, and these same picture badges unlock the various secured doors at the facility near the elevators and at the entrances to the shop floor via badge readers.

DCMEF implemented its PKI in 1999, using commercial products for CA and directory services. The CA is located in a separately secured data center, with a warm standby machine locked in a disaster recovery site in the Midwest. The warm standby machine does not have keying material. The emergency backup CA key is stored in a safety deposit box that requires the presence of two corporate officers or directors to access. The CA is administered by a specially cleared operations staff member who does not have access to the logging server, which ensures that that operations person cannot ask the CA to do anything (such as create certificates) without a third person seeing the event. The RA clients are scattered through human resources, but are activated with separate keys, not the HR representatives' normal day-to-day keys.

When new employees are hired, they are first put through a two-day orientation course. At this course, the employees fill out their benefits forms, tax information, and also sign the data security policy form. After signing the form, each employee is given individual access to a machine that uses cryptographic hardware support to generate a key pair for that user. The public half of the key pair is submitted to the organization's CA for certification by the human resources representative, who is serving as the RA, along with the new employee's role in the organization.

The CA checks to ensure that the certificate request is correctly formed and originated with the RA. Then, the CA creates and signs a certificate for the new employee, and returns the signed certificate to the human resources representative. The resulting certificate is stored on a smart card at that time, along with the private key. The private key is locked on the smart card with a PIN selected by the user (and known only to that user). DCMEF's CPS specifies a four-digit PIN, and prohibits use of common patterns like "1234" or "1111." Hence, each user selects four digits; those who select inappropriate PIN values are prompted to select again until their selection meets DCMEF policies.

A few last steps are required before the user is ready to go. First, a copy of each user's private key is encrypted with the public key of DCMEF's escrow agent and stored in the escrow database. Then, the HR representative activates the WWW-based program that stores the new employee's certificate in the directory server, along with the employee's phone number and other information, and adds the employee to the appropriate role entry in the authentication database server. After this step, other employees will be able to look up the new employee in the company electronic phone book, be able to encrypt e-mail to the new employee, and applications will be able to determine the information to which the employee should have access. After these few steps, the user is done generating key material.

The key generating machine is rebooted before the next new employee uses it. During this time, the new employee who is finished generating a key pair is taken over to a digital camera for an identification photograph. This photograph is printed onto the smart card, and the employee's identification number is stored on the magnetic strip on the back of the card to enable physical access to the appropriate parts of the building.

At this point, the new employees return to the orientation course, armed with their smart cards for building access loaded with credentials for authentication to the PKI. This entire process took less than 15 minutes per employee, with most of that spent typing in information.

The next portion of the orientation course is hands-on instruction on using the ERP modules. In a normal ERP implementation, users have to log on to their client workstation, to an ERP presentation server and, finally, to the application itself. In DCMEF, Inc., users need only insert their smart cards into the readers attached to their workstations (via either the serial port or a USB port, in this case), and they are logged in transparently to their local machine and to every PKI-aware application — including the ERP system. When the employees insert their smart cards, they are prompted for the PIN to unlock their secret key. The remainder of the authentication to the client workstation is done automatically, in roughly the manner described above. When the user starts the ERP front-end application, it expects to be given a valid certificate for authentication purposes, and expects to be able to look that certificate up in an authorization database to select which ERP data this user's role can access. Hence, after the authentication process between ERP application server and user (with the smart card providing the user's credentials) completes, the user has full access to the appropriate ERP data. The major ERP packages are PKI-enabled using vendor toolkits and internal application-level controls. However, it is not always so easy to PKI-enable a legacy application, such as DCMEF's shop-floor data manager. In this case, DCMEF could have chosen to leave the legacy application entirely alone, but that would have meant users would need to remember a different username and password pair to gain access to the shop-floor information, and corporate security would need to manage a second set of user credentials. Instead, DCMEF decided to use a gateway approach to the legacy application. All network access to the shop-floor data manager system was removed, and replaced by a single gateway in or out. This gateway ran customized proxy software that uses certificates to authenticate users. However, the proxy issues usernames and passwords that match the user's role to the shop-floor data manager. There are fewer roles than users, so it is easier to maintain a database of role-password pairs, and the shop-floor data manager itself does not know that anything has changed. The proxy application must be carefully designed and implemented, because it is now a single point of failure for the entire application, and the gateway machine should be hardened against attack.

The user credentials issued by HR expire in 24 months — this period was selected based on the average length of employment at DCMEF, Inc. Hence, every two years, users must renew their certificates. This is done via an automatic process; users visit an intranet WWW site and ask for renewal. This request is routed to human resources, which verifies that the person is still employed and is still in the same role. If appropriate, the HR representative approves the request, and the CA issues a new certificate — with the same public key — to the employee, and adds the old certificate to DCMEF's revocation list. If an employee leaves the company, HR revokes the user's certificate (and hence the user's access to applications) by asking the CA to add the certificate to the public revocation list. In DCMEF's architecture, a promoted user needs no new certificate, but HR must change the permissions associated with that certificate in the authorization database.

This example is not futuristic at all — everything mentioned here is easily achievable using commercial tools. The difficult portions of this example are related to DCMEF itself. HR, manufacturing, planning, and accounting use the PKI on a day-to-day basis. Each of these departments has its own needs and concerns that need to be addressed up front, before implementation, and then training, user acceptance, and updates must include each department going forward. A successful PKI implementation will involve far more than corporate information security — it will involve all the stakeholders in the resulting product.

### IMPLEMENTING A PKI: GETTING THERE FROM HERE

The technical component of building a PKI requires five logical steps:

1. The policies that govern the PKI, known as a Certificate Practice Statement (CPS), must be created.
2. The PKI that embodies the CPS must be initialized.
3. Users and administration staff must be trained.
4. Connections to secured systems that could circumvent the PKI must be ended.
5. Any other system integration work — such as integrating legacy applications with the PKI, using the PKI for operating system authentication, or connecting back-office systems including e-mail or human resource systems to the PKI — must be done.

The fourth and fifth steps may not be appropriate for all organizations.

The times included here are based on the authors' experience in designing and building PKI systems, but will vary for each situation. Some of the variability comes from the size of clients; it requires more time to build a PKI for more users. Other variability derives from a lack of other standards; it is difficult to build a PKI if the organization supports neither Windows NT nor UNIX, for example. In any case, the numbers provided here offer a glimpse into the effort involved in implementing a PKI as part of an ERP implementation.

The first step is to create a CPS. Creating a CPS involves taking a commonly accepted framework, such as the National Automated Clearing House Association guidelines, PKIX-4, or the framework promulgated by Entrust Technologies, and adapting it to the needs of the particular organization. The adaptations involve modification of roles to fit organizational structures and differences in state and federal regulation. This step involves interviews and extensive study of the structure and the environment within which the organization falls. Additionally, the CPS specifies the vendor for the PKI as well as for any supporting hardware or software, such as smart cards or directories. Hence, building a CPS includes the analysis stage of the PKI selection. Building a CPS normally requires approximately three person-months, assuming that the organization has in place certain components, such as an e-mail policy and Internet use policy, and results in a document that needs high-level approval, often including legal review.

The CPS drives the creation of the PKI, as described above. Once the CPS is complete, the selected PKI vendor and products must be acquired. This involves hardware acquisition for the CA, any RA stations, the directories, and secure logging servers, as well as any smart cards, readers, and other hardware cryptographic modules. Operating system and supporting software must be installed on all servers, along with current security-related operating system patches. The servers must all be hardened, as the security of the entire system relies to some extent on their security. Additional traditional information security work, such as the creation of intrusion detection systems, is normally required in this phase. Many of the servers — especially the logging server — will require hardware support for the cryptographic operations they must perform; these cryptographic support modules must be installed on each server. Finally, with the pieces complete, the PKI can be installed.

Installing the PKI requires, first, generating a "root" key and using that root key to generate a CA key. This generation normally requires hardware support. The CA key is used to generate the RA keys that in turn generate all user public keys and associated private keys. The CA private key signs users' public keys, creating the certificates that are stored on the directory server. Additionally, the RA must generate certificates for each server that requires authentication. Each user and server certificate and the associated role — the user's job — must be entered into a directory server to support use of the PKI by, for example, secure e-mail. The server keys must be installed in the hardware cryptographic support modules, where appropriate. Client-side software must be installed on each client to support use of the client-side certificates. Additionally, each client browser must be configured to accept the organization's CA key and to use the client's certificate. These steps, taken together, constitute the initialization of the PKI. The time required to initialize a PKI is largely driven by the number of certificates required. In a recent project involving 1000 certificates, ten applications, and widespread use of smart cards, the PKI initialization phase required approximately twelve person-months. Approximately two person-months of that time were spent solely on the installation of the smart cards and readers.

Training cannot be overlooked when installing a large-scale system such as a PKI. With the correct architecture, much of the PKI details are below users' awareness, which minimizes training requirements. However, the users have to be shown how to unlock their certificates, a process that replaces their login, and how to use any ancillary PKI services, such as secure e-mail and the directory. This training is usually done in groups of 15 to 30 and lasts approximately one to two hours, including hands-on time for the trainees.

After training is completed, users and system administration staff are ready to use the PKI. At this point, one can begin to employ the PKI itself. This involves ensuring that any applications or servers that should employ the PKI cannot be reached without using the PKI. Achieving this goal often requires employing third-party network programs that interrupt normal network processing to require the PKI. Additionally, it may require making configuration changes to routers and operating systems to block back door entry into the applications and servers. Blocking these back-doors requires finding all connections to servers and applications; this is a non-trivial analysis effort that must be included in the project planning.

Finally, an organization may want to use the PKI to secure applications and other business processes. For example, organizations, as described above, may want to employ the PKI to provide single sign-on or legacy system authentication. This involves employing traditional systems integration methodologies — and leveraged software methodologies — to mate the PKI to these other applications using various application programming interfaces. Estimating this effort requires analysis and requirements assessment.

As outlined here, a work plan for creating a PKI would include five steps. The first step is to create a CPS. Then, the PKI is initialized. Third, user and administrator training must be performed. After training, the PKI connections must be enforced by cutting off extraneous connections. Finally, other system integration work, including custom development, is performed.

## CONCLUSION

Security is an enabler for electronic business; without adequate security, senior management may not feel confident moving away from more expensive and slower traditional processes to more computer-intensive ones. Security designers must find usable solutions to organizational requirements for authentication, authorization, confidentiality, and integrity. Public key infrastructures offer a promising technology to serve as the foundation for E-business security designs. The technology itself has many components — certificate authorities, registration authorities, directory servers — but, even more importantly, requires careful policy and procedure implementation.

This chapter has described some of the basics of cryptography, both secret and public key cryptography, and has highlighted the technical and procedural requirements for a PKI. The authors have presented the five high-level steps that are required to implement a PKI, and have listed some vendors in each of the component areas. Obviously, in a chapter this brief, it is not possible to present an entire workplan for implementing a PKI — especially since the plans vary significantly from situation to situation. However, the authors have tried to give the reader a start toward such a plan by describing the critical factors that must be addressed, and showing how they all work together to provide an adequate return on investment.

### Additional Reading

1. Jonathan S. Held, Password Security, *Data Security Management,* April 2000, No. 83-01-11.
2. William S. Murray, Principles and Applications of Key Management, *Data Security Management,* June 1998, No. 83-10-50.

# Chapter 48
# Getting Started with PKI

*Harry DeMaio*

IN THE RECENT HISTORY OF INFORMATION PROTECTION, THERE HAS BEEN AN ONGOING PARADE OF TECHNOLOGIES THAT LOUDLY PROMISE NEW AND TOTAL SOLUTIONS BUT FREQUENTLY DO NOT MAKE IT PAST THE REVIEWING STAND. In some cases, they break down completely at the start of the march. In others, they end up turning down a side street. Is Public Key Infrastructure (PKI) just another gaudy float behind more brass bands, or is there sufficient rationale to believe that this one might make it? There are some very good reasons for optimism in this case, but we have been overly optimistic before.

This chapter examines PKI as objectively as possible, in hopes of arriving at some sort of consensus. To do that, one needs to know more than just the design principles. Many a slick and sophisticated design has turned embarrassingly sour when implemented and put into application and operational contexts. There are also the questions of economics, market readiness, and operational/technological prerequisites, all of which can march a brilliant idea into a blind alley.

## Approach and Preliminary Discussion

One can begin with a short review of the changing requirements for security. Is there really a need, especially in networking, that did not exist before for new security technologies and approaches? This chapter:

- Briefly describes encryption, public key encryption, and PKI
- Illustrates how well PKI satisfies today's needs from a design standpoint
- Delves into what is involved in actually making PKI a cost-effective reality
- Questions whether PKI is an exceptional approach or just one of many alternatives worth looking at

0-8493-1160-8/02/$0.00+$1.50
© 2002 by CRC Press LLC

## THE CHANGING WORLD OF NETWORKED SYSTEMS

Take a moment to compare a few characteristics of yesterday's and today's network-based information processing. If the differences can be summed up in a single phrase, it is "accelerated dynamics." The structure and components of most major networks are in a constant state of flux — as are the applications, transactions, and users that traverse its pathways. This has a profound influence on the nature, location, scope, and effectiveness of protective mechanisms.

Exhibit 1 illustrates some of the fundamental differences between traditional closed systems and open (often Internet-based) environments. These differences do much to explain the significant upsurge in interest in encryption technologies.

Clearly, each network is unique and most display a mix of the above characteristics. But the trends toward openness and variability are clear. The implications for security can be profound. Security embedded or "hard-wired" to the system and network infrastructure cannot carry the entire load in many of the more mobile and open environments, especially where dial-up is dominant. A more flexible mode that addresses the infrastructure, user, workstation, environment, and data objects is required.

An example: envision the following differences:

- A route salesperson who returns to the office workstation in the evening to enter the day's orders (online batch)
- That same worker now entering, on a laptop through a radio or dial-up phone link, those same orders as they are being taken at the customer's premises (dial-up interactive)
- Third-party operators taking orders at an 800-888 call center
- Those same orders being entered by the customer on a Web site
- A combination of the above

The application is still the same: order entry. However, the process is dramatically different, ranging from batch entry to Web-based E-commerce.

**Exhibit 1.  Open versus Closed Networks**

|  | Legacy/Closed Network | Modern Open Network |
|---|---|---|
| User environments | Known and stable | Mobile/variable |
| End points | Established | Dynamic/open |
| Network structure | Established/known | Dynamic/open |
| Processing | Mainframe/internally distributed | Multi-site/multi-enterprise |
| Data objects | Linked to defined process | Often independent |

In the first case, the infrastructure, environment, process, and user are known, stable, and can be well controlled. The classic access control facility and/or security server generally carries the load.

In the second (interactive dial-up) instance, the employee (one needs to verify that it is an employee) is still directly involved. However, now one has a portable device and its on-board functions and data, the dial-up connections, the network, the points of entry to the enterprise, and the enterprise processes themselves to protect if one wants to achieve the same level of control as in the first instance.

The third instance involves a third party and the network connection can be closed or open.

The fourth (Web-based) approach adds the unknowns created by the customer's direct involvement and linkage through the Internet to the company's system.

Finally, the fifth, hybrid scenario calls for significant compatibility adjustments on top of the other considerations. By the way, this scenario is not unlikely. A fallacious assumption in promoting Web-based services is that one can readily discontinue the other service modes. It seldom happens.

Consider the changes to identification, authentication, and authorization targets and processes in each instance. Consider monitoring and the audit trail. Then consider the integrity and availability issues. Finally, the potential for repudiation begins to rear its ugly head. The differences are real and significant.

## THE EVOLVING BUSINESS NETWORK

Remember, too, that most network-based systems in operation today have evolved, or in many cases, accreted into their current state — adding infrastructures and applications on demand and using the technology available at the time. Darwin notwithstanding, some of the currently surviving networks are not necessarily the fittest. In most of the literature, networks are characterized as examples of a specific class — open/closed; intranet/extranet; LAN/WAN/Internet; protocol-X or protocol-Y. While these necessary and valuable distinctions can be used to describe physical and logical infrastructures, one must remember that when viewed from the business processes they support — supply chain, order entry, funds transfer, patient record processing — most "business process" nets are technological and structural hybrids.

The important point is that today security strategy and architecture decisions are being increasingly driven by specific business requirements, not just technology. This is especially true in the application of encryption-related techniques such as PKI. Looking again at the order entry example above, the application of consistent protective mechanisms for a hybrid order entry scenario will undoubtedly require compatibility and interoperability across platform and network types unless the entire system is rebuilt to one specification. This seldom happens unless the enterprise is embarking on a massive reengineering effort or deploying major application suites like SAP or PeopleSoft.

## THE DIS-INTEGRATION AND RE-INTEGRATION OF SECURITY MECHANISMS

To be effective, a protective mechanism must appropriately bind with the object and the environment requiring protection. In open networks, the connection, structure, and relationship of the components are more loosely defined and variable. Therefore, the protective mechanisms must be more granular, focused, and more directly linked to the object or process to be protected than was the case with legacy systems. Formerly, protection processes operated primarily at a "subterranean plumbing" level, surfacing only in password and authorization administration and logons. Now the castle moat is being supplemented with "no-go" zones, personal bodyguards posted at strategic spots, food tasters, and trusted messengers.

Encryption mechanisms fit this direct, granular requirement, often ideally, because they can protect individual files, data elements (including passwords), and paths (tunneling and virtual private networks), and manage access management requirements. (Identification and authentication through encryption is easier than authorization.) But saying that encryption is granular is not the same as saying that a PKI system is interoperable, portable, or scalable. In fact, it means that most encryption-related systems today are still piece parts, although some effective suites like Entrust are on the market and several others (e.g., IBM SecureWay and RSA/SD Keon) are now just entering.

This "dis-integrated" and specialized approach to providing security functions creates a frustrating problem for the security professional accustomed to integrated suites. Now the user becomes the integrator or must use a third-party integrator. The products may not integrate well or even be interface compatible. At the 1999 RSA Conference in San Jose, California, the clarion call for security suites was loud and clear. We will discuss this topic again shortly but first, a short digression.

The reader is probably familiar with encryption, but a brief summary follows.

Encryption is a process for making intelligible information unintelligible through the application of sophisticated mathematical conversion techniques. Obviously, to be useful, the process must be reversible (decryption). The three major components of the encryption-decryption process are:

1. *The information stream* in clear or encrypted form.
2. *The mathematical encryption process* — the algorithm. Interestingly enough, most commercial algorithms are publicly available and are not secret. What turns a public process into a uniquely secret one is the encryption key.
3. *The encryption key.* The encryption key is a data string that is mathematically combined with the information (clear or encrypted) by the algorithm to produce the opposite version of the data (encrypted or clear). Remember that all data on computers is represented in binary number coding. Binary numbers can be operated upon by the same arithmetic functions as those that apply to decimal numbers. Thus, by a combining process of complex arithmetic operations, the data and key are converted into an encrypted message form and decrypted using the same process and same key (**WITH ONE CRITICAL EXCEPTION**).

Before explaining the exception, one more definition is required. The process that uses the same key to decrypt and encrypt is called symmetric cryptography. However, it also has several advantages, including exceptional speed on computers. It has a serious drawback. In any population of communicating users (n), in order to have *individually unique* links between each pair of users, the total number of keys required is n(n + 1)/2. (Try it with a small number and round up.) If the population of users gets large enough, the number of individual keys required rapidly becomes unmanageable. This is one (but not the only) reason why symmetric cryptography has not had a great reception in the commercial marketplace in the last 20 years.

The salvation of cryptography for practical business use has been the application of a different class of cryptographic algorithms using asymmetric key pairs. The mathematics is complex and not intuitively obvious, but the result is a pair of linked keys that must be used together. However, only one of the pair — the private key — must be kept secret by the key owner. The other half of the pair — the public key — can be openly distributed to anyone wishing to communicate with the key owner. A partial analogy is the cash depository in which all customers have the same key for depositing through a one-way door, but only the bank official has a key to open the door for extracting the cash. This technique vastly reduces the number of keys required for the same population to communicate safely and uniquely.

## ENTER PKI

If the public key is distributed openly, how does one know that it is valid and belongs with the appropriate secret key and the key owner? How does one manage the creation, use, and termination of these key pairs. That is the foundation of Public Key Infrastructure (PKI). Several definitions follow:

> The comprehensive system required to provide public key encryption and digital signature services is known as the *public key infrastructure* (PKI). The purpose of a public key infrastructure is to manage keys and certificates.
>
> — Entrust Inc.

> A public key infrastructure (PKI) consists of the programs, data formats, communications protocols, institutional policies, and procedures required for enterprise use of public key cryptography.
>
> — Office of Information Technology, University of Minnesota

> In its most simple form, a PKI is a system for publishing the public key values used in public key cryptography. There are two basic operations common to all PKIs:
>
> 1. Certification is the process of binding a public key value to an individual organization or other entity, or even to some other piece of information such as a permission or credential.
>
> 2. Validation is the process of verifying that a certificate is still valid.
>
> How these two operations are implemented is the basic defining characteristic of all PKIs.
>
> — Marc Branchaud

## THE DIGITAL CERTIFICATE AND CERTIFICATE AUTHORITIES

Obviously, from these definitions, a digital certificate is the focal point of the PKI process. What is it? In simplest terms, a digital certificate is a credential (in digital form) in which the public key of the individual is embedded along with other identifying data. That credential is encrypted (signed) by a trusted third party or certificate authority (CA) who has established the identity of the key owner (similar to but more rigorous than notarization). The "signing key" ties the certificate back to the CA and ultimately to the process that bound the certificate holder to his or her credentials and identity proof process.

By "signing" the certificate, the CA establishes and takes liability for the authenticity of the public key contained in the certificate and the fact that it is bound to the named user. Now, total strangers who know or at least trust a common CA can use encryption not just to *conceal* the data, but also to *authenticate* the other party. The integrity of the message is also ensured. If one changes the message once encrypted, it will not decrypt. The message *cannot be repudiated* because it has been encrypted using the sender's certificate.

Who are CAs? Some large institutions are their own CAs — especially banks (private CAs). There are some independent services (public CAs) developing, and government, using the licensing model as a takeoff point, is moving into this environment. It may become a new security industry. In the Netherlands, KNB, the Dutch notary service, supplies digital certificates.

As one might expect, there has been a move on the part of some security professionals to include more and more information in the certificate, making it a multi-purpose "document." There is one major problem with this. Consider a driver's license, printed on special watermarked paper, with one's picture and encapsulated in plastic. If one wanted to maintain more volatile information on it, such as current make of car(s), doctor's name and address, or next of kin, one would have to get a new license for each change.

The same is true for a certificate. Back one goes to the CA for a new certificate each time one wants to make a change. For a small and readily accessible population, this may be reasonable. However, PKI is usually justified based on large populations in open environments, and often across multiple enterprises. The cost and administrative logjam can build up with the addition of authorization updates, *embedded in the certificate*. This is why relatively changeable authorization data (permissions) is seldom embedded in the certificate, but rather attached. There are several certificate structures that allow attachments or permissions that can be changed independently of the certificate itself.

To review: the certificate is the heart of the PKI system. A given population of users who wish to intercommunicate selects or is required to use a specific CA to obtain a certificate. That certificate contains the public key half of an asymmetric key pair as well as other indicative information about the target individual. This individual is referred to as the "distinguished name" — implying that there can be no ambiguities in certificate-based identification; all Smiths must be separately distinguished by ancillary data.

**Where Are Certificates Used?**

Certificates are used primarily in open environments where closed-network security techniques are inappropriate or insufficient for any or all of the following:

- Identification/authentication
- Confidentiality
- Message/transaction integrity
- Non-repudiation

Not all PKI systems serve the same purposes or have the same protective priorities. This is very important to understand when one is trying to justify a PKI system for a specific business environment.

### How Does PKI Satisfy Those Business Environment Needs?

**Market Expectation.** As PKI becomes interoperable, scalable, and generally accepted, companies will begin to accept the wide use of encryption-related products. Large enterprises such as government, banks, and large commercial firms will develop trust models to easily incorporate PKI into everyday business use.

**Current Reality.** It is not that easy! Thus far, a significant number of PKI projects have been curtailed, revised, or temporarily shelved for reevaluation. The reasons most often given are:

- Immature technology
- Insufficient planning and preparation
- Underestimated scope
- Infrastructure and procedural costs
- Operational and technical incompatibilities
- Unclear cost-benefits

### APPARENT CONCLUSIONS ABOUT THE MARKETPLACE

PKI has compelling justifications for many enterprises, but there are usually more variables and pitfalls than anticipated. Broadside implementation, while sometimes necessary, has not been as cost-effective. Pilots and test beds are strongly recommended.

A properly designed CA/RA administrative function is always a critical success factor.

### CERTIFICATES, CERTIFICATE AUTHORITIES (CAs), AND REGISTRATION AUTHORITIES (RAs)

How do they work and how are they related?

First take a look at the PKI certificate life cycle itself. It is more involved than one might think. A digital certificate is a secure and trustworthy credential; and the process of its creation, use, and termination must be appropriately controlled.

Not all certificates are considered equally secure and trustworthy and this in itself is an active subject of standards and industry discussion. The strength of the cryptography supporting the certificate is actually only one discriminating factor. The degree to which the certificate complies with a given standard (e.g., X.509) is another criterion for trustworthiness. The standards cover a wide range of requirements, including content, configuration, and process. Spend a moment on process. The following is hardly an exhaustive list, but it does provide some insight into some of the basic requirements.

1. *Application*. How do the "certificate owners to-be" apply for a certificate? To whom do they apply? What supporting materials are required? Must a face-to-face interview be conducted, or can a surrogate act for the subject? What sanctions are imposed for false, incomplete, or misleading statements? How is the application stored and protected, etc.?
2. *Validation*. How is the applicant's identity validated? By what instruments? By what agencies? For what period of time?
3. *Issuance*. Assuming the application meets the criteria and the validation is successful, how is the certificate actually issued? Are third parties involved? Is the certificate sent to the individual, or in the case of an organization, some officer of that organization? How is issuance recorded? How are those records maintained and protected?
4. *Acceptance*. How does the applicant indicate acceptance of the certificate? To whom? Is non-repudiation of acceptance eliminated?
5. *Use*. What are the conditions of use? Environments, systems, applications?
6. *Suspension or revocation*. In the event of compromise or suspension, who must be notified? How? How soon after the event? How is the notice of revocation published?
7. *Expiration and renewal*. Terms, process, and authority?

## Who and What Are the PKI Functional Entities to Consider?

### Certification Authority (CA)

1. A person or institution
2. Trusted by others
3. Vouch for the authenticity of a public key
4. May be a principal (e.g., management, bank, credit card issuer)
5. Secretary of a "club" (e.g., bank clearing house)
6. A government agency or designee (e.g., notary public, DMV, or post office)
7. An independent third party operating for profit (e.g., VeriSign)
8. Makes a decision on evidence or knowledge, after due diligence
9. Records the decision by signing a certificate with its private key
10. Authorizes issuance of certificate

### Registration Authority (RA)

1. Manages certificate life cycle, including:
   a. Certificate directory maintenance

    b.   CRL (certificate revocation list(s)) maintenance and publication
2.  thus can be:
    a.   A critical choke point in PKI process
    b.   A critical liability point, especially as relates to CRLs
3.  An RA may or may not be a CA

### Other Entities

1. *Other trusted third parties.* These may be service organizations that manage the PKI process, brokers who procure certificates from certificate suppliers, or independent audit or consulting groups that evaluate the security of the PKI procedure
2. *Individual subscribers.*
3. *Business subscribers.* In many large organizations, two additional constructs are used:
   a. *The responsible individual* (RI). The enterprise certificate administrator
   b. *The responsible officer* (RO). The enterprise officer who legally assures the company's commitment to the certificate. In many business instances, it is actually more important to know that this certificate is backed by a viable organization that will accept liability than to be able to fully identify the actual certificate holder. (Author note: In a business transaction, the fact that I can prove I am a partner in Deloitte & Touche LLP who is empowered to commit the Firm usually means more than who I am personally.)

PKI policies and related statements include:

1. Certificate policy
2. Named set of rules governing certificate usage, with common security requirements tailored to the operating environment within the enterprise
3. Certificate Practices Statement (CPS):
   a. Detailed set of rules governing the Certificate Authority's operations
   b. Technical and administrative security controls
   c. Audit
4. Key management
5. Liability, financial stability, due diligence
6. CA contractual requirements and documents
7. Subscriber enrollment and termination processes

## THE CERTIFICATE REVOCATION LIST (CRL)

Of all the administrative and control mechanisms required by a PKI, the CRL function can be one of the more complex and subtle activities. The

CRL is an important index of the overall trustworthiness of the specific PKI environment. Normally, it is considered part of the RA's duties. Essentially, the CRL is the instrument for checking the continued validity of the certificates for which the RA has responsibility. If a certificate is compromised, if the holder is no longer authorized to use the certificate, or if there is a fault in the binding of the certificate to the holder, it must be revoked and taken out of circulation as rapidly as possible. All parties in the trust relationship must be informed. The CRL is usually a highly controlled, online database (it may take any number of graphic forms) from which subscribers and administrators can determine the currency of a target partner's certificate. This process can vary dramatically in terms of:

1. *Timing/frequency of update.* Be careful of the language here. Many RAs claim a 24-hour update. That means the CRL is refreshed every 24 hours. It does not necessarily mean that the total cycle time for a particular revocation to be posted is 24 hours. It may be longer.
2. *Push-pull.* This refers to the way in which subscribers can get updates from the CRL. Most CRLs today require subscribers to pull the current update. A few private RAs (see below) employ a push methodology. There is a significant difference in cost and complexity and, more importantly, the line of demarcation between the RAs and the subscriber's responsibility and liability. For lessened liability alone, most RAs prefer the pull mode.
3. *Up link/down link.* There are two transmissions in the CRL process: the link from the revoking agent to the CRL and the distribution by the CRL to the subscribing universe. Much work has been exerted by RAs to increase the efficiency of the latter process; but because it depends on the revoking agency, the uplink is often an Achilles' heel. Obviously, the overall time is a combination of both processes, plus file update time.
4. *Cross domain.* The world of certificates can involve multiple domains and hierarchies. Each domain has a need to know the validity status of all certificates used within its bounds. In some large extranet environments, this may involve multiple and multi-layer RA and CRL structures. Think this one through very carefully and be aware that the relationships may change each time the network encompasses a new environment.
5. *Integrity.* A major way to undermine the trustworthiness of a PKI environment is to compromise the integrity of the CRL process. If one cannot ensure the continued validity of the certificate population, the entire system is at risk.
6. *Archiving.* How long should individual CRLs be kept, and for what purposes?
7. *Liabilities and commitments.* These should be clearly, unambiguously, and completely stated by all parties involved. In any case of message

or transaction compromise traceable to faulty PKI process, the RA is invariably going to be involved. Ensure a common understanding.

As one might expect, CAs and RAs come in a variety of types. Some of the more common are:

1. *Full-service public CA,* providing RA, certificate generation, issuance, and life-cycle management [Examples: VeriSign, U.S. Postal Service (USPS), TradeWave]
2. *Branded public CA,* providing RA, certificate issuance, and life cycle management
3. *Certificates generated by a trusted party* [Examples: VeriSign and GTE CyberTrust; IDMetrix/GTE CyberTrust and Sumitomo Bank/VeriSign]
4. *Private CAs,* using CA turnkey system solutions internally [Examples: ScotiaBank (Entrust), Lexis-Nexis (VeriSign On-Site)]
5. *IBM Vault Registry*

There are also wide variations in trust structure models. This is driven by the business process and network architecture:

- Hierarchical trust (a classical hierarchy that may involve multiple levels and a large number of individual domains)
- VeriSign, Entrust
- X.509v3 certificates
- One-to-one binding of certificate and public key
- Web of Trust (a variation on peer relationships between domains)
- PGP
- Many-to-one binding of certificates and public key
- Constrained or lattice-of-trust structures
- Hybrid of hierarchical and Web models
- Xcert

There are a large number of standards, guidelines, and practices that are applicable to PKI. This is both a blessing and a curse. The most common are listed below. Individual explanations can be obtained from several Web sites. Start at the following site which has a very comprehensive set of PKI links: http://www.cert.dfn.de/eng/team/ske/pem-dok.html. This is one of the best PKI link sites available.

- X.500 Directory Services and X.509 Authentication
- Common Criteria (CC)
- ANSI X9 series
- DoD standards
- TCSEC, TSDM, SEI CMM
- IETF RFC — PKIX, PGP
- S/MIME, SSL, IPSec

- SET
- ABA guidelines
- Digital signatures, certification practices
- FIPS Publications 46, 140-1, 180-1, 186

**CA/RA Targets of Evaluation.** To comprehensively assess the trustworthiness of the individual CA/RA and the associated processes, Deloitte & Touche has developed the following list of required evaluation targets.

- System level (in support of the CA/RA process and certificate usage if applicable):
  — System components comprising CA/RA environment
  — Network devices
  — Firewalls, routers, and switches
  — Network servers
  — IP addresses of all devices
  — Client workstations
  — Operating systems and application software
  — Cryptographic devices
  — Physical security, monitoring, and authentication capabilities
- Data object level (in support of the CA/RA process and certificate usage):
  — Data structures used
  — Critical information flows
  — Configuration management of critical data items
  — Cryptographic data
  — Sensitive software applications
  — Audit records
  — Subscriber and certificate data
  — CRLs
  — Standards compliance where appropriate
- Application and operational level (repeated from above):
  — Certificate policy
  — Named set of rules governing certificate usage, with common security requirements tailored to the operating environment within the enterprise
  — Certificate Practices Statement (CPS):
  — Detailed set of rules governing the Certificate Authority's operations
  — Technical and administrative security controls
  — Audit
  — Key management
  — Liability, financial stability, due diligence
  — CA contractual requirements and documents
  — Subscriber enrollment and termination processes

## How Well Does PKI Satisfy Today's Open Systems Security Needs?

In a nutshell, PKI is an evolving process. It has the fundamental strength, granularity, and flexibility required to support the security requirements outlined at the beginning of this chapter. In that respect it is the best available alternative. But wholesale adoption of PKI as the best, final, and global solution for security needs is naive and dangerous. It should be examined selectively by business process or application to determine whether there is sufficient "value-added" to justify the direct and indirect cost associated with deployment. As suites such as Entrust and others become more adaptive and rich interfaces to ERP systems like SAP become more commonplace, PKI will likely become the security technology of choice for major, high-value processes. It will never be the only game in town. Uncomfortable or disillusioning as it may be, the security world will be a multi-solution environment for quite a while.

## What is Involved in Actually Making PKI a Cost-Effective Reality?

The most common approach to launching PKI is a pilot environment. Get your feet wet. Map the due diligence and procedural requirements against the organization's culture. Look at the volatility of the certificates that will be issued. What is their life expectancy and need for modification? Check the interface issues. What is the prospective growth curve for certificate use? How many entities will be involved? Is cross-certification a necessity? Above all else, examine the authorization process requirements that must coexist with PKI. PKI is not a full-function access control process. Look into the standards and regulations that affect your industry. Are there export control issues associated with the PKI solution one is attempting to deploy? Is interoperability a major requirement? If so, how flexible is the design of the solutions being considered?

The most popular approach to PKI today is the pilot project. This is not a "sandbox" or theoretical exercise. It usually involves putting an actual environment into play.

## CA PILOT CONSIDERATIONS

Type of pilot:

- *Proof of concept:* may be a test bed or an actual production environment
- *Operational:* a total but carefully scoped environment. Make sure there is a clear statement of expectations against which to measure functional and business results.
- *Inter-enterprise:* avoid this as a startup if possible, but sometimes it is the real justification for adopting PKI. If so, spend considerable time and effort getting a set of procedures and objectives agreed upon by

all the partners involved. An objective third-party evaluation can be very helpful here.

- Examine standards alternatives and requirements carefully — especially in a regulated industry.
- Check product and package compatibility, interoperability, and scalability VERY CAREFULLY.
- Develop alternative compatible product scenarios. At this stage of market maturity, a plan B is essential. Obviously, not all products are universally interchangeable. Develop a backup suite and do some preliminary testing on it.
- Investigate outsourced support as an initial step into the environment. While the company's philosophy may dictate an internally developed solution, the first round may be better deployed using outside resources.
- What are the service levels explicitly or implicitly required?
- Start internally with friendly environment. You need all the support you can get, especially from business process owners.
- Provide sufficient time and resource for procedural infrastructure development including CA policy, CPS, and training.
- Do not promise more than you can deliver!

### Is PKI an Exceptional Approach or Just One of Many Alternatives Worth Looking At?

The answer to this question depends primarily on the security objectives of the organization. PKI is ideal (but potentially expensive) for extranets and environments in which more traditional identification and authentication are insufficient. Tempting as it may be, resist the urge to find *the single solution*. Most networked-based environments and the associated enterprises are too complex at this moment for one single global solution. Examine the potential for SSL, SMIME, Kerberos, single-sign-on, and VPNs. If one can make the technical, operational, and cost-justification case for a single, PKI-based security approach, do so. PKI is a powerful structure but it is not a religious icon. Leave room for tailored multi-solution environments.

# Chapter 49
# Digital Signatures in Relational Database Applications

*Mike R. Prevost*

NOW THAT PUBLIC KEY ENCRYPTION AND ITS ASSOCIATED INFRASTRUCTURE (PKI) HAVE BECOME AN ACCEPTED FOUNDATION FOR SECURING THE ELECTRONIC WORLD, WE ARE SEEING A WEALTH OF NEW SECURITY PRODUCTS COME ON THE SCENE. However, it seems that many of these products are solving security problems related to the infrastructure upon which business applications run rather than the applications themselves. For example, virtual private network (VPN) products are beginning to support certificate-based authentication and public key-based key exchange. Secure sockets layor (SSL) is the standard for privacy and authentication on the Web. Although these types of technologies are completely necessary, they are all highly specialized and are invisible to the applications they are securing.

The nature of digital signature technology and its use in database-driven applications require a certain amount of application integration. It is this integration step that has been the primary technical stumbling block to the widespread use of digital signatures. PKI programming is still a "black art" known only to the few who have conquered its formidable layers of complexity. PKI integration projects have proven too costly and too risky for many application owners. As a result, organizations seem to be focusing on ways to add security to applications without performing complex integrations. However, as we move from securing our infrastructure to securing our applications, there is a growing genre of data security products that are making it easier to integrate security features such as digital signature into the applications themselves.

This chapter discusses the issues associated with integrating digital signature functionality into relational database applications. First, we discuss some concepts about digital signature and the role that digital signature plays in an application security strategy. Next we explain why relational

0-8493-1160-8/02/$0.00+$1.50
© 2002 by CRC Press LLC

database applications are different from other environments and discuss some of the pitfalls of various integration approaches. Then we outline an "application generic" solution to digitally signing data stored in relational databases that is very easy to integrate into applications.

## DIGITAL SIGNATURE CONCEPTS

In relational database applications, digital signatures are typically used to ensure data integrity and/or nonrepudiation (i.e., proof of origin). Since digital signatures are semantically similar to paper signatures, they are used to streamline business processes by reducing or entirely eliminating the need to print, sign, transfer, and store paper documents. The legal framework for holding signers accountable for documents they sign digitally is beginning to take shape.

Note that digital signature is only one element of a complete application security plan. Our focus on digital signature does not at all diminish the need for other technologies such as encryption, authentication, authorization, access control, firewalls, and intrusion detection. Digital signature does, however, provide important security services that are not addressed by other technologies.

### The Anatomy of a Transaction

When discussing application security, the term "transaction" is often used. This is a very vague term that brings to mind financial or business transactions. Sometimes the term "document" is used. For our immediate purposes, a transaction (or document) is any exchange between the user and the application that results in a change to data that is stored by the application. In database applications, the transaction data is stored in a relational database.

Exhibit 1 breaks a transaction into four steps. Each step has unique security requirements. This diagram will serve as a basis for illustrating how digital signatures fit into the overall security requirements of an application. The order of these steps may be different for some application architectures.

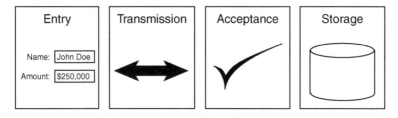

**Exhibit 1. Four Steps in a Transaction**

**Step 1: Data Entry.** Since transactions involve data, the data has to originate somewhere. This usually means that a user enters it on some sort of data entry screen. In this step, the application is probably concerned with data validation: ensuring that all required data fields are populated in a format that the application can understand. Applications may also want to prevent certain users from accessing certain data entry screens.

**Step 2: Data Transmission.** In many applications, transaction data is transferred across a network to a central application server or a database server. Applications may need to ensure that the transaction data is not altered during transmission. Also, the transaction may include sensitive information such as credit card numbers or other private personal information. It is also likely that applications may require assurance that the data is being transmitted to the intended recipient. The popular SSL protocol satisfies these requirements for Web-based applications. VPN technologies can provide these services also.

**Step 3: Acceptance.** At some point in the process, the application or application server "accepts" the transaction. That is, the transaction meets all the requirements necessary to be processed. Accepting a transaction may involve several elements.

- *Data Validation* — all required fields are entered in a format that the application can understand.
- *Integrity* — the data has not been altered during transmission to the application or database server.
- *Authentication* — the identity of the user has been firmly established.
- *Authorization* — the authenticated user has permission to perform this transaction.

**Step 4: Storage.** Since we are defining a transaction as an interaction between the user and the application that results in a change to the data stored in the database, the data must be stored. In many cases, a transaction requires that new data be written to the database. However, transactions might only change existing data. In either case, applications may need to ensure that the stored data is not changed, destroyed, or viewed by malicious or unauthorized users. These attacks can often be prevented by a strong access control mechanism and a good backup plan.

**Prevention versus Proof**

In the previous explanation, there is an element of transaction security that is missing. Let us examine what we do know at the acceptance stage (step 3).

- We know that all the required transaction data is entered in an acceptable format (validation).

- We know that the data has not been altered during transmission (integrity).
- We know that no one has viewed the data during transmission (privacy).
- We know the identity of the user performing the transaction (authentication).
- We know that the user has permission to perform the transaction (authorization).

It seems as though all the major security requirements have been met. The problem is that we know these things only during the brief period of time which the transaction is executed. Once the transaction is complete, this knowledge vanishes and cannot be reestablished because it cannot be stored along with the transaction data. However, digital signatures allow some of this knowledge to be captured and stored.

However, digital signatures do not protect data in the same way that other cryptographic techniques do. Digital signatures do not hide data from unauthorized viewers. This is provided by data encryption. Digital signatures cannot prevent data from being modified by external hackers or malicious insiders. This is provided by authentication and access control. Digital signatures simply allow an application to prove two things about the data they "protect":

- *Integrity* — the data has not been modified since it was signed.
- *Origin* — the identity of the signer can be cryptographically proven.

There is a significant difference between *preventing* changes to application data and being able to prove that the data has not been changed. This may seem like a fine line, but how do you *prove* that your access control mechanisms have not been compromised? It is much easier to prove that a security violation has occurred than it is to prove that one has not. If attempts to defraud your organization are detected, then the hacker has not done a good enough job.

If the transaction data is digitally signed, applications that rely on that data can prove that it has not changed and that it came from an authorized user. So, although digital signatures cannot prevent fraud from being attempted, they prevent attempted fraud from succeeding by giving applications the ability to detect fraudulent transactions.

The digital signature itself is a separate piece of data that must be stored with the transaction to facilitate this proof. The fact that digital signature impacts the data storage requirements of the application is another reason why digital signature functionality requires a tighter integration with the application than other security technologies.

## Paperless Business Processes

Exhibit 2 shows how digital signatures are typically used to implement a paperless process. In each step, the users are using an application that allows them to view and modify data that is stored in a central database. Note that each time a "document" is created or modified within the application, it is digitally signed. Each time that data is used, its signature is verified. This allows the relying user to be confident that the data in the database is genuine and was originated by an authorized user. The application performs the signing and verifying automatically whenever a document is stored or retrieved from the database. This enforces the security policy and prevents users from inadvertently skipping these steps. Since the application must know when to sign documents, when to verify them, and what to do when either of these operations fails, digital signature must be an integral part of the application's work flow logic.

## DATABASES ARE DIFFERENT

So far, we have discussed why digital signature is different from other security technologies. Relational database applications also have some unique qualities. These unique qualities require a unique approach to digital signature integration.

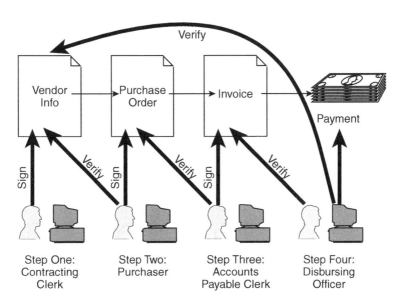

**Exhibit 2.    A Typical Paperless Business Process**

## What Is a Document?

Earlier, we discussed digitally signed "transactions." Often the term "document" is used to denote the data that is signed (see Exhibit 3). Each type of digital signature solution seems to define a document differently. For example, e-mail security products define a document as an e-mail and its attachments. There are security products that digitally sign word processing documents or spreadsheets. Other products digitally sign any type of file. Note that in each of these examples, even though a document may internally contain many discrete data elements, the document as a whole can be represented as a contiguous set of bytes.

Relational databases store their data much differently. Databases store structured data as opposed to unstructured data. This means that all the data elements that comprise a document must be known in advance before the first document is created. Databases use a concept called "normalization," which allows large amounts of structured data to be stored and searched efficiently. The data in a document is stored in tables. Tables are composed of rows and columns. The columns define the name (e.g., PRODUCT_NAME, INVOICE_NUMBER or PURCHASE_DATE) and type (e.g., CHARACTER, NUMBER, and DATE, respectively) of each data element. A row in a table, called a "record," contains the actual data values for each column in the table.

For our purposes a "document" is defined as the data in one or more rows from one or more columns of one or more tables in a relational database. That is, a document may span multiple database tables and may include only selected columns from those tables and may encompass more than one row per table. This sounds complex and it can be very complex. Databases are designed to efficiently handle large amounts of data that is related in complex ways.

Exhibit 4 shows a document in a format that makes sense to people. It is a very simplified purchase order from Gradkell Systems, Inc., to a company named LLED Computer Corporation. A purchase order is usually identified by a purchase order number. This is purchase order #123. It has four line

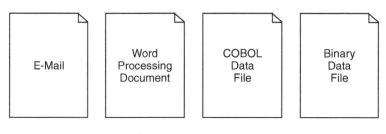

**Exhibit 3. Types of Documents**

| PURCHASE ORDER | | #123 |
|---|---|---|
| TO: LLED Computer Corporation<br>From: Gradkell Systems, Inc.<br>    4910 University Place | | |
| 1 | 4 Processor 800 Mhz Pentium III<br>PowerEdge Server w/Hed Hat Linux | $4,750.00 |
| 4 | 512 MB PC-100 DIMM Memory | $250.00 |
| 1 | SCSI RAID Controller | $1,750.00 |
| 3 | 18 GB 10,000 RPM SCSI Disk Drive | $1,250.00 |
| | **Total:** | $8,000.00 |

**Exhibit 4.  A Database Document Printed or Displayed by an Application**

items. Each line item has a quantity, description, and amount. The purchase order also has a total amount. Exhibit 5 represents how purchase order documents might be stored in a database.

Note that not all columns shown in Exhibit 5 are displayed in Exhibit 4. This is important because database applications may contain data that are

| Vendor | Vendor Code | Name | Payment Address | · · · |
|---|---|---|---|---|
| | DM | DELL Computer | 1 Dell Way, Round Rock | · · · |
| | PIZ | Dominos Pizza | Down the Street | · · · |

| Purchase Orders | P.O. Number | Vendor Code | Approver | Total | · · · |
|---|---|---|---|---|---|
| | 123 | DM | GGASTON | $25,764.25 | · · · |
| | 345 | PIZ | KGASTON | $27.50 | · · · |

| P.O. Line Items | P.O. Number | Item # | Qty | Description | Amount | · · · |
|---|---|---|---|---|---|---|
| | 123 | 1 | 1 | 4 Processor 600 . . . | $4,750.00 | · · · |
| | 123 | 2 | 4 | 256 MB PC-100 DIMM . . . | $250.00 | · · · |
| | 345 | 1 | 2 | Large Pepperoni + Cheese | $13.75 | · · · |

Highlighted rows pertain to Purchase Order #123.

**Exhibit 5.  A Database Document Stored in the Database**

used internally by that application but are not important to the business process. Examples of such data are internal flags that mark a document's position in a work flow (e.g., it has been entered, but approval is pending). It is not usually necessary to sign this type of data because it is not really part of the document. This data is used only to move the document through a process. If it is signed, the signature will be invalidated when the data changes. So it is important to be able to choose which columns to include in the signature rather than having to sign the entire row.

Note that the data that pertains to purchase order #123 is not a contiguous set of bytes. It is intermingled with other purchase orders (e.g., #345, a pizza order). Since digital signature algorithms operate on a contiguous set of bytes, the data must be retrieved from the database and formatted into a contiguous string of characters. This must be done exactly the same way each time. The result must be bit for bit the same every time or the signature will not verify. This is because the digital signature operation is performed on a block of data. At the level in the process where the cryptography is applied, the contents of the data have no meaning. The signing process sees the data only as an ordered collection of bits. The signature verification process simply answers the questions: Is this the data that was signed? Was it signed by the specified user?

The exactness with which data must be represented presents some special problems. Databases store numeric and date values in a special way and usually have a default format that is used to display these values. For example, if a date value was signed in the form "11:30 P.M. on 10 May 1999" but was verified in the form "1999-05-10 23:30:00," the signature will not verify because the data was changed. Actually, only the representation of the data has changed, but that representation was not bit for bit the same as it was when signed. The same is true of numeric data. The real number 47502.5 can also be represented as "$47,502.50." This becomes an issue when the default format used by the database to represent numeric and date values can be changed by a database administrator. These problems can be avoided if the format of the data is explicitly specified when the data is retrieved from the database.

## INTEGRATION APPROACHES: WHY IS APPLICATION INTEGRATION SO PROBLEMATIC?

When adding security features to applications, digital signature is fundamentally different from other security techniques. There are several reasons for this:

- Applications must trigger the signing and verification of documents at the appropriate points in the business process.

- Applications must be able to reject documents or stop processes when signature verification indicates that data has been altered since it was signed.
- The digital signature itself is an additional piece of information that must be stored by the application so that data integrity or nonrepudiation can be proven at a later date.

The additional application logic and data storage requirements necessary to correctly process digital signatures mean that digital signature functionality usually cannot be added to applications in a completely transparent manner.

**Integration Using Low-Level Cryptographic Toolkits**

The nuts and bolts of public key cryptography and PKI are extremely complex. The underlying cryptographic algorithms involve advanced mathematics and absolutely must be implemented correctly. The data formats used to encode data—usually ASN.1 (abstract syntax notation)—are very complex and require extensive low-level programming experience and a high degree of familiarity with ISO and ANSI standards. The logic associated with building and validating certificate chains presents a substantial learning curve. Fortunately there are cryptographic toolkits that handle much of this low-level processing.

However, cryptographic toolkits go only so far. Developers must still have a high level of familiarity with the data structures and algorithms used in digitally signing and verifying. Most cryptographic toolkits are based on the assumption that developers are using the C or C++ programming languages. Even when using toolkits such as these, developers who lack a comprehensive understanding of what is going on "under the hood" can cause disastrous security problems.

In addition to security problems, there are a host of other issues that have prevented organizations from taking this approach to application security integration. One reason is high risk. An organization may have plenty of application developers who are proficient in environments such as Visual Basic, Power Builder, Oracle Forms, Cold Fusion, JSP, ASP, etc. However it often does not have many developers who can be committed to the task of learning C/C++, PKI programming, and low level cryptographic toolkits. Even if an organization does have a wealth of "system level" developers, what are they going to do in 6 months when the digital signature feature is 90 percent complete and the developer leaves the company? The cost of integration and maintenance must be weighed against the cost of available third party solutions that do not require such a steep learning curve.

In many cases, "enterprise" databases have several "front ends" to the same data. Data may originate from a Web-based application and be processed internally by an application written in Visual Basic. Often, digital signature integration projects that use low-level toolkits result in a solution that is specific to one application or to one development environment. If the digital signature system works only in the Web interface, there may be no way of proving—using other applications—that no one has tampered with the data.

### Development Environments with Digital Signature Built In

An alternative approach to using low-level cryptographic toolkits is to completely rewrite the application using tools that have digital signature built in. For new systems this can work very well. For example, some electronic forms products have digital signature capabilities built in. These products perform very well when used to directly replace a paper system. The electronic forms can be made to look almost exactly like the paper forms, but do not have to be printed for signature purposes. Many of the packages also integrate with relational databases. They can use the database for both retrieval and storage of form data and they can use the database for form storage. However, these products are not general-purpose database front ends. Some products require their own database structure. Others have limited ability to integrate with existing database structures. They also store a copy of the data within the electronic form itself. So using such a product as a database front end comes with some storage, and thus performance, overhead. Electronic forms products usually have their own development environments and macro languages. This mean that converting an existing application to use digitally signed "electronic forms" usually amounts to a complete rewrite.

When it comes to digital signature, the electronic forms products work well as long as you are using the electronic form software to access the database. This is because the digital signature is stored within the electronic form itself. If, for example, a Visual Basic application was written that relied on the data in the database, the digital signature could not be verified. Even if the electronic form product included a programming interface that allowed the digital signature to be verified, the signature would be verified using the copy of the data stored in the electronic form, not the copy stored in the database. This is a very serious problem because the Visual Basic application is making "decisions" based on the data in the database, not the data stored in the electronic form. The verification of electronic form signature could succeed even if the data in the database were altered.

So development environments that include digital signature functionality usually come with some serious limitations when applied to relational databases. These limitations stem from the fact that they are not designed to be general-purpose database application development tools. They often do not use the database as their primary storage medium, but offer database support as an optional or auxiliary feature. Their digital signature features are not designed for use in other types of applications. These types of digital signature–enabled tools are "development environment-centric" instead of "data-centric."

## A GENERIC APPROACH TO DIGITAL SIGNATURE IN RELATIONAL DATABASES

As already mentioned, the current approach to securing database applications is to build a virtual "wall" around the database server. This wall is composed of network firewalls, encryption, strong authentication and authorizations, intrusion detection, etc. This works well and is complexly application independent. However, this strategy works at the database server level and falls short of providing verifiable data integrity and non-repudiation at the transaction (or "document") level. Digital signatures are the next step in application security, but digital signature technology is different because it requires a certain amount of application integration. To get to this next step, we need an application-independent system of digitally signing data stored in relational databases that requires as little application integration as possible.

### Basic Requirements for Digital Signature Integration into Database Applications

The following sections describe basic design goals for a generic database signing system.

#### No PKI Knowledge Required for Application Developers. Application developers should not have to become digital signature experts. Ideally they should not even need to understand what a digital signature is, other than that it is an operation that is performed on a certain document at a certain place in the business process. There are five application-specific items that a generic database signature system cannot determine:

- What type of operation needs to be performed (e.g., signing or verification)
- What type of document is being signed or verified (e.g., purchase request, invoice, time card, leave request, 401(k) participation form)
- Which specific document is being signed or verified (i.e., the "primary key" values that uniquely identify a single document)
- When in the business process to perform digital signing or verification
- What to do if an error occurs during signing or verification

All these items are known by the application developer and are similar to the types of information required by other operations in the application. For example, an application developer has to know that "purchase request number 123 needs to be signed when the user presses the submit button." Of course, the actual process is much more complex, but the application developer does not need to know the other details such as which columns in which tables are signed or where the signature data is stored.

**Does Not Require Modification of the Existing Database Structure.** If the digital signature system is to be application independent, it should not directly rely on the database structure of a certain application. Adding new tables should not be problem, however.

**Allows the Data That Is Signed To Be Specified.** Because databases do not store their data as contiguous sets of bytes, the data items that compose a document or transaction must be gathered from the database. The data that is signed has to be exactly the same when it is verified as when it was signed. Inasmuch as we want this system to be very easy to integrate, we do not want to burden the application developer with this task. Because the digital signature will be performing the data-gathering step, it must allow the data (tables and columns) to be specified. This specification should include information that defines how each data item is to be formatted (e.g., "1:00 P.M." or "13:00"). The specification should also be able to represent the "primary keys" of the document and the complex ways that the underlying tables are related to each other.

**Scalable and Does Not Introduce a Single Point of Failure.** The database server and the application server are both required by the application. The PKI adds a directory server. The digital signature system should not introduce any additional servers that could become a bottleneck or cause application processing to stop.

**Signature Storage Overhead Should Be as Small as Possible.** Database environments offer great advantages when it comes to the efficient storage of data. The de facto standard format for digital signature storage is PKCS #7, the cryptographic message syntax standard. This standard defines a data structure for cryptographic messages such as signed documents.

Most of the fields are optional, but a typical signed data message includes the signer's certificate, the other certificate authority (CA) certificates in the "chain," and a copy of the data that was signed. Essentially a PKCS #7 signed data message is a large "de-normalized" chunk of binary data. Because the database is a central data repository that is shared by the signer and the verifier, the certificates and the data do not need to be stored with each signed document. Because this data is being stored in a database, it can be "normalized." The certificates can be stored only once

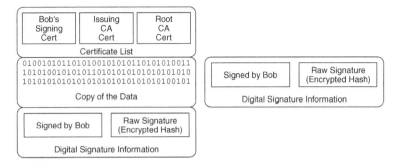

**Exhibit 6. A Typical PKCS #7 Signed Data Message versus One That Has Been Optimized for Storage in a Database**

and linked to the signed document via database relationships. A single certificate is about 600 to 1000 bytes in size. A typical PKCS #7 message contains about three certificates. The data portion, which is of indeterminate length, can also be removed from the PKCS #7 message because the data is already stored in the database and does not need to be stored again. As Exhibit 6 shows, normalization of the signature information greatly reduces the amount of signature storage overhead required by the digital signature system. The "optimized" PKCS #7 is about 300 bytes long versus more than 3000 bytes (assuming 1024 bytes of data) for the typical case. Storing less data per document also improves performance because less data has to traverse slow network connections.

## Abstracting the Digital Signature Process

Digital signature integration can be viewed as "gluing" digital signature functionality onto an existing application. The actual cryptographic operations and interaction with PKI components are performed by low-level cryptographic toolkits. The "glue" is a program library that "knows" how to interact with both the database and the cryptographic toolkit.

In Exhibit 7, the cryptographic toolkit knows only how to sign raw data. It does not know how to gather it from the database or how to store signature information in the database. The database-signing logic knows how to retrieve the purchase request data from the database and how to use the cryptographic toolkit to sign the data. It also handles formatting the signature data in a way that is optimal for storage in the relational database environment.

Essentially, the process of digitally signing data in a database is standardized and abstracted from the application so that the application developer does not have to know anything about it. The developer provides just enough information to get the process started. The rest is handled automatically.

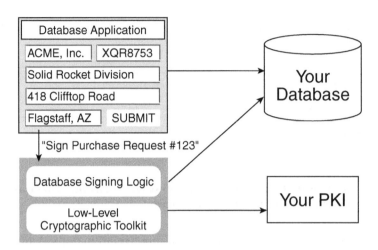

**Exhibit 7. The Process of Signing a Database "Document" Is Standardized and Removed from the Application Logic**

## SUMMARY

We have discussed some of the unique qualities of both digital signatures and relational databases. Digital signatures are different because they require that data be stored to support signature verification. Relational databases are different because they store data in a unique way. These two differences work together to make integrating digital signatures into relational database applications a complex and tedious task. The cost and risk of this crucial integration step has hindered the use of digital signatures in many applications. Until recently, there have been no digital signature products specifically designed for the database environment. Products such as DBsign from Gradkell Systems, Inc., are now available to vastly simplify the integration of digital signature security into relational database applications. Such products leverage the cryptographic and security expertise of specially trained third-party developers to drastically reduce the cost and risk associated with trying to tackle complex, highly technical integration projects in-house. For more information about DBsign or Gradkell Systems, please visit their Web site at www.gradkell.com.

# Chapter 50
# A Primer on Cracking: Part 1

*Edward Skoudis*

RECENT HEADLINES DEMONSTRATE THAT THE LATEST CROP OF HACKER TOOLS AND TECH-NIQUES CAN BE HIGHLY DAMAGING TO AN ORGANIZATION'S SENSITIVE INFORMATION AND REPUTATION. With the rise of powerful, easy-to-use, and widely distributed hacker tools, many in the security industry have observed that today is the golden age of hacking. This article describes the tools in widespread use today for compromising computer and network security. Additionally, for each tool and technique described, the article presents practical advice on defending against each type of attack. Part 1 of this article discusses network mapping and port scanning, vulnerability scanning, wardialing, network exploits, and denial-of-service attacks. Part 2 discusses stack-based buffer overflows, password cracking, backdoors, Trojan horses and rootkits, and defenses — intrusion detection and incident response procedures.

The terminology applied to these tools and their users has caused some controversy, particularly in the computer underground. Traditionally, and particularly in the computer underground, the term "hacker" is a benign word, referring to an individual who is focused on determining how things work and devising innovative approaches to addressing computer problems. To differentiate these noble individuals from a nasty attacker, this school of thought labels malicious attackers as "crackers." While hackers are out to make the world a better place, crackers want to cause damage and mayhem. To avoid the confusion often associated with these terms, in this chapter, the terms "system and security administrator" and "security practitioner" will be used to indicate an individual who has a legitimate and authorized purpose for running these tools. The term "attacker" will refer to those individuals who seek to cause damage to systems or who are not authorized to run such tools.

Many of the tools described in this chapter have dual personalities: they can be used for good or evil. When used by malicious individuals, the tools allow a motivated attacker to gain access to a network, mask the fact that a compromise has occurred, or even bring down service, thus impacting large masses of users. When used by a security practitioner with proper authorization, some tools can be used to measure the security stance of their own organizations, by conducting "ethical hacking" tests to find vulnerabilities before attackers do.

## CAVEAT

The purpose of this chapter is to explain the various computer underground tools in use today, and to discuss defensive techniques for addressing each type of tool. This chapter is not designed to encourage attacks. Furthermore, the tools described below are for illustration purposes only, and mention in this chapter is not an endorsement. If readers feel compelled to experiment with these tools, they should do so at their own risk, realizing that such tools frequently have viruses or other undocumented features that could damage networks and information systems. Curious readers who want to use these tools should conduct a through review of the source code, or at least install the tools on a separate, air-gapped network to protect sensitive production systems.

## GENERAL TRENDS IN THE COMPUTER UNDERGROUND

### The Smart Get Smarter, and the Rise of the Script Kiddie

The best and brightest minds in the computer underground are conducting probing research and finding new vulnerabilities and powerful, novel attacks on a daily basis. The ideas of and deep research performed by super-smart attackers and security practitioners are being implemented in software programs and scripts. Months of research into how a particular operating system implements its password scheme is being rendered in code, so even a clueless attacker (often called a "script kiddie") can conduct a highly sophisticated attack with just a point-and-click. This can occur even if the script kiddie does not understand the tool's true function and nuances, since most of the attack is automated.

In this environment, security practitioners must be careful not to underestimate their adversaries' capabilities. Often, security and system administrators think of their potential attackers as mere teenage kids cruising the Internet looking for easy prey. While this assessment is sometimes accurate, it masks two major concerns. First, some of these teenage kids are amazingly intelligent, and can wreak havoc on a network. Second, attackers may not be just kids; organized crime, terrorists, and even foreign governments have taken to sponsoring cyber attacks.

### Wide Distribution of High-Quality Tools

Another trend in the computing underground involves the widespread distribution of tools. In the past (a decade ago), powerful attack tools were limited to a core group of elites in the computer underground. Today, hundreds of Web sites are devoted to the sharing of tools for every attacker (and security practitioner) on the planet. FAQs abound, describing how to penetrate any type of operating system. These overall trends converge in a world where smart attackers have detailed knowledge of undermining our systems, while the not-so-smart attackers grow more and more plentiful. To address this increasing threat, system administrators and security practitioners must understand these tools and how to defend against them. The remainder of this chapter describes many of these very powerful tools in widespread use today, together with practical defensive tips for protecting one's network from each type of attack.

## NETWORK MAPPING AND PORT SCANNING

When launching an attack across a TCP/IP network (such as the Internet or a corporate intranet), an attacker needs to know what addresses are active, how the network topology is constructed, and which services are available. A network mapper identifies systems that are connected to the target network. Given a network address range, the network mapper will send packets to each possible address to determine which addresses have machines.

By sending a simple Internet Control Message Protocol (ICMP) packet to a server (a "ping"), the mapping tool can discover if a server is connected to the network. For those networks that block incoming pings, many of the mapping tools available today can send a single SYN packet to attempt to open a connection to a server. If a server is listening, the SYN packet will trigger an ACK if the port is open, and potentially a "Port Unreachable" message if the port is closed. Regardless of whether the port is open or closed, the response indicates that the address has a machine listening. With this list of addresses, an attacker can refine the attack and focus on these listening systems.

A port scanner identifies open ports on a system. There are 65,535 TCP ports and 65,535 UDP ports, some of which are open on a system, and most of which are closed. Common services are associated with certain ports. For example, TCP Port 80 is most often used by Web servers, TCP Port 23 is used by Telnet daemons, and TCP Port 25 is used for server-to-server mail exchange across the Internet. By conducting a port scan, an attacker will send packets to each and every port. Essentially, ports are rather like doors on a machine. At any one of the thousands of doors available, common services will be listening. A port scanning tool allows an attacker to knock on every one of those doors to see who answers.

Some scanning tools include TCP fingerprinting capabilities. While the Internet Engineering Task Force (IETF) has carefully specified TCP and IP in various Requests for Comments (RFCs), not all packet options have standards associated with them. Without standards for how systems should respond to illegal packet formats, different vendors' TCP/IP stacks respond differently to illegal packets. By sending various combinations of illegal packet options (such as initiating a connection with an RST packet, or combining other odd and illegal TCP code bits), an attacker can determine what type of operating system is running on the target machine. For example, by conducting a TCP fingerprinting scan, an attacker can determine if a machine is running Cisco IOS, Sun Solaris, or Microsoft Windows 2000. In some cases, even the particular version or service pack level can be determined using this technique.

After utilizing network mapping tools and port scanners, an attacker will know which addresses on the target network have listening machines, which ports are open on those machines (and therefore which services are running), and which operating system platforms are in use. This treasure trove of information is useful to the attacker in refining the attack. With this data, the attacker can search for vulnerabilities on the particular services and systems to attempt to gain access.

Nmap, written by Fyodor, is one of the most full-featured mapping and scanning tools available today. It supports network mapping, port scanning, and TCP fingerprinting, and can be found at http://www.insecure. org/nmap.

### Network Mapping and Port Scanning Defenses

To defend against network mapping and port scans, the administrator should remove all unnecessary systems and close all unused ports. To accomplish this, the administrator must disable and remove unneeded services from the machine. Only those services that have an absolute, defined business need should be running. A security administrator should also periodically scan the systems to determine if any unneeded ports are open. When discovered, these unneeded ports must be disabled.

### VULNERABILITY SCANNING

Once the target systems are identified with a port scanner and network mapper, an attacker will search to determine if any vulnerabilities are present on the victim machines. Thousands of vulnerabilities have been discovered, allowing a remote attacker to gain a toehold on a machine or to take complete administrative control. An attacker could try each of these vulnerabilities on each system by entering individual commands to test for every vulnerability, but conducting an exhaustive search could take years. To speed the process, attackers use automated scanning tools to quickly search for vulnerabilities on the target.

These automated vulnerability scanning tools are essentially databases of well-known vulnerabilities with an engine that can read the database, connect to a machine, and check to see if it is vulnerable to the exploit. The effectiveness of the tool in discovering vulnerabilities depends on the quality and thoroughness of its vulnerability database. For this reason, the best vulnerability scanners support the rapid release and update of the vulnerability database and the ability to create new checks using a scripting language.

High-quality commercial vulnerability scanning tools are widely available, and are often used by security practitioners and attackers to search for vulnerabilities. On the freeware front, SATAN (the Security Administrator Tool for Analyzing Network) was one of the first widely distributed automated vulnerability scanners, introduced in 1995. More recently, Nessus has been introduced as a free, open-source vulnerability scanner available at http://www.nessus.org. The Nessus project, which is led by Renaud Deraison, provides a full-featured scanner for identifying vulnerabilities on remote systems. It includes source code and a scripting language for writing new vulnerability checks, allowing it to be highly customized by security practitioners and attackers alike.

While Nessus is a general-purpose vulnerability scanner, looking for holes in numerous types of systems and platforms, some vulnerability scanners are much more focused on particular types of systems. For example, Whisker is a full-feature vulnerability scanning tool focusing on Web server CGI scripts. Written by Rain Forest Puppy, Whisker can be found at http://www.wiretrip.net/rfp.

### Vulnerability Scanning Defenses

As described, the administrator must close unused ports. Additionally, to eliminate the vast majority of system vulnerabilities, system patches must be applied in a timely fashion. All organizations using computers should have a defined change control procedure that specifies when and how system patches will be kept up-to-date.

Security practitioners should also conduct periodic vulnerability scans of their own networks to find vulnerabilities before attackers do. These scans should be conducted on a regular basis (such as quarterly, or even monthly for sensitive networks) or when major network changes are implemented. The discovered vulnerabilities must be addressed in a timely fashion by updating system configurations or applying patches.

### WARDIALING

A cousin of the network mapper and scanner, a wardialing tool is used to discover target systems across a telephone network. Organizations often spend large amounts of money in securing their network from a full frontal assault over the Internet by implementing a firewall, intrusion detection system, and secure DMZ. Unfortunately, many attackers avoid this route and instead look for other ways into the network. Modems left on users' desktops or old, forgotten machines often provide the simplest way into a target network.

Wardialers, also known as "demon dialers," dial a series of telephone numbers, attempting to locate modems on the victim network. An attacker will determine the telephone extensions associated with the target organization. This information is often gleaned from a Web site listing telephone contacts, employee newsgroup postings with telephone contact information in the signature line, or even general employee e-mail. Armed with one or a series of telephone numbers, the attacker will enter into the wardialing tool ranges of numbers associated with the original number (e.g., if an employee's telephone number in a newsgroup posting is listed as 555-1212, the attacker will dial 555-XXXX). The wardialer will automatically dial each number, listen for the familiar wail of a modem carrier tone, and make a list of all telephone numbers with modems listening.

With the list of modems generated by the wardialer, the attacker will dial each discovered modem using a terminal program or other client. Upon connecting to the modem, the attacker will attempt to identify the system based on its banner information and see if a password is required. Often, no password is required, because the modem was put in place by a clueless user requiring after-hours access and not wanting to bother using approved methods. If a password is required, the attacker will attempt to guess passwords commonly associated with the platform or company.

Some wardialing tools also support the capability of locating a repeat dial-tone, in addition to the ability to detect modems. The repeat dial-tone is a great find for the attacker, as it could allow for unrestricted dialing from a victim's PBX system to anywhere in the world. If an attacker finds a line on PBX supporting repeat dial-tone in the same local dialing exchange, the attacker can conduct international wardialing, with all phone bills paid for by the victim with the misconfigured PBX.

The most fully functional wardialing tool available today is distributed by The Hacker's Choice (THC) group. Known as THC-Scan, the tool was written by Van Hauser and can be found at http://inferno.tusculum.edu/thc. THC-Scan 2.0 supports many advanced features, including sequential or randomized dialing, dialing through a network out-dial, modem carrier and repeat dial-tone detection, and rudimentary detection avoidance capabilities.

### Wardialing Defenses

The best defense against wardialing attacks is a strong modem policy that prohibits the use of modems and incoming lines without a defined business need. The policy should also require the registration of all modems with a business need in a centralized database only accessible by a security or system administrator.

Additionally, security personnel should conduct periodic wardialing exercises of their own networks to find the modems before the attackers do. When a phone number with an unregistered modem is discovered, the physical device must be located and deactivated. While finding such devices can be difficult, network defenses depend on finding these renegade modems before an attacker does.

## NETWORK EXPLOITS: SNIFFING, SPOOFING, AND SESSION HIJACKING

TCP/IP, the underlying protocol suite that makes up the Internet, was not originally designed to provide security services. Likewise, the most common data-link type used with TCP/IP — Ethernet — is fundamentally unsecure. A whole series of attacks are possible given these vulnerabilities of the underlying protocols. The most widely used and potentially damaging attacks based on these network vulnerabilities are sniffing, spoofing, and session hijacking.

### Sniffing

Sniffers are extremely useful tools for an attacker and are therefore fundamental elements of an attacker's toolchest. Sniffers allow an attacker to monitor data passing across a network. Given their capability to monitor network traffic, sniffers are also useful for security practitioners and network administrators in troubleshooting networks and conducting investigations. Sniffers exploit characteristics of several data-link technologies, including Token Ring and especially Ethernet.

Ethernet, the most common LAN technology, is essentially a broadcast technology. When Ethernet LANs are constructed using hubs, all machines connected to the LAN can monitor all data on the LAN segment. If userIDs, passwords, or other sensitive information are sent from one machine (e.g., a client) to another machine (e.g., a server or router) on the same LAN, all other systems connected to the LAN could monitor the data. A sniffer is a hardware or software tool that gathers all data on a LAN segment. When a sniffer is running on a machine gathering all network traffic that passes by the system, the Ethernet interface and the machine itself are said to be in "promiscuous mode."

Many commonly used applications, such as Telnet, FTP, POP (the Post Office Protocol used for e-mail), and even some Web applications, transmit their passwords and sensitive data without any encryption. Any attacker on a broadcast Ethernet segment can use a sniffer to gather these passwords and data.

Attackers who take over a system often install a software sniffer on the compromised machine. This sniffer acts as a sentinel for the attacker, gathering sensitive data that moves by the compromised system. The sniffer gathers this data, including passwords, and stores it in a local file or transmits it to the attacker. The attacker then uses this information to compromise more and more systems. The attack methodology of installing a sniffer on one compromised machine, gathering data passing that machine, and using the sniffed information to take over other systems is referred to as an island-hopping attack.

Numerous sniffing tools are available across the Internet. The most fully functional sniffing tools include Sniffit (by Brecht Claerhout, available at http://reptile.rug.ac.be/~coder/sniffit/sniffit.html) and Snort (by Martin Roesch, available at http://www.clark.net/~roesch/security.html). Some operating systems ship with their own sniffers installed by default, notably Solaris (with the Snoop tool) and some varieties of Linux (which ship with tcpdump). Other commercial sniffers are also available from a variety of vendors.

**Sniffing Defenses.** The best defense against sniffing attacks is to encrypt the data in transit. Instead of sending passwords or other sensitive data in cleartext, the application or network should encrypt the data (SSH, secure Telnet, etc.).

Another defense against sniffers is to eliminate the broadcast nature of Ethernet. By utilizing a switch instead of a hub to create a LAN, the damage that can be done with a sniffer is limited. A switch can be configured so that only the required source and destination ports on the switch carry the traffic. Although they are on the same LAN, all other ports on the switch (and the machines connected to those ports) do not see this data. Therefore, if one system is compromised on a LAN, a sniffer installed on this machine will not be capable of seeing data exchanged between other machines on the LAN. Switches are therefore useful in improving security by minimizing the data a sniffer can gather, and also help to improve network performance.

## IP Spoofing

Another network-based attack involves altering the source address of a computer to disguise the attacker and exploit weak authentication methods. IP address spoofing allows an attacker to use the IP address of another machine to conduct an attack. If the target machines rely on the IP address to authenticate, IP spoofing can give an attacker access to the systems. Additionally, IP spoofing can make it very difficult to apprehend an attacker, because logs will contain decoy addresses and not the real source of the attack. Many of the tools described in other sections of this chapter rely on IP spoofing to hide the true origin of the attack.

**Spoofing Defenses.** Systems should not use IP addresses for authentication. Any functions or applications that rely solely on IP address for authentication should be disabled or replaced. In UNIX, the **r**-commands (**rlogin**, **rsh**, **rexec**, and **rcp**) are notoriously subject to IP spoofing attacks. UNIX trust relationships allow an administrator to manage systems using the **r**-commands without providing a password. Instead of a password, the IP address of the system is used for authentication. This major weakness should be avoided by replacing the **r**-commands with administration tools that utilize strong authentication. One such tool, secure shell (ssh), uses strong cryptography to replace the weak authentication of the **r**-commands. Similarly, all other applications that rely on IP addresses for critical security and administration functions should be replaced.

Additionally, an organization should deploy anti-spoof filters on its perimeter networks that connect the organization to the Internet and business partners. Anti-spoof filters drop all traffic coming from outside the network claiming to come from inside the network. With this capability, such filters can prevent some types of spoofing attacks, and should be implemented on all perimeter network routers.

### Session Hijacking

While sniffing allows an attacker to view data associated with network connections, a session hijack tool allows an attacker to take over network connections, kicking off the legitimate user or sharing a login. Session hijacking tools are used against services with persistent login sessions, such as Telnet, rlogin, or FTP. For any of these services, an attacker can hijack a session and cause a great deal of damage.

A common scenario illustrating session hijacking involves a machine, Alice, with a user logged in to remotely administer another system, Bob, using Telnet. Eve, the attacker, sits on a network segment between Alice and

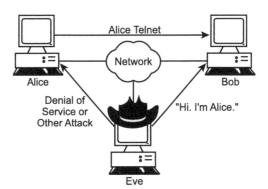

**Exhibit 1.   Eve Hijacks the Session between Alice and Bob**

Bob (either Alice's LAN, Bob's LAN, or between any of the routers between Alice's and Bob's LANs). Exhibit 1 illustrates this scenario in more detail.

Using a session hijacking tool, Eve can do any of the following:

- *Monitor Alice's session.* Most session hijacking tools allow attackers to monitor all connections available on the network and select which connections they want to hijack.
- *Insert commands into the session.* An attacker may just need to add one or two commands into the stream to reconfigure Bob. In this type of hijack, the attacker never takes full control of the session. Instead, Alice's login session to Bob has a small number of commands inserted, which will be executed on Bob as if Alice had typed them.
- *Steal the session.* This feature of most session hijacking tools allows an attacker to grab the session from Alice, and directly control it. Essentially, the Telnet client control is shifted from Alice to Eve, without Bob's knowing.
- *Give the session back.* Some session hijacking tools allow the attacker to steal a session, interact with the server, and then smoothly give the session back to the user. While the session is stolen, Alice is put on hold while Eve controls the session. With Alice on hold, all commands typed by Alice are displayed on Eve's screen, but not transmitted to Bob. When Eve is finished making modifications on Bob, Eve transfers control back to Alice.

For a successful hijacking to occur, the attacker must be on a LAN segment between Alice and Bob. A session hijacking tool monitors the connection using an integrated sniffer, observing the TCP sequence numbers of the packets going each direction. Each packet sent from Alice to Bob has a unique TCP sequence number used by Bob to verify that all packets are received and put in proper order. Likewise, all packets going back from Bob to Alice have sequence numbers. A session hijacking tool sniffs the packets to determine these sequence numbers. When a session is hijacked (through command insertion or session stealing), the hijacking tool automatically uses the appropriate sequence numbers and spoofs Alice's address, taking over the conversation with Bob where Alice left off.

One of the most fully functional session hijacking tool available today is Hunt, written by Kra and available at http://www.cri.cz/kra/index.html. Hunt allows an attacker to monitor and steal sessions, insert single commands, and even give a session back to the user.

**Session Hijacking Defenses.** The best defense against session hijacking is to avoid the use of insecure protocols and applications for sensitive sessions. Instead of using the easy-to-hijack (and easy-to-sniff) Telnet application, a more secure, encrypted session tool should be used. Because the attacker does not have the session encryption keys, an encrypted session cannot be hijacked. The attacker will simply see encrypted gibberish using Hunt, and will only be able to reset the connection — not take it over or insert commands.

Secure shell (ssh) offers strong authentication and encrypted sessions, providing a highly secure alternative to Telnet and rlogin. Furthermore, ssh includes a secure file transfer capability (scp) to replace traditional ftp. Other alternatives are available, including secure, encrypted Telnet or a virtual private network (VPN) established between the source and destination.

## DENIAL-OF-SERVICE ATTACKS

Denial-of-service (DoS) attacks are among the most common exploits available today. As their name implies, a denial-of-service attack prevents legitimate users from being able to access a system. With E-commerce applications constituting the lifeblood of many organizations and a growing piece of the world economy, a well-timed DoS attack can cause a great deal of damage. By bringing down servers that control sensitive machinery or other functions, these attacks could also present a real physical threat to life and limb. An attacker could cause the service denial by flooding a system with bogus traffic, or even purposely causing the server to crash. Countless DoS attacks are in widespread use today, and can be found at http://packet-storm.securify.com/exploits/DoS. The most often used network-based DoS attacks fall into two categories: malformed packet attacks and packet floods.

### Malformed Packet Attacks

This type of attack usually involves one or two packets that are formatted in an unexpected way. Many vendor product implementations do not take into account all variations of user entries or packet types. If the software handles such errors poorly, the system may crash when it receives such packets. A classic example of this type of attack involves sending IP fragments to systems that overlap with each other (the fragment offset values are incorrectly set). Some unpatched Windows and Linux systems will crash when they encounter such packets. The teardrop attack is an example of a tool that exploits this IP fragmentation handling vulnerability. Other malformed packet attacks that exploit other weaknesses in TCP/IP implementations include the colorfully named WinNuke, Land, LaTierra, NewTear, Bonk, and Boink.

### Packet Flood Attacks

Packet flood denial-of-service tools send a deluge of traffic to a system on the network, overwhelming its capability to respond to legitimate users. Attackers have devised numerous techniques for creating such floods, with the most popular being SYN floods, directed broadcast attacks, and distributed denial-of-service tools.

SYN flood tools initiate a large number of half-open connections with a system by sending a series of SYN packets. When any TCP connection is established, a three-way handshake occurs. The initiating system (usually the client) sends a SYN packet to the destination to establish a sequence number for all packets going from source to destination in that session. The destination responds with a SYN-ACK packet, which acknowledges the sequence number for packets going from source to destination, and establishes an initial sequence number for packets going in the opposite direction. The source completes the three-way handshake by sending an ACK to the destination. The three-way handshake is completed and communication (actual data transfer) can occur.

SYN floods take advantage of a weakness in TCP's three-way handshake. By sending only spoofed SYN packets and never responding to the SYN-ACK, an attacker can exhaust a server's ability to maintain state of all the initiated sessions. With a huge number of so-called half-open connections, a server cannot handle any new legitimate traffic. Rather than filling up all of the pipe bandwidth to a server, only the server's capacity to handle session initiations needs to be overwhelmed (in most network configurations, a server's ability to handle SYNs is lower than the total bandwidth to the site). For this reason, SYN flooding is the most popular packet flood attack. Other tools are also available that flood systems with ICMP and UDP packets, but they merely consume bandwidth; thus, an attacker would require a bigger connection than the victim to cut off all service.

Another type of packet flood that allows attackers to amplify their bandwidth is the directed broadcast attack. Often called a smurf attack, named after the first tool to exploit this technique, directed broadcast attacks utilize a third-party's network as an amplifier for the packet flood. In a smurf attack, the attacker locates a network on the Internet that will respond to a broadcast ICMP message (essentially a ping to the network's broadcast address). If the network is configured to allow broadcast requests and responses, all machines on the network will send a response to the ping. By spoofing the ICMP request, the attacker can have all machines on the third-party network send responses to the victim. For example, if an organization has 30 hosts on a single DMZ network connected to the Internet, an attacker can send a spoofed network broadcast ping to the DMZ. Each of the 30 hosts will send a response to the spoofed address, which would be the ultimate victim. By sending repeated messages to the broadcast network, the attacker has amplified bandwidth by a factor of 30. Even an attacker with only a 56-kbps dial-up line could fill up a T1 line (1.54 Mbps) with that level of amplification. Other directed broadcast attack tools include Fraggle and Papasmurf.

A final type of denial-of-service that has received considerable press is the distributed denial-of-service attack. Essentially based on standard packet flood concepts, distributed denial-of-service attacks were used to cripple many major Internet sites in February 2000. Tools such as Trin00, Tribe Flood Network 2000 (TFN2K), and Stacheldraht all support this type of attack. To conduct a distributed denial-of-service attack, an attacker must find numerous vulnerable systems on the Internet. Usually, a remote buffer overflow attack (described below) is used to take over a dozen, a hundred, or even thousands of machines. Simple daemon processes, called zombies, are installed on the machines taken over by the attacker. The attacker communicates with this network of zombies using a control program. The control program is used to send commands to the hundreds or thousands of zombies, requesting them to take uniform action simultaneously.

The most common action to be taken is to simultaneously launch a packet flood against a target. While a traditional SYN flood would deluge a target with packets from one host, a distributed denial-of-service attack would send packets from large numbers of zombies, rapidly exhausting the capacity of even very high-bandwidth, well-designed sites. Many distributed denial-of-service attack tools support SYN, UDP, and ICMP flooding, smurf attacks, as well as some malformed packet attacks. Any or all of these options can be selected by the attacker using the control program.

**Denial-of-Service Attack Defenses**

To defend against malformed packet attacks, system patches and security fixes must be regularly applied. Vendors frequently update their systems with patches to handle a new flavor of denial-of-service attack. An organization must have a program for monitoring vendor and industry security bulletins for security fixes, and a controlled method for implementing these fixes soon after they are announced and tested.

For packet flood attacks, critical systems should have underlying network architectures with multiple, redundant paths, eliminating a single point of failure. Furthermore, adequate bandwidth is a must. Also, some routers and firewalls support traffic flow control to help ease the burden of a SYN flood.

Finally, by appropriately configuring an Internet-accessible network, an organization can minimize the possibility that it will be used as a jumping-off point for smurf and distributed denial-of-service attacks. To prevent the possibility of being used as a smurf amplifier, the external router or firewall should be configured to drop all directed broadcast requests from the Internet. To lower the chance of being used in a distributed denial-of-service attack, an organization should implement anti-spoof filters on external routers and firewalls to make sure that all outgoing traffic has a source IP address of the site. This egress filtering prevents an attacker from sending spoofed packets from a zombie or other denial-of-service tool located on the network. Anti-spoof ingress filters, which drop all packets from an Internet claiming to come from one's internal network, are also useful in preventing some denial-of-service attacks.

# Chapter 51

# A Primer on Cracking: Part 2

*Edward Skoudis*

CHAPTER 50, OR PART 1, DISCUSSED NETWORK MAPPING AND PORT SCANNING, VULNERA-
BILITY SCANNING, WARDIALING, NETWORK EXPLOITS, AND DENIAL-OF-SERVICE ATTACKS.
This chapter, Part 2, discusses stack-based buffer overflows, password
cracking, backdoors, Trojan horses and rootkits, and defenses — intrusion
detection and incident response procedures.

## STACK-BASED BUFFER OVERFLOWS

Stack-based buffer overflow attacks are commonly used by an attacker to
take over a system remotely across a network. Additionally, buffer overflows
can be employed by local malicious users to elevate their privileges and gain
superuser access to a system. Stack-based buffer overflow attacks exploit
the way many operating systems handle their stack, an internal data structure used by running programs to store data temporarily. When a function
call is made, the current state of the executing program and variables to be
passed to the function are pushed on the stack. New local variables used by
the function are also allocated space on the stack. Additionally, the stack
stores the return address of the code calling the function. This return
address will be accessed from the stack once the function call is complete.
The system uses this address to resume execution of the calling program at
the appropriate place. Exhibit 1 shows how a stack is constructed.

Most UNIX and all Windows systems have a stack that can hold data and
executable code. Because local variables are stored on the stack when a
function is called, poor code can be exploited to overrun the boundaries of
these variables on the stack. If user input length is not examined by the code,
a particular variable on the stack may exceed the memory allocated to it on
the stack, overwriting all variables and even the return address for where
execution should resume after the function is complete. This operation,
called "smashing" the stack, allows an attacker to overflow the local variables to insert executable code and another return address on the stack.
Exhibit 1 also shows a stack that has been smashed with a buffer overflow.

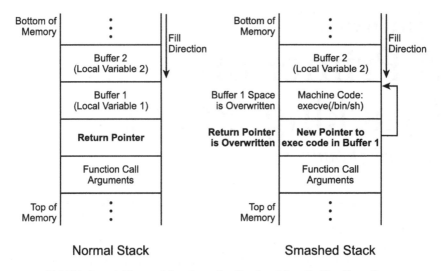

**Exhibit 1. A Normal Stack and a Stack with a Buffer Overflow**

The attacker will overflow the buffer on the stack with machine-specific bytecodes that consist of executable commands (usually a shell routine), and a return pointer to begin execution of these inserted commands. Therefore, with very carefully constructed binary code, the attacker can actually enter information as a user into a program that consists of executable code and a new return address. The buggy program will not analyze the length of this input, but will place it on the stack, and actually begin to execute the attacker's code. Such vulnerabilities allow an attacker to break out of the application code and access any system components with the permissions of the broken program. If the broken program is running with superuser privileges (e.g., SUID root on a UNIX system), the attacker has taken over the machine with a buffer overflow.

**Stack-Based Buffer Overflow Defenses**

The most thorough defense against buffer overflow attacks is to properly code software so that it cannot be used to smash the stack. All programs should validate all input from users and other programs, ensuring that it fits into allocated memory structures. Each variable should be checked (including user input, variables from other functions, input from other programs, and even environment variables) to ensure that allocated buffers are adequate to hold the data. Unfortunately, this ultimate solution is only available to individuals who write the programs and those with source code.

Additionally, security practitioners and system administrators should carefully control and minimize the number of SUID programs on a system that users can run and have permissions of other users (such as root).

Only SUID programs with an explicit business need should be installed on sensitive systems.

Finally, many stack-based buffer overflow attacks can be avoided by configuring the systems not to execute code from the stack. Solaris and Linux offer this option. For example, to secure a Solaris system against stack-based buffer overflows, the following lines should be added to /etc/system:

```
set noexec_user_stack=1
set noexec_user_stack_log=1
```

The first line will prevent execution on a stack, and the second line will log any attempt to do so. Unfortunately, some programs legitimately try to run code off the stack. Such programs will crash if this option is implemented. Generally, if the system is single purpose and needs to be secure (e.g., a Web server), this option should be used to prevent stack-based buffer overflow.

## THE ART AND SCIENCE OF PASSWORD CRACKING

The vast majority of systems today authenticate users with a static password. When a user logs in, the password is transmitted to the system, which checks the password to make the decision whether or not to let the user login. To make this decision, the system must have a mechanism to compare the user's input with the actual password. Of course, the system could just store all of the passwords locally and compare from this file. Such a file of cleartext passwords, however, would provide a very juicy target for an attacker. To make the target less useful for attackers, most modern operating systems use a one-way hash or encryption mechanism to protect the stored passswords. When a user types in a password, the system hashes the user's entry and compares it to the stored hash. If the two hashes match, the password is correct and the user can login.

Password cracking tools are used to attack this method of password protection. An attacker will use some exploit (often a buffer overflow) to gather the encrypted or hashed password file from a system (on a UNIX system without password shadowing, any user can read the hashed password file). After downloading the hashed password file, the attacker uses a password cracking tool to determine users' passwords. The cracking tool operates using a loop: it guesses a password, hashes or encrypts the password, and compares it to the hashed password from the stolen file. If the hashes match, the attacker has the password. If the hashes do not match, the loop begins again with another password guess.

Password cracking tools base their password guesses on a dictionary or a complete brute-force attack, attempting every possible password.

Dozens of dictionaries are available online, in a multitude of languages including English, French, German, Klingon, etc.

Numerous password cracking tools are available. The most popular and full-functional password crackers include:

- John-the-Ripper, by Solar Designer, focuses on cracking UNIX passwords; available at http://www.openwall.com/john/.
- L0phtCrack, used to crack Windows NT passwords, is available at http://www.l0pht.com.

**Password Cracking Defenses**

The first defense against password cracking is to minimize the exposure of the encrypted/hashed password file. On UNIX systems, shadow password files should be used, which allow only the superuser to read the password file. On Windows NT systems, the SYSKEY feature available in NT 4.0 SP 3 and later should be installed and enabled. Furthermore, all backups and system recovery disks should be stored in physically secured locations and possibly even encrypted.

A strong password policy is a crucial element in ensuring a secure network. A password policy should require password lengths greater than eight characters and the use of alphanumeric *and* special characters in every password, and force users to have passwords with mixed-case letters. Users must be aware of the issue of weak passwords and be trained in creating memorable, yet difficult-to-guess passwords.

To ensure that passwords are secure and to identify weak passwords, security practitioners should check system passwords on a periodic basis using password cracking tools. When weak passwords are discovered, the security group should have a defined procedure for interacting with users whose passwords can be easily guessed.

Finally, several software packages are available that prevent users from setting their passwords to easily guessed values. When a user establishes a new password, these filtering programs check the password to make sure that it is sufficiently complex and is not just a variation of the user name or a dictionary word. With this kind of tool, users are simply unable to create passwords that are easily guessed, eliminating a significant security issue. For filtering software to be effective, it must be installed on all servers where users establish passwords, including UNIX servers, Windows NT primary and backup domain controllers, and Novell servers (Jonathan Held, "Password Security," *Data Security Management,* April 2000, 83-01-11).

## BACKDOORS

Backdoors are programs that bypass traditional security checks on a system, allowing an attacker to gain access to a machine without providing a system password and getting logged. Attackers install backdoors on a machine (or dupe a user into installing one for them) to ensure they will be able to gain access to the system at a later time. Once installed, most backdoors listen on special ports for incoming connections from the attacker across the network. When the attacker connects to the backdoor listener, the traditional user ID and password or other forms of authentication are bypassed. Instead, the attacker can gain access to the system without providing a password, or by using a special password used only to enter the backdoor.

Netcat is an incredibly flexible tool written for UNIX by Hobbit and for Windows NT by Weld Pond (both versions are available at http://www. l0pht.com/~weld/netcat/). Among its numerous other uses, Netcat can be used to create a backdoor listener with a superuser-level shell on any TCP or UDP port. For Windows systems, an enormous number of backdoor applications are available, including Back Orifice 2000 (called BO2K for short, and available at http://www.bo2k.com), and hack-a-tack (available at http://www.hack-a-tack.com). (See also Christopher Klaus, "An Introduction to the Back Orifice 2000 Backdoor Program," *Data Security Management,* October 2000, 84-02-02.)

### Backdoor Defenses

The best defense against backdoor programs is for system and security administrators to know what is running on their machines, particularly sensitive systems storing critical information or processing high-value transactions. If a process suddenly appears running as the superuser listening on a port, the administrator needs to investigate. Backdoors listening on various ports can be discovered using the **netstat –na** command on UNIX and Windows NT systems.

Additionally, many backdoor programs (such as BO2K) can be discovered by an anti-virus program, which should be installed on all user desktops, as well as servers throughout an organization.

### TROJAN HORSES AND ROOTKITS

Another fundamental element of an attacker's toolchest is the Trojan horse program. Like the Trojan horse of ancient Greece, these new Trojan horses appear to have some useful function, but in reality are just disguising some malicious activity. For example, a user might receive an executable birthday card program in electronic mail. When the unsuspecting user activates the birthday card program and watches birthday cakes dance across the screen, the program secretly installs a backdoor or perhaps deletes the users' hard drive. As illustrated in this example, Trojan horses rely on deception — they trick a user or system administrator into running them for their (apparent) usefulness, but their true purpose is to attack the user's machine.

### Traditional Trojan Horses

A traditional Trojan horse is simply an independent program that can be run by a user or administrator. Numerous traditional Trojan horse programs have been devised, including:

- The familiar birthday card or holiday greeting e-mail attachment described earlier
- A software program that claims to be able to turn CD-ROM readers into CD writing devices (although this feat is impossible to accomplish in software, many users have been duped into downloading this "tool," which promptly deletes their hard drives upon activation)
- A security vulnerability scanner, WinSATAN (this tool claims to provide a convenient security vulnerability scan for system and security administrators using a Windows NT system; unfortunately, an unsuspecting user running this program will also have a deleted hard drive)

Countless other examples exist. While conceptually unglamorous, traditional Trojan horses can be a major problem if users are not careful and run untrusted programs on their machines.

### RootKits

A RootKit takes the concept of a Trojan horse to a much more powerful level. Although the name implies otherwise, RootKits do not allow an attacker to gain "root" (superuser) access to a system. Instead, RootKits allow an attacker who already has superuser access to keep that access by foiling all attempts of an administrator to detect the invasion. RootKits consist of an entire suite of Trojan horse programs that replace or patch critical system programs. The various tools used by administrators to detect attackers on their machines are routinely undermined with RootKits.

Most RootKits include a Trojan horse backdoor program (in UNIX, the */bin/login* routine). The attacker will install a new Trojan horse version of */bin/login,* overwriting the previous version. The RootKit */bin/login* routine includes a special backdoor userID and password so that the attacker can access the system at later times.

Additionally, RootKits include a sniffer and a program to hide the sniffer. An administrator can detect a sniffer on a system by running the **ifconfig** command. If a sniffer is running, the **ifconfig** output will contain the PROMISC flag, an indication that the Ethernet card is in promiscuous mode and therefore is sniffing. RootKit contains a Trojan horse version of **ifconfig** that does not display the PROMISC flag, allowing an attacker to avoid detection.

UNIX-based RootKits also replace other critical system executables, including **ps** and **du**. The **ps** command, emloyed by users and administrators to determine which processes are running, is modified so that an attacker can hide processes. The **du** command, which shows disk utilization, is altered so that the file space taken up by RootKit and the attacker's other programs can be masked.

By replacing programs like /bin/login, ifconfig, ps, du, and numerous others, these RootKit tools become part of the operating system itself. Therefore, RootKits are used to cover the eyes and ears of an administrator. They create a virtual world on the computer that appears benign to the system administrator, when in actuality, an attacker can log in and move around the system with impunity. RootKits have been developed for most major UNIX systems and Windows NT. A whole variety of UNIX RootKits can be found at http://packetstorm.securify.com/UNIX/penetration/rootkits, while an NT RootKit is available at http://www.rootkit.com.

A recent development in this arena is the release of kernel-level RootKits. These RootKits act at the most fundamental levels of an operating system. Rather than replacing application programs such as /bin/login and ifconfig, kernel-level RootKits actually patch the kernel to provide very low-level access to the system. These tools rely on the loadable kernel modules that many new UNIX variants support, including Linux and Solaris. Loadable kernel modules let an administrator add functionality to the kernel on-the-fly, without even rebooting the system. An attacker with superuser access can install a kernel-level RootKit that will allow for the remapping of execution of programs.

When an administrator tries to run a program, the Trojanized kernel will remap the execution request to the attacker's program, which could be a backdoor offering access or other Trojan horse. Because the kernel does the remapping of execution requests, this type of activity is very difficult to detect. If the administrator attempts to look at the remapped file or check its integrity, the program will appear unaltered, because the program's image *is* unaltered. However, when executed, the unaltered program is skipped, and a malicious program is substituted by the kernel. Knark, written by Creed, is a kernel-level RootKit that can be found at http://packetstorm.securify.com/UNIX/penetration/rootkits.

## Trojan Horses and RootKit Defenses

To protect against traditional Trojan horses, user awareness is key. Users must understand the risks associated with downloading untrusted programs and running them. They must also be made aware of the problems of running executable attachments in e-mail from untrusted sources.

Additionally, some traditional Trojan horses can be detected and eliminated by anti-virus programs. Every end-user computer system (and even servers) should have an effective, up-to-date anti-virus program installed.

To defend against RootKits, system and security administrators must use integrity checking programs for critical system files. Numerous tools are available, including the venerable Tripwire, that generate a hash of the executables commonly altered when a RootKit is installed. The administrator should store these hashes on a protected medium (such as a write-protected floppy disk) and periodically check the veracity of the programs on the machine with the protected hashes. Commonly, this type of check is done at least weekly, depending on the sensitivity of the machine. The administrator must reconcile any changes discovered in these critical system files with recent patches. If system files have been altered, and no patches were installed by the administrator, a malicious user or outside attacker may have installed a RootKit. If a RootKit is detected, the safest way to ensure its complete removal is to rebuild the entire operating system and even critical applications.

Unfortunately, kernel-level RootKits cannot be detected with integrity check programs because the integrity checker relies on the underlying kernel to do its work. If the kernel lies to the integrity checker, the results will not show the RootKit installation. The best defense against the kernel-level RootKits is a monolithic kernel that does not support loadable kernel modules. On critical systems (such as firewalls, Internet Web servers, DNS servers, mail servers, etc.), administrators should build the systems with complete kernels without support for loadable kernel modules. With this configuration, the system will prevent an attacker from gaining root-level access and patching the kernel in real-time.

## OVERALL DEFENSES: INTRUSION DETECTION AND INCIDENT RESPONSE PROCEDURES

Each of the defensive strategies described above deals with particular tools and attacks. In addition to employing each of those strategies, organizations must also be capable of detecting and responding to an attack. These capabilities are realized through the deployment of intrusion detection systems (IDS) and the implementation of incident response procedures.

An IDS acts as a burglar alarm on the network. With a database of known attack signatures, an IDS can determine when an attack is under way and alert security and system administration personnel. Acting as an early warning system, the IDS allows an organization to detect an attack in its early stages and minimize the damage that may be caused. (See also Eugene Schultz and Eugene Spafford, "Intrusion Detection: How to Utilize a Still Immature Technology," *Data Security Management,* October 1999, 84-10-28.)

Perhaps even more important than an IDS, documented incident response procedures are among the most critical elements of an effective security program. Unfortunately, even with industry-best defenses, a sufficiently motivated attacker can penetrate the network. To address this possibility, an organization must have procedures defined in advance describing how the organization will react to the attack. These incident response procedures should specify the roles of individuals in the organization during an attack. The chain of command and escalation procedures should be spelled out in advance. Creating these items during a crisis will lead to costly mistakes.

Truly effective incident response procedures should also be multi-disciplinary, not focusing only on information technology. Instead, the roles, responsibilities, and communication channels for the legal, human resources, media relations, information technology, and security organizations should all be documented and communicated. Specific members of these organizations should be identified as the core of a Security Incident Response Team (SIRT), to be called together to address an incident when it occurs. Additionally, the SIRT should conduct periodic exercises of the incident response capability to ensure that team members are effective in their roles. (See also Chris Hare, "CIRT: Responding to an Attack," *Data Security Management,* June 2000, 82-02-66.)

Additionally, with a large number of organizations outsourcing their information technology infrastructure by utilizing Web hosting, desktop management, e-mail, data storage, and other services, the extension of the incident response procedures to these outside organizations can be critical. The contract established with the outsourcing company should carefully state the obligations of the service provider in intrusion detection, incident notification, and participation in incident response. A specific service level agreement (SLA) for handling security incidents and the time needed to pull together members of the service company's staff in a SIRT should also be agreed upon.

## CONCLUSIONS

While the number and power of these attack tools continue to escalate, system administrators and security personnel should not give up the fight. All of the defensive strategies discussed throughout this chapter boil down to doing a thorough and professional job of administering systems: know what is running on the system, keep it patched, ensure appropriate bandwidth is available, utilize IDS, and prepare a Security Incident Response Team. Although these activities are not easy and can involve a great deal of effort, through diligence, an organization can keep its systems secured and minimize the chance of an attack. By employing intrusion detection systems and sound incident response procedures, even those highly sophisticated attacks that do get through can be discovered and contained, minimizing the impact on the organization. By creating an effective security program with sound defensive strategies, critical systems and information can be protected.

# Chapter 52
# Protecting Data and Systems from Internet Viruses

*Terinia Reid*

A COMPUTER VIRUS IS A PROGRAM DESIGNED TO REPLICATE AND SPREAD ON ITS OWN, USUALLY WITHOUT A PERSON'S KNOWLEDGE. Computer viruses spread by attaching themselves to another program — such as word processing or spreadsheet programs — or to the boot sector of a diskette. When an infected file is executed or the computer is started from an infected disk, the virus itself is executed. Often, it stays in memory, waiting to infect the next program that is run or the next disk that is accessed.

There exists a perception that there are benign viruses and malignant viruses. Considering that any type of virus typically causes a computer to perform abnormally, whether it results in damage or not, this author finds it difficult to class a virus as benign. However, the majority of viruses are harmless and do no real damage to a computer or files. A benign virus might do nothing more than display a message at a predetermined time or slow down the performance of a computer.

Destructive, or malignant, viruses, can cause damage to a computer system by corrupting files or destroying data. These viruses do not corrupt the files they infect; that would prevent them from spreading. Rather, they infect and then wait for a trigger date to do damage. Just because a virus is classified as malignant does not mean the damage it causes is intentional. Sometimes the damage is the result of poor programming or unintended bugs in the viral code.

## TYPES OF VIRUSES

### Boot Sector Infectors

All logical drives — hard disk and floppy — contain a boot sector, including disks that are not bootable. The boot sector contains specific information relating to the formatting of the disk and the data stored there. It also contains a small program called the boot program that loads operating system files. Boot sector viruses infect the boot program of the hard drive when an infected diskette is left in a floppy drive and the system is rebooted. When the computer reads and executes the boot sector program, the boot sector virus goes into memory and infects the hard drive. Later, when the user boots from the hard drive, the virus again gains control and can then infect each and every diskette used on the computer. Because every disk has a boot sector, boot viruses on a "data disk" that has no programs or operating system can infect computers.

Some symptoms of boot sector virus activity:

- Cannot launch Windows
- Computer cannot perform a disk-based setup
- Diskette errors
- Hard drive errors
- Non-system disk errors

### Macro Viruses (Most Common)

A macro virus is a piece of self-replicating code written in an application's macro language. Many applications have macro capabilities such as the automatic playback of keystrokes available in early versions of Lotus 1-2-3. The distinguishing factor that makes it possible to create a macro virus is the existence of auto-execute macros in the language (e.g., Microsoft Word/Excel).

An auto-execute macro is one that is executed in response to some event and not in response to an explicit user command. Common auto-execute events are opening a file, closing a file, and starting an application. Once a macro is running, it can copy itself to other documents, delete files, and create general havoc in a computer system. These things occur without the user explicitly running that particular macro.

Another type of hazardous macro is one named for an existing Word command. If a macro in the global macro file or in an attached, active template has the name of an existing Word command, the macro command replaces the Word command. For example, if one creates a macro named FileSave in the "normal.dot" template, that macro is executed whenever one chooses the Save command on the File menu. There is no way to disable this feature.

Macro viruses spread by having one or more auto-execute macros in a document. By opening or closing the document or using a replaced command, one activates the virus macro. As soon as the macro is activated, it copies itself and any other macros it needs to the global macro file "normal.dot." After they are stored in normal.dot, they are available in all opened documents. An important point to make here is that Word documents (.DOC files) cannot contain macros; only Word templates (.DOT files) can contain macros. However, it is a relatively simple task to mask a template as a document by changing the file name extension from .DOT to .DOC.

An example of a Word macro virus is the Nuclear macro virus with nine macros (AutoExec, AutoOpen, DropSuriv, FileExit, FilePrint, FilePrintDefault, FileSaveAs, InsertPayload, and Payload). It was the first macro virus known to cause damage, particularly to printouts and MS-DOS system files. Printing a document after infection may cause the following text to be appended to one's printout: "STOP ALL FRENCH NUCLEAR TESTING IN THE PACIFIC!" Also, once infected, it will attempt on April 5 to delete system files from one's root directory, MS-DOS will no longer start.

### File Infectors

These viruses attach themselves to or replace .COM and .EXE files, although in some cases they can infect files with the extensions .SYS, .DRV, .BIN, and OVL. This type of virus generally infects uninfected programs when they are executed with the virus in memory. In other cases, they infect programs when they are opened-using the DOS DIR command, for example — or the virus simply infects all of the files in the directory it was run from (a so-called direct infector). A sample:

> File: VIRS0779.TXT
> Name/Aliases: Smeg, Pathogen, Queeg
> Platform: PC/MS-DOS
> Type: Program.
> Disk Location: EXE application.
> COM application
> Features: Memory resident; TSR
> Polymorphic
> Damage: Overwrites sectors on the Hard Disk
> Size:
> See Also: Junkie
> Notes: Smeg and its variants are memory resident, polymorphic COM
> and EXE infectors

The Pathogen variant overwrites part of one's disk drive between the hours of 17:00 and 18:00 on Monday evenings. It then prints the following message:

> Your hard-disk is being corrupted, courtesy of PATHOGEN!
> Programmed in the U.K. (Yes, NOT Bulgaria!) [C] The Black Baron
> 1993-4.
> Featuring SMEG v0.1: Simulated Metamorphic Encryption Generator!

Smoke me a kipper, I'll be back for breakfast...'
Unfortunately some of your data won't!!!!!

### Virus Hoax

A virus hoax is an e-mail that is intended to scare people about a non-existent virus threat. Users often forward these alerts, thinking they are doing a service to their fellow workers, but this causes lost productivity, panic, and lost time. This increased traffic can soon become a massive problem in e-mail systems and cause unnecessary fear and panic. A sample of a virus hoax:

> Dear All,
> For your reference, take necessary precautions. If you receive an email with a file called California, do not open the file. The file contains WOB-BLER virus.

> WARNING
> This information was announced yesterday morning from IBM; AOL states that this is a very dangerous virus, much worse than "Melissa," and that there is NO remedy for it at this time. Some very sick individual has succeeded in using the reformat function from Norton Utilities causing it to completely erase all documents on the hard drive. It has been designed to work with Netscape Navigator and Microsoft Internet Explorer. It destroys Macintosh and IBM compatible computers. This is a new, very malicious virus and not many people know about it.

## HOW VIRUSES INFECT

Viruses, whether they are boot viruses, file viruses, or macro viruses, can employ none, one, or several of the following techniques to spread or conceal themselves.

**Multi-partite Viruses.** These often infect multiple targets instead of just one type of file or disk. For example, they will infect both files and boot records on hard disks, or both files and boot sectors on floppy disks.

**Polymorphic Viruses.** The polymorphic virus changes segments of its own code so that it looks like a different virus from one infection to another. This technique is employed by virus creators to make it more difficult for anti-virus (AV) software to detect them, inasmuch as detection software has a harder time of comparing the changing virus to its inventory of known viruses.

**Stealth Viruses.** These viruses actively conceal themselves from being discovered by AV software. There are two types of stealth virus:

- *Size stealth*. Once it infects a computer and becomes active in a computer's memory, a virus with size stealth capabilities monitors the opening and closing of all files. If it sees that a file it has infected earlier is about to be opened, it races to the file and un-infects it, so that the AV software does not know it has been infected. Once the file is closed, the virus then re-infects it. Another means these viruses have for hiding from AV software is by altering the disk directory data of a file to hide the additional bytes of an infecting virus. When possible, the virus may continue to infect any other files that are accessed on one's hard drive.

- *Full stealth.* Like a size stealth virus, a full stealth virus is memory resident and monitors all file activity. When it sees that an infected file is about to be opened, it redirects the call to an uninfected copy of the file that it made before infecting it. The virus stores the uninfected copy of the file at some other location on the hard drive for just this purpose.

These viruses actively conceal themselves while they are running in memory. If the anti-virus program does not scan in memory for these viruses, it will completely miss them when scanning files.

**Retro Viruses.** These viruses are designed to actively attack anti-virus software. They are anti-anti-virus viruses! They will attempt to delete anti-virus data files, corrupt anti-virus programs, and more.

**Triggered-Event Viruses.** These viruses activate based on some event. This event is known as a trigger event; hence, the characteristic name. An event can include a date, a certain keyboard action, or the opening of a particular file. The effect depends on the virus.

**Memory-Resident Viruses.** These viruses are copied to the computer's memory when its host program is executed. The virus no longer relies on the host program to remain active, as it stays active in memory, thereby infecting other files, until the computer is turned off.

**Non-Memory-Resident Viruses.** These viruses become memory resident when the host program is executed. The virus stays active in memory, infecting other files, until the host program is closed. It can only remain active while the host program is running.

**Encrypting Viruses.** These viruses are transformed into something that does not look like a virus in order to avoid detection by anti-virus software. The virus does this with special code that allows it to convert, or encrypt, itself into program code that is non-infectious. But in order to infect, the virus must re-convert, or decrypt, itself into the original virus code, also making it visible to anti-virus software.

**Combination Viruses.** These viruses can include one or more of the above characteristics, thus having a combination of characteristics. For example, a particular virus can be a polymorphic encryptor, which means that it combines both polymorphic and encryption characteristics.

## OTHER DESTRUCTIVE PROGRAMS

As the name implies, a Trojan horse program comes with a hidden surprise intended by the programmer but totally unexpected by the user. The Trojan is not really a virus, but rather a means of virus delivery. The virus masquerades as a legitimate program so that the user will not realize it is a virus. For example, one has downloaded from an online service what one thought was a game program; but when one executes it, it turns out to be virus that infects one's computer.

Recent example: W95.Babylonia. According to Symantec, the virus was originally posted to an Internet newsgroup inside a Windows help file named serialz.hlp. This file was claimed to be a list of serial numbers for "Warez" (pirated commercial software). But if the help file was opened, it exploited a little-known feature of Microsoft Windows that allows help files to contain executable programs. Merely opening the help file caused the Trojan horse program to be released within the computer system and begin wreaking mischief.

Worms are like viruses in that they do replicate themselves. However, instead of spreading from file to file, they spread from computer to computer, infecting an entire system.

Worms are insidious because they rely less (or not at all) upon human behavior in order to spread themselves from one computer to another. The computer worm is a program designed to copy itself from one computer to another, leveraging some network medium: e-mail, TCP/IP, etc. The worm is more interested in infecting as many machines as possible on the network, and less interested in spreading many copies of itself on a single computer (like a computer virus). The prototypical worm infects (or causes its code to run on) a target system only once; after the initial infection, the worm attempts to spread to other machines on the network. Following is an example of the recent ExploreZip worm virus that uses an e-mail message to spread:

> Hi (recipient name)
> I received your email and I shall send you a reply ASAP.
> Till then, take a look at the attached zipped docs.

After a user clicks on the attachment, the worm searches hard drives C through Z. It selects the Microsoft Word, Excel, and PowerPoint files, as well as source code files, and destroys the data on those files. When executed, the worm uses MAPI-enabled e-mail systems to automatically reply to received e-mail messages.

## VIRUS PROTECTION

Viruses can be controlled at the desktop, the file server, the gateway, and on e-mail servers. Desktop and server anti-virus applications allow for virus scan and detection on an ongoing and periodic basis, as well as each time a file is downloaded or a computer is booted. More and more, computer users have anti-virus software running full-time in the background, scanning all files and diskettes the moment they are accessed. As macro viruses proliferate, scanning e-mail attachments at the desktop is critical. To protect networks, monitoring attachments at the e-mail gateway is just as important.

Recommendations:

1. Avoid installing any unknown software (e.g., games, screen-savers, etc.).
2. Be careful of software auto-installations from unknown/untrusted Web sites.
3. Write-protect diskettes (ensure floppy is clean first).
4. Install and auto-scan all hard drives, floppy disks, files, and programs with an anti-virus product at all times.
5. On a regular basis, update the signature files for the anti-virus program (as viruses are created and identified, the fixes are included in signature files).
6. Be aware of strange computer system behavior, such as keyboard making strange noises, characters dropping from documents, etc.

## HOW TO REMOVE A VIRUS

If the infection is file based (e.g., macro), running an anti-virus scanner with up-to-date signatures should clean the file and restore it to normal working order. If the infection is boot sector or hard-drive related, to keep downtime short and losses low, do the minimum required to restore the system to a normal state, starting with booting the system from a clean diskette. It is very unlikely that one will need to low-level reformat the hard disk.

If backups of the infected files are available and appropriate care was taken when making the backups, this is the safest solution — although it requires a lot of work if many files are involved.

More commonly, a disinfecting program is used. If the virus is a boot sector infector, one can continue using the computer with relative safety if one boots it from a clean system diskette, but it is wise to go through all diskettes removing infection, because sooner or later, one may be careless and leave a diskette in the machine when it reboots. Boot sector infections on PCs can be cured by a two-step approach of replacing the MBR (on the hard disk), either by using a backup or by the FDISK/MBR command (from

641

DOS 5 and up), then using the SYS command to replace the DOS boot sector. Do not use FDISK/MBR for Monkey or any other virus that encrypts the MBR (Master Boot Record). Confirm the above steps with a computer technician before completing to ensure that the proper method is used.

**Additional Virus Information Web Sites**

www.symantec.com, Norton Antivirus
www.mcafee.com, McAfee VirusScan
www.cai.com, Computer Associates
www.caic.com, Computer Incident Advisory Capability
www.drsolomon.com, Dr. Solomon
www.f-secure.com, Formerly Data Fellows
www.stiller.com/vintro.htm

The above list is not intended as an endorsement for any product or manufacturer.

# Chapter 53
# Types of Firewalls
*E. Eugene Schultz*

A FIREWALL IS AN EXCELLENT SECURITY MECHANISM AND, WHEN APPROPRIATELY SELECTED AND IMPLEMENTED, CAN ESTABLISH A RELATIVELY SECURE BARRIER BETWEEN A SYSTEM AND THE EXTERNAL ENVIRONMENT. This chapter describes the types of firewalls that are available and presents the advantages and disadvantages of each type.

## PACKET FILTERS

The most basic type of firewall is the packet filter. It receives packets and evaluates them according to a set of rules that are usually in the form of access control lists. These packets may be forwarded to their destinations, dropped, or dropped with a return message to the originator describing what happened. The types of filtering rules vary from one vendor's product to another, but those most frequently applied are

- Source and destination IP address (e.g., all packets from source address 128.44.9.0 through 128.44.9.255 might be accepted, but all other packets might be rejected)
- Source and destination port (e.g., all TCP packets originating from or destined to port 25 — the simple mail transfer protocol, or SMTP, port — might be accepted, but all TCP packets destined for port 79 — the finger port — might be dropped)
- Direction of traffic (e.g., inbound or outbound)
- Type of protocol (e.g., IP, TCP, user datagram protocol, or internetwork packet exchange)
- The packet's state (i.e., SYN, meaning synchronize, or ACK, which is the acknowledgement that a connection between hosts has already been established)

Packet-filtering firewalls provide a reasonable amount of protection for a network with minimum complications. Packet-filtering rules can be extremely intuitive and thus easy to set up. One simple, but surprisingly effective, rule is to allow (i.e., accept) all packets that are sent from a specific, known set of IP addresses, such as hosts within another network owned by the same organization or corporation. Packet-filtering firewalls also tend to have the least negative effect on the throughput rate at the gateway compared with other types of firewalls. They also tend to be the most transparent to legitimate users. If the filtering rules are set up appropriately, users obtain their required access with little interference from the firewall.

However, simplicity has its disadvantages. The rules that packet-filtering firewalls implement are based on port conventions. If an organization wants to stop certain service requests (e.g., telnet) from reaching internal or external hosts, the most logical rule is to block the port (e.g., port 23) that by convention is used for telnet traffic. Blocking this port, however, does not prevent someone inside the network from allowing telnet requests on a different port that the firewall's rules leave open. In addition, blocking some kinds of traffic causes a number of practical problems. Blocking X-Windows traffic (which is typically sent to ports 6000 to 6013) on the surface seems to provide an effective security solution because of the many known vulnerabilities in this protocol. Many types of remote log-on requests and graphical applications depend on X-Windows, however, so blocking X-Windows traffic may thus restrict functionality, leading to the decision to allow all X-Windows traffic (which makes the firewall a less-than-effective security barrier).

In short, firewalling schemes based on ports do not provide the precise control that many organizations require. Moreover, packet-filtering firewalls are often deficient in logging capabilities, particularly in providing logging that can be configured to an organization's needs (e.g., to capture only certain events in some cases and, in others, to capture all events). They may also lack remote administration facilities that can save considerable time and effort. Finally, the process of creating and updating filtering rules is prone to logic errors that could result in easy conduits of unauthorized access to a network.

Like most other security-related tools, over time, many packet-filtering firewalls have become more sophisticated. Some vendors of packet-filtering firewalls offer programs that check the logic of filtering rules to discover any contradictions and errors. Packet-filtering firewalls also exist that offer strong authentication mechanisms, such as token-based authentication. Many products defend against previously successful methods to defeat packet-filtering firewalls. However, network attackers can send packets to or from a disallowed address or disallowed port by fragmenting the contents. Fragmented packets cannot be analyzed by a conventional packet-filtering firewall, so the firewall allows them through, where they are assembled at the destination host. In this manner, the network attackers can bypass firewall defenses.

Similarly, attackers have developed an attack in which the initial TCP packet sent has the acknowledge (ACK) rather than the synchronize (SYN) flag set in the header. Because SYN packets are used to establish connections, a conventional packet-filtering firewall is programmed, for efficiency, to analyze and apply filtering rules only to SYN packets. ACK packets can freely pass through the choke because they should be part of an established connection. However, some vendors have developed a state-conscious firewall, which is a special type of packet-filtering firewall, to prevent these types of attacks. By remembering the state of connections that pass through the firewall, a state-conscious firewall can prevent packet fragmentation and ACK packet-based attacks. Some state-conscious firewalls can associate each outbound connection with a specific inbound connection (and vice versa), creating simpler rules. Because the User Datagram Protocol (UDP) is connectionless and thus does not contain information about states, state-conscious firewalls are vulnerable to UDP-based attacks unless they track each UDP packet that has already gone through and determine which subsequent UDP packet sent in the opposite direction(i.e., inbound or outbound) is associated with that packet.

Many routers have packet-filtering capabilities and, therefore, can be considered a type of firewall. Using a packet-filtering router as the sole choke component within a gate, however, is not likely to provide effective security, because routers are more vulnerable to attack than are firewall hosts, and they generally do not log traffic efficiently. A screening router is difficult to administer, often requiring that a network administrator download its configuration files, edit them, and send them back to the router. The main advantage of screening routers is that they provide some filtering functionality with minor performance overhead and minimal interference to users, who may not realize the screening router's existence. One option for using packet-filtering routers is to employ them as external routers in a belt-and-suspenders topology. The security filtering by the external router provides additional protection for the firewall by making unauthorized access more difficult. Moreover, the gate has more than one choke component, providing multiple barriers to prevent an attack on an internal network and to compensate for configuration errors and vulnerabilities in any one of the choke components.

## APPLICATION-GATEWAY FIREWALLS

A second type of firewall handles the choke function of a firewall differently — by determining not only whether but how each connection through it is made. This type of firewall stops each incoming (or outgoing) connection at the firewall, and, if the connection is permitted, initiates its connection to the destination host on behalf of whoever created the initial connection. This type of connection is called a proxy connection. By using its database, which defines the types of connections allowed, the firewall either establishes another connection(i.e., permitting the originating and destination host to communicate) or drops the original connection. If the firewall is programmed appropriately, the process can be transparent to users.

645

An application-gateway firewall is simply a type of proxy server that provides proxies for specific applications. The most common implementations of application-gateway firewalls provide proxy services, such as mail, file transfer protocol (FTP), and telnet, so that they do not run on the actual firewall, which increases security. Each connection is subject to a set of specific rules and conditions similar to those in packet-filtering firewalls, except that the selectivity rules that application-gateway firewalls use are not based on ports, but on the to-be-accessed programs or services (regardless of which port is used to access these programs). Criteria, such as the source or destination IP address, however, can be used to accept or reject incoming connections. Application-level firewalls also determine permissible conditions and events when a proxy connection has been established. An FTP proxy can restrict FTP access to one or more hosts by allowing the Get command, for example, and, at the same time, preventing the Put command. A telnet proxy can terminate a connection if the user attempts to perform a shell escape or to gain root access. Application-gateway firewalls are not limited only to applications that support TCP/IP services, however. These tools can similarly govern conditions of usage for a variety of applications, such as financial or process control applications.

The two basic types of application-gateway firewalls are application-generic firewalls and application-specific firewalls. The application-generic type provides a uniform method of connection for every application, regardless of type. The application-specific firewall determines the nature of connections to applications on an application-by-application basis. Regardless of the type of application-gateway firewall, if properly configured, the resulting security control can be precise — considerably more than is possible with packet-filtering firewalls. If used in connection with appropriate host-level controls (e.g., proper file permissions and ownerships), application-gateway firewalls make externally originated attacks on applications difficult. Another important function of application-gateway firewalls is hiding information about hosts within the internal network from the rest of the world. Finally, a number of commercial application-gateway firewalls are available that support strong authentication methods, such as token-based methods (e.g., use of hand-held authentication devices).

Application-gateway firewalls are the best selling of all types of firewalls. Nevertheless, they have some notable limitations. Most significant, for every TCP/IP client for which the firewall provides proxies, the client must be aware of the proxy that the firewall runs on its behalf. Therefore, each client must be modified accordingly. A second limitation is that, unless one uses a generic proxy mechanism, every application needs its own custom proxy. In the case of proxies for widely used services, such as telnet, FTP, and HTTP, this limitation is not formidable because a variety of proxy implementations is available. Proxies for many other services are not available at the present time, however, and must be custom written. Although some application-gateway firewall implementations are more transparent to users than others, none is completely transparent. Some require users, who have initiated connections, to make selections from menus before they reach their destinations. Finally, most application-gateway firewalls are not easy to initially configure and update correctly. To use an application-gateway firewall to its maximum advantage, network administrators should set up a new proxy for every new application accessible from outside a network. Furthermore, network administrators should work with application owners to ensure that specific restrictions on usage are placed on every remote connection to each critical application from outside the network. Seldom, however, are such practices observed because of the time, effort, and complexity involved.

## CIRCUIT-GATEWAY FIREWALLS

As discussed previously, application-gateway firewalls receive connections from clients, dropping some and accepting others, but always creating a new connection with whatever restrictions exist whenever a connection is accepted. Although, in theory, this process should be transparent to users, in practice, the transparency is less than ideal. A third type of firewall, the circuit-gateway firewall, has been designed to remedy this limitation by producing a more seamless, transparent connection between clients and destinations using routines in special libraries. The connection is often described as a virtual circuit, because the proxy creates an end-to-end connection between the client and the destination application. An application-gateway firewall is also advantageous because, rather than simply relaying packets by creating a second connection for each allowed incoming connection, it allows multiple clients to connect to multiple applications within an internal network.

Most circuit-gateway firewalls are implemented using SOCKS, a tool that includes a set of client libraries for proxy interfaces with clients. SOCKS receives an incoming connection from clients, and if the connections are allowed, it provides the data necessary for each client to connect to the application. Each client then invokes a set of commands to the gateway. The circuit-gateway firewall imposes all predefined restrictions, such as the particular commands that can be executed, and establishes a connection to the destination on the client's behalf. To users, this process appears transparent.

As with application-gateway firewalls, circuit-gateway firewall clients must generally be modified to be able to interface with the proxy mechanism that is used. Making each client aware of SOCKS is not an overwhelming task, because a variety of SOCKS libraries are available for different platforms. The client must simply be compiled with the appropriate set of SOCKS libraries for the particular platform (e.g., UNIX or Windows) on which the client runs.

Circuit-gateway firewalls also have limitations. First and foremost, the task of modifying all clients to make them aware of the proxy mechanism is costly and time-consuming. Having a common interface to the proxy server so that each client would not have to be changed would greatly improve usability. Second, circuit-gateway firewalls tend to provide a generic access mechanism that is independent of the semantics of destination applications. Because, in many instances, the danger associated with specific user actions is dependent on each application, offering proxies that take into account application semantics would be more advantageous. (Invoking the Delete command to remove data in an application that reinitializes all parameter values by retrieving values from a database that is not accessible to users every time it is invoked is relatively safe. In other applications, however, being able to delete data is potentially hazardous.) In addition, SOCKS has several limitations. Most implementations of SOCKS are deficient in their ability to log events. Furthermore, SOCKS neither supports strong access authentication methods nor provides an interface to authentication services that could provide this function.

## HYBRID FIREWALLS

Although the distinctions between packet-filtering firewalls, application-gateway firewalls, and circuit-gateway firewalls are meaningful, many firewall products cannot be classified as exactly one type. For example, one of the most popular firewall products on the market is basically a packet-filtering firewall that supports proxies for two commonly used TCP/IP services. As firewalls evolve, it is likely that some of the features in application-gateway firewalls will be included in circuit-gateway firewalls, and vice-versa.

## VIRTUAL PRIVATE NETWORKS

An increasingly popular Internet security control measure is the virtual private network (VPN), which incorporates end-to-end encryption into the network, enabling a secure connection to be established from any individual machine to any other. At present, this technology is most commonly implemented in firewalls, allowing organizations to create secure tunnels across the Internet, as shown in Exhibit 1. Attackers who have planted one or more network capture devices along the route used to send packets between the firewalls do not gain any advantage from capturing these packets unless they can crack the encryption key — an unlikely feat unless an extremely short key is used. The chief disadvantage of the firewall-to-firewall VPN is that it does not provide an end-to-end tunnel. In this scheme, packets transmitted between a host and the firewall for that host are in cleartext and are thus still subject to being captured. Increasingly, however, vendors are announcing support for end-to-end VPNs, allowing host-to-host rather than only firewall-to-firewall tunnels.

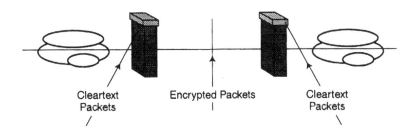

Cleartext　　　　Encrypted Packets　　　　Cleartext
Packets　　　　　　　　I　　　　　　　　　Packets

**Exhibit 1.　A Virtual Private Network**

Like any other type of Internet security control measure, VPNs are not a panacea. Anyone who can break into a machine that stores an encryption key can subvert the integrity of a VPN. VPNs do not supplant firewalls or other kinds of network security tools, but rather supplement the network security administrator's arsenal with capabilities that were not previously available. With the point-to-point tunneling protocol (PPTP) standard currently being widely implemented in VPN products (usually in firewalls with VPN support capabilities), the task of setting up secure tunnels is at least much less formidable than it had been until recently.

## CONCLUSION

The successful use of a firewall is dependent on the selection of an appropriate product. Packet-filtering firewalls accept or deny packets based on numerous rules that depend on the source and destination ports of packets and other criteria. This type of firewall is the closest option to a plug-and-play firewall solution, although it is also generally the easiest to defeat. Proxy-based firewalls, such as circuit-gateway firewalls, are generally more difficult to defeat, and the resulting virtual circuit connection is relatively transparent to users. However, circuit-gateway firewalls do not understand the semantics of applications and thus lack a certain amount of granularity of control. Application-gateway firewalls are also proxy-based, but connect a specific client to a specific application. Application-gateway firewalls can provide more granularity of control, but require that every application that proxies reach be modified, and they are generally less transparent to users than circuit-gateway firewalls.

# Chapter 54
# Assessing and Combating the Sniffer Threat

*E. Eugene Schultz*

To say that determining the real origins and magnitudes of threat is one of the most challenging problems facing information security (InfoSec) professionals is a gross understatement. The media, net news, and myriad other sources constantly remind us just how diverse the range of potential threats is. Internet security, intranet and extranet security, operating system-based security, information warfare, personnel security, and other important topics have all at one time or another received a disproportionate amount of attention in the 1990s, forcing InfoSec professionals to deal with these issues more than with many other competing issues. Addressing these issues is a sound strategy, but the proverbial winds of hype continually shift. All things considered, deciding what the real, relevant sources of InfoSec threat are, then assessing the resulting risk, and, finally, planning how to effectively control that risk have become more difficult than ever.

The inevitable result of all this justified attention on these diverse, sometimes sensational sources of InfoSec-related threat has been diminished attention to less dramatic, more seemingly routine sources of threat. One such source, the focus of this chapter, is network snooping or sniffing, in which network traffic is captured without authorization. Although most InfoSec professionals understand that such a threat exists, it is easy to fall into the trap of thinking that somehow the magnitude of this threat pales compared to the other, more exciting sources of threat. An organization is likely to have provisions in an InfoSec policy that prohibit the use of sniffers without proper authorization and that may even require periodic inspections to determine whether unauthorized sniffers exist. Furthermore, unless one works in a unit whose responsibilities include networking, one is not likely to be aware of the extent to which sniffers are deployed and exactly who has access to the data that sniffers capture. Of

0-8493-1160-8/02/$0.00+$1.50
© 2002 by CRC Press LLC

all the sources of potential loss due to unauthorized access to systems, illegal data transfers, etc., however, none is greater in most operational environments than the deployment of unauthorized sniffers. This chapter explores the nature of the sniffer threat, presents solutions for combating the risk, and suggests strategies for dealing with sniffer-related incidents should they occur.

## THE NATURE OF THE THREAT

### How Sniffers Work

To understand the threat that sniffers present first requires understanding how sniffers work. The manner in which sniffers operate depends on the type of network. In a shared media network such as a standard Ethernet, packets sent along a network segment travel everywhere along the wire. Any host connected to a segment is capable of capturing all sessions within that segment. For example, Exhibit 1 depicts a sniffer-capable host. It is able to capture any traffic that goes through the network segment, regardless of the particular neighboring host or other remote host to which that traffic is destined. In other types of networks (e.g., token-ring networks), sniffers are capable only of capturing sessions sent to or through a specific device or host, that is, either the physical sniffer itself or the host that houses a logical sniffer. Exhibit 2 depicts this scenario in a token-ring environment. Note that only the traffic traversing the side on which the sniffer is located can be captured by the sniffer.

### Types of Sniffers

The two types of sniffers are physical sniffers and logical sniffers. Physical sniffers are devices with built-in network interface hardware such that when they are installed on a network, they record all traffic. Logical sniffers are programs that run on host machines that also capture data traversing a network. In order for logical sniffers to function, the host machines that house them must have a network interface card that not only provides a physical interface to the network, but also provides packet capture functionality. This type of interface card, commonly known as a promiscuous network interface card, is built into some off-the-shelf systems, but must be installed in others.

Two types of promiscuous network interface cards exist. One can monitor all traffic going across a network segment. The other is capable only of capturing the traffic bound for or going through the host on which it is installed.

### The Concern

Why do unauthorized sniffers pose such a high degree of threat? In the hands of legitimate network administrators and other technical personnel,

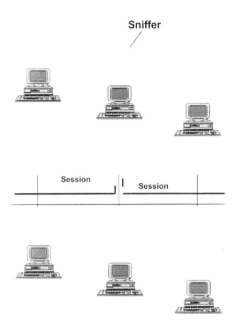

**Exhibit 1.  A Sniffer in a Shared Media Network**

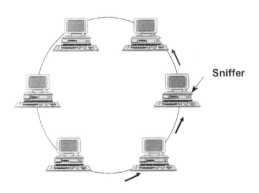

**Exhibit 2.  A Sniffer in a Token-Ring Network**

sniffers are an immensely valuable tool; sniffers help substantially in diagnosing and fixing networking problems (such as broadcast floods and locating points in a network in which traffic flow is disrupted). In the hands of unauthorized persons, however, sniffers are a potential security-related catastrophe waiting to happen because:

1. Many logins across networks in typical operational environments involve transmission of cleartext passwords. An intruder with access

to a sniffer can quickly learn the login names, passwords, and IP addresses of host machines on which login accounts exist by examining the first portion (the "header") of each log-in packet. The intruder can then establish a telnet or a similar connection to that host and attempt to log in. Unless captured passwords are obsolete (because, for example, the user whose password has been captured recently changed the password), the probability of the intruder's success in breaking into legitimate user's accounts is very high. Once the intruder breaks into an account, the intruder will have the access rights of the user whose account is now compromised, leading to the possibility of reading and copying files to which the user has access. Worse yet, the intruder now has a foothold (namely, user-level access) within a system and can attempt to use cracking tools and other methods that provide superuser access on this system. With superuser access, the attacker is able to read and copy any file stored on that system, and is in addition very likely to find attacking other machines with the network considerably easier.[1]

2. Data (including text within e-mail messages) is constantly sent from host to host within a typical network; sniffers can capture this data. If the data is not encrypted, unauthorized persons can read and copy the data. A reasonably high proportion of transmitted data in typical corporate network environments is business critical. The compromise of data such as information about pending patents, original engineering data, marketing and lease bid data, and other information can result in immeasurable loss in the hands of a competitor or other potentially hostile party. Consider also that this type of data compromise may not directly result in direct financial loss — a competitor may obtain critical information but not use it. The media may, however, learn of the incident involving data compromise or some other negative outcome, and then release stories that can damage an organization's image. The result may be substantial indirect loss through outcomes such as lowering customer confidence in products and services offered by that organization, stockholder lawsuits, etc.

## EXTENT OF THE PROBLEM

The full extent of unauthorized deployment of sniffers is (like so many other types of InfoSec-related problems) unlikely to be known or even reasonably estimated. The meaning of "unauthorized deployment" is in fact ambiguous at best; an intruder can, for example, gain access to a legitimately installed sniffer. Whereas the installer and others may have legitimate access, someone else's access to that sniffer may be unauthorized. In addition, sniffers for the most part are by nature clandestine — discovering them requires additional analysis and work that many organizations neglect.

Despite complications such as these, data about deployment of unauthorized sniffers is available. The following two case studies exemplify the range of incidents that can occur as a result of unauthorized sniffers.

### Case Study 1: Outbreak of Sniffer Attacks on the Internet

A widespread series of sniffer-based attacks on the Internet occurred between 1993 and 1995.[2] Attackers initially broke into host machines using automated attack scripts widely available over the Net, then exploited other vulnerabilities to gain superuser access using additional scripts. Superuser access allowed them to put unauthorized network sniffers in place. The intruders then connected to the hosts on which the logical sniffers were installed to gather log-in names and passwords, enabling them to break into additional hosts throughout the Internet. What was most noteworthy, however, was the fact that the intruders compromised hosts used by Internet service providers. These hosts were within subnets to which hub routers used in routing large volumes of Internet traffic were placed. In addition, these subnets had numerous leased line and dial-up connections. By placing sniffers on a host within the same network segment to which hub routers were connected, the attackers were able to capture all traffic that went in and out of the routers. Sniffers were often embedded in hacking toolkits that also removed indications of the intruders' activities from system logs.[3]

These attacks were devastating in that an organization could have a relatively secure, sniffer-free network that nevertheless could be compromised because of sniffers outside the network. A single user simply had to log in remotely to a machine within the network from a machine outside the network. When the traffic passed through a compromised Internet service provider's network, one or more sniffers captured passwords and other critical information. The practical significance is that sniffers within an organization's networks are only part of the total sniffer threat; sniffers *outside* an organization's network(s) can pose a significant security threat to that organization's security.

### Case Study 2: An Unauthorized Gateway-Based Sniffer in a Large Corporation

Several years ago, a technical staff member for a U.S.-based Fortune 100 company discovered an unauthorized physical sniffer. Unauthorized sniffers almost always spell trouble, but the location of this particular sniffer posed an especially high risk — it was attached to a high throughput link to the Internet immediately before (i.e., outside of) a firewall that screened incoming traffic. Whoever had planted this sniffer had the ability to capture all traffic coming into and out of this business-critical network. Soon after the sniffer was discovered and removed, an investigation ensued. Investigators determined that it had been installed by an employee who was working in collusion with another outside person in a scheme to sell corporate information. The sniffer had been in place for approximately three months before it was discovered.

The moral of this story is that physical sniffers placed anywhere can cause catastrophic results. Sniffers placed at gateways to critical networks, however, can potentially cause the greatest loss because they can capture all traffic (inbound and outbound) through the gateways. Sniffers attached to a network's backbone also entail significantly elevated risk because so much traffic traverses through the backbone.

Which pose a greater overall threat — physical or logical sniffers? Although physical sniffers pose a serious threat, they are separate, identifiable hardware devices that can be seen by someone who is physically present. Additionally, someone who is physically present at a location where network cabling (to which a physical sniffer must be attached) is accessible must install them. Someone who installs an unauthorized sniffer might be observed and subsequently reported. Furthermore, physical sniffers tend to be somewhat (but not prohibitively) expensive, making their purchase by the typical user somewhat unlikely. A more likely scenario, therefore, is unauthorized access to a physical sniffer purchased and installed legitimately by an organization, rather than the purchase and installation of such a device by a dishonest employee or contractor (although the latter possibility is nevertheless real and potentially catastrophic).

Logical sniffers in many respects comprise a more serious threat than physical sniffers. Many systems have built-in promiscuous interfaces; more commercial system administration tools than one might expect have built-in network traffic capture capabilities. Someone with access (authorized or unauthorized) to these tools could read or copy captured network traffic. Access to such tools is, however, not necessary; a perpetrator can simply gain remote access (in most cases, superuser access) to a target host, install a sniffing program, then wait until a sufficient amount of passwords or data is captured, and finally harvest the captured data. In many incidents, intruders have gone even further; they have replaced the entire kernel of a compromised system with a new, promiscuous kernel, thereby making discovery of the fact that the compromised system is now in promiscuous mode very difficult.[2]

For all practical purposes, however, the greatest threat associated with the use of logical sniffers is an everyday desktop user buying a promiscuous interface card and a sniffer program at a local computer store, then installing both on a desktop machine that connects to a corporate or other network. Commercial sniffer programs that run in environments such as DOS and Windows 95 now often cost less than $20. Sniffing in Macintosh environments is even easier; a sniffer program, Traffic Peek, is built into every Macintosh host. Windows NT 4.0 Server also offers a built-in logical sniffer, the Network Monitor (NM). Fortunately, access to this program is limited by default to administrators and also requires entry of a password.

In summary, the sniffer threat is indeed more serious than might superficially be apparent. Sniffers can be installed virtually anywhere network wires go.[4] Not only are there physical sniffers, but there are also logical sniffers, many of which can be installed by an average user without elevated privileges. In so many corporate, government, and academic environments around the world, passwords and data traverse networks in cleartext, making them perfect targets for sniffer attacks. Worse yet, only one sniffer installed in the proper location can capture a voluminous amount of data.

## SOLUTIONS

The sniffer threat is insidious. It should come as no surprise, therefore, that choosing suitable control measures is by no means easy or straightforward. The following solutions are the best currently known solutions.

**Policy.** Policy is the basis for all effective InfoSec measures. The first and most essential step, therefore, in dealing with the sniffer threat is to ensure that one's InfoSec policy contains provisions that prohibit the installation or use of sniffers (physical or logical) on any system or network without the written approval of cognizant management. Cognizant management may possibly include line management, business unit managers, InfoSec management, or some other management function. This policy should also specify who (employees only, employees and contractors, etc.) is allowed to install sniffers and read sniffer data; include provisions for protecting sniffer data from unauthorized disclosure; and specify consequences in case someone does not adhere to it.

**Encryption.** The most powerful, single technical solution to the sniffer threat is the widespread deployment of network encryption. Encryption forces those who deploy sniffers without authorization to be capable of breaking the encryption to read the contents of captured packets. Tragically, the major question with respect to deployment of encryption too often centers on the strength of encryption (e.g., 40-bit versus 128-bit encryption). The result is that encryption solutions are postponed, leaving systems and data at risk. Some encryption (no matter how weak) is better than none. Relaxation of U.S. encryption export policies makes implementing some kind of network encryption feasible in nearly every country.[5]

Implementing virtual private networks (VPNs) is an increasingly popular method of achieving encrypted network traffic flow. Sessions between hosts can be encrypted using either private or public key encryption, thereby establishing a secure "tunnel" between them. VPNs between firewalls or routers are now used routinely in corporate intranets and in other

657

critical network deployments. Although VPNs are generally effective in controlling the sniffer threat, the type of VPN deployed makes a significant difference in the overall effectiveness. VPNs that provide link encryption (as from one firewall to another) are not so effective in that transmissions are sent in cleartext everywhere but between the hosts that provide the link encryption (see Exhibit 3).

In contrast, VPNs that provide point-to-point (also known as end-to-end) encryption are more effective in that network transmissions are encrypted over every part of the route they traverse (see Exhibit 4).

Additionally, a problem common to both types of VPNs is that some vendors have deviated from the mainstream by developing their own proprietary Point-to-Point Tunneling Protocols (PPTP — the protocol that provides the encrypted sessions). Consequently, two hosts that support different implementations of PPTP cannot establish a secure tunnel.

**Employ One-Time Password Authentication.** In one-time password schemes, a password for a user is sent across the network once, and then changed the next time a password for that user is transmitted. Several different one-time password programs exist, but one of the most effective versions is Bellcore's commercial S/KEY tool. S/KEY allows the user to choose a particular password for a given number of log-ins, but never allows a cleartext password to be sent over the network. Instead, it encrypts every password transmission. Better yet, it encrypts each password differently[6] during each log-in attempt. Even if a sniffer captures passwords, the passwords will be encrypted. The encrypted versions will be very difficult to crack because no two cyphertext passwords sent over the network will be identical.

**Use Secure Ethernet Technology.** As mentioned previously, standard Ethernets are shared media networks. As such, they are ideal for perpetrators of sniffer attacks. Fortunately, a relatively new development — the secure

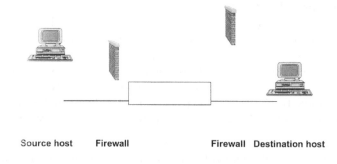

Source host     Firewall          Firewall   Destination host

**Exhibit 3.   A VPN with Link Encryption Between Firewalls**

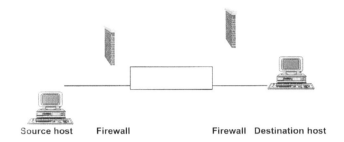

Source host    Firewall                Firewall  Destination host

**Exhibit 4.   A VPN with End-to-End Encryption**

Ethernet — limits the distribution of data sent over a network. Secure Ethernets send data only to the host that each packet header indicates is the destination host. In a secure Ethernet, an attacker would have to plant a sniffer on every host within a network segment to capture all sessions. The major limitation of secure Ethernet technology is that it works only locally; once network transmissions are sent outside of the local network in which this technology is implemented, the traffic may be subject to sniffer attacks if the destination networks have not implemented secure Ethernets. Still, secure Ethernet technology offers substantial improvement in ability to defend against the sniffer threat.

**Have System Administrators Regularly Inspect Hosts for Unauthorized Logical Sniffers.** In particular, have them look within gateways — routers are often the hosts on which logical (as well as physical) sniffers are installed without authorization because such a large volume of traffic generally goes through routers. Logical sniffers are often installed in public directories (including temporary directories) where anyone can add files and where the sheer number of files can make finding the executable and data files for the sniffer unlikely. Using integrity checking tools such as Tripwire (for UNIX hosts) can be helpful in identifying changes to existing files if someone replaces a legitimate file with a sniffer executable. Other clues that unauthorized logical sniffers may be in place are the presence of hidden files (such as . files in UNIX hosts and $ files in Windows NT hosts), often with unfamiliar names such as ., .., .X, or others. A well-known logical sniffer program in the UNIX arena is named "rootkt," although an attacker is likely to change this name to some name that is not so easily recognized. Entries in audit logs may show that a sniffer has been installed; similarly, checking for current processes that are running on each system may reveal the presence of unknown processes that capture network or host sessions. Scanning programs such as CPM (Check for Network Interfaces in Promiscuous Mode[7]) are useful in that they can be run on Sun Microsystems hosts to determine whether they are in packet-capturing mode.

Remember, however, that measures such as these help only with respect to the sniffer threat in local networks.

**Frequently Inspect for Unauthorized Physical Sniffers.** These sniffers can sometimes be very easy to detect. The fact that a desktop computer bearing a well-known sniffer manufacturer's name, such as Network General, is attached to the network is, for example, a dead giveaway that the computer is a sniffer. The presence of a hardware device that connects to a network cable via a vampire clamp — a type of interface that penetrates the cable's insulation where the clamp is attached — is a high probability indicator of the presence of an unauthorized physical sniffer. The most significant problems in discovering unauthorized physical sniffers are that homemade sniffer devices may not be so easily recognizable and also that sniffers can be hidden in difficult-to-access locations such as wiring closets and subflooring.

**Implement Secure E-Mail.** Secure e-mail programs can protect the privacy of e-mail messages by encrypting the contents. Both commercial and freeware programs of this nature are widely available. As mentioned previously, U.S. encryption export restrictions have recently been relaxed sufficiently to allow sufficiently strong encryption throughout the world.

**Prepare for and Plan to Use the IPv6 Protocol.** This emerging protocol consists of an authenticating header (AH) and encrypted session payload (ESP). The ESP portion keeps cleartext data from being transmitted over networks, making data safe from sniffers. IPv6 is currently an emerging technology; however, to use this technology requires that network applications be programmed to utilize it. As a real solution to the sniffer threat, therefore, this technology is still several years away. Nevertheless, initiating efforts to investigate and utilize IPv6 as soon as possible is an excellent strategy for dealing not only with the sniffer threat, but also a wide range of other threats.

**Employ Third-Party Authentication.** This type of authentication requires users to authenticate to an authentication server (usually through presenting some kind of token such as a smart card), then to authenticate using the normal system authentication procedures (namely by entering a log-in name and password). With third-party authentication, even if a perpetrator captures a user's cleartext password and attempts to log in using it, the log-in attempt will fail because the perpetrator will not possess the necessary token. As strong as this measure is, unfortunately, it provides only a partial solution to the sniffer threat in that it protects against password sniffing, but does not protect data transmitted over the network.

**Educate Users.** Educates users about the sniffer threat and help them understand the policy the organization has in place concerning sniffers.

The education and awareness effort should enable them to recognize and report illegal sniffers through proper channels. This effort can go a long way in the battle to combat unauthorized sniffers. The time and resources spent in training system and network administrators usually also have great benefits; the "gung-ho" administrator who installs sniffers with good intention but without proper authorization is in many respects the greatest source of danger.

## RESPONDING TO SNIFFER-RELATED INCIDENTS

Schultz and Wack[8] maintain that responding to incidents requires six distinct phases of activity, including:

- Preparation
- Detection
- Containment
- Eradication
- Recovery
- Follow-up

Of these stages, detection and containment are usually the most critical in a sniffer-related incident. Detection is critical because, as mentioned earlier, any system within a network can be capturing packets without anyone's knowledge other than the person who installed it. Additionally, sniffer incidents are often extremely difficult to contain. As in Case Study 2 above, a sniffer may be running for months before it is finally detected. By the time the sniffer is found, it may have captured tens of thousands or more cleartext passwords to systems that are now subject to immediate, unauthorized access.

If an unauthorized sniffer is discovered, the first thing one should do, if at all possible, is to perform a full backup of the system on which the sniffer runs. The backup will serve as evidence in case the organization initiates prosecution of the perpetrator(s). Additionally, by including all the sniffer's executables and data files, the backup may be useful in determining how the sniffer works, what data the sniffer has captured already, and (if one is lucky) clues concerning the identity of the person(s) who have written and installed the sniffer.[9] If the sniffer is a logical sniffer, one may be able to inspect the code to determine the file(s) to which the sniffer is writing data. Inspecting log-in IDs and passwords in such files will allow one to know which accounts in which systems are most likely to have been compromised. Have the system administrators of these systems inspect logs, log-in messages, etc. to determine whether these systems have been accessed without authorization; then take any necessary evasive measures (including, if circumstances warrant, initiating system shutdown procedures) to protect these systems and the data they store. Be sure at this point to also delete any sniffer-related files within any compromised system to prevent them from being accessed and used by others.

If an unauthorized physical sniffer is discovered, handle this device as you would any other piece of physical evidence.[10] Fingerprints on the sniffer device may enable law enforcement personnel to identify the perpetrator; be sure, therefore, to have someone who is an expert in computer forensics or law enforcement be in charge of evidence handling. As in the case of logical sniffers, inspecting the output of a physical sniffer may also enable one to determine the accounts and systems that are currently most at risk.

The next step is also an extremely important one. One should now initiate an effort to change all passwords on all hosts within any network on which a sniffer has been found or through which remote log-in traffic has passed. Although the user community is likely to be less than enthusiastic about this measure, it is the only logical course of action. One sniffer may have captured passwords for any other host in the entire network, allowing the perpetrator(s) easy and immediate access. Changing all passwords is the only way to be sure that any passwords that any perpetrators have "stockpiled" are now invalid and useless.

Performing incident response procedures correctly for sniffer-related incidents may not be as easy as it seems. Consider the following case study.

### Case Study 3: A Lesson Learned in Responding to a Sniffer Incident

During the massive outbreak of Internet sniffers from 1993 to 1995, a member of a national emergency response team traveled to a site in which several unauthorized logical sniffers were found. After analyzing the problem, this investigator deleted the sniffer programs, then logged in remotely as root (superuser) to a system at the site from which this team operated. Shortly afterward, this system — in addition to scores of others at the response team's site — was compromised. The investigator did not realize that additional, as yet undiscovered sniffers had been installed at the site at which the investigation was being performed. The root password to the investigator's system was transmitted in cleartext across a network segment in which an undiscovered sniffer had been installed. A perpetrator harvested this password, broke into the investigator's system as root, and planted still another sniffer on this system. This enabled the perpetrator to gather many passwords for machines at the investigator's site (in addition to a number of additional sites). The lesson learned from this series of unfortunate events is that sniffer attacks are not as easy to handle as one might suspect. One mistake, such as the one discussed in this case study, can proliferate these incidents out of control. Although the speed of response is critical, it is most important to carefully think through every step and action to avoid making the situation worse. This "lesson learned" is particularly applicable to organizations with many intranet and extranet connections.[11]

Finally, one should engage in a follow-up process to determine how the sniffer-related incident occurred and what measures (e.g., scanning hosts more frequently to see if they are in promiscuous mode) might have made the occurrence of such an incident less likely. One should also evaluate the response to the sniffer incident, identifying steps that could have been performed more efficiently and additional resources that would have been useful. One should revise incident handling procedures accordingly and, finally, write a report on the incident for future reference.

## CONCLUSION

The threat of unauthorized sniffers has long been recognized in the InfoSec community. Amid all the confusion generated by the news of new, more sensational threats, it is easy to overlook the sniffer threat. Overlooking the sniffer threat is a major mistake; in many respects, a well-placed, unauthorized sniffer could easily result in more loss and disruption to an organization than any other type of incident. The proliferation of logical sniffers on many platforms represents a serious escalation in the sniffer threat. Network attackers cannot only install sniffers on remote hosts, but even the most casual, inexperienced user can now buy an inexpensive logical sniffer and install it on a desktop machine to capture critical data and passwords transmitted across network segments.

Many potential control measures for unauthorized sniffers exist. These include getting the appropriate policy provisions in place, encrypting network transmissions, using one-time passwords, implementing secure Ethernet technology, regularly inspecting for both logical and physical sniffers, installing secure e-mail, implementing network applications that utilize the IPv6 protocol, using third-party authentication, and establishing an effective user education and awareness program that helps both users and system administrators understand and combat the sniffer threat. The appropriate subset of these measures depends on the particular business and other needs of the organization. However, ensuring that an appropriate policy exists is imperative, no matter what other measures are appropriate. Encryption is the best (although not necessarily the most feasible) technical solution. Additionally, the potential for a widespread outbreak of sniffer attacks dictates that an effective incident response program that includes the appropriate procedures for combating sniffer attacks be put in place.

**Notes**

1. Many system administrators set up trusted access mechanisms that allow them to easily move from one machine to the other in a network without having to authenticate themselves to each machine. These mechanisms often require that those who use them have superuser privileges on the machine from which trusted access is initiated. Although advantageous from the perspective of convenient access for system administrators, a perpetrator who gains superuser status in a single machine may also be able to exploit these mechanisms to gain unauthorized access to many other systems within the same network.
2. Schultz, E.E. and Longstaff, T.A. (1998). Internet Sniffer Attacks. In D.E. Denning and P.J. Denning (Eds.), *Internet Besieged.* Reading, MA: Addison-Wesley, pp. 137–146.
3. Van Wyk, K.R. (1994). Threats to DoD Computer Systems. Paper presented at *23rd International Information Integrity Institute Forum* (cited with author's permission).
4. Sniffers could also, in fact, be used to attack wireless networks if they are planted in any host connected to such networks.
5. Laws within countries such as France and Russia restrict the use of encryption within these countries.
6. The change in encryption is the same for both the sending and receiving host, so authentication is not disrupted.
7. Available from ftp.cert.org and other ftp and Web sites.
8. Schultz, E.E. and Wack, J. (1996). Responding to Information Security Incidents. In M. Krause & H.F. Tipton (Eds.), *Handbook of Information Security Management: 1996–97 Yearbook.* Boston: Auerbach, pp. S-53–S-68.
9. Authors of a sniffer tool will, for instance, write the sniffer code in a manner that manifests a particular style of programming. Software forensics experts may accordingly be able to identify the authors. In addition, the code may contain Internet addresses and other information that may enable investigators to determine the identity of any perpetrator(s).
10. Bernstein, T., Bhimini, A., Schultz, E.E., and Siegel, C. (1996). *Internet Security for Business.* New York: John Wiley & Sons.
11. An intranet is, for the purposes of this article, considered a group of internal networks that connect with each other. An extranet is a group of external networks that are linked together.

# Section X

# Operations and Post-Implementation Considerations

This section examines operational considerations for evaluating, monitoring, maintaining, and enhancing an Internet solution after it is implemented. The following chapters are included in this section.

"Supporting a Web Site" discusses approaches and techniques for supporting a Web site in the context of performance, ease of use, and ease of maintenance.

"Web Server Monitoring" explains the risks of running critical Web sites and how monitoring can reduce those risks. Different strategies are used for monitoring and executing tests on individual components of Web sites to ensure that the entire site is operating correctly.

"Web Traffic Analysis: Analyzing What Is Happening" offers approaches for measuring Web traffic patterns and forming conclusions that can improve flow and performance.

"Guaranteeing Internet Service Levels: TCP Rate Control" examines TCP rate-control technology and differentiates it from alternatives. This chapter covers technology's support for service levels, TCP packets, and traffic flow.

"MSPs: Monitoring and Managing E-Commerce" discusses MSP delivery architecture and provides criteria for selecting an MSP. Management service providers can supply IT infrastructure monitoring and management through remote tools and full-time staff.

"Using Intelligent Agents to Maximize the Benefits of the World Wide Web" shows how intelligent agents can facilitate searching, monitoring information changes, customizing information according to individual needs, and other information management for a better Web experience.

"Auditing a Corporate Web Site" provides rules for determining if a site is vulnerable from internal or external attacks. The chapter describes approaches for auditing a Web site and process tools.

# Chapter 55

# Supporting a Web Site

*Gilbert Held*

THE CONNECTION OF A WEB SERVER TO THE INTERNET IS COMMONLY ACCOMPLISHED VIA THE USE OF A LEASED LINE BETWEEN YOUR SERVER SITE AND AN INTERNET SERVICE PROVIDER (ISP). At your server site your Web server is normally connected to a local area network (LAN), and the LAN is connected to a router which in turn is connected to the leased line routed to the ISP. Exhibit 1 illustrates the previously described method used to connect a Web server to the Internet.

In examining Exhibit 1 it is important to note that some ISPs will provide a router and arrange for the installation of a leased line for a single monthly fee. If the ISP is also a communications carrier it can provide both the leased line and the router, which may result in a slight reduction in the total monthly cost due to the elimination of a middleman. Examples of ISPs that are also communications carriers include AT&T, MCI, Sprint, and several of the local Bell Operating Companies (BOCs).

The router provides the ability to move traffic destined to a different network off the LAN hub to the ISP, which forwards data to the Internet. Similarly, the router also accepts inbound data and places such data onto the local network via a connection to the hub. Most ISPs allow customers to purchase a router; however, they will only guarantee support for certain products. This means that if you obtain a non-supported product and a problem arises, the ISP will not be able to test the connection from its location to your router's wide area network interface.

The actual leased line can range in scope from a Dataphone Digital Service (DDS) 56 Kbps line to a fractional T1 operating in increments of 56 or 64 Kbps up to 784 Kbps, or a full T1 operating at 1.544 Mbps. Thus, the actual cost for communications will vary based upon the type of transmission facility installed. Although most ISPs bill monthly based upon the transmission capacity of the leased line, several ISPs introduced a new type of measured transmission service during 1996. One example of this measured service is offered by BBN Planet which will install a T1 line and bill your organization based upon the average utilization of the transmission facility over a 24-hour

0-8493-1160-8/02/$0.00+$1.50
© 2002 by CRC Press LLC

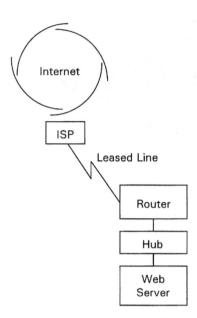

**Exhibit 1.   Connecting a Web Server to the Internet**

per day period on a monthly basis. Although this measured usage billing mechanism can provide significant savings for organizations that need the ability to support periodic surges in network traffic from a relatively low base of usage, if you have a consistent high level of usage a more conventional fixed rate plan may be more appropriate.

Returning to Exhibit 1, note that the Web server is shown as only one of two devices connected to the LAN hub, with the other device being the router. This type of connection represents a communications-isolated connection to the Internet since there is no possible access from the Internet to other corporate computers that may reside on an internal corporate network. Since many organizations either have other devices connected to the network to which the Web server is connected, or use a multiport router to connect multiple networks to the Internet via a single Internet communications connection, security then becomes a very important issue to consider.

## SECURITY ISSUES

Almost all routers include a filtering capability that can be used to enable or disable the flow of packets based upon source address, destination address, and the TCP "well-known" port. Here the term "well-known" port represents a numeric that identifies the type of application data being transported within a TCP packet. For example, a value of 25 is used for the Simple Mail Transport Protocol (SMTP) used to transport electronic mail, while a value of 80 is used for the HyperText Transport Protocol (HTTP) used to transport Web browser data. Thus, by configuring the router to disable all traffic on TCP port 25 you could disable the flow of electronic mail.

Although router filtering is useful, it cannot prevent repetitive attacks against your computer resources. For example, if your Web server is also configured to support the file transfer protocol (ftp), a hacker could guess an account name by repetitively using the entries in an electronic dictionary to first obtain an account name, and could then reuse the dictionary to discover a password associated with the account. Preventing this so-called dictionary attack, as well as providing additional levels of security beyond router filtering, requires the use of a firewall.

## THE FIREWALL OPTION

Exhibit 2 illustrates the use of a firewall to protect an internal corporate network connected to the Internet by the use of a two-LAN port router. In this example the Web server can be considered to reside on the public access network while the corporate internal network obtains protection from the use of a firewall.

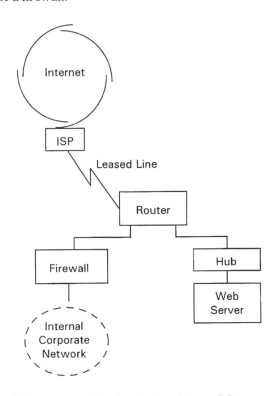

**Exhibit 2.   Using a Firewall to Protect an Internal Corporate Network**

The actual cost of a firewall can range from approximately $2,500 to well over $30,000, with the more expensive products providing authentication, encryption, and a digital signature capability, features not included in low-cost products. In addition to the one-time cost of the firewall, most vendors market a separate yearly maintenance fee that provides support and software upgrades. Concerning the actual configuration and operation of a firewall, it can require a minimum of a day or two to set up. Thereafter, the level of support will vary based upon the dynamics of the organization. If your organization frequently changes policies and rules, you can expect a member of your communications staff to be devoted to reconfiguring and testing the firewall. If your organization rarely changes rules and policies once they are established, you can probably expect an existing employee to devote only a few hours every few weeks to maintaining the firewall. Now that we have an appreciation for the communications involved in supporting a Web site, let us focus on the hardware platform.

## Hardware

A Web server can be established on a variety of platforms, ranging from older Intel 486 computers to the latest Sun Microsystem Solaris workstations, Intel Pentium and Pentium Pro, and Digital Equipment Corporation's Alpha-based systems. Although Sun Solaris-based computers probably represented the majority of Web server platforms established during 1994 and 1995, the introduction of Pentium and Pentium Pro microprocessors and Microsoft's Windows NT Server resulted in the "Win-Tel" combination of Windows NT Server operating on an Intel-based Pentium or Pentium Pro becoming a very popular platform.

Most organizations establishing a Web presence look upon themselves as explorers charting virgin territory since there is no practical method to anticipate usage. This means that an effective hardware platform will represent one that is expandable to satisfy an increased level of usage if the site should grow in popularity. One commonly used type of platform is a multiprocessor server with a Redundant Array of Inexpensive Disks (RAID) storage subsystem. In early 1997, ARL, DEC, Dell, and IBM offered multiprocessor-capable motherboard systems that could support 2, 4, 6, and eventually 8 Pentium or Pentium Pro processors. Thus, if a single Pentium Pro should prove inadequate, additional processors can be added instead of having to consider the use of a UNIX-based minicomputer or a mainframe. Concerning disk storage, most multiprocessor-capable servers support RAID storage subsystems that include drive-bys: additional drives can be easily installed while the server continues to operate. Due to the modular design of most modern Web server hardware platforms, upgrades can usually be accomplished in hours instead of days. Thus, hardware support can usually be accomplished by existing personnel. Unfortunately, this is usually not the case with software, which will be examined next.

## Software

There are three areas that must be considered when planning support requirements for software: the operating system, server software, and applications software.

## Operating System

Most modern operating systems now are changed on almost a yearly basis. Since few organizations are comfortable with simply upgrading their OS without prior testing, many organizations first upgrade a test platform and test that software upgrade for a period of time prior to migrating the upgrade to their production computer. Web servers are no exception to this test first policy, which means you may have to consider acquiring a test server if your organization plans to test software prior to installing new products on a production server.

The value of a test platform was recently noted by a series of problems associated with a service pack for a popular operating system. This service pack, which represents a minor release designed to correct bugs, introduced a new one that caused Web servers to freeze. Fortunately, several organizations noted this problem on their test servers and did not apply the service pack release to their production servers.

The personnel support required for the operating system to include maintaining administrative accounts usually requires only a few hours per week and may be able to be performed by existing personnel. The real effort that will more than likely require additional employees involves support for Web server software and the application programming effort involved in creating and maintaining Web pages on the server.

## SERVER SOFTWARE

The installation and operation of a Web server software program is normally a relatively simple, non-time consuming process. What turns this process into a half-to-full-time position is when access controls are added to different directories on the Web server and have a dynamic environment that requires frequent backups. Under such circumstances an employee may be required to devote a considerable amount of time to maintaining Web accounts, performing tape backups onto a backup server, and performing other administrative actions. Quite often many organizations will assign hardware, operating system, and Web server support to one individual on a full-time basis and designate a second employee as a backup.

## APPLICATION PROGRAMMING

The scope of the application programming effort required to support a Web server can vary considerably based upon the type of Web pages to be constructed, whether or not CGI scripts and JAVA applets will be used, and the presence or absence of a database server that will be linked electronically to the Web server. A simple Web site that uses only HyperText Markup Language (HTML), to create static Web pages that are only periodically changed, may only require the effort of one person to create and maintain application software on the Web server. As the complexity of the Web site increases, the level of support can increase in tandem. In fact, based upon the experience of this author in installing, configuring, and managing approximately 30 Web sites, you can expect the necessity to add a full-time programmer to support the creation and testing of JAVA applets, and another person for database queries. Thus, a commercial Web site that requires the establishment of accounts and uses CGI scripts, JAVA applets, and an electronically linked database server could require at least four full-time staff members to support all software-related activities. One person would maintain the operating system and Web server software, while three additional employees would be assigned to the application programming development effort.

## RECOMMENDED COURSE OF ACTION

It is important to note that no two Web sites, unless they are mirrored, are equal. This means that the level of support required to install, configure, operate, and maintain a corporate presence on the World Wide Web can vary from organization to organization based upon the type of server being operated, the level of Web page design, and the possible linkage of the server's pages to a back-end database. Thus, readers should view the information presented in this chapter as general guidelines that can be used to note the potential level of support associated with communications, hardware, and software aspects associated with establishing and maintaining a Web server. In addition, this chapter indicates the various options for communications, hardware, and software to be considered, which will have a bearing on the total cost associated with a Web site. By carefully considering the requirements and evaluating those requirements against the information presented in this chapter, one can determine the general level of support and cost associated with establishing and maintaining a Web site. This in turn will allow noting the true shape of the iceberg in terms of cost and support, instead of just noting the proverbial "tip of the iceberg"!

# Chapter 56
# Web Server Monitoring
*Pete Welter*

THIS CHAPTER INTRODUCES WEB SERVER MONITORING, explaining the importance of monitoring, describing monitoring concepts, and discussing various types of monitoring. A set of common Web server problems are enumerated, along with methods of monitoring to detect and/or prevent these conditions. Finally, automated monitoring systems are discussed, along with two of their primary advantages — immediate notification of problems, and the gathering of historical data. Although the focus of this chapter is on Web server monitoring, the concepts generalize for other types of Internet servers, including Mail, News, FTP, and application servers.

## THE IMPORTANCE OF MONITORING

In today's information age competition, a well-designed and smoothly operating Web site provides a distinct competitive advantage. On the Internet, the only hard currency is attention. A Web site that fails to deliver its content, either in a timely manner or at all, causes visitors to quickly lose interest, wasting the time and money spent on the site's development. Ensuring that all of the elements of a Web site are functioning properly is critical to maximizing a company's Web investment. If an irate customer call (or even good-natured e-mail) provides the first indication of a Web site failure, then many other potential users have certainly been turned away.

When the inevitable failures do occur, minimizing downtime reduces the impact of the problems. Failure of a corporate Web site quickly transforms visitors from potential customers to disinterested passers-by. One of the primary advantages of a corporate Web site is its ability to reach customers around the world 24 hours a day, seven days a week. A broken Web site does not fulfill that potential.

Intranet Web server failures sever important lines of intracompany communication. Common and prolonged failures can change a corporate culture to depend less on these highly effective communications tools, thus minimizing the return on Intranet investments.

0-8493-1160-8/02/$0.00+$1.50
© 2002 by CRC Press LLC

## THE GOALS OF WEB SERVER MONITORING

After a Web site has been designed, created, and deployed, it must be maintained and operated. Web server monitoring performs several functions critical to the smooth day-to-day operation of a Web site. Monitoring:

- Verifies that all components of the Web site are functioning properly
- Enables quick and accurate diagnosis of problems that do occur
- Measures performance to quantify the user experience and to provide hard data for capacity planning
- Aids in predicting possible problems or needs for increased resources

Because of the distributed nature of the Internet, failures can occur at many points, some of which are outside of a Web administrator's control. Exhibit 1 shows a simplified view a single Web page request; note the number of complex components that are required to fulfill the request. Being able to quickly ascertain which components are functioning and which have failed can dramatically reduce the time taken to diagnose the problem. Once the Web site is back up and functioning, hard data can be used to inform customers and management of the causes of a given failure.

Monitoring can prevent problems by revealing patterns of resource usage and performance that might otherwise go undetected. For example, full disks typically cause a host of problems for applications and operating

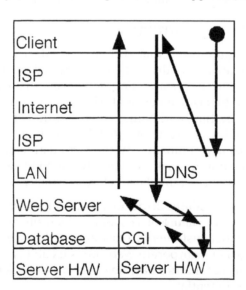

**Exhibit 1. Typical Web Page Request. Each Section Represents a Major Component in a Typical Internet/Web Server Architecture, Starting from the Client (Browser) and Progressing Over the Network to the Web Server.**

systems. Simply knowing that a disk is nearing capacity may save a Web administrator hours of time fixing the problems caused by a full disk, not to mention heading off the inevitable flood of user reports.

## MONITORING STRATEGY

A "monitor" is a test, typically a diagnostic command or emulation of actual use of the system, whose results are recorded so that they can be stored and/or acted upon. Monitoring systems or processes check services and components on a periodic basis, frequently enough to catch failures in a timely manner, but not so often as to significantly impact system resources. Monitoring systems typically consist of a set of monitors, mechanisms for alerting administrators if failures occur, and a historical log of data collected by the monitors. The focus of various monitor types covers a broad spectrum, from "deep" monitors that simulate user actions and that test many components of a Web site simultaneously, to "shallow" monitors that measure a single aspect of a single component.

Tests performed by deep monitors involve a large number of components (see Exhibit 2), and often simulate a typical user transaction; results are measured in "user units," such as the number of seconds to complete a common task. Deep monitors indicate whether a large set of components that provide a given service are functioning properly (in which case the performance data represents what a user would see) or if something is wrong with at least one of the components (although a precise diagnosis may be difficult). One common example of a deep monitor is a monitor that periodically attempts to retrieve a URL, recording any errors that may occur and the amount of time the retrieval took. This procedure can be performed manually, using a browser to retrieve the page, or automatically, using a monitoring system. Other examples of deep monitoring include filling in and submitting a series of Web forms (a common E-commerce activity), sending and receiving an e-mail message, or downloading a file from an FTP server.

In contrast, shallow monitors test one or more aspects of a single component of the system (see Exhibit 3). Shallow monitors indicate precisely when a given component has problems, but often lack the context of real system usage. Measurements from these monitors are typically in the units of the component being monitored: for example, bytes per second, or CPU utilization percentage. The following are examples of shallow monitors:

- Ping Monitor — tests whether a machine is reachable over the network, and whether the target machine is functioning well enough to send a simple reply
- Domain Name Server (DNS) Monitor — tests whether a machine's name (for example, www.freshtech.com) can be mapped into a network address

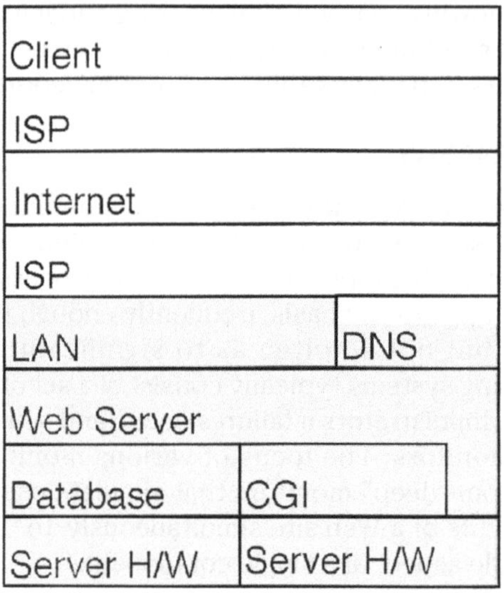

| Client | |
|---|---|
| ISP | |
| Internet | |
| ISP | |
| LAN | DNS |
| Web Server | |
| Database | CGI |
| Server H/W | Server H/W |

**Exhibit 2.  Deep Monitoring Coverage for a URL Monitor. Shaded Areas Are Covered, Meaning That a Failure in Any of the Components Will Be Detected by Testing the URL.**

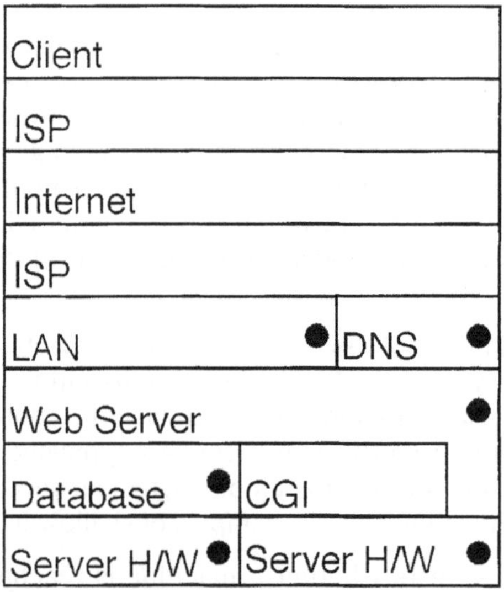

| Client | |
|---|---|
| ISP | |
| Internet | |
| ISP | |
| LAN ● | DNS ● |
| Web Server ● | |
| Database ● | CGI |
| Server H/W ● | Server H/W ● |

**Exhibit 3.  Shallow Monitoring Coverage, Which Uses Monitors Focused on Specific Parts of the Architecture**

- Process Monitor — ensures that a process is still active and using an acceptable amount of system resources
- CPU Monitor — measures the utilization of the CPU to flag chronic overloading
- Memory monitor — measures memory usage and paging activity

In practice, a combination of deep and shallow monitors gives the most effective and understandable picture of a Web site's current state and allows the quickest diagnosis of problems. To create good overlapping coverage for the deep URL test, a URL monitor can be combined with several shallow monitors such as a process monitor, DNS monitor, a CPU monitor, and several ping monitors. The URL monitor verifies that a page can be retrieved from the server in a timely manner, while the process monitor verifies that the Web server process is still running. The CPU monitor ensures that processing resources on the server are not overloaded, while the DNS monitor tests whether the host name portion of the URL can be resolved. Finally, the ping monitors check network connectivity between the Web server and the router, the ISP, the backbone, and several remote sites on the Internet (Exhibit 4).

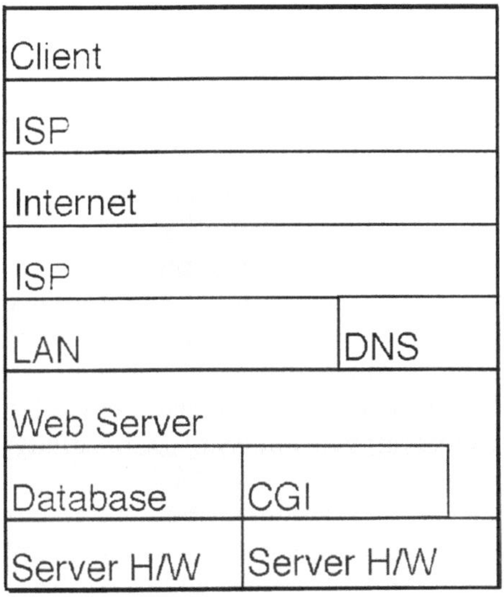

| Client | |
|--------|--|
| ISP | |
| Internet | |
| ISP | |
| LAN | DNS |
| Web Server | |
| Database | CGI |
| Server H/W | Server H/W |

**Exhibit 4. Local Monitoring Coverage Showing the Ability to Cover the Local Components Well, Decreasing in Effectiveness in Testing the Network Components**

## INTERNAL VERSUS REMOTE MONITORING

Remote monitoring is testing done by machines that are outside a site's internal network. An example of a remote monitor would be a monitoring machine in New York that fetched a public Web page from a Web server in San Francisco. Internal monitoring occurs on a Web server itself, or from a machine on the internal network. The advantages of internal monitoring are

- It is closer to the source of addressable problems — internal monitoring keeps confounding factors such as ISP or backbone failures from obscuring site-specific problems (see Exhibit 4). Because of the finer granularity of measurements possible, more precise problem diagnosis can be achieved. Problems detected by internal monitoring can generally be corrected by people at the site because they control the machines and the networks.
- It allows automatic corrective actions to be taken — internal monitors, especially those running on the servers they are monitoring, have the direct access required to take actions. Remote monitors usually do not have the security access required to initiate actions.
- It is more reliable — internal monitoring does not depend on other networks to monitor and deliver data.
- It is easier to administer — internal monitoring software and configuration are on directly accessible machines.

Remote monitoring has its own set of benefits.

- It provides truer access time measurements — access time measurements taken remotely are a truer reflection of the end user's experience than measurements taken from internal machines
- It detects configuration errors that affect external users — configuration errors in Web servers, firewalls, proxy servers, and routers may permit access from internal machines to internal sites, but may prevent legitimate external users from reaching a Web site.
- It detects problems with ISP and backbone links — testing connectivity from sites out on the Internet can also help detect failures in ISP or backbone links which may be affecting users' ability to access the Web site (Exhibit 5).
- It serves as a backup monitoring system. A catastrophic event could crash and/or disable all of the machines at a site. Without some monitoring from the outside, this failure would not be detected.

## COMMON WEB SITE PROBLEMS

Although a detailed treatment of Web site problems could itself comprise an entire chapter, Exhibit 6 will cover the most common points of failure for a Web site, and how monitors can be set up to detect them. These fall into three general categories:

| Client | |
|---|---|
| ISP | |
| Internet | |
| ISP | |
| LAN | DNS |
| Web Server | |
| Database | CGI |
| Server H/W | Server H/W |

**Exhibit 5.  Remote Monitoring Coverage. A Large Number of Components Are Covered by a Remote Monitor, Although if an Error Occurs, Pinpointing the Problem Component Can Be Difficult.**

1. The client cannot connect to any Web sites.
2. An error occurs at the Web server and is returned to the user.
3. The connection times out or fails.

This discussion will proceed from the points architecturally most distant from the Web server (and hence less under an administrator's control), and move toward the Web server itself (top to bottom in Exhibit 6).

## AUTOMATED MONITORING SYSTEMS

There are several ways to implement a Web monitoring strategy. Most simply, a person or group of people can manually check various aspects of the Web site on a periodic basis. Self-monitoring is better than relying on visitors to do the monitoring; however, people can forget, and they probably will not be around 24 hours a day. The results of manual monitoring are rarely recorded in a form that permits historical and quantitative analysis. Information gathered by hand also does not generally get broadly disseminated, so the status of the site is only known to a few people.

Automated monitoring tools run these tests 24 hours a day, seven days a week. These tools exist in a large number of forms: commercial products, shareware, freeware scripts, and home-grown solutions. A number of commercial remote monitoring services also exist. They all share the common abilities of periodically measuring some aspects of the system and recording these data. Most have a variety of shallow monitors, some also allow

681

**Exhibit 6.     Common Web Site Problems**

| Problem/Failure Point | Symptoms | Monitors |
|---|---|---|
| Client software or machine | Client machine crashes, or cannot connect to any Web site | None |
| Network connection between client and Internet | Client cannot connect to any external Web sites, can connect to machines on their internal network | Ping monitors from an internal machine to major ISPs and routers |
| Internet backbone connection | Some clients can connect, other cannot, or the connections are very slow | Ping to remote locations on Internet that use different backbones, remote ping and URL monitoring to Web server |
| Server ISP connection | All remote clients cannot connect, or connections are slow, although connections from internal machines work OK | Ping all routers between server and the Internet, some remote locations, and remote ping and URL monitoring |
| Document file is missing or HTML link is broken | Web server returns a "document missing" (404) error. | Local or remote URL monitor |
| Document file has improper permissions | Web server returns a "forbidden" (401) error | Local or remote URL monitor |
| CGI or other server-side process broken | Web server returns a "server error" (501 or 500) error, Web page displays error message or improper output (when HTTP headers or HTML are returned), or "no data" is returned | Local or remote URL monitor, with HTML content matching |
| DNS is misconfigured | "Host not found" error returned to remote and internal clients | Use nslookup-type monitor, or other monitor that requires a name lookup, such as a ping or URL monitor |
| DNS configuration has not been propagated | "Host not found," or wrong host, returned to remote clients, but internal clients are OK | Use remote nslookup-type monitor, or other remote monitor that requires a name lookup, such as a ping or URL monitor. |
| Firewall is misconfigured | Remote clients cannot connect, internal clients connect OK | Use remote monitor for each service that will be accessed through the firewall |
| Service process, such as HTTP (Web), FTP, database, etc. is down | One or more services do not function, others work OK | Use a deep monitor for each service of interest to verify proper operation |

**Exhibit 6.    Common Web Site Problems (Continued)**

| Problem/Failure Point | Symptoms | Monitors |
| --- | --- | --- |
| Services are performing inadequately | Services time out, or perform too slowly | Monitor CPU and memory (paging) usage for each service of interest, monitor performance of system overall |
| Web server or back-end services/applications have occasional errors | An error condition is being triggered in the server that may not be detectable externally. | Monitor service/application log files for error messages |
| Web server returns "Server Busy" errors | Too many simultaneous connections to a Web server | Monitor service periodically to detect patterns and determine whether additional resources are warranted |
| Web server crashed | Machine is totally unreachable | Remote ping or other network monitors, or ping monitors from other internal machines |
| Server is overloaded | Client requests time out frequently | Use deep monitors for each service, with reasonable timeout limits. Also monitor system resources, such as CPU and memory for the system and key processes, to correlate with performance of service |

deeper levels of monitoring. By keeping historical records, trends that will lead to problems can be nipped in the bud. Knowing that a disk is nearing capacity allows some quick file cleaning or additional storage to be added, before the system comes to a screeching halt.

## MANAGING PROBLEMS WHEN THEY OCCUR

After the detection of a problem, the persons responsible for the equipment or function in question should be notified, typically via e-mail or pager messages. The faster the notification, the greater the chance that the problem can be fixed without affecting customers or users. When implementing a notification scheme, remember that if the scheme can be disabled by the same problems that are being monitored, notification may not succeed.

For example, if e-mail is used to trigger a pager message, and the e-mail server, or the connection to the e-mail server, has problems, the pager message will not get sent. Also consider the "cry wolf" syndrome; if alerts are sent out too often, and for unimportant events, then when real problems occur the chances of the notification being ignored are high.

Notification is fine; automatically correcting problems is even better. A hung Web server process can be automatically restarted, a nearly full disk can have temporary files automatically erased, or a flaky machine can be automatically rebooted. Automatically fixing as many problems as possible ensures minimum down time, and reduces the need for human intervention.

## COLLECTING AND USING HISTORICAL DATA

Historical data allows the correlation of several sets of monitor readings, leading to a quicker diagnosis of problems. For example, if the CPU utilization of the Web server machine is very high, then failures to retrieve URLs during that period of time may be related to Web server overload rather than the failure of the Web server process itself.

Historical data can also uncover trends that are useful in preventative maintenance. If a disk space usage monitor indicates a disk is filling up, steps can be taken to determine the root cause well before the problem becomes critical. Cyclical patterns of usage may also be revealed. A nightly maintenance process might be creating temporary files that bring the disk perilously close to capacity, and then delete those files before anyone notices.

Here is a real-world example that illustrates the usefulness of having a history of a server's performance. A Web administrator who had been running automated monitoring software was sure that something was wrong with the monitoring setup — requests for Web pages from his server were shown as timing out at the top of every hour, and he had not heard any complaints from his users. However, later on that week, when he had a chance to try out his site manually with a browser, sure enough, at the top of the hour, the server response was incredibly slow (as in minutes to load a Web page). It turned out that a scheduled job was being run on the hour, and its resource requirements slowed the server to a crawl. Without historical data, the few percent of users who would have eventually reported this problem would have had to give quite accurate time information for this pattern ever to have been found.

## CONCLUSION

If you have taken the time and money to create and maintain a Web site, then monitoring can protect that investment from the inevitable failures and performance problems that accompany the complex array of software, hardware, and network connections that comprise Web servers on the Internet.

**References**

Nemeth, E., Snyder, G., Seebass, S., and Hein, T.R., *UNIX System Administration Handbook,* Prentice-Hall, Upper Saddle River, NJ, 1995.

Spainhour, S. and Spainhour, V., *Webmaster in a Nutshell,* O'Reilly and Associates, Sebastopol, CA, 1996.

Welter, P., Why is my web site down? *Sys. Admin.,* April, 1998.

# Chapter 57

# Web Traffic Analysis: Analyzing What Is Happening on Your Site

*Michael McClure*

THE WEB TRAFFIC ANALYSIS MARKET BARELY EXISTED A FEW SHORT YEARS AGO AND IS ALREADY A MULTIMILLION DOLLAR SEGMENT OF THE E-BUSINESS INDUSTRY. Web traffic analysis growth is being driven by the growth of the World Wide Web and the desire to know as much as possible about visitors through self-identification, registration, and Web server logs. International Data Corporation predicts that the Web traffic analysis market will break $100 million by the year 2002.

Web traffic analysis tools take Web server traffic information and try to make sense of it so intelligent business conclusions can be drawn. Simple things like how many total files were requested can be easily calculated and reported. By looking for multiple requests from the same computer during the same timeframe, more complex things can be calculated, like the number of total visitors and visits that were made to a site. By adding other information to the analysis, such as advertising information, ad impressions and click-through rates also can be calculated.

Two types of Web traffic analysis are described below: Web log analysis and Web mining.

## WEB LOG ANALYSIS — TRADITIONAL WEB TRAFFIC ANALYSIS

Web log analysis software reports basic traffic information based on Web server log files. Tools in this category use calculations and assumptions to create a maximum number of log data relationships for inclusion in reports.

Traditionally, the main purpose for Web log analysis has been to gain a general understanding of what is happening on the site. Web masters and system administrators who are responsible for keeping the site up and running often want to know how much traffic they are getting, how many requests fail, and what kinds of errors are being generated. This information is typically used for Web site management purposes.

Recently Web log analysis has become more popular with Web marketers. By adding information such as advertisement names, filters, and virtual server information, log data can be further analyzed to track the results of specific marketing campaigns. Product managers and marketers who are responsible for allocating budgets in the most efficient manner require this type of information to make intelligent business decisions. Web log analysis can be used to answer questions like:

- What companies are visiting your site?
- What pages are the most and least popular?
- What sites are your visitors coming from?
- How much bandwidth does your site utilize?

## WEB MINING — ADVANCED WEB TRAFFIC ANALYSIS

Rather than look at Web traffic data as its own island of information (Exhibit 1), Web mining integrates Web traffic information with other databases in the corporation such as customer, accounting, profile, and E-commerce databases. The resulting reports not only use advanced relationships between log data, but also draw from these external databases as well.

The main purpose of Web mining is to analyze online investments of the entire enterprise, in an effort to maximize return. Executive management and Chief Information Officers are typical candidates for this type of information.

Many Web miners base their offers on visitor profiles and, more importantly, create new products that match the results of their analysis. Web mining is typically used to answer more complex Web-related questions like:

- How do visitors' demographic and psychographic information correlate with their Web site browsing behavior?
- What is your Web site's return on investment?
- Which advertising banners are bringing the most qualified visitors to your site?
- Which sites refer the highest number of visitors who actually purchase?

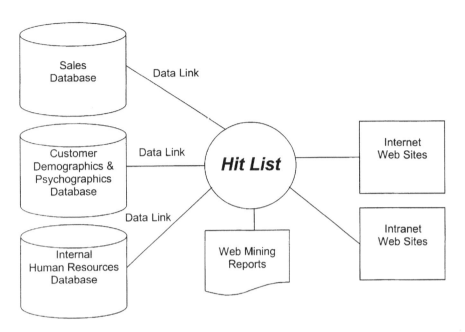

**Exhibit 1.  Web Mining Tools Integrate Web Traffic Data with Other Corporate Data from Sales, Customer, and Human Resources Databases.**

### An Overview of Web Traffic Analysis Software

To accomplish its goal, Web traffic analysis software must be able to collect Web traffic data from multiple Web sites, store it into a data warehouse, integrate it with other sources of information, and then analyze and report the results quickly and accurately. The ideal Web traffic analysis system is also both completely programmable and extensible to support customization and scalability with the enterprise. This section presents an overview of the technology typically used to accomplish each of these tasks. Good Web traffic analysis software is available today and ranges in price from free to more than $20,000. The most popular packages are priced at around $300.

### DATA COLLECTION

Web traffic analysis tools must first be able to collect Web traffic information, often from multiple Web sites deployed throughout the world. This can be accomplished through reading Web server log files or more recently through TCP/IP packet sniffing techniques.

## Web Server Log Files

Web server log files are undoubtedly the most common sources for Web traffic information. Behind every Web site is a Web server, whose purpose is to respond to visitors by locating and sending the requested files. After each request, the Web server logs the results of the exchange in a "log file." A typical log file is ASCII-based and contains information about which computer made the request, for which file and on which date.

These log files contain useful Web traffic information. By looking for multiple requests from the same computer during the same timeframe, conclusions can be drawn about the total number of visitors and visits that were made to a site.

## Data Collection through Packet Sniffing Technology

Packet sniffing technology has recently been introduced into the traffic analysis market which eliminates the need to collect and centralize log file data entirely. This technology gets its information directly from the TCP/IP packets that are sent to and from the Web server.

The advantage here is

- Data is collected in real time rather than being read in from a log file after the fact. This keeps the data warehouse up-to-date on a continuous basis.
- Data is continuously being read into the data warehouse rather than being collected from huge log files. This increases the data warehouse capacity.
- Companies with distributed Web servers can easily and automatically collect information in a centralized data warehouse. This solves the problem of collecting all the latest log files from sites located throughout the world.

Packet sniffing technology (Exhibit 2) watches network traffic going to and from the Web server and extracts information directly from the TCP/IP packets. The data collector must be installed on a computer located on the same network segment as the Web server that it is supposed to monitor, in order to "see" the network traffic as it goes by. Most packet sniffing tools are priced over $10,000.

## DATA INTEGRATION

For Web mining applications, Web traffic data must be linked to other traditional business and marketing databases within the company. These databases might include E-commerce, profile, accounting, and customer registration databases, for example.

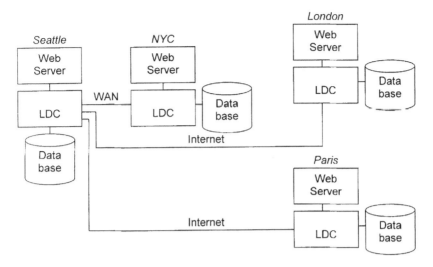

**Exhibit 2.** **Packet Sniffing Allows for Multiple Distributed Web Servers to Send Traffic Information over the Internet to a Centralized Data Warehouse. Here, Live Data Collectors (LDCs) Are Used in New York, London, and Paris to Form a Data Warehouse in Seattle.**

A typical way to perform this is through the computer IP address, as all requests to your Web server will include this information. Once you link an IP address to a particular company or person, you will be able to correlate future visits from the same IP address. This method is not perfect, however, as it is common for IP addresses to be shared among multiple users. This is done by larger organizations, such as Microsoft, as well as by Internet Service Providers such as America Online.

A more accurate method of creating this link is through the use of "cookie" technology. This ensures that the same computer is connected to your site, independent of the IP address that is used to make the connection. Both cookies and computer IP addresses are covered in more detail in the next sections.

## DATA REPORTING AND ANALYSIS

This is a typical area that Web traffic analysis tools overlook. It is important to keep in mind that the end goal of Web traffic analysis is to allow for online investments to be quickly analyzed and business decisions to be made. These reports, therefore, must include real data that can be acted on, rather than just reams of detailed technical information. If you cannot easily analyze this information, put it in a presentation-quality format, and quickly get it to the right decision maker, then there is not much purpose to collecting the information in the first place.

A quality Web traffic analysis package will include features like multi-level filtering and remote reporting, and will support multiple output formats. These features make Web traffic information easy to obtain for everyone in the organization.

## EXTENSIBLE AND PROGRAMMABLE

The final essential feature for Web traffic analysis tools is the ability to easily program the tool to integrate it with other Web applications you may have, or extend its capabilities. This is a key requirement for any organization that has had to wrestle with a tool that could not grow with the organization's needs and eventually needed to be replaced — an extremely painful and expensive process.

The ability to program a tool, through a standard scripting language, makes it easy to add custom functions. This might be used, for example, to remotely administer advertisements through user-created ASP pages.

Beyond programmability, the ability to add plug-ins is a requirement if you need to purchase or integrate your own custom functions. This can be used to extend data collection capabilities to other file types such as advertising servers and streaming-media logs, for example. It can also be used to create custom output types that might be necessary for proprietary data analysis systems.

### Some Important Web Traffic Analysis Concepts

To better understand Web traffic analysis software and what visitor information can be obtained from a Web site server, it is useful to have a basic understanding of how a Web server collects and logs visitor data.

To illustrate this, we will use the Marketwave Web server as an example. When visitors enter the URL "http://www.marketwave.com/default.htm" into a Web browser, they are asking the Marketwave Web server to send a file to them called default.htm which is located in the root directory. The Marketwave server responds to this request by sending the file and logging the results of the exchange in a server "log file."

In Marketwave's case, the default.htm file has references to two other HTML files and 23 other graphic files, which are needed to fully display the page. These files will also be automatically sent by the Marketwave Web server to the computer making the request and will be logged by adding lines to the Marketwave Web server log file. This means that a visit to the Marketwave home page will result in 26 total files (3 HTML files and 23 graphic files) being transferred and 26 lines being added to the server log files.

This example illustrates some key definitions that are imperative to understand when analyzing Web sites:

- *Hit or Request.* A "Hit" or "Request" refers to an individual file request made to the Web server. This can be measured very precisely by simply counting the number of lines contained in the Web server log file. Measuring requests, however, is not a very accurate measure of Web site popularity, as each visit to a site can generate large numbers of file requests. The way a Web site is designed and the number of graphics it has will both significantly affect the number of file requests a site receives. In the example above, there are 26 requests.
- *Page View.* A better measurement of site traffic can be found by counting page views. A page view is simply the transfer of a specific HTML file. Page views can also be measured precisely by simply counting the number of requests for HTML files. Page views are a better measurement of Web site popularity, but are still imprecise when multiple HTML files are required to display a page (when using frames on a site, for example). In the example above, there are three page views, due to the use of frames on the Marketwave home page.
- *Visitor.* A visitor is defined simply as a unique computer "IP address." This measurement is less precise, due to the fact that IP address are sometimes shared by many people, as is the case with large corporations and online service organizations. This precision can be improved by using other information as well, such as the browser type or a persistent cookie (more on this technology later). Visitors are a much better measurement of gross Web site traffic than page views or requests. In the above example, there is only one visitor.
- *Visit.* A visit is a collection of requests that represent all the pages and graphics seen by a particular visitor at one time. The total number of visits is usually more than the total number of visitors because each visitor can visit the site more than once. Visits are more difficult to measure precisely, because there is no way to be certain that a series of requests actually belongs to the same person, or, for that matter, to the same person during the same visit. Measuring visits is also a good gauge of gross Web site traffic popularity. In the example above, there is only one visit.

It is important to realize that measuring Web site popularity is an imperfect science. The art of good Web traffic analysis includes the ability to draw business conclusions using data that is imperfect. Having an understanding of the data, how it is collected, and what limitations exist, is key to drawing the proper business conclusions. As demonstrated in our example, one must understand and trade off between PRECISION (Requests and Page Views are precise but less accurate) and ACCURACY (Visits and Visitors are more accurate, but less precise) before drawing conclusions.

## MORE DETAILS ON LOG FILES

This section is included to provide the detailed background needed to understand how Web traffic data is collected and analyzed. A typical Web server log file is ASCII based and contains information about which computer made the request, for which file. Additional information can be recorded including the date, the browser type, the requesting computer's IP address, any error codes, and the referring site, to name a few.

## LOG FILE FORMATS

Different Web servers record this information in different log file formats. Most formats have similar information — they simply store it in different ways. Common log file formats include NCSA, W3C, Microsoft IIS, and O'Reilly. Here is a portion of a log file from the Marketwave Web site. This file was created by Microsoft's Internet Information Server, Version 4.0, which stores its log output in W3C format.

This log file shows 54 log files entries (requests), 10 HTML file requests (page views), and one unique IP address (visitor). Let us analyze it in more detail and explain each piece of the data to demonstrate what can be learned from this information.

The first thing to notice is that there are 18 unique fields (columns) in this log file, each representing a different piece of the Web traffic puzzle. In this respect, Web log analysis is a lot like music composition — there are only a few basic pieces of information (notes) to build from, yet by putting this information together in different ways, it is amazing what can be derived.

## LOG FILE FIELD DEFINITIONS

The definitions of these fields are as follows:

- *Request date.* This is the date that the request was made of the server.
- *Request time.* This is the time the request was made of the server. Some Web servers will include the time, as well as the offset from Greenwich Mean Time. If you are analyzing data from multiple Web sites located around the world, you will want to account for date and time-zone changes.
- *Request IP address.* This is the IP address of the computer that made the request. Every computer on the internet has a unique IP address so that other computers can find and connect to it. An IP address is made up of a series of four numbers separated by dots (206.129.192.10). Because humans have a difficult time remembering long strings of numbers, the Internet Domain Name System (DNS) was created, allowing these IP address to be associated with more readable domain names (e.g., market-wave.com).

- *Authenticated user name.* This is for sites that require a user to fill in a name and password before accessing a page. Whatever the visitor types in as his or her username is added to this field in the log file. This is typically used to restrict content on your site to only a few select users who know the password.
- *Server name.* This is the name of the server that responded to the request. It is useful for individually tracking multiple sites that are hosted on one computer (called virtual servers). For example, a publishing company might have a different Web site for each of its magazines, but host them all through one computer and one Web master. The term virtual server comes from the fact that there is only one computer behind the scenes, but to the outside world there appears to be multiple "virtual" Web sites, one for each magazine. This field allows the publishing company to analyze each site individually, as well as create aggregate statistics for the entire Web operation.
- *Computer name.* This is the name of the computer that responded to the request. It is useful for larger sites that require more than one computer to handle the number of requests being made (sites like Netscape, Microsoft, and Yahoo). This field could be used to calculate the "load" on each of the Web server computers and help determine when it is time to add additional resources or perform "load balancing" among the computers.
- *Server IP address.* This is the IP address of the server that responded to the request. In Marketwave's case, the Web server's IP address is 206.129.192.10, which is the computer hosting the Marketwave Web site.
- *Method.* This is the method that was used to respond to the request. GET is the most common command to retrieve HTML documents. Another commands you may see include HEAD, which is used to retrieve just the header portion of a file, and POST, which passes data to the server directly without being displayed in the URL (usually for security reasons).
- *Requested file name.* This is the path and file name that was requested relative to its root directory location on the Web server.
- *Query string.* This field includes any "query" text that was entered along with the URL. For example, in the URL "http://www.marketwave.com/default.htm?MWUID=info@marketwave.com" the text after the ? (MWUID=info@marketwave.com) is referred to as a query string. You will notice these strings used on dynamically generated sites like search engines and may sometimes see them embedded in hyperlinks to better track marketing campaigns. By intelligently using query strings, you can improve the trackability of your site.
- *Error code.* This is the Web server error response code. A "successful" request (meaning the visitor's browser loaded the entire HTML/GIF/JPEG, etc.) generates a response code of 200. Codes in the 200

and 300 range are generally OK, while codes in the 400 range are bad and in the 500 range are really bad. Server codes are grouped into ranges as follows:

— 200 Range — successful delivery of the requested file
— 300 Range — successful re-direct to another file
— 400 Range — failure to deliver the file
— 500 Range — server error

- *Bytes received.* This is the number of bytes of data that were received by the Web server.
- *Bytes sent.* This is the number of bytes of data that were transferred to the client during the visit.
- *Time taken.* This is the time the server took to respond to this request.
- *Version.* This is the format and version number of the request protocol, in this case HTTP, Version 1.0. A protocol is simply the "language" that computers use to communicate with one another. HTTP is the standard protocol of the Web and stands for HyperText Transfer Protocol. Another protocol you may run into is FTP, which stands for File Transfer Protocol.
- *Agent.* This is a code that identifies which browser and operating system made the request. "Mozilla/4.04" refers to the Netscape browser, and Win95 refers to the operating system, which in this case is Windows 95.
- *Cookie.* This is any cookie information from the browser (more on this later).
- *Referring page.* This is the page and site our visitor was on immediately prior to making this request. This is very useful information if we want to determine how visitors are finding our site.

### INTERPRETING THE LOG FILE

Looking at our example log file tells us quite a bit about what is happening with our Web site. The first line is a request for the Marketwave home page (default.htm). We notice a couple of useful pieces of information in this line, including the referring site (www.uu.se) and the referring page /software/analyzers/access-analyzers.html. This immediately tells us that this visitor came from a site based in Sweden (from the .se extension) and indicates that this site probably has a link to the Marketwave site on the /software/analyzers/access-analyzers.html page. If we go to this site ourselves, we find out that this is a university and the page in question has lots of links to different Web traffic analysis software packages.

The error code of 304 is also interesting. It tells us that this visitor already had access to cached version of our home page. Rather than send the file again, the Marketwave Web server responds with a status 304, indicating to the visitor's browser that it should go ahead and use the version of the page it already has.

The next 25 requests are all related to the home page. These are the additional 2 HTML frames and 23 graphics files (GIFs) that make up the remainder of the Marketwave home page. Notice that all of these requests resulted in an error code of 304, meaning that this visitor already had up-to-date copies of these files available. No files needed to be exchanged to display the Marketwave home page, frames, and graphics, as this computer has been to our site before and has our pages cached locally.

The next request is for a file called hitlist/live/default.htm. Odds are, this visitor clicked on a link to the Hit List Live page. This resulted in an error code 200, meaning the file was transferred and received success-fully. The next 21 lines are the frames and graphics associated with the Hit List Live page. Notice that all of them were transferred successfully (error code 200) and the file sizes range from a few hundred Kbytes to almost 5000 Kbytes.

The next request was for a file called /downloads/frames-default, which is the Marketwave download page. Great! This prospect hit our home page, then hit our Hit List Live page, and then went right to the download page. You can't ask for much more than that from a Web site!

As can be seen, a lot of information is available in the log file. Under-standing how your Web site is designed will really help with interpreting these data. If you didn't know that the Marketwave home page used frames, for example, you might think that the first three lines of the log file refer-enced three separate pages on the site. By knowing how the site is designed and looking at the data in the Web server log file, we can start to draw conclusions about visitors who can to the site.

## Don't Waste Your Time Manually Interpreting Log Files!

Don't misinterpret the intent of the previous section! I highly recom-mend that you DON'T waste your time manually trying to interpret your log files. There are plenty of good software packages on the market that will do this job for you, including many of them that are offered free of charge. You can get a reasonably complete list by going to any search engine and look-ing for "Web traffic analysis" or "log file analysis."

The intent of the last section was to give you enough of an understand-ing of what is happening in the background of this process so that you can better interpret the results you get from these packages. As with any type of data analysis, understanding what is behind the data is a key part of interpreting the results. The more details you understand, the better choices you will make when buying Web traffic analysis software and the better job you will do interpreting the results.

### Getting Fancy with Web Traffic Information

The last section shows how simple conclusions can be drawn directly from the information in the log file. With this information alone we could easily calculate things like:

- Which browsers and operating systems are the most common (through the agent field)
- How many bytes are being transferred by the server (through the bytes sent field)
- Which files and directories are the most popular (through the requested file names)
- What sites are visitors coming from (through the referring pages)

But wait! With a little more work, there is still more information we can add to this analysis.

### CONVERTING IP ADDRESSES BACK TO DOMAIN NAMES

We know this particular visitor was using a computer connected to the internet with IP address 193.237.55.144. Remember that every IP address has a corresponding domain name associated with it and these are linked through the Domain Name System (DNS). When a visitor entered www.marketwave.com into their browser, it was the DNS system that converted this name into the appropriate IP address (206.129.192.10) so that the computers could connect with each other. We can use the DNS system in reverse (called a reverse DNS lookup) to convert our mystery visitor's IP address back into a domain name. In this case, after doing a reverse DNS lookup, we find that the IP address 193.237.55.144 belongs to the domain issel.demon.co.uk. With this information we surmise that our visitor was using a computer owned by a company name Issel (due to the first part of the domain name) which is based in the U.K. (due to the .uk extension in the domain name).

You can either have your Web server perform this DNS conversion for you, or have your Web traffic analysis software do it. I generally recommend that you have your Web traffic analysis software do it, so you do not slow your Web server with this task. In addition, if someone else hosts your site, you may not have a choice in the matter, as most service providers do not want to slow their servers down to perform reverse DNS lookups. That's OK. Simply get the log files from your provider and have your Web traffic analysis software do it for you.

### CONVERTING FILE NAMES TO PAGE TITLES

A well-designed site will have a title (using the TITLE HTML keyword) for every page on the site. Rather than simply report the file names that were requested, we can easily look at these files and determine the corresponding page names. In general, page names are much more human-friendly in terms of communicating information. By simply extracting the page names from the files that are listed in our Web server logs, we can end up with a report that contains actual page names, rather than simply the file names themselves.

## CALCULATING VISITORS AND VISITS

If we make a simple assumption that any log file entry with same IP address and same browser is probably the same visitor, we can easily calculate the number of visitors on our site. Note that this assumption is not perfect, as it is certainly possible that two different visitors happen to have the same IP address and browser type (from an online service provider for example). In general, however, this is unlikely to happen enough to significantly change the results of your analysis.

We can also calculate the number of visits to the site by assuming that if we do not see any more requests from that same visitor in 30 minutes, that the visit has ended. If we then see that same IP address and browser sometime in the future, we can assume that the same visitor is back for a second visit.

## PATH ANALYSIS

By linking log file entries and then sorting by time and date, we can also start to see the path that a visitor took through the site. This is what we did in our example above. The log file shown only included requests from IP address 193.237.55.144 on 7/19/98. If we did this for each individual visitor, we would be able to calculate the most popular paths taken through the site as a whole.

## GROUPING INFORMATION

By grouping information together, we can start to draw conclusions. For example, if we group all Netscape Browser and all Microsoft Browser information together we could calculate which company's browser was the more popular on our site. Using this same technique with referrer information, and looking for any referring URL with the word "Yahoo" in it, we could see how many of our visitors came from Yahoo as a whole.

## COUNTRIES

By looking at the extensions on our visitors domain names, we can also estimate where in the world our visitors are coming from. Example extensions include:

.ca — Canada
.au — Australia
.se — Sweden
.uk — United Kingdom

## FILTERING INFORMATION

By filtering information, we can answer very specific questions about the site. For example, to calculate how many visitors we got from Microsoft this week, we would only look at information from this week, and only look at visitors that have the word "Microsoft" contained in their domain name. This could be compared to our overall traffic to determine what percentage of our visitors presumably work for Microsoft.

## CORRELATING INFORMATION

By correlating and cross-tabbing information, we can answer questions like, "Of the visitors I get from Germany, how many of them use Microsoft Windows 98 as their operating system?" This kind of detailed information can be useful for both site management and marketing segmentation purposes.

## QUERY STRING PARSING

A piece of information we have glossed over is the query string field, which was blank in our example above. Query strings are typically used on database-driven sites and consist of all of the data at the end of a URL (usually delimited with a "?"). For example, the following referring URL is from Yahoo: http://search.yahoo.com/bin/search?p=Web+Traffic+Analysis.

By looking at the data after the "?" we see that this visitor searched for "Web Traffic Analysis" on Yahoo before coming to our site. Yahoo encodes this information with a query parameter called "p" and separates each search keyword with the "+" character. In this example, "p" is called the query parameter and "Web," "Traffic," and "Analysis" are each referred to as parameter values.

This information would normally be stored via the query field in the log file, and by looking at it in detail we can draw conclusions about what our visitors was searching for before hitting our site. This is useful information when trying to design the site to come up higher on the list of search engines, or when trying to determine what visitors are looking for before coming to our site.

## VIRTUAL SERVERS

If you host multiple sites, another useful piece of information is contained in the site name field. By using this information intelligently, we could perform a separate analysis for each of the sites that you host. This would tell you which of your sites is responsible for the most traffic.

## ADDING COOKIES INTO THE PICTURE

Another field we glossed over was the cookie field, which is a topic that has received much attention and debate in the press. Up to this point, we have not actually been tracking people, but are instead tracking Internet (IP) addresses as they come to our site. Cookies were invented to attempt to do a better job of tracking people, rather than simply IP addresses.

This technology was developed by Netscape and is really pretty ingenious. A cookie is merely a unique identifying code that the Web server gives to the browser to store locally on the hard drive during the first visit to the site. The intent of a cookie is to uniquely identify visitors as they come to the site.

Cookies benefit Web site developers by making individual "requests" much more trackable, which results in a greater understanding on how the site is being used and, therefore, a better Web site design. Cookies also benefit visitors by allowing Web sites to "recognize" repeat visitors. For example, Amazon.com uses cookies to enable its "one-click" book ordering. Since the company already has your mailing address and credit card on file, it does not make you reenter all of this information to complete the transaction. It is important to note that the cookie did not obtain this mailing or credit card information. This information was collected in some other way, typically by the visitor entering it directly into a form contained on the site. The cookie merely confirms that the same computer is back during the next visit to the site.

Unfortunately, cookies remain a misunderstood and controversial topic. Contrary to many beliefs, a cookie is not an executable program, so it cannot format your hard drive or steal private information from you (note that languages like Java CAN do either of these things, but for some reason Java does not get the negative "security" press that cookies do). The second objection regarding cookies is that some people feel that it is a violation of their resources to be forced to store information on their computers for the benefit of the Web site's owner. In reality, the amount of disk space that a cookie takes up is trivial. Regardless of how you feel about cookies, modern browsers all have the ability to turn this feature off and not accept cookies.

If your site uses cookies, this information will show up in the cookie field of the log file and can be used by your Web traffic analysis software to do a better job of tracking repeat visitors.

Now comes the time to put all this log file information together into a readable report that we can draw conclusions from. Next is an example report showing the types of information that can be obtained from simply running your log files through a typical Web traffic analysis program.

## WEB MINING — GOING BEYOND WEB SERVER LOG FILES

As mentioned at the beginning of this chapter, Web mining can be used to incorporate other information along with Web server log files into your analysis. This allows for information to be correlated to Web browsing behavior, such as accounting, profile, demographic, and psychographic information. Complex questions like the following, therefore, can be addressed:

- Of the people that hit our Web site, how many purchased something?
- Which advertising campaigns resulted in the most purchases (not just "hits")?
- Do my Web visitors fit a certain profile? Can I use this for segmenting my market?

As an example of this technology in action, we will again use the Marketwave Web site (www.marketwave.com). When you download a Hit List product from our Web site, we ask you to register it. During this registration process we ask you for information including your name, company, phone number, e-mail address, and state/country. This information (along with your IP address, the date, and the product you downloaded) is automatically stored in a contact management software package. All Marketwave personnel use this centralized database to handle any interactions we have with you. This includes our sales, marketing, public relations, and support departments.

Our contact management database is linked to the Hit List Web traffic database through "DataLink" technology using your computer's IP address as the key field. Combining Hit List information with sales and marketing data opens up a whole realm of one-to-one marketing possibilities. In our case, every time we see your computer (the same IP address) on our site, we can pull up your registration information and take appropriate action. Often, this action is personalized to your particular situation.

One of the first things we do with the information we collect from you is to sort it by territory and send it to our worldwide distribution network (Exhibit 3). On a daily basis, we automatically e-mail a report to the appropriate Marketwave personnel. This report shows Web activity for the previous day, as well as product downloads. We sort these by territory to make it easy for our territory managers to personally follow up on the leads in their area. We also link our database of actual contact names and phone numbers into the report, rather than only including domain names which, by themselves, are not as useful to our distribution channel.

## TRACKING E-BUSINESS SALES

Marketwave recently added the ability to order Hit List directly from our Web site using a credit card. Our marketing department and management

**Exhibit 3.** **A Worldwide Distribution Report of Top Sales Prospects Who Hit the Web Site Yesterday (Jana Winslow — VP, Domestic Sales)**

| Company | Contact | E-Mail | Telephone | Visits |
|---------|---------|--------|-----------|--------|
| Microsoft | Seth Longo | Sethl@microsoft.com | 206-962-1200 | 3 |
| Tango Designs | Suzanne Gayaldo | Sgayaldo@dirk.tango.net | 509-323-6027 | 3 |
| Intel | Sanford Arnold | Sa@intel.com | 212-865-8584 | 2 |
| Lucent | Larry Rubin | Larry_rubin@lucent.com | 201-386-4200 | 2 |
| Volvo | Yasim Kinneer | Ykinner@vd.volvo.se | 206-765-1008 | 2 |
| ESPN | Michael Louis | Orioles@espn.com | 203-585-2000 | 1 |
| USDA | Tom Bianchi | Tommyb@dc.usda.gov | 202-548-2435 | 1 |
| Apple | Mark Sojic | Mark@apple.com | 301-255-7500 | 1 |

*Note:* This information has been generated by matching Web traffic data stored in the Hit List database with information stored in the Marketwave customer registration database.

staff now receive a daily report with e-business information in DOLLARS (not just hits, page views, or visits). This is accomplished by linking to our E-business database. The report shows how many online sales were made the previous day and how many dollars were involved. More importantly, we also report on the number of sales that were not completed and who they were. This helps us track down prospects who had trouble with the online ordering process, as well as those who simply need a bit more information before making a purchase decision.

### The Way We Manage Our E-Mail Campaigns

When we release new product versions, we first go back and market to our existing installed base of users. Generally, this is done through e-mail. In this e-mail, we add a link that looks something like: http://www.marketwave.com/default.htm?CAMPAIGN=date&MWUID=email.

The query string characters you see in this URL after the "?" are for tracking purposes. In this case, the campaign you are responding to (CAMPAIGN) is filled in with today's date and your Marketwave User ID (MWUID) is your e-mail address. When people click on this URL, these parameters end up in the query field of the log file. This means that we cannot only find out how many visitors we got as a result of our marketing efforts (through the CAMPAIGN parameter), but we can also tell who those visitors were (through the MWUID parameter).

### Measuring Marketwave Print Advertising

In addition, Marketwave directs visitors to our site through print advertising campaigns. These ads point people to our Web site for more information on our product and free evaluation software. The URLs we give in our print ads usually look something like: http://www.marketwave.com/adname.

This allows us to measure how many people responded to the campaign, by simply looking for how many people came from this URL. For example, by adding an entry page filter set to "adname*" to any of our reports, we would be able to see how many visitors we had to the site that clicked on the above URL.

I suggest keeping "adname" to just a few characters, as many people will not type long strings of text into their browsers. Also, like most marketing information, the data we get are not perfect. Many of our visitors will not type the "/adname" portion of the URL into their browser, so your actual response rate is probably higher than what is reported through your Web traffic analysis software.

### Measuring Marketwave Banner Advertising

Marketwave also is currently running multiple banner advertising campaigns. We also use query strings to track these. When we submit the ads to the sites we want to run them on, we also submit click-through URLs for each ad that look something like these:

> http://www.marketwave.com/default.htm?AdName=ad1&
> AdSource=sitename1
> http://www.marketwave.com/default.htm?AdName=ad2&
> AdSource=sitename1
> http://www.marketwave.com/default.htm?AdName=ad2&
> AdSource=sitename2

We then run reports filtering on AdName as the query parameter when we want to know how each ad is doing relative to another (ad1 vs. ad2). To compare our ad sites, we use filters that look for different AdSource as the query parameter (sitename1 vs. sitename2). This data is only are used to make future advertising decisions, but also to check the validity of the data we get from the sites we choose to do business with.

### Measuring Return on Investment

The ultimate measure of an advertising campaign is return on investment. On a periodic basis, we report the cost of each of our ad campaigns and impressions. This is then compared to our E-business database to calculate a total return for any particular campaign.

We then shift our promotional budget toward those ad campaigns that perform the best for us — in dollars returned, not visitors returned. As you may already suspect, it is not always true that the least advertising CPM (cost per thousand impressions) is the best value.

## OTHER EXAMPLES OF WEB MINING TECHNOLOGY

This section demonstrates some other real-world applications that Web mining technology is currently being used for within other major corporations.

### Qualifying Leads

Web mining can be used to not only collect and distribute leads, but also qualify them as well. For example, imagine using the Dun and Bradstreet SIC database to integrate corporate information along with your Web traffic information. Leads could be sorted by territory, then by company size, and distributed worldwide to the proper sales territory. This process can be completely automated, distributing Web leads as often as you would like.

In addition, this data can be used in a marketing report showing what pages are the most popular by industry (SIC code), as shown in Exhibit 4. This information could then be used to better target site information to particular industries.

**Exhibit 4.   Most Popular Pages by SIC Code**

| Page Name | SIC Code | Total Requests |
|-----------|----------|----------------|
| Home Page.htm | 3454 — Manufacturing | 4090 |
| | 5466 — Software | 3000 |
| | 8745 — Real Estate | 3500 |
| Pricing Page.htm | 0343 — Construction | 10,057 |
| | 2354 — Insurance | 1300 |
| Ordering Page.htm | 6404 — Banking | 3700 |
| | 2111 — Manufacturing | 2300 |
| Reseller Page.htm | 9999 — Financial Services | 3516 |
| | 6854 — Telecommunication | 5400 |

*Note:* Shows which pages are most commonly requested by companies with the following SIC codes and SIC descriptions.

### Performing Marketing Segmentation

When combined with a profiling system, Web mining can be used to perform marketing segmentation. This allows Web marketers to better target campaigns and messages to each target group.

For example, an online music company using a profiling system could easily create reports detailing the differences in browsing behavior based on age ranges. They might find that most of their actual purchasers are in their 20s (Exhibit 5). An understanding of what information was attractive to other visitors would be invaluable in designing the Web site to appeal to a wider audience. This information could then be used to expand content and quickly direct visitors to the right place.

| Exhibit 5. | Report Showing Browsing Profiles by Age Range per Page | |
|---|---|---|
| **Page Name** | **Age Range** | **Requests** |
| Home Page | 0:9 | 1 |
| | 10:19 | 3 |
| | 20:29 | 23 |
| | 30:39 | 13 |
| | 40:49 | 11 |
| | 50:59 | 8 |
| | 60:69 | 3 |
| Product Page | 0:9 | 1 |
| | 10:19 | 4 |

*Note:* Shows the age ranges, in 10-year increments, of visitors to each page.

## FEATURES USERS LOOK FOR IN WEB TRAFFIC ANALYSIS TOOLS

If you are in the market for a good Web traffic analysis software package, this section covers specific features you should consider when comparing tools.

### Basic Log Analysis Features (The Basic Stuff)

**Product Architecture.** We start with product architecture, as it is probably the single biggest difference in the leading Web traffic analysis tools and significantly impacts what can be done with the product. Some tools parse log file information directly into memory and then produce reports, all in one step. Others, first create a database of Web traffic information, then use this database to create Web traffic reports.

The main advantage of the "parsing" approach is speed for the *first* report, as writing data to a database is a step that is completely avoided. The main disadvantage of this approach is flexibility. Every change you need to make to a report (like a simple filter or query) will require that you reread all the log files and recreate a report from scratch. Not only does this take time, but it also eliminates the possibility of using the product with extremely high-traffic sites.

The main advantage to the database approach is that once a database has been formed, detailed reports can be generated by making simple queries to this database. In addition, having these data available is *fundamental* to the ability to perform one-to-one marketing and Web mining. Using a standard database opens up a realm of possibilities to effectively data mine your Web traffic information. This allows Web visitation information to be integrated into the rest of your organization, rather than having Web traffic analysis be its own island of information within your company.

**Reporting Speed.** When comparing Web traffic analysis tools for speed, I have two suggestions:

1. Make sure you are comparing "apples to apples." Some products do not store their results in a database and do not perform IP address lookups. For an "apples-to-apples" comparison, make sure you store the results and turn on IP-lookup capability, if it is available.
2. Make sure you compare multiple reporting sessions rather than simply running one report. Products that parse log files into memory will be faster on the first pass, as they do not store any data, so save the time of this step. The downside to this is that a *second* report with a simple change (like a filter or query) will require that you re-read all the log files and recreate the report from scratch.

**Predefined Reports/Elements.** This is the No. 1 requested feature by users — predefined reports that already perform the most common analysis tasks. Look for products that already include reports on advertising, marketing, technical analysis, proxy server, long-term trends, virtual server, and management summaries.

**Flexible Filtering.** Look for products that make it easy to get more detailed information, usually through the use of filters. Overview reports are fine, but you will soon find yourself asking for more detailed data, like how many visitors am I getting from each of the search engines? Sophisticated filtering includes the ability to apply filters to individual reports and individual reporting elements.

**Easy Creation of New Reports and Customization of Existing Reports.** Look for products that are easy to use and are intuitive, especially when creating your own reports. You want to spend your time analyzing the data, not creating the report.

**Report Output in Common Formats Like HTML, ASCII, CSV, Word Processor and Spreadsheet Formats.** Look for a product that produces reports in the formats you need and use. Another nice feature is the ability to automatically post reports on a network or Web site.

**Support for Multiple Web Servers.** Make sure the product reads and understands all of the Web server formats you use in your organization. Often companies will have multiple formats around the world that will need to be combined for reporting purposes.

**Automated Event Scheduling.** Look for a solution that lets you automate the creation and distribution of reports. For example, you may want a daily report to be created every night and automatically e-mailed to your sales force.

**Automatic LAN and FTP Retrieval of Compressed Log Files.** If you have Web site located remotely, look for a product that can automatically retrieve compressed log files from any FTP site or LAN.

**Language Manager for Customization.** Look for support for foreign language as well as support for company-specific terminology.

### Advanced Log Analysis Features (The Fancy Stuff)

**Search-Engine Keyword Reporting.** Look for software that intelligently uses the query string information. This is useful for tracking marketing campaigns, as well as understanding what visitors are searching for both on and off your site.

### Advertising Banner Campaign Analysis

If you run advertising campaigns, look for the ability to track them through measurement of impressions and click-through rates. In addition, you may consider a package that can link to your accounting database, so that results can be measured in terms of expenses and revenues generated, as opposed to just "Hits."

**Virtual Server Reporting.** If you run multiple sites, look for a package that can report on individual (real or virtual) servers separately. This allows you to understand how each server and site is doing.

**Detailed Visitor Path Analysis.** Some packages include the ability to analyze the most common paths that visitors take through the site. This is useful for optimizing the site to direct visitors toward certain areas, such as the ordering page or the technical support page.

**Link Checking Capability.** Web traffic analysis can highlight any error or broken links that visitors are encountering. This is useful for Web masters to understand the details of what errors users are encountering on the site.

**Remote Reporting with Security Manager.** Remote reporting allows any authorized user to obtain Web traffic information with nothing more than an Internet connection and browser. This makes it easy to get data to the people who need it, without having to install custom software or design individual reports for them. Making Web traffic data easily accessible to the nontechnical business specialists will improve an organization's efficiency in a distributed decision-making environment.

**Database-Driven Site/Query Reporting.** If you run a database-driven site, you will need the ability to parse your query strings into the parameters and values that are called from the integrated database. When combined with DataLink, query parsing results of dynamic site activity can be linked back to tables within the actual dynamic site generator to provide more meaningful information, such as a page title or content description.

**Custom Columns and Calculations Including User-Defined Variables and Formatting.** Much like a spreadsheet, look for the ability to add a column to any report table with custom calculations and formatting. This could be used by an ISP, for example, to calculate customer bills based on bytes transferred and display the result in dollars. When combined with DataLink, billing rates could even be read from another database.

## Web Mining Features (The Really Fancy Stuff)

**Plug-In Architecture for Extendability.** If you have custom needs, you should look for the ability to extend the software to perform the tasks you wish.

**Web Mining for Combining Web Log Data with Information from Other E-Business Databases.** This means that Web traffic information does not have to be yet another island of data within your organization. For example, reports can incorporate detailed customer information like real names, e-mail addresses, and phone numbers. For complex users, look for SQL statement support for ultimate information flexibility. This allows more complex questions to be answered based on Dollars and ROI, rather than just Hits and Visits.

**Integrated Programming Language and Editor.** Many companies will need the ability to customize their Web traffic analysis tool to meet specific needs or integrate with other E-business applications. Look for extendability through a standard programming language such as Visual Basic and Visual C++.

**Remote Administration from Any Connected Computer.** If you work for a larger organization, consider the ability to administer your software from any network connection. This makes maintenance and administration in distributed environments extremely easy from any location.

**Real-Time Data Collection via TCP/IP Packet Sniffing and Web Server Plug-Ins.** Packet sniffing eliminates the need to collect and manage multiple distributed server log files by automatically collecting traffic information in real time directly from the TCP/IP network packets. The resulting database is always up to date and available for reporting. The benefit here is not only the real-time aspects of data reporting, but also the complete elimination of log file administration. This feature is especially useful for companies with multiple Web sites located throughout the world. Packet sniffing allows data to be collected and stored in a centralized data warehouse, completely automatically and in the background.

## CONCLUSION

The Internet is the most significant technology the world has seen since the computer and has the potential to revolutionize business and marketing techniques. If you are serious about your online investment, the first step is to get a better understanding about who is visiting your site and what they are looking for.

Knowing this information allows you to make better business decisions by catering to your best customers and delivering the information they are looking for. With today's powerful Web traffic analysis software, this analysis can be performed easily and inexpensively.

# Chapter 58
# Guaranteeing Internet Service Levels: TCP Rate Control

*Bob Packer*
*Pat Thomas*

THE TRANSMISSION CONTROL PROTOCOL (TCP) PROVIDES CONNECTION-ORIENTED SER-
VICES FOR THE PROTOCOL'S APPLICATION LAYER; THAT IS, THE CLIENT AND THE SERVER
MUST ESTABLISH A CONNECTION TO EXCHANGE DATA. TCP transmits data in segments encased in IP datagrams, along with checksums used to detect data
corruption, and sequence numbers to ensure an ordered byte stream. TCP
is considered to be a reliable transport mechanism because it requires the
receiving computer to acknowledge not only the receipt of data, but its
completeness and sequence. If the sending computer does not receive
notification from the receiving computer within an expected timeframe,
the segment is retransmitted. TCP also maintains a flow control window to
restrict transmissions. The receiver advertises a window size, indicating
how many bytes it can handle.

In summary, TCP provides the following reliability checks:

- Acknowledges receipt of packets; retransmits when dropped packets
  are detected
- Resequences segments, if necessary, if they arrive out of order
- Tosses packets if data becomes corrupted during transmission
- Discards duplicate segments
- Maintains flow control to manage a connection's transmission rate

0-8493-1160-8/02/$0.00+$1.50
© 2002 by CRC Press LLC

## THE BANDWIDTH CHALLENGE

TCP/IP was primarily designed to support two traffic applications: FTP and Telnet. With the growth of the Internet, network applications and user expectations have changed. Today, with more high-speed users and bursty, interactive Web traffic, greater demand is placed on networks, causing delays and bottlenecks that impact a user's quality of service. Many of the features that make TCP reliable contribute to performance problems, including:

- Retransmitting when the network "cloud" drops packets or delays acknowledgments
- Backing off when it infers congestion exists (Conventional TCP bandwidth management uses indirect feedback to infer network congestion. TCP increases a connection's transmission rate until it senses a problem and then it backs off. It interprets dropped packets as a sign of congestion. The goal of TCP is for individual connections to burst on demand to use all available bandwidth, while at the same time reacting conservatively to inferred problems to alleviate congestion.)

TCP uses a sliding-window flow-control mechanism to increase the throughput over wide area networks. It allows the sender to transmit multiple packets before it stops and waits for an acknowledgment. This leads to faster data transfer because the sender does not have to wait for an acknowledgment each time a packet is sent.[1] The sender "fills the pipe" and then waits for an acknowledgment before sending more data. The receiver not only acknowledges that it got the data, but it advertises how much data it can now handle — that is, its window size.

TCP's slow-start algorithm attempts to alleviate the problem of multiple packets filling up router queues. Remember that TCP flow control is typically handled by the receiver, which tells the sender how much data it can handle. The slow-start algorithm, on the other hand, uses a congestion window, which is a flow-control mechanism managed by the sender. With TCP slow-start, when a connection opens, only one packet is sent until an ACK is received. For each received ACK, the congestion window increases by one. For each round-trip, the number of outstanding segments doubles until a threshold is reached.

In summary, TCP uses flow control determined by client and server operating system configurations, distances, and other network conditions. As will be seen in subsequent chapter sections, TCP Rate Control provides rate control explicitly configured in user-defined policies.

## BANDWIDTH MANAGEMENT APPROACHES

When faced with bandwidth constraints, a number of solutions come to mind. This section addresses the following potential solutions, focusing on their advantages and limitations:

- Adding bandwidth
- Using queuing schemes on routers
- Upgrading Web servers
- Defining precise control (the TCP Rate Control solution)

### Adding Bandwidth

An obvious approach to overcoming bandwidth limitations is to add more bandwidth. As technology trends demonstrate, this is a short-term solution; as soon as bandwidth is increased, it is consumed. So, one is back to where one started — trying to more efficiently manage the bandwidth that one has.

### Using Queuing Schemes on Routers

For the most part, network devices have kept pace with evolving high-speed technology. Routers provide queuing schemes such as weighted fair queuing, priority output queuing, and custom queuing in an attempt to prioritize and distribute bandwidth to individual data flows so that low-volume applications, such as interactive Web applications, do not get overtaken by large data transfers, typical of FTP traffic.[2-4]

Router-based queuing schemes have several limitations, including:

- Routers manage bandwidth passively, tossing packets and providing no direct feedback to end systems. Routers can only use queuing — that is, buffering and adding delay — or packet tossing to try to control traffic sources.
- Router queuing is unidirectional, that is, outbound traffic only.
- Queuing results in chunkier traffic and erratic performance because multiple, independent TCP sources compete for bandwidth, ramping up and backing off; and queues accumulate at the access link. Queuing, especially "weighted fair queuing," does not work well for chunky flows because packets arriving in chunks tend to be discarded.
- Routers do not allow one to set guaranteed rates for specific traffic types.
- Routers cannot prevent "brown-outs"; that is, they do not provide admission-control policies to dictate what happens when a link is oversubscribed.

- Rate specification is imprecise. One cannot specify high-speed and low-speed connections separately and one cannot specify speed in bits per second.
- Traffic classification is too coarse. A router cannot classify traffic by URL, treating all flows the same at the Web site.

### Upgrading Web Servers

On the Web server end, hardware improvements, server software, and HTTP have caused the bottleneck to move away from the server, and out to the access link. As illustrated in Exhibit 1, congestion occurs when data from a LAN's large pipe is passed to a smaller pipe on the WAN.

### Defining Precise Control: The TCP Rate Control Solution

Traffic, by nature, consists of chunks of data that accumulate when multiple independent sources of data are combined. These data chunks tend to form at access links where speed conversion is handled. This is where TCP Rate Control makes a difference.

Imagine putting fine sand, rather than gravel, through a network pipe. Sand can pass through the pipe more evenly and quickly than chunks. TCP Rate Control conditions traffic so that it becomes more like sand than gravel. These smoothly controlled connections are much less likely to incur packet loss and, more importantly, the end user experiences consistent service.

As in the next section, TCP Rate Control takes advantage of TCP mechanisms to overcome TCP deficiencies and offer predictable performance. Where TCP relies on indirect network feedback from tossed packets to infer congestion, TCP Rate Control provides direct feedback to the transmitter by detecting a remote user's access speed and network latency and correlating these data with aggregate flow information. This results in smoothed traffic flow.

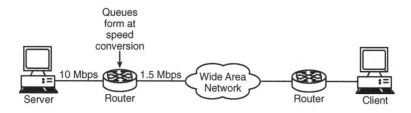

**Exhibit 1.   Access Link Bottleneck**

## HOW TCP RATE CONTROL WORKS: RATE CONTROL VERSUS FLOW CONTROL

TCP Rate Control maintains state information about individual TCP connections, giving it the ability to provide direct, quality-of-service feedback to the transmitter. In addition, one can define TCP Rate Control policies to explicitly manage different traffic classes and partition bandwidth resources to meet one's business needs. As a result, one gains precise control of one's service levels.

TCP Rate Control provides several key functions that differentiate it from other bandwidth-management solutions:

1. Controls the end-to-end connection, eliminating burstiness, so users experience smooth, even data displays
2. Classifies traffic for precise control and can even classify by a specific application or URL
3. Allocates bandwidth according to one's policies (features are discussed in more detail in the following sections)

### Controls the End-to-End Connection

TCP Rate Control uses two methods to control the rate of TCP transmissions:

1. It detects real-time flow speed and then delays acknowledgments going back to the transmitter.
2. It modifies the advertised window size in the packets sent to the transmitter. TCP Rate Control changes the end-to-end TCP semantics from the middle of the connection. It calculates the round-trip time (RTT), intercepts the acknowledgment, and holds onto it for the amount of time that is required to smooth the traffic flow without incurring retransmission time-out (RTO). It also supplies a window size that helps the sender determine when to send the next packet. To see how this rate control mechanism works, refer to Exhibit 2 and the following data flow example.

**A TCP Rate Control Data Flow Example.** Exhibit 2 shows how TCP Rate Control intervenes and paces the data transmission to deliver predictable service. The following steps trace the data transfer shown in Exhibit 2.

1. A data segment is sent to the receiver.
2. The receiver acknowledges receipt and advertises an 8000-byte window size.

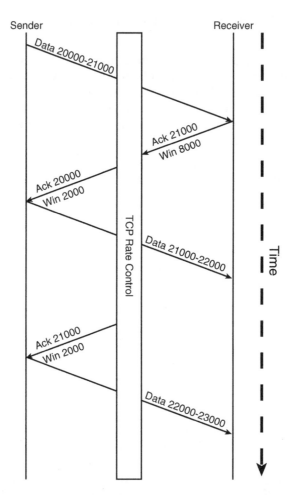

**Exhibit 2.   TCP Rate Control Manages the Connection**

3. TCP Rate Control intercepts the ACK and determines that the data must be more evenly transmitted. Otherwise, subsequent data segments will queue up and packets will be tossed because insufficient bandwidth is available, as defined by this flow's policy.
4. TCP Rate Control sends an ACK to the sender, calculated to arrive at the sender to cause the sender to immediately remit data; that is, the ACK sequence number plus the window size allows the sender to transmit an additional packet.

**Smooth Traffic Flow with TCP Rate Control.** Without the benefit of TCP Rate Control, multiple packets are sent; an intermediate router queues the packets; and when the queue reaches its capacity, the router tosses packets, which must then be retransmitted. Exhibit 3 shows bursty traffic when TCP

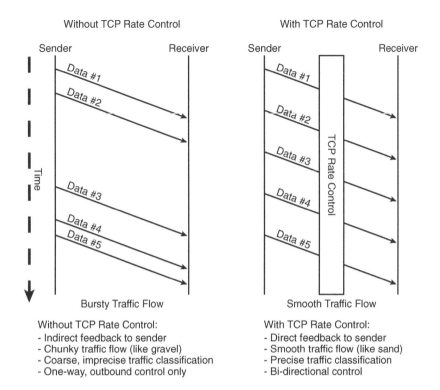

**Exhibit 3.    Traffic Behavior: Before and After TCP Rate Control**

Rate Control is not used, and evenly spaced data transmissions when TCP Rate Control intervenes. *Note:* Independent of access-link congestion problems, traffic chunks are more prone to packet loss than evenly spaced traffic.

## Classifies Traffic for Precise Control

TCP Rate Control uses a hierarchical tree structure to classify traffic. One can identify the characteristics of the traffic types one wants to control, such as traffic from a particular application (like Web traffic) or even a specific URL. One need not classify all network traffic — only the traffic that affects one's business' quality of service. TCP Rate Control classifies a traffic flow by traversing the traffic class tree, attempting to match the flow to one of the classes defined. The final step in the classification process maps a flow to a policy. The policy defines the type of service one wants a traffic class to get, for example, a guaranteed rate.

TCP Rate Control offers rich traffic classification by:

- Providing classification for specific applications and URLs, giving one precise control

- Maintaining a traffic class hierarchy to manage priorities and enable policy inheritance
- Ordering traffic classes automatically, yet allowing one to flag specific classes as exceptions, overriding the natural tree-search order

**A Web-Access Scenario.** Anyone using a Web browser to access information on the World Wide Web communicates on the Internet using HTTP (HyperText Transfer Protocol) over TCP. HTTP traffic tends to be bursty because HTTP transfers data for each user request. A typical Web-browsing session is shown in Exhibit 4.

## Allocates Bandwidth

After creating traffic classes for the traffic types one wants to control, one defines policies, which are the rules that govern how TCP Rate Control allocates bandwidth. Then, one applies the policies to appropriate classes.

As TCP Rate Control processes a traffic flow, it matches the flow to one of the classes in its tree structure and uses the class-assigned policy to set the quality of service for the flow. A traffic flow can be either a connection or an individual URL.

TCP Rate Control offers three policy types: rate-based, priority-based, and never-admit-that-you-configure-to-control-bandwidth. The following sections describe how TCP Rate Control determines how to divide bandwidth in accordance with the rules one has defined.

**Assigning Rates for a Traffic Class.** Designed to smooth bursty traffic, rate-based policies allow one to reserve bandwidth by assigning a guaranteed rate for a traffic class. The guaranteed rate sets a precise rate, in bits per second, for a connection. If bandwidth is available, the connection can use some of the unused or excess rate, according to the policy settings one has defined.

**Controlling Admissions.** One can define what should happen if a traffic class's total guaranteed rate gets used up. For example, if the next connection for a class needs a guaranteed rate and no bandwidth is available, TCP

**Exhibit 4.   A Typical Web-Browsing Session**

| User Action | TCP Rate Control Action |
|---|---|
| 1. Click on a button to select a specific URL. | 1. Classifies the traffic flow by URL — Is it an index? Is it an HTML file? Is it a GIF? |
| | 2. Maps the traffic class to a policy — the rules for rate control. |
| | 3. Smoothes the data transfer, giving the user an even, nonbursty data display. |

718

Rate Control can handle the bandwidth request by either refusing the connection or Web request, redirecting the request, or squeezing the connection into the existing bandwidth pipe.

**Scaling Bandwidth to Connection Speed for Efficient Bandwidth Use.** TCP Rate Control monitors a connection's speed and adjusts bandwidth allocation as the connection speed changes. Low-speed connections and high-speed connections can be assigned separate guaranteed rates so that TCP Rate Control can scale bandwidth usage accordingly. For example, during a typical Web session, the wait period between clicks does not consume bandwidth, so TCP Rate Control frees bandwidth to satisfy other demands.

**Prioritizing Bandwidth Allocation.** One can use priority-based policies for traffic that do not require a guaranteed rate, but that one still wants to manage along with competing traffic. Priority-based policies are ideal for non-bursty traffic, for which one does not need to reserve a guaranteed rate. One assigns a priority (0 to 7) to a traffic class so that TCP Rate Control can determine how to manage the aggregate flow. One does not need to classify all traffic. Any traffic that one has not classified is treated as priority-based traffic with a priority of 3.

**Denying Access.** In some cases, one may want to deny access to users — perhaps traffic from a particular IP address. One can control access using a never-admit policy, which one can configure to always refuse access or redirect the user to another URL.

## TCP Rate Control Bandwidth Allocation Order

TCP Rate Control uses the policies one has defined to determine how to allocate bandwidth. When determining bandwidth allocation, TCP Rate Control takes into account all bandwidth demands — not just the individual traffic flows. As shown in Exhibit 5, bandwidth is allocated based on the following basic allocation scheme:

1. Traffic flows that have assigned guaranteed rates are satisfied first.
2. All other traffic — both traffic with assigned policies and unclassified traffic — competes for the remaining or excess bandwidth.
3. Excess bandwidth is allocated based on the priorities one has set in priority-based policies.

Note that a flow may have both a guaranteed rate and some excess rate, as it is available. One determine an application's priority. For example, one could set PointCast connections to use excess rate at a low priority to keep it from interfering with revenue-generating activities (see Exhibit 4).

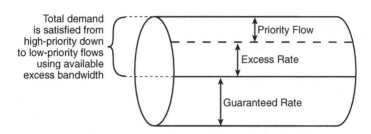

**Exhibit 5.   Bandwidth Allocation**

**How TCP Rate Control Allocates Bandwidth: The TCP Rate Control Advantage.** TCP Rate Control provides patent-pending technology that enables one to explicitly control TCP/IP bandwidth to keep one's network under one's own control. This technology offers the following unique bandwidth management features:

- Explicit bits-per-second rate control, providing the ability to specify guaranteed rates and to define how total bandwidth should be allocated
- Smoothed traffic flow — that is, evenly paced transmissions — eliminating the burstiness associated with Web traffic and ensuring consistent quality of service
- Precise traffic classification — even by URL or by application type
- Bi-directional traffic control, unlike routers, which control outbound traffic only
- Direct feedback to sender about transmission rate and flow status, rather than the indirect feedback provided by routers
- Admissions control for brown-out protection

**Notes**

1. Stevens, W. R., *TCP/IP Illustrated,* Vol. 1: *The Protocols,* Addison-Wesley Longman, Reading, MA, 1994, 455.
2. Recent work in network engineering indicates that traffic has self-similar or fractal properties. This implies that queuing problems at access links are far worse than would be predicted by traditional Poisson modeling.
3. Paxson, V. and Floyd, S., "Wide Area Traffic: The Failure of Poisson Modeling," *IEEE/ACM Trans. Networking,* Vol. 3, No. 3, June 1995.
4. Erramilli, A., Narayan, O., and Willinger, W., "Experimental Queuing Analysis with Long-Range Dependent Packet Traffic," *IEEE/ACM Trans. Networking,* Vol. 4, No. 2, April 1996.

# Chapter 59

# MSPs: Monitoring and Managing E-Commerce

*Yash Shah*

THE E-COMMERCE INDUSTRY IS STILL EVOLVING, WITH FORRESTER RESEARCH PREDICTING THAT E-COMMERCE REVENUE WILL TOP $1.3 TRILLION BY 2004. IT professionals continue to develop applications that streamline business-to-business (B2B) transactions or speed up data exchange. These new applications, coupled with existing B2B technology and the staggering number of E-commerce companies and customers, place enormous demands on a company's IT infrastructure. E-commerce initiatives can push a company's bandwidth, hardware, and software beyond their limits. Overextending IT capabilities sets the stage for costly system failures and dwindling customer loyalty.

In E-commerce, even a few seconds of Web site downtime can result in thousands of potential customers lost forever, and a significant drop in expected revenue. After spending time and money deploying their information technology (IT) infrastructures, E-businesses often think they have invested in uptime for their Web sites. But all they have really bought is the hardware and software to power their sites. What is missing is often the expertise and manpower to manage these infrastructures to ensure that all components perform reliably.

Firewalls, World Wide Web servers, load balancers, operating systems, and publishing databases are among the many components required to generate Web content. IT managers must ask several questions to determine whether their E-commerce infrastructure is operating correctly:

- How are the servers sitting on the infrastructure edge performing?
- How are the connectivity, bandwidth, and caching performing?
- How is the end-to-end transaction performing from a customer's perspective?
- How is security?

While many management software providers offer products to answer such questions, they are expensive and complicated, and require full-time IT staff to operate. Totally outsourcing the project is another option, but many companies fear losing control of their IT assets.

Enter the management service provider (MSP), a new industry player that can help companies stabilize their complex IT infrastructures to deliver maximum uptime, while enabling their IT staff to focus on the heart of the business: developing vital E-commerce applications. MSPs can answer the questions above with remote monitoring tools and a full-time staff to keep track of a company's IT assets around the clock.

Like an air traffic controller, MSPs can guide the safe operation of a client's IT infrastructure from afar, and prevent it from crashing. Through a subscription model, MSPs give businesses a set of eyes into their IT infrastructures by monitoring, tracking, and reporting on the infrastructure's health. E-commerce companies can use this information to enhance their IT infrastructure availability and reliability.

Moreover, MSPs provide E-commerce IT managers with a single view of their IT infrastructure. This complete view of every infrastructure component, including both co-located E-commerce systems and the back-office IT environment, eliminates reactive firefighting based on fragmented information from disparate monitoring systems.

MSPs can increase an IT staff's value to its company by relieving it of the daily routine of monitoring and tracking IT environment performance. Rather than worry about monitoring infrastructure health, IT staff members can instead develop new E-commerce capabilities, implement best practices, and focus on strategic projects like planning and change management.

## THE MSP ADVANTAGE

MSPs can help companies manage problems that occur everywhere in the infrastructure, including applications, networks, databases, systems, and E-business architectures. IT staffs can gain management control over their entire infrastructure through MSP services that automatically correlate management information to help them prevent downtime and improve performance. By monitoring, notifying, tracking, and reporting on every IT infrastructure component, MSPs enable companies to address potential problems before they occur. MSPs provide these services remotely by combining a centralized monitoring infrastructure with distributed monitoring systems strategically located across the Internet.

Fast provisioning of network and systems management is a crucial MSP advantage. By contrast, traditional software deployments are not only costly and time-consuming, but IT managers risk encountering a system failure until the monitoring technology is in place.

## MSP DELIVERY ARCHITECTURE

Although it is an emerging market, the MSP industry already has a broad range of providers that offer a variety of specialized services. Some MSPs focus on monitoring and management services for the entire IT infrastructure. Others specialize in monitoring select segments of the IT environment, such as networks and Web sites. Whatever their focus, MSPs generally have a similar model for delivering their service.

MSPs gather information about their clients' IT environment through a delivery architecture featuring monitoring servers that are strategically placed throughout the infrastructure, and a network connection to transfer that information to the MSP. MSPs use highly available servers, providing full redundancy so they can continuously monitor infrastructure components and help clients ensure optimal performance. Often loaded with an intelligent agent, the servers gather performance data based on a predetermined set of thresholds. They then feed that information to the MSP delivery network.

The network must have a secure connection through the firewall into the company's infrastructure so that the MSP can access the performance and availability information. MSPs can work with their clients to determine the best path for information exchange, whether it is a direct Internet connection, Frame Relay, a virtual private network (VPN), or point-to-point connectivity.

If the MSP monitors the client's network remotely, it will transfer the data to an off-site network operations center (NOC). The MSP has the staff and software tools to correlate the data and put it into a format that the client can use to make informed decisions about the IT infrastructure. The MSP will then make that information available to the IT manager as instant notifications via e-mail, or page and reports via a Web portal.

To obtain the most comprehensive view of all of the IT assets, an IT manager should have the MSP tie in the performance data from the company's entire IT infrastructure. IT managers use this information to see how the total environment is operating, and react and plan accordingly. In addition, an E-commerce company's IT manager may require that an MSP provide monitoring services for IT assets be co-located at a hosting partner's facilities.

## THE CRUCIAL SINGLE VIEW

Many E-commerce companies, however, do not have a single view of their IT and E-commerce infrastructure performance. In fact, the high-tech industry appears to be promoting the use of different monitoring tools for different corporate operations. These might include one for E-commerce and one for the back-office IT infrastructure. This could be an enormous mistake. Unless IT managers have established some form of data exchange between the two systems, they will not have a clear view of their overall IT infrastructure health.

For example, a B2B Web exchange that trades precious metals might experience internal e-mail problems that slow transaction processing on the Web site. If the company has separate monitoring systems for the exchange and for its back-office IT infrastructure, the IT manager may not quickly see the cause-and-effect relationship between the two systems. Because each monitoring system generates a different set of performance information from different databases, the IT staff must address the problems independently through a reactive firefighting mode.

If the same company had one comprehensive MSP monitoring system for both functions, the IT staff could react more quickly because the integrated information would automatically point to the correlation between the two problems. Even if the company had two different MSPs monitoring its Web exchange and its back-office infrastructure, a preestablished data exchange between the two services would be able to quickly identify the problem's root cause. This single view of the entire infrastructure not only allows companies to predict when their infrastructures could fail, but also enables them to react quickly when these problems arise.

## WHAT TO LOOK FOR

When choosing MSPs, IT managers should learn about each prospective MSP's delivery architecture and monitoring and quality assurance processes. Failure to do so could mean that an IT manager does not receive the type of information needed to make solid decisions.

Most importantly, an MSP must have the type of delivery infrastructure that will provide companies with timely information for predicting system performance and ensuring good customer experiences. This architecture must be highly available so that it can handle the large amount of data moving between the MSP and the client. Everything from the servers to the network connections and the network itself must have the bandwidth capacity to deliver the performance information that a client expects. In addition, the delivery architecture must be highly redundant to ensure that the MSP infrastructure provides monitoring and management services on a 24×7 basis.

Security is also paramount. A reliable MSP should have an externally validated security infrastructure that safeguards a client's vital information as it passes from the client's IT infrastructure to the MSP's NOC and back. In addition, MSPs should be able to provide their clients with on-demand scalability. For example, if a client acquires a company and needs to immediately add 1000 servers to its list of monitored components, an MSP should have the capacity and scalability to essentially flip a switch and provide these services instantly. Delaying deployment of additional component monitoring services could lead to unexpected infrastructure problems that could in turn hamper a client's ability to serve its customers.

In general, IT managers should ask prospective MSPs about the kind of processes they have in place to ensure that their IT infrastructures run optimally. To ensure that its client's IT environment runs optimally, MSPs must first ensure that their own infrastructures do not fail. An MSP must stay one step ahead of its client to effectively monitor the client's IT infrastructure. IT managers will want to know what kind of quality assurance testing the MSP performs to keep its systems running, and possibly whether the MSP has earned any quality certifications.

Having chosen an MSP, the IT manager should work with the MSP to identify which components within the company's infrastructure the MSP should monitor. Then, the IT manager and the MSP should develop a format for receiving the performance data that best suits the IT manager's needs. This means determining how the MSP should present the data, and to whom within the company this data should be sent.

## CONCLUSION

Many E-commerce companies are finding that they are paying for their IT deployments twice: once for the technology and a second time for the staff and tools to monitor its performance. MSPs provide IT managers with an affordable and efficient means of ensuring that their IT assets remain highly available and reliable. They give IT managers the information they need to make informed decisions about infrastructure performance and planning. They also enable companies to get more value from their IT staff members, who no longer need to spend much of their time monitoring and managing the IT environment. The result is that the company delivers great customer experiences and increases profitability.

# Chapter 60
# Using Intelligent Agents to Maximize the Benefits of the World Wide Web

*Barbara J. Haley*
*Kelly Mega Hilmer*

ORGANIZATIONS THAT INVEST MUCH TIME AND EFFORT IN INFORMATION SYSTEMS THAT SUPPORT UNIQUE MANAGEMENT NEEDS ARE INCREASINGLY INTEGRATING THE WORLD WIDE WEB (WEB) INTO THEIR IS PORTFOLIO. Although countless articles and books have espoused the Web's promise to provide information and commercial opportunities to the business community, several current limitations make the Web fall short of expectations.

Recently, intelligent agents have become practical solutions for addressing these limitations. The use of intelligent agents is important for Web developers, IS and business managers, and organizations interested in maximizing the benefits of the Web as an information tool while minimizing the time, costs, and frustration associated with Web use. After describing how the Web nominally supports management information needs, this chapter illustrates how five types of intelligent agents address the current Web weaknesses that managers may encounter.

## WEB-SUPPORTED INFORMATION NEEDS

Managers are unique systems users because of the wide variety of tasks they perform, the diversity of information they require, and the dynamic nature of their decision-making environment. The literature on executive information systems, for example, illustrates that executives require special systems that

- Are custom tailored to individual executives

0-8493-1160-8/02/$0.00+$1.50
© 2002 by CRC Press LLC

- Extract, filter, compress, and track critical data
- Access and integrate a broad range of internal and external data
- Are user friendly and require minimal or no training
- Are used directly by executives without intermediaries
- Present graphical, tabular, and textual information

Over the years, systems have evolved to address these requirements and provide executives with effective tools for accomplishing management tasks. The Web appears to be yet another innovative way to address such needs. A broad range of internal and external data is accessible from Web sites within an organization and from external sites located around the world. Managers can use the available graphical packages to navigate the Web without assistance. Web browsers also present information in creative ways, taking advantage of graphics, sound, and video.

### Limitations of the World Wide Web

Information overload, constant updating and reshuffling of information, and minimal support for novice users are some of the current problems that reduce the Web's value to managers. The lack of Web regulation and control combined with rapid growth have contributed to an abundance of information. Because this information changes constantly with little order or customization, it is difficult for managers to locate information efficiently, especially because they typically navigate this chaos with minimal or basic computer skills. As managers increase their Web use, organizations will become more concerned about these problems.

### CAPABILITIES OF INTELLIGENT AGENTS

Intelligent agents, also called software agents, are software programs that help find, organize, and present information that is custom tailored to a meet a manager's needs. The programs are relatively autonomous; they are not attached to a particular software application and do not need a user for activation. Agents always are ready to perform a specified action according to preset user parameters. In addition, advanced agents learn trends and user preferences, and they can analyze information to support decision making.

Agents address a variety of problems. They are designed to save time, perform mundane tasks, fulfill requests tailored to specific needs, and manage data. To some people, these agents serve as personal data assistants, addressing diverse information requirements. But, unlike a human assistant who needs sleep and occasional days off, an agent addresses customized needs around the clock.

There are many types of agents, and a multitude of classification schemes have been suggested to help understand what intelligent agents can do. In general, agents vary in terms of three dimensions: agency, mobility, and intelligence. These dimensions respectively refer to the autonomy of the agent's performance, the amount an agent traverses through networks, and how much an agent can learn or adapt to user requests. Agents can perform several functions, including

- Weeding out unnecessary data
- Alerting to specific conditions
- Matching requesters with requests, while maximizing resources
- Routing, creating, updating, and destroying data
- Identifying trends and combining information from different sources
- Performing administrative functions

Some examples of agents include those for filtering e-mail, scheduling appointments, locating information, making travel arrangements, and paying bills. It has been suggested that agents will someday perform the tasks of a knowledge worker throughout the day, making human executive assistants unnecessary.

## USING WEB AGENTS TO MEET MANAGEMENT NEEDS

The World Wide Web has five primary shortcomings:

- Too much information
- Changing information
- Unordered information
- Lack of support for novice users
- Minimal customization

The increasing use of agents on the Web has resulted in a growing number of creative and helpful agent solutions that address these shortcomings. The following sections present five types of Web agents—search engine, monitor, publisher, guide, and personal assistant—each of which addresses a major Web shortcoming and supports several management needs.

### Using Search Engines to Reduce Information Overload

The ease of creating Web pages has triggered the proliferation of Web pages representing users, organizations, and topical issues. Burgeoning numbers of new companies providing skills and services promote further production of Web pages. Unfortunately, the proliferation of data available on the Web makes it difficult for managers to find useful information.

To address this problem, intelligent agents called search engines seek information and present results based on prespecified criteria. Search engines extract, filter, and compress critical data from a broad range of internal and external sources. Most search engines have similar interfaces in which a manager enters some criteria (e.g., *subject* = *stock market AND date*= *1996*). After the search is invoked, a list of Web page addresses are displayed for further investigation. Some search engines provide options that set a time limit for the search, the number of addresses to be displayed at one time, and the amount of detail to include in the output.

One search engine, SavvySearch (www.cs.colostate.edu/~dreiling/smart-form.html), is considered a metasearch tool that provides a convenient interface, available in multiple languages, to several other search engines. The manager enters criteria for a search and selects options that expand or limit the search output. This metasearcher ranks a list of available search engines (e.g., Alta Vista [www.altavista.digital.com/], Lycos [www.lycos.com], and Yahoo [www.yahoo.com]) and transfers the search request to selected engines. The selection is based on the query, topic area (e.g., Web resources, news, or entertainment), estimated Web traffic, anticipated response time of the other search engines, and the load on the SavvySearch computer.

### Using Monitors to Keep Up with Changing Information

Not only is there an abundance of information on the Web, but the information is also changing constantly. Many Web pages contain information that is regularly added to, deleted, or modified. The location of these Web pages changes as well; servers, directories, and file names move and disappear, frustrating managers who reference invalid links.

Monitor agents accommodate the problems created by dynamic information. These agents let managers track critical data by looking for changes on the Web and communicating these changes to the manager. Instead of relying on people to determine when information becomes obsolete, a manager can count on monitor agents to flush out changes as information evolves and provide direct notification of them.

Both Specter Communications (www.specter.com) and First Floor Software (www.firstfloor.com) offer agents that search the Web for updates on selected sites. WebWatch from Specter Communications, for example, checks selected sites automatically and highlights modifications. A manager can have WebWatch monitor competitor sites for market changes, for instance. Managers who use WebWatch can view downloaded Web sites offline at their convenience. WebWatch has filtering capabilities similar to search engines that allow the agent to traverse the Web looking for changed Web sites, while the program resides on a personal workstation and updates Web bookmarks (i.e., listings of Web site addresses). Such an agent helps managers keep pace with the ever-changing business world.

### Using Publishers to Make Sense of Unordered Information

Information on the Web is unordered, redundant, and uncategorized. Unlike a library, which offers a well-defined process for searching for information, the Web offers no standard approach for meeting information needs. Therefore, intelligent agents that custom-tailor information to individual executives while accessing and integrating a broad range of internal and external data are highly desirable.

Publisher agents do just that. Although they have access to large amounts of information, they present to a manager only the topics and types of information that have been prespecified, often in a variety of presentation formats.

For example, PointCast Network (www.pointcast.com) provides a personalized newspaper to users of the software. First, managers select the topics that they want to read about. This could include headline news, stock quotes, weather, sports, or industry and company news. Based on a manager's interests, hundreds of articles are filtered, integrated, and "pointcasted" to the manager to read at his or her convenience. The text is accompanied by weather and stock price quotes presented graphically in maps and charts.

### Using Guides to Maneuver Novice Users through the Web

Users can access the Web with a Web connection and basic computer skills. Browsers, such as Netscape and Mosaic, take advantage of Windows's point-and-click environment and graphical interface to further facilitate Web use. With ease comes the surge of novice users, including managers, rushing to encounter the global electronic network. This results in the continual need to maintain ease of use.

Some software agents on the Web, called guides, learn user habits and preferences and adapt to individual needs. This is beneficial for managers who are Web novices, because an adaptive and easy-to-use interface requires minimal training and can be used directly by the manager without an intermediary. The more managers can rely on guides to lead Web experiences, the more time they have to focus on the content and significance of information they encounter.

ZooWorks (www.zoosoft.com) from Hitachi is a guide that remembers and sorts each Web site that a manager views. This information is placed in a personal index for future access. The index organizes and structures Web viewing and provides an easy way to locate past sites by keywords, a date, or a range of dates. Because it manages Web information more effectively, ZooWorks helps managers spend their time using information rather than searching for it.

### Using Personal Assistants to Customize Web Information

Diverse visitors stop by organizational Web sites, and different types of people peruse individual Web pages. Because there are myriad purposes for visiting a Web site, a Web page needs to be flexible enough to change to serve each purpose. A financial manager of a company, for example, would be interested in different information than a marketing manager.

When managers locate pages of interest, the information needs to be presented in a useful, understandable way. Personal assistants help present tabular, textual, and graphical information that has been custom-tailored to manager needs. Agents such as BroadVision, Inc.'s One-to-One product (www.broadvision.com) work to make Web pages more relevant to individual users by customizing them based on a user's demographics and usage patterns. Instead of viewing static, general information, managers can interact with personalized Web pages that have been customized through a learning process. For example, a financial manager may see stock quotes and links to financial news articles when entering the company Web site, whereas a marketing manager may be linked to sales information and recent promotions.

## LIMITATIONS OF WEB AGENTS

Although Web agents add great value to the growing number of managerial Web experiences, they do have some limitations. First, agents can be resource intensive; they often must be monitored and their activity needs to be harnessed. If an agent makes a large number of requests in a short amount of time, servers may slow down to a crawl or crash. Some Web servers opt to boycott agent activity and technically prevent agents from interaction. Agents that reside on user machines must be updated and regularly maintained to ensure continued usefulness. In addition, although search engines provide a good starting point for locating information, general searches can result in too much or irrelevant information. Without proper intervention, agents used to reduce information overload can aggravate the problem.

## CONCLUSION

Managers who increasingly use the Web to support their information needs can use the searching, monitoring, and customizing capabilities of intelligent agents to address Web limitations. By custom-tailoring information to individual executives; extracting, filtering, compressing, and tracking critical data; and accessing and integrating a broad range of internal and external data, these software programs help support basic management information needs.

As intelligent agents mature, their minor limitations will be overcome. In the future, as organizations integrate the Web into their technology plans, they will have to increasingly rely on intelligent agents to ensure effective Web use.

**Bibliography**

1. Bottoms, D., Agents of change, *Ind. Week*, 243(16), 49–54, 1994.
2. IBM white paper, intelligent agent strategy http://activist.gpl.ibm.com:8, 1995.
3. McKie, S., Software agents: application intelligence goes undercover, *DBMS*, 8(4), 56–60, 1995.
4. Watson, H. J., Rainer, R. K., and Koh, C. E., Executive information systems: a framework for development and a survey of current practices, *MIS Q.*, 13–30, March 1991.

# Chapter 61
# Auditing a Corporate Web Site

*Mark G. Irving*

PART OF THE AUDIT PROCESS IS DETERMINING HOW SECURE THE WEB SITE IS FROM UNAU-THORIZED ACCESS. Unauthorized access can occur from the inside as well as outside the organization. As a matter of fact, employees inside the organization commit the majority of fraud and other white-collar crimes. The need to protect company assets and customers' confidential information goes without saying. One's customers are counting on their credit card numbers and other personal information being protected from prying eyes. Some questions to ask relating to Web site security follow.

1. Are intranet and Internet pages stored in separate locations on the same server, or are they stored on independent servers?
2. Is anti-virus protection software being run on Internet, intranet, firewall, and e-mail servers? Are the current virus pattern files being updated routinely? What types of files are being scanned (only executable or all files)? Is active virus scanning being performed? Are virus logs being reviewed and infected files cleaned?
3. Is the Internet server in front of the firewall? Is anyone granted access to any computers behind the firewall (customers, hackers, etc.)? If they are allowed access, then find out why this is necessary. If this access is not required, have this hole plugged.
4. Are corporate intranet pages stored behind the firewall and secured properly from unauthorized access by employees?
5. Are access logs reviewed periodically and violations dealt with by the appropriate authorities? Are security permissions updated regularly to be sure terminated employees' access is revoked. Also, are access rights adjusted for employees who change jobs?
6. Does a secure transaction interface exist for E-business transactions? (Specifically, when customers enter credit card and other sensitive information, proper safeguards should be in place to protect this information.)

0-8493-1160-8/02/$0.00+$1.50
© 2002 by CRC Press LLC

Now that some preliminary questions have been presented about the Web site being reviewed, one can delve into the process of auditing a Web site.

## AUDITING

When actually performing the audit of a corporate Web site, there are several items one should address. Considerations need to be made as to which methods and tools will best help accomplish this task. The following sections describe some of the available techniques.

**Interviews.** Talking with key personnel is a good method for gaining a sense of how the Web site has been constructed and is being maintained. Where in-person interviews are not practical, a questionnaire or phone interview can be performed. It generally helps to have a scripted format to follow. This maintains consistency in one's line of questioning when contacting multiple Web administrators at different sites. It also helps to keep one on track, and makes sure that nothing is omitted during the interview. One can use the same questions provided in the questionnaire for interviews (see Exhibit 1).

**Sample.** One will also want to verify that information received during an interview is consistent with actual practices. As most Web sites are too large to review all pages, usually a sample needs to be selected. The sample should be representative of the total universe being reviewed. However, there should also be an effort made to review higher risk pages (E-commerce and frequently accessed pages). Thus, one's sample may be a combination of stratified, random, and judgmental.

**Review Page Content.** Interact with the Web site online, just as a user would. Check the pages being reviewed. Look at the pages for content. As an auditor, use some judgment as to whether the content on a page is appropriate.

**Review HTML Source Code.** Look at the code behind the page. Just looking at the page without looking at the programming behind it is not enough. There can be a lot going on behind the scene that is not apparent without looking at the actual HTML and scripts programming (see Exhibit 2).

Some of the things to check for within the source code are:

- Scripts and applets written in Java, ActiveX, CGI, XMA that perform suspicious functions, such as capturing information about one's computer, downloading code to one's PC, etc.
- Hidden code links (backdoors) that take one to a different site
- Commented out code containing trails that may be helpful to hackers

**Exhibit 1.    Sample Web Page Questionnaire**

**GENERAL**
1.  On what platform(s) do external Web pages reside? (Sun, PC, Mac, other)
2.  Are there guidelines/standards for setting up Web pages? (Get a copy)
3.  Are test and production in separate areas for Web page development? (Yes/No)
4.  Are pages tested and reviewed before being moved to production? (Yes/No)
5.  How are updates to Web pages handled? (Describe)
6.  Are previous versions of pages kept? (Yes/No)
7.  Who approves Web pages before they are published?
8.  How often are Web pages updated?
9.  Are out-of-date information and old URLs removed? (Yes/No)

**SECURITY**
10.  Do internal and external Web pages reside on the same server? (Yes/No)
11.  How are external published pages secured from update over the Internet?
12.  How are the pages in the Intranet protected from access from the outside?
13.  Are the pages inside or outside the firewall?
14.  Is virus protection software used on your Web server? (Yes/No)

**BACKUP and RECOVERY**
15.  Do written procedures for backup and recovery exist? (Yes/No)
16.  How often are onsite and offsite backups tested?
17.  How often are the procedures reviewed and updated?
18.  If there are any Web pages identified as mission critical, have they been included in the Business Contingency Plan?

**MISCELLANEOUS**
19.  Do you have any concerns or other information you wish to add?

---

- Lack of program documentation, also called meta information (author, date created, last updated, software used to create page)

## TOOLS

One can use several tools during the audit. They are described in the following sections and referenced in the Resources section of this article.

**Questionnaire.** The questionnaire in Exhibit 1 can be used in conjunction with interviews (described in auditing techniques above). It can be very useful in obtaining information from key individuals who are at remote locations. Questionnaire formats help capture important facts quickly and can easily be summarized into a statistical package to look for trends, present information by percentage, etc.

**WYSIWYG Viewer.** This is not only useful to the developer in preparing Web pages, but also to the auditor. WYSISWYG or "What You See Is What

**Exhibit 2.    HTML Source Statements to Review**

| | |
|---|---|
| <! -- > | Comments are contained between these two tags; used for documenting purposes<br>• Check for any commented-out HTML code that may contain links<br>• Check for confidential information<br>• Check for information that could help a hacker gain access<br>Example: <! -- The password for accessing the root directory is .... --> |
| <META> | Provides information about the document, such as: source, content, date last updated, and misc. comments<br>• Check for confidential information<br>• Check for information that could help a hacker gain access<br>Example: <meta name="steal_passwords" content="/scripts/steal_passwords.asp"> |
| <SCRIPT LANGUAGE= | Jumps to executable scripting languages, such as: Java, ActiveX, XML, etc.<br>• Check for what scripting languages are being used<br>• See if any of these are being hidden from the user: (_blank, ONMOUSEOVER, <img>)<br>• May require help from a programmer<br>Example: <script language="JavaScript"> |
| </APPLET> | For running Java Script applet programs<br>• See what applets are being run; verify that they are valid<br>• May require help from a programmer<br>Example: </applet open backdoor> |
| <A>_blank </A> | The "_blank" option hides this link; blank-tagging<br>• Used in several commands: <A>, <BASE>, <LINK>, <FORM><br>• See that links are valid<br>Example: <A> _blank </A> |
| <INPUT TYPE= "hidden"> | Defines hidden input field<br>• See what is being hidden; verify this is valid<br>Example: <input type= "hidden"> |
| ONMOUSEOVER | If action occurs, execute statement; ONMOUSEOVER is one example<br>• Check for any code executed with "ON" parameters; see what is executed<br>• Other "ON" parameters: ONCLICK, ONDBCLICK, ONMOUSEDOWN, ONMOUSEUP, ONMOUSEOVER, ONMOUSEMOVE, ONMOUSEOUT, ONKEYPRESS, ONKEYDOWN, ONKEYUP<br>Example: ONMOUSEOVER |

You Get" viewers allow one to look/edit the layout of a Web page in the same format that it appears when accessed through a Web browser. The one difference is that special tagging symbols are shown to represent actions. Such items as image anchors, tables, frames, links to other locations, pages and scripts, etc. are easy to identify.

**HTML Viewer.** This will enable the auditor to look at the actual source code used to generate a Web page. All of the commands, parameters, and links are visible. Many of these viewers display text in different colors, fonts, and other richtext format attributes, to highlight various functions of the coding. The more sophisticated viewers can also format the code — indenting related commands to make the code easier to read.

**HTML Reference Guide.** Get a hold of a good HTML reference guide. This is an invaluable tool in assisting the auditor to determine what the commands do, their format, and parameters. There are examples of how to use the commands and how to use them in conjunction with other commands. It is quick way to build a general knowledge base of HTML, be introduced to coding concepts, and be exposed to the technical buzzwords. Going forward in the audit, one will refer back to this frequently.

**Web Developer.** Use the expert, the Web master. One will be an expert in HTML going in or coming out of a Web page review. Relying on the knowledge base of an HTML/Java programmer can make the difference in uncovering potential exposures. An experienced Web master can go through HTML code efficiently, isolate vulnerabilities, and correct them. Share Exhibit 2 with the Web master. The HTML source statements listed in this document are where some of the more common vulnerabilities can reside. A conscientious Web master also wants a clean and secure Web site.

**Anti-Virus Software.** This is a preventative tool. Verify that the Web server is running real-time anti-virus software. Also, make sure current virus pattern updates are being installed to check for the latest viruses. Review the virus software logs to see if any viruses were detected and what actions were taken if any were found. The last thing a company wants to do is start infecting customer PCs.

**Findings.** Some of the more common findings that one encounters include:

1. *Inappropriate material:* This can range from inflammatory or slanderous statements about competing organizations or personal opinions that are not in line with the company's position, to offensive language and graphics.
2. *Access to sensitive information:* Information used for developing may *not* have been removed. Comments may contain sensitive information like IP addresses, URL links, user ID and passwords, programmer notes, etc. Also, some code used for testing may not have been removed.
3. *Unresolved links:* This occurs when a Web page being referenced has been removed. The link no longer exists. The message displayed is: *(404 Not Found — The requested URL was not found on this server).*

This issue can be avoided by proper testing of pages on a regular basis to ensure all links exist.

4. *Untimely or inaccurate information:* Old information, misspellings, and misinformation all fall into this category. Proper review, approval, spellchecking, and proofreading remedy this.
5. *Weak security:* Access by inappropriate personnel to alter Web pages is the primary example here. However, access to statistical information, such as Web counters, can be another cause for concern. Information, such as IP addresses and URLs can provide useful information to a hacker.
6. *Consistent theme not readily apparent:* This is more a housekeeping item, but shows that the Web development process may not be centralized or using standardized procedures across the organization.

## ESTABLISHING A WEB PAGE POLICY

One measure addresses all of the problems mentioned above: establishing a corporate Web page policy. Developing a good corporate Web page policy and adhering to it are the best protection and methodology for implementing consistency. Be sure to address all of the areas listed below in the policy:

1. Standards for the development, maintenance, and review of a Web site
2. Standards for viewers, publishing, authoring tools, permissions, graphics, format, content, performance, reviewing, approving, conformance to *The Associated Press Style Book* for copy, etc.
3. Security over Web pages, Web tools, statistics, etc.
4. Review of security logs
5. Perform backups/recovery procedures
6. Use of virus protection software

## SUMMARY

There are many issues to keep in mind while reviewing a Web site. Web technology is continually evolving, with more sophisticated scripts, automatic updates to linked corporate databases, etc. More and more companies are joining in the process daily. Business-to-business Internet relationships are cropping up with additional security issues not covered in this article. This type of audit will require revisiting in the future because of the ever-changing environment of Web design.

**Books and Articles**

1. Holzschlag, Molly E. *Laura Lemay's Guide to Sizzling Web Site Design,* Software edition; Lemay, Laura, Series Editor, Sam.net Publishing, 1997. ISBN 1-57521-221-8.

2. Holzschlag, Molly E. and Oliver, Dick. *Teach Yourself HTML 4.0 in 24 Hours,* 2nd edition; Sam.net Publishing, 1997. ISBN 1-57521-366-4.
3. Menkus, Belden. Auditing the Effectiveness of the Design of a Web Page, *EDPACS,* June 2000, CRC Press LLC.
4. Dallas, Dennis A. Perl and CGI for Auditors (74-15-03), *EDP Auditing,* Feb/March 2000, Auerbach Publications, CRC Press LLC.

### Web Sites

1. http://lne.com/lemay/
2. http://irvmdfcp.webjump.com/
3. http://fodors.com/
4. http://electicodyssey.com/

### Tools

1. Microsoft Frontpage Express, Version 2.02.1118; Copyright 1995-97; Microsoft Corporation.
2. Claris Homepage, Claris Corporation.
3. Internet Explorer, Microsoft Corporation.
4. Netscape Communicator, Netscape/AOL, Inc.

The author expresses his thanks to Elden Filby, CISA, Lead Information Systems Auditor at Minnesota Power, Inc., for his input and time reviewing this article.

# Section XI
# Appendices

# Appendix A
# Internet Development Resources

**APPLICATION DEVELOPMENT**

**CAST**

| | |
|---|---|
| Address: | 500 Sansome St., Suite 601, San Francisco, CA 94111 |
| Phone: | (415) 296-1300 |
| Fax: | (415) 296-1313 |
| Web site: | www.castsoftware.com |
| Sales contact name: | Jeff Katz |

**Description Summary.** CAST (EuroNM "7289") is a software company committed to simplifying the complexity of software engineering through Application Mining solutions. Application Mining is suitable for IT professionals, while Data Mining is for business managers. By facilitating an understanding of the internal structure of applications, Application Mining gives IT directors — and their teams — a greater mastery of the software and truly superior responsiveness to change. CAST has more than 200 employees spread across four offices in the United States and in nine major European cities.

**Hamilton Technologies, Inc.**

| | |
|---|---|
| Address: | 17 Inman Street, Cambridge, MA 02139 |
| Phone: | (617) 492-0058 |
| Fax: | (617) 492-1727 |
| E-mail: | sales@htius.com |
| Web site: | http://world.std.com/~hti |
| Sales contact name: | Hannah Gold |

**Product: 001 (pronounced "double oh one")**

| | |
|---|---|
| Pricing: | seat and component based |
| Hardware requirements: | UNIX (HP, Sun, RS6000, Alpha), Windows (NT) |

Software requirements:    Developer Package for hardware environment
of choice, which includes C compiler and GUI
environment (Motif or Windows)

**Description Summary.** Hamilton Technologies, Inc. (HTI) was founded in 1986 to provide products and services to modernize the system engineering and software development process in order to maximize reliability, lower cost, and accelerate time to market. HTI's flagship product, 001, is based on HTI's Development Before The Fact (DBTF) formal systems theory used to develop systems in terms of System Oriented Objects (SOOs). This paradigm integrates systems and software engineering disciplines and transforms the software development process away from an inefficient and expensive curative process to a preventative, more productive, reliable process.

001 is a completely integrated systems engineering and software development environment. It can be used to define, analyze, and automatically generate complete, integrated, and fully production-ready code for any kind of software application with significantly lower error rate and high reusability. Because 001 has an open architecture, it can be configured to generate (or interface to) systems at all levels including those for hardware platforms, software platforms, programming languages, databases, operating systems, Internet systems, embedded systems, communication protocols, GUIs, and legacy code of choice.

Here are some of the properties and features that make the 001 tool suite environment unique:

- *Always number one when put to the test,* no matter how large or complex the system.
- *Inherently reusable,* all 001 developed systems are system-oriented objects (SOOs)
  — No interface errors
  — All objects are under control and traceable
- *Formal but friendly language.* The same language is used for defining any part of a system at any phase of development.
- *Integrated seamless design and development environment.*
- *Executable specification simulation.*
- *Integrated metrics for predictive systems* with a mechanism to trace from requirements to code and back again.
- *100 percent automatic code generation.* 001 automatically generates complete, integrated, fully production ready-to-run code for any kind of system whether it be GUI, database, communications, real time, distributed, client server, multi-user, or mathematical algorithms.
- *001's generator is accessible to be tailored for a user's own brand of generated code.* Once configured, 001 will automatically regenerate the

new system to reside on that environment. Complete flexibility is provided to the user to define his or her own primitive type interfaces to chosen API's which 001 integrates with 001's formal definitions.

- *Maintenance performed at the blueprint level.* The user never needs to change the code, only the specification, and then the user regenerates only the changed part of the system.
- *GUI environment tightly integrated* with development of an application.
- *Automatic testing.*
- *Automatic documentation.* 001's generator is able to automatically document reports for all phases of development because its documentation environment is tightly integrated with the formal definition of the system.
- *Completely defined and generated* with itself.

## Interwoven, Inc.

|  |  |
|---|---|
| Address: | 1195 W. Fremont Ave., Suite 2000, Sunnyvale, CA 94087-3825 |
| Phone: | (408) 774-2000 |
| Fax: | (408) 774-2002 |
| E-mail: | info@interwoven.com |
| Web site: | www.interwoven.com |

## Product: TeamSite

|  |  |
|---|---|
| Pricing: | by server and seat |
| Hardware requirements: | NT or Solaris-based server |
| Software requirements: | any Web server |

**Description Summary.** Interwoven TeamSite is the first and only open, scalable system developed specifically to manage the development and deployment of the large, dynamic Web sites. Teamsite, an Enterprise Web Production system, supports Web content management, software configuration management, and workflow for enterprise Web development.

Product feature list:

- *Openness* — leverages existing IT investments, compatible with all tools and content
- *Ease of use* — empowers all contributors, from authors to IT professionals
- *Performance/scalability* — manages sites containing hundreds of thousands of files
- *Branching* — enables massively parallel development on hundreds of simultaneous Web projects.
- *InContext QA* — provides each Web contributor a complete, fully functional copy of the site in which to develop and stage content.

- *Accommodates rapid change* — Only TeamSite can handle the realistic challenge of Enterprise Web Production for a site with 50,000 files and a team of 100 developers who have to build and release the Web site every two hours. No other product can scale to meet these demands.
- *Deployment* — Interwoven OpenDeploy provides a secure and configurable solution for deployment of Web content to any number of production servers.

## Speedware Corporation

| | |
|---|---|
| Address: | 9999 Cavendish Blvd., St. Laurent, QC, H4M 2X5, Canada |
| Phone: | (514) 747-7007 |
| Fax: | (514) 747-3380 |
| E-mail: | webmaster@speedware.com |
| Web site: | www.speedware.com |

## Product: Visual Speedware

Hardware/Software
requirements:  Visual Speedware is available for Windows 95, Windows NT, HP-UX, and MPE/iX. Requires Visual Basic 5.0

**Description Summary.** Visual Speedware is the first true multi-user development environment built on Microsoft Visual Basic. With Visual Speedware, you can create and deploy complex, robust, graphical client-server applications quickly and efficiently. Visual Speedware significantly reduces the time and cost of developing your applications and helps you use client and server resources intelligently.

Product feature list:

- *Scaling VB to the enterprise* — integrating Visual Basic with Speedware server-side technology offers a single, comprehensive working environment and extends the processing power of VB applications, scaling them up from the PC platform to back-end servers such as Windows NT, UNIX and MPE.
- *Cutting development time* — simplifies application development by offering time-saving wizards and by letting you create client and server components in one process using one tool.
- *Eliminating deployment costs* — Auto-Deployment feature distributes the application client components from server to end-users.
- *Controlling logic partitioning* — allows the developer to control which parts of the application logic are executed on the client and which on the server.

- *Leveraging existing systems* — Visual Speedware lets you plug Windows applications into a Visual Speedware client or legacy applications into the server component.

## Product: Speedware Autobahn

Hardware/Software
requirements: Speedware Autobahn is available for Windows 95, Windows NT, HP-UX, AIX, Solaris, and MPE/iX. Requires Web server software.

**Description Summary.** Speedware Autobahn is a complete development environment for creating new Web applications and Web-enabling existing, mission-critical applications for Internet, intranet, and extranet environments. Autobahn is based on an *n*-tier scalable Application Server that openly supports all Web technologies.

Product feature list:

- *Industry's highest level of security* — secure access to Web-based applications. Autobahn combines three distinct internal security features to ensure users are securely connected to their server-based applications.
- *Robust state management* — no other product handles state-oriented applications more completely. Autobahn's architecture enables permanent and persistent binding between users and applications.
- *Scalable distributed computing* — two types of scalability: scaling software architecture to a large number of simultaneous users and hardware architecture to incorporate multiple machines.
- *Web-enabling existing applications* — offers a variety of methods for tightly integrating legacy systems into Web-based applications, breathing new life into existing applications.
- *Easily integrate other web technologies* — supports an open Web architecture to facilitate the integration of current and future Web technology without having to regenerate applications.

Product: Media

Hardware/Software
requirements: client-supported platforms include Windows 95 and Windows NT. Server-supported platforms include Windows NT and UNIX (HP 9000, RS/6000 and Sun Solaris).

**Description Summary.** Media lets you access, graphically display, and analyze unlimited quantities of up-to-the-minute data with lightning speed — and it is simple to deploy and maintain. Media is available for both Windows and the Web.

Media/M, a multidimensional online analytical processing (MOLAP) tool, accesses data from its own compact, multimatrix, multidimensional database, offering unmatched performance. Media/MR is a hybrid online analytical processing (HOLAP) tool that rapidly accesses high-level aggregates from its multidimensional database and vast amounts of detailed data directly from any relational database.

Product feature list:

- *Excellent performance* — precalculate aggregates in Media's compact multimatrix MDDB. cache results of relational queries on the server, and share them between users.
- *Analytical flexibility* — slice and dice, drill down, perform sophisticated calculations, forecast, etc.
- *Real-time data* — real-time access to detailed data from your RDBMS or data warehouse.
- *High data capacity* — dynamic dimensions do not limit you to a predefined multidimensional structure.
- *Leverages data warehouse* — connects to all relational database management systems (RDBMSs), and supports all schemas.
- *Easy development* — Dictionary Wizard guides you through the rapid construction of your multidimensional model by proposing indicators and dimensions.
- *Low maintenance* — metadata-driven keeps the multidimensional model in sync with the underlying RDBMS.

**Product: Esperant**

| | |
|---:|---|
| Version number: | V4.1 |
| Pricing: | from U.S. $595.00 per user |
| Hardware/Software requirements: | IBM compatible PC running Windows 95 or NT |

**Description Summary.** Esperant is the fastest, most productive way to put corporate information into the hands of decision makers. Esperant is a powerful ad hoc query and reporting tool that empowers users with accurate information — the basis for sound business decisions.

The point-and-click interface removes the need to learn complex data structures or SQL. Only Esperant can generate the robust SQL you need to handle the widest range of business queries. Its patented SQL Expert ensures correct results. Esperant is available for both Windows and the Web.

Product feature list:

- *Intuitive, powerful queries* — English-like queries, transparent joins from multiple-data sources, batch scheduling, custom prompted queries

- *Complete reporting and charting* — drag-and-drop live-data report formatting. Customizable report templates, OLE2 support, 24 chart and graph types
- *Desktop integration* — export query results to spreadsheets and word processors. Executive Desktop for one-click access to queries and reports. Programmable integration through OLE Automation.
- *Flexible administration* — transform complex database structures into business terms. Import database structures from the RDBMS catalog. Full hierarchical security with inheritance.
- *Aggregate aware* — a collection of tables can be marked as an Aggregate Set and displayed to the end user as a single category.
- *Partitioned Set capability* — useful for applications that store identical fields in different tables, such as different time periods.

## AUDIO

### Voxware, Inc.

| | |
|---|---|
| Address: | Lawrenceville Office Park, P.O. Box 5363, Princeton, NJ |
| Phone: | (609) 514-4100 |
| Fax: | (609) 514-4101 |
| E-mail: | vox@voxware.com |
| Web site: | www.voxware.com |
| Sales contact name: | Jeff Hill |

### Product: Custom Compression and Signal Processing SDKs

| | |
|---|---|
| Version number: | Varies |
| Description summary (two paragraphs): | (see below) |
| Product feature list: | Contact Voxware |
| Pricing: | contact Voxware |
| Hardware requirements: | Pentium class microprocessors or a variety of DSPs and RISC chips |
| Software requirements: | Windows, Unix, Java, and others |

**Description Summary.** Voxware's voice compression and VOIP software development kits offer users state-of-the art compression, voice-activity detection, comfort noise generation, frame loss concealment, automatic jitter buffer minimization, and other technologies accessible by well-documented and easy-to-use APIs. Voxware specializes in technologies that maximize the quality of real-time voice communications over PC-to-PC links via the Internet and intranets. Voxware's SDKs handle packetization and other network interface functions, as well as PC sound system interface, and data sampling conversion. They are available in window NT, windows 95, and many versions are offered in other operating systems and with Java interfaces.

## CONSULTING/SOLUTION PROVIDERS

### Buchanan Associates

| | |
|---|---|
| Address: | 125 E. John Carpenter Fwy., Suite 1200, Las Colinas, TX 75062 |
| Phone: | (888) 730-2774 (U.S.); (888) 747-0474 (Canada) |
| Fax: | (972) 869-3975 (U.S.); (905) 501-0068 (Canada) |
| E-mail: | info@buchanan.com |
| Web site: | www.buchanan.com |
| Sales contact name: | Jim Buchanan |

**Description Summary.** Buchanan Associates is a leader in offering information technology solutions. The firm is headquartered in Irving, Texas, with regional offices in Toronto (Canadian headquarters), Dallas, Houston, Denver, Wichita, Chicago, and Detroit. Buchanan Associates is a technology company in the people business. That means we bring you experienced, professional consultants, engineers, project managers, and technical specialists for almost any kind of information technology project. We offer solutions around three technology disciplines, E-Business, network services, and end-user services.

### Cambridge Technology Partners

| | |
|---|---|
| Address: | 20 Richmond St. East, Suite 700, Toronto, ON |
| Phone: | (416) 350-7600 |
| Fax: | (416) 350-7700 |
| E-mail: | jeffrey.wright@ctp.com |
| Web site: | http://www.ctp.com/ |
| Sales contact name: | Jeffrey Wright |

**Description Summary.** Cambridge Technology Partners provides management consulting and systems integration services to transform clients into E-businesses. Working in collaboration with Global 2000 and high-velocity middle-market companies, Cambridge combines a deep understanding of New Economy issues with integrated, end-to-end services, and a proven track record of shared risk and rapid, guaranteed delivery. Cambridge has more than 4000+ employees and more than 40 offices in 19 countries worldwide. Cambridge employs a rapid development methodology that features an iterative approach to bring key client users, executives, and IT professionals to achieve consensus on the business case, strategic objectives, and functionality of a business solution. Cambridge primarily offers a fixed-price, fixed-time model with client involvement at all stages.

### Clarity Systems Limited

| | |
|---|---|
| Address: | 2 Sheppard Ave. East, Suite 800, Toronto, ON, M2N 5Y7 |

|  |  |
|---|---|
| Phone: | (416) 250-5500 |
| Fax: | (416) 250-5533 |
| E-mail: | mnashman@claritysystems.com |
| Web site: | claritysystems.com |
| Sales contact name: | Mark Nashman |

**Description Summary.** Clarity Budget Web, a product that leverages Microsoft Internet Explorer 5.01 or higher, is a multifeatured budgeting solution that supports all types of planning applications, such as Expense Planning, Revenue Planning, HR Planning, Capital Asset Planning, Cash Flow Forecasting, What-If Modeling, and Long Range Planning.

Clarity Systems specializes in implementing business intelligence solutions, with specific expertise in budgeting and planning applications. As a result, Clarity Systems has implemented budgeting applications for many Fortune 500 organizations across North American.

## International Communications, Inc. (has joined Lionbridge Multilingual Content Management)

|  |  |
|---|---|
| Address: | 492 Old Connecticut Path, Framingham, MA |
| Phone: | (508) 620-3900 |
| Fax: | (508) 620-3999 |
| E-mail: | info@intl.com |
| Web site: | www.intl.com or http://www.lionbridge.com/ |

### Product: Localization and translation services

|  |  |
|---|---|
| Version Number: | Localize into more than 22 different languages |

**Description Summary.** International Communications specializes in the localization of software, Web sites, marketing materials, and interactive media. Committed to helping leaders in the IT industry achieve success in overseas markets, the company utilizes leading-edge tools and provides customized solutions for complex projects. U.S. offices are located in Boston, Chicago, San Francisco, and Seattle. Overseas offices are in Beijing, Paris, and Rendsburg, Germany.

## QLogitek

|  |  |
|---|---|
| Address: | 155 Rexdale Blvd. Suite 801, Toronto, ON, M9W 5Z8 |
| Phone: | (416) 741-1595 |
| Fax: | (416) 741-4833 |
| E-mail: | info@qlogitek.com |
| Web site: | www.qlogitek.com |
| Sales contact name: | Musarait Kashmiri |

**Description Summary.** QLogitek is an E-Business Solutions provider. This includes ASP application development, hosting, systems integration, and technology migration. Qlogitek's flagship L'eBIZ application is a supply chain management system that focuses on order management and fulfillment at the time of writing. L'eBIZ is also a framework for developing a variety of Web portals and private trade exchanges on the Microsoft technology platform.

## QUEUE Systems, Inc.

| | |
|---|---|
| Address: | 600 Alden Rd., Suite # 606, Markham, ON L3R 0E7 |
| Phone: | (905) 940-8132 |
| Fax: | (905) 940-9234 |
| E-mail: | klee@queuesystems.net |
| Web site: | www.queuesystems.net |
| Sales contact name: | Lee, managing director |

**Description Summary.** QUEUE Systems, established in 1989, is a multidisciplinary consulting firm that provides complementary resources in its IT consulting, placement agency, and new media divisions. This includes customized software development, systems integration, E-commerce implementation, permanent/contract recruiting, electronic marketing and Web site design.

## Sapient

| | |
|---|---|
| Address: | One Memorial Drive, Cambridge, MA 02142 |
| Phone: | (617) 621-0200 |
| Fax: | (617) 621-1300 |
| E-mail: | info@sapient.com |
| Web site: | www.sapient.com |

**Description Summary.** Sapient is a leading business and technology consultancy that assists clients to successfully deploy technology solutions that deliver explicit, high-value business results. Founded in 1991, Sapient employs more than 2600 people in offices in Atlanta, Austin, Cambridge (MA), Chicago, Dallas, Denver, Düsseldorf, Houston, London, Los Angeles, Milan, Munich, New Delhi, New York, San Francisco, Tokyo, Toronto, and Washington, D.C. Sapient is included in *Standard & Poor's (S&P) 500 Index Directory*.

## SYR Systems, Inc.

| | |
|---|---|
| Address: | 250 Consumers Road, Suite 402, North York, ON M2J 4V8 |
| Phone: | (416) 502-9400 |
| Fax: | (416) 502-8371 |

E-mail:   selim@syrsystems.com
Web site:   www.syrsystems.com
Sales contact name:   Selim ElRaheb

**Description Summary.** SYR Systems Inc.'s mandate is to provide architecture and custom software solutions that meet real business needs and offer high performance, flexibility, reliability and high return on investment. SYR Systems Inc. has established a reputation in the Canadian application software development market as a company with exceptional ability to build high performance systems, using the range from Web, Client-Server to Mainframe technologies. These technologies were recognized as revolutionary and have provided the potential for corporations to build robust, high quality systems at a significantly accelerated rate. Also, in combination with excellent underlying design techniques, these technologies have proven to be substantially easier to maintain.

## E-COMMERCE

### Art Technology Group

Address:   25 First St., 2nd floor, Cambridge, MA 02141
Phone:   (617) 386-1000
Fax:   (617) 386-1111
E-mail:   info@atg.com
Web site:   www.atg.com

**Description Summary.** Dynamo Application Server and Dynamo Profile Station offer the only market-proven E-commerce solution for rapidly developing, deploying, and running extensive personalization-driven Web sites. Ranked the number one personalization solution by Forrester Research, Dynamo Application Server and Dynamo Profile Station are designed specifically to tackle the management of online relationships by applying personalization to every user experience.

Dynamo Application Server 3.5 ("Dynamo") and Dynamo Profile Station 3.5 ("Profile Station") provide enterprises with the platform and tools required to rapidly build and deploy scalable, high-volume Web applications utilizing dynamic HTML page generation, real-time user profiling, and personalized content delivery. Built to run together, Dynamo and Profile Station offer the industry's first true personalization engine that enables Web sites to track visitors, dynamically target content, and tailor each user's visit in real time. The Dynamo product suite provides the engine for managing online customer relationships and drives several of the busiest personalization-driven E-commerce sites on the Web today, including Sony (www.station.sony.com) and BMG Music Service (bmgmusicservice.com). Techical specs, hardware requirements, etc., can be found at http://www.atg.com/industry/products/d3/ and http://www.atg.com/industry/products/profile/.

## CyberCash, Inc.

| | |
|---|---|
| Address: | 2100 Reston Parkway, Suite 430, Reston, VA 22091 |
| Phone: | (703) 620-4200 |
| Fax: | (703) 620-4215 |
| E-mail: | info@cybercash.com |
| Web site: | www.cybercash.com |
| Sales contact name: | Richard K. Crone |

### Product: Electronic Cash Register for Internet payments; credit card, electronic check and electronic cash

| | |
|---|---|
| Version Number: | 3.0 |
| Hardware requirements: | all platforms |
| Software requirements: | all platforms |

**Description Summary.** CyberCash is introducing a new Internet payment architecture for our Cash Register that will make it easier to integrate storefronts, operate payment services, and enjoy upgrades to new services, standards, and options as they become available. With the CR3 Series, we lower the technical and financial hurdles to secure Internet payments.

The CyberCash CashRegister connects a storefront or Web site to the CyberCash payment services, enabling businesses to accept secure, real-time payments at their Web site.

Product feature list:

- Secure credit card transactions (including both SSL and SET)
- CyberCoin service, for cash payments from $0.25 to $10
- PayNow electronic check service, for interactive billing applications

## ICentral, Inc.

| | |
|---|---|
| Address: | 5252 N. Edgewood Drive, Provo, UT 84601 |
| Phone: | (801) 373-4347 |
| Toll-free: | (888) 373-4347 |
| Fax: | (801) 373-7211 |
| E-mail: | info@icentral.com |
| Web site: | www.shopsite.com |
| Sales contact name: | Jan Johnson, VP marketing |

### Product: ShopSite Pro

| | |
|---|---|
| Hardware/Software requirements: | These system requirements are for the average functional store. |

Operating systems:

— OpenLinux, Linux, Free BSD, or BSDI on Intel
— Solaris on SPARC shipping; Solaris on Intel coming soon
— NT and IRIX coming soon
— 6 MB RAM
— 10 MB hard drive space (up to 25 MB may be required to install only)

Hardware platforms must be running:

— Stronghold, Netscape, or any NCSA-compatible, secure Web server software
— PERL 5.003 or greater Sendmail

Client-side (Web site developer or merchant):

— Netscape browsers or Microsoft Internet Explorer, versions 3.0 or later, running on the user's system of choice (PC, Mac, or UNIX)

Client-side (shopper):

— Browser of choice

**Description Summary.** ShopSite Pro is a secure, online store creation and management application designed to meet the needs of site developers and merchants who are seeking to build a professional yet affordable storefront. In addition to its site creation and management tools and secure shopping basket, ShopSite Pro includes real-time credit card authorization, a site search engine, and an Associates Tracking program.

Product feature list:

• Ported to several Unix OS and NT
• Client-side, any platform that supports a standard browser
• Foreign language support
• Unlimited simultaneous shoppers
• Online help
• Payment information encryption
• E-mail notification of orders
• Auto shipping and tax calculation
• First Virtual payment system
• Customizable order system
• Easily indexed by search engines
• Sales stats
• Traffic Stats
• Page creation/site management tools
• Direct media upload
• Media library manager

- Database upload
- Order database download
- Credit card authorization
- Stats plus
- Associates tracking
- Site search
- Large database handling tools
- Interface to other applications
- SmartTags
- Discount calculation
- Automatic product upsell
- Global database editing

**Product: ShopSite Manager**

Hardware/Software
requirements: These system requirements are for the average functional store.

Operating systems:
— OpenLinux, Linux, Free BSD, or BSDI on Intel
— Solaris on SPARC shipping; Solaris on Intel coming soon
— NT and IRIX coming soon
— 16 MB RAM
— 10 MB hard drive space (up to 25 MB may be required to install only)

Hardware platforms must be running:
— Stronghold, Netscape, or any NCSA-compatible, secure Web server software
— PERL 5.003 or greater Sendmail

Client-side (Web site developer or merchant):
— Requires Netscape browsers or Microsoft Internet Explorer, versions 3.0 or later, running on the user's system of choice (PC, Mac, or UNIX)

Client-side (shopper):
— Browser of choice

**Description Summary.** ShopSite Manager is for the small- to medium-sized business manager who wants to begin marketing and selling products on the Internet, or who currently has a Web site, but wants to take the next step of selling products online.

For Web site designers, it reduces the many tedious tasks involved in maintaining a Web site, allowing them to concentrate on pure design. It empowers merchants, not only allowing them to make day-to-day merchandising changes without impacting the site designer. For the do-it-yourself merchant, this person can use ShopSite Manager and build an entire site without knowing HTML.

Product feature list:

- Ported to several Unix OS and NT
- Client-side, any platform that supports a standard browser
- Foreign language support
- Unlimited simultaneous shoppers
- Online help
- Payment information encryption
- E-mail notification of orders
- Auto shipping and tax calculation
- First Virtual payment system
- Customizable order system
- Easily indexed by search engines
- Sales stats
- Traffic stats
- Page creation/Site management tools
- Direct media upload
- Media library manager
- Database upload
- Order database download
- Credit card authorization

### Product: ShopSite Express

Hardware/Software
requirements: These system requirements are for the average functional store.

Operating systems:
— OpenLinux, Linux, Free BSD, or BSDI on Intel
— Solaris on SPARC shipping; Solaris on Intel coming soon
— NT and IRIX coming soon
— 16 MB RAM
— 10 MB hard drive space (up to 25 MB may be required to install only)

Hardware platforms
must be running:
— Stronghold, Netscape, or any NCSA-compatible, secure Web server software

— PERL 5.003 or greater Sendmail

Client-side (Web site developer or merchant):

— Requires Netscape browsers or Microsoft Internet Explorer, versions 3.0 or later, running on the user's system of choice (PC, Mac, or UNIX).

Client-side (shopper):

— Browser of choice

**Description Summary.** ShopSite Express is a shopping basket software application that allows a site developer to build a site using his or her HTML tool of choice, then quickly and easily add Order and Checkout buttons to the Web site. Shoppers can click on these buttons and place an order in the secure shopping basket.

ShopSite Express offers a simple point-and-click, fill-in-the-blanks interface. Enter product information (name, price, ordering options) into ShopSite Express through the browser interface. After configuring tax and shipping (so it will be calculated automatically for shoppers), click on the Create Links button and ShopSite will automatically generate Order and Checkout buttons for each product in the ShopSite database. These buttons can be drag-and-dropped onto the HTML editing window.

Product feature list:

- 25-product limit (no real-time credit card handling capabilities, but can capture and store credit card information securely in the orders database for manual processing later)
- Ported to several Unix OS and NT
- Client-side, any platform that supports a standard browser
- Foreign language support
- Unlimited simultaneous shoppers
- Online help
- Payment information encryption
- E-mail notification of orders
- Auto shipping and tax calculation
- First Virtual payment system
- Customizable order system
- Easily indexed by search engines
- Basic sales stats

## E-MAIL MANAGEMENT

### GFI FAX AND VOICE

Address:    105 Towerview Court, Cary, NC 27513

Toll-Free:   (888) 243-4329
Fax:   (919) 388-5621
E-mail:   sales@gfifax.com
Web site:   http://www.gficomms.com
Sales contact name:   Nick Galea

### Product: Emailrobot for Exchange/SMTP

Software requirements:

— Windows NT server, Windows NT workstation, or Windows 95
— Microsoft Exchange Server or an SMTP/POP3 mail server
— ODBC compatible database such as Microsoft Access or SQL server
— Internet Explorer 3.02 or higher

**Description Summary.** Emailrobot manages and automates corporate/Web site e-mail such as sales@yourcompany.com and info@yourcompany.com. Integrating seamlessly with Microsoft Exchange Server and SMTP/POP3 mail servers, Emailrobot enables companies to archive, distribute, track, search, report and automate their e-mail. Emailrobot has full support for ODBC databases, including MS Access and SQL server. A free evaluation version can be downloaded from http://www.gficomms.com.

Product feature list:

- Distribute corporate e-mail among mail agents
- Track e-mails and their status with tracking numbers
- View communication histories ("e-mail threads")
- View reports on e-mail response times and other e-mail statistics
- Archive Web form output into any ODBC database
- Send out scheduled personalized mailings/replies, e.g., sales follow-up and payment reminders
- Automate any e-mail process using Wizards/VBscript
- Full integration with your mail server

### Product: Emailflow for Exchange/SMTP

Hardware requirements:   32 MB Memory, 100 MB free disk space
Software requirements:

— Windows NT server or workstation
— Microsoft Exchange Server or SMTP/POP3 mail server
— ODBC compatible database, such as Microsoft SQL server or MS Access
— To run VBscript code — Internet Explorer 4.01

**Description Summary.** Emailflow for Exchange/SMTP is a revolutionary workflow software application that integrates seamlessly with your e-mail system and does not require any proprietary client software. This has many advantages such as easier installation, transparent workflow process, no need for training, and a lower TCO. Furthermore, you can extend the workflow process to include your customers and suppliers. For more information and a free evaluation version, please visit our Web site at: http://www.gficomms.com.

Product feature list:

- Run "client-side" applications through HTML mail
- Use any ODBC database as a work-flow information store
- Launch flows through e-mail at scheduled intervals
- Server load balancing and clustering
- Powerful reporting features
- Load balance work flow tasks among users and use roles for tasks
- Industry standard development APIs: ODBC, MAPI, and VBscript
- Competitive pricing and low TCO

## Product: FAXmaker for Exchange

Hardware requirements:    one or more of the following fax devices:
- Class 1 or 2 fax modem (class 2 recommended)
- ISDN internal adapters (EICON DIVA Pro 2.0, EICON DIVA Server Bri, AVM B1)
- Brooktrout analogue TR114 fax boards

Software requirements:
- Windows NT server 4.1
- Microsoft Exchange Server 4.0/5.0/5.5

**Description Summary.** FAXmaker for Exchange is a fax connector for Microsoft Exchange Server, licensed to carry the *Designed for Microsoft BackOffice* logo. FAXmaker for Exchange enables users to send and receive faxes straight from Outlook just as if they were e-mail. FAXmaker offers advanced features at extremely competitive prices. More information and a free evaluation version can be downloaded from http://www.gfifax.com.

Product feature list:

- Automatic inbound delivery (CSID, OCR, DID/DTMF, Line)
- Outlook integration
- Send fax as e-mail
- Exchange integration
- Word mail merge faxing
- Windows fax printer driver
- Fax broadcasting

- ISDN support
- Office 95/97 attachments
- Call accounting/reporting
- Text API

Product: FAXmaker for Networks

Hardware requirements:   one or more of the following fax devices:
— Class 1 or 2 fax modem (class 2 recommended)
— ISDN internal adapters (EICON DIVA Pro 2.0, EICON DIVA Server Bri, AVM B1)
— Brooktrout analogue TR114 fax boards

Software requirements:
— Windows NT server/workstation or Windows 95

**Description Summary.** FAXmaker for Networks is a fax server that runs on Windows NT/95 and enables users to send and receive faxes straight from their desktop. FAXmaker offers advanced features at extremely competitive prices. More information and a free evaluation version can be downloaded from http://www.gfifax.com.

Product feature list:

- Automatic inbound delivery (CSID, OCR, DID/DTMF, Line)
- Windows fax printer driver
- Fax broadcasting
- ISDN support
- Office 95/97 attachments
- Call accounting/reporting
- Text API
- DDE toolkit

## Product: FAXmaker for SMTP

Hardware requirements:   one or more of the following fax devices:
— Class 1 or 2 fax modem (class 2 recommended)
— ISDN internal adapters (EICON DIVA Pro 2.0, EICON DIVA Server Bri, AVM B1)
— Brooktrout analogue TR114 fax boards

Software requirements:
— Windows NT server/workstation, Windows 95
— SMTP/POP3 mail server

**Description Summary.** FAXmaker for SMTP integrates seamlessly with SMTP/POP3 mail servers enabling users to send and receive faxes straight from their favorite e-mail application just as if they were e-mail. FAXmaker offers advanced features at extremely competitive prices. More information and a free evaluation version can be downloaded from http://www.gfifax.com.

Product feature list:

- Automatic inbound delivery (CSID, OCR, DID/DTMF, Line)
- Windows fax printer driver
- Integration with POP3 clients
- Send fax as e-mail
- Fax broadcasting
- ISDN support
- Office 95/97 attachments
- Call accounting/reporting
- Text API
- Word mail merge faxing

## HOSTING

### Data Return Corporation

| | |
|---|---|
| Address: | Millennium Center, 222 W. Las Colinas Blvd., Suite 450, Irving, TX 75039 |
| Phone: | (416) 931-7953 |
| Toll-free: | (800) 767-1514 |
| Fax: | (972) 409-6884 |
| E-mail: | sdabous@datareturn.com |
| Web site: | www.datareturn.com |
| Sales contact name: | Stephen Dabous |

**Description Summary.** Recognized by Microsoft as the Windows 2000 Global Hosting Partner of the Year, Data Return assists companies in deploying Microsoft .NET technologies. This involves testing applications prior to deployment, shortening implementation timeframes, rapidly scaling application infrastructures, and improving application monitoring capabilities. Data Return — A Higher Standard of Managed Hosting.

## JAVA DEVELOPMENT

### Tower Technology Corporation

| | |
|---|---|
| Address: | 1501 West Koenig Lane, Austin, TX 78756 |
| Phone: | (512) 452-9455 |
| Toll-free: | (800) 285-5124 |
| Fax: | (512) 452-1721 |
| E-mail: | tower@twr.com |

Web site: http://www.twr.com
Sales contact name: sales@twr.com

## Product: TowerJ

Hardware requirements: Sparc, Intel, PA/RISC, RS/6000, MIPS, or Alpha
Software requirements: Solaris, WindowsNT, AIX, HP-UX, IRIX, Linux, or Digital UNIX

**Description Summary.** TowerJ is a full "open" native deployment compiler for Java. It includes a global system–optimizing compiler, high-performance object aware run time, and tools for building and performance tuning server-side Java applications. TowerJ creates compact high-performance, self-contained executables for a range of server-class computer platforms from standard Java bytecode. Using TowerJ, software developers can get the full benefits of the Java language without having to sacrifice execution performance or cross-platform compatability. TowerJ supports "Write Once, Compile Anywhere" allowing consistant high-performance execution of a broad range of server platforms.

TowerJ allows companies to reduce server hardware costs, reduce deployment support costs, significantly improve application server performance and throughput, enhance software quality through more maintainable designs and architectures, reduce the costs associated with software performance tuning, and improve end-user satisfaction. TowerJ has been specifically designed and implemented to support the requirements of high-activity, high-availability, process-intensive, business-critical, server-side Java applications. Software groups developing and deploying the Java applications driving the Internet, intranet, and extranet sites for E-Commerce and Net-Business should have TowerJ on their short list of Java deployment tools.

Product feature list:

- Global system optimizations
- Structure and flow analysis
- Automatic dependency analysis
- High speed object dispatcher
- User configurable runtime
- Native and bytecode dynamic updating
- Serialization, reflection and JNI support
- Incremental compilation
- Native Threads support on selected platforms
- Ultrafast synchronization
- Fast scalable performance
- Graphical project manager

## Packeteer, Inc.

| | |
|---:|:---|
| Address: | 10495 N. De Anza Blvd., Cupertino, CA 95014 |
| Phone: | (408) 873-4400 |
| Toll-free: | (800) 697-2253 |
| Fax: | (408) 873-4410 |
| E-mail: | info@packeteer.com |
| Web site: | www.packeteer.com |
| Sales contact name: | info@packeteer.com |

### Product: PacketShaper 1000

**Description Summary.** PacketShaper 1000 is the branch office bandwidth management device that allocates bandwidth over WAN connections for branch offices and remote sites. The PacketShaper 1000 enables network managers to ensure bandwidth allocation and priority for vital business applications across WAN links with speeds up to 384 Kbps. With the PacketShaper 1000, network managers have a cost-effective way to allocate bandwidth and assign traffic priority, allowing them to maximize WAN efficiency, improve application performance, and simplify network management.

Product feature list:

- TCP rate control technology
- Web browser Interface
- Traffic Discovery
- Graphs of Bandwidth Usage
- Top Talkers and Top Listeners

### Product: PacketShaper 2000

**Description Summary.** PacketShaper 2000 is the IP bandwidth management solution that enables ISPs and corporate IT managers to control bandwidth allocation over expensive wide-area network (WAN) and Internet connections at speeds up to 10 Mbps Ethernet. PacketShaper 2000 allows network managers to prioritize business-critical traffic over less important traffic, such as external push applications. This enables network managers to improve the performance of vital applications, increase transactions per second, optimize bandwidth usage, and improve customer satisfaction.

Product feature list:

- TCP rate control technology
- Web browser interface
- Traffic discovery
- Graphs of bandwidth usage
- Top talkers and top listeners

## Product: PacketShaper 4000

**Description Summary.** PacketShaper 4000 is the carrier-class IP bandwidth manager for ISP, corporate data center, and Fast Ethernet LAN environments. PacketShaper 4000 supports WAN connections up to 45 Mbps (DS-3) and can be deployed at expensive access connections to maximize bandwidth efficiency, ensure high quality-of-service (QoS) for multiple classes of service, and improve application performance.

Unlike queuing-based quality-of-service schemes, PacketShaper 4000 explicitly allocates bandwidth by controlling the rate at which the end systems communicate. All traffic identified by PacketShaper is mapped to a specific bandwidth-allocation policy, ensuring that each flow can receive a defined minimum rate guarantee. Aggregate traffic classes can be assigned a burstable partition that efficiently shares excess available bandwidth at defined, prioritized weights. Packeteer's TCP rate-control technology communicates to each end-system in a connection, eliminating the need for queuing and subsequent packet loss, while increasing WAN efficiency. As a result, PacketShaper eliminates disruption associated with bursty traffic and improves application performance. The PacketShaper 4000 can be deployed on Fast Ethernet LANs or WANs supporting up to T3/E3 connections — wherever access costs are highest and bandwidth is most expensive.

Product feature list:

- TCP rate control technology
- Web browser interface
- Traffic discovery
- Graphs of bandwidth usage
- Top talkers and top listeners

## SECURITY

### Certicom Corp.

| | |
|---:|---|
| Address: | 1400 Fashion Island Blvd., Suite 1050, San Mateo, CA 94404-7062 |
| Phone: | (650) 312-7960 |
| Toll-free: | (800) 561-6100 |
| Fax: | (650) 312-7969 |
| E-mail: | info@certicom.com |
| Web site: | www.certicom.com |
| Sales contact name: | Sales and Marketing at (650) 312-7960 |

**Description Summary.** Certicom's product line, based on elliptic curve cryptography (ECC), includes Security Builder (SDK) software developer's Toolkit version 2.0 and SSL Plus SDK from Consensus Development

Corporation (a Certicom company), as well as embedded systems and integrated circuits.

Security Builder SDK 2.0 Certicom's security builder SDK sets a new standard in security, efficiency, and flexibility. The cryptographic Toolkit contains the primitives required to create fast, strong, and compact information security based on ECC for any application. Available for all major operating systems, Security Builder SDK dramatically reduces bandwidth requirements and delivers high throughput, minimizing server bottlenecks and enabling security in client devices or software with modest computing resources. With this standards based SDK, developers are amazed at how quickly security can be integrated into any application.

Functions of Security Builder SDK 2.0. For electronic commerce and other internet and wireless applications and devices, Security Builder provides information security services such as digital signature generation and verification, encryption/decryption, and key management. For more details, contact Certicom at 1-800-561-6100.

**FINJAN SOFTWARE**

| | |
|---|---|
| Address: | 2860 Zanker Road, Suite 201, San Jose, CA 95134 |
| Phone: | (408) 324-0228 |
| Toll-free: | (888) FINJAN.8 |
| Fax: | (408) 324-0229 |
| E-mail: | info@finjan.com |
| Web site: | http://www.finjan.com |
| Sales contact name: | Robert Tas, Vice President of Sales |

**Product: SurfinGate**

**Description Summary.** SurfinGate 4.0 is essential for any business using the Internet, extranet, or intranet for daily business transactions. Its unique patent pending Content Inspection technology for Java and ActiveX, and smart filtering for JavaScript, Visual Basic Script, Cookies and more, helps protect the enterprise beyond traditional firewall filtering. Besides supporting digital signature block or allow based on signature, SurfinGate 4.0 inspects even the signature-allowed applet code content. Central Management and administration make SurfinGate 4.0 truly easy to use and deploy, easing the network administrator routine. For large enterprises, SurfinGate 4.0 ensures high performance and ability to scale.

**Product: SurfinShield Corporate**

**Description Summary.** SurfinShield Corporate is the first centrally controlled mobile code security for the desktop, providing real-time security for its user. SurfinShield Corporate includes Finjan's DMZ (demilitarized zone) to run applets in a separate memory space from the browser. The DMZ provides an extra layer of security supporting the Java Security Manager and Finjan's Xbox (a security manager for ActiveX). The centralized management console allows network administrators to manage anyone connected to the corporate network, whether in-house or at remote locations. SurfinShield Corporate includes the ability to send instantaneous security alerts to the network — should one desktop encounter a control or applet containing a security breach, the rest of the organization will be instantly protected.

### Xcert International, Inc.

|                      |                                                              |
|----------------------|--------------------------------------------------------------|
| Address:             | 1001-701 W. Georgia St., PO Box 10145 Pacific Centre, Vancouver, BC V7Y 1C6 |
| Phone:               | (604) 640-6210                                               |
| Fax:                 | (604) 640-6220                                               |
| E-mail:              | info@xcert.com                                              |
| Web site:            | http://www.xcert.com                                        |
| Sales contact name:  | Alex Chen                                                    |

### Product: Sentry CA

Hardware requirements:

— CPU: Pentium 133 MHz
— RAM: 64 MB
— Disk space (CA software): 50 MB
— Disk space (per user): 4 KB

Software requirements:

— Windows NT
— Solaris 2.5 (Sparc and x86)
— HP-UX 10.20
— OSF/1 (Digital Unix) 4.0
— IRIX 5.3
— BSDI

**Description Summary.** Sentry CA harnesses Xcert's expertise in public key infrastructure to provide solutions for information security and Internet-based electronic commerce. Sentry CA provides organizations with the tools to implement either secure intranets or private networks over the Internet. Whether your organization is a small work group or a multinational corporation, the Sentry CA provides a highly efficient and manageable PKI architecture that scales in a robust and reliable manner.

Product feature list:

• Strong authentication
• Secure Web access

- Secure e-mail
- Nonrepudiation

## VPN

### FreeGate Corp.

| | |
|---:|:---|
| Address: | 1208 E. Arques Ave., Sunnyvale, CA 94086 |
| Phone: | (408) 617-1000 |
| Toll-free: | (800) 280-8816 |
| Fax: | (408) 617-1010 |
| E-mail: | info@freegate.com |
| Web site: | www.freegate.com |
| Sales contact name: | lstiff@freegate.com |

### Product: FreeGate Remote VPN software

Hardware requirements:    FreeGate Multiservices Internet Gateway

**Description Summary.** Enables telecommuters to dial into a local ISP to access corporate information or services as if they were sitting at their desks in the main office. Virtual Services Management (VSM) tools ease the administration and management of a virtual private network of remote users for smaller businesses or organizations with limited IT staff and resources by providing a single, simplified point of administration from which common services — e-mail, name directories, Web access, firewalls, file sharing, and access control — are delivered across locations.

Product feature list:

- Supports Microsoft's Point-to-Point Tunneling Protocol (PPTP, available with Windows clients) on the remote user's desktop or laptop system.
- A PPTP server in the FreeGate system authenticates the remote user, then opens an encrypted path through which traffic flows as if through the LAN (subject to the LAN's security policies).
- Future plans call for implementation of the Layer 2 Tunneling Protocol (L2TP), now in the standardization process.

### Product: FreeGate Branch VPN software

Hardware requirements:    FreeGate Multiservices Internet Gateway

**Description Summary.** Gives branch office users access to e-mail, directories, and other corporate information as if they were behind the firewall on the headquarters LAN. Virtual Services Management tools ease the administration and management of virtual private networking for organizations and smaller businesses with limited IT staff and resources by providing a single, simplified point of administration from which common services — e-mail, name directories, Web access, firewalls, file sharing, and access control — are delivered across multiple branch locations.

Product feature list:

- Class-of-service policies such as access privileges and priorities are applied as if the branch users were physically at headquarters.
- Security is implemented through the industry-standard IP Security (IPsec) protocol, which provides DES encryption, authentication, and key management.

### Product: FreeGate Extranet VPN software

Hardware requirements:    FreeGate Multiservices Internet Gateway

**Description Summary.** Opens up a corporate network selectively to customers, suppliers, and strategic business partners, with users having access to a limited set of information behind the corporate firewall. Virtual Services Management tools provide a single, simplified point of administration from which common services — e-mail, name directories, Web access, firewalls, file sharing, and access control — are delivered across multiple locations.

### WEB MONITORS

### Freshwater Software, Inc.

| | |
|---:|---|
| Address: | 1965 N. 57th Court, Boulder, CO 80301 |
| Phone: | (303) 443-2266 |
| Toll-Free: | (888) 443-2266 |
| Fax: | (303) 545-9533 |
| E-mail: | info@freshtech.com |
| Web site: | http://www.freshtech.com |
| Sales contact name: | Chris Anderson (chris@freshtech.com) |

### Product: SiteSeer

| | |
|---:|---|
| Hardware requirements: | Monitor with 256 colors |
| Software requirements: | Netscape or Internet Explorer browser |

**Description Summary.** Web administrators face the constant challenge of determining what kind of experience their Web site visitors are having. Are they able to get to the Web site? Are all the pages there? How long do they have to wait for a page to download? Freshwater Software's SiteSeer service offers a cost-effective solution to this problem.

With SiteSeer you can verify that your Web pages can be retrieved from outside your system and receive notification of errors via e-mail, pager, or SNMP trap. SiteSeer can detect ISP reliabilty problems, test forms and their associated processes, and verify that a page's contents include a specific string of text. Results of the monitored sites are compiled into daily and weekly management reports. SiteSeer Gold allows a greater variety of monitors, and Global SiteSeer can retrieve your Web pages from locations around the globe, verifying that your site can be accessed worldwide.

### surfCONTROL Division

| | |
|---|---|
| Address: | JSB, 108 Whispering Pines Drive, Suite 115, Scotts Valley, CA 95066 |
| Phone: | (408) 438-8300 |
| Toll-free: | (800) 572-8649 |
| Fax: | (408) 438-8360 |
| E-mail: | stevep@surfcontrol.com |
| Web site: | www.surfcontrol.com |
| Sales contact name: | Steve Purdham |

### Product: the surfCONTROL Family

Ensuring Internet Access is Business Access

Hardware requirements:　NT System
Software requirements:　NT4

**Description Summary.** surfCONTROL is a family of products designed for business which deliver the essential management tools to monitor, control, report, and manage "who can do what, when and how" with Internet Access. surfCONTROL protects productivity, bandwidth, security, and reputation by ensuring Internet Access is Business Access.

Product feature:　Family of products that can monitor and report Internet Access as well as control Access using Business Rules.

### Sequel Technology

| | |
|---|---|
| Address: | Lincoln Executive Center, Building III, 3245 146th Place SE, Suite 300, Bellevue, WA 98007 |
| Phone: | (425) 556-4000 |
| Toll-free: | (800) 973-7835 |
| Fax: | (425) 556-4042 |
| E-mail: | sales@sequeltech.com |
| Web site: | www.sequeltech.co, |

### Product: Sequel NetAccess Manager

**Description Summary.** With Sequel NetAccess Manager, you can identify, understand, and control Internet and intranet activity on your network, on an individual, group, or company basis. Sequel NetAccess Manager filters and logs all Internet activity at critical filter points including firewalls, proxy servers, and routers, and consolidates this information to produce clear, easy-to-understand reports. With this valuable information you can then define and enforce policies and strategies that will ensure the most productive use of your network:

Product features list:

- Perform network trend analysis and capacity planning to reallocate or upgrade network resources.
- Allocate usage costs back to individual departments.
- Develop and enforce usage policies using sophisticated access control functions.
- Run audit reports on individual usage of the Internet and corporate intranet to identify potential security breaches and limit legal liability.

## WEB SERVER

### Resonate, Inc.

|  |  |
|---|---|
| Address: | 465 Fairchild Drive, Suite 115, Mountain View, CA 94043 |
| Phone: | (650) 967-6500 |
| Fax: | (650) 967-6561 |
| E-mail: | sales@resonate.com |
| Web site: | www.Resonate.com |

### Product: Central Dispatch

|  |  |
|---|---|
| Hardware requirements: | Solaris SparcStation, HP/UX, AIX PowerPC, or NT; 4.x PentiumPro |
| Software requirements: | Solaris 5.5.1, HP/UX 10.20, AIX 4.2.x, or NT 4.x |

**Description Summary.** Software-based solution enabling multiple Internet servers to act as a single, scalable, reliable, and easily managed Internet server system. Servers in a central Dispatch site are accessed via one or more Virtual IP (VIP) addresses and appear to clients as a single Internet site. Servers can be co-located (on one or more IP subnets) or distributed geographically, providing support for heterogeneous NT/UNIX environments, multiple departmental networks, and firewall architectures. Content can be replicated on multiple servers for highest availability, segregated by type (e.g., CGI scripts, graphics files, HTML pages, etc.) or by subject (e.g. */memberlogin/*) to minimize response times for client requests.

## Product: Global Dispatch

Hardware requirements:   Solaris SparcStation or NT 4.x PentiumPro
Software requirements:   Solaris 5.5.1, or NT 4.x

**Description Summary.** By gathering and using latency, load, and availability information, Global Dispatch directs client requests to the physical POP most suited to respond. Global Dispatch integrates into a Domain Name Server (DNS) architecture, resolving a virtual host name (such as www.coolstuff.com) into the IP address of a physical POP. When a client's local DNS makes an address resolution request for a virtual host name, Global Dispatch responds with the IP address of the most available physical POP based on latency and old information it receives from Global Dispatch agents installed at each POP.

## webMethods, Inc.

Address:   3375 University Drive, Suite 360, Fairfax, VA 22030
Phone:   (703) 352-0047
Fax:   (703) 352-0370
E-mail:   sales@webmethods.com
Web site:   http://www.webmethods.com
Sales contact name:   sales@webmethods.com

## Product: B2B Integration Server

**Description Summary.** webMethods' B2B Integration Server is the first and only XML-based solution that automates the exchange of data between applications, Web sites, and legacy data sources.

The Business-To-Business (B2B) Integration Server architecture is an innovative application integration and deployment platform that facilitates secure information exchange between disparate business applications. An XML-based remote procedure call (XML-RPC) provides the integration framework under which both Web and local data can be seamlessly integrated.

The B2B Integration Server enables companies to host and publish a set of business services, such as PlaceOrder or TrackShipment, that enable the application-to-application exchange of data and information sources via the Web. These services are encapsulated and accessed via an XML-RPC mechanism that uses XML for both the description of the business procedure interface, and the message format for the transferred data.

Unlike proprietary E-commerce systems, the B2B Integration Server uses standard Web protocols, specifically HTTP and XML, ensuring current and future interoperability. The B2B Integration Server can also translate messages in accordance with the language of a submitted request. For example, the Server can receive an XML message request formatted using the tags of a particular document type definition (DTD), perform the required business logic, and send an XML reply in the same format — even though the business logic has no specific knowledge of the tags being used.

Product feature list:

- Nonproprietary
- Based 100% on open standards of the Web
- Integrates your supply chain over the Web
- Automates procurement
- Manages distribution channels, order processing, and logistics
- Aggregate content, news, and business intelligence
- XML-based technology that you can use now
- The only solutions that work with existing HTML, so your corporate developers do not require expertise in XML
- Ease of use and simple to rapidly integrate Web data with any application
- Cross-platform flexibility, including Windows 95, Windows NT, Solaris, AIX, Linus, HPUX, Digital Unix, OS/2, and Macintosh
- Support for Java, C, C++, Visual Basic, PowerBuilder, Javascript, Active X, SAP, Baan, and PeopleSoft
- Communication with any back-end Web program via CGI, NSAPI, ISAPI and other common Web server interfaces
- Built-in change management features to insulate your applications from changes to Web resources

# About the Editor

Sanjiv Purba holds a Bachelor of Science degree from the University of Toronto and has more than 16 years of relevant information technology experience. He is Practice Director for Microsoft Consulting Services — E-Solutions in Canada. Prior to joining Microsoft, Mr. Purba was a Senior Manager with Deloitte Consulting and leader of their object-oriented practice.

Mr. Purba has extensive industry experience, with a focus on the financial and retail industry sectors. As a consultant, Mr. Purba has gained relevant experience in other industries, such as telecommunications, travel and tourism, manufacturing, and entertainment. He has served in a variety of roles in large organizations, including developer, senior developer, business analyst, systems analyst, team leader, project manager, consultant, senior architect, senior manager, director, and acting vice president.

Mr. Purba is the author of six information technology (IT)–related textbooks. He is also editor of *High-Performance Web Databases* and *The Data Management Handbook*, both published by Auerbach. Mr. Purba has authored more than 100 IT articles for *Computerworld Canada*, *Network World*, *Computing Canada*, *DBMS Magazine*, *Hi-Tech Career Journal (HTC)*, and the *Toronto Star*. Mr. Purba is past editor of *ITOntario*, a publication of the Canadian Information Processing Society (CIPS). He has also written fantasy and science-fiction graphic novels.

Mr. Purba is a regular speaker at industry symposiums on technical and project management topics. He has lectured at universities and colleges for the past 16 years, including Humber College, the University of Toronto, and Ryerson Polytechnic University. He recently hosted an IT forum on a television program in the Toronto area.

Prior to joining Deloitte Consulting, Mr. Purba ran his own computer consulting business, Purba Computer Solutions, Inc., during which time he consulted with Canadian Tire, Sun Life Assurance Company of Canada, and IBM in a variety of roles, including senior architect, facilitator, and project leader.

Mr. Purba also served as a senior architect and senior consultant with Flynn McNeil Raheb and Associates, a management consulting firm, for five years prior to owning his own business. During that time, he consulted with such organizations as IBM, ISM, The Workers Compensation Board, Alcatel, and the Ministry of Education.

Mr. Purba enjoys weight lifting, aerobics, karate, tae kwon do, tae bo, movies, and charity work.

# Index

# N

# Q

# R

T - #0209 - 101024 - C0 - 234/156/44 [46] - CB - 9780849311604 - Gloss Lamination